Eighth Edition

An Introduction to the Bible

A JOURNEY INTO THREE WORLDS

Christian E. Hauer, FSA, FRSA
Professor of Religious Studies (Emeritus)
Westminster College

William A. Young
Professor of Religious Studies (Emeritus)
Westminster College

PEARSON

Boston   Columbus   Indianapolis   New York   San Francisco   Upper Saddle River
Amsterdam   Cape Town   Dubai   London   Madrid   Milan   Munich   Paris   Montréal   Toronto
Delhi   Mexico City   São Paulo   Sydney   Hong Kong   Seoul   Singapore   Taipei   Tokyo

Editorial Director: Craig Campanella
Editor in Chief: Dickson Musslewhite
Publisher: Nancy Roberts
Editorial Project Manager: Nicole Conforti
Editorial Assistant: Nart Varoqua
Director of Marketing: Brandy Dawson
Senior Marketing Manager: Laura Lee Manley
Senior Managing Editor: Maureen Richardson

Production Manager: Fran Russello
Cover Design: Suzanne Behnke
Composition/Full-Service Project Management: Element LLC/Suganya Karuppasamy
Printer/Binder: Courier Companies, Inc.
Cover illustration: The Lindisfarne Gospels, Cotton MS Nero D. IV (seventh century C.E., Latin), folio 211, first text page of the Gospel of John. The Granger Collection.

Library of Congress Cataloging-in-Publication Data

Hauer, Christian E. (Christian Ewing)
 An introduction to the Bible: a journey into three worlds/Christian
E. Hauer, William A. Young.—8th ed.
  p. cm.
 Includes bibliographical references and index.
 ISBN-13: 978-0-205-05165-6
 ISBN-10: 0-205-05165-0
1. Bible—Introductions.   I. Young, William A., 1945– II. Title.
 BS475.3.H38 2012
 220.6'1—dc23

                                     2011019621

10 9 8 7 6 5 4 3

www.pearsonhighered.com

ISBN-13: 978-0-205-05165-6
ISBN-10: 0-205-05165-0

For Chris, Sr., Ann Lee, Liz, John, and Anna
and Art, Rhoda, Sue, Rachel, and Matthew

CONTENTS

ABBREVIATIONS OF THE BOOKS OF THE BIBLE

Acts	Acts of the Apostles	Jude	Jude
Am.	Amos	1 Kgs.	1 Kings
1 Chr.	1 Chronicles	2 Kgs.	2 Kings
2 Chr.	2 Chronicles	Lam.	Lamentations
Col.	Colossians	Lev.	Leviticus
1 Cor.	1 Corinthians	Lk.	Luke
2 Cor.	2 Corinthians	Mal.	Malachi
Dan.	Daniel	Mic.	Micah
Dt.	Deuteronomy	Mk.	Mark
Ec.	Ecclesiastes	Mt.	Matthew
Eph.	Ephesians	Nah.	Nahum
Est.	Esther	Neh.	Nehemiah
Ex.	Exodus	Num.	Numbers
Ezek.	Ezekiel	Ob.	Obadiah
Ezra	Ezra	1 Pet.	1 Peter
Gal.	Galatians	2 Pet.	2 Peter
Gen.	Genesis	Phil.	Philippians
Hab.	Habakkuk	Philem.	Philemon
Hag.	Haggai	Pr.	Proverbs
Heb.	Hebrews	Ps.	Psalms
Hos.	Hosea	Rev.	Revelation to John
Is.	Isaiah	Rom.	Romans
Jas.	James	Ru.	Ruth
Jer.	Jeremiah	1 Sam.	1 Samuel
Jg.	Judges	2 Sam.	2 Samuel
Jl.	Joel	Song	Song of Songs (Solomon)
Jn.	John	1 Th.	1 Thessalonians
1 Jn.	1 John	2 Th.	2 Thessalonians
2 Jn.	2 John	1 Tim.	1 Timothy
3 Jn.	3 John	2 Tim.	2 Timothy
Job	Job	Tit.	Titus
Jon.	Jonah	Zech.	Zechariah
Jos.	Joshua	Zeph.	Zephaniah

FOREWORD

What! Another introduction to the Bible? Isn't that what Koheleth had in mind when he wailed, "Of the making of books there is no end …?" The answer to the first question is, indeed yes. The reply to Koheleth's plaint is: There are books and books. This book is one he would not, or at least should not, have complained about. In the field of textbooks, the difference between books and books is the difference in attitude of the author or, in this case, authors. Some write what they are certain is the definitive statement, the last (not the latest) word in the field. The student is swept away and buried under an avalanche of absolute certainties. Others, and such is the case with this volume, offer a forthrightly relativistic approach: This is what is known and this is how we have come to know it. Tomorrow something may turn up—an archaeological find, or a brilliant literary analysis—that may set some (some, but not all) of what we have written on its ear. They have prepared for that possibility, and they want you to be prepared for it as well.

Perhaps the best way to sum up the attitude pervading this work is to quote the old Latin phrase *vade mecum,* walk along with me, for that is its invitation. Come along, and together let us see what there is to be learned about one of the most influential collections of literature ever put together, the Bible. Let us see what there is to be learned and how we can learn it. The program this book provides is straightforward and clear: the three worlds of the Bible, the historical, the literary, and the contemporary. Under these three headings, the authors first approach the context of the Bible, its place within the known historical past of the ancient Near and Middle East; what the archaeological and literary remains of ancient civilizations tell us about the traditions and events reported in the Bible, and what it tells us about them. They then turn to the Bible as a literary event and examine its own history, and the history claimed for it by various schools of thought. While they have not ventured too far from the beaten tracks of contemporary scholarly opinion, they have been fair and honest in their assessments. Finally, they have turned their attention to the contemporary role of the Bible. What can it, what does it, mean to us, and how does it touch and affect the lives of those who stand in some connection, positive or negative, near or remote, to it?

In each instance, the authors are at pains to help the reader understand how these three worlds have come into being and how they interrelate. The technical language of scholarship has not been eschewed, but it is meticulously explained so that the insights and methods that lie behind the terms are given their due. The student, the reader, is given every consideration as well. The illustrations, maps, charts, and tables are designed to complement the text so that the biblical worlds take on a concrete presence; they are not words alone.

What lies behind this volume is, I am certain, a conviction on the authors' part that students are important, teaching is important, and the Bible is important. Those who use this text will, I am confident, come to the same conclusions.

Lou H. Silberman
(1915–2006)

We retain this foreword by the late Prof. Silberman, written for the first edition of this book, as a token of our affection and respect for a gifted scholar, inspiring teacher, and exemplary mentor. Prof. Silberman was Hillel Professor of Jewish Literature and Thought at Vanderbilt University (1952–1980) and, at the time of his death, visiting professor at the Center for Middle Eastern Studies at the University of Arizona.

PREFACE

An Introduction to the Bible: A Journey into Three Worlds is an introductory text for college students and general readers who have had little or no previous exposure to the academic study of the Bible. The three worlds are the *historical world* out of which the Bible emerged and through which it came to us; the *literary world* (or worlds) created by the Bible itself; and the *contemporary world* in which we read and try to understand the Bible.

The first two worlds are likely to be strange and possibly confusing for a person entering them for the first time. The historical world involves not just the history of events to which the Bible alludes. It also encompasses the original historical context surrounding the Bible; the literary history of the Bible, which means the writing, collection, copying, passing on, and interpretation of the books through time; and the process through which the books became Scripture. The literary world is equally complex. The Bible is not so much a book as it is a library. The biblical collection contains various types of literature.

Like someone traveling in a foreign country for the first time, a student embarking on an initial study of the Bible deserves an orientation before beginning the journey. Chapter 1 can be compared to an orientation to the geography, customs, and language of a new country. We will acquaint you with the basics about each of the three worlds into which you will be venturing. Chapter 2 is like the practical preparation a student about to go abroad receives concerning such matters as how to rent a room, get to the bathroom, use the telephone, or travel on trains. We will introduce you to the methods of analysis used in the academic study of the literary and historical worlds of the Bible and to some of the ways the Bible is interpreted in the contemporary world.

However, as is the case with travel, orientation is no substitute for the journey itself. In Chapters 3 through 15, we will guide you through the literary and historical worlds of the Bible and raise questions that stimulate you to consider the contemporary worlds of the various books.

We have tried hard to avoid the latest academic jargon. Where technical terms were necessary for clarity, we tried to state clearly what they mean.

In our discussions of the literary and historical worlds, our intent was to describe, not to evaluate. We hope that persons of a variety of religious backgrounds, or no religious background, will feel comfortable with our descriptions. Our purpose was to create a basis for people of various convictions about the Bible to examine its literary and historical worlds. This will, we hope, create a common ground for meaningful discussion of the contemporary world. Often, when people engage in conversation about the Bible without such a foundation, they end up talking past one another.

An Introduction to the Bible combines two of the major recent trends in biblical scholarship with more traditional concerns of biblical study. One new trend is the application of social scientific models and general history of religion models in biblical study. The second is intrinsic literary interpretation of biblical texts. We have tried to make a very clear distinction between literary inquiry and historical study. On the basis of our classroom experience, we have found that introductory students benefit from an approach that keeps the historical and literary worlds separate. It will become obvious to even the most naive reader that this dichotomy cannot and should not be pushed too far. We have also tried to make greater use of recent research in Jewish studies than is common in introductory texts, particularly in our treatment of postexilic Israel and the New Testament period.

Ideally, a student should read the entire section of the Bible along with the discussion of it. We hope that the general reader, uncoerced by the time limits of an academic schedule, will be able to do just that. At the very least, our analyses of certain materials will require students to consult those particular passages. We have very deliberately tried to write a book that introduces the Bible without becoming a substitute for reading the Bible itself. Our reason for this is quite simple. No secondary text, however excellent, can replace the experience of the primary text itself. A book about Shakespeare is no substitute for *Hamlet*, nor is a book about the Bible a substitute for Genesis.

We are gratified that the first seven editions of *An Introduction to the Bible* have been well received by students and teachers alike. We are humbled that a project that originated twenty-five years ago is still garnering positive responses. In this new, eighth edition, we have once again benefited from the constructive suggestions of a number of readers. Our intention has been to update and enhance our presentation of the three worlds of the Bible, without changing the basic approach.

WHAT'S NEW TO THIS EDITION?

- A number of new illustrations and maps throughout the 8th edition provide engaging pedagogical aids for instructors and students.
- The Introduction (Chapters 1 and 2) has been streamlined to make the process of becoming oriented to the three worlds of the Bible and the methods of studying them more accessible for students.
- At the outset, the importance of interpretation of the Bible in the contemporary world is highlighted with discussion of the ongoing controversy surrounding same-sex marriage and the dispute as to whether Islam and the *Qur'an (Koran)* are compatible with religions based on the Bible.
- Important new developments in archaeological research related to the Bible are discussed, such as whether archaeology helps answer the question, "Did God have a wife?" and the continuing controversy over the "James Ossuary," an ancient burial box alleged to contain the bones of a brother of Jesus.
- The descriptions of the Pharisees and the relationship between the Essenes and the community that produced the Dead Sea Scrolls have been updated.
- Several topics related to the study of Jesus and the New Testament gospels are given new attention, among them the importance of understanding Jesus of Nazareth as a first-century Jew, the meanings of the titles associated with Jesus, and the stereotypes of Judaism found in recent biblical scholarship. A brief overview of the life of Jesus is added to the discussion of the "historical Jesus."
- New examples enhance discussion of the impact of the Bible in contemporary American culture, including the dispute regarding the teaching of Intelligent Design alongside the theory of Evolution, various perspectives on the Bible and climate change, new efforts to encourage study of the Bible and its influence on Western culture in public schools, and interpretations of the Bible in the blockbuster movie *Avatar* (2009) and the hit animated series "The Simpsons."
- A thoroughly revised and updated annotated bibliography provides students and teachers with a wealth of sources for further study of the three worlds of the Bible. It also offers an updated list of movies and documentary films related to the Bible, with information on how to obtain them, and a revised list of Internet gateway sites for serious study of the Bible.

ACKNOWLEDGMENTS

Any major publishing project involves the work of many persons. We would like to express our particular appreciation to the following: Wayne Spohr, former Prentice Hall field editor; Nicole Conforti and the rest of the Prentice Hall Religion and Philosophy editorial staff; and production editors. We would also like to thank David Torbett, Marietta College; J. Brabban, Chowan University; Shannon Grimes, Meredith College; Cheryl Rhodes, Coastal Carolina University and University of South Carolina; and Gerald Vigna, Alvernia University, for their helpful reviews of the eighth edition. We would also like to thank the reviewers of earlier editions for their insightful comments.

The late Professor Lou Silberman generously provided the foreword. Professor Robert Seelinger, Messrs. Dan Engle and Bill Wilson, and the late Rev. Arthur Young and Rhoda Young assisted with photographic illustrations. Liz Hauer, former interlibrary loan librarian at Reeves Library, Westminster College, Fulton, MO, provided access to documentary sources otherwise unavailable in central Missouri. The interlibrary loan staff at Stephens College in Columbia, MO was very helpful in obtaining resources for the eighth edition. Our Westminster College colleagues in Classics, Dr. Robert Seelinger and Dr. Victor Leuci, provided helpful references.

The Scripture quotations in this publication are from the New Revised Standard Version of the Bible, copyright © 1989 by the Division of Christian Education of the National Council of the Churches of Christ in the USA, and used by permission. All rights reserved.

It would be quite impossible in this limited space to acknowledge the contributions of all those scholarly colleagues whose works, and whose comments and advice on our own research, made the book possible. Nor can gratitude be restricted to merely our own generation or even our own century. However, we do wish to acknowledge the special debt of gratitude we owe to those teachers whose instruction, encouragement, and example contributed to our lives in a singular fashion. Chris particularly remembers the late Dean John Keith Benton, and the late Professor J. Philip Hyatt, and the late Professor Lou H. Silberman. Bill particularly remembers the late Professor John Gammie, and Professors Edward F. Campbell, Jr., and J. Kenneth Kuntz. Chris also expresses appreciation of a decade-long collaboration with the late Professor John Page (anthropology) in the Westminster College Field Archaeology Project, and many helpful discussions of the theory and method of archaeology and anthropology that flowed therefrom.

Both authors also acknowledge happy associations (albeit at different times) with field excavation projects of the Institute of Archaeology of Tel Aviv University, and the opportunity to learn from the late Professor Anson Rainey and Professor David Ussishkin.

Finally, each of us wishes to thank his coauthor, whose encouragement, cooperation, and personal scholarly contribution made the production of this volume and revisions through the decades a great deal easier and a whole lot more fun than a job this size has any right to be. Any errors in this work are his fault!

Christian E. Hauer, Jr.
William A. Young

Chapter 1

The Three Worlds of the Bible

An Orientation

Gay Marriage Rally. A 2008 rally in Sacramento, California, protests passage of a proposition banning gay marriage in the state. Both supporters and opponents of legalizing same-sex marriage claim the Bible supports their position.   *Source:* Karin Hildebrand Lau/Shutterstock

INTRODUCTION

Why Study the Bible?

The Jewish (Hebrew) and Christian Bibles are ancient. Some portions of the Hebrew Bible (or Old Testament, as it is known to Christians) may well have been committed to writing over three thousand years ago. The most recent books in the New Testament portion of the Christian Bible are just a century or so short of two thousand years old. In the twenty-first century, why should we study such seemingly archaic writings?

For many readers, the answer is obvious. The Bible is fundamental to their identity as Jews or Christians. They consider the Bible a sacred text and are committed to living their lives on the basis of the values they find in their version of the Bible. According to Professor Stephen Prothero of Boston University polls show that two-thirds of the American people believe that the Bible holds the answers "to all or most of life's basic questions."[1] Around the world, in synagogues and churches, millions encounter the Bible weekly in worship. The year for them is marked by deeply meaningful ritual observances based on stories found in these texts, such as the Jewish Passover, Rosh Hashanah, and Yom Kippur, or the Christian Easter and Christmas. The Bible is also held in deep respect by Muslims, who consider central biblical characters such as Abraham, Moses, and Jesus to be prophets of God.

However, there are other less obvious reasons the Bible should be studied today. These are particularly relevant for readers who have little or no connection with the Bible as a sacred text, but they are also important for those who have a spiritual association with the Bible. The ongoing impact of the Bible is evident in everyday life. One of the most intimate of human activities—the naming of babies—draws on the Bible. In 2009 five out of the most popular names for boys (Noah, Ethan, Jacob, Caleb, and Lucas) and four of the most frequently chosen names for girls (Sophia, Madeline, Abigail, and Chloe) in the United States had biblical roots or associations. Common expressions such as "let there be light," "falling on one's sword," and "handwriting on the wall," to name just a few, come from the Bible.

Moreover, in addition to its direct, religious significance, the Bible continues to have a profound influence on the political and legal institutions—as well as art, literature, and music—of modern cultures.

Here are two examples of the continuing impact of the Bible. You will find a much fuller discussion of the ongoing legal, political, and cultural influence of the Bible in the final chapter (see Chapter 16).

In August 2010 a federal judge ruled a California law banning same-sex marriages unconstitutional. Enacted in a referendum of voters in 2008, the law was in response to a ruling by the California Supreme Court that allowed for marriages of gays and lesbians in the state. The federal court ruling has been appealed, and the case likely will reach the U.S. Supreme Court.

Opinion polls in 2010 show the American public evenly divided on this hotly contested issue, in which interpretation of the Bible plays a central role. Many of those who oppose same-sex marriage claim that it is a clear violation of the Biblical teaching that God has sanctified marriage as only between a man and a woman, citing passages such as Gen. 1:24 and Mk. 10:7. To change the understanding of marriage expressed in the Bible, they contend, erodes the moral foundations of the family, which is a central pillar of society. Supporters of same-sex marriage respond by saying the Bible's limited view of marriage reflects the culture in which the Bible was written and no longer applies today.

---

[1]Stephen Prothero. *Religious Literacy: What Every American Needs to Know–And Doesn't*. San Francisco: HarperOne, 2008. Ironically, despite this claim, most Americans know little about the Bible, as Prothero demonstrates. For example, less than half of Americans can name the first book of the Bible.

They point out that the Bible was once used as warrant for laws in which women were considered to be the property of their husbands and to prohibit interracial marriages. Just as modern societies recognize that these attitudes should be rejected, so should discrimination against same-sex couples, they claim, arguing that they should be given the opportunity to commit themselves to one another in the bonds of marriage. Why, they ask, should the living out of the Bible's teaching of unconditional love, symbolized in the marriage covenant, be limited to heterosexual couples?

Also in August 2010 a church in Florida announced that on the ninth anniversary of the September 11, 2001 attacks on the World Trade Center and Pentagon by Islamic extremists, its members would burn copies of the holy book of Islam, the Qur'an. Once again, the Bible was at the center of a modern controversy. According to the church's pastor, Islam is an evil religion and the Qur'an is a demonic book. The burning of the Qur'an, he claimed, was the modern equivalent of the burning of books of magic described in the Bible (Acts 19:19). While the burning of the Qur'an was being justified on biblical grounds, other interpreters of the Bible emphasized similarities in the Islamic holy book and the Jewish and Christian Bibles, calling for greater understanding and respect among the three religions. They pointed out that God's promises to Abraham and the patriarch's obedience (see Chapter 3) are so prominent in the sacred texts of all three religions that they are known collectively as the Abrahamic religions. Moreover, they claimed, the three texts focus on the one God who created the universe, shows love for all humanity, has spoken through prophets, and calls humans to treat one another and all creation with justice and compassion. The same tension was evident in the summer of 2010 in the impassioned debate over whether an Islamic cultural center and mosque should be built two blocks from "Ground Zero," the site of the World Trade Center bombings.

As you will learn, the reality of the Bible's ongoing religious influence and these two examples of the Bible's impact in twenty-first century culture illustrate one of the "three worlds" of the Bible upon which this text is based, the one we call the "contemporary world," the world in which the Bible is read and interpreted today. In addition, there are two other "worlds of the Bible" to which you will be introduced in this book—the "literary" and the "historical" worlds.

What Are the "Three Worlds" of the Bible?

Every book is written from a point of view. Our perspective, as authors, is that the best way to introduce readers to an academic study of the Bible is to take them on a journey into the Bible's "three worlds." The first step in that journey is to clarify what we mean by these three worlds of the Bible: the literary, historical, and contemporary. That is what we will do in this chapter. In the next chapter, we will describe the various methods developed to explore each of these worlds. Be aware that these first two chapters are challenging. You may feel weighed down, like a traveler who has packed too much for a trip and is worried about how to carry it all. However, the chapters will not disappear when you read them through for the first time. They will remain accessible throughout your journey into the Bible's three worlds, which will begin in Chapter 3. We encourage you to refer back frequently to these chapters as you read through the rest of the book.

So what are the "three worlds" of the Bible? If you have read the Preface, you already know, but since most readers jump right into the first chapter, we will introduce them here more fully.

The *literary world* of the Bible is simply the text itself, apart from anything outside the text. We mean the world (or, better, worlds) created by the words on the page, by the stories, songs, sayings, letters, and the myriad other types of literature that make up the Bible. All good literature (and the Bible is, among other things, good literature) creates in readers' minds magnificent, mysterious, and often moving worlds that take on a reality of their own, whether or not they represent anything real outside the pages. If you are (or were in your younger years) a fan of J. K. Rowling's *Harry Potter* series, or if you enjoy J. R. R. Tolkien's *Lord of the Rings*, you know precisely what we mean. These books (and the movies based on them) are wildly popular because of their ability to create self-contained, enchanting worlds into which readers (and viewers) are invited to journey. Similarly, approached from this perspective, the Bible creates literary worlds for readers that beckon them to enter.

Here is an example of what we mean by the literary world. The first two chapters of the very first book of the Bible, Genesis, create fascinating worlds as they portray one of the grandest of all mysteries: the origins of the heavens and the earth. Note, for example, the building to a crescendo in the first chapter of Genesis through the repetition of the creative command by a mysterious, unseen voice, "And God said, let there be …" or the moving image of the LORD God picking up clods of earth (*adamah* in Hebrew) and breathing life into them to create the first human (*adam* in Hebrew). Such close observation of the intricate literary qualities of biblical texts (note the wordplay!) leads to an appreciation of their fascinating literary worlds. To assist you in journeying into the literary world of the Bible, we will provide a general introduction to the Bible as literature in this chapter and to methods of studying the Bible from this perspective in the next.

If the literary world is the "world within the text," the *historical world* of the Bible is the world "behind the text" or "outside the text." It is the context in which the Bible came to be written, translated, and interpreted over time, until the present. In studying the historical world of the Bible, we look for evidence outside the text that helps us answer questions such as who wrote this text, when was it written, to whom was it written, and why was it written. We also probe the text itself for evidence that links it to historical times, places, situations, and persons.

For example, to journey into the historical world of Genesis 1–2 is to develop an understanding of who might have written these chapters, why, where, when, and how. As you will learn in Chapter 3, scholars have unearthed creation texts from various ancient Near Eastern cultures that provide critical background information for understanding the historical world of these chapters. And the Genesis texts provide clues themselves that illuminate their original historical worlds.

The historical world of a biblical text also includes the complex story of its becoming part of the Bible as we know it and its interpretation until the present. What can we learn about how Genesis 1 became part of the Bible? How, for example, was it joined with Genesis 2, a quite distinct text, and the rest of the material making up the first section of the Hebrew Bible, known as the Torah? And how has this text been understood throughout the ages? How was it interpreted by early Christian writers (see, e.g., the first chapter of the Gospel of John)? Or, how did the advent of modern science affect interpretation of the "six days of creation" described in Genesis 1?

This brief description of the historical world suggests its complexity. To prepare you for your journey into this multifaceted world, we will provide, in this chapter, an overview of the history of the writing and interpretation of the Bible. In Chapter 4 you will find an introduction to the Bible's original historical context, the ancient Near East in general, and ancient Israel in particular, from approximately 2000 B.C.E. to 200 C.E.[2] In Chapter 2 we will outline the various methods scholars have developed to study the different dimensions of the historical world of the Bible.

In addition to the literary and historical worlds of the Bible, the worlds "within the text" and "behind or outside the text," you are invited to journey into a third world, the *contemporary world* of the Bible, the "world in front of the text" or "the world of the reader."[3] In one sense, there are as

---

[2] Throughout the text we will use the more general B.C.E. (Before the Common Era) and C.E. (Common Era), rather than the Christian terms B.C. (Before Christ) and A.D. (Anno Domini—in the year of the Lord), to designate dates. This is in keeping with current style in academic writing and with our commitment to a descriptive, rather than confessional, approach to the study of the Bible.

[3] For a fuller description of the three worlds, see W. Randolph Tate. *Biblical Interpretation: An Integrated Approach*, 3rd ed. Peabody, MA: Hendrickson, 2008.

many contemporary worlds of the Bible as there are readers, for each of us brings our own particular concerns and questions to the text. They inevitably shape our reading experience. We are all interested in answering the question of whether the Bible in general, or particular texts, has any relevance to our personal lives. For example, some readers today experience Genesis 1:29 as a personal challenge to commit to a vegetarian diet. Can you see why?

In another sense, each age has its own unique set of questions and approaches to understanding what the Bible means. For example, contemporary readers in many cultures bring to their reading of Genesis 1:27 attitudes and expectations concerning gender roles different from those of readers in earlier times, and their different perceptions affect how they interpret this passage. It is also important to note that different cultural experiences create different contemporary worlds for readers of the Bible. In a culture influenced strongly by modern science, readers bring different understandings of the natural world to a reading of Genesis 1–2 than do readers whose approach to nature is more traditional.

To orient readers to the contemporary world, we, in this chapter, look more closely at the shared concerns readers in modern Western cultures bring to the Bible and at the broader question, "Is the Bible true?" In the next chapter, we will survey the various methods of reading the Bible with an emphasis on the contemporary world of readers and the different uses of the Bible today. Throughout the book, at the end of each chapter, we will provide case studies and questions designed to challenge readers to explore the contemporary world of the Bible for themselves.

AN ORIENTATION TO THE LITERARY WORLD

The Jewish and the Christian Bibles

The word *Bible* derives from the Greek *biblia*, which means "books." The Bible is not a single book but rather a collection of writings. It is a library of diverse pieces of literature that were collected together as the Scripture of the Jewish and Christian communities. "Book" really meant "a scroll" in the ancient world. The Bible was originally a collection of scrolls. With the development of the codex (leaf-book), a number of books could be bound together in a single volume, and the Bible encompassed in one or more such volumes.

The Jewish Bible and the Christian Bible are not identical. For the Jewish community, the Bible is composed of twenty-four books divided into three sections (see Table 1.1): Torah (Law), Prophets (divided into Former Prophets and Latter Prophets), and Writings. An acronym drawn from the first letters of the Hebrew name for each section (*Torah, Neviim, Ketuvim*) yields the name often applied to the Jewish Bible: Tanak (or Tanakh). We will use the word *Tanak* as our primary way of describing this collection. A second name widely adopted today for the *Tanak* is *Hebrew (or Jewish) Bible*, and we will use it on occasion.

"Old Testament" is the usual Christian designation for the first half of the Christian Bible. Therefore, we will use "Old Testament" only when referring to the first section of the Christian Bible. Among Christian groups, however, there is disagreement concerning the contents of the Old Testament. Some Christian churches (Roman Catholic, Eastern Orthodox, and a few Protestant groups) add six or seven additional books (plus additions to the books of Esther and Daniel) to the twenty-four books of the Tanak. These additional works are called the *Deuterocanon* (second canon) by these groups and the *Apocrypha* (hidden writings) by other Protestant groups, whose Old Testament has the same contents as the Tanak, although arranged somewhat differently. Table 1.1 illustrates these differences.

The Christian community added twenty-seven early Christian writings to the Old Testament, which they had formerly called simply *Scripture*. The addition became known as the *New Testament*.

TABLE 1.1 The Books of the Jewish and Christian (Roman Catholic and Protestant) Bibles

Tanak (Hebrew [Jewish] Bible)	Old Testament		New Testament
	Roman Catholic	Protestant	
Torah (Torah*)	**Pentateuch**	**Pentateuch**	**Gospels**
Genesis (*Bereshith**)	Genesis	Genesis	Matthew
Exodus (*Shemoth**)	Exodus	Exodus	Mark
Leviticus (*Wayiqra**)	Leviticus	Leviticus	Luke
Numbers (*Bemidbar**)	Numbers	Numbers	John
Deuteronomy (*Debarim**)	Deuteronomy	Deuteronomy	
			Acts of the Apostles
Prophets (Neviim*)	**Historical books**	**Historical books**	**Letters of Paul**
Former			
Joshua (*Yehoshua**)	Joshua (Joshue**)	Joshua	Romans
Judges (*Shofetim**)	Judges	Judges	1 and 2 Corinthians
	Ruth	Ruth	Galatians
Samuel (*Shemuel**)	1 and 2 Samuel (1 and 2 Kings**)	1 and 2 Samuel	Ephesians
	1 and 2 Kings (3 and 4 Kings**)	1 and 2 Kings	Philippians
Kings (*Melakim**)	1 and 2 Chronicles (1 and 2 Paralipomenon**)	1 and 2 Chronicles	Colossians
		Ezra and Nehemiah	
	Ezra and Nehemiah (1 and 2 Esdras**)		1 and 2 Thessalonians
	Tobit*** (Tobian**)		
	Judith***		1 and 2 Timothy
	Esther (with additions***)	Esther	Titus
	1 and 2 Maccabees*** (sometimes placed after prophets)		Philemon
	Poetry and Wisdom	**Poetry and Wisdom**	
	Job	Job	
	Psalms	Psalms	
	Proverbs	Proverbs	
	Ecclesiastes	Ecclesiastes	
	Song of Songs (Canticle of Canticles**)	Song of Solomon	
	Wisdom of Solomon***		
	Ecclesiasticus*** (Wisdom of Jesus the Son of Sirach**)		
Latter	**Prophets**	**Prophets**	**General Epistles**
Isaiah (*Yeshayahu**)	Isaiah (Isaias**)	Isaiah	Hebrews
Jeremiah (*Yirmeyahu**)	Jeremiah (Jeremias**)	Jeremiah	James
		Lamentations	1 and 2 Peter
Ezekiel (*Yehezqel**)	Ezekiel (Ezechiel**)	Ezekiel	1, 2, 3 John
	Daniel (with supplements***)	Daniel	Jude
			The Revelation to John
Scroll of the Twelve (*Tere Asar**)	Hosea	Hosea	
	Joel	Joel	
	Amos	Amos	

Tanak (Hebrew [Jewish] Bible)	Old Testament		New Testament
	Roman Catholic	Protestant	
	Obadiah (Abdias**)	Obadiah	
	Jonah (Jonas**)	Jonah	
	Micah (Micheas**)	Micah	
	Nahum	Nahum	
	Habakkuk (Habucuc**)	Habakkuk	
	Zephaniah (Sophonias**)	Zephaniah	
	Haggai (Aggeus**)	Haggai	
	Zechariah (Zacharias**)	Zechariah	
	Malachi (Malachias**)	Malachi	
Writings (Ketuvim*)			
Psalms (*Tephillim**)			
Job (*Iyyob**)			
Proverbs (*Mishle**)			
Ruth (*Ruth**)			
Song of Solomon (Songs) (*Shir Hashirim**)			
Ecclesiastes (*Qoheleth**)			
Lamentations (*Ekah**)			
Esther (*Ester**)			
Daniel (*Daniel**)			
Ezra–Nehemiah (*Ezra–Nehemyah**)			
Chronicles (*Dibre Hayamim**)			

*Hebrew name.

**Traditional name in the Latin Vulgate.

***Deuterocanon (Apocrypha).

Notes: The Protestant Churches are those with roots in the Reformation that led them to break from the authority of the Roman Catholic Church. They recognize as canonical only those books in the Old Testament that are found in the Tanak. These include such modern churches as the Lutheran, Presbyterian, Baptist, and Methodist. However, like the Roman Catholic Church, the Church of England and other churches of the worldwide Anglican Communion (including the Episcopal Churches of America) also accept as part of their Old Testament the books of the Deuterocanon. These churches are in continuity with the pre-Reformation Church of England and therefore typically do not include themselves in the "Protestant" grouping. On the Deuterocanon (Apocrypha), see the section "Canonization" and Chapter 10.

The Eastern Orthodox Churches recognize what has been called a "third" Old Testament canon. Although not all the linguistic–ethnic churches in the Orthodox family (e.g., Greek, Syriac, Coptic, Russian, Ethiopic) agree, the most common canon among likely Orthodox readers of this book (affirmed by the Holy Synod of the Greek Orthodox Church) includes the books of the Roman Catholic Old Testament and, in addition, 1 Esdras (3 Ezra), the Prayer of Manasseh, 3 and 4 Maccabees, and Psalm 151.

Overview of the Tanak

In this section and the next, we will provide a general overview of the literary worlds of the Tanak and the New Testament. Fuller discussion of the types of literature in the Bible in general is found in Chapter 2. The literary characteristics of particular books will be highlighted in later chapters.

The first nine books of the Tanak (Genesis through Kings) have a narrative framework, recounting a story that begins with the creation of the heavens and the earth by God, continues with the formation and flourishing of the nation Israel, and concludes with the chaos of the destruction of ancient Israel.

The Torah (Genesis, Exodus, Leviticus, Numbers, and Deuteronomy) begins with a prehistory (Genesis 1–11), including accounts of cosmic origins, the first humans, a disastrous flood, restoration after the flood, and the spread of humanity. The central historical narrative of the Tanak begins with the ancestral stories (Genesis 12–50). We follow a divinely directed Abraham and Sarah and their descendants on a journey to the land of Canaan, and eventually into Egypt, where they become slaves to Pharaoh. The literature of Genesis is explored more fully in Chapter 3.

In the subsequent narrative, Moses leads an enslaved people out of Egypt (Exodus 1–18), climaxing in a dramatic encounter with God at Mount Sinai in which they enter into a covenant with the LORD, followed by a two-year stay at Mount Sinai (Ex. 19:1–Num. 10:10). Then follows a tension-filled forty-year journey through the wilderness, until the tribes of Israel stand on the verge of entering the land of promise. In the context of the sojourn at Sinai, we find extensive bodies of ritual and legal material in the form of a series of collections (such as the Book of the Covenant in Ex. 20:22–23:33 and the Holiness Code in Leviticus 17–26).

The last book of the Torah (Deuteronomy) serves as a transition to the next section of the Tanak, as Moses recounts to the people the journey on which God has led them, exhorts them to keep the law given by God, and prepares them for life in the land they are about to enter. Further discussion of the literature in Exodus, Leviticus, Numbers, and Deuteronomy is found in Chapter 4.

The section of the Tanak known as the Former Prophets (Joshua, Judges, Samuel, and Kings) recounts the dramatic story of the often violent settling of the land of Canaan by the tribes of Israel under the leadership of Joshua (Joshua 1—Judges 2), the exploits of heroic leaders known as judges who emerge to defend the tribes when they are threatened (Judges 3–21), the emergence of a unified polity, the capture of Jerusalem and the creation of a nation of Israel under King David and his son Solomon, the building of the Temple in Jerusalem, the division of the nation into the Kingdoms of Israel (in the north) and Judah (in the south), and finally the conquest of the two kingdoms by the Assyrian and Babylonian empires, culminating in the destruction of the Temple and the beginning of the exile in Babylon (Samuel, Kings). Throughout the Former Prophets, the story is told from the perspective introduced in the Book of Deuteronomy, that the nation prospers when leaders and people are faithful to the law God has revealed to them at Sinai. Hence, this section of the Tanak is often called the Deuteronomistic History by scholars. The literary qualities of these books are a topic in Chapter 5.

Each of the books of the Latter Prophets (Isaiah, Jeremiah, Ezekiel, Book of the Twelve) includes collections of the utterances and writings of the prophets, usually in poetic form, and sometimes stories about the prophets. The first three are usually called the major prophets; the Book of the Twelve encompasses the minor prophets. "Major" and "minor" refer to length, the organizing principle for collecting the prophetic books. The longest of the books (Isaiah) is placed first, while the shortest are all grouped together in the Book of the Twelve. Chapter 6 will feature a discussion of the themes and types of prophetic literature.

The final section of the Tanak, the Writings, is a quite diverse collection of literature. It includes religious poetry (Psalms and Lamentations), love poetry (Song of Songs), conventional wisdom sayings and poems (Proverbs), and skeptical wisdom (Ecclesiastes and Job). The basic characteristics of biblical poetry will be introduced in Chapter 2. Chapters 7 and 8 describe the various types of literature found in these books.

In addition, the Writings includes a group of historical books (Chronicles, Ezra, Nehemiah), called by scholars the Chronicler's History. These books revisit the story of the formation and collapse of the nation Israel, already introduced in the Former Prophets, and extends it to the return after the Babylonian exile, focusing on the rebuilding of the Jerusalem Temple, the wall of the city, and the renewal of the covenant with God. Ruth and Esther are short stories about heroic women who play crucial roles in the life of Israel. In Jewish tradition, five of the books in the Writings (Ruth, Esther, Song of Songs, Ecclesiastes, and Lamentations) are grouped together as the Megilloth, or festival scrolls, and assigned to be read at important religious holidays. The remaining book in this section (Daniel) is the only fully apocalyptic book in the Tanak. It includes visions of a dramatic end time and the beginning of a new age, the kingdom of God. The literary qualities in all these works are more fully discussed in Chapter 9.

We should note that in the Christian Old Testament the books of the Tanak are divided and rearranged after the Torah (or Pentateuch). Some of the books (Samuel, Kings, Ezra–Nehemiah, and Chronicles) are divided into two books in the Old Testament, Lamentations follows Jeremiah, and the Book of the Twelve is broken into separate books (Hosea, Joel, Amos, Obadiah, Jonah, Micah, Nahum, Habakkuk, Zephaniah, Haggai, Zechariah, and Malachi). As a result, there are thirty-nine distinct books in the Old Testament, in contrast to the twenty-four of the Tanak.

The historical books are collected together in the Old Testament (with Ruth and Esther included), followed by the poetic and wisdom books. At the end of the Old Testament are the prophetic books, with Daniel included in this grouping. Those books that look ahead to a new beginning for Israel are the culmination of the collection, creating a more effective transition to the New Testament.

The deuterocanonical (or apocryphal) books reflect the same literary variety as the Tanak. Tobit, Judith, additions to Esther, and First and Second Maccabees are placed with the historical books. Tobit and Judith are short stories, recounting the exploits of heroic figures. Maccabees extends the historical narrative begun in the Tanak. Edifying tales (Susanna and Bel and the Dragon) and poems (The Prayer of Azariah and the Song of the Three Men) are added to Daniel in the Deuterocanon. A fuller discussion of these books is found in Chapter 10.

Overview of the New Testament

The New Testament begins with four works known as gospels (Matthew, Mark, Luke, and John). Each is a narrative of the life and teachings of Jesus of Nazareth, proclaiming him to be the Christ, which means the anointed one (messiah) who fulfills the promises made by God to Israel, and the Son of God. The four gospels feature the relationship of Jesus with the twelve apostles and other close followers (including women), miracles of Jesus, parables and other teachings, and especially "passion narratives" recounting the final days in the life of Jesus, climaxing in his crucifixion and resurrection from the dead. As we shall see in Chapter 12, "gospel" (meaning "good news") is a unique type of literature, and each of the four New Testament gospels has its own distinct literary features and interpretation of the significance of Jesus. Because the Gospels of Matthew, Mark, and Luke share a common structure and point of view, they are called by scholars the synoptic ("with the same perspective") gospels, to distinguish them from the quite distinct Gospel of John.

The gospels are followed in the New Testament by a historical narrative (Acts of the Apostles) recounting the spread of the Christian gospel from Jerusalem to Rome and the growth in numbers of the followers of Jesus Christ. Acts focuses on the role of the twelve apostles of Jesus, especially Peter, and another apostle, Paul, who was commissioned by the risen Christ. As will be made clear in Chapter 13, the consensus of scholars is that the Gospel of Luke and Acts of the Apostles are two volumes in a connected historical narrative of the birth of Christianity.

Thirteen of the twenty-seven New Testament books are letters attributed to the Apostle Paul, who was instrumental in the spread of the Christian gospel beyond Israel into the Mediterranean world (although scholars disagree over which are "authentic" letters, actually written by Paul). As we shall see in Chapter 14, the Pauline letters typically follow the form of correspondence common in the Greek-speaking world of the first century C.E. In most of these letters (Romans, First and Second Corinthians, Ephesians, Philippians, Colossians, First and Second Thessalonians), Paul addresses Christian communities dotted around the Mediterranean Sea. He (or in some cases, perhaps, another early Christian leader associated with the Apostle) writes to churches he has visited or plans to visit. He gives thanks for the people's faithfulness, exhorts them to hold firm to the gospel and live as disciples of Jesus Christ, chastises them for their failings, and clarifies his understanding of the meaning of the coming and expected return of Jesus. Philemon is addressed to a friend of Paul.

Three of the letters attributed to Paul (First and Second Timothy, Titus) are addressed to other Christian missionaries and are usually called the Pastoral Letters because of their concern with leadership in the Christian churches. The other New Testament letters (Hebrews; James; First and Second Peter; First, Second, and Third John; Jude) are more general tracts on Christian themes than correspondence addressed to particular communities of Christians or individuals. They are named for either the type of audience (Hebrews) or the claimed author. The author of the Letter of James has been traditionally identified as the brother of Jesus and leader of the Christian church in Jerusalem. Peter is the apostle of Jesus prominent in the Gospels and Acts. Jude is another of the brothers of Jesus. It is generally assumed that the "John" of the first letter is not the elder identified in the other two Letters of John. The literary features of all these letters are discussed more fully in Chapter 15.

The final book of the New Testament (the Revelation to John) is, like the Book of Daniel, an apocalyptic work featuring visions of the end of the present age and, with the triumphant return of Jesus Christ, the beginning of a new age. Its literary qualities are also explored in some depth in Chapter 15.

Central Themes of the Bible

Since the Jewish and Christian Bibles are not single books but collections of works, they have a variety of literary themes, as we shall see when we discuss them in subsequent chapters. However, considered as a whole, both the Jewish and Christian Bibles have central themes woven throughout the separate books. In the most general terms, both focus on the involvement of the Creator of the universe in the unfolding story of life, especially human life. Both begin in the Book of Genesis with the origins of the cosmos and quickly move to a story revolving around God's special relationship with human beings in general and the nation of Israel in particular. It is a story of God's faithfulness, the fulfillment humans enjoy when they respond with obedience to the way of life to which God calls them, the pain and anguish humans suffer when they are disobedient, and the hope that God will not give up on rebellious humanity.

In the Tanak a central theme is God's special relationship with the people of Israel, founded first on God's promise made to a couple named Abraham and Sarah that their descendants will become a great nation with a land of their own and that through this nation (which became known as Israel) all the peoples of the earth will be blessed. Because of this special relationship, the people of Israel are expected to follow the path God reveals to them through another central figure, Moses, and reaffirmed by a number of other agents at various points in the story of the nation. However, Israel's leaders and people fail to keep these expectations, and the Tanak recounts the tragic story of God's judgment as Israel breaks up. Yet, the underlying theme of God's faithfulness reappears in a variety of contexts, creating a sense of hope that God will not abandon his recalcitrant people.

The Christian Bible reorganizes the books of the Tanak as the "Old Testament" so that at their culmination the focus is on the hope that God will act in a new and decisive way to redeem Israel. From that perspective, the New Testament is the story of a "new Israel," formed not from the physical descendants of Abraham but from all people who respond faithfully to God's new revelation. That new manifestation is, of course, Jesus Christ. Therefore, the New Testament begins with the story of the life, death, and resurrection of Jesus in its first four books (the Gospels) and follows with the account of the formation of a new community of faith founded on faith in Jesus, proclaimed not only to be the fulfillment of God's promises to Israel but the one through whom all humans are brought back to a right relationship with the Creator. The New Testament ends by looking to the return of Jesus and the creation of a "new heaven and new earth" in which the harmony God intended at the beginning will finally be realized.

AN ORIENTATION TO THE HISTORICAL WORLD

Introduction

In focusing on the historical world of the Bible, the "world behind the text," we will consider several dimensions separately throughout this book: the story of the composition of the Bible as a literary text, the story of the translation and interpretation of the Bible over the centuries, and the story of the contexts out of which the Bible emerged. In this section we will discuss each of these facets of the historical world separately.

We call the first, the story of the writing of the Bible, the literary history (not to be confused with "literary world") of the Bible. Any literary text comes into existence in a series of distinct stages. The composition of this book began with our classroom experience teaching introductory courses

Mt. Hermon. Melting snow from Mt. Hermon (9,232 ft.), located north of Israel at the southern end of the Anti-Lebanon range, feeds the Jordan and Litani Rivers. According to the Book of Joshua (11:3, 17; 12:1, 5: 13:5, 11) Mt. Hermon was the northern limit of the conquest of Canaan by the armies of Israel under Joshua's leadership. *Source:* www.BibleLandPictures.com/ Alamy

on the Bible. Each of us committed to writing down our ideas on how to study the Bible and their application to the books of the Bible. Much of what we wrote began as classroom conversations with students. Next, we reviewed each other's written contributions and combined them into a unified manuscript. Our publisher supervised the editing of the manuscript and published it in the form you are holding in your hands. Your instructor decided to use the book, and you are engaged in a process of reading and interpreting the text in your class. Similarly, contemporary scholars believe the Bible passed through a lengthy process of composition. For example, parts of the Genesis accounts of creation likely began orally, as stories told centuries before the final version we find in Genesis 1–2 was committed to writing. At this oral stage, we find legends, songs, and sayings told by storytellers, clan leaders, and other "tradents" (tradition bearers) as they are known. Next, the two separate accounts of creation in these chapters were likely written down. These "sources" were then combined into the form that became the chapters we find in the Bible. At some point, these chapters were added to others in Genesis, and eventually the five scrolls or books of the Torah were created as a distinct literary entity. The other two sections of the Tanak were joined to the Torah to create a "canon," the Jewish Bible (see the following section). The process continued with the addition of the New Testament to the Tanak (known to Christians as the Old Testament).

Even as the Bible was being composed as a written text, the second phase of the historical world was unfolding, recounted in the story of the translation and interpretation of the Bible. For example, as we have noted, the account of creation in Genesis is interpreted in the New Testament in texts such as the first chapter of the Gospel of John. After the biblical collection was closed, the interpretation of the Bible continued through the centuries until the present. Indeed, there is probably no text more interpreted than the Bible!

The Bible was written in several ancient languages. The Tanak was composed mostly in Hebrew, but with sections in a language similar to Hebrew, known as Aramaic. The New Testament was written in Greek. We have no single, original ("autograph") Hebrew, Aramaic, or Greek texts of the Bible. Rather, historians are faced with the challenge of reconstructing the most authentic text in the original language from the copies that have survived, as well as copies of ancient translations in Greek, Syriac, Latin, and so on. This process may be called textual history. The story of the translation of the Bible from the original languages into other languages is also part of its historical world.

A final dimension of the historical world of the Bible involves treating the Bible as one source among others in the process of reconstructing the historical context out of which the Bible emerged. Fortunately, archaeologists have unearthed a wealth of evidence that deepens our understanding of the history of the biblical period. For example, as you will see in Chapter 3, we have a number of creation texts from the cultures surrounding ancient Israel that illuminate for us the context of Genesis 1–2.

In this chapter, we will establish a foundation for study of these several dimensions of the historical world by describing, in general, the canonization of the Bible, its textual history, the translation of the Bible into English, and the interpretation of the Bible through the centuries. In Chapter 2 we will present the various methods used in studying the literary history of the Bible and in reconstructing the Bible's historical context. In Chapter 4 we will provide additional background on the historical context of the Bible, with overviews of the general geography and history of the ancient Near East and ancient Israel.

Canonization

How did we end up with the Tanak and the Christian Bible as we have them today (see Table 1.1)? Why were some Jewish and Christian writings included in these collections and others not? The term *canon* (which in another context can mean the laws of a religious body) is used to refer to the collections of writings deemed authoritative by a religious community. It comes originally from a Greek word meaning "rule" or "standard." A sacred canon typically establishes the standards a religious community draws on in assessing what is true and what is right for believers. Therefore, when speaking of the Bible we need to distinguish between the Jewish and Christian "canons," and within the Christian canons, among the canons recognized by different churches. A canon is considered "open" if more writings are being added to the collection, and "closed" if no more are being included.

Canonization (which can also mean the process in the Roman Catholic Church through which a saint is determined) refers in this context to the process by which a set of books came to be viewed as having sacred authority. Scholars today agree that canonization occurred over a long period of time. There were no definitive Jewish of Christian councils that formally endorsed a final canon, as scholars once thought. Since there is no one accepted view on how and why canonization occurred, we are able to give here only a very general overview of the process.

The canonization of the Tanak most likely occurred in three phases, reflecting the three divisions of the Hebrew canon (Torah, Prophets, and Writings). The five books of the Torah (Genesis, Exodus, Leviticus, Numbers, and Deuteronomy) were apparently set apart and considered authoritative not before the sixth century B.C.E. but not much after the fourth century B.C.E. The context was the period after the Babylonian Exile, which ended in 538 B.C.E., when the gathering of the traditions of the people of Israel was essential to the preservation of a sense of communal identity and purpose.

The gathering together of the section known as the Prophets, including both the historical books known as the Former Prophets (Joshua, Judges, Samuel, and Kings) and the books associated with the figures known as prophets, called the Latter Prophets (Isaiah, Jeremiah, Ezekiel [called the "major prophets"], and the Scroll of the Twelve [also known as the "minor prophets"]), probably was completed by the second century B.C.E. Ezekiel seemed to have been the most controversial among those considered for inclusion.

There is a reference to three divisions of the Tanak in the Wisdom of Jesus the Son of Sirach (see Chapter 10), written about 132 B.C.E. However, the final section of the Jewish canon, the Writings (which eventually included the Books of Psalms, Job, Proverbs, Ruth, Song of Solomon [Songs], Ecclesiastes, Lamentations, Esther, Daniel, Ezra–Nehemiah, and Chronicles) was probably not closed until well after the destruction of the Jewish Temple in Jerusalem in 70 C.E. First-century C.E. rabbis (teachers) who had established an academy at the village of Yavneh (Jamnia) may have been influential in this phase of the canonical process. However, the once widely accepted view that a council was held at Yavneh about 90 C.E. to close the Hebrew canon is no longer accepted by most scholars. Among the Writings, the suitability of the Song of Solomon, Ecclesiastes, and Esther for the canon was most hotly debated among rabbis. The rabbis apparently argued over which of these books "defiled the hands," meaning that, like the Torah scrolls, they should be considered sacred. Indeed, just which books should be included in the Writings continued to be disputed for several centuries.

Although it eventually became the collection accepted in the Jewish community, the Tanak or Hebrew Bible was not the only version of the Jewish canon. As early as the third century B.C.E., Jews who spoke Greek had begun to use their own translations of the books of the Tanak and add to them other works written in Greek but not found in the Hebrew Bible. This distinct Greek collection became known collectively as the *Septuagint* (from the Greek for "seventy" [abbreviated as LXX], based on the tradition that seventy elders were the translators). For example, the Wisdom of Solomon and Ecclesiasticus (Wisdom of Jesus the Son of Sirach) were Greek texts found in the LXX, but not the Tanak. Some of the Greek versions of the books of the Tanak (e.g., Jeremiah and Daniel) were different from their Hebrew counterparts. For many Jews in the Hellenistic or Greek-speaking world, the Septuagint rather than the Tanak was most authoritative.

The earliest reference to the three-fold canon in Christian writings is Luke 24:44, where the Gospel describes the risen Jesus referring to the Law, Prophets, and Psalms (the first book in the Writings). Most scholars date the Gospel of Luke to ca. 85–90 C.E. (see Chapter 12).

The books of the New Testament were written in Greek, and the numerous quotations from the books of the Jewish canon found in the New Testament typically follow the wording of the Septuagint. Therefore, it is likely that the Jewish canon most widely accepted in the early Christian Church was the Septuagint. However, with a single exception, the New Testament writers quote only the books of the Tanak, not any of the additional works found in the Septuagint as Scripture. This supports the notion that the Hebrew canon may have been the "Bible" in the earliest Christian Church.

Controversy over which works should be included in the Christian Old Testament continued long after the Tanak was set, as Table 1.1 illustrates. The Roman Catholic and Eastern Orthodox Churches recognize somewhat different Old Testaments, while most Protestant bodies accept as authoritative for the Old Testament only the books of the Hebrew canon and consider the other books accepted by the Roman Catholic and Eastern Orthodox Churches as apocryphal ("hidden, obscure") or part of a Deuterocanon ("second canon"). When the Protestant reformers decided to exclude the books of the Old Testament not found in the Hebrew canon, the Roman Catholic Council of Trent (1546) reaffirmed the rejected books as canonical.

The canonization of the New Testament began with the preservation of the sayings of Jesus and stories about him in the communities that proclaimed him as Christ and Lord. Gradually, these were collected and adapted, creating the works known as gospels (see Chapter 12). The four "canonical" gospels (Matthew, Mark, Luke, and John) were most likely completed in written form between 70 and 100 C.E.

Even before the gospels were written, a man known to Christian tradition as the Apostle Paul was composing letters to Christian communities he had either established or intended to visit (see Chapter 14). These letters were apparently read publicly in churches and collected. By 100 C.E. it is very possible that seven of the thirteen letters attributed to Paul in the New Testament (Romans, First and Second Corinthians, Galatians, Philippians, First Thessalonians, Philemon) had been gathered as a collection and achieved wide authority among many Christian churches.

Early in the second century C.E., one Christian theologian, Marcion, claimed that only the Gospel of Luke and some of the letters of Paul should be authoritative for Christians. He rejected the Jewish canon entirely. However, his views were not accepted by the majority of Christian leaders. Four gospels, not one, were endorsed, perhaps as the result of a compromise among groups of churches that favored one or the other of them. Other "noncanonical" gospels, such as the Gospel of Thomas, were not deemed appropriate as a guide for Christians and were not included in the New Testament (see Chapter 15).

By 200 C.E. the four gospels, the thirteen letters attributed to Paul (the seven listed above and Ephesians, Colossians, Second Thessalonians, First and Second Timothy, and Titus), and other works (the Acts of the Apostles, the First Letter of Peter and Jude, and the First Letter of John) were very likely authoritative for many Christian communities. However, the authority of other writings that were to become part of the New Testament canon remained in dispute.

It was not until 367 C.E. that, in a letter written by Athanasius, bishop of Alexandria, Egypt, we have clear evidence that the New Testament canon, with its twenty-seven books, was closed, at least for most Christians. Even then, controversy continued. Some Christian communities recognized other books not on Athanasius's list. For example, a fifth-century text includes two letters associated with Clement, a late first-century bishop of Rome, in its version of the New Testament canon. A book focusing on Christian ethics and ritual known as the Didache ("teaching") was also widely accepted as was a work known as Hermas (or the Shepherd of Hermas), a series of visions, commandments, and parables focused on the theme of repentance. Works on Athanasius's list that remained in dispute included the Letters of James, Second Peter, and Second and Third John as well as the Revelation to John.

As this overview demonstrates, canonization was gradual and controversial. Some interpreters today suggest that various faith communities (not to mention individuals) have their own effective canons, manifested both in the biblical books they draw on in their worship and reflection most frequently and in those they omit or de-emphasize. For example, some today stress biblical books and passages that focus on the "end times," while others ignore them because of their different interpretations of their relevance in the twenty-first century.

Textual History

A textual history of the Bible focuses on the copying of the Bible in its original languages—Hebrew and Aramaic (for Tanak), and Greek (for the New Testament)—and the translation of the Bible into other languages. One principal concern is to reconstruct the "original" texts (called *autographs*) of the Bible. None of the original copies of biblical books have survived. We are dependent on manuscripts in the original languages copied from earlier manuscripts ("texts") and early translations from the original languages into other ancient languages (called *versions*). These "witnesses" must be meticulously compared with one another in the effort to determine the most probable original reading of the text.

Until the late 1940s, the oldest complete Hebrew manuscript available for textual study of the Tanak dated from around 1000 C.E. The only other evidence came from the early translations, principally into Greek, Aramaic, and Latin. The main Greek translation preserved was the Septuagint, which was begun in the third century B.C.E. In the late 1940s, the discovery of a set of ancient scrolls in caves along the shore of the Dead (Salt) Sea made available an important new body of textual evidence. These scrolls, which include at least portions of every book of the Tanak except Esther (see Chapter 10), give us Hebrew manuscripts fully a thousand years older than those previously available.

The Shrine of the Book, Jerusalem. A special building was constructed at the Israel Museum, Jerusalem, to house the Dead Sea Scrolls and other important archaeological finds from the caves of the Judean wilderness. It is designed to suggest both the caves and the jars in which some of the scrolls were found. The great Isaiah scroll, a complete manuscript of the Book of Isaiah, is displayed here, topped by a replica of a scroll spindle. *Source:* David Harris/Israel Museum Jerusalem

The textual history of the New Testament is also complex, with at least 5,000 known hand-written Greek manuscripts, 10,000 manuscripts of ancient versions, and thousands of quotations in early Christian writings. There may be as many as 200,000 differences in readings among all these sources. Fortunately, nearly all of these differences are of minor significance in determining the basic meanings of the texts. The earliest textual evidence for the New Testament comes from fragments of papyri (paper made from reeds) that date to the second century C.E. These have all been discovered within the past 150 years. Manuscripts written in capital Greek letters (called *uncials*) constitute the basic and longer known body of evidence, although their importance was not appreciated until the nineteenth century. The most important are known as *Codex Sinaiticus, Codex Vaticanus* (both fourth century), and *Codex Alexandrinus* (fifth century). Other manuscripts, written in a smaller, cursive style (and called *minuscules*), date from the ninth century C.E. and later.

Textual history is the domain of specialists knowledgeable in the ancient languages and texts. Thanks to the skills of such scholars, the texts of the Tanak, Deuterocanon, and the New Testament can be reconstructed with great confidence. Readers today should know that good modern translations rest on critical texts that the final author–editors of biblical books would recognize as very close to the works that left their hands.

History of the Translation of the Bible into English

The Bible has been translated into most of the languages of larger Jewish and Christian communities throughout history. Because students using this work are probably dependent on an English translation in their study, we will survey the basic stages in the development of the English Bible. The great Saxon King Alfred patronized a translation of the Bible into Anglo-Saxon. The first complete English version of the Bible dates to around 1382 and is the work of John Wycliffe, who worked from the Latin Vulgate translation rather than the original Hebrew and Greek. Although it was enthusiastically received by the public in England, church and state authorities responded by banning Wycliffe's Bible and condemning to death any who used it. Nevertheless, 170 copies have survived.

About 150 years later, William Tyndale translated the New Testament and parts of the Old Testament from the original languages. Denied support by the Bishop of London, Tyndale received funds from a London civic official. He had to complete his work in Germany due to church pressure. When the translation reached England, it was attacked by church authorities, who said that it would lead to vice, corruption, and moral depravity. Only a few copies of the original Tyndale translation have survived. However, until the advent of modern translation, all English versions of the New Testament were essentially revisions of Tyndale's work.

The first complete English Bible to be printed was translated by Miles Coverdale and published, with the apparent blessing of King Henry VIII, in 1535. Coverdale then published the Great Bible (1539) under the license of the king and with a foreword by the Archbishop of Canterbury, Thomas Cranmer. It was ordered to be set up in each church, to the dismay of many priests, for people noisily crowded around it during services. The negative reaction of many church leaders caused King Henry to restrict Bible reading to members of the aristocracy. Under King Henry's daughter, the Catholic Mary Tudor, Cranmer and other advocates of the Great Bible were executed, and Coverdale was forced to flee. However, the Great Bible gained popularity and was revised by Protestant refugees from Mary's persecution as the Geneva Bible (1560) and the Bishops' Bible (1568).

In response to the growing popularity of English translations, Roman Catholic leaders joined together in support of a new English version, the result being the Douay Version (1606–1610).

In an effort to bring unity to an increasingly divided English church, King James I ordered a new translation of the Bible by the best scholars in the land. Apparently, forty-seven were involved, divided into several working groups. The result was a work based on the Tyndale–Coverdale versions, but with greatly heightened literary polish. The new Bible was not immediately accepted, but gradually the King James Bible (Authorized Version, 1611) acquired the status as the most widely used English Bible among Protestants.

In the nineteenth century, important new manuscripts of the Bible in the original languages were discovered, making new translations desirable. A revision of the Authorized Version (AV), based on new evidence, was produced by an interdenominational group of scholars in England and published as the Authorized Revised Version in 1885. An American revision, called the American Standard Version, appeared in 1901.

The discovery of papyrus letters and other everyday documents of Greco-Roman life showed that the Greek of the New Testament was nonliterary and conversational. This sparked a surge of translations in the twentieth century that attempted to use a simpler style than the AV. For example, in 1976 the United Bible Societies published the Bible in *Today's English Version.*

A revision of the 1885 and 1901 Standard Versions was carried out in America during the 1930s and 1940s and published in 1952 by the National Council of the Churches of Christ in America. Intended to embody the best results of modern scholarship while retaining the classic English style of the King James Version, the Revised Standard Version (RSV) was an immediate success and continues to be widely used. A committee of Roman Catholic scholars deemed the RSV appropriate for Catholic use. An ecumenical edition was issued in which Catholic authorities requested only the insertion of a note in the gospels defending the doctrine of the perpetual virginity of Mary. A continuing Standard Bible Committee of outstanding scholars periodically revises the RSV to keep it current with recent findings. It is dominated by Protestant scholars representative of the member churches of the National Council of Churches. However, it also includes representative Roman Catholic, Eastern Orthodox, and Jewish scholars. The committee produced a complete revision of the RSV entitled the New Revised Standard Version (NRSV) in 1989. According to the chairman of the committee, Bruce Metzger, the translators were guided in their revision by the maxim "as literal as possible, as free as necessary."

The discovery of the Dead Sea Scrolls was another impetus for new translations. In the past few decades there have been a number of new English translations by scholars, none of which has yet attained the popularity of the AV or the RSV and NRSV. These include the New English Bible (1970), prepared by British scholars in an effort to produce a literary translation as suited to the twentieth century as the AV was to the seventeenth; the New American Bible (1970), prepared by members of the Catholic Biblical Association and sponsored by the American bishops; the Jerusalem Bible (1966), an English translation from a French version produced by Catholic scholars; and the New American Standard Bible (1975), a revision of the 1901 version quite popular among some Protestant groups. A revised edition of the AV in modern English was issued in 1979 as the New King James Version. Another modern translation of the Bible from the original languages begun in the 1960s and widely used by contemporary Christians is the New International Version (NIV). The most recent revision of the NIV appeared in 2011.

The Jewish Publication Society in the United States produced an excellent English translation of the Tanak in 1917. The same organization launched a new translation project in the 1950s. The Torah appeared in 1962, the Prophets in 1978, and the Writings in 1982.

For students not familiar with the original languages, it is often fruitful to compare several alternative readings of difficult passages in the modern translations to see the possible range of meanings.

A problem for biblical translators is that different names for God were used in the Hebrew Bible. The general term for god in Hebrew and other similar languages is *El.* The traditions of the Tanak use this singular form and the plural form (*Elohim*) as designations for the God of Israel, as well as for other divine beings. Translators reflect this difference by translating *Elohim* as "God" when it refers to the Israelite deity and "gods" when it denotes other divine beings.

Another divine name presents more difficult problems for translators. It is the proper name for the deity used in the Hebrew Bible, usually transliterated into English as *Yahweh*. The problem is that the earliest Hebrew manuscripts were written without vowels. Thus, the proper divine name appeared as YHWH. By the time vowel signs were added to the Hebrew manuscripts of the Tanak, the custom had developed of not pronouncing the proper name of the deity. Instead, wherever YHWH appeared in the Scripture, the Hebrew word *Adonai* (Lord) was pronounced in its place. Early translations adopted this act of reverence. Thus, YHWH was read in Greek as *Kyrios* and in Latin as *Dominus*. The major English versions have followed this custom. However, Hebrew has several words of respect that may be translated "lord." To make clear where the proper divine name was used in the original Hebrew, most editions of the English Bible set the initial L in large capitals and the rest in smaller caps, yielding LORD wherever YHWH appears. We will follow this convention by using LORD wherever YHWH appears in the Hebrew text.

The term *Jehovah* appears in some translations and has become a popular name in English for the God of Israel. This form probably originated when scribes attached the vowels from *Adonai* to YHWH in Hebrew manuscripts to remind readers to say Adonai when they saw YHWH. Early translators mistook YHWH written with the vowels from Adonai as the intended name and wrote the combination to yield "Jehovah."

History of the Interpretation of the Bible

The historical world of the Bible also includes the interpretation of the Bible from the time of its writing until the present. Interpretation began even as the Bible was being written. Later books of the Tanak explained the significance of earlier writings. For example, Daniel 9 is an interpretation of the references to the seventy years of punishment after the destruction of Jerusalem in Jer. 25:11–12, 29:10. In Nehemiah 8, Ezra is described as not only reading the "Book of the Law" (presumably the Torah or some part of it) but also explaining what he read.

In the New Testament there are over 1,600 citations of the Old Testament. Because many in the earliest Christian communities believed they were living in the final years before the beginning of a new age of history, it is not surprising that the Old Testament was viewed as full of prophecies now being fulfilled. Because Christians believed Jesus was the Messiah (Christ) of Israel announced in the Tanak, the New Testament often sees predictions about Jesus in Old Testament passages and shows how they have been fulfilled.

Another type of New Testament interpretation of the Old Testament is typology, in which Old Testament persons, events, or things are seen as having counterparts in the new age that began with the coming of Jesus Christ. For example, Christ is called the New, Second, or Last Adam (e.g., 1 Cor. 15:45). Related to this is allegorical interpretation, in which an Old Testament narrative is said to have a hidden meaning that relates to a Christian theme. For example, Paul claims in Gal. 4:21–31 that the relationship between Sarah and Hagar (Genesis 16) was an allegory for the conflict between the slavery of the old covenant and the freedom of the new. The New Testament also collects quotations from the Old to illustrate given themes (e.g., Rom. 3:10–19).

Before, during, and after the New Testament period, Jewish scholars (rabbis) were developing their own methods of interpreting the Tanak. In general, interpretation was for the purpose of either *halakah* (understanding the meaning of a text as it relates to observance of authoritative custom) or *haggadah* (amplifying the text for devotional and inspirational purposes). Set rules to govern halakic interpretation were developed, but haggadic interpretation was freer. The rabbis believed that Scripture could have a multiplicity of meanings unless a matter of halakah was involved, and there

Martin Luther (1483–1546). A statue in front of the Frauenkirche in Dresden, Germany, honors the Protestant Reformer Martin Luther who played a critical role in the history of interpretation of the Bible. In addition to placing renewed importance on the authority of the Bible, he translated it from the original languages into German so that it could be more widely read and studied. *Source:* 50u15pec7a70r/Shutterstock

they debated what the one meaning was. As one rabbi wrote, interpreting Jer. 23:29, "just as a rock is split into many splinters, so also may one biblical verse convey many meanings."

In subsequent centuries interpreters typically stressed one of the following four levels of meaning in Scripture—literal, allegorical, moral, or mystical. For example, medieval Christian scholars interpreted Jerusalem in the Bible as either the earthly city (literally), the church (allegorically), the soul (morally), or the heavenly city of God (mystically).

The Protestant Reformation in Christianity caused an explosion of interest in the Bible among ordinary people. Reformers such as Martin Luther (1483–1546) and John Calvin (1509–1564) said that, approached with faith, the Bible yields to ordinary readers the living Word of God. The Bible, they said, is the preeminent authority for believers. Both of them stressed the plain meaning above the allegorical or the mystical sense, unless the passage in question was clearly meant to be taken as symbolic. Two of the results of the Reformation were translations of the Bible into the language of the people and commentaries intended for general audiences.

In response to the Reformation, the Roman Catholic Church reasserted at the Council of Trent (1545–1563) an interpretation of Scripture that stressed the authority of the church. After the Reformation, a movement called Protestant Scholasticism developed the doctrine of the *inerrancy* of Scripture to counter the Catholic emphasis on tradition. Inerrancy means that the Bible was dictated by God to human writers in a manner that overrode the human personality of authors. Therefore, the interpretation of Scripture must come from Scripture and not from the church or other human agency, for that would dilute its divine meaning. For the first time, *literal* meaning was equated with the view that the Bible is the actual, direct word of God. This approach to interpretation is called *literalism*.

The Enlightenment of the seventeenth and eighteenth centuries, which stressed reason as the test of truth, brought renewed emphasis on rational interpretation of Scripture. The Jewish philosopher Baruch Spinoza (1632–1677) argued that the Bible must be interpreted using rational and scientific principles. In particular, he said that an interpreter must take into account the original historical situations in which the biblical authors wrote. Especially in the nineteenth century, the *critical movement* (called *higher criticism* or *historical criticism*) burst forth with profound impact.

Scholars devoted themselves to the effort to reconstruct the history of the composition of Scripture, setting aside in the process such traditional notions as the view that Moses wrote the Pentateuch. In general, this movement, which continues to be very influential today, is based on the assumption that the task of interpretation is to place a document in its most likely original historical context. It tries to determine when and how the books of the Bible were written, to whom they were written, and why they were written. This approach draws on as many sources of evidence as possible about the Bible and the times in which it was written.

Throughout the latter decades of the nineteenth century and to the present, proponents of literalism have reacted strongly against "higher criticism" when they feel it threatens full appreciation of the Bible as the "Word of God." Because of their belief in the divine authorship of Scripture, they challenge the basic assumption of "higher criticism" that the Bible should be studied like other literature. "Literal interpretation" continues to be very influential, and resistance to "historical criticism" is evident in many religious communities.

In addition to the reaction against "higher criticism" on religious grounds, many scholars who recognize the important contributions of historical criticism to serious interpretation of the Bible have challenged its almost total dominance of academic study of the Bible. They point out that texts should be interpreted not only historically but also from the perspective of their inherent literary qualities and the ways in which they are understood by readers today. One result has been the development in biblical scholarship of methods of study that focus on the text itself, apart from its historical contexts. Analysis of what we call here the "literary world" of the Bible has been influenced by methods of literary analysis grouped together under the title *new criticism* or *formalism*. It focuses on "close readings" of biblical texts, emphasizing the various literary styles and techniques present in them. Still other recently developed approaches in the academic study of the Bible emphasize the role readers play in interpreting literature. Finally, influenced by recent developments in the social sciences (especially in sociology and anthropology), some modern biblical scholars have applied new approaches to the historical project of reconstructing the original contexts in which the biblical texts were written.

In the next chapter, we survey in more detail the various methods of interpretation within what has been traditionally called "historical criticism," approaches that highlight the literary and contemporary worlds of the Bible, and the new "social scientific" study of the historical world of the Bible.

As we have now seen, the historical world of the Bible has a number of possible realms. Given the limitations of an introductory text, we will not be able to devote separate attention to each area in every chapter. Subsequent chapters will focus on the original historical contexts of biblical books and the reconstruction of biblical history.

AN ORIENTATION TO THE CONTEMPORARY WORLD

Throughout the history of interpretation of the Bible, readers have been affected by the times in which they lived. Their approach to Scripture was significantly determined by the concerns and assumptions of the cultures and communities of which they were a part. We are no different. We must be aware that, as we study the Bible, our understanding is guided by the contemporary world. This is not to say that all modern readers read the Bible the same way. Within the contemporary world are a variety of different realms, some diametrically opposed. For example, a student who is a member of a Jewish or Christian community that takes a literalist approach to Scripture will read the Bible in a way considerably different from a student who comes from a nonreligious background or one in which the Bible is not seen as the literal word of God. Muslim, Buddhist, Hindu, or Humanist readers will have their own perspectives.

However, there are issues unique to the modern world that affect the questions we raise as we study Scripture, whatever our presuppositions. For example, the scientific theory of evolution has raised questions for the contemporary interpreter of Genesis 1–2 that are unique to the modern world. Interpreters disagree on how to answer these questions, but no modern reader of Genesis is completely unaffected by them.

Nor can a reader of the Bible today be divorced from the reality of the threats of the proliferation of nuclear weapons to unstable governments, nuclear devices in terrorist hands, and catastrophes in peaceful nuclear installations. These threats condition how we view biblical passages on war, peace, and the end of the present age of history, as well as the Bible in general. The dawn of a new millennium has also inspired questions about the relevance of sections of the Bible dealing with the end of the current age.

In addition, no one today is immune from the threat of international terrorism. That some are motivated by their interpretation of sacred texts to take thousands of innocent lives, as in the terrorist attacks of September 11, 2001, is an unsettling realization. Given these events, how should we understand the biblical texts describing total annihilation of enemies as well as those calling for an attitude of compassion toward those who attack you?

The worlds of science and technology, with their emphasis on natural causes and effects, invariably elicit questions with which the contemporary person wrestles in reading of the involvement of God in history and nature. Likewise, the conflict among modern political systems and the various liberation movements shape our understanding of the biblical prophets, the sayings of Jesus on wealth, and the description of the lifestyle of the early Christians in the Book of Acts.

The ecological crisis (the threatened human destruction of the balance of life in the natural world) has heightened awareness of biblical texts, such as the first chapters of Genesis, which touch on the human as well as divine relationships to nature. Likewise, concern over past and present oppression and subordination of women has led to special interest in the role of women in the Bible and in interpretation of the Bible. Among other issues contemporary readers bring to their reading of the Bible are concerns about abortion, capital punishment, and racism.

The now familiar picture of the earth as a small blue marble floating in a sea of black, which was taken from space by astronauts, is a graphic symbol of the new consciousness that is emerging.

The 9/11 Terrorist Attacks. The disturbing image of a World Trade Center tower in New York City burning after being struck by a commercial jet hijacked by terrorists on September 11, 2001, evokes profound questions in the quest to understand the contemporary world of the Bible. *Source:* Ken Tannenbaum/Shutterstock

We are more aware than ever before of the interdependence and fragility of life on "spaceship Earth." This new, global perspective is bound to affect our reading of the Bible in ways that are just now beginning to take shape.

So far, we have viewed the contemporary world of the Bible as the determiner of the concerns modern readers bring to reading it. There is another way to look at this world. The only situation to which the Bible speaks is the present. This is to raise the question of the relevance of the Bible to the twenty-first century, and of the uses to which the biblical text is put today. These will be discussed in the next chapter.

The most commonly asked question about the Bible today is probably "Is the Bible true?" The answer depends, of course, on what is meant by "truth." Today we tend to assume what might be called a "referential" understanding of truth. From that perspective, a statement is true if it refers to something that can be verified empirically. Is there evidence in the "real world" to support the statement or not? Assuming the referential approach to truth, the answer to the question "Is the Bible true?" depends on whether evidence outside the Bible can be found to support what it says. For example, approached referentially, the "truth" of stories about figures such as Abraham and Sarah in Genesis, and David and Bathsheba in Second Samuel depends on whether supporting evidence can be found to corroborate the existence of these persons and the events described in the associated texts. Did Abraham and Sarah really exist? Did they actually migrate from Mesopotamia to Canaan? Particularly in an academic setting, the "referential" understanding of truth is very important, and so it will be in this text.

However, "truth" has other meanings than the referential. Statements that are referentially "false" or at least "unverifiable" may be "true" in other respects. To simplify, let us acknowledge at this point just one other understanding of truth, that which might be called "symbolic." The symbolic truth of stories such as those previously mentioned depends not on whether they "actually happened," but on their ability to shed light on fundamental questions about the meaning of life. From this perspective, the "truth" of the narrative about David and Bathsheba depends not on whether it actually happened as described in the text, but on the insights communicated about basic questions of human nature and the divine–human relationship. Regardless of one's approach to the question of the "referential" truth of the Bible, reflection on the contemporary relevance of the Bible is surely enhanced by looking as well for the "symbolic" truth in biblical texts.

Our approach to the contemporary world in this text is to pose case studies and questions for reflection and discussion at the end of each chapter. In that way, we hope to avoid imposing our interpretation and to let the different points of view of readers come to bear. Our assumption is that reflection and discussion, informed by a study of the literary and historical worlds of the Bible, will be most fruitful.

THE PROBLEM: JOURNEYING INTO THE FIRST TWO WORLDS

In studying the Bible, it is possible to become trapped in one of the three worlds we have now identified. There is the danger of subjectivity for those unable to look beyond the contemporary world. If this world only is included in a study of the Bible, it can become a mirror for our own attitudes and prejudices. In the nineteenth century a number of biographies of Jesus were written. But as Albert Schweitzer, who was not only a missionary to Africa but also an eminent New Testament scholar, showed, most of these biographies portrayed Jesus as the reflection of the biases of the author. To a romantic writer, Jesus was an idealist; to a political radical, he was a revolutionary. Needless to say, we must be careful to avoid forcing Scripture into the mold of our own preconceptions.

A reader can also become locked into the historical world. As we have noted, it is extremely important to become aware of a text's context. But the Bible is literature, with meanings not necessarily dependent on historical setting. For example, some scholars have become so wrapped up in trying to determine the original contexts of the Psalms that they have neglected them as poems with meanings apart from the situations in which they first appeared.

Similarly, the literary world can become a place to hide from the hard questions of historical context and contemporary impact. The Book of Job, for example, should be viewed not only as a literary masterpiece, which it is, but also in terms of the context of the Wisdom Movement of Israel and the ancient Near East and from the perspective of modern events that spotlight the question of the relationship between God and evil, such as the various holocausts of modern history.

The challenge we face is to set aside (or at least be aware of) our own questions, concerns, and preconceptions, shaped by our experience of the contemporary world, long enough to travel into the world of the text itself and into the historical world in which the text came into being and through which it has passed. If we are diligent and patient in this effort, we will be rewarded with a more informed basis from which to make judgments about the relevance of the Bible today. This is not an easy journey; no one likes to travel without at least some baggage. There are no certain safeguards to avoid becoming trapped in one of the worlds. Healthy doses of humility and self-criticism are the best antidote. Let us now gear up for the journey with an introduction to the methods of studying the first two worlds of the Bible and a discussion of its uses in the contemporary world.

Summary

The approach followed in this introduction to the Bible is to distinguish three worlds of the Bible for study: literary, historical, and contemporary. By *literary world* we mean the biblical texts themselves. To describe this world ("the world within the text") is to relate the images, stories, insights, and questions we, as readers, see in these texts.

By *historical world* we mean the events, places, and people that form the context in which the Bible was written, transmitted by copyists and translators, and interpreted through the ages. To study the historical world ("the world behind or outside the text") is to use evidence within as well as outside the biblical texts themselves to better understand when, why, how, where, and by whom they were composed. To focus on these tasks is to work on the *literary history* of the Bible. In addition, study of the historical world of the Bible involves using the biblical texts as historical sources in an effort to reconstruct the general history of Israel and the ancient world.

By *contemporary world* ("the world in front of the text") we mean the assumptions, points of view, and questions modern readers bring to the Bible whenever they encounter it; the ways in which the Bible confronts and challenges us today; and the various uses to which the Bible is put in the present by individuals and communities.

In this chapter, we introduced you to the three worlds through an overview of the types of literature in the Bible; the history of the Bible's composition, translation into English, and interpretation; and the issues at stake as modern readers confront the Bible. Finally, we warned of the dangers of too much emphasis on one of these worlds to the exclusion of the others.

The three worlds approach is a tool, not an end in itself. The Bible, after all, is not neatly divisible. We recognize that a unified reading of the Bible, blending literary, historical, and contemporary concerns, is best. The challenge to any student of the Bible is to develop a mature, holistic understanding of what is unquestionably one of the most important and influential collections of writings in human history. Our conviction is that a journey into the three worlds of the text will assist a serious student in reaching that goal.

The Contemporary World

Case Study

A Discussion among Friends

A group of friends (Mary, John, and Joyce), who are in an Introduction to the Bible class together and have all read Chapter 1, are talking about whether the Bible is relevant to life in the twenty-first century and the value of the "three worlds" approach to which they have been introduced.

Mary says she is certain that the Bible has no relevance to the world today because it was written in an entirely different, prescientific world. "Of what use," she says, "is a book that resorts to supernatural explanations for everything, such as God creating the heavens and the earth, dividing the Red Sea, and raising a corpse from a grave? We know now that the world operates according to natural causes and effects. We would be better off if we left the Bible on the shelf and used our own minds to solve problems. If looking at the Bible in its literary and historical contexts exposes the Bible as unrelated to life today, I'm all for it."

John counters angrily, "Mary, if you believed, as I do, that the Bible is the inspired Word of God, you would know that not only is the Bible still relevant in the twenty-first century, it is the answer to every single problem we face. It is because so many have turned from the literal truth of the Bible that we are in the horrible mess we're in. I think that dividing the Bible into these three worlds will only confuse the plain meaning of God's word. God inspired the biblical authors to write without error,

and, through the Spirit, God can open our eyes to the truths of Scripture. That's all we need to know in order to understand how God is speaking to us through the Bible."

Joyce says, "I think you are both right, but you're both also wrong. Just because the Bible was written in a pre-scientific world, Mary, does not mean it is irrelevant today. Your position assumes that brains are a modern invention. However, it's a mistake, John, to think that the Bible has an answer for every problem, or even to assume that all its answers are still best for us today. I know the Bible condones slavery and the treatment of women as property. Does that mean slavery and viewing women as objects to be owned are still acceptable today, just because the Bible says so? And, even if we grant your theory of the literal truth of the Bible, you still have to use reason to apply it to modern situations, don't you? I really do think that the truths of the Bible are best seen through a process that includes studying the original contexts in which the various books were written and also taking seriously the type of literature you're reading. I'm really looking forward to learning more about the Bible's literary and historical worlds. I think they'll help me understand its relevance today."

With which of the friends do you most agree and why? How might each position be more fully developed to be convincing? Are there other possible positions regarding the contemporary relevance of the Bible?

Questions for Discussion and Reflection

1. What is your attitude toward the Bible as you begin this study? Have you studied the Bible previously? If so, in what context(s)? What questions do *you* bring to a study of the Bible?
2. With which of the English translations of the Bible mentioned in this chapter are you familiar? Obtain several different translations and compare their different versions of the same biblical passages (e.g., Genesis 1–2, Psalm 23, John 1:1–14). How might consulting various translations assist you in the study of the Bible?
3. It has been said that individual readers of the Bible have *private canons*, that is, biblical books and passages that they personally find most meaningful. If you have such a canon, what passages does yours include? As you study the Bible, note any texts that you find compelling enough to include in your own canon.

4. How are contemporary concerns over such issues as the ecological crisis, war, women's rights, abortion, euthanasia, sexual orientation, and hunger and homelessness likely to affect the ways in which we read the Bible today? How do peoples' attitudes toward the Bible affect the ways they approach these issues? How does your understanding of the Bible affect your position on the two issues discussed in this chapter: same-sex marriage and relationships between Islam, Judaism, and Christianity?

5. In a recent collection of essays on the question "Is the Bible true?" the authors made the following assertions.[4] With which statement(s) do you agree and/or disagree?

   a. "Whoever ... thinks that he understands the Holy Scripture, or any part of them, but puts such an interpretation on them that does not tend to build up [the] twofold love of God and our neighbor, does not understand them as he ought." (Citing St. Augustine, 354–430 C.E.)

   b. "... the truth of Scripture implies that we submit ourselves to its teachings. We trust it to guide our lives."

   c. "... Scripture is true because it discloses to us the living Word of God, that is Jesus Christ."

   d. "We must pay attention to the history behind the text, as well as to the realities of our own culture, [to understand] the truth of Scripture today."

   e. "... the root notion [in the Bible] of truth is that of something's measuring up—that is, measuring up in being or excellence. ... For example, is the exclamation 'Oh, the depth of the riches both of the wisdom and knowledge of God' a 'true exclamation?' Is the expression 'The Lord is my shepherd; I shall not want' a true expression of confidence. Does it measure up?"

   f. The truth of the Bible "... is generated in the give-and-take interaction between text and interpreter; it is not a timeless property of the text that awaits discovery by the passive reader."

6. Do you agree that there are "traps" into which the readers might fall as they study the Bible? Which of the three "worlds" described in this chapter might you be most likely to focus on, to the exclusion of others? Do you agree that, as you begin a study of the Bible, it is important to be aware of one's own questions, concerns, and preconceptions?

---

[4]Alan G. Padgett and Patrick R. Keifert, eds. *But is it All True? The Bible and the Question of Truth.* Grand Rapids, MI: Eerdmans, 2006. The citations are from pp. 71, 4, 5, 42–43, 82.

Chapter 2

Preparing for the Journey

An Orientation to the Methods of Biblical Study

Biblical Archaeology—Excavating the Buildings of Caesarea. Herod the Great built a magnificent seaport on the Mediterranean coast in the first century B.C.E. and named it Caesarea to honor Caesar Augustus. According to the New Testament Book of Acts, the Apostle Paul began and ended several of his missionary journeys in Caesarea and was brought to the city to stand trial in a Roman court. *Source:* PhotoStock-Israel/Alamy

In Chapter 1 you received an orientation to the literary, historical, and contemporary worlds of the Bible. You know what the three worlds are, but how are you to navigate your way through them? In this chapter you will encounter an overview of the various methods developed by scholars of the Bible to illuminate the literary, historical, and contemporary worlds. Together, Chapters 1 and 2 will serve as references to which you will want to return as you journey through the Bible's fascinating worlds.

First, we will examine the type of study appropriate to a journey into the literary world, the "world within the text." The goal of this approach is to understand the meanings of the literature itself. Therefore, we call this type of study *intrinsic*. The assumption of intrinsic study is that biblical texts create unique worlds through their language. The goal is to recreate through description, as faithfully as possible, the dynamics of these worlds. Because each interpreter inevitably reads texts from a certain point of view that cannot be completely divorced from the description, and because the biblical texts are rich and multifaceted, intrinsic study yields not one, but many possible readings of texts. From the perspective of intrinsic study, there is no one right or wrong description of the world of a text, but rather readings that are more or less faithful to what is actually created by the literature. Thus, the primary criterion for judging literary analysis is the text itself. In this chapter, we will clarify two methods of interpretation associated with study of the literary world (*formal criticism and rhetorical criticism*) and outline specific steps that may be taken in an introductory analysis of this world.

Study of the historical world of the Bible draws on evidence outside the Bible to reconstruct the history of which the biblical text is a part. It also utilizes the evidence found in the Bible to develop and test historical theories. We call this type of study *extrinsic* because it relates to the world outside the text. We will first focus our attention on the study of the history of the writing and collection of the books of the Bible. We will survey the following methods utilized in recreating what might be called the *literary history* of the Bible: *traditions criticism, form criticism, source criticism, redaction criticism, textual criticism*, and *canonical criticism*. We will then discuss the general historical method appropriate for using the Bible as a source for the study of the history of the periods in which it was written, emphasizing application of techniques drawn from *anthropology* and *archaeology*.

A principal value of extrinsic study is that it helps us understand what the Bible meant when it was written by exploring how it was written, for whom it was written, and what situations motivated the writing. Like intrinsic study, extrinsic study can distort texts. Zealous interpreters sometimes describe contexts that the available data do not support when other investigators check them out. The test for extrinsic study is to ask how well the reconstructed context suggested by the interpreter "fits" the available evidence—inside and outside the Bible. Your task as a reader in assessing our historical interpretation will be to analyze whether the contexts we describe are supported by the evidence we present. As with all extrinsic interpretation, we are stating what we consider the most probable reconstructions. You must ask whether we make too much or too little of the evidence.

Finally, we will discuss methods of studying the contemporary world of the Bible. We will touch briefly on several approaches developed in recent decades that strongly emphasize the role of the contemporary reader in interpreting texts: *reader-response criticism, deconstructionist criticism, liberation criticism*, and *feminist criticism*. In this chapter, we will also distinguish various uses to which contemporary readers put biblical texts: *theological, devotional, ethical, liturgical*, and *political*. Evaluation of claims about the contemporary world of the Bible is challenging and must be done carefully and respectfully. On the one hand, in a free society each reader has a right to his or her understanding of the impact of a biblical text. On the other hand, in any society that promotes the open pursuit of truth, each of us has a responsibility to subject our interpretations to the scrutiny of other readers. Hopefully, the questions at the end of this and other chapters will encourage that process.

INTRINSIC STUDY: JOURNEYING INTO THE LITERARY WORLD

Introduction

Methods of study that focus on the intrinsic worlds of biblical texts share the assumption that any text creates a world of its own. Adapting the principles of the twentieth-century school of literary analysis known as *formal* (or *new*) *criticism*, some biblical scholars have sought to describe carefully and, in some cases, meticulously those literary qualities that make each text unique. Some biblical scholars who focus on study of the literary strategies present in particular (especially poetic) texts call their method *rhetorical criticism*. In the "close readings" associated with formal study, emphasis is placed on the use of literary techniques common to all literature (such as key words, themes, and motifs) and literary devices (such as metaphors, hyperbole, and irony). Formal critics of the Bible also look for those literary features particularly characteristic of biblical literature.

Our assumption is that the place to begin an intrinsic study is with recognition of formal literary features such as genre, theme, and (surface) structure.

We have identified the following steps appropriate to an initial examination of the literary world of a biblical text:

1. establishing the boundaries of the text being studied;
2. distinguishing the type(s) of literature found in the text;
3. observing the prose and poetic qualities of the text;
4. searching for the theme(s) of the text;
5. identifying the "surface" structures of the text;
6. presenting an integrated reading of the text.

1. ESTABLISHING THE BOUNDARIES   A photographer can stand in one place and use one camera to take a variety of pictures of the same subject merely by changing the lens of the camera. In the same way, an interpreter of the Bible describing its literary worlds can present a variety of readings simply by narrowing or widening what is in view. It makes considerable difference whether the world being described is the entire Bible (Jewish or Christian), one section (such as the Torah), one book (such as Genesis), one collection of literary units within the book (such as Genesis 1–11), one single literary unit (such as Gen. 1:1–2:4), or one passage within the unit (such as Gen. 1:26–31). It is legitimate to study any of these worlds and to try to describe its unique characteristics. However, the more limited the boundaries, the more specific and detailed the description can be. Sometimes it is fruitful to compare two worlds, such as the two different accounts of creation in Genesis 1 and Genesis 2 (see Chapter 3).

In reading an intrinsic study of a biblical text, be aware of the limits of the world being described. In this work, our primary attention will be on books of the Bible and the major collections of literary units within them. However, we will sometimes change the lens and look for characteristics of sections of the Bible (such as the Torah), and sometimes even venture comments on the Bible as a whole. On a smaller scale, we will sometimes examine individual literary units as examples of recurrent types. For more detailed discussions of individual passages, readers should consult commentaries on the books, such as those recommended in the Annotated Bibliography.

2. DISTINGUISHING THE TYPE OF LITERATURE   Intrinsic study also describes the types of literature present in the world being analyzed. As a framework for this step, we will outline some of the forms of literature found in the Tanak and the New Testament.

In the Hebrew Bible we encounter many different types of literature, among them myths, legends, historical narratives, short stories, sermons, genealogies, chronicles, songs, meditations, oracles, blessings and curses, legal sayings and codes of law, prophetic sayings, proverbial sayings, poetic dialogue, and apocalyptic visions (see Table 2.1).

TABLE 2.1 Examples of Types of Literature in the Tanak

Type of Literature	Definition	Example(s) in the Tanak
Myth	Foundational story establishing values, meaning, goals	Stories of origins of cosmos, humanity (Genesis 1–2)
Legend	Story about characters or events presented as historical, but not closely verifiable	Stories of ancestors of Israel (Genesis 12–25); stories of heroes (Book of Judges)
Historical narrative	Developed accounts of past events and people	Accounts of kingdoms of Judah and Israel (Books of Samuel, Kings)
Short story	Stories with sustained plot, developed through closely connected scenes	Stories of Joseph (Genesis 37–50); Ruth, Esther
Sermon	Address by individual speaking of God and God's involvement in human life	Appeals by Moses to heed God's commandments (Deuteronomy)
Genealogy	List of names showing line of descent of people in a family, clan, tribe, or nation[*]	Table of nations (Genesis 10); descendants of Shem (Gen. 11:10–26); descendants of Levi (Ex. 6:16–25); Adam to descendants of Saul (1 Chr. 1:1–9:44)
Chronicle	Account of past events or persons presented as a list, usually using a formula	Various books of the acts of the kings, alluded to in Kings (1 Kgs. 11:41–42, 14:19–20)
Song	Poetic composition in praise of God; may have been put to music or performed	Songs of Moses and Miriam (Ex. 15:1–22); Song of Hannah (1 Sam. 2:1–10)
Meditation	Poetic reflection on a theme	Times and seasons (Ec. 3:1–9); justice of God (Psalm 73)
Oracle	Utterance from an authoritative source (in the Tanak, God) regarding what is to happen	Oracles of Balaam (Numbers 23–24); oracles against the nations (Isaiah 13–23)
Blessing	Effective pronouncement of well-being, introduced by the formula "Blessed be . . ."	Blessings of Moses (Dt. 28:1–14)
Curse	Effective pronouncement of disaster, introduced by the formula "Cursed be . . ."	Curses of Moses (Dt. 27:14–26, 28:15–19)
Oath	Ritual assurance, with conditional curse pronounced against oneself	Oath of a woman suspected of adultery (Num. 5:19–22)

[*]Some anthropologists think it is important to distinguish between linear and segmented genealogies. Linear genealogies are concerned about inheritance. Segmented genealogies tell us who was kin to whom at a particular time, and hence who we should be friendly with (and maybe who not).

Although today we use the term *myth* to speak of stories that are assumed to be false, we must set that definition aside if we are to understand the myths in the Bible and in other ancient literature. In general, myths are stories about actions of divine beings. In the Bible there are allusions to myths of this type, such as the reference to the deeds of the "sons of God" in Gen. 6:1–4. However, because the Bible acknowledges only one deity, the use of myths (which dominate other ancient Near Eastern religious texts) is restrained. Rather than developing new myths, the Bible adapts the myths of other cultures to its unique view of God. For example, as we shall see, Genesis 1 adapts a myth about creation that was common in the ancient world to a belief in one all-powerful creator. Myths often answer some of the most basic human questions, such as why are we here? Where are we going? What is the meaning of life—and of death? To call a text a myth does not mean that it is false, but rather that it is a story centering on divine action outside the realm of history. Because the Bible is primarily historical in its orientation (i.e., concerned about the world of time and space), myths are usually adapted to historical settings. For example, as we shall see, Exodus 15 adapts a myth of divine combat to a historical situation.

Many modern interpreters of religious literature use the concept of myth in a more general sense, to refer to any narrative that establishes the worldviews for people whether or not divine beings are involved. From this perspective, myths are foundational stories that establish basic values, goals, meanings, and acceptable modes of living. The interpreter who applies this broader understanding will see many myths in the Bible. For example, the stories about the ancestors of Israel in the Torah establish models of faith and practice for the people who preserved them. And the gospel accounts of Jesus might be called mythic in the sense that they provide paradigms for disciples of Jesus to follow. Although we recognize the validity of this understanding of myth, in this textbook we use *myth* in the narrower, more traditional sense just explained.

The common definition of a *legend* is an account regarded as historical, but not verifiable. Unlike myths, legends focus on human characters (but often with divine involvement). Formally, legends focus on a single event or series of events, and on a single character, pair of characters, or family. Sometimes, legends are combined into *cycles* to tell a connected story. Although concrete in form, legends often have broader implications. One type of legend focuses on ancestors who reflect in their lives the qualities the people descended from them either have or should have. The stories of the ancestors in Genesis (see Chapter 3) include such legends and cycles of legends. Other legends explain why something is the way it is. They are called *etiological legends* (legends about origins). For example, the account of the Tower of Babel in Genesis 11 is an etiological legend that explains why there are so many languages. *Hero legends* describe the exploits of memorable leaders, such as the deliverers known as "judges" (see Chapter 5).

Historical narratives are developed accounts of events and people of the past. The historical narratives of the Bible deal with events and people in the development of the nation Israel (Tanak) or early Christianity (New Testament). Critical history is an invention of the European Enlightenment (seventeenth and eighteenth centuries). There are no historical narratives in the Bible or any other ancient writings in the modern sense; that is, accounts that intend an objective, verifiable description of the past. In the Bible, historical narratives always relate the past in order to highlight an underlying meaning, usually in terms of the divine purpose. For example, the historical narrative in the early chapters of Exodus describes the deliverance of the descendants of Jacob from Egypt from the perspective of God's plan for these people. Disasters, such as the Babylonian conquest of Judah narrated in Second Kings, are presented as divine judgment on the sins of the rulers and people. Historical narrative weaves other types of literature into accounts of the past—legends, songs, stories, sayings, and so on.

The *short stories* of the Bible are distinguished from legends in that they are narratives in which a sustained plot is developed through a series of closely connected scenes. They are not historical narratives, because, although they may relate to questions of history, they move behind the scenes to focus on a more individual story. Their style is more refined and polished than the usual historical narrative. Typically, short stories do not present the deity as an onstage actor. The stories teach a moral or religious "lesson" or "lessons" in an entertaining manner. Among the short stories of the Bible are the Joseph story in Genesis 37–50 and the stories of Ruth, Esther, and, possibly, Jonah.

A *sermon* is an address by an individual that speaks of God and the divine involvement with, and purposes for, people. Sermons usually exhort people to action and challenge people to be obedient to God. In the Tanak, Deuteronomy takes the form of a series of sermons by Moses.

Genealogies are lists of names purporting to record the pedigree of an individual or the relationship among families, clans, tribes, or nations. Genealogies linking Adam ultimately to Abraham are found in Genesis 1–11, creating continuity in this collection of literary units.

Chronicles, like historical narratives, give accounts of past events and persons. However, unlike historical narratives, chronicles simply list, usually using a formula, the events and persons, with no attempt to highlight underlying causes or meanings. The Books of Chronicles are, in fact, more historical narrative than chronicle. In Kings, short excerpts from chronicles and references to the chronicles (i.e., royal court records) are used as a source for the narrative (e.g., 1 Kgs. 14:29).

The types of literature described so far tend toward prose. The rest that we will discuss are more poetic. *Songs* are poetic compositions that give indication of having been put to music or performed. For example, Exodus 15 is presented as a victory song used at the time of the Exodus from Egypt.

Meditations are long poems that do not seem to have been sung, but rather seem to reflect on various themes. Some meditations are on the Torah (such as Psalms 1 and 119). Other poems reflect on the nature and role of Wisdom (e.g., Proverbs 8 and Job 28), times and seasons (e.g., Ec. 3:1–9), old age (e.g., Ec. 12:1–8), the justice of God (e.g., Psalm 73), or creation (e.g., Job 38–39).

Oracles are utterances or pronouncements from an authoritative source about what is going to happen in the near or distant future, introduced by a formula. In the Tanak, oracles are from God. There are many prophetic oracles introduced by the formula "Thus says ..." (see Chapter 6), and a few are scattered elsewhere (as in Numbers 23–24).

Blessings and their opposite, *curses*, are also pronouncements with the formulaic introduction "Blessed be . . ." or "Cursed be . . . ." They announce well-being or disaster for persons or groups. Blessings and curses are rooted in the belief that, once uttered, they carry effective power that cannot be revoked, because they invoke the power of the divine. An example of a blessing formula is Dt. 28:6; a curse is found in Dt. 27:15–26. One recurrent type of blessing, developed into an extended poem, is the deathbed testament in which a father blesses his children (Genesis 49). *Oaths* were conditional curses pronounced against oneself to ensure the truth of a statement or the performance of an action (Ruth 1:17). The accused in a legal case might be released on taking an oath if evidence was not conclusive.

In the New Testament we find many of the same types of literature as in the Tanak. There are no *myths*, as such, in the New Testament. However, some contend that the Gospel of John adapts a myth in its portrayal of Jesus and that the Resurrection accounts and the story of the Transfiguration of Jesus are mythic. There is also dispute over which New Testament accounts should be called *legends*. The birth narratives about Jesus in Matthew and Luke seem to be the strongest candidates. The only sustained *historical narrative* is the Book of Acts, although the Passion narratives in the gospels might also be so considered. *Sermons* are found throughout the Book of Acts (e.g., 2:14–36).

There are *genealogies* of Jesus in Mt. 1:1–17 and Lk. 3:23–38. *Songs* in the New Testament are usually hymns in praise of God (Lk. 1:46–55) or Christ (e.g., Col. 1:15–20). There are no legal codes in the New Testament, but *legal sayings* are found in the Sermon on the Mount (Mt. 5–7). Although sometimes called a hymn, the prologue to the Gospel of John (1:1–18) might also be considered a *meditation* on the Word (logos) of God made flesh. The gospels have a number of *proverbial sayings* attributed to Jesus (such as Mt. 5:13–15). The beatitudes in the Sermon on the Mount (Mt. 5:3–12) are a *blessing* formula. The Book of Revelation includes *apocalyptic visions*.

However, the New Testament also introduces new types of literature (see Table 2.2). There is no precedent in the Tanak for the two most dominant literary forms of the New Testament: *gospel* (Chapter 12) and *letter* (Chapter 14). Within the gospels and letters of the New Testament, there are several other types of literature not encountered to any significant extent in the Tanak. Many of the teachings of Jesus in the gospels are in the form of *parables*, brief narratives that forcefully illustrate a point. There are but a few such narratives in the Hebrew Bible (as in 2 Sam. 12:1–6). However, parables and other sorts of anecdotes were a favorite teaching device of the rabbis of Jesus's time and later. Another common Rabbinic literary form, the *midrash*, is found in a number of New Testament books. The midrash cites or alludes to an authoritative text (in this case, from the Tanak) and applies it to a new situation. For example, in Galatians 3, Paul cites and comments on a series of passages from the Tanak. Another type of midrash is the allegorical interpretation of the story of Hagar and Sarah (found in Gal. 4:21–31). A third type of midrash is the typological interpretation, in which a correspondence is drawn between a former and a later person or event. For example, in Rom. 5:12–21, the Christ is compared and contrasted with the first man, Adam. The midrash form is also found elsewhere in the New Testament (e.g., Acts 13:16–41 and Mt. 8:16–17). In the letters, we find other literary forms not paralleled much in the Tanak. Paul also adapts *lists of virtues and vices* similar to those found in Greek ethical treatises (e.g., Col. 3:5–17).

3. OBSERVING THE LANGUAGE   In addition to distinguishing the type of literature, an intrinsic study requires sensitivity to the nature of the language of the biblical text. Because the Bible was written in languages quite different from modern English, students dependent on translations need to make a special effort to become familiar with the characteristics of biblical language that can be observed in translation.

The basic distinction to be made is between poetic and prose styles. This distinction should not be too closely drawn, because the style of biblical language defies such neat categorization. Often it is difficult to say whether a text is poetry or prose. Rather than thinking of them as categories, we should think of the distinction as two points on the same continuum. Some texts have language that tends toward the *poetic* side; others have a style that tends toward *prose*. The reader must be aware that language tending toward the poetic will be more symbolic in nature, and must be analyzed accordingly.

Poetry can be distinguished from prose by the regularity of its style. Prose language tends to have sentences of irregular length and rhythm. In general, poetic language observes conventions that give it uniformity of line length and rhythm (although the rhythm or meter of biblical poetry remains largely an unsolved mystery).

The principal convention of biblical poetry has come to be known as *parallelism*. It might better be called *balancing, seconding,* or *extending*. Biblical poetry is almost always composed of two-line (sometimes three-line) units in which the elements of the second (and third) line(s) balance the elements of the first by reasserting, strengthening, or in some other way completing them. For example, Ps. 24:3 asks:

TABLE 2.2 Examples of Types of Literature in the New Testament

Type of Literature	Definition	Example(s) in the New Testament
Historical narrative	Developed accounts of past events and people	Arrest, trial, and stoning of Stephen (Acts 6:8–15, 7:54–8:1a)
Sermon	Address by individual speaking of God and God's involvement in human life	Stephen's speech at his trial (Acts 7:1–53); Peter's summary of the gospel (Acts 10:34–43)
Genealogy	List of names showing line of descent of people in a family, clan, tribe, or nation	Descent of Jesus from Abraham and David (Mt. 1:1–17) and Adam (Lk. 3:23–38)
Song	Poetic composition in praise of God or Christ	Song of Mary (*Magnificat*) (Lk. 1:46–55), Phil. 2:6–11, Co. 1:15–20
Meditation	Poetic reflection on a theme	The Word (Logos) made flesh (Jn. 1:1–18)
Blessing	Effective pronouncement of well-being, introduced by the formula "Blessed are . . ."	The beatitudes (blessings) (Mt. 5:1–12, Luke 6:20–23); blessing of Peter (Mt. 16:17)
Curse	Effective pronouncement of disaster, introduced by the formula "Woe to . . ."	Lk. 6:24–26, 11:42–52
Proverb	Short saying, observing how life is and/or should be; often drawn from everyday life	Gal. 6:7–8
Parable	Metaphorical saying or very short story with a figurative meaning in addition to a literal sense; often with a central point	The sower (Mk. 4:3–8, Mt. 13:3–8, Lk. 8:5–8); prodigal son (Lk. 15:11–32)
Gospel	Literally, "good news." Narrative proclaiming God's saving work in the life, death, and resurrection of Jesus	Matthew, Mark, Luke, John
Letter	Literary communication, greeting and instructing a group of Christians often after or in place of a personal visit by the sender	The letters of Paul (e.g., Romans, Galatians, Philippians)
Midrash	An allusion to an authoritative text (the Tanak, in the case of the New Testament), applying it to a new situation	Promise to Abraham (Gal. 3:6–18); allegory of Hagar and Sarah (Gal. 4:21–5:2); the new Adam (Rom. 5:12–21)
List of virtues/ vices	Attributes describing either excellence or deficiency of character	Phi. 4:8, 2 Pet. 1:5–7, Col. 3:5–17
Vision	Account of sights usually hidden, as of God on the heavenly throne or of a coming new age	Rev. 4:2–11, 21:1–22:9, 2 Cor. 12:1–4
Myth[*]	Foundational story establishing values, meaning, goals	Stories of the passion (Crucifixion and Resurrection) of Jesus in the gospels
Legend[*]	Story about characters or events presented as historical, but not closely verifiable	Birth stories of Jesus (Mt. 1:18–2:18, Lk. 2:1–40)

[*]There is a controversy over whether myths and legends are among the types of literature found in the New Testament. For example, the stories of the Passion of Jesus and his birth are considered historical narratives by some scholars.

> Who shall ascend the hill of the LORD?
> And who shall stand in his holy place?

Notice how the second line balances the first, by repeating the thoughts in different words. The phrase "Who shall ascend" is balanced by "Who shall stand," and "hill of the LORD" is repeated as "his holy place."

Biblical poetry is composed then of *thought units*—words or phrases—that are structured in two (sometimes three) lines of roughly equal length. There is no rhyming. Rather, the lines are related through balancing of thought units.

Sometimes, as in the example from Psalm 24, the thought units of the first line are balanced by their repetition, in the same order, in the second line. In other couplets the second line contrasts the thought of the first, as in Pr. 20:29:

> The glory of youths is their strength,
> but the beauty of the aged is their gray hair.

Another type of balancing is *stair-like*; one part of the line is balanced in the second, but the thought is developed further. Psalm 74:23 is an example:

> Do not forget the clamor of foes,
> the uproar of adversaries
> goes up continually!

As this example shows, parallelism often has a function other than simply patterning the language. Here the notion of the rising clamor of enemies is expressed in the building, crescendo effect of the verse. It is not enough merely to categorize the type of parallelism in a biblical poem. It is important to ask how the balancing contributes to the world being created.

The larger sections of biblical poems, consisting of groups of two- or three-line units, are often called *stanzas* or *strophes*. There is no set length for the stanzas of biblical poems, although they are usually short. Sometimes a refrain marks the end of a strophe, as in Psalm 107 (vv. 8–9, 15–16, 21–22, 31–32). On occasion, there is an acrostic (alphabetic) arrangement of strophes, in which each stanza begins with a subsequent letter of the Hebrew alphabet (e.g., Psalm 119). Usually, changes in strophes are more subtly indicated by changes in subject or grammar. A reader should examine a poem to determine the stanzas in it. Each presents a scene that blends together to paint a world of words and images. By the way, selah, found in many psalms, does not seem to demarcate stanzas. We wish we knew its meaning!

As we shall see in our analyses of some biblical poems, there is often a parallelism among the stanzas of a poem, with one balancing another. (See, e.g., our discussion of Psalm 8 in Chapter 7.)

In one sense, biblical poems are like musical compositions. The arrangement is really not linear. Rather, there is a concentric ordering in which themes emerge, slip away, and then come together again. Or, similarly to paintings, poems create pictures, using words instead of lines and colors. Like a picture, a poem may have a subject, but not one that can be reduced to a neat summary. One might say that poems are like butterflies—if you try to pin them down, they die.

Because biblical poetry draws on the stock of images of ancient Israel and the ancient Near East, some of the poems need clarification. For example, "pit" is not a hole in the ground, but a metaphor for *sheol*, the dwelling place of the dead. Water imagery is often a way of speaking of the chaos that opposes the divine ordering of life and therefore threatens humanity.

The use of graphic language, including metaphor and simile, is as typical of ancient Near Eastern poetry as it is of English poetry. "As a lily among brambles, so is my love among maidens," sings the Song of Songs (2:2). Like balancing, this can be appreciated in translation. Unfortunately, many of the poetic devices of biblical poetry are lost in translation. Biblical poems make frequent and effective use of alliteration (repetition of sounds at the beginning of words or syllables), paronomasia (word plays), assonance (repetition of sounds in accented vowels), and onomatopoeia (words that sound like what they describe). Other devices, such as irony, can be noticed in translation.

Biblical poetry was meant to be spoken and heard. Even in translation its impact can be felt. When you read biblical poems, do so aloud. Try to capture the mood or feeling you find in them.

The other type of language to be observed in the Bible is *prose*. This is used principally in historical narratives and stories. It is also found in legends, myths, sermons, gospels, and letters. We can generally discern in prose a movement of thought from A to B to C, more so than in poetry. The reader observes a flow to prose and tries to understand the place of individual scenes in that movement. In narratives, a tension is usually established, heightened, and perhaps mitigated in succeeding moves until it attains a climax; then in some way it is resolved. This basic pattern can be observed again and again in biblical stories and historical narratives.

By modern standards, biblical prose is very simple and straightforward. In describing or narrating scenes, biblical stories get right to the point. There is a minimum of the background information and asides, so typical of modern stories. Biblical narrative does not very often present what characters are thinking or feeling. In fact, the biblical narrator does not intrude into the story at all (again unlike modern stories). The plot is developed through straightforward descriptions of actions, or, frequently, through reported dialogue of characters. The pace is quick. Stories are brought rapidly to a climax through a series of juxtaposed scenes, sometimes with little or nothing to connect them. For example, in the gospels, Jesus seems to "jump" from place to place with the focus on the action within the scenes rather than on the connections among them.

Given the terseness and brevity of biblical prose and its refusal to look into the thoughts and feelings of characters, readers must infer motives and intentions. Instead of telling us about the divine plan to create the nation Israel, the narrative simply begins with the LORD speaking to Abraham (Gen. 12:1–3). From this utterance, one infers the divine intention. And instead of telling us that Abraham was a man of faith, the narrative follows the divine address simply by stating what Abraham did, which implies his faith.

Another characteristic of biblical narrative prose is *foreshadowing*. Often the outcome of a story is indicated at the beginning (as when Rebecca learns that her younger son Jacob will supplant his older brother Esau). The action then revolves around how everything falls into place to bring this about. Often there is a tangled web of events that makes the outcome seem impossible. There are also interludes that heighten the tension, usually just as it seems the inevitable will be thwarted.

An important characteristic of biblical prose and poetry is *repetition*. Key words, phrases, and scenes recur, giving an indication of something to which the poem or story wants to draw our attention. Repetition also serves to build tension or add a nuance by balancing two elements. An obvious example is Psalm 150, which reverberates with the call to "Praise!" no less than twelve times. The prologue to the Book of Proverbs (1:2–6) leaves no doubt that the concern of the book is with "wisdom," but it contains a number of subtle nuances on the meaning of "wise" and "wisdom." The ancestor narrative repeats the scene of a patriarch's wife being taken by a foreign ruler no less than three times (Gen. 12:10–13:1, 20; 26:1–11), but with a different twist each time. Within a story, the repetition of a word is a clue to a central concern of the narrative, as, for example, the repetition of the word *blessing* in the Jacob story in Genesis.

Having made the distinction between poetry and prose, and described some of the major characteristics of each, we should reiterate the point with which we began. This distinction should not be pushed too far. Much prose has a poetic quality in the Bible, and much poetry has the character of prose. Nevertheless, asking whether a text is more poetic or more prose-like can be helpful in trying to understand its world.

4. SEARCHING FOR THEMES   In an intrinsic reading of a text, an interpreter should look for the theme or themes. A theme is an organizing motif that dominates a literary unit. It is not the same as the subject of a unit, but rather is a perception of how the subject is handled. In other words, a *theme* is an interpreter's word for what is seen to be dominant. It is the interpreter's responsibility to show how the perceived theme accounts for the work as it is.

An example of a theme should help to clarify this tool of intrinsic study. A reader might ask, "What is the theme of the Pentateuch?" One study suggests that it is:

> the partial fulfillment—which implies also the partial non-fulfillment—of the promise
> to or blessing of the patriarchs. The promise or blessing is both the divine initiative in a
> world where human initiatives always lead to disaster and a re-affirmation of the primal
> divine intentions for man.[1]

The themes of particular books can also be perceived. For example, the principal theme of the Song of Songs has been stated as "the paradox of love in the world."[2] In some cases, a book may even state its own theme. The theme of Paul's letter to the Romans, for example, might be drawn from 1:16, where Paul states that the gospel is the "power of God for salvation to everyone who has faith, to the Jew first and also to the Greek."

In an introductory study, the identification of themes can be a very helpful way for readers to enter the literary world of the Bible.

Related to themes, but distinct, are *motifs*. These are images that recur in texts but do not constitute the theme. Observing the principal motifs in a text is often important. For example, in the story of Joseph in Genesis, clothes, and their being put on and taken off, is a recurrent motif.

5. IDENTIFYING THE STRUCTURES   The language of texts forms patterns that can be observed, which then become maps to their literary worlds. We have already begun to discuss structure in talking of the phenomenon of parallelism or balancing, by which poetic language is patterned. In alluding to types of literature, we have also begun to speak of structures, for each literary form has a typical structure. We should discriminate between *typical structures*, that is, patterns shared by literature of a certain type (e.g., hymns), and *unique structures*, which are the individual patterns of separate texts. We will identify a unique structure when analyzing the literary world of Genesis 1 in the next chapter.

We should also discriminate between what might be called the formal or surface structures of texts, either typical or unique, and what have come to be known as *deep structures*. These are the implicit structures in the texts that manifest culturally determined or universal patterns of life and thought. In recent decades, a movement called *structuralism* has developed, and many structuralist interpretations of biblical texts have been attempted. They go beyond the scope of an introductory study (see the Annotated Bibliography).

---

[1]David J. A. Clines. *The Theme of the Pentateuch*. Sheffield, England: Journal of the Study of the Old Testament, 1978, p. 29.

[2]Marcia Falk. *Love Lyrics from the Bible: A Translation and Literary Study of the Song of Songs*. Sheffield, England: Almond Press, 1982, p. 97.

6. PRESENTING AN INTEGRATED READING   The final step in an intrinsic study is offering a reading of the text being interpreted, drawing together observations gathered from the steps just discussed as well as others. The point of intrinsic study is not merely to analyze texts but also to offer synthetic readings of them. Therefore, in our intrinsic discussions of biblical literature, we will not "run through" the steps of intrinsic study. Rather, we present synthetic readings that draw on the various insights of this type of research.

EXTRINSIC STUDY: ENTERING THE HISTORICAL WORLD

There are two types of extrinsic study of the Bible, one that focuses on the historical development of the literature itself and another that uses the Bible as a historical source (along with others) in an effort to reconstruct the history of the biblical period. They are obviously related. However, in the first area of extrinsic study, a variety of specific methods of analysis have developed.

Those methods that attempt to reconstruct the stages in the development of biblical texts can be identified as *literary history*. Although they do overlap, each type of "criticism," as it is called, focuses on a different stage in the history of biblical literature: the oral or preliterary stage, the written sources, the editing of sources into their final written form, the transmission of texts in their original languages, and the canonizing of texts.

To reconstruct the history of the biblical period, we will use the empirical method of historiography. We will draw especially on the discipline of archaeology.

Literary History

Two methods of extrinsic study aim at uncovering the earliest stage in the composition of the Bible. *Traditions criticism* seeks to reconstruct the development of individual elements (traditions) within texts to find their point of origin and to trace how they have been adapted as they have been transmitted. Although traditions criticism carries an interpreter into the written stages in the circulation of traditions, the central concern is the preliterary stage, in which traditions circulated orally. That tradition (the handing over or passing on of stories, beliefs, and practices) was important in the development of the Bible is evident in such texts as Dt. 6:20–25, where a father is instructed to pass on the Exodus tradition as an explanation of why it is important to keep the Torah, and 1 Cor. 15:1–11, where Paul writes about receiving the tradition about the Resurrection of Jesus and passing it on in his preaching.

A second method utilized in studying the early stages of the literary history of the Bible is known as *form criticism*. In contrast to the intrinsic analysis of types of literature, form critics look for clues to the context in which the text most likely functioned at the time of its writing and even earlier, at an oral stage. For example, the lament, a literary form common in the Book of Psalms (e.g., Psalms 13 and 74) and other books of the Tanak (e.g., Lamentations), implies and illuminates a ritual setting in which a personal or communal crisis is being acknowledged and mourned.

New Testament form critics have studied the gospels to determine the situations in the life of the early Christian community in which particular types of literature may have developed. For example, a form common in the gospels is the "pronouncement story" in which Jesus is confronted with a question and makes a "pronouncement" on the topic (as in Mark 12:13–17, when Jesus is asked whether it is lawful to pay taxes to the Roman emperor). The implied "life situation" may have been a dispute probably common in Christian communities over whether their loyalty to Christ should take precedence over their obligation to the Roman government.

Form criticism is most effective when there is clear confirmation of the relationship between a form and its life situation, as in the connection in the Book of Joel (in the Scroll of the Twelve) between the lament form and a ritual fast. Some scholars question the method of form criticism beyond these limited situations, because its reasoning can be circular. A form is used to postulate a life situation, and the hypothetical life situation is then drawn on to interpret the form. From the perspective of empirical history, to claim a literary form as the only evidence for a historical event is merely speculative.

Source (or *documentary*) *criticism* is a type of analysis that seeks to identify the various written sources used in the writing of the Bible, as part of the effort to reconstruct the history of the literature. The first result of this type of study was the so-called *documentary hypothesis*, which claims that behind the Pentateuch in its final form were a series of written sources and/or cycles of oral tradition combined. We will discuss this hypothesis in detail in Chapter 3. For the New Testament, source criticism has resulted in hypotheses about the sources used by the writers of the gospels (see Chapter 12) and other books.

While form criticism focuses on the life situations in which biblical texts originally emerged, and source criticism analyzes the written sources the author(s) of the text drew on in writing the text, the literary historical method known as *redaction criticism* addresses the final stage in which the text is edited. "Redaction" means "editing," so redaction critics look for evidence of the work of an editor who has combined sources together to create a text or added material to an existing text. This evidence can be helpful in analyzing the point of view of the editor(s) of a text and/or the situations to which the text as edited was most likely addressed.

Perhaps the clearest and best example of the value of redaction criticism is its application to the final stages in the composition of two of the New Testament gospels—Matthew and Luke. As we shall describe more fully in Chapter 12, source critics have determined that the authors of the Gospels of Matthew and Luke almost certainly used the Gospel of Mark and a collection of sayings of Jesus as sources. Redaction critics have been able to learn much about the perspectives from which the Gospels of Matthew and Luke were written and the contexts in and for which they were composed by comparing and contrasting how their authors drew differently on these two principal sources—Mark and the "Sayings Source."

Redaction critics also pay close attention to the introductions, conclusions, and "seams" between sections of a text for they often reveal the perspective of the text's editor. For example, the authors of Matthew and Luke preface their accounts of the ministry of Jesus with distinct stories of his birth. These introductions, added by the author/editor of each gospel, yield valuable evidence for understanding their unique perspectives.

While redaction criticism has proven more helpful in the study of the literary history of the New Testament, it has also been applied to the Tanak. For example, source critics have determined that the editors of the Chronicles most likely used the books of Samuel and Kings, or perhaps the sources on which they were based, as written sources.

Redaction criticism is most valuable in cases in which there is comparative evidence to demonstrate that sources have been edited. Elsewhere, to interpret the text as being edited is more speculative.

Textual criticism examines the transmission of works once they have been written and seeks to reconstruct the most likely original texts. This method and its results have already been discussed in Chapter 1.

Canonical criticism examines works in terms of their place in the collections deemed authoritative in the Jewish and Christian communities. The historical process did not end when books were written, but continued as they were selected and ordered canonically. For those within the communities that consider the Bible authoritative, this opens the door to seeing the Bible not merely as literature but also as Scripture. Even for those who do not recognize the authority of the Bible, canonical criticism is a reminder that the whole is more than the sum of its parts.

The Bible as a Source for History

THE EMPIRICAL HISTORICAL METHOD   The American comedian Jack Paar used to end his monologues with the question, "How was that?" To which a disembodied voice would respond, "As compared to what?" This is an illustration of the concept of *control*, which is fundamental to all scientific inquiry. Control means the introduction of a standard that permits ideas and evidence to be evaluated in an orderly manner. It is the cornerstone of any *empirical* method, that is, one that depends on observable evidence. The use of control prevents subjective preference from displacing objective discussion. Generally speaking, control permits investigators to keep their bearings.

The most fundamental question that historians seek to ask and to answer is, "What actually happened?" One may also ask how and why events transpired as they did, and question their significance for future developments. Historians may also reflect on the meaning of events for the participants, for people of a later time, or for our understanding today.

Historians ordinarily apply a form of the empirical method in the following manner. They develop a hypothesis, a statement of what may be the case (or, in history, what may have been the case). Then they examine the available evidence. In historical research, evidence (or data) often means documents. But the historian studying the ancient world (including the biblical period) must take into account archaeological data as well. Both positive and negative evidence are examined, and then judgments concerning the truth or falsity of the hypothesis are made. Alternatively, a historian can survey the available evidence and ask what the most likely explanation for its existence is. That is, the historian might try to frame an explanatory hypothesis that does the best possible job of fitting the evidence into a meaningful pattern.

HISTORICAL ANTHROPOLOGY   One element of the empirical method increasingly utilized in the historical study of the Bible is the use of models borrowed from the social sciences, particularly sociology, social psychology, and anthropology. The advantage they provide for biblical history is a variety of models of human behavior valid in different cultures. This is especially true of anthropology. We shall use anthropological models in addressing issues in biblical history, so the method we are using might also be called *historical anthropology* in some contexts. But these models, however appealing in their own right, must be warranted by evidence relevant to the topic at hand to merit empirical standing. The empirical method results in probable, not absolute, conclusions. There is always the possibility that new evidence will prove an accepted hypothesis false; suggest new, more probable, hypotheses; or raise totally new issues. The appeal of this method is always to "public information," that is, data that can be evaluated by anyone who has developed the basic skills and information required to study the subject at hand.

HISTORICAL REVISIONISM   Historians and other scholars who present views that differ markedly from commonly accepted positions are sometimes called "revisionists." If revisionist views are accepted by a majority of scholars, they become the new orthodoxy. Revisionists perform a valuable service to their disciplines even when their views are rejected because they prevent smugness and oblige persons with more traditional views to reexamine the basis of their conclusions. Sometimes traditional views are modified because of a revisionist critique even when the revisionist thesis, as such, is rejected.

The most vigorous revisionist movement in biblical studies today may be a group of scholars who argue that the historical books of Tanak were edited so late that they could contain no valid historical information about earlier periods. They differ on the cutoff date. Some would exclude the ancestral ("patriarchal") age, others the Exodus age and the settlement in Canaan, others the United Monarchy, still others the entire age of the Judean and Israelite kingdoms. Some members of this group of scholars also seem to reject or explain away archaeological data. Because they reject so much information that is accepted (with various degrees of reservation!) by other scholars, they have been dubbed "minimalists." Others outside their circle call them "nihilists." Recent minimalist interpretations have gone to the point of radically revising paleographic/epigraphic tables and widespread consensus concerning archaeological data, although they have not previously been among the more prominent experts in these fields. Some of the most distinguished professional archaeologists have been among the more vehement critics of minimalist theories, suspecting that many minimalists do not understand archaeology and its methods and do not respect its findings.

Recent discoveries seem to have further undercut the minimalist position. For example, archaeologist Eilat Mazar discovered a substantial stone wall in the City of David dated on ceramic evidence to the eleventh to tenth century B.C.E. This discovery has also stirred controversy, and Mazar's question, "Did I find King David's palace?" is clearly speculative. More conservative archaeologists refer to her discovery as "the large stone structure." From the standpoint of historical research, whether or not the stone work can be attributed to David, the important point is that there was, again contrary to minimalist doctrine, a government capable of producing works of monumental architecture during the age of the United Monarchy.[3]

BIBLICAL ARCHAEOLOGY   The area of scholarship known as archaeology is a form of historical inquiry. It may be defined as the study of human cultures through the disciplined investigation of their material remains. It is conventionally divided into prehistoric archaeology, the archaeology of preliterate cultures, and historical archaeology, which means that historical archaeology may be assisted in its inquiries by texts. *Biblical archaeology* is a branch of historical archaeology concerned with the study of the biblical world. It thus centers on the land of Israel. But from the very outset it must include the entire Fertile Crescent (see Chapter Four). The Middle East as a whole enters its purview with the Persian period, and the eastern Mediterranean world with the conquests of Alexander during the latter stages of the history underlying Tanak. During the age of Classical Judaism and

---

[3] Eliat Mazar. "Did I Find King David's Palace?" *Biblical Archaeology Review*, 32:1 (January–February 2006), 18–27, 70.

Archaeological Technique—Excavating Pottery. An archaeologist carefully prepares to remove a pot uncovered during the excavation of the Canaanite city of Ashkelon located on the coast of the Mediterranean Sea, near the city of Gaza. According to Jdg. 1:28, Ashkelon was conquered by the tribe of Judah when the Israelites occupied Canaan. *Source:* Richard T. Nowitz/Photo Researchers, Inc.

the New Testament, its purview expanded to Rome and the western Mediterranean world. Some scholars who seem uneasy with the word *biblical* have proposed alternative names, but none does justice to the scope of the inquiry. The bottom line is, biblical archaeology, like any other branch of archaeological inquiry, should exemplify the most rigorous and up-to-date methods of the discipline. The word *biblical* does not make it any less scientific than other modern archaeology. Indeed, some attacks on biblical archaeology are essentially expressions of secular humanist dogmatism.

It is no exaggeration to say that archaeology has revolutionized biblical studies over the past century and a half. Before the advent of modern archaeology in the nineteenth century, the Bible was the only text available in the West that reached into deep antiquity, prior to classical Greece. Archaeology revealed the cultures of Israel's predecessors and neighbors, some only names beforehand. The recovery of the literatures of other ancient Middle Eastern cultures has cast a great deal of light on the understanding of the Bible. Archaeology has revealed the glories of the Egyptian empire and of the great empires of Mesopotamia, as well as the more modest material culture of ancient Israel. The historical and literary discussions in this book are enriched by archaeological findings.

Archaeology in biblical lands concentrated for many years on the sites of cities, with their monumental architectural features. More recently, biblical archaeologists have turned to the investigation of smaller sites and to "environmental archaeology," the study of ancient life in its total ecological context. This has led to a much fuller understanding of how people lived, including what they ate and what parasites made them sick.

Excavation of occupation sites is the most typical activity of archaeologists. This digging is done carefully and systematically according to a controlled plan. The excavation area is typically defined by a grid survey, and the excavator attempts to follow the layers, or strata, created by successive human occupational activity. The goal is "three-dimensional recording" of all architectural features, artifacts, and environmental samples so that they can be understood in their original context. This spatial context also implies a temporal context, since one generally goes back in time as one goes down through the strata (although erosion or earlier digging may create localized dislocations). The fact that the styles of most human artifacts change through time means that an archaeological stratum may be dated by the artifacts found in it, especially pottery (and coins, after they were invented). The greatest care is always essential. "Archaeology is destruction" is an archaeologist's proverb. You can only dig a locus once, so you need to do it right the first time!

Archaeological Technique— Pottery Reconstruction. Careful study of the evolution of pottery styles in ancient Israel has created a "ceramic chronology" used by archaeologists to date the levels of a site. Here a shattered pot discovered in the ancient biblical city of Lachish is being carefully reconstructed from the broken pieces ("shards"), so that its style can be determined. *Source:* William A. Young

Archaeologists also conduct larger-scale surveys to study settlement and land use patterns, and so on. Archaeological findings must be carefully recorded in notes, sketches, scale plans, and drawings and photographs, and artifacts carefully labeled, if they are to have any scientific value. Much of the most important work goes on after the dig, when the records are collated and artifacts studied and perhaps subjected to various laboratory tests. (Carbon dating is the one scientific test used in archaeology that seems to be widely known. But there are many others, described in most archaeology textbooks.) Finally, the results must be reported in scholarly journals and books so that the results can be used and interpreted by other scholars.

New archaeological discoveries or new interpretations of older finds, some with profound implications for our understanding of biblical history, are announced almost every year. For example, in 2010, a new theory concerning the origins of the alphabets in which the languages of the Bible (Hebrew, Aramaic, and Greek) are written was advanced by Dr. Orly Goldwasser, Professor of Egyptology at the Hebrew University in Jerusalem.[4]

At a site today called Serabit el-Khadem located deep in the mountains of the southern Sinai peninsula, an Egyptian turquoise mine flourished during the reigns of the Pharaohs Amenemhet III (*ca.* 1853–1808 B.C.E.) and Amenemhet IV (*ca.* 1808–1789). At the site was a temple dedicated to Hathor, the Egyptian goddess of turquoise. On the path leading to the temple were stone pillars with inscriptions invoking the protection of Hathor and other deities on the workmen and traders who came to the mine from Egypt to the south and various "Asiatic" cultures, including the Canaanites, to the north. Most of the inscriptions are in Egyptian hieroglyphics. However, some are in a new form of writing, a set of simple pictograms representing sounds, mostly adapted from the hieroglyphs, called Proto-Sinaitic by scholars. According to Prof. Goldwasser, the signs were likely developed by Canaanite workers at Seraphis who were unable to read or write Egyptian hieroglyphs.

According to Prof. Goldwasser and experts on ancient writing who have studied them, these inscriptions may be the first evidence of the creation of the alphabet, a writing system with fewer than 30 signs and straightforward rules associating signs with the sounds produced by consonants (vowels came later). By contrast, to read the hieroglyphs of Egypt and wedge shapes impressed in clay (cuneiforms) of Mesopotamia, the two systems prevalent at the time, required knowledge of hundreds of signs and complex rules. With the alphabetic system, writing would no longer be under the control of professional scribes and would become available to many more people.

The alphabetic system took many centuries and other influences to evolve in various forms. However, if this theory is correct, all three of the languages of the Jewish and Christian Bibles (Hebrew, Aramaic, and Greek) were among the heirs of what may be called a "democratic" system of writing developed by Canaanite workers engaged in dangerous work in a desolate area, who were invoking divine blessing and protection.

Another theory based on interpretation of archaeological finds dating back decades has recently gained wide attention, especially among those interested in issues related to gender in biblical times. The theory, popularized by American archaeologist William Dever, relates to his proposition that in ancient Israel a distinction existed between "elite" or "priestly" religion and "popular" or "folk" religions. According to Dever "elite" religion dominated the class that wrote the Tanak and took a mostly monotheistic perspective, condemning worship of any god other than the Israelite deity Yahweh. "Folk" religion is not represented as clearly in the Tanak (except where it is denounced), but is manifest in a variety of archaeological finds. In making the claim that has drawn the most attention, Dever draws on a growing body of archaeological research to defend the theory,

[4]Orly Goldwasser. "How the Alphabet Was Born from Hieroglyphs." *Biblical Archaeology Review*, 36:2 (March/April 2010). Available online at www.bib-arch.org/bar.

first developed in the 1960s, that most Israelites worshipped a number of gods, including a goddess, consort of the god Yahweh, often called Asherah. In other words, in the folk religion of ancient Israel, "God had a wife."[5]

The fact that archaeological finds are sometimes valuable has created an international industry consisting of clandestine diggers, smugglers, and shady antiquities dealers in addition to a network of legitimate dealers around the world. The purchasers of what might be called undocumented, and in some cases illicit, antiquities are usually private collectors. However, some prominent museums have been caught with objects of dubious pedigree, and there have been celebrated lawsuits in which museums have been obliged to return objects to the country of origin. The looting of antiquities sites is a worldwide phenomenon.

The value of artifacts has also led to the creation of faked artifacts. The most spectacular alleged forgery in recent biblical archaeology is the so-called James Ossuary. Ossuaries are small stone boxes used to store bones after a body has decayed in order to allow the burial space to be reused. Many were inscribed with the names of those whose bones they contained. Ossuaries were common in Israel during the first century of the common era. In 2002 an ossuary emerged bearing the inscription "James son of Joseph, brother of Jesus."

The implicit New Testament connection of the James Ossuary created an immediate international sensation, and it was soon claimed that it provided the first physical link to the family of Jesus. The box was put on display and made the subject of a television documentary (see Chapter 16). The Israel Antiquities Authority (IAA) responded to it by carefully examining the ossuary scientifically and concluded that while the box came from the first century, the inscription was a modern hoax. However, other scholars challenged the findings, and the ongoing debate resulted in a series of publications.[6]

In 2005 five men, among them respected antiquities collectors, were charged with forging the James Ossuary and trying to pass it off as the actual burial box of the brother of Jesus. Prosecutors claimed they had uncovered an international criminal network making millions or dollars in forged antiquities. Prominent scholars were named as complicit in the conspiracy. Six years later the trial was still dragging on in the Jerusalem District Court, with only two of the five defendants remaining and many of the original charges retracted. Archaeologists and other scholars have testified, both defending and challenging the ossuary's authenticity.

USES OF THE TEXT: TRAVELING INTO THE CONTEMPORARY WORLD

Several specific methods have been developed recently, stressing the role readers play in determining the meaning of texts. They illustrate the attention now being given to redefining our understanding of the "contemporary world" of the Bible.

---

[5]William G. Dever. *Did God Have a Wife? Archaeology and Folk Religion in Ancient Israel.* Grand Rapids, MI: Eerdmans, 2008. See also Raphael Patai. *The Hebrew Goddess,* 3rd ed. Wayne State University Press, 1990 (first published 1967); Mark S. Smith. *The Early History of God: Yahweh and the Other Deities in Ancient Israel.* Grand Rapids, MI: Eerdmans, 2002.

[6]See, for example, Hershel Shanks and Ben Witherington. *The Brother of Jesus: The Dramatic Story and Meaning of the First Archaeological Link to Jesus and His Family.* San Francisco: HaperSanFrancisco, 2003; Nina Burleigh. *Unholy Business: A True Tale of Faith, Greed, and Forgery in the Holy Land.* New York: Smithsonian Books/Collins, 2008; and Ryan Byrne and Bernadette McNary-Zak, ed. *Resurrecting the Brother of Jesus: The James Ossuary Controversy and the Quest for Religious Relics.* Chapel Hill: University of North Carolina Press, 2009. Shanks and Witherington consider the James Ossuary authentic, while the other volumes conclude that it is a fake. For the most recent developments in the James Ossuary controversy, see http://jamesossuarytrial.blogspot.com.

Reader-response (or *reception*) *criticism* argues that the meaning of a text is not a given, residing in the text itself or in its historical context, but in the unique interaction between a particular reader (or group of readers) in a particular situation with the text. These critics emphasize the dynamics of "the reading experience" and point out that readers are often required to "fill the gaps" in a text, to interpret not only what is present but also what is missing.

One of the most controversial types of modern interpretation is known as *deconstruction* (or *poststructuralism*). From our perspective, it is a methodology appropriate to the "contemporary world." Those who practice "deconstruction" resist any one definition of the method (and indeed often refuse to call it a "method"), and its critics complain vigorously about the incomprehensibility of the writings of deconstructionists, so the following description is at best a hint at its complexity. Emphasizing the ambiguity in both texts and the interpretation of texts, "deconstructive" critics argue that readers actually create their own texts in their encounters with literature. Thus, the idea of fixed texts and "canons" of authoritative literature with set meanings must be "deconstructed," replaced by awareness that all texts have an "excess of meaning" that continually spills over as they are encountered by particular readers. Deconstruction theory also includes the contention that classical literature produced in Western culture (including the Bible) is built on binary oppositions (such as soul/body, male/female, white/nonwhite, and rational/irrational) in which the first term is assumed to be superior to the second. Therefore, deconstructionists seek to break through these oppositions by seeking out and emphasizing the marginal elements within texts and bodies of literature. Influenced by this theory, interpreters challenge the idea that there are classical texts such as the Bible and works of Shakespeare that deserve to be studied on their own merits. They turn instead to the writings of oppressed peoples—minorities and women, for example. In "classical" texts, such as the Bible, they look for the marginal elements, the seemingly absurd and irrational, which are devalued in traditional critical interpretation.

Deconstructive readers also assert that *texts* are not limited to written works. Anything that "signifies" is a text. From this perspective, virtually anyone or anything is a text, for everything signifies. Some deconstructive critics speak of *intertextuality*, which means that, for each reader, any "text" is actually a constantly changing web of many texts (including, as one of these texts, the reader's own experience). Readers create their sense of meaning in relation to this fluid network of texts.

By *liberation criticism* we mean approaches to interpreting the meaning of the Bible from the context of one or more oppressed groups in the world today. All forms of liberation criticism affirm that the Bible takes the side of those who are victims of oppression and calls for their liberation. They contend that interpretation of the Bible must emerge from and speak to the actual experience of the weak and powerless. For example, a number of liberation critics have written in the context of the experience of the poor in Latin America. Others speak from the perspective of other oppressed communities. Another branch of liberation criticism approaches the Bible from the perspective of African Americans. All movements within "liberation theology," as this method is also called, emphasize that the criterion for evaluating all reading of the Bible is *praxis* ("action"). In other words, study of the Bible must lead to involvement in God's work of liberating the poor from oppression.

Another emerging group of methods for studying biblical texts, which might be considered as a branch within liberation criticism but is also widely considered an independent school, is called *feminist criticism*. All forms of feminist criticism share the conviction that the Bible itself, and virtually all interpretations of the Bible, have, until recent times, reflected the ideology of (white) male dominance (patriarchy). Feminist critics may use various forms of extrinsic and intrinsic analysis in their work, but they are united in the goals of exposing patriarchy in the Bible and its interpretation, and finding alternatives that support the dignity and equality of women, children, and racial–ethnic minorities. This agenda places feminist criticism, in general, within the contemporary world of the Bible.

One feminist scholar has identified five contemporary perspectives among those who emphasize the patriarchal context in which the Bible was written[7]:

1. ***Rejectionist:*** The Bible must be rejected as a source of authority for contemporary society because of its unrelentingly negative attitude toward, and portrayal of, women. Contemporary interpreters must expose the patriarchy of the Bible and point the way to new sources of inspiration that take a positive perspective toward women.

2. ***Loyalist:*** Since the Bible is the Word of God, it cannot by nature be oppressive, because God is not oppressive; when the Bible is used to support the submission of women today, the fault is with the interpreter, not the text. Interpreters should recognize and emphasize that the basic themes in the Bible support gender equality, despite the patriarchal perspectives evident in particular texts.

3. ***Revisionist:*** A positive perspective toward women is evident not only in general themes but also in particular biblical texts. However, the crucial role of women, often evident in the Bible, has been obscured by the ancient patriarchy at the time the Bible was written and also by the androcentric attitude of interpreters throughout history. Contemporary interpreters must, at times, be willing to "read between the lines" of the predominantly patriarchal biblical text to recover a portrayal of women that is healthy and empowering.

4. ***Sublimationist:*** There is, in biblical symbolism, a glorification of the feminine, found in imagery for God, Christ (in the New Testament), and also people of faith (e.g., Israel as the bride of God in the Tanak or the Christian Church as the bride of Christ in the New Testament).

5. ***Liberationist:*** This approach joins with the perspective mentioned above to emphasize that the biblical proclamation of God's liberation of the oppressed peoples includes freeing women from patriarchal domination.

Another important dimension of the reading of the Bible in the contemporary world is the question of the various uses of the Bible. Religious texts, such as the Bible, have typically been put to at least two types of uses. These might be described as the *theological* and the *devotional.* The theological is the derivation of authoritative religious teaching from the text, as when theologians derive the doctrine that the world was created out of nothing from the biblical accounts of creation, or the doctrine of the Trinity from the New Testament language about the relationship between God the Father, Jesus, and the Holy Spirit. The devotional use of religious texts may be either communal or individual, but its purpose is personal and experiential rather than intellectual. That is, persons are led to some sort of religious experience or insight through devotional study. The Bible is also frequently used in the development of *ethical* teachings. The Bible includes numerous direct ethical guidelines, such as the injunction found in both the Tanak and New Testament to "love your neighbor." In addition, interpreters find implicit instruction on virtually every ethical issue, from birth control to euthanasia. However, it must be noted that advocates of variant ethical perspectives contend that the Bible supports their positions.

In addition to theological, devotional, and ethical uses, some religious texts are suited to *liturgical* use, that is, use in worship. Lessons from the Bible are read in Jewish and Christian services. Psalms and other sections of Scripture may be sung, chanted, or read. At the most intense level, biblical texts may serve as the basis for the recreation of the events they describe. For example, the Jewish Passover makes liturgical use of the biblical account of the deliverance from Egypt so that worshippers can sense themselves in the same situation as those who were a part of the original Exodus.

---

[7]Carolyn Osiek. "The Feminist and the Bible: Hermeneutical Alternatives." *Feminist Perspectives on Biblical Scholarship*, ed. Adela Yarbro Collins. Chico, CA: Scholars Press, 1985, 97–105.

The Christian sacrament of Holy Communion (the Eucharist, or the Lord's Supper) makes liturgical use of New Testament passages to reenact the Passover meal Jesus ate with his Disciples before he died. Liturgical use can "remember"; it can also "anticipate." Both Passover and Communion have dimensions of looking ahead to a time of future deliverance, giving participants a foretaste of the Messianic Age or the Kingdom of God.

Another use of the Bible may be called *political.* Whenever interpreters appeal to Scripture to support a particular action by, for, or against governing authority, they are using the Bible politically. For example, opponents of abortion have used the Bible to support action aimed at ending legalized abortions. And proponents of government action to assist the hungry and homeless have drawn on the Bible to support their positions.

All these uses of the Bible that attempt to derive a contemporary meaning from texts have their proper place. They "misfire" when their uses or appropriate places of application are confused. There will be no deliberate theological, ethical, devotional, or political use of the biblical texts in this work because our concern is to describe objectively the literary and historical worlds of the Bible. However, we recognize that these questions are important and of great interest to many readers. Therefore, we will conclude each chapter with questions for reflection and discussion, some of which will raise issues of theological and devotional interpretation. If this book is being used in a group setting, we suggest that the various views of all participants as to the proper theological and devotional interpretation of texts be heard and respected. However, on questions of literary and historical interpretation, we suggest you be less cordial. You can, and should, discuss vigorously various alternative literary and historical interpretations of texts, those in this work and others. But the bottom line in descriptive study is "What does the *evidence* support?" That should always be the question.

We have now surveyed the three worlds of the Bible and the methods appropriate to studying them. We have distinguished the literary, the historical, and the contemporary worlds and charted a course for entering them. Now let us begin the journey.

Summary

Having introduced the reader to the literary, historical, and contemporary worlds of the Bible in Chapter 1, in Chapter 2 we outlined the methods of study appropriate to these worlds. We called examination of the literary world *intrinsic study,* since the focus is *within* the biblical texts themselves. We described two recently developed methods that focus on texts themselves: formal criticism and rhetorical criticism. We then identified the steps appropriate to an introductory study of the literary world. In an intrinsic study, one must establish the boundaries of the text being described, distinguish the type(s) of literature within the text chosen for analysis, pay attention to the poetic or prose character of the text, identify the theme(s) present as appropriate, and analyze the structure of the text. The goal of intrinsic study is a synthetic reading of the text, drawing together the various observations made of the text itself.

Study of the historical world is *extrinsic,* focusing on the relationship between the text and evidence *outside* the text. Scholars have developed a number of methods of study useful in reconstructing the history of the composition of the Bible. In this chapter, we briefly described each of these methods and its role in reconstructing the *literary history* of the Bible: traditions criticism, form criticism, source criticism, redaction criticism, textual criticism, and canonical criticism. In this chapter, we also discussed the way in which historians use the *empirical method* and the insights of the social sciences (especially *anthropology*) in an effort to reconstruct the historical world of the Bible. We focused special attention on the discipline of *biblical archaeology.*

Finally, in this chapter we identified several methods of study appropriate to the contemporary world of the text (reader-response criticism, deconstruction, liberation criticism, and feminist criticism) and some of the contemporary uses of the Bible—theological, devotional, ethical, liturgical, and political. We encouraged readers to engage in open, respectful discussion of the various meanings of the Bible for contemporary life. Our hope is that the descriptions of the literary and historical worlds of the Bible in the remaining chapters will provide helpful background information for such discussion. We intend the questions at the end of each chapter to provoke both individual reflection and group discussion of the contemporary world of the Bible. These questions are suggestions and certainly do not exhaust the possible issues serious readers may wish to raise about the meanings of the Bible for our time.

The Contemporary World

Case Study

The Three Worlds of Psalm 150

To develop a better sense of the method of studying the Bible adopted in this book, read Psalm 150, and reflect on/discuss its literary, historical, and contemporary worlds. Referring to some of the biblical commentaries mentioned in the Annotated Bibliography would be helpful, but first, try to draw on your own initial understanding of the various methods of study introduced in this chapter, with the help of the following observations.

To appreciate the literary world of Psalm 150, discuss its poetic style (note the effect of poetic balancing in the psalm, the series of imperatives, and its musical imagery), the central theme of the poem (how does it answer questions of praising God in terms of where, why, how, and who?), and its structure (note the enclosing frame created by the repetition of a phrase creating a sense of order, but also its open-ended quality as an extended call to praise).

A discussion of the literary history of the psalm might include the question of why this psalm was placed at the end of the Book of Psalms, especially when it has an open ending. Try also to draw on what you find in the psalm and in commentaries to understand the manner of worship in ancient Israel. What were the instruments described? Where was the sanctuary described and what occurred there?

After a literary and historical study of Psalm 150, engage in reflection on/discussion of its contemporary world. What guidance does the psalm offer for structuring contemporary worship services? Do you see any implications for addressing the contemporary environmental crisis in the way the psalm describes the extent of the congregation praising God?

Here are a few other texts you might use as a basis for developing initial familiarity with the "three worlds" approach to the study of the Bible: Genesis 12:10–20, Amos 1–2, Mark 1:1–15, and Philippians 2:1–11.

Questions for Discussion and Reflection

1. This chapter introduced you to an array of methods of studying the three worlds of the Bible. Do you think it is important to have a clearly defined "method" when you study the Bible? At this initial stage of your study, which of the methods described in this chapter do you find most intriguing and most confusing?
2. Have you had experience in "intrinsic" study of the Bible or other literature? Do you agree that approaching the Bible "intrinsically" will enhance your understanding of the Bible as literature? Practice a little "intrinsic" analysis on an art form you have recently experienced and enjoyed: a movie, a song, or a book.

Try to describe the "world" created by this art form, without reference to anything outside the piece.
3. Have you had experience in "extrinsic" study of the Bible or other literary texts? Try raising some "extrinsic" questions about the same art form you used in your experiment with "intrinsic" analysis. What do you know about how it was composed, who created it, why it came into being, its intended "audience," and how it might be interpreted by different persons?
4. To begin to develop a sense of the complexity of the "literary history" of the Bible, try reconstructing the "literary history" of a story in a daily newspaper. What

stages might the story pass through between the events reported and the actual publication of the paper?

5. A prominent twentieth-century biblical scholar once said, "I cannot take the Bible literally, but I do try to take it seriously." What do you think this interpreter meant by this distinction? Are there types of literature that need to be taken literally in order to be taken seriously? If so, is the Bible this type of literature?

6. What has been your experience with any of the following "uses" of the Bible—theological, devotional, ethical, liturgical, and political? Which do you think is the most important "use" of the Bible today? Have

you observed situations in which you felt the Bible was "misused?"

7. What is your initial response to the various methods mentioned in this chapter of studying the contemporary world of the Bible? Do you think they might assist in understanding the contemporary significance of biblical texts? On the other hand, are you concerned that they might cause confusion about what the Bible means today?

8. Look further into the controversy regarding the "James Ossuary" and formulate your own position on whether it is authentic or a hoax.

Chapter 3

Origins

The Book of Genesis

Great Ziggurat of Ur. Located in southern Mesopotamia, Ur was an important city from Sumerian times. The ziggurat was a great earthen pyramid or artificial mountain used in rituals to symbolically connect heaven end earth. Shrines were situated on top and at the base. A ruined ziggurat may underlie the Tower of Babel story in Gen. 11:1–9. Genesis 11:27–31 identifies "Ur of the Chaldeans" as Abraham's ancestral home. *Source:* Courtesy of the Penn Museum, image #AAAFOAW0.

The Book of Genesis is an account of the creation of the universe (Genesis 1–2), the origins of human communities (Genesis 3–11), and the beginnings of the people set apart by God (Genesis 12–50). The focus gradually narrows from the entire cosmos to one couple, Abraham and Sarah, and then begins to widen again. In this chapter, we will examine the literary and historical worlds of each of these sections before raising questions related to the contemporary world of Genesis.

PREHISTORY: COSMIC ORIGINS (GENESIS 1–2)

The Literary World: Balance in Genesis 1–2

The theme of the first two chapters of Genesis is the creation of the heavens and the earth by the one God. A subtheme is humankind's special place in this creation. However, there is not one creation account, but two, different in both content and style. To describe the literary world of Genesis 1–2 is to compare and contrast these two narratives.

The first account (1:1–2:4a) is patterned as six "days" of creation followed by a seventh day on which the creator rests. Then, there is a transitional statement (2:4b) that sums up the first account and introduces the second. In the second account (2:4b–25), creation is described again, with the focus on the origins of humanity and other living creatures.

There are significant differences in the content of the two creation stories. In Genesis 1 the order of creation is light, heaven, earth, vegetation, sun, moon, stars, sea creatures, birds, land animals, and humanity. In Genesis 2 the stage is entirely the earth. In this second story the creation of humanity precedes the creation of vegetation and animal life. In Genesis 1 the creation of humanity is a single act, with the suggestion that male and female were created simultaneously. In Genesis 2 the creation of man and that of woman are separate acts. In the first chapter creation is preceded by watery chaos and begins when these waters are divided. In the second chapter the precreation situation is a dry desert; creation begins with the land being watered. In the first account the creator is identified simply as God (Elohim). God is present in the account only through the commands that cause the creative acts to occur. In the second account the creator is called Lord God (YHWH Elohim), adding the proper name of the deity to the general designation. YHWH Elohim is intimately involved in the happenings; creation is a hands-on experience for the deity. Like a potter, the deity forms man from clods of earth. YHWH Elohim breathes the breath of life into man and shows concern about man's solitude. Like a surgeon, the deity takes a rib from man to make a helper suitable for him. A careful reader will find other differences in the content of the two chapters.

The two accounts also differ stylistically. The first is precisely choreographed. The days are numbered, like the scenes of a drama. Each day is carefully patterned, beginning with the divine utterance ("And God said …") and ending with a refrain ("It was evening and it was morning …") and, on all but one day, the phrase "And God saw that it was good," or, on the sixth day, "very good." Each act of creation results in a pair of opposites: darkness and light, night and day, evening and morning, water and sky, sea and dry land, sun and moon, grass and trees, birds and sea creatures, beasts of the field and creeping things of the earth, and human male and female.

The six days of creation are likewise balanced into a pair of three-day sets. In the first set a context is established for creation. In the second set the actors appear, climaxing with the entrance of the lead character on the earthly stage—humankind. The following table shows how Genesis 1 is structured:

Setting	Characters
Day 1: light	Day 4: luminaries
Day 2: sea and heaven	Day 5: sea creatures and birds
Day 3: dry land	Day 6: land animals and humankind

Before creation, there was a formless chaos. After creation, there is an orderly cosmos. It is not rigid and static. There is process within it. It is a lawful universe that does not require periodic divine intervention to keep it on track. Further, God has placed within it his human agents, formed in his own creative image and charged to enhance the level of order. At this point the creator rests, and in so doing sanctifies a humane institution, the Sabbath day of rest for both humans and domestic animals.

The second account (2:4b–25) has a narrower focus and a much different style. It is a story, not a description. Everything takes place more or less at once, "in the day that the LORD God made the heavens and the earth." There is no ordering, no balance, no careful symmetry. Man is created; then the creator goes about developing a place for him (the Garden), food, and companions. There is spontaneity in this account, as though the creator is pursuing an experimental process. In the first account the divine architect-engineer lays out the blueprints and watches as the commands are carried out, saying as each step is completed, "That's just the way I planned it!" In the second account the divine artist starts with a central theme (man), and then fills in the background to complete the picture. In the first account there is no real tension; everything is in its place, balanced and harmonious. In the second account tensions are quickly established. The man is commanded not to eat the fruit of one of the trees of the Garden. He is alone, in need of companionship. The second tension is resolved with the creation of woman. But the first tension is left unresolved. Will man and woman eat the forbidden fruit? The way is opened to the next, connected scene.

The following table summarizes some of the key differences in the two Genesis accounts of creation:

	Genesis 1:1–2:4a	Genesis 2:4b–25
Initial condition	Wet	Dry
Name for deity	God	LORD God
Creation	By command of a removed, divine CEO	Hands-on involvement of divine artist
Order	Humans last	Humans first
Humanity	Male and female together	First male, and then female
Style	Repetition of "And God said …" with description of what was created each day in balanced format	Story, with unfolding plot

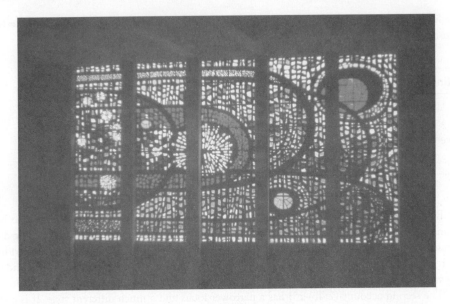

Chaos to Cosmos. This modern stained-glass window interprets the creation narrative of Genesis 1. The burst of light at the center symbolizes God's first creative word, "Let there be light" (Gen. 1:3). The culmination is the orderly universe, which God pronounced "very good" (Gen. 1:31). Smaller light bursts suggest the creation of more distant galaxies. *Source:* Dr. Christian E. Hauer Jr., FSA

To the modern reader, schooled to look on contradictions as errors, the two different creation accounts cause a dilemma. If there are two, which is correct? However, this perspective imposes a foreign standard on biblical literature. As noted in Chapter 2, two of the basic techniques of both biblical poetry and prose are repetition and balancing. This is the way emphasis and nuance are achieved. To include two accounts of creation is to emphasize the importance of cosmic origins. To set different accounts side by side is to give a broader perspective, which reflects the ambiguity in trying to speak of such a basic mystery as the creation of everything. By itself each account is narrow. Is the creator as austere and distant as Genesis 1 implies, or as intimate and casual as Genesis 2 suggests? The two accounts together give a balanced view of the creator, and the order and harmony of Genesis 1 is balanced with the trial-and-error world of Genesis 2. Do we not experience the creation in both ways, at different times? A modern writer would probably blend the accounts to form a single, qualified version. To respect the literary world of Genesis 1–2 is to recognize how the two separate accounts complement and balance each other.

The Historical World: Creation Accounts of the Ancient Near East

LITERARY HISTORY The different creation accounts in the first two chapters of Genesis provide evidence for literary historians that the editor who produced the final version of Genesis used at least two sources. The most widely accepted theory about the multiple sources that were combined in the editing of Genesis (and other books in the Pentateuch) is called the "documentary hypothesis." On the basis of changes in vocabulary and style, proponents of this theory maintain that there are several sources evident in the Pentateuch (or Hexateuch, the first six books of the Bible). One of the first indications of different sources recognized was the alternation of divine names. For example, the two names for the deity in the two accounts of creation (Elohim in the first and YHWH [Yahweh]

Elohim in the second) are seen as evidence of at least two (but probably three) sources from different authors behind the final text.

The most commonly held version of the documentary hypothesis is that there are four sources in the Pentateuch, three of which are evident in Genesis. These sources are known by the first letters of the names assigned to them by scholars: J, E, P, and D. Because of the importance of this theory in the literary historical study of the Pentateuch, each of the hypothetical sources will be introduced at this point.

The source usually assumed to have been the first written is called *J (Yahwist)* because the divine name Yahweh (spelled with a "J" in German and so labeled by the German biblical scholars who first stated the theory) appears in it. From this perspective, the second creation narrative is from the "J" source. Most literary historians contend that "J" was a product of the literary "golden age" in Judah, the southern kingdom of ancient Israel (see Chapter 4), the time of King Solomon or shortly thereafter (tenth–ninth century B.C.E.). According to this theory, the "J" narrative in Genesis 1–11 is found in 2:4b–4:26; 6:1–8; 7:1–5, 7, 10, 12, 17–19, 22–23; 8:2b–3a, 6, 8–12, 13b, 20–22. There is a very personal, anthropomorphic description of Yahweh in the "J" narrative (e.g., walking in the garden [Gen. 3:8]).

"J" also emphasizes the role of women (e.g., Eve in the Garden of Eden and the wives of the patriarchs [Sarah, Rebekah, Leah, Rachel] in Genesis 12–37). The narrative clearly focuses on Judah, the tribe to which King David belonged, linking the founding fathers and mothers in Genesis to sites in Judah and describing the boundaries of the land promised to Abraham (Gen. 15:18) with the extent of the Kingdom of David. Many scholars believe that "J" was written by a member of the royal court of David or Solomon, who was commissioned to tell the story of Israel from the time of cosmic origins to the creation of the Davidic dynasty.

The minority view of the "minimalist" school (see Chapter 1) is that "J" was a late work, written after the Babylonian invasion of Judah and destruction of the Davidic monarchy and added as part of a postexilic preface to the Book of Deuteronomy.

According to most supporters of the documentary hypothesis, the next source written is called *E (Elohist)* because it favors the divine name "Elohim." (In the "E" narrative, the divine name Yahweh does not appear until it is revealed to Moses.) No independent examples of the "E" source are found in Genesis 1–2 (although many scholars assume that it was combined with the "J" account, rendering in Genesis 2 what they call the "JE" creation story). Examples of "clearly" Elohistic texts later in Genesis include 20:1–17, 21:8–34, and 22:1–19. It is usually assumed that "E" was composed in the Northern Kingdom of Israel about a century or so after "J." In the "E" source, the deity often communicates through dreams and is therefore more indirectly involved in human affairs than in the "J" source.

Because the evidence of "E" is fragmentary in comparison to the three other hypothetical sources, some scholars have argued that rather than being a full narrative, like "J," "D," and "P," it is better understood as a collection of oral traditions instead of a written source.

The hypothetical *D (Deuteronomist)* source likely refers to the bulk of the material found in the present book of Deuteronomy, and therefore does not figure in our discussion at this point. According to most scholars, "D" (see Chapters 4 and 5) was probably written during the time of King Hezekiah and/or King Josiah of the Southern Kingdom (eighth–seventh century B.C.E.).

Some in the so-called "minimalist" school take the position that "D" is actually the oldest of the sources of the Torah and that "D" is evident in some passages in Genesis, Exodus, and Numbers.

The last of the "four sources" is called *P (Priestly Writer)* because of its interest in matters of worship and law associated with the priesthood. Like "E," "P" prefers the divine name Elohim and must be distinguished from "E" on other grounds. Its style is more formal than "J" and "E," and its view of the deity is more majestic. The first creation account is assumed to have come from the hand of "P." Other sections of Genesis 1–11 assigned to "P" include 5:1–27 and 11:10–27. Proponents of the documentary hypothesis point out that the story of Noah and the great flood seems to combine two versions, one from "J" (or "JE") and another from "P." The story seems to begin, for example, with two accounts of the cause of the flood, one from "J" (6:1–8) and another from "P" (6:11–22). Most proponents of the documentary hypothesis speculate that the "P" source was written in the postexilic period, perhaps in the fifth century B.C.E.

According to this theory, an editor (redactor), often designated "R," combined these sources to form the final narrative. Some think that "P" was the redactor, others that the redactor was an independent person or school. The documentary hypothesis remains the dominant theory about the literary history of the Pentateuch. However, many scholars have challenged its sometimes quite arbitrary divisions of the literature and the circularity of its arguments. (The assumptions about the characteristics of the source are used as evidence for identifying texts that come from the source.) Literary historians increasingly speak of "strands" of oral tradition, rather than written "sources," as the components that were combined in the final version.

Many ancient peoples developed creation accounts. These were not meant to be bad substitutes for science; rather they were statements about the meaning of the cosmos and the status of things in it. Often, they justified some political or social order.

The stories told by Israel's predecessors and contemporary neighbors presupposed polytheism (belief in many gods), and often lodged creation in a dispute or struggle among the gods. The world, after it was created, remained infused with divinity. In the Babylonian *enuma elish,* the cosmos was formed when Marduk, the patron god of Babylon, killed Tiamat, the threatening dragon of watery chaos, and divided her corpse to form the dome of heaven and the dry land. Marduk's victory justified his headship

TABLE 3.1 Apparent Parallels between Genesis 1 and the Babylonian Creation Epic (Enuma Elish)

Genesis 1	Babylonian Creation Epic
Precreation chaotic waters	Precreation chaotic waters
God (Elohim) creates by speaking (1:3, 6, 9, 14, 20, 24, 26)	Ea (god of all living creatures) creates by speaking
Six days of creation followed by divine rest on the seventh	Six generations of gods followed by divine rest
Creation begins with light on first day (1:3)	Creation begins with light in first generation
Dome (firmament) created through separation of precreation waters on second day (1:6–8)	Dome (firmament) created through separation of Tiamat in second generation
Dry land created on third day (1:9–10)	Kishar, god of earth, created in third generation
Lights in sky created on fourth day (1:14–19)	Anu, god of sky, created in fourth generation
Creation ends with humanity on the sixth day (1:26–27)	Creation ends with humanity in the sixth generation

Note: Those scholars who emphasize the parallels between the creation account in Genesis 1 and the Babylonian Creation Epic note the above similarities. Other scholars claim the similarities have been overemphasized and fundamental differences overlooked.

of the pantheon and Babylon role as the imperial city. The sun, moon, stars, and so forth, and the various natural phenomena were regarded as gods and goddesses or their abodes (see Table 3.1).

The status of humanity in these narratives is often problematic. In *enuma elish* and the *Atrahasis Epic* (another Mesopotamian story), humans were created to be the slaves of the gods, providing offerings so the gods (and the ruling class, including the priests) would not have to work. These accounts were often closely tied to the annual agricultural fertility cycles, and they suggested that the cosmos might come unhinged without the repeated creative acts of the gods, sustained by the cultic acts of humans. Events in the human realm had to be foreshadowed by divine actions in the spirit world.

The Israelites used the combat–creation theme as a poetic metaphor (see Chapter 8), but not in their creation narratives. Their creation accounts do, however, share common motifs with their cultural matrix. Creation begins in chaos (water in Genesis 1, desert in Genesis 2). Tiamat, the Babylonian chaos dragon, may underlie the Hebrew word *tehom* (translated as "deep," Gen. 1:2), although the Hebrew version is simply water. The flat earth and heavenly dome of Babylonian cosmology persist, but the Hebrew accounts are monotheistic. The one God creates a stable material universe requiring no ritual supports. Humanity holds a high status in both Israelite accounts; indeed, it shares with God in creative activity. Male and female exhibit God's image and likeness in Genesis 1. The center of focus shifts from the spirit realm to the plane of human experience. The climactic event, the goal of the narrative, in both Israelite accounts is the creation of a humane institution. In Genesis 1 it is the Sabbath, the universal day of rest for people and domestic animals. In Genesis 2 it is marriage. The Israelite stories thus reinforce the world-affirming optimism and humanitarianism characteristic of the Torah traditions (see Table 3.1).

PREHISTORY: COMMUNAL ORIGINS (GENESIS 3–11)

The Literary World: Separation in Genesis 3–11

THE GARDEN OF EDEN (GENESIS 2–3) In a word, *harmony* is the theme of Genesis 1–2 as a whole. As a result of divine creation, there is harmony between the creator and the principal creation—humankind—between humanity and nature (expressed, e.g., in the pun involved in the creation of man [*adam* in Hebrew] from the ground [*adamah*]) and between male and female (expressed in the unity implied in 1:26 and more explicitly in 2:24). The one source of tension in the harmonious creation is the prohibition against eating the fruit of the tree of knowledge of good and evil (2:17).

That tension is exploited in the next scene, which can be considered part of the Garden of Eden story begun in Chapter 2 (3:1–24). The harmony of creation is broken by the rebellion of humankind, and the result is alienation and separation. As is the case with Hebrew narrative style, the story moves very quickly. With no introduction, the action begins. The serpent, identified only as the most subtle of the wild creatures in the Garden, plays the role of the trickster. Tricksters in literature are figures who use psychological ploys and distortions to encourage others to do what they know they should not. They are not so much evil as they are devious manipulators of others. In this case, the trickster exploits the human desire to be "like the gods" or "like God." That is apparently what "knowing good and evil" means, although the phrase is admittedly ambiguous. Many commentators feel that "knowing good and evil" is like saying "knowing it all." This perspective has been denied to humankind, yet humans are unwilling to accept the limitation.

With the serpent as catalyst, the desire to be "like God" proves too strong to resist, so the woman and then the man eat the forbidden fruit. The result is the replacement of harmony with separation. First, there is estrangement between the man and the woman; they become aware of their nakedness, are ashamed, and hide. Next, there is separation from the LORD. The man and woman try unsuccessfully to hide from the deity and deny their guilt. The man blames God for giving him the woman. This leads to a heightening of the tension between man and woman (She made me do it!) and introduces a distance between humankind and the animal world (The serpent is to blame!). Finally, the harmony between humankind and the earth is disrupted. "Cursed is the ground because of you; in toil you shall eat of it all the days of your life" (3:17). As a result of their disobedience, the man (now called Adam, "everyman") and the woman (now called Eve, "lifegiver") are expelled from the Garden. The original harmony is irrevocably broken, it seems. And humankind is aware of the basic source of alienation in human life—death (3:19). The elements of the story can be outlined as follows:

> **Catalyst:** The serpent tempts the woman.
>
> **Rebellion:** The woman and man eat the forbidden fruit.
>
> **Confrontation:** The man and woman hide, but the LORD finds and confronts them.
>
> **Rationalization:** The man blames the woman (and, by implication, God); the woman blames the serpent.
>
> **Result (alienation):** The harmony of humankind with the creator and with nature, and the harmony of male and female, is broken.

Despite the swift reaction of the LORD to this act of disobedience, and despite the pervasive sense of alienation, a new tension is introduced that balances the negative tone. Despite their estrangement, there is a glimmer of persistent harmony between man and woman. The man names the woman Eve because she is the mother of all living. They leave the Garden together, not apart. Even though the LORD expels the pair from the Garden, lest they exploit their newfound knowledge and eat of the tree of life and become immortal, he clothes them, suggesting that the LORD still has compassion for humanity. And although the pair has experienced a sort of "spiritual death" as a result of eating the fruit, the LORD does not kill them, as the original command had implied.

Professor Carol L. Meyers notes that literary analysts classify stories such as these in Genesis, Chapters 2–11, into two categories: archetypes (stories that illustrate typical patterns of behavior) and prototypes (stories that set in motion a chain of causes that replicate the original action, and that are referred back to as prototypical in later narratives).[1] She points out that from the standpoint of the Torah, the Garden of Eden story is an archetype. It shows people behaving rebelliously toward God, a bad human trait that turns up all too frequently. But later texts dealing with human rebellion do not refer back to it as a cause of later rebellion.

An observation on the history of interpretation of Genesis 2–3 follows from this comment on its literary type, illustrating how studies of the literary and historical worlds of texts often overlap. The influential Christian theologian, St. Augustine (354–430 C.E.), whose understanding of the Greek in which the New Testament was written was limited, read the Latin translation of Rom. 5:12 to mean that the sin of Adam was a prototype—it caused others to sin. Augustine's interpretation gave rise to the Christian doctrine known as "original sin," the view that sin is inherited by all subsequent humans after Adam and Eve. In the Apostle Paul's original Greek in Rom. 5:12, it seems clear that Paul understood Adam's sin to be an archetype. Death spread to all people because *all* people sinned rather than as a direct result of the sin of Adam and Eve. In other words, sin is humanity's first and most persistent copycat crime.

---

[1]Carol L. Meyers. *Discovering Eve: Ancient Israelite Women in Context.* New York: Oxford University Press, 1991.

CAIN AND ABEL (GEN. 4:1–16)   The next story is the account of two brothers, Cain (a farmer) and Abel (a herdsman). It, too, is a story of alienation. Here, the *catalyst* is the LORD's unexplained preference for Abel's offering over Cain's. It probably just meant that Abel's burned better. Despite this external motivation, a comment makes clear that the real problem is not the LORD's preference, but Cain's inability to master sin. The *rebellion* is fratricide; Cain murders Abel. There is a *confrontation* by the LORD, but Cain offers a *rationalization:* Am I my brother's keeper? The result is *alienation* for Cain: from nature (4:12), from other people (Cain will be a fugitive), and from the LORD (4:15). However, again there is a qualification. To protect Cain from being slain while he wanders, the LORD places a mark on him, a "brand" to warn whoever might try to do violence that Cain belongs to the creator. The links among the narratives are genealogies that connect the stories from creation onward (Gen. 5:1–32; 10; 11:10–32).

THE FLOOD (GENESIS 6–9)   The next extended narrative, the Flood story (Chapters 6–9), follows the same pattern we have observed in the earlier stories. The pace is quickened. The sons of God (divine beings) are the culprits, indicating that rebellion has spread to the divine realm. They saw the daughters of men (*catalyst*) and had intercourse with them (*rebellion*). This sets the stage for the observation that humankind is completely evil. The *confrontation* is an inner one for the LORD, who must admit the mistake of having brought these rebellious creatures into existence. The consequences are severe. *Alienation* has run its course; now there is a complete reversal in the creation process. Creation has been so disrupted by rebellion that a new start is necessary. In this story the *qualification* becomes the central element. The blameless Noah will be spared, along with representatives of the animal kingdom. In a graphic return to precreation chaos, the chaotic waters burst through the firmament and rise up from below. That sets (or resets) the stage for a new beginning. Dry land again "emerges," and a new command to be fruitful and multiply is given. The new creation is marked by a covenant between God and all flesh and a promise not to destroy life again with a flood. Yet the hope of a fresh start is quickly shattered by Noah's curse on a grandson for something his father did while Noah was passed out drunk.

An Artist's Rendition of Noah's Ark. According to the Book of Genesis (Chapters 6–9), God commanded Noah to build an ark in order that his family and pairs of animals might survive the great flood brought by God to punish human sin. *Source:* photobank.kiev.ua/Shutterstock

THE TOWER OF BABEL (GEN. 11:1–9)   In the final story in the Prehistory, the Tower of Babel (11:1–9), there is again a *catalyst* (one language), an act of *rebellion* (building the tower in the heavens, a ziggurat, to facilitate human access to and control of the heavenly realm), a *confrontation* ("Come, let us go down!"), a *rationalization* (lest we be scattered), and the resultant *alienation* (confusion of languages). The story humorously mocks human arrogance. The grand project to take heaven by storm is, in reality, so trivial that YHWH must go down and take a closer look to see what is going on. The punishment is thus for hubris, not for mounting a potentially successful revolution. What is missing is any indication of divine compassion qualifying the alienation.

THE THEME OF GENESIS 1–11   Considering Genesis 1–11 as one literary unit (the Prehistory), we can observe a general theme. It is the tension between the harmony present in the created order and the alienation that occurs as a result of the human refusal to accept the prescribed limits of creation. The estrangement deepens until God decides to start over again, but even the purging of creation does not work, for the one blameless man does not turn out to be as righteous as billed. As alienation grows, the divine compassion balances it, until the failure of the new beginning after the Flood. With the confusion of human languages, there is no sign of divine mercy. As the Prehistory ends, the question of the continued place of humankind in God's creation is open. Having tried and failed twice to have a harmonious creation, with humankind as lead actor, perhaps God will find someone else to play the part or will simply give up on the whole mess.

The Historical World: Setting the Stage for History

The Prehistory sets the stage for history and tries to render comprehensible the Israelite understanding of nature and history. This does not beg the question of the ultimate historicity of some of the traditions in Genesis 1–11. Some of them may, in fact, have roots in historical objects and events. The mark of Cain (4:15) may well have been a Kenite tribal tattoo. The list of heroes who lived before the Flood (Chapter 5) has a counterpart or predecessor in a list of Sumerian kings who lived before a flood and who, like the biblical heroes, lived to substantial ages. The etymology of Babel in Gen. 11:9 seems to connect it with Babylon, and a ruined Mesopotamian ziggurat (temple pyramid) seems to constitute the physical basis of the story.

One of the dramatic news bulletins generated by early Mesopotamian archaeology was the discovery of silt deposits at various locations, patently the work of great floods, which were quickly associated with Noah's flood.

The *Gilgamesh Epic,* with a flood interlude narrated to the hero by Utnapishtim, the Babylonian Noah, probably has Sumerian roots. Another Sumerian story, in which the Noah figure was named Ziusudra, has also come to light. The Atrahasis Epic offers yet another Mesopotamian flood story. The biblical flood story, which itself is a composite of traditions, almost certainly traces back to Mesopotamian origins. The sort of horizon-to-horizon flooding presupposed by the Noah story simply has no archetype or precedent in the experience of people living in Israel, a country lacking the huge rivers and the broad valleys or deltas required for such a phenomenon. The Israelites must have brought this tradition with them as they moved southward from Mesopotamia, or acquired it from Mesopotamian sources at a later time. The story may coalesce a folk memory of a succession of great floods of the sort experienced in Mesopotamia, or it may embody the memory of one particularly catastrophic flood. In any case, the Noah story is grounded in history in the sense that its authors were not creating it out of whole cloth but, rather, were reworking an ancient folk tradition that itself rested on actual human experience.

Noah's flood reentered the headlines when respected marine geologists William Ryan and Walter Pitman published their findings about the Neolithic catastrophe that formed the Black

Sea as it has existed since.[2] Runoff from melting glaciers fifteen thousand years ago raised the level of the Mediterranean Sea to the point that its waters invaded the Bosporus valley and cascaded into the former freshwater lake beyond. Water levels rose six inches per day, inundating former farms, villages, and ports. In an illustration of the literary historical method of *traditions history* (see Chapter 2), the authors speculate that accounts of the unparalleled disaster spread to Mesopotamia, where they became the basis of the Sumerian, Babylonian, and ultimately the Israelite flood stories, as well as to Europe. Folk memories of such an event, when it seemed that the fountains of the Great Deep, the primordial nether ocean, had indeed burst forth may indeed underlie the various flood epics. But the floods of Ziusudra, Utnapishtim, and Noah abated. The Black Sea is still there.

Oceanographer and deep sea explorer Robert Ballard, of *Titanic* fame, and his colleagues have now entered the picture, so further discoveries of ancient shipwrecks and drowned villages surely lie ahead. But even if the Neolithic catastrophe lies in the deep substrata of the flood stories, most folklorists and archaeologists continue to believe that the early Mesopotamian archaeologists got it right. The flood stories as they come down to us were inspired by successive horizon-to-horizon floods in the Tigris–Euphrates valley that rose but then abated so normal life could resume.

However, in the final analysis, given the current state of evidence, we simply cannot talk about history when discussing Genesis 1–11. No drawing or description of a Kenite tattoo survives. The long-lived hero kings cannot be anchored in any historical contexts. The ruined ziggurat cannot be pinpointed. Which flood or floods, and when or precisely where, cannot be specified. Thus, not all materials that ground in history are necessarily historical. These stories do not seem to function in a historical fashion, to convey information about people and their experiences in space and time. Rather, the stories in Genesis 1–11 seem to be trying to answer basic questions about why things are as they are. The technical term for this type of story is *etiology*. An etiological story explains the origin of something, in response to the perennial human question "why?" For example, why is there hostility between the human and the divine, between human beings and nature, and among humans? The story of the Garden of Eden relates the reason. Why are there so many languages? The Tower of Babel provides an answer. Searching for a historical context for Genesis 1–11 leads not to actual events, but to the human longing to know why things are as they are—what they *mean*, not their efficient causes—and to Israel's need to know why the creator of the universe decided to become involved with Abraham and his descendants.

Ancient creation/origin stories also affirm the rightness of institutions and states of affairs in the world. The Babylonian *enuma elish* story grounds the Babylonian empire, the Marduk cult of Babylon, and the sorry status of the majority of humanity in the actions of goddesses and gods at creation. A high status for the totality of humanity, the masses as well as the ruling classes, is established only in the Israelite narratives. The egalitarian aspects of Torah, not the pretensions of kings, priests, and magnates, are thus grounded in creation. The Israelite state, the holy city of Jerusalem, and its temple all emerge in the course of human history. However, two humane social institutions, the Sabbath (seventh) day of rest (history's first wage–hour legislation) and marriage, are established at creation by the Israelite accounts.

There has been a great deal of literary historical study of the sources used in the composition of Genesis 1–11. This section is a composite of at least two literary strata, the "J" and "P" previously noted. The alternation of the divine names YHWH and Elohim, differences in literary style and interest, and otherwise inexplicable repetitions and contradictions all point in this direction. For

---

[2]William Ryan and Walter Pitman. *Noah's Flood: The New Scientific Discoveries about the Event that Changed History.* New York: Simon & Schuster, 1998.

example, repetitions in the flood narrative can be interpreted as evidence of the weaving together of "J" and "P" versions of the story. The following will suffice to illustrate this widely accepted theory. The flood account begins with an introduction from the "J" strand (6:5–8) in which Yahweh is described as "sorry that he had made humankind on the earth, and it grieved him to his heart." This accords with the portrayal of Yahweh in personal, intimate imagery seen throughout "J." Contrasted with the pervasive human wickedness is Noah, who "found favor in the sight of the LORD." Then follows another introduction (6:9–13), in which "P" describes Noah as a "righteous man" who "walked with Elohim (God)" at a time when "all flesh had corrupted its ways on the earth."

There seem also to be two versions of how many animals Noah brought onto the ark he was instructed to build. "P" says a pair of each species (6:19–20) while "J" mentions seven pairs of clean and a single pair of unclean animals (7:2–3). "J" apparently assumed that the clean animals would be slaughtered and eaten, while "P" assumed that the clean/unclean distinction would come with the Mt. Sinai legislation. Therefore, from the "P" perspective Noah sailed a vegetarian ship! Indeed, the "P" account of creation says that humans are given fruits and vegetables to eat, but no mention is made of God giving humans animals as a food source (1:29).

In describing the cause of the flood, "J" speaks of "forty days and nights" (7:4, 12) while the version in "P" is that the waters crested after 150 days (7:24). While "J" describes the flood more naturalistically as the result of rain, "P" appeals to the imagery of its creation account in Genesis 1, with the opening of windows in the dome (firmament) created to hold back the chaotic precreation waters (7:11).

After the flood, "J" describes Noah building an altar to Yahweh, on which some of the clean animals are sacrificed. Again, in very personal imagery, Yahweh smells the "pleasing odor" of the sacrifice and says "in his heart" that he will never again curse the ground because of human evil (8:20–21). The version in "P" is of a restoration of creation, with a repetition of the command given in 1:28 to "be fruitful and multiply and fill the earth" (9:1). Now, however, according to "P," humans are given animals to eat (9:3).

ORIGINS OF THE PEOPLE OF GOD (GENESIS 12–50)

The Literary World: Promise and Journey in the Ancestor Legends

The Prehistory has set the scene. In Genesis 12 we center in on the lead characters in the subsequent drama. The Prehistory also establishes the basic dilemma (human rebellion) and foreshadows the resolution (divine mercy) in the narrative, but it leaves the situation in a seemingly hopeless state.

Against this background Gen. 12:1–3 establishes a new theme, which will, in some respects, dominate the biblical narrative throughout. In a word, that theme is *promise*. It is the promise of the LORD, first expressed to a Mesopotamian named Abram (whose name is later changed to Abraham), and his wife, Sarai (later changed to Sarah). With the barest of introductions to the man Abram, the promise is immediately brought to center stage:

> Now the LORD said to Abram, "Go from your country and your kindred and your father's house to the land that I will show you. I will make of you a great nation. I will bless you, and make your name great, so that you will be a blessing. I will bless those who bless you, and the one who curses you I will curse; and by you all the families of the earth shall be blessed." (12:1–3)

This three-fold promise of a land (see also 12:7), progeny (a great nation), and blessing (not only for the nation formed from Abram but also through this nation for others) is the thread woven throughout the stories of the patriarchs and matriarchs (the "first fathers" and "first mothers" of Israel): Abraham and Sarah (Genesis 12–25), Isaac and Rebekah, Jacob and Rachel (Genesis 26–36), and Joseph (Genesis 37–50). This theme also connects these ancestral stories with what follows. Throughout the narrative, the promise is renewed, endangered, and reaffirmed in an intricate web of scenes.

Related to this primary theme is a secondary one: *journey.* The story of the promise is told as a series of journeys—Abraham to Canaan; Jacob to Paddan-aram and back; Joseph (and the rest of his family) to Egypt; Moses to Midian and back; the tribes of Israel out of Egypt, through the wilderness to the border of Canaan, and finally into the promised land.

We have chosen to describe these materials as "the ancestor narratives," rather than the traditional term, "patriarchal narratives." By so doing, we recognize the crucial role of women in the stories.

The family system was indeed patriarchal and the inheritance system patrilineal. Nevertheless, beside each patriarch stands an equally chosen wife without whom the promises cannot be realized. On the practical level, women in this culture had a fair amount of independence. Rachel did "man's work," keeping her father's sheep (Gen. 29:1). Sarah laughed at God, lied to God about it, and survived to have her baby (Gen. 18:12–15). Although the men conducted the negotiations, Rebekah made the final decision about her marriage (Gen. 24:57–61). Women took the initiative in matters that involved their sons and husbands. Female status probably declined through time with the adoption of settled farming life and, particularly, with the emergence of a male-dominated complex social and political polity.

ABRAHAM AND SARAH (GENESIS 12–25)   Even before the promise is given to Abram, a tension in its fulfillment is introduced, foreshadowing the major concern of the first ancestral narrative. Sarai is barren (11:30). How can the LORD make of Abram (meaning "father of many") a great nation when he is already seventy-five years old and his wife is unable to have children? As they later recognize, there is more than a little bitter humor in their situation.

We gain insights into biblical characters through their words and deeds; unlike the characters in modern literature, we are rarely given access to their thoughts or feelings. In Abraham's case, his actions speak. Despite the seeming absurdity of a childless septuagenarian becoming the father of a great nation, he leaves his own country without question and heads off for a new land. Through his actions we are told that Abraham is a man of faith, willing to trust the word of a deity previously unknown to him. Abraham is also clever. His wife Sarah—and the promise—is endangered when the "beautiful" Sarah is taken to Pharaoh's house while they are in Egypt. With foresight, Abraham has told her to claim to be his sister, so that the Egyptians will not kill him (12:10–20). To make the point of the patriarch's cunning (and the LORD's protection) more forcefully, the wife–sister motif is repeated in the Abraham story (20:1–18). Abraham is also materially successful (13:2). He is a good host (Genesis 18) and a mediator among men (Genesis 13).

Abraham is also portrayed as a military hero, successfully leading a small guerrilla force against an alliance of raiding kings (Genesis 14). Thus, he is not a crazed wanderer who follows divine voices through the desert. He is a skilled, successful, and wise leader. Because Abraham symbolizes the nation that remembers him as "father of the country," this characterization is part of the development of a positive Israelite self-image.

Most of the Abraham narrative is devoted to portraying Abraham as a man willing to trust the LORD totally. In Genesis 15 the promise is renewed, Abraham responds in faith (15:6), and the promise is sealed with a covenant ceremony. Even though Abraham still has no heir, he trusts the LORD to fulfill the promise. The scene is repeated in Genesis 17, for emphasis, but this time the deity is called El Shaddai (God Almighty), and the sign of the promise is circumcision. The promise (called here a *covenant;* see Chapter 4) is said to be "everlasting," that is, unconditional. Finally, after years of waiting, a son, heir to the promise, is born—Isaac (Genesis 21).

When his faith is tested, Abraham endures. In one of the most sublime stories in the Bible, Abraham is told by God to sacrifice Isaac, with no explanation why (Genesis 22). There is no hint of reluctance by Abraham to kill his son and, thereby, the promise. Not until Abraham demonstrates his willingness to take Isaac's life is the boy saved. This story functions to make crystal clear the depth of Abraham's devotion to God. His loyalty to God conditions every other loyalty, but he is not passive in his relationship with the deity. He is willing to challenge the LORD's plan to destroy Sodom and Gomorrah and to bargain for the salvation of the people (18:22-33).

The traditions generally portray Abraham as an admirable person. He is, above all, a paradigm of faith and piety, an aspect of his character that is celebrated in later Jewish, Christian, and Islamic tradition. When the LORD and his angels came calling incognito, Abraham was the model of hospitality(18:1-8), a theme elaborated in Jewish lore. He gave Lot the choice of range for his herds, proving himself the generous chieftain (13:8-13). When Abraham fought the four kings to liberate Lot and the captives and booty of the Cities of the Plain and kept nothing (though he paid tithes to Melchizedek), he proved himself the heroic and magnanimous warrior (14:1-24). But faith wavered when he signed on to Sarah's scheme to get a child by surrogate motherhood by Hagar, and something like cruelty emerged when he gave in to Sarah's blandishments and expelled Hagar and her child (16:1-16). Finally, he comes across as a scheming, if desperate, rogue when he passed Sarah off as his sister—and into Pharaoh's harem (12:10-20). His life was at forfeit, but the faithful Abraham shows himself not to be above self-serving behavior that endangers his wife.

The character of Sarah is also developed in the story. She is a woman who, at age seventy-five, remains beautiful. But she does not rely on her attractiveness. She uses her wits to try to assure that the promise will be fulfilled (16:1–6). Like her husband, she shows skepticism about their having a son in their old age (18:9–15). In this collection of vignettes about Abraham and

Abraham and Isaac. One of the most moving stories in the Book of Genesis (22:1–19) is the account of Abraham's willingness to sacrifice his son Isaac in response to God's command. At the climax of the story (illustrated in this statue), an angel intervenes to stop the sacrifice since Abraham has passed what many interpreters call an ultimate test of faith in God. Christian interpreters see a foreshadowing of God's sacrifice of his son, Jesus, in the story. *Source:* Zvonimir Atletic/Shutterstock

Sarah, we see not flat, lifeless characters who walk through a divinely ordained drama like robots, but complex persons, with strengths and weaknesses, to whom a promise is given, put in jeopardy, and renewed.

ISAAC AND REBEKAH AND JACOB AND RACHEL (GENESIS 25–36)   In the ancestral narrative, the stories of Isaac, Abraham's son, and Jacob, Isaac's son, and their wives are woven together. Isaac is a transitional figure. The stories in which he is the central character repeat, and therefore connect him with, similar incidents in the life of Abraham (Genesis 26). Jacob looms larger. The story of Jacob serves to balance the Abraham narrative and to prepare the way for the Joseph story, as we shall see.[3]

As in the Abraham cycle, Isaac's wife (Rebekah) is barren (25:21). But unlike Sarah, Rebekah does not have to wait years for a son. The problem is almost the opposite. Twins are born, creating a conflict as to who shall be the principal heir. Because Esau is the first to emerge from the womb, he has the right of the firstborn—a double portion of the inheritance and the office of family head. The basic tension in the story is introduced when we are told of an oracle received by Rebekah: "The elder shall serve the younger" (25:23). And at birth, the infant Jacob ("supplanter") is already trying to fulfill the oracle, grabbing his older brother's heel.

The friction between the brothers is compounded by their opposite natures. Esau is a ruddy, hairy outdoorsman. Jacob is a smooth-skinned, contemplative boy who likes to stay inside. Esau is a fool, willing to sell his birthright for a bowl of pottage. Jacob is clever, taking advantage of his brother's hunger to buy the birthright. Later, prompted by his manipulative mother, Rebekah, he exploits his father's age and blindness to steal the blessing intended for Esau. Abraham was introduced as a man of faith who trusted God. Jacob is introduced as a conniver who collaborates with his mother in deceit. They are unwilling to trust God to fulfill the divine promises.

Now Jacob's journey begins, in prudent flight from Esau's wrath (not in faith, like Abraham). It takes him to the home of his Uncle Laban in Paddan-aram and back home again. It is a journey not only of time and space but also within Jacob himself. Ultimately, his journey transforms him. In Abraham and Jacob we have two ancestor types: one whose faith is evident at the outset and the other for whom the journey to trust in God is a slow, agonizing process.

In his initial flight, Jacob has an encounter with the LORD at a place that he names Bethel (House of God). There the LORD gives him the promise made to his father and to Abraham. Jacob's response is to place a condition on his trust in the LORD (28:20).

In his years with Laban, Jacob is tested. First, the tables are turned on the deceiver, and the deceit ironically turns on the matter of birthright. Jacob has fallen in love with Laban's younger daughter Rachel ("ewe"), but, after working seven years to earn the right to marry her, he is tricked by Laban into marrying the firstborn Leah ("cow"). The right of the elder daughter to marry first is the basis of a comeuppance for Jacob. But Jacob is not only clever but also persistent. He works another seven years to marry Rachel. Through hard work, and the clever use of magic, Jacob becomes wealthy at his father-in-law Laban's expense. And the promise of a "great nation" begins to seem realistic as twelve sons are born to Jacob.

---

[3]For observations on the literary world of Genesis 26–36, we are indebted to Michael Fishbane. *Text and Texture: Close Readings of Selected Biblical Texts.* New York: Schocken Books, 1979, pp. 42–62.

Now the journey starts to be reversed. In a series of scenes that balance step by step the journey away from home, Jacob returns to Canaan. On the way, Rachel demonstrates her cunning by stealing her father's household gods, a symbol of family leadership.

The unresolved tension in the story is the conflict between Jacob and Esau. As Jacob prepares to meet his brother, hoping that he can win his favor through gifts, the climax in his inner journey is reached. He has another encounter with the divine, near a border, this time in a wrestling match near the Jabbok River (32:22–32). After an all-night struggle, the fight is a draw. Jacob receives the blessing he has demanded, but he is also given a new name, Israel, which means "he who strives with God" or "God strives," and a limp in his walk. These indicate that Jacob has changed. There are a number of levels of meaning in this story of Jacob's wrestling match, but in its present context it indicates that in an encounter with God (symbolized in the name Jacob gives to the place, *Peniel,* which means "face of God"), Jacob has undergone a transformation. He resolutely limps out to encounter his brother.

In a clever twist, when Jacob meets Esau, it is the "fool" Esau who takes the initiative in reconciling the hostility between the brothers. Esau's warm reception moves Jacob to recognize that "to see your face is like seeing the face of God" (33:10). He has not earned Esau's favor; yet Esau has accepted him with open arms. Apparently that causes Jacob to realize something about the God he has been attempting to manipulate and the nature of the relationship he should have with the deity. In another clever reversal, Jacob bows down before his brother.

After an interlude, the journey of Jacob continues (Genesis 34) with a return to Bethel, the site of his first encounter with the LORD. Now Jacob is a man of faith. He puts away all foreign gods and builds an altar. Here at Bethel, the change in Jacob is reaffirmed as again he receives the

Cave of the Patriarchs. Located in Hebron in the modern nation of Israel, this complex of shrines (also known as the Cave of Machpelah or the Sanctuary of Abraham) is honored as the burial site of the ancestors of the people of Israel: Abraham and Sarah, Isaac and Rebekah, and Jacob and Leah. The site is considered sacred by Jews, Christians, and Muslims. *Source*: David Rabkin/Shutterstock

name Israel. In the final scene of Jacob's journey, Jacob and Esau together bury their father, who has been lingering all these years on his deathbed, waiting for the conflict between his sons to be resolved.

The structure of the story of Jacob is that of a story within a story, what we might call an *envelope structure*. The story of Jacob's relationship with Esau is the frame, or envelope, for the story of his stay with his Uncle Laban. Despite the fact that the narrative is composed of a series of seemingly independent legends about Jacob, it has been woven together into a carefully crafted composite around the theme of the journey of Jacob. Jacob's journey balances Abraham's. Abraham's journey is that of a man of faith, whose faith is tested; Jacob's journey is of a man who comes to faith after finally seeing the face of God in his brother's compassion.

JOSEPH AND HIS BROTHERS (GENESIS 37–50) From a literary perspective, the Joseph narrative is much more integrated than the earlier ancestral stories. Instead of individual incidents woven together, the story is a sustained tale with clear plot development. It has been called the first example in the Bible of a short story or novella. In the Joseph story, the dominant promise theme moves into the background. The deity, who plays such a crucial role in the Abraham and Jacob stories, speaking from time to time, moves offstage. There are no indications of God's playing a direct role in the Joseph story. Nevertheless, a principal conclusion in the story is that the divine intention underlies the web of events in this drama of conflict among brothers.

We are introduced to Joseph as a spoiled, arrogant, and foolish seventeen-year-old. Favored by his father, he is naturally despised by his older brothers. And when he foolishly tells his brothers of his dream that they will serve him, they hate him all the more. Not surprisingly, when they have the chance, they plot to get rid of him, first deciding to kill him, and then (at Judah's urging) making a profit from their crime by selling him into slavery.

Then follows an interlude involving Judah (Chapter 38), in which Judah is tricked by his daughter-in-law Tamar into fulfilling the kinship responsibilities he has been neglecting. As in the Jacob story, this interlude interrupts the principal story just as the tension is heightening. Although unrelated to its setting, it plays a crucial role in foreshadowing later developments, as we shall see.

Once in Egypt, Joseph is tested. He is tempted by his master's wife and imprisoned unjustly, but remains steadfast throughout. Although the LORD is not directly involved in the story, the narrator points out "the LORD was with him" (39:2, 23). Using his ability to interpret dreams, but attributing the power to the LORD, Joseph wins release from prison and quickly rises to power as a high official in Pharaoh's administration. The distance Joseph has come from his family is symbolized by his marrying an Egyptian wife and taking an Egyptian name.

Now the reversal begins. Joseph does not journey home (like Jacob); instead, his family journeys to him. Driven by famine, the brothers are forced to go to Egypt, paralleling the forcing of Joseph into Egypt. Like Joseph, they are tested by being unjustly accused and imprisoned. Unwittingly, they fulfill the dream by bowing before Joseph but show they are unchanged by claiming to be "honest men." One brother (Simeon) is endangered, as Joseph had been, and apparently they are willing to leave him in prison. Now the tension is at its height. How can reconciliation occur when the brothers have not changed? Once again, they come to Egypt, and now Joseph places them in precisely the same situation they had been in with him years earlier. The fate of the youngest, favored brother (now Benjamin) is in their hands. They can leave him to die if they choose. But now Judah, who had contrived to sell Joseph and had learned his lesson from Tamar about fulfilling kinship responsibility, takes the initiative (as did Esau in the Jacob story). He asks to take Benjamin's place in prison. With this act of compassion, the way to resolution is opened, and the journey is completed as Jacob and his sons are reunited in Egypt, where they settle in the land of Goshen.

Genesis ends with the promise to Abraham renewed but not yet fulfilled. The descendants of Abraham are still few in number. They are now living outside the land promised to Abraham. In the journeys of Abraham, Jacob, and Joseph, the narrative introduces several types of persons of faith. However, if the promises to the ancestors are to be fulfilled, there will have to be a journey of the people.

The Historical World: The Ancestors in History

FINDING THE ORIGINAL CONTEXT   The narratives concerning the ancestors Abraham and Sarah, Isaac and Rebekah, Jacob and his family, and Joseph seem more characteristic of ordinary human experience than those encountered in the Prehistory. The people who move through the stories are recognizably human, and they exhibit consistent character and at times even signs of growth, as the literary analysis has shown. Thus, readers might get the subjective impression that when we move into the ancestral narratives we come into the realm of history.

But subjective impressions, however strong, fall far short of historical demonstration. Is there any firm data showing that the ancestral narratives are historical in nature?

Scholars have come to a general consensus concerning the political history of the ancient Near East during the Bronze Age (see Table 3.2). However, outside of the Bible itself, there is no

TABLE 3.2 Political Situations in the Ancient Near East before the Exodus

Date (B.C.E.)	Egypt	Canaan (Palestine)	Mesopotamia
3200		Proto-urban culture (Jericho)	
2800	Old Kingdom (c. 2900–2200)	Seminomadic Invasions	Sumerian ascendancy (c. 2800–2360)
2400	First Intermediate Period (c. 2200–2100)		Empire of Akkad (c. 2360–2180)
2000	Middle Kingdom (c. 2206–1950)		Sumerian resurgence (c. 1950–1750)
1800	Second Intermediate Period, Hyksos rule (c. 1700–1550)	Ancestral Period (?)	Old Babylonian Dynasty (c. 1830–1530)
			Hammurabi (c. 1728–1686)
1600	New Kingdom (c. 1550–1100)	City states under Egyptian control	Hittite invasion and decline of Babylon
	Hyksos expulsion (c. 1550–1525)		
	Thutmose III (1490–1435)		
1400	Amarna era (c. 1400–1350)	Weakening of Egyptian authority; Habiru Active	Old Assyrian Empire (c. 1356–1197)

direct evidence that the Israelite patriarchs and matriarchs existed. Some researchers profess to be able to connect the four kings of Genesis 14 with Bronze Age monarchs. Others believe that the recently discovered Ebla archives name the "cities of the plain" in the form and order known from the Abraham story in Genesis. But both of these findings have been vigorously disputed by other scholars familiar with the data. Even if verified, neither of these propositions, among others that have been advanced, would confirm that the Abraham of the narratives ever existed.

Archaeological data do seem to illuminate the ancestor narratives, particularly in terms of marriage and inheritance customs. The storytellers of ancient Israel had no way of recovering or reconstructing forgotten customs of the past. That certain customs appear in the narratives suggests that they were contained within traditions handed down from an earlier period. This is illustrated by references to a type of surrogate motherhood known from archaeological discoveries. Both Sarah, the wife of Abraham, and Rachel and Leah, the two wives of Jacob, compensated for periods of personal infertility by giving their slaves to their husbands to bear children. This was important in a world where offspring constituted a person's retirement annuities. The Torah provided for young widows under the levirate law (Dt. 25:5–10) and permitted polygamy and concubinage. It had no provision for surrogate motherhood. Had it done so, there would have been no grounds for the Samson and Samuel birth stories (Jg. 13:1–25; 1 Sam. 1:1–28).

The importance of Rachel's theft of her father's household gods is similarly illuminated. The ancestors are portrayed as *de facto* YHWHistic monotheists. The images *were* taken by a wife, not by the hero himself. The significance of the theft, beyond the opportunity for a bit of humor, is not clear in the Israelite story. Bronze Age Mesopotamian custom made possession of the family gods the sign of the firstborn, the next family head. Rachel was thus feathering her husband's, and her own, nest.

Much of our knowledge of family law in the Bronze Age comes from adoption papers. In a culture where family ties were paramount and land title was closely tied to family (and clan) membership, adoption was used by men without male heirs to provide for their old-age security and for the continuity of family and property. Because real property was frequently not transferable outside the kinship circle, adoption was also used to secure loans with real property.

A comparison of this material with the Jacob stories, especially Genesis 29–31, shows many close parallels in the customs. It has even been suggested that Laban adopted Jacob before he had sons of his own. Jacob's departure, and Rachel's theft of the household gods, would then be connected with the birth and growth to maturity of Laban's natural sons, with a consequent decline in Jacob's family status (Gen. 31:1–2). Adoption is not a factor in the Abraham–Sarah–Hagar tale, but it is likely that customs we know from adoption contracts were a part of the general complex of family law and customs through many parts of Bronze Age culture.

The general location of the ancestors in the environing culture is also consistent with what is known of Bronze Age society in Mesopotamia and the Levant. It was a feudal and largely agrarian society. Documents from various times and places in that world contain references to a people who are called *habiru* or *'apiru*. The resemblance of these words to *Hebrew* is quite obvious. These habiru appear as outsiders ("men without a master"), persons who do not have a place in the stratified social order. In times of disorder they appear as raiders and cohorts of rebels. The biblical word *Hebrew* comes from a root meaning to "cross over," a likely term for people who came from someplace else and lacked a proper knowledge of and respect for boundaries. In this connection, down to the rise of the monarchy, the term *Hebrew* may not have been a compliment among the Israelites themselves (e.g., see 1 Sam, 13:3; 14:21, and Gen. 39:14). In the earlier biblical traditions, the Israelites do not use the term among themselves, but only to identify themselves to outsiders, as outsiders use it to designate them. They see themselves as "strangers and sojourners." They use land in Canaan, but they do not own it; Abraham has to buy the cave of Machpelah for a family burial place (Gen. 23:1–20). The Israelites do not consider intermarriage with the indigenous population of Canaan to be a good thing (Gen. 24:1–67, 26:34–35, 27:46–28:9).

The ancestor narratives begin with a migration, but this does not mean the people were pure nomads like the Bedouin Arabs today. When the ancestors moved, it was for an immediate reason to seek water or pasturage or to escape famine.

Where in the Bronze Age did the Israelite ancestors fit? Until recently there was a fairly strong consensus in favor of the middle Bronze Age (*c.* 2000-1500 B.C.E.). This view is now being questioned with increasing frequency. Some scholars date the ancestral period earlier. Some argue that the ancestral stories did not originate until after 1000 B.C.E. and are not historical.

However, as we will see in the next chapter, there *is* compelling, if not incontrovertible, evidence for dating the Exodus from Egypt in the thirteenth century B.C.E. Any reconstruction of ancestral history should therefore begin with the most firmly anchored event, and that is the Exodus. Israel Finkelstein has presented archaeological survey evidence that a pastoral-nomadic culture arose in the highlands of Canaan following the collapse of Middle Bronze Age urbanism there, and persisted through the late Bronze Age.[4] He was trying to understand changes in highland subsistence strategies, not to "prove" the ancestor narratives. However, the situation he described would supply an appropriate sociological setting for the lifestyle portrayed in the ancestor narratives. The open frontier of such a world would permit the infiltration of "strangers and sojourners" from various quarters. All this makes the first centuries of the late Bronze Age (*c.* 1500-1200) the most likely chronological setting for the ancestral period. This is, at best, a historical possibility, although not a certainty.

ANCESTRAL RELIGION   A careful reader of the ancestor stories notices that alongside the typical names for the deity, YHWH (LORD) and Elohim (God), there are some other names: God Almighty (El Shaddai) in Gen. 17:1, 28:3, 35:11, and 48:3; God Most High (El Elyon) in Gen. 14:18–20; and God of Seeing (El Roi) in Gen. 16:13, for example. These names all include the divine name El with various epithets. Archaeological research has shown that *El* was the general Semitic name for the "father of the gods" (like Zeus in Greek mythology). El could be addressed by a variety of epithets, often reflecting different sanctuaries.

It may be that the different divine names mentioned reflect ancestral contact with Canaanite religion. We know from later periods that Israelite writers adapted Canaanite mythology to speak of the LORD. That practice may have begun earlier. Or it may be that the ancestors were polytheistic, and that the references to belief in and worship of one god are anachronistic. The revolutionary factor in ancestral religion may have been not the worship of a single god but the close ties between the deity of the ancestral clan and the ancestor. In a time when gods were thought of as localized beings, often dwelling in one temple, the ancestors apparently believed in a deity who journeyed with them and was related to them not via a sanctuary but through a covenant.

CONCLUSION   Taking into account all we have observed, we can conclude that the ancestor stories are authentic folk memories passed down from the Bronze Age, probably the late Bronze Age. The precise nature of these materials, whether accounts of actual exploits, tribal activities narrated under the name of eponymous heroes, etiological tales, or whatever, must be determined by the analysis of

---

[4]Israel Finkelstein. *The Archaeology of the Israelite Settlement.* Jerusalem: Israel Exploration Society, 1989.

each story in question. Individual analysis is also needed to distinguish the accretions added as the stories were transmitted. It is certainly not unreasonable to assume both that some of the ancestors of Israel were remembered in some circles in Israel and that the memories of them were used to advance Israelites' understanding of the world around them.

Summary

The Bible begins with a portrait of cosmic and human origins, as the backdrop for the story of the ancestors of the nation Israel. Genesis 1–11 constitutes a Prehistory to the story of Israel, which begins with the ancestor narratives (Genesis 12–50). Genesis is part of the Torah or Pentateuch, the first section of the Tanak.

From a literary perspective, two creation accounts in Genesis 1–2 combine to give a balanced picture of the mystery of origins. Examined historically, these two accounts seem to be the product of different writers or schools. Study of their original context leads the reader to other ancient Near Eastern accounts of origins, from which these stories seem to draw imagery, even while they interpret the meaning of creation in unique ways.

We detected a recurrent literary pattern in Genesis 3–11. The human breaking of the divinely created order causes a tension between harmony and alienation. Historical study suggests that although some of the traditions in Genesis 3–11

have roots in history, their principal function is to set the stage for history.

Our literary analysis of Genesis 12–50 stressed the themes of promise and journey. A three-fold divine promise of land, progeny, and blessing comes first to Abraham and Sarah, and then to Isaac and Rebekah, Jacob and his wives, and Jacob's twelve sons. Each of these first ancestors of Israel pursues a journey, with both external and internal consequences. The weight of evidence in the search for the original historical context of the ancestors seems to point to the late Bronze Age (after 1500 B.C.E.). A careful reading of Genesis 12–50 reveals hints of the religion of the ancestors of ancient Israel, although the significance of these clues is far from clear.

Questions of origins are timeless, equally as fascinating to us as to those who first heard and read the stories of Genesis. We turn now to questions about the relationship between Genesis and contemporary discussions of origins.

The Contemporary World

Case Study

A Conversation with a Professor

In a biology class, your professor says that modern science has demonstrated that when it comes to teaching us about origins, the biblical Book of Genesis has been proven wrong because its theory about how things came to be does not hold up to

scientific scrutiny. She invites anyone who would like to discuss this statement to drop by her office. You decide to take her up on the offer. Would you agree with your professor's assertion or challenge it? Drawing on what you have learned about the literary and historical worlds of the Genesis accounts of origins in this chapter, what points would you make to your professor about its scientific validity?

Questions for Discussion and Reflection

Note: The ten-part PBS-TV series *Genesis,* produced by Bill Moyers and first aired late in 1996, is a highly engaging, provocative series of conversations among biblical scholars and other sensitive readers about some of the stories in the Book of Genesis. The series provides an excellent resource for an extended discussion of issues raised in this first book of the Bible.

1. *Read Genesis 1–2: Cosmic Origins:*

   a. Much in the news recently has been a theory known as "intelligent design." "ID" theory holds that the natural world has abundant evidence of design by a supernatural creator. Proponents of this theory claim that nature is full of examples of "irreducible complexity" that could not have been produced by a series of successive modifications as advocates of evolution maintain. ID does not relate directly to the account of origins in Genesis. However, ID does harmonize with the fundamental claim of Genesis that the universe was brought into existence by an intelligent designer (God). According to proponents of ID, advocates of the competing theory of evolution by natural selection among randomly generated variables cannot explain away the evidence of intelligent design.

   One of the principal advocates of intelligent design, biochemist Michael Behe, cites the flagella (whip-like structures) found on bacteria as an excellent example of irreducible complexity. He writes in a special report on the issue in a 2002 edition of the journal *Natural History* that the flagella of bacteria are "outboard motors that bacterial cells can use for self-propulsion.... Dozens of different kinds of proteins are necessary for a working flagellum. In the absence of almost any of them, the flagellum does not work or cannot even be built by the cell" (cited in www.actionbioscience.org/evolution/nhmag. html#behe/miller). Behe and other advocates of intelligent design would like the theory to be included alongside the competing evolutionary theory in discussions of origins in science classrooms.

   Intelligent design and its claim that nature is replete with examples of "irreducible complexity" that evolutionary theory cannot explain have been widely challenged by most other contemporary scientists. For example, biochemist Kenneth Miller responds to Behe's claim that the flagella of bacteria could not have evolved. In a companion essay in the same *Natural History* special edition, Miller writes, "Behe's contention that each and every piece of a machine, mechanical or biochemical, must be assembled in its final form before anything useful can emerge is just plain wrong. Evolution produces complex biochemical machines by copying, modifying, and combining proteins previously used for other functions ...

   A small group of proteins from the flagellum does work without the rest of the machine—it's used by many bacteria as a device for injecting poisons into other cells. Although the function performed by this small part when working alone is different, it nonetheless can be favored by natural selection."

   The controversy over whether ID should be considered a legitimate scientific alternative to "evolution through natural selection" has come to public attention in debates over whether ID should be introduced in public school science classrooms. The dispute came to a head in a federal court case in which the Dover, PA, school board was sued by parents who objected to a board mandate that high school biology students be informed of the controversy and directed to a source that advocated ID (see Chapter 16). The judge in the case ruled that ID was actually a veiled attempt to promote the religious belief in a supernatural creator rather than a theory that can be scientifically tested. In his opinion, the judge wrote that requiring ID to be introduced in a public school science classroom violates the U.S. Constitution's prohibition of government "establishment" of religion. Despite these and other court rulings and the broad consensus among today's scientists that ID is not a valid scientific theory, the dispute continues and merits discussion in the context of the contemporary world of Genesis 1–2.

   With regard to the relationship between Genesis 1–2 and the most widely accepted scientific theories of origins (including the "Big Bang" theory of the origin of the known universe and the theory of evolution through natural selection), at least three positions are possible: seeing the two as enemies, strangers, or collaborators. That is, Genesis 1–2 can be seen as in conflict with modern science (since they offer conflicting answers to the same questions), as unrelated to modern science (since the two deal with fundamentally different questions), or as complementary to these scientific theories (since, although dealing with different questions, the two enhance one another). With which of these three positions do you most agree? Or would you describe the relationship between Genesis 1–2 and modern science in a different way?

   b. Some readers identify these passages and their interpretation as one of the root causes of the modern environmental crisis. What, if anything, in the text might be interpreted as condoning human despoiling of the environment? Do you find positive environmental themes in the passage?

c. Are the "two creation stories" ambiguous on the issue of gender relations? Is there gender equality in one and inequality in the other? What effect has this text had (or should it have) on the contemporary discussion of the role of women in society?

2. Read Genesis 3: The Garden of Eden:

a. Focus on the portrayal of the principal characters in this narrative: the serpent, the LORD God, the man (Adam), and the woman (Eve). Reflect on and/or discuss each of the characters. How might the following adjectives apply to each of the characters: cunning, deceitful, mysterious, bold, curious, rebellious, aloof, compassionate, inconsistent, and arrogant? Think of other appropriate descriptions. Do you find in the portrayal of the characters insights into human nature? What does the story imply about the divine/human relationship?

b. Some readers take the story literally, as a description of actual events, while others assume it to be a myth. What difference does such a decision make for the contemporary relevance of the story? Christian readers have traditionally understood these chapters to be the story of the "original sin." Do you find evidence of "sin" in the story? If so, what is the "sin?"

c. Some feminist readers reject the story because they find its portrait of Eve misogynist (characterized by hatred of women). Do you think the story portrays Eve negatively? If so, should it be dismissed as irrelevant or challenged as injurious to women today? In what sense might Eve be considered to be the exemplary character in the story, a role model for modern women?

3. Read Genesis 25–36: Isaac and Jacob:

a. Once again, after reading the story, reflect on and/or discuss the portrayal of the leading characters: Jacob, his brother Esau, their mother Rebekah and father Isaac, Jacob's wives Leah and Rachel, Jacob's uncle Laban, the mysterious wrestler in Genesis 32, and, of course, God. Choose and discuss adjectives that might be applied to each.

b. Do you think Jacob undergoes a process of transformation, as is suggested in the reading offered in this chapter? Other readers do not think Jacob changes in the story.

c. As in the other ancestor stories, the ancestors are not portrayed as "perfect" people; yet they still served God's purposes in important ways. Do you find contemporary significance in this insight?

d. Compare the role of dreams in the story with your own understanding of dreams, or modern theories of the significance of dreams, with which you may be familiar.

e. Try to take one or more of the perspectives of a feminist reader (see Chapter 2) as you consider the story. Are women in this story consistently portrayed as subservient to men? Do any of the women in the story act decisively to defend themselves and their families? In a discussion of the portrayal of women in Genesis, you might also consider the story of Tamar in Genesis 38.

f. How would you respond to those who argue that polygamy should not be outlawed in contemporary society because it is sanctioned in the Bible, as is evident in the ancestor narratives in Genesis?

Chapter 4

Covenant

Exodus, Leviticus, Numbers, and Deuteronomy

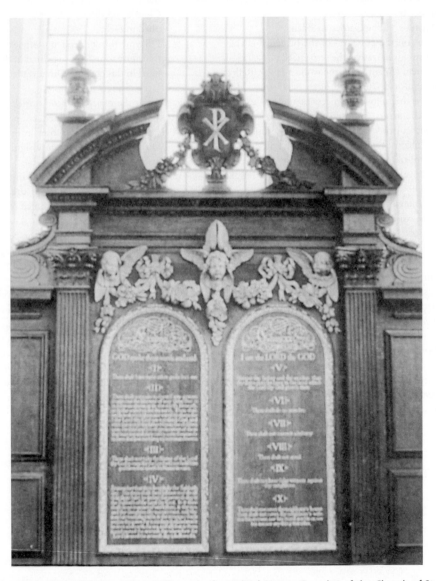

The Winston S. Churchill Memorial and Library in the United States. Reredos of the Church of St. Mary, the Virgin, Aldermanbury, Westminster College, Fulton, Missouri. The Ten Commandments are inscribed above the altar of this seventeenth-century London parish church reconstructed on the Westminster College campus in the 1960s. *Source:* Dr. Christian E. Hauer, Jr., FSA

In the remaining four books of the Pentateuch, the theme of fulfillment of the ancestral promise continues to dominate the narrative. At the beginning of Exodus, the first element of the three-fold promise of progeny, land, and blessing is well on the way to fulfillment. With the deliverance of the people from bondage in Egypt and the subsequent wandering in the Sinai wilderness, attention turns to the second element—the promise of a land. With the covenant at Sinai and with the speech of Moses in Deuteronomy, the theme of blessing is central. At the end of the Pentateuch, each of the promises is on the verge of fulfillment. Within the framework of the narrative, there are several types of literature—legends, poems, legal codes, and speeches.

We have titled this chapter "Covenant" because of the centrality of this theme in these four books. Indeed, covenants are important throughout both the Tanak and New Testament.

There are two basic types of covenants in the Bible. One is essentially a promise made by God, in which a divine plan for a people is revealed, as we have seen in the divine promises made to Noah and all living creatures (Gen. 6:18; 9:9, 11–17) as well as Abraham and Sarah and their descendants (Gen. 15:18; 17:2, 4, 7–11, 13, 19, 21).

The other is an agreement between parties establishing a relationship in which each takes on obligations. It may be a pact between people, as when Jacob and his father-in-law Laban reach a mutual agreement to resolve a conflict (Gen. 31:43–54; *cf.* Gen. 21:27, 32; 26:28; 31:44). This reciprocal type of covenant may also be between God and humans. The most important covenant of this type is the Sinai (Mosaic) Covenant, which is at the center of the books to be considered in this chapter. According to the Sinai Covenant, God made a commitment to the people of Israel that is conditional. The Israelites must fulfill the commandments of the covenant if they expect God to remain faithful to them.

As we shall see, both types of covenants recur throughout the Bible. The promissory type is seen again in the Davidic Covenant in which the LORD vows to keep the heirs of King David on the throne of Judah forever (2 Sam. 7:8–17; *cf.* Ps. 89:19–37). The conditional form is central both to the narrative of the formation and fall of the nations of Israel and Judah in the books of Samuel and Kings and to the prophets of ancient Israel who pronounced judgment based on the people's failure to be obedient to the Sinai Covenant (see Chapter 6). However, the prophets also draw on the promissory covenant when they proclaim a future restoration of the people of Israel and a new age of universal peace and justice. Indeed, the tension between the promissory and conditional forms of covenant is one of the most important dynamics in the Tanak.

The concept of "covenant" is also at the heart of the Christian Bible, in which the "old" covenant between God and Israel is contrasted with the "new" covenant with all humanity believed to have been established through Jesus. From this perspective, the promises of God to Abraham and David are fulfilled in Jesus, as are the obligations stipulated in the Sinai Covenant fulfilled through faith in Jesus Christ. This is symbolized in the Christian community's redesignation of the Tanak as the Old Testament (Covenant) and the remainder of its canon as the New Testament (Covenant).

In addition to the covenant theme, the books to be discussed in this chapter have a fascinating variety of literary features, and we will examine a representative sampling of them: the role of irony in Exodus 1–18, the genre of law codes, and the structuring of the Book of Deuteronomy. These books also raise a number of important historical questions such as: How did the Exodus take place and who was involved? When were the law codes included and when were these books actually written? Was Deuteronomy, or a portion of it, the lawbook found in the Jerusalem Temple in the seventh century B.C.E.? What is the literary history of this material? How does the law found in these books compare with similar legislation in other ancient cultures? These questions concern us in our historical analysis.

Before proceeding, it is appropriate to provide further background for our study of the historical world of the Bible by describing the geography in which biblical history occurred and summarizing the histories of the great empires of the ancient Near and Middle East and of ancient Israel.

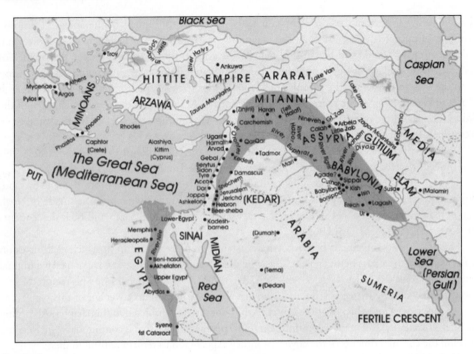

Fertile Crescent

GEOGRAPHY OF THE ANCIENT NEAR EAST AND ISRAEL

At its greatest extent, the land of the Bible includes the area from what is now Turkey in the north to Egypt in the south, and from Italy in the west to Iran in the east. More specifically, the geographic area with which we are concerned is the narrow strip of land at the east end of the Mediterranean Sea. The larger area was the arena of the empires of the ancient world—Egyptian, Assyrian, Babylonian, Persian, Greek, and Roman. The smaller area, known as Canaan or Israel, and to modern geographies as Palestine, was a land bridge across which these empires passed during military campaigns and trade excursions. This area is a coastal corridor connecting the continents of Asia and Africa.

To the north and east lay the empires of Mesopotamia (the land between the Tigris and the Euphrates rivers). Here, at different times, the Babylonians (in southern Mesopotamia) and the Assyrians (in northern Mesopotamia) flourished, exercising dominance over the area. To the south, beyond the Sinai Desert, was Egypt, located along the banks of the Nile. The area from Egypt through Palestine into Mesopotamia is called the Fertile Crescent. Western civilization was born within this crescent-shaped swath of arable land, sandwiched between sea and desert.

The land called Palestine was known by a variety of names in the ancient world. In some texts it was called Canaan. In the Bible it is often "the land of Israel." The name *Palestine,* which derives from "land of the Philistines," was applied to the whole area by the Romans in the second century C.E.

Although small in size (150 miles from north to south and an average of 60 miles from east to west, about the size and shape of Vermont), Palestine has many contrasting features. The land is divided by two north–south mountain ranges that are intersected by east–west valleys, creating four geographic regions: the coastal plain, the central highlands, the Jordan Rift, and the transjordanian highlands.

The coastal plain, along the shore of the Mediterranean, is narrow in the north but broadens in the south as the coast swings to the west. The plain begins in the north at Tyre and continues until it is broken by Mount Carmel, where the important Jezreel Valley begins. This triangular-shaped, very fertile plain (also known as the Plain of Esdraelon or Megiddo) is the only valley that cuts across Palestine all the way from the coast to the Jordan Valley. Thus, it was heavily traveled and of great strategic importance in ancient times. It was controlled by the city of Megiddo. South of Mount Carmel lies the Plain of Sharon, a forested area during the biblical period. At the south end of Sharon was Joppa, Jerusalem's seaport. To the north, Herod the Great built another port, Caesarea, which during New Testament times was the official center for the Roman governor of the province of Judea. The southern stretch of the plain was named after the Philistines, who inhabited it and controlled five main cities (the Pentapolis): Gaza, Ashdod, Ashkelon, Gath, and Ekron. Through these plains ran a road as important as any modern highway—the Way of the Land of the Philistines or the Way of the Sea (Via Maris). It was the major thoroughfare between Egypt and Mesopotamia and therefore of great commercial and strategic importance.

Between the southern coastal plain and the central highlands is a range of low hills (the Shephelah). Through this area, full of olive and sycamore trees, ran a series of valleys that led toward Jerusalem. Therefore, it was full of important and often fortified cities during the Israelite period—Lachish, Beth-shemesh, Gezer, and Beth-horon, to name a few.

The central highlands are the spine of Palestine, formed by a mountain range that begins with the Lebanon range to the north and continues all the way to the desert, broken completely only by the Jezreel Valley. The northern part of this region is Galilee. The northern part ("upper Galilee") was sparsely populated and isolated in the biblical period. The southern part, "lower Galilee," was much less isolated. Nazareth is located in the southern foothills, near Sepphoris, the Roman capital of the province.

The area around Mount Ephraim became known as Samaria. It was fairly populous during the age of the Tanak and the New Testament period, and contained important cities such as Shechem, Tirzah, Dothan, and Samaria.

Further south was Judah. Bounded by steep slopes along east and west, Judah was defensible and relatively isolated. Although crops could be grown in some areas, the rocky terrain was more

The Jordan Rift Valley. A deep depression known as the Jordan Rift, with the Jordan River flowing through its upper half, runs from north to south in Israel. "Jordan" means "that which goes down" in Hebrew, and the winding river drops throughout its course, sometimes rapidly. *Source:* Bumihills/ Shutterstock

suitable for vine culture and for grazing sheep and goats. Judah's major road was along the east slope, and along this road were the important cities of Hebron, Bethlehem, and Jerusalem.

South of Judah lay the Negev (which in Hebrew means "dry land" or "south"), a wilderness area suitable for dry farming and pastoralism. During the biblical period, Beersheba was the main town and marked the traditional southern boundary of Israel (Dan was the northern). In the first century B.C.E. and the first century C.E., the Nabateans, with their capital at Petra, ruled in this area.

The Jordan Rift is a huge geological fault between the two mountain ranges. It is a deep depression running from the Lebanon and Anti-Lebanon mountain ranges in the north (the Beqa Valley) to the Dead Sea (1,300 ft. below sea level) in the south and beyond. It is dominated in the upper half by the Jordan River (from the Hebrew for "descend"). The Jordan begins in several streams near the foot of the snow-peaked Mount Hermon and flows through a swampland (called Lake Huleh) into the Sea of Chinnereth (also called the Sea of Tiberias or the Sea of Galilee). Near

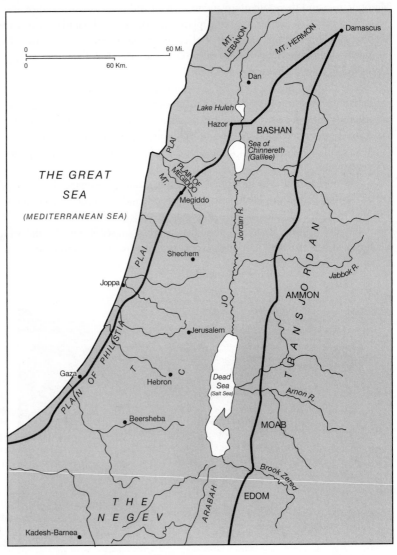

**The Major
Geographic Divisions
of Palestine**

Lake Huleh was the important city of Hazor. Along the shore of the Sea of Galilee (which is actually a freshwater lake) lay the important New Testament cities of Capernaum and Tiberias. The sea is surrounded by steep hills that create a funnel effect for the winds that can quickly whip up into a serious storm on the water.

South of the Sea of Galilee is the Jordan Valley, which in biblical times was full of dense vegetation and predatory animals. The most important cities of the valley were Bethshan, at the juncture of the Jordan and Jezreel valleys, and Jericho, near the Dead Sea. The Jordan River enters into the Dead Sea (also known as the Salt Sea or Sea of the Arabah), the lowest point on earth. Because the sea has no outlet, its waters evaporate, leaving a salty brine in which no marine life can survive. Along the banks of the Dead Sea, the Judean mountains are pocketed with caves. On the northwest edge of the sea lies the ancient site of Qumran, where most of the Dead Sea Scrolls were found. The Jordan Rift continues south of the Dead Sea, forming the Arabah and the Gulf of Aqabah in the Red Sea. At the southern end of the 100-mile-long Arabah was the seaport of Ezion-geber (the modern Elath), from which sea trade was carried out, with the copper mined in the region a prime commodity.

The mountains across the Jordan to the east (the transjordanian highlands) form a plateau. This area was divided into four districts by four streams. From north to south these were Bashan, Gilead, Moab, and Edom. A group of trade routes ran the length of this plateau (e.g., the King's Highway).

HISTORY OF THE ANCIENT NEAR EAST

The great empires of the ancient Near and Middle East developed in the valleys of the Nile in Egypt, the Tigris and Euphrates in Mesopotamia, and the Indus in India. These river valleys were all suited to large-scale irrigation agriculture, which leads to urban civilization. During the period known to archaeologists as the Bronze Age (*c.* 3300–1200 B.C.E.), great urban cultures arose in each of these valleys (see Table 4.1). We shall pass over the Harapan (Indus Valley) Civilization because it was in decline before the biblical period was well under way and because (despite some trade relations) it was peripheral to the cultures in which biblical history transpired.

TABLE 4.1 Archaeological Periods in the Ancient Near East

Stone Age

Paleolithic (100000–8000 B.C.E.)

Mesolithic (8000–5500 B.C.E.)

Neolithic (5500–4000 B.C.E)

Chalcolithic (4000–3300 B.C.E.)

Bronze Age

Early Bronze (3300–2000 B.C.E..)

Middle Bronze (2000–1500 B.C.E..)

Late Bronze (1500–1200 B.C.E..)

Iron Age

Iron I (1200–900 B.C.E..)

Iron II (900–600 B.C.E..)

Iron III (600–300 B.C.E..)

Egypt

The culture along the Nile exhibits one of the longest unbroken strains of ethnic and cultural continuity in the world. From the time of the Old Kingdom to the Muslim Conquest of the seventh century C.E., Egypt had basically a single civilization. There was change and adaptation (especially with the infusion of Greek culture after the conquest of Alexander in the fourth century B.C.E.), but things Egyptian remained recognizably so for over three thousand years.

Egypt is sometimes called the *gift of the Nile*. Indeed, the habitable land is a narrow strip along the Nile with desert on either side. Egyptian agriculture depended on the annual Nile floods and on irrigation from the river. Egypt was a difficult land to invade, and there were relatively few infusions of new populations. But the activities of the great empire did enrich Egypt's population with people of varied heritages. Only once during the entire Bronze Age was Egypt successfully invaded. The conquerors were Asiatics (the Egyptian name for people to the northwest, from Sinai and beyond). They became known as *Hyskos* ("aliens"). The Hyskos kingdom in lower (northern) Egypt lasted from about 1700 to 1550 B.C.E.

The native Egyptian dynasty that followed forced out the invaders and brought the Egyptian empire to its apogee. The brilliant pharaoh Thutmose III (1490–1435) campaigned northward and extended his dominion to the Euphrates. Once again, under Ramses II (1290–1224), Egypt projected its power that far northward, only to be blocked by the Hittites. Sheshonk I's invasion of Israel (*c.* 920) marked the last successful Egyptian incursion into Asia. Egyptian influence declined during the first millennium B.C.E., although the empire remained a power to be reckoned with until the Persian Conquest (sixth century).

Biblical Geography from Space. Gemini XI astronauts took this photograph in which the Red Sea (bottom) and the Gulf of Aqaba (right) frame the Sinai Peninsula. The Wadi Arabah extends northward to the Dead Sea. Further north, the Jordan River flows from the Sea of Galilee to the Dead Sea. The lands of Israel and Philistia are in the upper left; the lands of Edom, Moab, and Ammon (modern Jordan) to the right. Egypt spreads across the bottom while Phoenicia (modern Lebanon), Syria, Asia Minor (modern Turkey), and Mesopotamia (modern Iraq) lie at the top. An edge of the Mediterranean Sea is at the upper left.   *Source:* NASA/Johnson Space Center

Egyptian culture was permeated with an optimism rooted in elaborate hope for an afterlife. There was an opulent lifestyle for the rich, yet ordinary people seemed to fare well in Egyptian society in most periods. The slave-driven hordes building the pyramids are a product of Hollywood imagination. It is more likely that the great pyramids were built by agricultural workers during slack seasons.

Egypt had a large and generally benevolent pantheon of deities. Not surprisingly, a sun god headed many of the early local pantheons. Later Amon–Re (actually a combination of two sun gods) and the falcon-headed Horus emerged as central deities. Khonsu (the moon god) and Nut (the sky goddess) joined Amon–Re to form the divine triad of the great cultic center at Thebes. Still later Osiris, god of the underworld, and his wife, Isis, became central deities. The pharaoh was considered to be the son of Amon and thus himself a god. Pharaohs generally enjoyed great popular affection.

Mesopotamia

Whereas the Nile floods were beneficent, the floods of the Tigris and Euphrates were dangerous and destructive, a fact reflected in Mesopotamian mythology. Mesopotamia was much more open to foreign influences than Egypt. Conquests by warrior aristocrats who installed themselves atop the existing hierarchy were fairly common. Still more common was the peaceful diffusion of cultural innovations.

The basic character of Mesopotamian civilization was laid down by Indo-Aryan people, the Sumerians, in the early Bronze Age. They may have been displaced by Semitic peoples. "Semitic" is a term coined by scholars to refer to people with similar languages and cultures in the ancient world, within the area between Africa and what is now Iran. The languages included Akkadian, Hebrew, Aramaic, and Arabic.

Pyramids of Giza. The pyramids, monumental tombs for great early pharaohs of Egypt, are the best known symbols of the wealth and power of the Egyptian Empire. This group was constructed for pharaohs of the Fourth Dynasty (2600–2480 B.C.E.), and includes the Great Pyramid of the legendary Cheops. Pyramids later gave way to elaborate tombs tunneled into the cliffs of the Valley of the Kings west of Thebes for the burial of pharaohs and other persons of high status, including royal women. *Source:* Sculpies/Shutterstock

Mesopotamia was the seat of great empires from late in the third millennium B.C.E. onward. Often, there was more than one great power between the rivers or on the fringes, and several of these have bequeathed artifacts and records that illuminate the earliest biblical traditions. But prior to the encompassing Persian conquests of the sixth century B.C.E., the major northern influences on biblical history were three: the Hittites, the Assyrians, and the Babylonians.

The mutual exhaustion caused by the confrontation between the Hittite and Egyptian empires, climaxing in the Battle of Kadesh in about 1286 B.C.E., set the stage for the rise of the nation of Israel. Assyria became the dominant influence in the Near East from the ninth to the seventh centuries. Less durable was the neo-Babylonian Empire that replaced the Assyrian, only to perish at the hands of the Persians in the middle of the sixth century.

Persia was not really a Mesopotamian empire because it arose in what is now Iran. But Mesopotamia was the center of Persia's wealth and power, and Babylon was its hub during its dominance in the sixth and fifth centuries. Babylon was also the center of operations of the Macedonian conqueror Alexander during the fourth century. The death of Alexander and the division of his empire to some extent recreated the situation of the pre-Persian world. The Seleucids of Babylonia and Syria and the Ptolemies of Egypt vied for control of the lands between. This unsettled situation continued until Rome moved east. For biblical history the crucial date is 63 B.C.E., when the Roman general Pompey occupied Jerusalem.

Mesopotamian civilization had more influence on Israel than Egyptian culture. Like the Israelites, most Mesopotamians were Semites, and during most of biblical history the empires of Mesopotamia were the dominant power. The Bible traces the origins of the people of Israel to Mesopotamia, whereas in Egypt they were resident aliens.

Like the Egyptian culture, the Mesopotamian was feudal in organization. Unlike Egypt, there was no optimistic hope of an afterlife. The souls of the dead were thought to go to a disembodied existence in the underworld, the fate of all, rich and poor, alike. Unlike the Egyptian pharaohs, the Mesopotamian kings were not considered divine. At best, the king was thought to be the adopted son of the chief god and an agent of the gods.

Assyria was one of the most militaristic powers in history, directing a great deal of energy to the development and use of the technology of war. The Assyrians showed great cruelty to the people they conquered. Their practice was to decimate the societies they conquered through exiling the most important people, if they had not died in battle, and taking other people as slaves.

From the very beginnings of biblical history, the lands between Egypt and Mesopotamia were pawns in the power games of these empires. It was only when the great empires were in a temporary eclipse early in the Iron Age (c. 1100–850 B.C.E.) that Israel and its neighbors flourished. Otherwise, Egypt was the dominant power through the second half of the second millennium, and Mesopotamian empires (first Assyrian, and then Babylonian) dominated in the first millennium, until the Persians took over.

From the Assyrian and Babylonian conquests of Israel and Judah in the eighth and sixth centuries to modern times, excepting the brief Maccabean interlude, the land of Israel was under the control of a succession of empires. It was not so much their resources that made Israel and the other lands between the empires so important; rather, it was their strategic location on the routes of trade and conquest that were essential to control.

HISTORY OF ANCIENT ISRAEL

The history of the people of Israel most likely begins sometime during the second millennium B.C.E., when their ancestors (remembered in the stories of the patriarchs and matriarchs preserved in Genesis [see Chapter 3]) left Mesopotamia and moved to the area we call Palestine (see Table 4.2). This is called the *ancestral period*. Sometime between the fourteenth and twelfth centuries, their descendants,

TABLE 4.2 Major Social and Cultural Periods in the History of Israel

The Ancestral Period (disputed, perhaps *c*. 1750–1500 or 1500–1200 B.C.E.)

The Mosaic Period (disputed, perhaps *c*. 1350–1300 B.C.E.)

The entry of the Exodus group into Canaan (disputed, perhaps between 1300 and 1200 B.C.E.)

The period of the Judges (*c*. 1200–1020 B.C.E.)

The United Kingdom (*c*. 1020–922 B.C.E.)

The Divided Kingdom (*c*. 922–721 B.C.E.)

The Judean Kingdom (*c*. 721–587 B.C.E.)

The Babylonian Period (*c*. 587–539 B.C.E.)

The Persian Period (*c*. 539–333 B.C.E.)

The Hellenistic Period (*c*. 333–63 B.C.E.)

The Roman Period (63 B.C.E. to end of the biblical period)

who had migrated into Egypt, were enslaved, later escaped, and returned to Palestine through the Sinai Desert. Because of the role attributed to Moses, this is often called the *Mosaic period*.

Then follows the occupation of the land of Canaan (Palestine). Not all later Israelites were descended from the Exodus group led by Moses, itself a somewhat mixed company according to the biblical narrative. But it was they who gave emerging Israel its normative origin traditions. During the twelfth and eleventh centuries, the tribes of various origins that made up the people of Israel were apparently loosely organized, joined together by kinship claims and by a commonly held allegiance to their covenant with God. Charismatic leaders emerged to head coalitions of tribes against common enemies. Because these leaders are called judges in the Bible, this is known as the *period of the Judges*.

In the eleventh and tenth centuries the tribes gradually organized themselves into a state-level society, with a centralized bureaucracy under a king (Saul, David, and then Solomon). This is the period of the United Kingdom. A period called the Divided Kingdom followed, with a division of the land into two nations—Israel in the north and Judah in the south. The Divided Kingdom continued until Israel was conquered by the army of Assyria (completely by 722 B.C.E.) and Judah was dominated by the Babylonians (by 589–587 B.C.E.).

Then followed the Babylonian Exile, when the Judean king and many other leaders were forced to live in exile in Babylon. When the Persians replaced the Babylonians, there was a return of some leaders to Palestine, beginning the period called the *Persian period*. The Babylonian Exile began a phase of Jewish history called the *Diaspora* (Dispersion), in which Jews established communities outside Palestine.

The Persian period continued from about 539 to 333 B.C.E., when the Macedonian conqueror Alexander the Great gained control of Palestine. This began the Hellenistic (Greek) phase. Alexander's successors, the Egyptian Ptolemies and the Mesopotamian Seleucids, eventually took control of Palestine in turn. The vicious repression practiced by the Seleucids sparked a revolt among Jews, headed by a family called the Hasmoneans, or the Maccabees. Their victory led to the creation of an independent Jewish state in the second century B.C.E., which lasted until the Romans took over in 63 B.C.E.

Throughout the New Testament period, Rome continued to maintain control over Palestine and the Mediterranean world. All of the New Testament was written against the backdrop of the *Roman period*. Several events are especially important. During a Jewish revolt in 70 C.E., Jerusalem was leveled by the Romans, a traumatic event in both Jewish and Christian history. This was about forty years after the death of Jesus. Paul had conducted his missionary activity and written his letters in the 40s and 50s.

During the development of the Christian Church and the period of the writing of the New Testament, there existed relative toleration, interspersed with periods of persecution of Christians by Roman authorities (e.g., in the 60s under Nero, possibly in the 80s and 90s under Domitian, and twenty years later under Trajan). The period before the 70s is usually called the *apostolic age*, and the period after that, which continued until the middle of the second century, is called the *postapostolic age* of Christian history.

LET MY PEOPLE GO (EXODUS 1–18)

The Literary World: Pharaoh a God?

The narrative in Exodus 1–18 tells the story of the enslavement of Jacob's descendants in Egypt by a Pharaoh who "did not know Joseph" (1:8); the birth, early career, and commissioning of Moses by God, who reveals for the first time (to the characters in the story) the special name YHWH (LORD); the confrontation of Moses, and his brother Aaron, with Pharaoh and the demand to "let my people go"; the ten plagues visited on the recalcitrant Pharaoh and his people; and the miraculous deliverance of the fleeing Hebrews from Pharaoh at the Red Sea.

The story gives us an opportunity to observe the role of irony in a biblical tale, especially in the portrayal of Pharaoh, whose attempts to oppress the people of Israel and keep them from escaping are thwarted at every turn. Pharaoh lays heavy burdens on the people; they multiply all the more. He plots to kill the sons of the Hebrews, but he is outsmarted by Hebrew midwives. His own daughter adopts Moses, causing Pharaoh to take to his bosom the very one who will cause his demise. Pharaoh is victimized by the series of plagues that climaxes in an ironic reversal of his plot to kill the sons of the Hebrews. It is Egyptian children who die as a result of Pharaoh's treachery. Finally, Pharaoh and his best warriors are humiliated by the motley collection of slaves. In the final reversal, the oppressor himself is crushed.

When we remember that Pharaoh was accorded divine status in Egypt, the ironic portrayal takes on deeper significance. This is more than the humiliation of a human despot; it is the deflation of the claim of divinity for the Egyptian king. The real contest dramatized in Exodus 1–18 is between the LORD and a pretender to divine power. The narrative and the victory song (Exodus 15) leave no doubt who is the victor:

> Sing to the Lord, for he has triumphed gloriously;
> the horse and rider he has thrown into the sea! (15:21)

Mighty Pharaoh is powerless in comparison with the true divine warrior and king. With his heart hardened by the LORD, he is little more than a helpless pawn in the drama.

Irony in Exodus 1–18 is not confined to the portrayal of Pharaoh. Moses is not exempt. His first decisive act of leadership of his people—killing an Egyptian who is beating one of the Hebrews (2:11–12)—is immediately undercut by suspicion of his motives by other Hebrews. Their reaction foreshadows the recurrent motif in the Torah narrative of the people complaining to Moses about his leadership. Another example of irony is the strange incident that occurs as Moses returns to Egypt to carry out the LORD's commission. With no explanation, we are told, "At a lodging place on the way the LORD met him [Moses] and sought to kill him" (Ex. 4:24). Why would the LORD try to kill the one he has just chosen to lead his people from slavery? The irony of this incident serves to add a touch of mystery to the story. Just when it seems the LORD's ways are clear and intelligible, the narrative shocks us into realizing they are not.

These observations must serve as one of the few hints we will be able to provide of the rich irony pervading biblical literature. The general effect of irony is to enliven the literature with humor, surprise, and mystery.

From a literary perspective, the LORD is a character, not only in the Exodus narrative but also throughout the Bible.[1] In these chapters, we are introduced to one of the most pervasive characterizations of the LORD in the Tanak: God as Divine Warrior without equal. The stage is set for the problematic and troubling theme of holy war, in which the biblical writers will portray Israel's battles against enemies as the LORD's wars and the utter annihilation of foes as an expression of obedience to God. As we will note in our historical discussion in the next chapter, the genocidal conquest of Canaan by the Israelites, found especially in the Book of Joshua, may very well reflect the perspective of an author or editor intent on giving an idealized and ruthless account of a ritually pure army led by their divine commander in an idealized campaign rather than a record of actual events. As many have observed, historical study can at times serve to balance and correct conclusions reached on the basis of intrinsic literary analysis alone.

The Historical World: The Exodus in History

Literary historians agree that the Song of the Sea (Exodus 15) is one of the oldest texts in the Hebrew Bible because of the archaic character of the poem's language and style. In addition, the Song seems to draw on the structure and imagery of the Canaanite myth of the god Ba'al (Lord), who destroys the chaotic forces personified as the god Sea (Yamm) in order to reestablish cosmic order after it has been disrupted. In Exodus 15, the LORD shatters Pharaoh's army, with the imagery of chaotic waters being

Seder Cup and Plate. The Festival of Passover celebrates the liberation of Israelite slaves from Egyptian bondage. A special plate arrayed with the most important symbolic elements of the Seder, the Passover banquet, is traditionally placed near the seat of the leader to facilitate explanations of their significance. Each celebrant receives four cups of wine (mixed with water, so no one will get drunk, and with spices to maintain the flavor). A fifth cup of wine is poured for the prophet, Elijah, herald of the Messiah. Jesus' last supper with his disciples was a Seder according to the Gospels of Matthew, Mark, and Luke.   *Source:* MG photos/Shutterstock

---

[1]For a provocative literary analysis of God as a character in the Hebrew Bible, see Jack Miles. *God: A Biography.* New York: Random House, 1995.

overcome (v. 8). Just as Ba'al is installed in a mountain palace after his victory and proclaimed the cosmic king, the LORD is established in His sanctuary, from which He will reign eternally. The earthly sanctuary on its mountain is the parallel of the heavenly abode of the divine king. Stylistically, the "stair-like parallelism" evident in the building imagery in verses 7, 11, 16–17 is commonly found in the Canaanite myth.

Feminist interpreters have pointed out that in the Canaanite myth the goddess Anat is Ba'al's fellow combatant, and imagery associated with her in the Canaanite myth is applied to the LORD in the Song of the Sea, in effect collapsing the god and goddess into the single character of the LORD.

Adaptation of Canaanite mythology is found in a number of other books in the Hebrew Bible, especially the Psalms (e.g., 74:12–15) and the prophetic books (e.g., Isaiah 51:9–11). As in the Song of the Sea, the recurrent pattern is to relate the exploits of Ba'al and Anat in Canaanite myth to the LORD's involvement in historical events, especially the exodus from Egypt. In so doing, fundamental events in the creation of the nation Israel, such as the deliverance from bondage in Egypt, are given cosmic significance.

Israelite folk memory recalled the Exodus and the manifestation of the LORD at Mount Sinai (Exodus 19–20 and following) as a single complex of events. Indeed, these events became the charter of Israel's national existence, and the reference point for understanding the meaning of Israel's life and its relationship with God. However, placing these events (if they are indeed historical) within the context of ancient Near Eastern history (see Table 4.3) has challenged generations of interpreters.

Some literary historians have argued that not all circles in Israel shared this full complex of traditions. When we examine the establishment of Israel in the land of Canaan in the next chapter, it will become clear why this might well be the case. At this stage, we need only observe that the group that experienced the Exodus became the bearer of Israel's national traditions. These traditions became the common property of all those who came to think of themselves as Israelites, whether or not they had a real ancestor who had followed Moses in the wilderness. Thus, in rabbinic practice, converts to Judaism immersed themselves as a part of their ritual of induction, recreating the experience of passing through the waters of the sea. Similarly, all the events surrounding American independence are the property of every American citizen, whether native or naturalized.

TABLE 4.3 Political Situations in the Ancient Near East during the Period of the Exodus and Occupation of Israel

Date (B.C.E.)	Egypt	Canaan (Palestine)	Mesopotamia
1300	New Kingdom continues; Egyptian Revival, Seti 1 (c. 1305–1290)	Israelite Exodus	Assyrian dominance continues until c. 1197
	Ramses II (c. 1290–1224), Battle of Kadesh with Hittites (c. 1286)	Wilderness wandering	
	Merneptah (c. 1224–1200), War with Sea Peoples (c. 1220–1175)	Israelite occupation	
1200	Ramses III (c. 1183–1152)	Invasion of Sea Peoples (Philistines and others)	Assyrian decline
	Egyptian decline	Period of the Judges (c. 1200–1020)	Brief Assyrian revival (c. 1116–1078)
1100		Philistine pressure on Israelite tribes	
		Samuel	

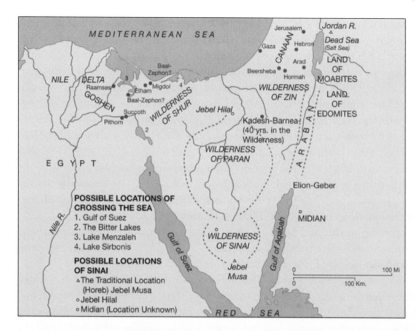

Possible Routes of the Exodus

Looking beneath the recognizably stylized aspects of the narrative concerning the Exodus, a plausible sequence of events can be seen. Perhaps abetted by natural misfortunes, a group of Hebrew slaves won manumission from their imperial master. Led by their advocate, Moses, a Hebrew with knowledge of Egyptian ways, they began their journey northeastward out of Egypt. But a contingent of Egyptian frontier guards, whether on orders of a central government that had changed its mind or on their own initiative, pursued the escapees. A fortuitous thunderstorm prevented immediate capture. Then, at a crucial moment, the lightly shod Hebrews escaped through a body of water shallowed by the wind. The Egyptian chariots foolishly pursued for the kill, but the wind changed, the tidal flow shifted, and, in a moment of panic, the chariots turned into the resurgent flood.

All discussions of the Exodus are obliged to recognize that the topography of Suez–Sinai has been modified by the digging of the Suez Canal. Several candidates have been advanced as the possible location of the Exodus. One is Lake Timsah in the central Suez. Another is the nearby Great Bitter Lake, now incorporated like Timsah, in the Suez Canal. Another possibility is a "northern" route. The southern arm of Lake Menzaleh is one prominent northern candidate; Lake Sirbonis offers another. Other proposals have included the northernmost neck of the Gulf of Suez, where wind and tidal behavior (before dredging for the Suez Canal) permitted crossings. It is said that during his Egyptian campaign, Napoleon tried a crossing at Suez, only to barely escape the fate of Pharaoh's chariots when the wind and tide turned. The northern neck of the Gulf of Elath has also been proposed. However, this gulf is almost certainly too distant from Egypt.

If we could pinpoint the location of the sacred mountain, the location of the Exodus might be easier. But for the ancient Israelites, the mountain of God was movable. When Solomon built the Temple in Jerusalem, the holy mountain moved from the wilderness to Jerusalem. Israelite folk memory is vague on Mount Sinai's original location. Most interpreters are inclined to accept the traditional location in southern Sinai at what is now Jebel Musa (for which there is no plausible pre-Christian evidence) or a more modest peak near Kadesh Barnea in north central Sinai. Others think the traditions point toward a location in the land of Midian to the east, south of Edom. The southern Exodus route would best serve this theory.

We must admit that a consistent and plausible case can be made for the northern, the central, or the southern Exodus routes, and the biblical account of the stages of Israel's journey to the mountain of God squared with one of the Sinai identifications. The popular view of modern biblical scholars that the name for the body of water that was crossed means in Hebrew "Sea of Reeds" supports the notion that a relatively shallow reed-grown lake or bay was involved. However, this language may be pressed too vigorously by scholars looking hard for evidence to support their reconstructions, for the term has been understood throughout history to mean Red Sea. Certainly, a shallow point in the sea is probable. The southern location on the Gulf of Suez (an arm of the Red Sea) may have the most historical probability.

There still seems to be a fairly strong consensus among knowledgeable historians as to the date of the Exodus, although it is not as widely held as it once was. It rests on reasoning out the most probable conclusion from both biblical tradition and archaeology. Genesis 15:12–16 and 1 Kings 6:1 appear to presuppose an exodus in the fifteenth century B.C.E., and Gen. 15:13 a lengthy enslavement in Egypt. But, on careful reading, the Genesis passages are less clear. It is only with the rise of the Israelite monarchy that the chronological references in the Tanak can be correlated with the modern calendar with any degree of precision.

It was noted earlier that some scholars wish to put the Israelite descent into Egypt in the Hyksos period as the most likely time for an Asiatic, Joseph, to rise in the service of Pharaoh. However, foreigners were in important Egyptian governmental positions at other periods. Some would associate the Pharaoh who did not remember Joseph, and hence enslaved the Israelites (Ex. 1:8), with the expulsion of the Hyksos. Others associate the Exodus itself with the Hyksos expulsion.

But the Hyksos episode does not exhaust the sort of upheavals that could bring "new people" to the fore or dash down others in radical changes of government and policy in middle to late Bronze Age Egypt. Amenhotep IV (Akhnaton) of the dynasty XVIII, who lived from 1364 to 1346, presided over a great cultural revolution in Egypt (including an experiment in monotheistic religion) called the *Amarna Age,* after the modern name of his new capital city. Discovery of the archives of the ruined palace at Tel el-Amarna have revealed a diplomatic correspondence from supposed vassal kings in Canaan. These *Amarna Letters* portray a region in turmoil. It was each against all, all against each, all after Egyptian foreign aid, and the Habiru on the prowl. Some have conjectured that the Israelite invasion under Joshua belongs at this time, but data do not support this view. A counterrevolution late in the reign of Akhnaton, or at the accession of the famed Tutankhamun, ended the Amarna experiment and achieved a temporary accommodation between old and new, while rebuilding the military and shoring up the empire. Tutankhamun was succeeded by his loyal vizier, the elderly Ay. A scheme to marry King Tut's young widow to a Hittite prince to solidify the dynasty and make peace with the northern empire failed. General Horemheb, who despised Tut and Ay, usurped the throne but failed to establish a dynasty. Then, dynasty XIX under Seti I appeared. Many could rise and fall in such times.

The biblical narratives require a time for the Exodus when there were extensive building activities in the Nile delta, because that is where the Israelites were supposed to have been when the Exodus began. They also require that the Egyptian court be located nearby, because Moses and Aaron seemed to get back and forth handily between the Hebrew labor camps and Pharaoh's court. The early thirteenth century B.C.E. meets this requirement, because during dynasty XIX there was an infrastructure for imperial campaigns in Asia headquartered in the delta region. At the other end, the third ruler of dynasty XIX, Merneptah, claimed in a victory hymn to have inflicted grief on "Israel" during an Asiatic campaign. The inscription dates to about 1208 B.C.E., indicating that, by this time, somebody called Israel was on the loose in Canaan.

The biblical traditions say that Moses led the Exodus group in the wilderness for forty years, the conventional Hebrew figure for a generation. Then he yielded to Joshua, who led the second generation of the Exodus company across the Jordan River into the land of Canaan. Clear-cut destruction layers dating to the mid to late thirteenth century have been found at some of the towns said to have been captured by Joshua. Other sites not mentioned in the Joshua narrative suffered a similar fate at about the same time. The rebuilding of these sites tended to be cruder and more modest. New villages sprang up in previously unpopulated areas. This, along with changes in pottery types, suggests that a different, culturally less sophisticated group was responsible for the destructions and for the new villages. Archaeological surveys of occupation patterns in the Transjordan seem to accord with a thirteenth-century date. According to the Book of Numbers, Moses and his band encountered armed resistance as they moved through the Transjordan on their way to Canaan. Although currently under scrutiny, archaeological surveys of this area seem to indicate that this type of opposition would have been more likely in the thirteenth century than one or two centuries earlier, because of relative population densities in the Transjordan.

Exodus 13:17 says that Moses did not lead the Israelites "by way of the land of the Philistines … for God thought, 'If the people face war, they may change their minds and return to Egypt.'" That is, Moses avoided the more direct and heavily traveled coastal route to Canaan, for at the Egyptian end, it would have been well supplied with checkpoints and fortifications, and further along (assuming a thirteenth-century date), there would have been the chance of encountering Egyptian–Hittite friction and the first ripples of the incursion of the Sea Peoples (including the Philistines).

These data constitute a strong if not compelling case for an early thirteenth-century B.C.E. date for the Exodus. Plausible hypotheses locating the Exodus a century or two earlier can be argued, but no alternative hypothesis can muster such a large body of converging and cumulative data in its favor.

Ronald Hendel has developed a thesis that reinforces our "three worlds" model, showing how a literary tradition (the Exodus story) interacts with historical experience.[2] Hendel notes that the Exodus story would resonate with a broad range of people in the region over an extended period of time. The pharaoh in the story is not named. He is an archetype, the model of the evil oppressor. Many groups experienced oppression under the pharaohs of the XVIII–XX dynasties as Egyptian armies marched to the north, taking war prisoners and other slaves and deportees who were brought to Egypt. Egyptian vassal rulers in Canaan sent male and female slaves as a form of tribute. There were also tales of signs and wonders, including a devastating plague during the late XVIII dynasty that some regarded as the handiwork of a god from Canaan. Finally, Moses, the central character of the Exodus traditions, was a mediating figure, a Semite with an Egyptian name, married to a Midianite woman, and associated with the landless tribe of Levi. These considerations are not direct arguments for the historicity of the Exodus. But they do suggest how such traditions, whatever their origin, could become a central focus for the diverse people who came to constitute historic Israel.

YOU SHALL BE MY PEOPLE, AND I SHALL BE YOUR GOD (EXODUS 19–50, LEVITICUS, NUMBERS)

The Literary World: Covenant and Law

THE SINAI COVENANT   As the people camp near the holy mountain, Moses ascends and encounters the LORD. He is told to remind the people how the LORD delivered them from the Egyptians and brought them to this place, and then to say, "Now therefore, if you obey my voice and keep my covenant, you shall be my treasured possession out of all the people. Indeed, the whole earth is mine, but you shall be for me a priestly kingdom and a holy nation" (Ex. 19:5–6).

---

[2]Ronald Hendel. "The Exodus in Biblical Memory." *Journal of Biblical Literature,* 140:4 (Winter 2001), 601–622; "A Book of Memories." *Bible Review,* XVIII:4 (August 2002), 38–45, 52.

This is the heart of what became known as the *Sinai Covenant*. Unlike the earlier covenants, it is not an unconditional promise by God to the people. It is a conditional agreement, dependent on allegiance to the LORD and faithfulness to the covenant. The Sinai Covenant introduces the way to fulfillment of the third element of the ancestral promise: blessing. Through obedience to this covenant, the descendants of Abraham will be blessed, and through them, others will be blessed. It should not be difficult to understand why observance of the stipulations of the Sinai Covenant became so central to the self-understanding of the nation Israel (and later, to Judaism). These commandments were considered Torah (the instruction or law delivered by God as the basis for the ordering of human life). They were thought to be the heart of the Books of Moses (the Pentateuch) and of the entire Tanak.

In the final form of the Pentateuch, the stipulations of the covenant given through Moses at Mount Sinai continue (with one narrative interruption in which the covenant is broken and reaffirmed—Exodus 32–34) from Exodus 20 to the entire book of Leviticus and until Numbers 10. For a variety of reasons it is dubious that *all* this legislation was given to Moses at this time. Much of the law has the ring of later institutions and practices (such as extensive legislation concerning the priesthood and elaborate worship); it is probably grouped here for the sake of validating its authority.

TYPES OF LAWS   To analyze the legislation from a literary point of view, let us first focus on the form of particular laws. There are two basic types of laws in the Sinai legislation. One is an unconditional command or prohibition (called absolute, or *apodictic law*). It is legislation. "You shall have no other gods before me" (Ex. 20:3) and "Honor your father and mother" (20:12) are examples. The other basic form is conditional law (called case, or *casuistic*). It is "common law." It includes an "if …" or "when …" (describing a situation) with the required or prohibited action. For example, "If you lend money to my people, to the poor among you, you shall not exact interest from him" (Ex. 22:25).

The first type of law demarcates categories of actions to do or avoid in order to maintain the type of social order God desires. The second type identifies specific situations that can threaten social harmony, and it identifies what to do or not do in these situations in order to maintain or restore balance. Often the action mandated in conditional law is to "pay back" an injured party (see, e.g., Ex. 22:14). If the reparation is the same as the action, the law is called a *talion,* stated, for example, in general terms in Ex. 21:23–24. Still another legal form is the curse (and its counterpart, the blessing), in which a general punishment (or state of well-being) is invoked for specific types of action.

The specific law is often elaborated when given, either to make it more specific or to provide a motive for obeying it. For example, after prohibiting "graven images" (Ex. 20:4, RSV), the law makes the prohibition more specific ("You shall not bow down to them or serve them"), and then explains the motive ("For I the LORD your God am a jealous God …"). Frequently, the motive is based on assumptions about who God is and what God has done (e.g., Ex. 20:11). Other motives appeal to general principles of respect for human life and the minimal conditions of living.

LAW CODES   Individual laws are combined in the Pentateuch as legal collections or codes with their own particular orientations. Grouped together in the Sinai setting, they are given equal authority as stipulations of the covenant, regardless of when they may have been composed.

Most basic is the ethical *Decalogue (Ten Commandments),* which appears first in Ex. 20:1–17. Its fundamental significance is underlined by its being placed first and by its subsequent repetition in Dt. 5:1–21. In these ten apodictic laws are found the essence of what it meant for ancient Israel to keep the covenant. The ten laws are divided into four that establish the parameters of the people's relationship with the LORD and six that set forth the boundaries of human relationships. Although seemingly negative ("Thou shalt not …"), they are actually "permissive." They establish the broad area within which Israel may find a harmonious life, establishing respect for the LORD and respect for human life, within and outside the family, as that framework.

The first appearance of the Decalogue is followed immediately by a collection of mostly casuistic laws, known as the *Covenant Code* or *Book of the Covenant* (Ex. 20:23–23:33). These laws seem to make more specific some of the Ten Commandments. Exodus 20:23–26, for example, specifies in what ways the LORD is to be worshipped if there are to be no graven images, and 21:15 and 17 indicate what should happen to those who do not respect their parents. The code establishes the rights of slaves (21:1–11); specifies how violence shall be controlled (21:12–32); states how property shall be respected (21:33–22:17); establishes a ritual calendar around a weekly sabbath, a sabbath year every seven years, and three-yearly festivals—Unleavened Bread in the spring (note that Passover is expressly not mentioned), First Fruits of the wheat harvest in the summer (the same as Pentecost or the Feast of Weeks, Shavuot), and Ingathering in the fall (the Feast of Booths, Sukkot) (23:10–19). This collection assumes a settled, agrarian style of life, which the Israelites did not begin until they entered the land of Canaan, and some of the laws (e.g., against nakedness at the altar) seem to be reactions against worship practices of the resident Canaanites.

After the Covenant Code is given, a ceremony is held to seal the covenant (24:1–18). The blood of a sacrificial animal is thrown by Moses on the altar and the people, and Moses reads the *Book of the Covenant* to them.

Another early code, usually called the *Ritual Decalogue,* is found in Ex. 34:10–26. Except for the Ritual Decalogue, the next collection of laws continues, with one narrative interruption, from Exodus 25 to Numbers 10. Because of the dominant concern with matters of worship and the priesthood, this lengthy corpus has been called by interpreters the *Priestly Code.* However, to consider this long block of material a unity obscures the variety within it. For example, Leviticus 17–26 can be considered a separate collection of laws that revises much of the Covenant Code. Because of a basic concern with the "holiness" of the people (e.g., Lev. 19:2), Leviticus 17–26 is called the *Holiness Code.*

Many literary historians set apart Leviticus 17–26 as distinct from the rest of the Book of Leviticus and consider it a separate law code for several reasons. First, its views of holiness (the state of being set apart, made sacred by God) contrasts with the other chapters. In the rest of the book, holiness is associated with the sanctuary; in these chapters the land promised by God is the context for holiness. Moreover, in the remainder of Leviticus, holiness is linked to priests and Nazirites (those who have taken a special vow or been devoted to the service of the LORD by their parents [*cf.* Num. 6:1–21; 1 Sam. 1:1–11; Jg. 13:1–7]), while in the Holiness Code, all the adults in the land (including resident aliens) are admonished to be holy. The emphasis in these chapters is the life of holiness associated with the keeping of the commandments of the Sinai Covenant. Second, the section begins with the introductory formula of a law code, as the LORD addressing Moses and telling him to say to the people of Israel: This is what the LORD has commanded (17:1–2). It ends with the formulaic conclusion of a code (26:46), even though the book continues with other legislation. Finally, the recurrent phrases "I am the LORD your God" and "I am the LORD; I sanctify them" seem to suggest unity.

However, other scholars question whether Leviticus 17–26 should be considered a separate literary unit. They point out that this section of Leviticus is connected thematically with the preceding chapters. They also observe that Leviticus 25–26 is distinct from the other chapters in the "code."

The themes addressed in the Holiness Code include the slaughtering of animals (17); sexual relations, including the controversial sections on same-sex relations among men (18); ritual and moral holiness (19), including admonitions to "love your neighbor as yourself" (19:18) and to love

Michelangelo's Moses. This statue by renowned Italian Renaissance artist Michelangelo Buonarroti (1475–1564) is located in the Church of San Pietro in Vincoli in Rome, Italy. Completed in 1515, it portrays Moses with horns (an ancient symbol of wisdom and authority) as was customary in depictions in medieval Europe. The representation of Moses with horns is based on the version of Exodus 34:39–35 in the Latin Vulgate. The Hebrew text of these verses, reflected in modern translations, uses words meaning "radiance" rather than horns, indicating that the face of Moses shone after his encounter with God on Mt. Sinai.   *Source:* Imagestalk/Shutterstock

the alien who resides with you as yourself "for you were aliens in the land of Egypt" (19:34); penalties for the violations of the mandate for holiness, including death for breaking the prohibition against homosexual acts; the holiness of priests (21); holy offerings (22); appointed festivals, including the Sabbath, Passover, Unleavened Bread, Weeks, Booths, and the Day of Atonement (23); the ritual lamp, bread, and punishments for speaking contemptuously of God (24); the Sabbatical year (a year of rest for the land) and Year of Jubilee (every fiftieth year, which is, among other things, a year of cancellation of debts and freedom for indentured servants) (25); and rewards for obedience and penalties for disobedience (26).

When Moses ascends the mountain again after the ratification ceremony, he receives an elaborate set of instructions on the building of an ark (container) for the tablets of the covenant. The Ark of the Covenant was also considered a symbolic throne for the LORD. In addition, an elaborate lampstand, an altar table, and a "tabernacle" to house them are mandated, with instruction for the priests who will conduct worship there. The priests will come from the family of Aaron. It stretches the most fertile imagination to see all of this happening in the Sinai Desert, and much of the description seems to be of the later Temple of Solomon in Jerusalem. Again, having this legislation (Exodus 25–31) in the Sinai setting gives it special authority.

The other major collection of law in the Tanak is delivered by Moses as part of his speech in Deuteronomy 12–26 and is called the *Deuteronomic Code.*

The Historical World: Law in the Ancient Near East

Common understanding concerning rules of behavior, notions of how to deal with rule breakers, and techniques for solving tensions caused by extreme forms of misbehavior (especially homicide, which can lead to acts of vengeance and feuds) are characteristic of almost all human social groups.

Such systems have often been administered by family heads, tribal notables, a shaman or other cultic figure, or a special sort of arbitrator. Law in this simple sense is probably as old as living in communities. The formal codification of law and certainly the development of legal institutions and means for enforcing law and order accompany the emergence of social stratification and governmental organization.

Law codes are some of the earliest documents to survive from the ancient Near East. The code of the famous early Babylonian emperor Hammurabi (1728–1686 B.C.E.) was the first to come to the attention of modern scholars and remains the best known. But it is predated by the Sumerian code of Ur-Nammu (*c.* 2050), the code of King Bilalama of the city of Eshnunna (*c.* 1920), and that of Lipit-Ishtar of Isin (*c.* 1875), all from Mesopotamia. These codes are compilations of laws and, hence, stand within a long process of development. Hammurabi's code reflects the background of a rigidly stratified society. The laws recognize degrees of social standing. The severity of the penalty for various transgressions (including medical malpractice!) increases with the status of the victims of the transgressions.

Not all legal documents were law codes. Contracts, including adoption contracts and slave acquisitions, have survived, as well as deeds and records of lawsuits. Various parts of the Tanak preserve a similar variety of legal documents and practices. Micah 6:1–8 reflects the literary form of a lawsuit. Job 31 is an oath of clearance of the sort a person would take to establish innocence before a court. Jeremiah 32:6–15 provides a great deal of information about property transfers and deeds. Ruth 4:7–12 portrays a transfer of the levirate marriage obligation (*cf.* Dt. 25:5–10).

Our literary analysis has shown that several major codes are embodied in the Torah, all of which seem to be compilations of material that grew up over a period of time. Actually, it is a bit misleading to speak of these compilations as *law codes.* They do contain what we today would regard as legal material. But they also contain religious rubrics, medical and public health protocols, rules for maintaining ritual purity (or resolving ritual pollution), obscure taboos (like the prohibition against weaving linsey-woolsey fabric [Dt. 22:11]), and many other items. Ancient law codes may not have been intended to be exhaustive bodies of law like the codes of modern states. Rather, they may have been handbooks for judges, giving them a variety of models on the basis of which they could deal with the more extensive range of issues that would ultimately come before them.

Law was administered in premonarchic Israel by tribal elders, village elders, or both, and by specialists whose particular skills or special charisma were widely recognized. The forensic activities of some of the judges and of the holy man Samuel are reminiscent of the anthropological description with which we began this section. As Israelite culture became more organized, important cultic centers and the gate courts of fortified towns and cities became the sitting places of sacerdotal and lay courts, respectively. Another legal judicial layer was created by the monarchy, but no royal decrees have survived, to our knowledge. Deuteronomy suggests a possible appellate court system with a high court in Jerusalem for the most difficult cases.

The monotheism of the Israelite Torah tradition and its inclusion of relatively rare (for that age) absolute law do not constitute its sole distinctions. Also notable is its persistent commitment to egalitarianism. This can be explained by its roots in the relatively egalitarian tribal culture of the premonarchic period. But all of Israel's great Torah compilations were "published" after the Israelites had developed a more stratified society and a state-level (monarchic) political organization. This aspect of the Torah tradition was not in the interests of the more prestigious circles in later Israelite society. Still, its survival and the persistence of prophetic condemnations of Torah infidelity point to the enduring influence of loyalty to the LORD's Torah in Israel's life.

A LOOK BACK, A LOOK AHEAD (DEUTERONOMY)

The Literary World: The Farewell Address of Moses

Throughout history many great leaders have given farewell addresses in which they sum up what has happened during their term of service, give advice for the future, and symbolically pass the mantle of leadership to a successor. In its final literary form, the first thirty chapters of Deuteronomy are structured as the farewell speech of Moses to the people of Israel as they stand ready to cross over the Jordan River and enter the land of Canaan. This speech includes the three elements of historical review, advice for the future, and concern for succession. To the speech are added two poems (Deuteronomy 32–33) and a historical conclusion (Deuteronomy 31, 34), which links the entire Pentateuch to the subsequent narrative. The speech is divided by three separate introductions (1:1–5; 5:1; 29:1).

There are a number of theories concerning the literary structure behind the speech format. We will mention only two. It is possible to see most of Deuteronomy as a reflection and "updating" of much of the Book of Exodus:

Exodus	Deuteronomy
1–18: Egypt to Sinai	1:1–4:43: Sinai to Moab
19:1–20:21: Covenant and Ten Commandments	4:44–5:22: Covenant and Ten Commandments
20:22–23:33: Book of the Covenant	12–26: Deuteronomic Code
24: Concluding Ceremony	27–28: Concluding Ceremony

In addition, similarities have been noted between the structure of Deuteronomy and the form of a treaty between a dominant nation and its vassal states (called the *suzerainty treaty*) common in the ancient Near East from about 1500 to 700 B.C.E. In these treaties, the suzerain (principal nation) agrees to protect the vassal, provided the conditions of the treaty are met. The treaties generally included the following elements:

1. preamble identifying the suzerain and vassals;
2. historical prologue noting the suzerain's protection of the vassal;
3. general principles;
4. detailed obligations imposed on the vassal;
5. directions as to the deposit of the treaty and future public reading;
6. lists of witnesses (gods);
7. curses that would result from disobedience and blessings that would accrue if the treaty obligations were followed.

Deuteronomy can be interpreted as an adaptation of this form to the covenant between the LORD (the suzerain) and Israel (the vassal):

1. preamble and historical prologue (Deuteronomy 1–4);
2. general principles (Deuteronomy 5–11);
3. detailed obligations (Deuteronomy 12–26);
4. curses and blessings (Deuteronomy 27–30);
5. provision for deposit and public reading (Deuteronomy 31–34).

Because the LORD is the only God, according to Deuteronomy, there can be no other divine witnesses, so that element is not present.

The language of Deuteronomy is markedly different from any we have so far encountered. It has the ceremonial style encountered today in many sermons and political speeches. The sentences are more involved than those to which we have grown accustomed. Formulas (such as "Hear, O Israel …") are repeated, and a few central points are emphasized again and again. Deuteronomy seems to be framed in the splendid rhetorical prose of Judah's professional scribes of the eighth to seventh century B.C.E.

All of the Israelite traditions tend to be egalitarian and humanitarian in outlook. Deuteronomy is even more so. The Covenant Code ordered manumission for male (but not female) Hebrew slaves after seven years (Ex. 21:2–11). Deuteronomy extends the rule to female slaves and requires the owner to provide an endowment to give the former slaves a start in the free life (Dt. 15:12–18). It also established a welfare system funded by the tithe (national religious tax [Dt. 14:28–29]) and prescribed a limited monarchy that placed the monarch under the law (Dt. 17:14–20). Equal justice for all, including aliens, is a given of Israelite law.

The Historical World: The Lawbook in the Temple

According to 2 Kings 22, in the eighteenth year of King Josiah of Judah (621 B.C.E.), Hilkiah, the chief priest, found the "book of the law" in the Temple during repairs and gave it to the royal secretary. When the king heard what this scroll said, he was distraught. If this was indeed the Torah, the express teaching of God, both he and his people were potentially in a great deal of trouble. Neither they nor their immediate ancestors had observed its teachings. Its authenticity had to be ascertained at once. A very-high-level delegation was dispatched to consult the person who must have been the most highly regarded prophetic figure in the realm, Huldah, the prophetess. Much of the news was bad. She informed the royal commission that the scroll was indeed authentic, and Judah was doomed for transgressing its teaching. The doom was mitigated on Josiah's behalf. Because of his piety, the doom would strike only after his death.

Josiah's response was decisive. Perhaps in an effort to head off the threatened doom of his people, his own death notwithstanding, he launched an extensive and radical religious reformation. The local sacrificial shrines throughout Israel were closed, and prominent ones such as the royal shrine at Bethel were deliberately and grossly desecrated. All sacrificial worship was centralized in the Jerusalem Temple, from which every trace of pagan religious influence was expunged.

Since the early nineteenth century, biblical scholars have debated whether the "book of the law" found in the Temple was the Book of Deuteronomy or a portion of it. The reasons, still considered compelling by most interpreters, are that the major interests of Deuteronomy (centralization of worship, the removal of pagan elements from the temple, and the incorporation of the provincial priesthood in the central shrine) were the key elements in Josiah's reform. Indeed, the remark of 2 Kings 23:9 that the provincial priests did not repair to Jerusalem is one of those offhand asides that catches the historian's notice. They were, according to Deuteronomy 18:6–7, expected.

That something like Josiah's reform was in fact executed is now witnessed by archaeology. For example, excavations at Arad in Judah have shown that during the time of Josiah a wall was constructed through the middle of the nave of the Solomonic shrine at Arad, rendering any sort of worship there impossible (the altar had been closed earlier by Hezekiah). This accords with the biblical tradition that Manasseh repealed many of his father Hezekiah's reforms, setting the stage for his grandson Josiah's more radical actions.

Josiah was a Davidic zealot like his great-grandfather, Hezekiah, dedicated to restoring the independent Davidic kingdom from Dan to Beersheba. It is not surprising that both these kings were religious reformers as well. Political and religious revitalization movements frequently go hand in hand. It is equally unsurprising that the Deuteronomic reform foundered after Josiah's death. A pro-Egyptian cabal gained sway in the Jerusalem court, creating an atmosphere hostile to revitalization and independence.

Summary

The books of the Torah after Genesis (Exodus, Leviticus, Numbers, and Deuteronomy) form a narrative of the deliverance (exodus) of the heirs of the ancestral promise from slavery in Egypt, their wandering in the wilderness of Sinai, and the making of a covenant with the LORD. The narrative includes extensive teaching concerning how the people of the covenant are to conduct themselves and climaxes in a long farewell address by their leader, Moses.

In this chapter we first provided additional historical context (supplementing Chapter 1) with a description of the geography of the ancient Near East and Israel and overviews of the histories of ancient Egypt, Mesopotamia, and Israel. We then highlighted the role of the literary device of irony in Exodus 1–18, the literary shape of the Sinai Covenant and the laws of the Pentateuch, and the structure of Deuteronomy. We also advanced hypotheses on some of the principal historical issues arising from the narrative: the nature and date of the Exodus from Egypt, the ancient Near Eastern context for the laws of the Pentateuch, and the relationship between the Book of Deuteronomy and a "book of the law" reputedly found in the Temple of Jerusalem in 621 B.C.E.

Exodus and Covenant not only are constitutive themes in the Bible but have also played important roles in the self-understanding of Jewish and Christian people through the centuries. The following questions will focus discussion and reflection on the continuing impact of these and other themes from this section of the Tanak.

The Contemporary World

Case Study

Can Holy Land Be Shared?

A group of Israeli and Palestinian college students are discussing the section of the Bible studied in this chapter as it relates to the prospects for peace between their two peoples. How might knowledge of the literary and historical worlds of these books assist them in a discussion of their contemporary significance? For example, how might the central theme of God's liberation of oppressed people from bondage be understood in a way that offers hope to both Israelis and Palestinians? And how might awareness of the particular historical contexts in which these books were written illuminate potential dangers in applying them uncritically to the contemporary political situation? Is there any way to resolve the conflict between those Israelis and Palestinians who view the land as holy, a gift by God to their separate peoples that cannot be shared with the other side?[3]

Questions for Discussion and Reflection

1. *Read Exodus 1–18: Let My People Go:*
   a. Discuss and/or reflect on the portrayal of the principal characters in this narrative: Moses, his brother Aaron, the unnamed Pharaoh, and God. Once again, choose adjectives for each. What

   might this story have to say about leadership in the contemporary world?

   b. Other, less frequently mentioned female characters seem to play decisive roles in this narrative. Consider, for example, the Hebrew mid-

---

[3]See William A. Young. "Constructing the Holy Land: The Uses of Sacred Texts in the Palestinian-Israeli Conflict," *Proceedings of the Central States Regional Meeting of the Society of Biblical Literature and American Schools of Oriental Research*, vol. 6 (Spring 2003), 5–24.

wives, Shiprah and Puah, in 1:15–22; Pharaoh's daughter in 2:5–10; the mother of Moses and Miriam, sister of Moses (Exodus 2:4, 15:20–21); and Zipporah, the Midianite wife of Moses (Exodus 4:24–26). What insights applicable to the contemporary world do you find in the decisions made by these women?

c. Do you agree that the dominant theme in this narrative is that God acts to liberate oppressed people? If so, does this theme still have relevance today? How might different readers understand this theme of liberation? Consider, for example, a person living in poverty as a result of an unjust economic situation, a person living in a war-torn country, or a person living in relative affluence in the United States who feels a sense of emptiness in life.

d. How might different readers (e.g., a Jew, a Christian, a Muslim, a Buddhist, a Hindu, a non-religious person) understand the contemporary meaning of the story of the Passover in Exodus 11–13 differently?

e. Some of the Europeans who first occupied the North American continent used the imagery in this story in reflecting on their situation. They believed that God had led them to the land and, in giving it to them, displaced Native Americans, as God had led the ancient Israelites into the land of Canaan, uprooting the Canaanite peoples. They came to view the European occupation of America as the creation of a "new Israel," with America having a divinely ordained mission in the world. Do you think this understanding of the United States is still held by American citizens and leaders today? If so, does it affect American policies?

2. *Read Exodus 19–24: The Sinai Covenant:*

a. Are "covenants" necessary for societies and other human groups to function effectively? Make a list of the "covenants" (agreements) that affect you and your family, both those you yourself have entered into and those made by others, including national and international agreements. Which of these covenants is most important? Why? Which are less influential in your life? Why?

b. In 2003 an Alabama Supreme Court justice sued in federal court to overturn a ruling that a large stone monument inscribed with the biblical Ten Commandments must be removed from the state courthouse. The judge had placed the monument in the courthouse to remind attorneys, judges, and the public that the laws of Alabama are based on the Ten Commandments. A suit was brought by the American Civil Liberties Union on behalf of Alabamians who considered the judge's action a violation of the U.S. Constitution prohibition of government sponsorship of religion. If you were a federal court judge ruling on the case, how would you decide and what would be your reasons? (***Note:*** See Chapter 16 for a discussion of the Ten Commandments controversy.)

c. What, if any, relevance should Exodus 20:13 and 21:22–24 have in the contemporary discussion of the morality of abortion?

d. What, if any, relevance should the principle of "life for life, eye for eye, tooth for tooth, etc." (Exodus 21:23–25) have on the debate over capital punishment today?

e. Should adultery be considered a crime? If so, in what circumstances?

3. *Read Deuteronomy 6:1–25, 20:1–20, 30:1–20:*

a. Deuteronomy 6:4–9 (called the *shema'* after the first word in Hebrew) is the first of several verses from the Tanak repeated twice daily in traditional Jewish worship. What do you suppose makes this verse so central? Deuteronomy 6:4–5, along with Leviticus 19:18, was cited by Jesus of Nazareth as central to Torah (Mark 12:28–31). Do you find in these verses the essence of religion? Why or why not?

b. Deuteronomy 20 is a text often referred to in discussions of the Bible's perspective on war. What types of war does this text justify? Are the guidelines still relevant for the conduct of war, or were they limited to the particular situation described? Some have argued that the development of nuclear weapons has made war essentially obsolete in the modern world. Do you agree? Some have cited 20:19 as evidence of a concern for the nonhuman world that has relevance as we cope with environmental challenges today. Does it apply?

c. If a gifted speaker stood up before an audience in your community and challenged hearers to "choose life," what images might come to most listeners' minds? What would be the source of their images? What does the phrase "choose life" mean as it is used in Dt. 30:19? Is there tension between the two understandings of "choose life?"

4. *Read Leviticus 18–19:*

    a. How might a study of the historical world of these stipulations about sexual relations impact interpretation of the contemporary significance of the guidelines?

    b. In 2003 a gay man, who acknowledged having a partner with whom he had lived in a committed relationship for over a decade, was installed as a bishop in the Episcopal Church in the United States. In response, a nondenominational church in Missouri ran a newspaper ad saying, "Don't like gay bishops? We don't either. Come to a church that honors the Word of God." With which, if either, action do you agree? What, if any, relevance should Leviticus 18:22 and 19:17–18 have in the debate over whether gays and lesbians should serve as ministers or priests in Christian churches? Does historical and literary study of the passages assist in determining their relevance to this contemporary dispute?

    c. What other guidelines, if any, in these two chapters do you think should figure in contemporary morality?

Chapter 5

The Nation Israel

Joshua, Judges, First and Second Samuel, First and Second Kings (The Former Prophets)

The Siege of Lachish (701 B.C.E.). The Assyrian emperor Sennacherib captured the great Judean citadel of Lachish during his war against King Hezekiah (2 Kgs. 18:13–19:37). A stone relief depicting the battle and its aftermath in collapsed spatiotemporal perspective surrounded the throne room of his palace in Nineveh. The visage of the emperor on the relief was defaced, apparently during the coup in which he was assassinated and the palace was burned.   *Source:* The Trustees of The British Museum/Art Resource, NY

The Pentateuch ends with the promise to the ancestors unfulfilled. The descendants of Abraham have become numerous, but they are a wandering band, not a great nation. The people have been blessed by the LORD, who has delivered them from Egyptian slavery and entered into a covenant relationship with them, but their name is not yet great, nor have they become a source of blessing for other nations. And, at the end of the Pentateuch, they are still at the border of the promised land. It is not yet theirs.

The next section of the Tanak, the Former Prophets, continues the narrative that began in Genesis 12, telling the story of the people of Israel from their entry into the land promised to the ancestors to their exile from that land.

The books of the Former Prophets hold to the position that obedience to the LORD leads to blessing and disobedience leads to disaster for the nation and for individuals. Because this point of view is presented so forcefully and so clearly in Deuteronomy, many modern interpreters feel that the Former Prophets and Deuteronomy form what they call the *Deuteronomistic History*. They claim the history of this period was edited by a hypothetical school or editor called the *Deueronomist*, who took a perspective on events based on the theology of the Book of Deuteronomy: when the people of Israel are obedient to God's ways, they flourish; when they reject God's path, they suffer. Although this theory has come under criticism, it is still the dominant one among literary historians who study this material.

We cannot attempt a thorough analysis of the literary and historical worlds of the Former Prophets. Rather, we will present overviews, and then focus on particular literary units as examples of the whole and on specific historical questions such as: How did the tribes of Israel occupy the land of Canaan? How did Israel develop from a group of tribes to a state-level society? What was the "empire" of David and Solomon like? How and why did the United Kingdom divide? How and why did Israel (the Northern Kingdom) and Judah (the Southern Kingdom) fall victim to outside aggression?

THE OCCUPATION OF CANAAN (JOSHUA AND JUDGES)

The Literary World: Balance in Joshua 1–12 and Judges 1–2

The Books of Joshua and Judges tell an overlapping and sometimes conflicting story of the occupation of the land of Canaan by the tribes descended from the sons of Jacob, and of the situation that followed among the tribes. Our emphasis in this section will be to show how these two books balance each other. What may seem to a modern reader to be contradictions between Joshua and Judges may instead reflect complementary narrative patterning, a technique we have already observed in Genesis 1–2 (see Chapter 3).

In the Book of Joshua all Israel, led by Joshua in strict obedience to the LORD, conquers the entire land of Canaan (Joshua 1–12). In this account of the occupation, God continues to be portrayed as Divine Warrior, who has charted the plan for the war. The LORD clearly intends the utter destruction of the people of Canaan. Enacting the directive given by the LORD to Moses in Deuteronomy to "not let anything that breathes remain alive" in the towns given to the people as their inheritance (Dt. 20:16), Joshua's army conducts what must be described as a genocidal campaign. In the defeat of Hazor, for example, the army "did not leave any who breathed" and the comment is added that "as the LORD had commanded his servant Moses, so Moses commanded Joshua, and so Joshua did; he left nothing undone of all that the LORD had commanded Moses" (Jos. 11:14–15). Then the land is distributed among the tribes, in accord with the assignments made by Moses in Numbers (Joshua 13–21), and the men of the tribes who had settled in the Transjordan leave the army and go home (Joshua 22). Joshua, like Moses before him, gives a farewell address in which he reiterates the warning that success for the people depends on allegiance to the LORD and His commandments (Joshua 23). Finally, Joshua gathers all the tribes together at Shechem for a covenant renewal ceremony (Joshua 24). According to the Book of Joshua, the occupation of the land of Canaan is the story of an obedient people led by a faithful leader.

Although the Book of Judges begins with the harmonizing note "After the death of Joshua . . . " (1:1), it is soon obvious that 1:1–2:5 is another account of some of the same events covered in Joshua, but from a much different perspective. In 2:7, Joshua is still alive, so 1:1 must on internal grounds be considered an editorial attempt to link Judges with Joshua. Whereas Joshua 1–12 portrays "all Israel" rumbling through the whole land like General Sherman's army through Georgia, the first two chapters of Judges speak of individual tribes (focusing on Judah in the south and Joseph in the north) taking different areas and having great difficulty dislodging the inhabitants. In fact, the account lists those areas not conquered alongside the cities taken. In some cases the very same city that Joshua identifies as having been conquered by "all Israel" is linked to a tribe or clan in Judges (e.g., Hebron in Jos. 10:36–37 and Jg. 1:9–10).

These conflicting accounts create a historical problem to which we will soon turn: How *did* the tribes occupy the land? However, from a literary point of view, the two contrasting accounts function much like the two creation accounts in Genesis. Just as the first creation account describes creation as the carefully orchestrated carrying out of the divine plan, Joshua is an account of the occupation of the land as God intended. And just as this account of a perfect creation is balanced by the more haphazard, spontaneous version of the second account, Joshua's version of the occupation is balanced by the more chaotic version of Judges. Joshua 1–12 is a patterned description of the taking of the land just as God intended; Jg. 1:1–2:5 is a less idealized, less ordered account. As the conclusion to the Judges account suggests, it was the disobedience of the people that led to a chaotic situation (Jg. 2:2), just as it was the rebellion in Eden that was ultimately responsible for the disruption of the created order.

The Goddess *Asherah*. Worship of the goddess Asherah, wife of the Canaanite deity El, represented in small clay images discovered in the excavations of various biblical cities, is condemned in the Tanak (e.g., Dt. 16:21, Mic. 5:12–13). However, some archaeologists have concluded that inscriptions from ancient Israelite sites link the Israelite god Yahweh with Asherah (or Astarte), suggesting that in certain forms of popular religion Yahweh may have been pictured with a wife. *Source:* www.BibleLandPictures.com/Alamy

Megiddo. Connecting the Valley of Jezreel to the east and the coastal plain to the west, the city of Megiddo occupied a strategic location, guarding a narrow pass and an important trade route. It was the site of a number of key battles, including one fought between the Kingdom of Judah, under King Josiah, and Egypt in 609 B.C.E. In the New Testament *Armageddon* (derived from the Hebrew for "Mount Megiddo") is the site of the final battle at the end of history. Tel Megiddo has been extensively excavated, yielding important evidence for the reconstruction of the history of ancient Israel. *Source:* Vblinov/Shutterstock

The Historical World: How Did the Israelites Occupy Canaan?

Three major hypotheses have been posited by modern biblical historians to account for the Israelite emergence in Canaan. The great American archaeologist W. F. Albright and his followers offered a sort of *blitzkrieg* model that followed the schematic history of the book of Joshua and was supported by some archaeological evidence. The great German scholar, Albrecht Alt, developed a *peaceful infiltration* hypothesis that accords more closely with the narrative in Judges and that also comports with a substantial amount of archaeological evidence. Another prominent American scholar, George Mendenhall, first tentatively proposed a *peasant revolt* hypothesis, although in the context of a more elaborate view. Another American, Norman K. Gottwald, developed straight out the notion that Israel originated in a revolt of Canaanite peasants against their aristocratic Canaanite overlords. There is little direct literary evidence for this hypothesis, and some archaeological data seem to tell against it.

We take the position that the origin of Israel as portrayed in the biblical traditions was an involved historical process and therefore unlikely to be explained by a single simple model. Our approach to the question of the Israelite emergence in Canaan is to work out a synthesis of the complex biblical traditions, and then to test this picture with the "control" provided by archaeological evidence.

Beneath the stylized, "all-Israel" account in Joshua, there is an indication that more than a ritualistic blitzkrieg was involved. The inhabitants of Gibeon tricked Joshua into a treaty of amity (Joshua 9), and no fighting is recorded in the neighborhood of Shechem, where Joshua conducted his great covenant renewal ceremony (Jos. 8:30–35; *cf.* Joshua 24). In the ceremony itself, "sojourner" as well as "homeborn" Israelites are mentioned (8:33, 35). The Book of Joshua also recognizes that not all possible territory was conquered (13:1–7; 23:4–6). Judges notes that others besides Joshua (e.g., Caleb in the south) were involved as leaders. Judges 1:19–2:5 lists unconquered Canaanite centers. In the rest of the Book of Judges the struggles described with the Canaanites are on a tribal level, although some "judges" led coalitions of tribes. Judges 1:16 records the settlement of Moses' in-laws, the Kenites

(Midianites), among the Judeans, and 4:11, 17, and 5:24 locate one Kenite family much farther north. But not all the information is in the Former Prophets. Numbers 14:39–45 describes an abortive assault on Canaan from the south, set in the lifetime of Moses. Exodus 12:38 mentions a "mixed multitude" that accompanied the Exodus group out of Egypt. These data from the biblical text itself, more examples of *narrative honesty,* make it clear that a facile reading of the text does not do it justice.

We begin our hypothesis by proposing that the Exodus group must have been relatively modest in size. Exodus 1:15 assumes that two midwives could see after the women's needs at the time of Moses' birth. The population could hardly have skyrocketed in the subsequent generations, particularly since one generation was spent on migrating. This band probably included elements of the Joseph tribes (eventually split into Ephraim and Manasseh), the tribe of Levi, and possibly others, but it also had acquired additional adherents (a mixed multitude) who were not biological descendants of Jacob–Israel.

The Exodus group, led by Joshua, entered the lands west of Jordan near Jericho in the middle of the thirteenth century B.C.E. They brought with them the traditions of the Exodus and the Sinai Covenant. They met a varied reception as they migrated toward the central highlands. Some settled on unoccupied marginal land. In some instances they were obliged to fight indigenous people.

**Traditional Locations of the
Tribes of Israel**

In others, local inhabitants entered into treaty relationships with them. In yet other instances, they seemed to move in peacefully among the indigenous population, as at Shechem (Jos. 8:30–35). In the process, additional peoples became parties to the Sinai Covenant. Some might have been members of the traditional twelve tribes who had not sojourned in Egypt but had remained in Canaan. Some might have otherwise claimed kinship (see Gen. 25:1–6) or some sort of special relationship from the past (as suggested by the various treaties and covenants made by the ancestors). Others were previously unrelated Canaanite groups (Gibeon in Jos. 9:3–27) or *habiru* (the sojourners of Jos. 8:33, 25), making common cause with a group that seemed to be on a roll. All adopted fidelity to the LORD as patron of their covenant relationship, whatever their previous allegiance may have been.

The activities of Joshua and other leaders during the thirteenth and twelfth centuries gave the expanding group of YHWHistic tribes a firm footing in the land of Canaan, but Canaan was hardly yet Israel. As the book of Judges shows, the Israelites were at times dominated by the Canaanites. At times they were independent. *But never did they decisively dominate the Canaanites.* We should recognize in reading these accounts that *no judge was a national leader.* Most led a single tribe or a coalition of neighboring tribes. The song of Deborah (Jg. 5:14–17) condemns some nearby tribes as slackers while praising those who supported Deborah and Barak, but more distant tribes, including the great southern tribe of Judah, are not even mentioned.

The indigenous urbanized population continued to control most of the great walled cities, which meant that they also controlled most of the lowlands constituting the agricultural hinterland of these cities. Although Jg. 1:8 claims a Judean conquest of Jerusalem, the city was still a Jebusite stronghold when David captured it. The Israelites were settled mostly in the hills and mountains (or in the semi-arid Judean Negev), lands suited to subsistence farming, vine culture, and the husbandry of ruminants but not to the extensive feudal agricultural practices of the Canaanite city–states. The situation could hardly be described as one of symbiosis, but it was one that permitted peaceful coexistence. Friction probably arose when some Canaanite ruler (or Midianite raider) looked at the Israelites in their unfortified villages with their tribal form of social organization as sheep to be sheared. Except in these circumstances, neither the Israelites nor the Canaanites particularly needed or wanted what the other had. The Israelites were strong enough, when properly aroused and led, to convince greedy neighbors that the return on taking or raiding them was not worth the cost. The Canaanite armies were suited to fighting one another or, in conjunction with the forces of an imperial overlord (Egypt), against other empires (the Hittites). They were not designed to hunt guerrillas in the hills. This balance persisted until about 1100 B.C.E., when burgeoning Philistine power upset the balance once and for all.

How does this account, framed so far on the basis of literary evidence, square with archaeological data? We noted in Chapter 4 that some sites in traditional Israelite territory seem to have been violently destroyed in the mid to late thirteenth century B.C.E., the most congenial time for the Exodus–Wilderness–Occupation series of events. These sites, and others vacant since the early Bronze Age, were occupied by people who utilized both a different pottery tradition and a different architectural tradition, a cruder one than their predecessors in both instances. The Book of Joshua says that Hazor was the only city that stood on a mound that Joshua burned (i.e., the only major fortress city), although lesser fortified towns are claimed for his bag. The excavation of Hazor has revealed evidence of a massive destruction in the thirteenth century. The Book of Joshua also says Joshua took Lachish (10:31–32). The thirteenth-century Canaanite city of Lachish had no defensive wall, as recent excavations have shown.

Jericho remains the most celebrated of Joshua's victories. But from the standpoint of archaeological evidence, Jericho is one of the most problematic sites for reconstruction of the first stages of the Israelite occupation. There is no evidence that the city was occupied during the thirteenth century.

Less dramatic than war, burning, and destruction, but certainly at least as important for our historical understanding, is archaeological evidence that a substantial part of the Israelite settlement was a peaceful infiltration into vacant land rather than an armed invasion. Both in the hill country and in the Judean Negev, a substantial portion of the "new people," as identified by their pottery, architecture, and subsistence strategy, settled on land that had for some time been unoccupied.

We have noted Finkelstein's hypothesis concerning pastoral nomadism in the Canaanite highlands during the late Bronze Age. He went on to show that this mode of life was jeopardized when trade relations between highland pastoralists and lowland grain farmers were disrupted by the incursions of the Sea Peoples. The highlanders were obliged to settle down and pursue a mixed subsistence farming strategy, growing cereal grains and so on, but continuing to keep sheep and goats, which were well adapted to the environment and which produced milk products, wool, and organic fertilizer. Vineyards and olive trees were also well adapted to some highland areas. This change of strategy initiated the rapid multiplication of small agrarian villages in the highlands during the late Bronze Age–early Iron Age transition. The new strategy permitted the highlands to support a larger population, and there was probably natural growth. Much of this population, says Finkelstein, was sedentarizing pastoralists and their descendants, but there were probably immigrants in addition, like the Exodus group. There was land available in the highlands and the Negev, unoccupied since the early to middle Bronze Age.[1]

Finally, how does our reconstruction fit with anthropological observations? The Book of Judges concludes with the observation, "In those days there was no king in Israel; all the people did what was right in their own eyes" (Jg. 21:25). The Israelites are pictured as living in villages, with a tribal social organization and no major intertribal institutions. The most that one might expect is some sort of tribal league, although it would have been a very loose one, based on claims of kinship and common loyalty to the LORD. Such an association usually functions only when there is a common interest at stake, and only to that extent. This is what one sees in the Book of Judges. Such an association does not function very efficiently. These observations are illustrated in Judges 19–21, the story of the sin of Gibeah.

Also typical of a tribal culture is charismatic leadership, persons "empowered" with natural leadership gifts. The judges are nothing if not charismatic leaders. This type of leadership functions most effectively when people are galvanized by the coincidence of a crisis and a leader. However, no one fades more quickly than a charismatic leader who cannot maintain success.

The military behavior of the Israelites is also consistent with what we would expect from anthropological models. The fighting force was essentially the able-bodied men mustered by families and clans. Such an army cannot maintain itself long in the field and lacks the equipment to conduct sustained operations. The judges usually went for a quick and decisive action, often involving surprise or ambush.

Tribal society is also generally egalitarian. There is no elaborate or rigid status system. Many of the most fundamental traditions of the Israelite Torah were laid down in this period, and they are reflected in the law codes and oracles of the later prophets. Much of the ideological tension in later Israelite society would grow out of conflict between the egalitarian tradition of its formative tribal culture, hallowed in the Sinai Covenant teachings, and the pretensions of the higher orders generated by the emergence of a more complex, stratified society. Archaeology joins literature in giving evidence of this tension. Monumental architecture appeared in Israel with the monarchy, but residential housing remained basically egalitarian down to the ninth or eighth century B.C.E.

---

[1]Israel Finkelstein. *The Archaeology of the Israelite Settlement.* Jerusalem: Israel Exploration Society, 1989.

FROM TRIBES TO STATE (JUDGES, SAMUEL)

The Literary World: A Cycle of Legends about Heroes

After its version of the occupation of Israel (1:1–2:5), most of the rest of Judges (2:6–16:31) is a collection of legends about heroes among the tribes who demonstrated their leadership by delivering people from oppression at times of crisis. We would call them *charismatic heroes*, but it is the stereotypical phrase that connects the legends that gave them their "title." Typically, after telling of the exploit, the text says that the hero "judged Israel _____ years." So they are called *judges*, although, except for Deborah, few are portrayed exercising a judicial or administrative function. A few judges are simply named, without being identified with any act of deliverance (10:1–5; 12:8–15), giving rise to the label *minor judges* to distinguish them from the more prominent *major judges*, and to fanciful theories about their role among the tribes. The remainder of the Book of Judges is not about judges at all, but instead relates incidents explaining why the tribe of Dan migrated from south to north and why a punishment was inflicted on the tribe of Benjamin in a tribal civil war (Judges 17–21).

As an example of one of the legends about the charismatic heroes called judges, let us analyze the story of Ehud in Jg. 3:12–30. Ehud was a member of the tribe of Benjamin (which means literally "son of the right"), whose warriors were renowned for their military prowess. Ehud was left-handed. He arose as a hero at a time of oppression at the hands of the nation Moab, just across the Dead Sea from Benjaminite territory. Under the obese King Eglon (a term suggesting the Hebrew word for calf), Moab had taken Jericho and had stationed an occupying army of at least ten thousand men in Israel.[2] Ehud was to deliver Israel by "killing the fatted calf" and leading a massacre of the Moabite occupation force as they tried to flee for home after hearing about the death of their leader. The story of how Ehud accomplished all this is full of sarcasm and lowbrow humor directed against Eglon and the Moabites, which would have undoubtedly delighted an Israelite audience listening to it.

The clever Ehud prepares for his dastardly act by making a small two-edged sword, which he puts on his right thigh under his cloak, aware that a quick motion with his left hand toward his right side would not alarm his unsuspecting victim. Ehud is careful not to arouse suspicion. He goes to Eglon to deliver tribute and starts for home. All alone, without any Israelite soldiers, he turns around at the stones near Gilgal (symbol of Israel's claim by divine right to the land; see Jos. 4:20) and goes back with a "secret message" for the king. Because the Hebrew word for *message* also means *thing*, there is a clever double entendre. The gullible king falls for the trick and sends his attendants away. There may be sexual nuances intended in the expression "came to" the king, for this is an idiom frequently used to indicate sexual contact. This may explain why Eglon so foolishly and excitedly sends his attendants away and why they are so reluctant to disturb him. Eglon is so eager for his "secret message" that he either misses or ignores the insult Ehud pays him by addressing him as "King" rather than with the address protocol would indicate—"My lord."

Alone in Eglon's private roof chamber, Ehud repeats the play on message–thing, this time identifying the source as God. Out of reverence for the one from whom the message comes, or out of excitement, the fat king stands up to receive it. In a flash Ehud delivers the message–thing, and the king's rolls of fat close over the sword. In his death throes the king's anal sphincter muscle relaxes and the "dirt came out." The scatological humor climaxes as Ehud makes his escape while the king's attendants, seeing the locked door and probably smelling the odor, decided the king is relieving himself and should not be disturbed.

In the subsequent battle the Moabites are portrayed as mirroring their king. They too are fools, for they rush toward home through the fords of Jordan that provide the Israelites excellent opportunities

---

[2]Or "ten brigades" or "ten musters."

for ambush. In a sarcastic play on words, the story says that the ten thousand Moabites killed were all "strong, able-bodied men." In Hebrew the word *strong* also means *fat*. The fat Moabites were subdued (literally, "laid low"), just like their corpulent king.[3]

Although the other legends of the judges are not so raucous in their humor, they are nonetheless all popular folk tales about memorable people: Deborah ("Honey Bee") and Barak ("Lightning") in Judges 4–5, Gideon (Judges 6–8), Jephthah (Judges 11–12), and Samson (Judges 13–16). As in the ancestral legends, the portrayal of the judges as heroic figures does not mean they are beyond reproach. For example, Jephthah takes the life of his own daughter because he has foolishly vowed to the LORD that he will kill the first person who greets him if the LORD grants him victory over his enemies. Unfortunately, his only daughter comes out to meet him when he returns from the battle (Jg. 11:29–40). Samson's passion for the beautiful Delilah is his undoing (Judges 16). All of these stories are woven together as a cycle, with a clearly stated theme introducing them (2:11–3:6). The theme is a pattern that is repeated in the stories:

1. The people turned from the LORD and served other gods.
2. The LORD became angry and allowed them to be oppressed.
3. The LORD raised up judges to deliver them.
4. When the judge died the people turned again to evil, and the cycle began again.

This pattern is illustrated in the otherwise vague story of Othniel (3:7–11), and then used as a framework for the other tales. We have already observed a cyclical pattern in the shaping of legends, as in the Prehistory of Genesis 1–11.

First Samuel begins with the story of another hero who is associated with judging: Samuel (1 Samuel 1–12). Samuel's judging, however, seems to involve the administration of justice (7:13–20), and he is not portrayed as a war hero like most of the judges in Judges. Samuel is a transitional figure between the loosely organized situation of Judges and the emergence of Israel as a state under a king. However, he too is a charismatic hero who plays a role in the deliverance of the people from a threat.

The next focal character, Saul, is also a charismatic hero and a transitional figure. He is a Benjaminite who emerges, like the judges, as a deliverer at a time of oppression. As a result, he is named king by the people (1 Sam. 11:1–15). However, this story is balanced against other traditions concerning Saul's rise to power that suggest a certain ambiguity in Israel's remembrance of him. In one of these, Samuel anoints Saul not as king, but as "prince" (1 Sam. 9:1–10:16). Another pictures a reluctant Saul being chosen king by lots (1 Sam. 10:17–27). These accounts reflect a balanced attitude toward kingship. Just who wanted a king and why is obscured in these accounts of the first king of Israel, and that is presumably a purposeful clouding of the issue. The narrative portrays Saul in tragic terms. He is rejected by God for a seemingly minor sin (1 Sam. 13:7–15). He is quickly overshadowed and driven to depression by the more charismatic David. He is called "king" but without the support or administration to govern effectively. He was a victim of his times.

The Historical World

The equilibrium between Israel and its Canaanite neighbors was upset by the activities of the Philistines, who appeared in Canaan during the twelfth century B.C.E. or perhaps earlier. They were part of the "Sea Peoples" from the Aegean region. Although defeated by the Egyptians when they attempted to enter the Nile Delta, the Philistines became rulers of the "Philistine plain," probably

---

[3]Based on Robert Alter. *The Art of Biblical Narrative*. New York: Basic Books, 1981, pp. 37–41.

with Egyptian sanction. They also ruled Bethshan, which controlled traffic around the southern end of the Sea of Galilee into the Jezreel valley.

The Philistines rapidly assimilated the culture of Canaan, probably because they were not very numerous. They were a warrior aristocracy, replacing the previous Canaanite warrior aristocracy. Their serfs probably could not tell the difference, but their neighbors soon could. Although they did not *introduce* iron to the Near East, they did have an advanced metals technology that allowed them to make superior weapons. The Philistines also had a more adaptive political system than the Canaanite city–states, organizing themselves under a national council, "the Lords of the Philistines." And they made astute use of heavy infantry, well-armed and protected foot soldiers who, in man-to-man combat, were invincible.

All this was bad for the Israelites. Concentrated as they were in the less productive hill country, they were relatively out of reach of the chariot-based armies of the principal Canaanite cities. But the Philistine infantry could march any place an Israelite could walk, and the Israelite citizen–soldier was neither trained nor equipped to confront such formidable adversaries. The Philistines probably did not want to take the Israelites' lands, but only to milk them for tribute and tolls. The Samson tales (Judges 13–16) show Israel's low estate. Poor Samson had no success trying to raise an army against the Philistines; the fearful Judahites even bound him and turned him over to the enemy. The Philistines were the probable cause of the migration of Dan northward (Judges 18). Even the Holy Ark of the Covenant could not give the Israelites victory over the Philistines (1 Samuel 4). First Samuel 7 credits Samuel with great success against the Philistines. He could win a guerrilla assault, but he could not drive them home. When Saul became king, there was a Philistine garrison and custom station at Geba, in the heart of the Benjaminite hill country (1 Sam. 13:3).

Anthropologists observe that states tend to rise when an area becomes *circumscribed* or impacted. This can happen in two ways. Either the population grows to the point that the habitable environment is pressed to the limits of its carrying capacity or social developments have the effect of closing people in.[4] At the time the Israelites began to emerge as self-conscious people in Canaan, the indigenous population was organized into city–states, with no good reason to try to incorporate the Israelites. There was plenty of land in the hill country and the Negev for the Israelites to practice subsistence agriculture; they had no need for a state-level organization. However, the more aggressive Philistines did attempt to annex Israelite holdings, and they had the means to do it. Thus, Philistine activity created *social circumscription*. The choice for the Israelites was submit or organize to resist. The latter required more than the guerrilla warfare of the Israelite tribal militias; a trained standing army was needed to fight the Philistines.

To raise a standing army requires a reorganization of society with the emergence of social stratification, the warrior class on top in league with bureaucrats and priests who organize the social system. That is, it requires a system of centralized control. States emerge in stages. That is what happened in Israel. In anthropological terms, Saul's kingdom appears to have been more like a *chiefdom*, an intermediate development, than a state-level monarchy. Abner, his uncle, was the only cabinet minister, and the ministry of war was the only government department. There is no evidence that Saul was able to institute a tax system. He depended on tribute not collected by force (1 Sam. 10:27)—but one cannot be sure how voluntary these gifts were—and expropriated Canaanite property (1 Sam. 22:7). If the fortress–palace excavated at the site of ancient Gibeah was in fact Saul's, its limited size accords with the literary data. Nevertheless, Saul took the essential first step on the road to statehood and created the catalyst for further advance. He recruited a standing army, organized into three battalions. Despite his inner turmoil, Saul carried on his duties, as he understood them,

---

[4]Robert Carneiro. "A Theory of the Rise of the State." *Science*, 169 (1970), 733–738.

with fortitude. He secured the central heartland of Benjamin and Ephraim against Philistine exploitation and brought the great southern tribe of Judah more fully into a total Israelite structure than it had ever been before. Overextended in the field, he fell before the Philistines at Mount Gilboa (1 Samuel 31). But his achievements survived his death and the demise of his kingdom–chiefdom. They were part of his legacy to David, a fact that should not be overshadowed by David's rather more monumental accomplishments.

FROM STATE TO EMPIRE: THE UNITED KINGDOM (SECOND SAMUEL, FIRST KINGS 1–11)

The Literary World: David and Solomon

The Book of Second Samuel focuses on the rule of David, first as king of the southern half of the territory of Israel (1–4), and then as king over the United Kingdom of Judah and Israel (5–24). The narrative weaves together a record of the achievements of David and a behind-the-scenes look at the intrigue of his court, particularly in Chapters 9–20.

First Kings begins with the death of David and the ascendancy of Solomon (1 Kings 1–2). It then portrays the reign of Solomon, renowned for his wisdom (1 Kings 3); his administration (1 Kings 4); his building projects, including the Temple (1 Kings 5–9); and his wealth and success in trade (1 Kings 10), but with a fatal flaw (1 Kings 11).

One section of this narrative (2 Samuel 9–20; 1 Kings 1–2) is often considered a single literary unit because of its unity of style and theme. It is called the *Succession Narrative* (SN) (because the underlying question is, "Who will succeed David as king?") or simply the *Court History of David*. Whether or not it was ever a single literary unit, it is one of the most polished sections of the Tanak's narrative and well worth our careful attention. The SN is an example of the literary form called the Hebrew short story or novella.

The narrative begins against the background of 2 Samuel 7, the promise of the LORD to David, delivered by the prophet Nathan that, "your house and your kingdom shall be made sure forever before me; your throne shall be established forever" (7:16). In broader perspective, this *Davidic Covenant*, based on the promise of the LORD that there will always be a Davidic king, introduces a new tension. With the ancestral promises of people, land, and blessing having been at least partially realized, the promise to David replaces them as the "goal" toward which the biblical narrative is moving. It is a concern of both the Hebrew Bible and the New Testament, and it is a recurrent interest in the literature that arose after the Tanak but before the New Testament. How will the promise of a Davidic king be kept, especially after the destruction of Jerusalem and the exile of the house of David? The full scope of this promise leads to the hope for a messiah (anointed one) who will arise from the line of David as a new king and restore Israel to Davidic glory. More immediately, the promise raises the question of how the Davidic dynasty will begin. Which of the sons of David will inaugurate his father's everlasting kingdom?

The SN itself opens in Chapter 9 with a scene highlighting the ambiguity of David's character. David takes into his home Meribbaal,[5] the crippled son of Jonathan, the only remaining heir of Jonathan's father, King Saul. The motives are obviously mixed. David's compassion for his friend's son may be genuine, but so is his desire to keep tabs on the only survivor of a rival dynasty.

---

[5]This was probably his real name. It means "is my lord" (*cf.* the genealogy of 1 Chr. 8:34). Hostility toward Canaanite worship is reflected by the change of the name from Meribbaal to Mephibosheth ("he who [spreads] shame") in 2 Sam. 4:4; 9:1–13, *et passim.*

Michelangelo's David. The most famous statue of King David, rendered by famed Italian Renaissance artist Michelangelo Buonarroti (1475–1564) between 1501 and 1504, shows David ready for (or perhaps after) his battle with the Philistine warrior Goliath (1 Sam. 17:1–58). The original of the statue is in the Accademia Gallery in Florence, Italy.   *Source:* Wjarek/Shutterstock

The stage is then set for the most famous incident of the SN—David's affair with the beautiful Bathsheba. We see from this story that the most important events in the court of the king are not always the most public. At the level of public affairs, this is a time of war against a neighboring nation, Ammon. A description of the war (10; 12:26–31) serves as the frame for the private events that overshadow the public in their long-term significance.

The scene opens innocently enough. Confined to Jerusalem while his commander Joab leads the war against the Ammonites, a restless king is strolling on the roof of the palace. His eye catches a beautiful woman, whom he does not know, bathing on a nearby roof. The narrative then moves quickly, as though the events flow together spontaneously. When David learns that the woman is Bathsheba, wife of one of his mercenaries, Uriah the Hittite, who is fighting in the war, David acts. He orders Bathsheba brought to him; they go to bed, and she becomes pregnant. The deed has the marks of a spontaneous act of passion. It could have ended there. But the act has consequences that begin the unraveling of David's rule. Whether out of concern for Bathsheba, fear of blackmail, or both, David now acts to cover up the sin. He brings Uriah home from the front and instructs him to go home, obviously so that he will have intercourse with Bathsheba and cover up the king's act. Ironically, Uriah, a foreigner, shows himself more faithful to the law of the LORD than David, whom the LORD has chosen to be king. Uriah refuses to violate the taboo against intercourse by soldiers consecrated for war (see 1 Sam. 21:4–5), and he refuses to sleep in his own bed while his comrades are sleeping in the field. Even when David gets him drunk, Uriah's integrity does not waver!

Now the tragic consequences of David's violation of the Torah begin to play themselves out. Greater sin follows on lesser. In desperation, David orders Joab, his commander, to place Uriah in the hardest of the fighting, where he will surely be killed. Joab enthusiastically obeys, sacrificing elite troops to accomplish the murder of Uriah. When the news of Uriah's death reaches him, David says, "the sword devours now one and now another . . . " (2 Sam. 11:25), as though Uriah's death were mere chance. It is difficult to imagine a more cynical statement.

The cover-up is complete when David marries Bathsheba. A son is born, and that seems the end of it. It appears that a king can use his great power any way he pleases, even in violation of the law he has sworn to protect. But this is not the end. We are told that the LORD sent the prophet Nathan to David. Interestingly, David's compassion and sense of justice are used to condemn him. When told a parable of a rich man who arrogantly takes a poor man's only ewe lamb, David renders judgment without hesitation. He deserves to die! He *shall* pay! David has unwittingly determined his own fate. "*You* are that man," says Nathan. With hindsight on the tragedies that were to befall David and his family, the narrative offers a theological explanation. It is David's sin that is at the root of the tragic events that now unfold.

As a result of his sin, David's first son by Bathsheba dies. The last scene in this story is the obverse of the first. A once proud and cynical king is now a humbled mourner, lying on the ground helpless beside his dying son. Yet David is not broken. When the boy dies, he ends his fast and returns to the palace to resume his responsibilities. He bears the burden of his guilt, but he is able to lay it to rest and continue on. The last word is that even out of tragedies such as this, good can come. A second son is born, Solomon, successor to David, who brings the nation Israel to the pinnacle of its glory.

The remainder of the SN weaves a tangled web of intrigue, passion, and power plays. Solomon slips into the background as the tragedy of David's kingship unfolds in a series of devastating blows. David's son Amnon mirrors the sin of his father, raping his half-sister Tamar. When an indecisive David refuses to respond, Tamar's brother Absalom takes vengeance himself, killing Amnon. This sparks hostility, which leads to a rebellion by Absalom, the flight of David, and, ultimately, the death of Absalom at the hands of Joab. The cry of David when he learns of his son's death is a tragic reversal of his cynical response to the death of Uriah. Now he feels the pain deeply, crying, "O my son Absalom, my son, my son Absalom! Would I had died instead of you, O Absalom, my son, my son!" (2 Sam. 18:33).

Finally, Solomon reenters the drama. With a cold political acumen that is in tension with his earlier moral earnestness, Nathan manipulates Solomon's rise to power. Neither king nor prophet can claim total righteousness! Given the right circumstances, anyone can fall victim to arrogance and deceit. A now feeble and impotent David, ironically warmed by a young virgin whose status does not change while she serves the king, confused by the wiles of Nathan in collaboration with Bathsheba, fulfills an oath he had never made to name Solomon his successor. His final words to his successor are an ironic combination of advice to follow the law of Moses and requests for ruthless retribution against Joab and others. To the end David is fully human—vain, sensitive, manipulative, arrogant, forgiving, humble, and repenting.

In contrast with earlier narratives, the SN portrays a diminished public role for the deity. Never does the LORD directly intercede with miracles or with direct revelation to principal characters. Here the LORD speaks only through the parables of prophets and acts indirectly or not at all. Only two asides in the story suggest divine involvement (2 Sam. 12:24–25 and 17:14). In this sense the story is a *secular tale*. The complex flow of events is a result of human decision and actions. There is an observable skein of causes and effects that are set in motion by David's affair with Bathsheba. Humans are clearly free to decide, but they are also held accountable for their actions by a moral law of cause and effect not unlike the law of karma in Indian philosophy. For David, Amnon, Absalom, Joab, and others, violence begets violence. Although the role of the LORD is muted, this is not to say the deity has been written out altogether. The narrative reflects a more subtle view of divine involvement. In a way not comprehensible to human minds, through events calculated by human arrogance to thwart the divine law, the plan of the LORD for the blessing of people is at work nonetheless. At the end, the promise to David is intact. It is the LORD who has the last word. These points, of course, are not made abstractly. That is not the style of the Hebrew narrative. Yet for the careful reader, they are there to discern.

The Historical World

There is more literary evidence in the Bible for the reigns of David and Solomon than for virtually any other period of biblical history. However, a historical analysis of this period must be more than a review of the history of the United Kingdom in Samuel and Kings, supplemented by additional material from the two Books of Chronicles and observations from archaeological and anthropological research. Following the death of Saul, a combination of appropriate circumstances and Davidic military and political skill made Israel a power to be reckoned with, not a pawn in the games of empires. The achievements of David were consolidated under Solomon, so that this period was the "glory age" for Israel as a nation–state, even a mini-empire.

Many of the "minimalist" literary critics (see Chapter 1) regard the entire history of the Israelite monarchy as fiction, the product of romantic apologists or worse, tendentious propagandists, of the Persian period. Some of the most spirited assaults on the standard history of Israel are directed against the narratives of the United Monarchy. David is dismissed as a fictitious founder—hero of a sort known from other cultures, although the historicity of those legendary heroes (such as King Arthur) is vigorously defended by respectable scholars. The recently discovered ninth-century Aramean "House of David" inscription from Tel Dan is perhaps the most important archaeological evidence for the early emergence of the Jerusalem dynasty, if not the founder himself. Foreigners knew and used the title less than a century after David's probable lifetime. Since the publication of the Tel Dan inscription, other scholars have proposed that "House of David" may be found on other ninth-century inscriptions, including the Mesha stone.

The Stepped Stone Structure is a massive retaining structure, stabilizing a steep hillside in the City of David (Jebusite and early Israelite Jerusalem, the fortified late Bronze Age–early Iron Age town). It may be taken as an example of how archaeology sometimes creates as many problems as it solves. Parts of it were exposed by Dame Kathleen Kenyon in the 1960s, but not enough to permit a full interpretation. The entire structure was exposed by Prof. Yigal Shiloh's City of David dig. It appears to have helped support a significant building, perhaps the palace citadel. Shiloh initially announced that Iron I pottery beneath the stonework established a Davidic date. This would be very important, because few, if any, monumental structures from the reign of David have been found. More recent archaeological interpreters have argued on the basis of other putative ceramic evidence that the structure may be earlier, or perhaps several centuries later, than the Davidic age. Apparently, Dame Kenyon typically saved a few types of sherds and dumped the rest, so conclusions based on the number of sherds in her store are dubious. But she also noted that the various terraces and retaining walls on the unstable slopes of the City of David, subject to damage from both seismic activity and heavy rainfall runoff, required successive repairs. It would not be surprising to find an admixture of pottery under such circumstances, particularly with the Stepped Stone Structure, which was also overbuilt with houses and other structures on its downhill end. It may be hoped that current intense discussions among archaeologists will resolve the enigma so this great masonry monument may be understood in its proper historical context.

Archaeologists have noted for some time that the Israelite monarchy of the divided kingdom, centered in Samaria, was in absolute terms wealthier and more powerful in the ninth century than the united monarchy of the tenth century, although the international political situation may have put David and Solomon in a relatively more influential position. More recent surveys suggest that it was not until the eighth century that the Judean polity centered in Jerusalem developed the organization and infrastructure that Israel had possessed a century earlier. Both ethnic and environmental factors were involved in this. The state formation process is linear in nature, going from chiefdom to rudimentary state to fully developed state and possibly to empire. The state formation process in the highlands of Israel and Judah was, so to speak, "jump started," being caused by social rather than environmental circumscription, as we have noted. Further, suzerainty in antiquity seems to have been personal in nature. Fealty was owed to the king, not to an abstract entity such as the "kingdom of Israel," or "the British Empire." (Note the cry of the rebels in 1 Kgs. 12:16: "What share do we have in David?—Look now to your own house, O David.") Under these circumstances it is quite plausible that a relatively rudimentary polity centered in the Judean highlands might establish suzerainty over a relatively wide area. The Former Prophets do not lead one to expect monumental building from the time of David (so a Davidic Stepped Stone Structure would be particularly exciting). Monumental building was attributed to Solomon. Archaeologists had assigned the great gates at Hazor, Megiddo, and Gezer to Solomon's reign, but others now argue that they come from the ninth century, rendering the Solomonic assignment problematic. Solomon's greatest Jerusalem projects were on and immediately adjacent to the Temple Mount where both Muslim and ultra-orthodox Jewish passions render archaeological work impossible. The Temple Mount platform was enlarged by Herod's builders and perhaps by the Hasmoneans before them. Thus, the area of the tenth-century royal compound may lie beneath it, if it was not obliterated by Herodian excavations.

The volume of inscriptional evidence and archival tablets from Assyrian and Babylonian sources that name Israelite and Judean rulers and that narrate events recounted in the books of Kings increases as one moves from the ninth on down to the eighth, seventh, and sixth centuries B.C.E. The challenge to the minimalists is to explain away, or perhaps more accurately, to wish away, a substantial body of archaeological data. Most rigorous empirical historians would conclude that the Former Prophets, though not without difficulties, offer a reliable outline of the history of Israel and Judah.

DAVID   Son of a notable Judean family, David appeared in Saul's court as a talented young soldier with great popular appeal who became commander of the royal bodyguard, closest friend of crown prince Jonathan, and son-in-law of the king through his daughter Michal. David was to some degree the victim of his own success. Whether or not Saul ever heard of the stories that Samuel had anointed David in boyhood to be king, replacing him, he began to suspect that David had designs on his crown. Worse yet, Jonathan seemed quite content to see it happen, and Michal connived to save David from her father's hand.

The narrative, with an obvious pro-Davidic slant, portrays David as loyal to a fault but finally obliged to flee for his life. After a brief refuge in Philistia, where he feigned madness to save his life, David became a fugitive in the hills of his native Judah. Some of his own kinsmen and an assorted company of fugitives and malcontents rallied to his standard and constituted the nucleus of the legendary "Mighty Men," the professional heavy infantry that proved the instrument of David's triumphs.

Saul perceived David with an armed company as an even greater threat to security than before and came after him with his professional army. David eluded pursuit and, according to the traditions, eschewed several golden opportunities to kill Saul. Meanwhile, he used his outlaw band to defend his Judean kinsmen from the Philistines and other assorted enemies.

David at length withdrew into Philistine territory to escape Saul's tenacious pursuit and took his troops into the service of Achish, king of Gath, who in return gave David the border town of Ziklag as his personal hold. David used the opportunity to play a double game. He exterminated Judah's enemies on his raids and told Achish he was raiding against Judah.

The news of Saul's death led David to bestir himself from his Philistine exile. Each step reflected his native political genius. He had exercised great care all along to ingratiate himself with his Judean kinsmen by defending them against predatory incursions, by sharing the booty of his own

Waterfalls at Ein Gedi. Located near the Dead Sea, *Ein Gedi* ("Goat Spring") is mentioned in 1st Sam. 24:1–22 as the place where King Saul encountered the young David after David had fled when he learned Saul was seeking to kill him. Today *Ein Gedi* is an Israeli national park and nature reserve. *Source:* Vblinov/Shutterstock

raids with Judah's elders, and by sparing them the embarrassment of choosing between Saul and him. Except for his appearance at the Aphek muster (1 Sam. 28:1–2; 29:1–11), he had carefully avoided assuming the role of an active rebel and visibly eschewed regicide. When an Amalekite adventurer appeared to claim credit for Saul's death, David dealt him an assassin's proper desserts. With similar effect, David congratulated the men of Jabesh Gilead for rescuing Saul's desecrated corpse from the walls of Bethshan. A total cynic could attribute David's actions to opportunism, but he was a complex person with complex motives.

Prompted by a favorable oracle, David marched his six hundred professional warriors from Ziklag up to Hebron, the principal town of Judah. (Israel, as yet, had no proper cities.) The elders of Judah, not surprisingly, acclaimed him king over their tribe. The stage was now set for internecine conflict. David's long-range intention to be king over all Israel was by this time obvious to most observers. The upshot was a dynastic war between the house of Saul and the house of David, with the balance turning in David's favor. Joab's murder of Saul's commander Abner and Saul's son Ishbaal's murder by two of his own henchmen threatened to derail David's plans. But he absolved himself in a way that actually advanced his interests (2 Sam. 3:6–4:12). In due course, the elders of the northern Israelite tribes showed up in Hebron to acclaim David and anoint him king over the rest of Saul's former dominions.

David acted quickly to solidify his kingdom. Hebron was too far south and too closely identified with Judah to be a proper capital for all Israel. Nor was a northern location wise. Instead, he seized the formidable Jebusite stronghold of Jerusalem, astride the watershed highway between Judah and Benjamin and a neutral site in relation to tribal rivalries.

"Warren's Shaft," connected to the Bronze Age tunnel system for bringing water from the Gihon spring into Jerusalem, had been assumed by many since its nineteenth-century discovery to

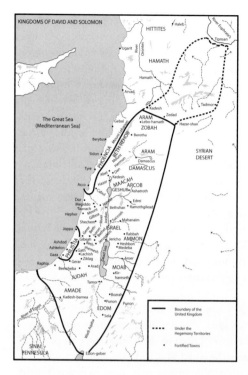

David's Kingdom

be the avenue by which Joab and David's elite commandos gained surprise access to the city. Recent investigations suggest that it was not connected with the tunnels open in the tenth century. But this does not change the fact that the water tunnels were the means by which David's troops scored their victory. The route, but not the method, is altered. And the high quality of the military intelligence that made it possible remains impressive.

Since the Battle of Gilboa seven years earlier, the Philistines had been strangely silent. But David's capture of Jerusalem jarred them into action. They sent a force against Jerusalem, but David escaped. Assuming that he was still in Jerusalem, they twice laid siege to the city, permitting David on both occasions to hit them from an unexpected quarter. He pressed his second pursuit into Philistia itself and exacted a toll that probably ensured his ultimate victory.

David made a generous peace with Philistia. Its territory was limited to the lands surrounding its pentapolis on the southern coastal plain, but it retained its own governments under treaty alliances with David. He also proceeded to recruit mercenary battalions for his own army from among the recently defeated Philistines.

The lowland city–states and their rich farmlands and orchards, whether ruled by native Canaanites or by Philistines, fell into David's lap with the defeat of Philistia. Under David, the land of Canaan finally became the land of Israel. He completed the conquest begun by Joshua. No one in the west was disposed to challenge his Mighty Men, the professional heavy infantry battalion, or perhaps by this time battalions, that had brought down the proud might of Philistia. To the northwest, in Phoenicia, Hiram of Tyre entered friendly and mutually beneficial treaty relationships with David.

However, things were not so tranquil east of the Jordan valley. Warfare somehow erupted between Israel and Moab. Moabite provocation can be suspected because David uncharacteristically inflicted a vicious atrocity on the defeated enemy, executing two-thirds of his prisoners. With the Moabite war David stumbled onto the slippery path of empire, subjecting the territory of another people. In the process, he reaped a harvest of suspicion among the other peoples of Transjordan, leading to wars against Ammon, Aramea (Syria), and Edom, and to additional conquests.

Under David the religion of the LORD became a state religion, centered in the royal capital of Jerusalem. As noted, anthropologists have shown that national religious institutions develop only when a state-level organization that both needs and supports them has arisen. David apparently elevated the Levites, zealots for YHWH, to the status of a national priesthood. This Davidic patronage was reciprocated by Levitical loyalty to the royal house. It was not until the time of David that such a situation was obtained in Israel. David was a modest monarch. He did not saddle his kingdom with the costs of ambitious building projects. His standing army was not very large, centering on the relatively inexpensive heavy infantry. His strategic approach did not require large, fortified cities. The royal bureaucracy, though larger than Saul's, still lay within very limited bounds. The flow of war booty through the first half of his reign would have spared Israel and Judah the burden of heavy taxation. Still, unlike Saul, David was capable of extracting taxes when they were needed and perhaps of conscripting the militia with unrivaled thoroughness. He put conquered peoples to forced labor, but it is not clear whether he instituted forced labor for his own people, as Solomon later did.

In spite of the relatively light burden that David's administration constituted, the later years of his reign were troubled by revolutions led by his own sons. The narrative attributes this unrest to the sin of David. Historians must look for proximate causes. Tribal rivalries from the past persisted. The northern tribes never embraced the Davidic dynasty the way Judah did. Absalom's campaign to gain popular support suggests that David's administration, able in war, was inept in peace. Finally, Jerusalem and the former Canaanite enclaves were the personal holdings of the conquering monarch. Monarchy had come into being in Israel as a response to the Philistine menace. It might seem a dispensable luxury once that threat was eliminated.

SOLOMON   Tradition remembers Solomon for two things, his wisdom and the building of the Jerusalem Temple. The wisdom for which Solomon was remembered was the ancient counterpart of a university education in business and public administration. Royal bureaucrats in the ancient Near East were schooled in such wisdom. Indeed, Solomon gave Israel a modern executive organization, including reorganization of the kingdom into tax districts that cut across traditional tribal boundaries and were capable of raising the revenue and the forced labor to support a splendid royal superstructure. On the second item, Solomon spent twice as long constructing his own palace as he did the LORD'S house, although the subsequent importance of the Temple defies estimate. Solomon did not stop with the Jerusalem building projects: the palace, the Temple (his court chapel), an armory, and others. Modern archaeology has revealed impressive Solomonic fortifications and splendid administrative structures, including palaces for the local governors and extensive storage magazines, at such important centers as Hazor, Megiddo, and Gezer. Small frontier outposts such as Arad, overlooking the marches to Edom, received proportional attention. Where comparison with earlier, modest Davidic installations is possible, as at Megiddo, the contrast is tremendous.

Militarily, Solomon opted for a more traditional imperial establishment than the small, highly mobile professional field army of David. This required an extensive system of fixed fortifications, a large chariot force based in the lowland fortress cities, as well as an infantry. All this was costly to sustain.

Solomon also launched a state-owned trading enterprise that took advantage of Israel's strategic location on the main overland arteries between Africa and Asia. He entered into a merchant marine venture with Hiram of Tyre, which seemed to concentrate on luxury trade. Whether successful or not, Solomon's policies were undoubtedly costly. Despite tribute from foreign territories, Israel itself was obliged to support the imperial establishment with taxes, including forced labor. Some Canaanite inhabitants were reduced to permanent slavery.

On the one hand, Solomon's reign was a time of peace and prosperity, a golden era for those in a position to enjoy it. Only one large-scale military operation is recorded (2 Chr. 8:3–4). The story of the visit of the Queen of Sheba suggests an international reputation for wisdom and splendor. However, there were signs of trouble. Outside Israel Solomon seemed unable to maintain David's control of the empire. Further, the rise of the aggressive Sheshonk to power in Egypt spelled trouble. After Solomon's death Sheshonk took advantage of the revolt led by his former guest, Jeroboam, and mounted a campaign that ravaged the land.

Internally, important factions were seriously disaffected before the end of Solomon's long reign. Tribal rivalries were worsened by Solomon's apparent policy of giving his native Judah a tax advantage. The heavy burden of taxation and forced labor alienated the elders and people of the northern tribes. Solomon's taste for splendor miffed the Levitical priesthood (Dt. 17:14–20), and both they and the emergent prophetic party (see Chapter 6) were disenchanted with Solomon's practice of making diplomatic marriages and then permitting his foreign brides to practice their religions in Jerusalem. The king was suspected of not only condoning but also participating in the abominable practices. Surely Solomon in all his wisdom could not have realized how his actions were robbing his court of two of its most important sources of support! The prophets had helped to create the monarchy and exalt the house of David. The zealously YHWHistic Levitical priests had been David's instrument for unifying his kingdom through propagation of a royal cult. Had Solomon left an heir as astute as he himself was supposed to be, the situation might have been salvaged. But such was not to be the case.

FROM EMPIRE TO EXILE: THE DIVIDED KINGDOM (FIRST KINGS 12–22, SECOND KINGS)

The Literary World: The Patterning of History in Kings

The Books of Kings might best be called a historical overview of the period from the end of the reign of David in 961 B.C.E. to the destruction of the Southern Kingdom of Judah in 587 B.C.E. (see Table 5.1), with a postscript concerning the release of the exiled King Jehoiachin from prison in Babylon some years later.

The narrative assumes that readers have access to the chronicles on which this sketch is based, such as the Book of Acts of Solomon (1 Kgs. 11:41), the Book of the Chronicles of the Kings of Israel (1 Kgs. 14:19), and the Book of the Chronicles of the Kings of Judah (1 Kgs. 14:29). The purpose is not a detailed account of events but a survey that reveals the pattern evident in the story of this period and highlights crucial moments. Because the aforementioned sources are now lost, historians are frustrated by the lack of data about the kings who followed Solomon. From a literary point of view, the schematic presentation gives us a fairly clear view of the patterning of history.

One important internal indication of the patterning in Kings is the repeated use of a formula that summarizes and assesses the reigns of the kings. It first appears in 1 Kgs. 11:41–43, applied to Solomon. The formula includes a reference to another historical source, a statement about the length of the subject's reign, and the naming of his successor. This is preceded by an identification of the "fatal flaw" in Solomon's reign, which was the cause of the rupture of the United Kingdom,

TABLE 5.1 Political Situations in the Ancient Near East during the Period of the Monarchy in Israel

Date (B.C.E.)	Egypt	Israel		Mesopotamia/Syria
1000	Weakness continues	United Kingdom (c. 1020–922) Samuel Saul (c. 1021–1000) David (c. 1000–961) Solomon (c. 961–922)		Assyrian decline continues in Mesopotamia
		Southern Kingdom (Judah)	*Northern Kingdom* (Israel)	Assyrian resurgence begins (c. 935)
900	Revival (935–725) Sheshonk I (c. 935–914) Invasion of Judah (c. 918)	Rehoboam (922–915) Abijah (915–913) Asa (913–873)	Jeroboam I (922–901) Baasha (900–877) Omri (876–869)	Benhadad I (Syria) (c. 880–842) Battle of Qarqar (853)
	Decline	Jehoshaphat (873–849) Joash (837–800)	Ahab (869–850) Jehu (842–815)	Hazael (Syria) (c. 842–806) Shalmaneser III (Assyria) receives tribute from Jehu (841)
800		Amaziah (800–783) Uzziah-Azariah (783–742)	Jehoahaz (815–801) Jehoash (801–786) Jeroboam II (786–746)	Assyrian decline (800–750)
750				Assyrian Expansion begins (c. 750)
		Jotham (742–735) Ahaz (735–715) Samaria falls to Assyria (722)	Menahem (745–738) Hoshea (732–724)	Syro-Israelite alliance (735) Syris falls to Assyria (732) Assyrian kings: Tiglath-Pileser III (745–727) Shalmaneser V (727–722) Sargon II (722–705) Sennacherib (704–681)
		Hezekiah (715–687)		
700	Thebes falls to Assyria (663)	Lachish falls (701) Manasseh (687–642) Josiah (640–609)		Invades Judah (701)
		Jehoiakim (609–598) Jehoiachin (598–597) First deportation (597) Zedekiah (597–587) Fall of Jerusalem (587) Second deportation (587)		Rise of Neo-Babylonian Empire begins (c. 627) Fall of Assyria (610) Battle of Carchemish (605) Nebuchadnezzar of Babylon (605–562)

according to the narrative. Solomon forsook the LORD and worshipped other gods. He failed to obey the LORD "as David his father did" (1 Kgs. 11:31–40).

Each subsequent king of the Southern Kingdom (Judah) and the Northern Kingdom (Israel) also receives a report card followed by a summarizing formula. Jeroboam, the first king of the north after the split, had been promised "a sure house (dynasty), as I built for David" if he was obedient to the LORD, but he too fell victim to idolatry and "unlike David" was not faithful to the covenant (1 Kgs. 14:7–11). Because of the sins of Jeroboam, the promise of a dynasty is invalid and the Northern Kingdom will eventually be destroyed, the narrative announces (1 Kgs. 14:15–16). Under Rehoboam, Solomon's successor in Judah, idolatry continued, we are told. A note about royal and Temple treasures that Rehoboam handed over to Pharaoh Sheshonk of Egypt to spare Jerusalem is juxtaposed, suggesting again the outcome when the people are not obedient to the LORD.

Every king of the north is given a negative assessment, generally with the note that he followed in the sins of Jeroboam. Most kings of Judah are chastised, like Solomon and Rehoboam, with comments to the effect that "his heart was not true to the LORD his god, as the heart of David his father." Only two southern kings, Hezekiah (2 Kgs. 18:3–7) and Josiah (2 Kgs. 22:2), are given really high marks. Both, we should note, championed reforms aimed at removing idolatry from the Temple in Jerusalem and keeping the commandments of the LORD. Their positive evaluation is stated in terms of their walking in the way of David. Other kings of the south—Asa, Jehoash, Azariah, and Jotham—are given qualified approval. They did what was right, except they did not remove the high places (shrines outside Jerusalem).

The twin concern in the narrative's evaluation of kings is restriction of worship outside Jerusalem and obedience to the "statutes and commandments of the LORD." Because these same concerns are so dominant in Deuteronomy, this is often taken as evidence of a "deuteronomic" historian's hand. However, as there is no such identification in the text, this theory goes beyond strict literary analysis and is the proper concern of literary history.

Another indication of the patterning of history in Kings is the role of prophets. We have already witnessed the crucial part played by the prophet Nathan in the story of David. In the sections on Solomon and Jeroboam, another prophet—Ahijah—figures prominently (1 Kgs. 11:29–39; 14:1–16), first announcing judgment on Solomon for his sins, and then on Jeroboam for his. Another prophet is mentioned in passing in a similar role—Jehu (1 Kgs. 16:1–7). Then the overview of the reigns of the kings is interrupted by an extended narrative on the prophet Elijah (1 Kgs. 16:29–19:21; 21), who was active in Israel. The king at the time, Ahab, becomes the secondary character in the story. In the chapter not concerned with Elijah, another unnamed prophet dominates the action (1 Kings 20).

In 1 Kings 22, the prophet Micaiah is the focus of a fascinating story. The basic plot is a conflict among a true prophet who says one thing, false prophets who say something else, and a king who ignores the advice of the true prophet and pays the price. After the Micaiah interlude, Elijah reappears and is succeeded by Elisha (2 Kings 1–2; 4–13), with overviews of the kings interspersed. Also in Second Kings, the role of the prophet Isaiah of Jerusalem is highlighted (2 Kings 19). So crucial are the prophets to the narrative that, beginning with Ahijah's announcement of the division of Israel and Judah (1 Kgs. 12:15), every significant act of destruction in the narrative is foretold by a prophet, creating a pattern of prophecy and fulfillment. In this way all disasters, including the greatest—the Babylonian Exile—are linked to covenantal disobedience, with the people warned by the LORD via prophets of the consequences of their actions. The Word of the LORD is the implicit source of the pattern the narrative is relating.[6]

---

[6]Leonard L. Thompson. *Introducing Biblical Literature: A More Fantastic Country.* Englewood Cliffs, NJ: Prentice Hall, 1978, pp. 124–127.

The ending of Kings gives us still another indication of the patterning of history. Both Israel and Judah have been conquered by foreign nations. The Temple has been destroyed. For failure to be obedient to the law of the LORD, a terrible price has been paid. Yet the narrative does not end without a glimmer of hope. The postscript (2 Kgs. 25:27–29) says that the Davidic king has been freed from prison and is being treated well in Babylonian exile. The promise to the house of David is in jeopardy but not lost.

The ancestral promise is in similar straits. By the end of Kings, many of the people are separated from the land. Israel–Judah is no longer a great nation, and the people are not blessed by the LORD. The reason, the narrative wants us to understand, is clearly discernible. Moses warned that disobedience would lead to destruction and exile, to curse rather than to blessing. It did. Yet there is still hope. The promise to the Davidic house is still alive, and the Sinai Covenant has not been invalidated.

The Historical World

The institution of kingship was only a century old when Solomon died. Some living adults could remember a time before Solomon's efficient redistributive system began its exactions. Empires ordinarily solve their economic problems by forcing the provinces to pay for their mistakes. The empire had begun to creak even in Solomon's lifetime, and a substantial proportion of his revenues had to be raised from domestic sources. But Israel was not a wealthy nation to begin with. Production cannot be intensified beyond a certain point, no matter how efficient the tax system.

Solomon's death about 922 B.C.E. found Jerusalem, a personal hold of the royal house, and Judah, the royal tribe, ready to acknowledge the dynastic principle. They accepted the middle-aged crown prince, Rehoboam, as king. But Rehoboam still had to be confirmed by an assembly of tribal

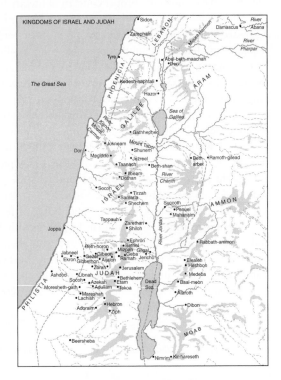

Israel and Judah

elders at Shechem before he could be recognized as king of all Israel. Jeroboam, son of Nebat, who had heard of Solomon's death while in exile in Egypt, showed up at the Shechem meeting armed with the prior warrant of prophetic support. Rehoboam was confronted by a restive assembly, protesting Solomon's exploitative policies and demanding a less rigorous order. Rehoboam listened to the wrong advisors. He pledged his reign to harsher, not milder, policies. Restive tribesmen thus became active rebels. Solomon's great fortress cities availed little for counterinsurgency. His chariots proved an ineffective weapon for keeping order in the hill country.

Rehoboam, in desperation, mustered the militias of Judah and Benjamin, which alone remained loyal, in hopes of suppressing the revolt. The prophet Shemaiah warned against fratricidal warfare, and the militia went home. The Shechem assembly anointed Jeroboam king over the northern tribes, now the kingdom of Israel, and Rehoboam was left to rule over a Southern Kingdom, which included the tribes of Judah and Benjamin. This period of chaos opened the door for a campaign by Pharaoh Sheshonk. Archaeological evidence shows that Sheshonk directed more of his destruction against the kingdom of his former guest, Jeroboam, not surprisingly, as it was larger and stronger than Judah. His purpose was to eliminate the Israelites as a check on his Asiatic policy. The Davidic empire was no more. Where once a sturdy and more or less unified kingdom had stood, two smaller kingdoms weakened by foreign invasion and border skirmishes now surveyed one another across hostile frontiers.

The Northern Kingdom was the larger, stronger, and more populous. It had the best agricultural land. The most important strategic points and fortress cities lay within its borders (such as Hazor, Megiddo, and Gezer) along the main transport route, the inland extension of the Way of the Sea. Shechem, later overshadowed by Samaria, was an important city in the central hill country.

The Northern Kingdom really had no fixed capital in its early decades. The royal residence was most often at Tirzah. Israel gained a permanent capital and royal citadel when Omri built the new city of Samaria, a fortress so formidable that the Assyrian army, mightiest in the ancient world, required three years to capture it. Archaeologists have discovered not only massive fortifications but also evidence of the opulent lifestyle of the Israelite court.

Dynastic instability was characteristic of the Northern Kingdom. The existence of a professional army with ambitious generals was a destabilizing element. The usual course of things was for a strong king to die in bed or in battle. Soon thereafter, his dynastic heir would be assassinated by a senior military officer who would make himself king. The process would be repeated, unless the usurper himself fell to another conspirator first. Only two northern ruling houses, those of Omri and Jehu, extended through four reigns. Omri and Ahab were probably the strongest and most able of the northern monarchs. Archaeological findings suggest that, in absolute terms, the kingdom of Omri and Ahab was richer and stronger than the Davidic–Solomonic polity. However, in relative terms, they confronted much more formidable adversaries than did their predecessors. Assyrian records referred to Israel as "the house of Omri" in the century following the demise of his dynasty. Jeroboam II's reign was the most tranquil, largely because Egypt and Assyria were minding their own business for a change.

The more exposed and strategic situation of the Northern Kingdom probably meant that it could not avoid entanglement in international power politics, with the shifting fortunes and ultimate doom involved. Judah, though smaller and poorer, might have avoided that ruinous game in her mountain terrain and played the role of an ancient Switzerland. But its best kings could not resist the temptation to try to restore the Davidic kingdom and, in the process, run afoul of the games empires play. Its worst kings seemed to be addicted, inept players of those games. Even so, Judah survived its stronger northern neighbor by a century and a half.

Royal stability characterized Judah. The Davidic dynasty ruled nearly uninterrupted to the end of the kingdom, even beyond. Jerusalem was Judah's capital throughout, to the fall of the kingdom, and it has remained so in fact or in ideal for the Jewish people.

Three periods of international crisis punctuated the history narrated in the Former Prophets: the Aramean wars of the mid-ninth century, the Assyrian conquests of the mid-eighth to the mid-seventh centuries, and the Babylonian conquests of the late seventh to early sixth centuries.

Israel and the Aramean kingdom of Damascus (Aramean is often translated "Syrian") were the prime adversaries of the ninth-century wars. David had beaten the Arameans to the punch in the tenth century, but a century later they came into their own. Omri was the architect of the success Israel enjoyed during the Aramean wars, nurturing an alliance with Judah in which the Judeans became *de facto* vassals and cementing an alliance with the Phoenician city–states through a diplomatic marriage between his son Ahab and Jezebel, princess of Sidon. One example of Israel's strength comes from an inscription of the Assyrian emperor Shalmaneser III. When the resurgent Assyrians came adventuring southward, the little Levantine states buried the hatchet temporarily. An alliance of kings met the Assyrian army at Qarqar (853 B.C.E.) in northern Syria and fought it to a standstill. By Shalmaneser's estimates, Ahab of Israel supplied over half of the allied chariots.

One of the most interesting archaeological documents relating to the Hebrew Scriptures comes from this period. It is an inscription from Mesha, king of Moab, that recounts the events narrated in 2 Kgs. 3:4–27 from the Moabite perspective. Neither of the divided kingdoms ever bid fair to restore the Davidic empire, although Israel sometimes dominated Moab, and Judah ruled Edom.

The rebellion of Jehu, instigated by a prophetic faction, brought down the Omride dynasty and made a shambles of Omri's diplomatic achievements. Not only did the mad chariot general Jehu exterminate the Omride line, but he also massacred the king of Judah and his brothers when they crossed his path, accomplished the murder of Jezebel, and slaughtered worshippers of the Phoenician god Ba'al in Samaria. Bereft of allies, Jehu is shown on the "Black Obelisk" of Shalmaneser III, bowed to the ground and offering tribute to the same Shalmaneser against whom Ahab had launched two thousand chariots.

Aerial View of Lachish. Located in the foothills of Judah, Lachish (the modern *Tel ed-Duweir*) was an important biblical city, said to have been captured by the army of Joshua (Josh. 10:1–32), devastated by the Assyrians in 701 B.C.E. (2 Kgs. 18:13), and attacked by the Babylonians (Jer. 34:7). *Source:* www.BibleLandPictures.com/Alamy

The baleful effects of Jehu's folly were mitigated for Israel by external forces. Assyria greatly weakened Damascus, and then obligingly went into a period of quiescence. This paved the way for the long, peaceful, and prosperous reign of Jeroboam II in Israel and its counterpart in Judah under Uzziah (or Azariah). The reigns of these two kings constituted a sort of golden age, and their deaths marked its end, for within a decade the resurgent Assyrians were embarked on a century of unprecedented conquest.

Much of the remaining history narrated in the Former Prophets will be examined (though not chronologically) in our account of the Latter Prophets. We will thus conclude our treatment here with a sequential summary, referring the reader to the next chapter for more details.

Israel and Aramea (Syria) tried to organize a coalition to oppose Assyrian expansion, as Ahab and his allies had done a century earlier. They went to the extent of war against Judah (the Syro-Ephraimitic War of 735 B.C.E., Ephraim being another name for the Northern Kingdom) to compel cooperation. But the scheme misfired. Damascus fell to the Assyrian Tiglath-Pileser III's legions in 732, and Samaria to Sargon II in 722, after a three-year siege.

Judah had a brief renaissance under the nationalist reformer, Hezekiah, who reconstituted the Davidic kingdom under the nose of Assyria. Many historians believe that "Hezekiah's tunnel," built in his time, was explicitly intended to secure Jerusalem's water supply against an expected Assyrian siege. He overreached himself and paid the price. Assyria pressed on in the next century to do what no Asiatic group had done in the millennium since the Hyksos—conquer and rule Egypt. The long reign of Manasseh in Judah, the abject and obedient vassal of Assyria and Judah's worst king in the eyes of the editors of the Former Prophets, filled the middle years of the seventh century.

An Anglo-Israeli team of scholars performed a radiometric analysis to date materials collected from "Hezekiah's tunnel."[7] The dates all focus on the period around 700 B.C.E., the time of Hezekiah, for the construction. This is important on a couple of counts. It confirms the previous judgment of historians. A few years ago, writers known collectively as "minimalists" proposed redating the tunnel and its inscription to the late Hellenistic period on paleographic grounds. That is now proven to be manifestly mistaken. Finally, the inscription (now in a museum in Ankara, Turkey, but soon to be returned to Jerusalem) is a chronological anchor for the study of ancient writing in Israel and surrounding areas. Dating it to the time of Hezekiah lends support to this convention.

The beginning of Assyria's sudden collapse, precipitated by the Medo-Babylonian alliance, coincided roughly with the coming of age of the former boy-king, Josiah, in Judah. Probably an active ally of Babylon himself, Josiah was another Hezekiah, a reforming nationalist whose writ ran from Dan to Beersheva. He died in 609 B.C.E. at Megiddo, possibly by treachery, in a futile attempt to prevent Pharaoh Necho II's equally futile expedition to shore up the last remnants of Assyria.

The Judean monarchy itself became an imperial pawn following Josiah's death. The Egyptians deposed Josiah's acclaimed heir Jehoahaz and installed Jehoiakim. He maladroitly offended Babylonian interests and died just in time to avoid Nebuchadnezzar II's invasion of his realm in 597. His heir, Jehoiachin, reigned only long enough to effect a prudent surrender and go away to lifetime exile in Babylon, initially as a prisoner, accompanied by many prominent Judeans. Nebuchadnezzar elevated Jehoiachin's uncle, Zedekiah, to king, but that worthy allowed himself to be swayed by pro-Egyptian interests and rebelled against Babylon, to his own ruin and that of his kingdom (587).

Our literary analysis has already recounted the hopeful note on which the Former Prophets end. Jehoiachin had been elevated to a place in the court of the Babylonian emperor, Evil Merodach, about 561. But Jerusalem was still in ruins, and the other prominent Judeans exiled during the Babylonian campaigns remained in exile.

---

[7]Amos Frumkin, Aryeh Shimron, and Jeff Rosenbaum. "Radiometric Dating of the Siloam Tunnel, Jerusalem." *Nature*, 425:11 (September 2003), 169–171.

Summary

The Former Prophets (the Books of Joshua, Judges, First and Second Samuel, First and Second Kings) form a connected narrative recounting the creation and destruction of the nation Israel. The perspective from which the story is told stresses that obedience to the LORD results in blessing, whereas disobedience leads to tragedy. Because this is the theme of the Book of Deuteronomy, many interpreters call the narrative the *Deuteronomic History*.

Our literary discussion of the Former Prophets described the balance between Joshua 1–12 and Judges 1–2, complementary accounts of the occupation of the land of Canaan by the Israelites. We then observed closely one of the hero legends in the Book of Judges, the exploits of Ehud in Jg. 3:12–20. We also noticed the pattern that weaves the tales of the judges together. We next examined one of the most refined literary units in the Tanak—the story of the transition from King David to his son Solomon. Finally, we identified the patterning of history in the Books of Kings

through repeated formulas and the recurrent role of prophets.

These books are a rich resource for the historian seeking to reconstruct key periods in the history of ancient Israel. In this chapter we defended the hypothesis that the occupation of Canaan by the Israelites was a complex process that included elements of violent destruction and peaceful occupation and assimilation. We also discussed the evidence concerning the rise of a state-level society in Israel and the reigns of the only two monarchs of the United Kingdom— David and Solomon. We then described the division of Israel into a Northern Kingdom (Israel) and a Southern Kingdom (Judah), and the defeat of Israel by the Assyrians and the vanquishing of Judah by the Babylonians. With many leaders in exile in Babylon, Israel's independent status was ended, but for the Hasmonean interlude in the second to first centuries B.C.E. (see Chapter 10). We turn now to questions of contemporary significance arising from our analysis of the Former Prophets.

The Contemporary World

Case Study

The War on Terrorism

After nearly three thousand people were killed in the attacks by Islamic extremists on September 11, 2001, the United States, Great Britain, and other nations launched what has become known as the "War on Terrorism." The war began with an invasion of Afghanistan, where a radical government headed by the Taliban ("students") had given refuge to a terrorist network known as al-Qaeda ("the base") headed by a Saudi Arabian named Osama bin Laden. In 2003, the war was expanded with the invasion of Iraq, governed by Saddam Hussein, who was alleged to be developing weapons of mass destruction that could fall into the hands of terrorists. The Hussein regime was toppled, but at the time of this writing violence and political instability continue to create chaos in the nation and greater instability in the region. The Taliban is in resurgence

in Afghanistan, copying techniques developed in the Iraqi insurgency. In 2010 the United States and other nations greatly increased troop strength in an effort to regain control of provinces dominated by the Taliban and other insurgents. By August 2010, over 6,400 U.S. and coalition military personnel and many thousands of civilians in Afghanistan and Iraq had died in the conflicts.

The Islamic extremists who have engaged in acts of terror claim to be carrying out God's command that Muslims who are attacked and oppressed must respond with *jihad*. *Jihad* is an Arabic word that means "struggle" and refers to the duty of Muslims to struggle to be obedient to Allah (God) and resist evil. The "greater *jihad*" refers to the individual Muslim's obligation to resist temptation and act righteously on the personal level. The "lesser *jihad*" means the duty of Muslims collectively to take up arms to resist all aggressors who have invaded a Muslim country and/or oppressed Muslims.

What relevance, if any, do you find in the books studied in this chapter to the contemporary War on Terrorism? Some see the modern conflict as nothing less than a "holy war" in which once again the LORD, the divine warrior, who led Israel into battle against its foes is on the side of the United States and its allies in the war not only to defeat but also to annihilate terrorism and terrorists. Others caution against such interpretations, warning that to draw on imagery of "holy war" in the contemporary conflict is to use the same absolutist logic as the terrorists. They point out that Jewish rabbis have long maintained that the legislation regarding "holy war" in the Torah (e.g., Deuteronomy 20) applied only to the war against the Canaanite nations, which no longer exist. How might literary and historical study of these books be relevant to relating them to the contemporary War on Terrorism?

Questions for Discussion and Reflection

1. *Read Joshua 1–12 and Judges 1–2: The Occupation of Canaan:*
   a. Are you troubled by the portrayal of God as a divine warrior who seems to sanction genocical war against the people of Canaan? The story of the conquest of Canaan in Joshua 1–12 may be an "idealized" narrative, written to encourage later Israelites to remain obedient to their covenant with God, rather than as an account of what actually happened in the occupation of Canaan by the tribes of Israel. Does this observation affect your understanding of the portrayal of God?
   b. Some factions on both sides of the long dispute between Israelis and Palestinians claim that the land one calls Israel and the other Palestine is a holy land given to them by God. For these groups, God has commanded them to drive the infidels of the other side from the land. Does this situation exemplify the dangers of interpreting sacred texts literally, and applying them directly to contemporary conflicts, as these factions do?
   c. Discuss the portrayal of Rahab in Joshua 1–2. How do her actions compare with those of other women you have encountered thus far in the biblical text? What impressions of the role of women in the Bible are you developing? What is the contemporary significance of characters such as Rahab?

2. *Read Judges 4–5: Deborah—Mother of Israel:*
   a. There are two versions of the story of Deborah: one a prose account in Judges 4; the other, the victory song in Judges 5, is one of the oldest poems in the Hebrew Bible. What different perspectives on the same events do you find in these two different texts?
   b. Imagine you are a reporter writing a story on Deborah. What would your headline be? How would you describe her role and status as a leader? How would you reconcile the patriarchal context in which she lived with her power and authority?

3. *Read Second Samuel 9–20, First Kings 1–2: The Court History of David:*
   a. After having read this story, which most modern interpreters consider a single literary unit, reflect on and discuss the main characters: David, Bathsheba, Nathan, Joab, and Absalom. What adjectives come to mind in describing them? Are there any "sympathetic" characters? What, if any, "timeless" qualities do you find in the story?
   b. Second Samuel 13 describes what would today be called "acquaintance rape." Discuss the reactions of each of the characters in this troubling story. Given the unfortunate frequency of similar acts of sexual violence today, you may be aware of one or more cases. Discuss what can be done to address the problem of acquaintance rape today.
   c. This story suggests that "what goes around, comes around" or "you reap what you sow." Has that been your experience?
   d. The story of David and Bathsheba (2 Samuel 9–11) illustrates what happens when the attempt is made to cover up wrongdoing. What modern incidents illustrate the perils of covering up misdeeds for political leaders? Why is it so difficult for humans in general, not just politicians, to face up to their shortcomings and failures?

Chapter 6

Covenant Advocates

The Prophets of Ancient Israel

(The Latter Prophets)

The Cyrus Cylinder. The inscription of this clay cylinder is an early example of political propaganda. It claims that Cyrus's conquest of Babylon was instigated by Marduk, the chief god of Babylon, to liberate the country from an unworthy tyrant and to restore right religious practices. Cyrus is pictured as the true friend of the gods and people of Babylon. He figures prominently in the postexilic history of the people of Israel. *Source:* Erich Lessing/Art Resource, NY

In modern parlance a *prophet* is someone who predicts future events before they occur, and *to prophesy* is simply to predict. The first step in understanding the prophets of ancient Israel and the *prophetic books* is to set aside this definition, for although biblical prophets often spoke of the future, their concern was not prediction *per se.* Their predictions were usually conditional, encouraging people to follow the way of Torah. The prophets were not so much *foretellers* as *forthtellers* who spoke the word of the LORD to people of their own time. The Hebrew word for prophet (*nabi*), which appears over three hundred times in the Hebrew Bible, probably means "one who announces" or perhaps "one who is called."

PROPHECY AS A SOCIAL PHENOMENON

Every human culture has had techniques for establishing contact with holiness, that is, with the realm of reality beyond the ordinary, everyday world of time and space. Anthropologists call this realm the *spirit world.* Human attempts to communicate with the spirit world usually fall into two categories. On the one hand, there are persons who seem to have an inborn talent or gift for moving between the world of normal wakefulness and the world of the spirits, gods, and ancestors. Anthropologists call such persons *shamans.* On the other hand, there are all the manipulative techniques, the professional skills that give access to the spirit realm and its wisdom. Here one would place the medicine man or woman, who can use spells, drugs, and other means to go where the shaman moves naturally, and all the methods utilized by priests, soothsayers, fortune tellers, spirit mediums, and augurs.

Ancient Near Eastern cultures witnessed both phenomena. Indeed, archaeologists have found model livers (similar to those used in modern biology classes) used to instruct fledgling augurs. There is also ample documentation for the more charismatic sort of seer, whose contact with the spiritual was more spontaneous.

Many passages in the biblical prophetic books refer to the hand or spirit of the LORD being on the prophet, in a form of shaman-like possession. The Hebrew phrase often translated "oracle of the LORD" literally means "burden of the LORD." Other important prophetic passages suggest that the prophets found themselves in the court of the LORD, surrounded by the heavenly council (e.g., 1 Kings 22).

These data suggest that the prophets of ancient Israel should be associated with the spontaneous, charismatic side of religious behavior. This may be troublesome for modern interpreters, who might prefer biblical personages to be more staid and conventional. It seemed already to be a problem in the biblical period, for association with prophets and prophetic behavior was sometimes deemed inappropriate for persons from "nice" families (1 Sam. 10:11–12; 19:24).

The precise form of Israelite prophetic behavior is less clear. As we have seen, the Hebrew term for prophet, *nabi,* seems to support the notion that prophets were speakers who carried messages from the divine realm to the earthly. The forms of behavior recognized as appropriate to the reception and delivery of prophetic oracles probably differed from time to time and from place to place.

Prophets were perceived as useful persons to have about. Other means of consulting the spirit realm had serious limitations. Lots could generally say only yes, no, and maybe. Omens and auguries were notoriously vague, and oracles were ambiguous. A prophet in direct communication with the spirit realm could elicit a discursive response. In addition, given the common folk belief in the effective power of word formulas (as in blessings and curses), the prophet could also be a dangerous person to have around. The word spoken by the prophet was the Word of the LORD. It was a causal force. Not surprisingly, prophets were themselves considered holy. Even when they were hated, they were not often killed. Deuteronomy does decree death for the prophet who seduces Israel to follow strange gods (13:1–5; 18:20). It appears that the "presumptuous" prophet who speaks words not commanded by God may be safely ignored (18:18–22). But the criterion of a true word is that it comes true! In most cases, the issue would be moot by the time the evidence was in. Deuteronomy's efforts illustrate the difficulty of dealing rationally and bureaucratically with charismatic phenomena (*cf.* Jer. 23:18–22).

Some prophets were associated with shrines and the Temple, and these are called *cultic prophets.* Others were members of the court—*royal prophets.* Some belonged to guilds or bands. Both Samuel and Elisha headed such bands, and Isaiah of Jerusalem had disciples. The term *sons of the prophets* usually designated these prophetic bands. Some prophets apparently went "on the road," showing up at important local festivals (as did Samuel). Some seemed to be in private practice. Some, such as Amos, were not professionals. Prophecy was an avocation they did not choose. Some prophets, such as Jeremiah and Amos, claimed an explicit call from God to a prophetic mission.

The word "spoken forth" by the prophet might be as commonplace as Samuel's information to Saul about the fate of his father's herd of lost asses, and it was frequently a response to everyday inquiries. But Samuel also anointed and denounced kings, and Elijah, Elisha, and Nathan felt themselves commissioned to make and unmake monarchs. Nathan, Gad, Isaiah, and Jeremiah advised kings. A number of prophets announced oracles bearing on matters of high policy.

The prophets mentioned in the Bible (see Table 6.1) were a minority, perhaps a maverick minority, of the prophets who flourished in ancient Israel. The biblical prophets understood themselves not merely as having access to the spirit world but also   as ambassadors of the divine court to the earthly seats of power. It is in this role that they can be seen as advocates of the Mosaic covenant, the holy treaty that formalized the special relationship between the LORD and Israel. Of course, diplomacy is a two-way street. Like good ambassadors, prophets also interpreted the case of the government to which they were accredited to the chancery of the Sovereign. Thus, prophets made intercession to God on behalf of Israel, and they were believed to have special powers in this regard.

Each of the prophets had particular points of interest and emphasis, to judge from the surviving materials. Still, as covenant advocates, they all shared in common an uncompromising demand for justice and righteousness, that is, for the creation on earth among God's people of those conditions representing the divine intentions as made explicit in the Torah—a religiously faithful people living under a decent government that sought to create a just and humane social order.

Given their source of authority, it is not surprising that the biblical prophets vigorously denounced the veneration of other gods, whether it was for political purposes (as when the king agreed to place objects associated with other gods in the Temple to cement diplomatic ties with another government) or devotional ends (as when individual Israelites turned to other gods to try to ensure an abundant harvest). *Ba'al* was the object of the greatest prophetic ire. The term *Ba'al* is both a name and a title (meaning "lord") associated with a number of Canaanite deities. They were all fertility gods associated with myths reflecting the yearly cycle of agriculture. The fact that some of the Canaanite religious festivals involved both orgiastic drinking and sexual license put the *Ba'al* cult at cross-purposes with the Torah's demands for both covenant loyalty and moral behavior. The concern of Torah and prophet was not so much proper belief as right practice.

Prophets concerned themselves with the future, in an ambassadorial sense. They brought messages warning what would happen if covenant abuse continued. That is, their predictions were addressed to immediate circumstances. For example, when Isaiah spoke the oracle to King Ahaz about the birth of a child named Immanuel ("God with us"), which is preserved in Is.7:14, he was addressing the situation of the time. The theological use of this text by the New Testament to see a prediction of the coming of Jesus lies outside the bounds of historical method to judge. All interpretations that claim to see in prophetic texts specific predictions of a far future age fall into the same category. They may be legitimate readings from a theological or devotional perspective, but they are outside the purview of historical analysis.

TABLE 6.1 The Prophets of Ancient Israel Beginning with Elijah

Prophet/Location	Approximate Dates	Ruler(s)
Elijah/Israel (1 Kings 17–19; 2 Kings 1–2)	850	Ahab of Israel (869–850)
Micaiah/Israel (1 Kings 22)	850	Ahab of Israel (869–850)
Elisha/Israel (2 Kings 2–10)	825	
Amos/Israel	750	Jeroboam II of Israel (786–746)
Hosea/Israel	740–730	Jeroboam II of Israel and others
Isaiah of Jerusalem (Isaiah 1–39)	742–695	Jotham of Judah (742–735)
		Ahaz of Judah (735–715)
Micah/Judah	730–701	Hezekiah (715–687)
		Manasseh (687–642)
Zephaniah/Judah	630–622	Josiah of Judah (640–609)
Jeremiah/Judah	627–580	Josiah, Jehoahaz (609)
		Jehoiakim (609–598)
Habbakuk/Judah	605–600	Jehoiachin (598–597)
		Zedekiah (597–587)
Ezekiel/Babylon	593–570	Nebuchadnezzar of Babylon (605–562)
Second Isaiah/Babylon (Isaiah 40–55)	540	Nabonidus of Babylonia (556–539)
		Cyrus of Persia (550–530)
Haggai/Jerusalem	520	Zerubbabel of Judea (520–518)
		Darius I of Persia (522–486) Zechariah/Jerusalem
Third Isaiah/Jerusalem (Isaiah 56–66)	515 (?)	
Joel/Jerusalem	400–350 (?)	
Obadiah	?	

Later, the hope of a restored Davidic ruler came to be associated with the term *messiah.* Messiah is a transliteration of the Hebrew word *mashiah,* which was translated into Greek as *christos,* from which we derive "Christ," one of the titles associated with Jesus of Nazareth (see Chapter 11). A brief summary of the evolution of the word *messiah* may help to clarify some of the confusion about its usage. In general, in the Tanak, the Hebrew word *mashiah* (messiah), which means simply "anointed," refers to someone who has been anointed with oil. Both kings and priests in ancient Israel were anointed at their induction. By extension, it may apply to anyone empowered by God for a particular task. For example, in Lev. 4:3, 5, the term appears to designate an "anointed priest." Most frequently in the Tanak it is used to speak of kings who perpetuate the Davidic dynasty (Ps. 89:20, 38, 51). Although *mashiah* later came to be associated with the hope that God would lift up an ideal king to restore the Davidic dynasty and the Israelite nation, it is important to note that none of the prophetic books of the Tanak use the term with this specialized meaning. In fact, as we shall see, in Is. 45:1 it is applied to the Persian king Cyrus, and in Hab. 3:13 it seems to refer to the people of Israel as anointed by God. Although the early Christian community adopted *christos* as a title for Jesus, drawing on imagery associated with *mashiah* present in postbiblical Jewish literature, we must be careful not to read this developed meaning into earlier texts. In the Tanak itself there really is no clear expectation of *a* "messiah." The development of "messianic thinking" in Israel is much more complex, as we shall see when we examine the Jewish literature between 200 B.C.E. and 100 C.E. (see Chapter 10).

There is one major exception to the rule of immediacy in prophetic prediction. Some oracles forecast an age when the divine promises to Israel will be realized. Some foretell blessings for all nations (e.g., Is. 2:1–4 and Mic. 4:1–4). Before the Babylonian Exile, which marked the practical end of the Davidic dynasty, prophets in Judah might speak of an ideal king of David's line, unlike the less-than-ideal monarchs they had to deal with. Isaiah 9:2–7, 11:1–10, and 32:1–8 may be concerned with such an ideal Davidic king.

After the Exile there was no court and, thus, no need for ambassadors. Later rabbinic interpretation held that prophetic inspiration ceased in the time of Ezra. Regardless, the role of prophecy diminished with changes in circumstance, and, over the long haul, prophecy itself faded. But for popular religion, the spirit of prophecy was maintained, especially in the hope of a restored age of glory, which would be announced by the return of Elijah (Mal. 3:1; 4:5–6). Popular religion still recognized prophets down into the New Testament period.

THE PROPHETS AND THEIR TIMES

The Origins of Prophecy

When did prophecy arise in Israel? In one sense, prophecy was always present, for the charismatic aspect of religion has been shown to be as old as religion itself. The evidence for prophecy as a distinct, recognized phenomenon begins to appear in materials associated with the Philistine oppression that led to the rise of the Israelite state and its monarchy. Given the nature of the evidence, the question of whether later generations would have recognized as prophets earlier heroic figures (such as Abraham, Moses, and Deborah), so designated in the Tanak, must be left open.

Samuel is the first individual figure portrayed in the Bible who exhibited the characteristics of what was later deemed prophecy. He headed, and sometimes was accompanied by, a band of "sons of the prophets," a prophetic guild of which he was the head, or "father." Samuel anointed kings, delivered divine oracles, and conversed with God concerning the destiny of Israel, all prophetic functions.

The "historical" books (the Former Prophets and Chronicles) contain a variety of traditions bearing on a number of other prophets. Together with the Levitical priests, these prophets are portrayed as great zealots of Mosaic religion.

Saul had no developed bureaucracy, but two prophets are associated with David's entourage. Gad the Seer was a part of David's wilderness company (1 Sam. 22:5) and served as the intermediary during the Jerusalem years, when a plague following David's census was interpreted as evidence of divine wrath (2 Sam. 24:1–25). The other, Nathan, appeared to be a central figure in the Jerusalem court. He is shown first approving, and then forbidding, David's project to build a temple for the LORD in Jerusalem. He is credited with the great oracle that was the foundation of the messianic hope (2 Sam. 7:1–19). The story of Nathan's condemnation of David for his sin against Uriah the Hittite (2 Sam. 11:1–12:26) is a classic confrontation between the prophet as covenant advocate and the king. Nathan was the key figure in the palace coup that quashed Adonijah's attempt to take the throne and that led to Solomon's accession (1 Kgs. 1:1–53). According to Chronicles, Nathan wrote an important source document on the reigns of David (1 Chr. 29:29) and Solomon (2 Chr. 9:29).

Prophetic activity was also associated with the disruption of the Israelite kingdom. Ahijah planted seeds of sedition in the mind of the young bureaucrat Jeroboam with a graphic, enacted oracle (1 Kgs. 11:26–40). Shemaiah persuaded Rehoboam not to launch a fratricidal war at the time of Jeroboam's revolt (1 Kgs. 12:21–25).

Elijah and Elisha

The Aramean wars of the ninth century were the occasion for another upsurge of prophetic activity. The prophets played an ambivalent role in these events. On the one hand, they appear as Israelite patriots, helping Ahab and his sons against their external enemies. On the other, they condemn the entire house of Ahab, apparently for policies that were the handiwork of Ahab's queen, Jezebel, princess of Sidon.

The two principal prophets associated with this period in the narrative are Elijah, called the Tishbite (ordinarily associated with the region of Gilead), and his follower and successor, Elisha, son of Shaphat, from the tribe of Issachar. Micaiah ben Imlah is the central figure in a single, fairly long narrative unit in 1 Kings 22, which is packed with information about the prophetic phenomenon, and which may reveal the deuteronomic (Levitical) historians' attitude toward some aspects of prophecy.

Elijah is portrayed as a person of remarkable strength and energy, whose rude and unusual costume (2 Kgs. 1:8) may symbolize a rejection of settled agrarian life, and, above all, urban life. Elijah appears as the adversary of King Ahab, but his real target was the patronage of the Ba'al cult by Queen Jezebel. The Elijah cycle (1 Kings 17–21; 2 Kgs. 1:1–2:18) ends with his being taken up to heaven by a whirlwind, while horses and chariots of fire interpose between Elijah and his chosen successor, Elisha. That Elijah (like Enoch; see Gen. 5:21–24) was supposed not to have experienced death like ordinary people sets the foundation for the growing role he was to play in later Jewish lore. The earliest evidence of the growth of an Elijah tradition is Mal. 4:5–6, where he is to be the herald of the day of the LORD. Thus, he became the forerunner of the Messiah. The tradition continued to develop in the New Testament. The gospels portray John the Baptizer as Elijah to Jesus's David. In the Jewish Passover celebration a cup set out for Elijah stands as a powerful symbol of the hope of a coming messianic age.

Unlike the prophets of the Latter Prophets, Elijah and Elisha were portrayed as wonder workers. Both performed feeding miracles and resuscitated dead children. Elisha headed a band of sons of the prophets; Elijah was addressed as "father," so he may have preceded in the position.

The final recorded act of Elisha marks a turning point in Israelite prophecy. After executing Elijah's revolutionary commission in Damascus by instigating the murder of the sick King Benhadad by his servant Hazael, Elisha sent one of his disciples to anoint General Jehu king in place of Joram (Jehoram), a son of Ahab. In the event, Jehu went berserk, making common cause with the Rechabites, the most radical religious element in Israel, and launching an unprecedented bloodbath that almost led to the extermination of the Davidic line in Jerusalem and the prophets' Samaritan adversaries (see Chapter 5). Elisha's reaction to the excesses of his former client is not recorded. A later response is. The eighth-century prophet Hosea condemned the Jezreel bloodbath in unconditional terms (Hos. 1:4–5).

Prior to these events, Israelite prophets appeared as revolutionary activists. Samuel made Saul king, and then tried to break him in favor of David. Prophets played a role in the division of the kingdom on both sides of the border. Elijah slaughtered prophets of Baal, and Elisha brought down dynasties. But after Jehu's bloodbath, the prophets seemed to recoil from such direct revolutionary action. By the time the cycles of tradition in the earliest section of the Latter Prophets emerged, the prophets seem to have settled into a less violent diplomatic role, serving as advocates rather than activists.

The Latter Prophets

The next period, from which a substantial body of prophetic material survives, marks yet another major change in Israelite prophetic traditions. The earliest collections of substantial prophetic oracles, many in poetic form, have been preserved in the scrolls of the Latter Prophets and issue from the mid to late eighth century B.C.E. This period witnessed the decline of the "tarnished" (in the eyes of the prophets) golden age of Jeroboam II in Israel and Uzziah (Azariah) in Judah and the rise of Assyria to regional dominance. The last prophet to receive substantial attention in the Former Prophets is Isaiah, whose name also appears in one of the major scrolls of the Latter Prophets. A number of prophets, other than those discussed here, are referred to in the Former Prophets and the Chronicler's History. A number of the references are anonymous. Only a few refer to prophets known from the Latter Prophets (Isaiah, Jeremiah, Jonah).

PROPHETIC SPEECH AND PROPHETIC LITERATURE

Unlike many other biblical books, where a pattern of organization is evident, if not to the casual reader then to the careful student, the prophetic books seem to have no ordering to them in most cases. So the most secure starting point in a literary overview of the prophetic books is the individual literary units, the prophetic sayings and narratives.

Let us first examine the narratives found in prophetic books. One type of story found in several of these works is the *call narrative* (Isaiah 6; Jeremiah 1; Ezekiel 1–3; Amos 7). The subject is the initial encounter of the prophet with the LORD, presumably as a form of validating the prophet's credentials as someone designated by the LORD as a messenger. The story in Isaiah 6 is an especially vivid, first-person description of a vision of the LORD seated on the heavenly throne, surrounded by an entourage of angelic beings who are proclaiming the divine sovereign's holiness (6:3). Their three-fold repetition (Holy, Holy, Holy) is the Hebrew way of saying that the LORD is *the* holiest. The prophet then describes how he was overwhelmed by a feeling of unworthiness at being in the presence of the LORD, but one of the angelic beings symbolically cleansed him and the voice of the LORD commissioned him with a message for the people of Israel. In the call narratives a basic pattern is observable:

> The LORD appears or speaks.
>
> Prophet expresses unworthiness.
>
> Prophet is reassured.
>
> The LORD commissions prophet.

Other types of narratives include reports of visions received by prophets (e.g., Am. 7:1–9; 8:1–3; 9:1–4; Ezekiel 8–11; 37; 40–48). Probably the most famous prophetic vision narrative is Ezekiel's account of seeing a valley of dry bones come to life when he prophesies to them (Ezek. 37:1–14). The visions are frequently symbolic messages rather than clairvoyant pictures of specific happenings. Ezekiel's vision symbolizes what will happen to the house of Israel. Although they are languishing in exile ("dead bones"), with no hope for a new life, the LORD will give them hope and a new life, restoring them to their own land (37:11–14). It is a secondary application of the vision narrative to say that it predicts resurrection after death for individuals.

Another form of prophetic narrative relates *symbolic actions* performed by the prophet as a visual statement to the people of the divine will. For example, when the prophet Jeremiah bought land at Anathoth near Jerusalem, it was a symbol of his confidence in the LORD's promise to restore Judah after the Exile (Jer. 32:1–44). Other examples of symbolic actions by prophets are found in Isaiah 20; Jeremiah 35; Ezekiel 4–5; 12; and Hosea 1; 3:1–5. In all cases, the prophet is directed by the LORD to carry out an action that seems strange, in order to draw attention to himself and thereby be heard.

Also in the prophetic books are narratives describing *dramatic encounters with kings,* similar to those we have already seen in the Former Prophets. Directed by the LORD, the prophet goes to the monarch or is summoned to the court for consultation. He delivers to the king a message either directly or through a symbol. For example, during the Syro-Ephraimitic wars, the LORD sent Isaiah to King Ahaz to reassure him, first directly, and then, when the king apparently ignored him, with a sign: the birth of a child named Immanuel (Isaiah 6–8). Other encounters between prophet and king are related in Isaiah 36–39 (paralleled in 2 Kgs. 18:13–20:19) and in Jeremiah.

Still another type of prophetic narrative is the account of the *persecution of the prophet* by opponents who have been unsettled by his announcement of judgment (e.g., Jer. 20:1–6; 26:1–4; 36–45).

The narrative sections of the prophetic books amount to only about 20 percent of the content. Most of the prophetic literature is poetry, ranging from very brief utterances, such as the saying of Amos:

> Hear this word that the Lord has spoken against
> you, O people of Israel, against the
> whole family which I brought up out of the
> land of Egypt:
> "You only have I known
> of all the families of the earth;
> therefore I will punish you
> for all your iniquities." (3:1–2)

to quite lengthy prayers, songs, and poems (such as those found in Isaiah 40–55). Some of these poetic forms are unique to the prophetic books; others are adapted from other settings.

For the most part, the prophetic books are collections of *prophetic oracles,* that is, sayings in which the prophet announces a message of the LORD. Frequently the oracle is introduced by a formula: "Thus says the LORD," or "Hear the word of the LORD." However, the message that follows might be one of a variety of types. Most common is the *oracle of judgment.* It might be a denunciation in a situation of present faithlessness, or it could be announcement of a future punishment. Usually a present indictment is combined with the announcement of coming results. For example, the Book of Amos begins with a series of oracles of this type (1:3–2:8).

Other prophetic sayings are *admonitions to repentance,* such as the straightforward oracle in Jer. 3:12: "'Return, faithless Israel,' says the LORD." Some exhortations add a warning of what will happen if they are ignored (e.g., Jer. 4:3–4). Another basic type of prophetic saying announces a *future deliverance* of the people, sometimes juxtaposed with an oracle of judgment (e.g., Is. 1:26 added to 1:24–25). Some prophetic sayings reflect the influence of wisdom literature. For example, the oracles in Am. 1:3–2:8 adapt the numerical saying form of wisdom teaching (*cf.* Prov. 30:15–31) to a prophetic context. In Jer. 17:5–11 we find a group of proverbs adapted to a prophetic setting.

Besides these basic types of prophetic oracles, prophetic books include more developed sayings. One of these is the *woe oracle,* which generally has three elements, as illustrated in Hab. 2:6–8:

announcement of distress (2:6);

reason for distress (2:7);

announcement of doom (2:8).

Other examples of woe oracles can be found in Mic. 2:1–5 and Zeph. 2:5–7.

Another developed prophetic saying is the *covenant lawsuit,* in which the LORD is portrayed as bringing Israel to court, accusing the nation or its leaders of violation of the stipulations of the Sinai Covenant, stating the evidence, and announcing the punishment. The prophet plays the role of prosecuting attorney. Hosea 4 provides a good example of this form of prophetic speech:

Summons (4:1a)	To the people of Israel
Charge (4:1b–2)	A general accusation of covenant dereliction, followed in this case by a specific allegation of violations amounting to the breaking of specific commandments of the Decalogue
Evidence (4:3–6a)	The upheaval in nature caused by the covenant violation followed by the specific behavior of priests and prophets
Verdict (4:6b–10)	Priests, prophets, and people to be punished

Other covenant lawsuits can be found in Mic. 6:1–8 and Is. 3:13–26.

In addition to sayings, prophetic literature includes other poetic forms, adapted from other types of literature. For example, Is. 5:1–7 adapts the popular form of a harvest song into an allegory about the LORD'S relationship to Israel and Judah. Ezekiel 19:2–14 is a dirge or funeral song. The laments and hymns common in the Psalms (see Chapter 7) are also found in prophetic literature. Jeremiah especially utilizes the *lament of the individual* in his "confessions," cries of anguish to the LORD (11:18–12:6; 15:10–21; 17:14–18; 18:18–23; 20:7–13; 20:14–18). Amos 4:13, 5:8–9, and 9:5–6 are short hymns in praise of the LORD (called *doxologies*) that stand out amid the oracles of doom dominating the book. In Isaiah 40–55 the hymnic form predominates. These chapters include the longest, and probably the most sophisticated, poems in the prophetic literature. For example, 40:12–31 is a carefully crafted hymn utilizing rhetorical questions to elicit praise of the LORD as the all-powerful creator of the universe, leading to an affirmation of the LORD as the source of strength for those who wait on the creator.

Prophetic poetry, like other poetry of the Tanak, is rich in imagery, which unfortunately loses some of its force for modern readers unaware of its meaning. For example, we find imagery drawn from myths that would have been familiar to ancient Israelites but that are foreign to modern readers. When Is. 51:9 asks the LORD:

Was it not you who didst cut Rahab in pieces,
who pierced the dragon?

the imagery is that of a mythic battle between the divine king and the forces of chaos, which results in order and fertility. The statement is directed to the LORD as an appeal for God as divine warrior to conquer current enemies as the LORD had once vanquished these cosmic agents of chaos. Rahab and Tannin ("Dragon" or "Sea Monster") are two of the numerous names by which the divine foes are known in Semitic mythology.

Prophetic poetry is also rich in the use of such devices as alliteration, assonance, and parono-masia, which are lost to students unfamiliar with Hebrew. Isaiah 5:7, for example, loses its poetic force when the reader is not made aware of the paronomasia (wordplay) present:

He [the LORD] expected justice [*mishpat*],
but saw bloodshed [*mispah*],
righteousness [*sedaqa*],
but heard a cry [*seaqa*]!

Good commentaries will clarify such imagery and point out poetic devices that depend on a knowl-edge of Hebrew.

However, much of the poetic imagery is accessible in translation. Careful attention to it will reward the sensitive reader. There is nothing esoteric about the metaphors the prophet Amos uses to condemn the social injustice of his day. You do not need to know that Bashan was a fertile area well adapted to raising cattle or need to understand the meaning of Harmon (no one in fact does!) to grasp the force of the imagery Amos used to indict the women of Samaria in 4:1–3. Nor does the reader need to know a great deal about ancient Near Eastern religions to feel the satirical irony in the poem about idols in Is. 44:9–20.

PROPHETIC THEMES: COVENANT, JUDGMENT, REDEMPTION

In addition to an orientation to the forms of prophetic discourse, an introduction to prophetic literature should at least attempt to sort out some of the basic themes recurrent in the prophetic books. Any such summary risks oversimplification, but it can also be a helpful framework within which to consider each particular prophet.

All of the prophets assume the special relationship between the LORD and Israel expressed in the Sinai Covenant. They frequently base their indictment of the people and leaders of the nation on violations of the covenant. The prophets are *covenant advocates* or *covenant mediators,* who remind the nation of its responsibilities because of its special relationship with the LORD (see Am. 3:2).

Because the LORD has chosen Israel and entered into a covenant with this nation, the divine expectations for Israel are more rigid. On the other hand, because of this special covenantal relationship, the LORD is more reluctant to destroy the nation. Thus, the covenant creates a tension reflected in the movement in prophetic literature between the announcement of judgment on Israel for covenant abuse and the announcement of restoration of the nation or some part of it. The intimate relationship between the LORD and Israel is expressed in a number of images: parent–child (Hosea 11), owner–vineyard (Isaiah 5), shepherd–flock (Is. 40:11), potter–clay (Jeremiah 18), and, frequently, husband–wife (Jer. 2:1–7). The term often used to describe the LORD's basic attitude toward Israel, and what the LORD expects from them as covenant partners, is *hesed,* translated into English as "steadfast love" (NRSV), "mercy," "compassion," "faithfulness," "devotion," or "grace." It is because of *hesed* that the LORD cannot let Israel go (see, e.g., Hos. 2:16–20; Jer.3:12; Is. 54:7–8).

The basic prophetic tension is heightened by the rebellion of Israel (and other nations), which leads inevitably to punishment. One of the most graphic images of Israel's rebellion is Jeremiah's portrayal of Israel as a camel or wild ass in heat (2:23–25). More common is the image of Israel as a prostitute (e.g., Ezek. 16:8, 15). For virtually every prophet, this rebellion is the subject, with inevitable punishment, often described as total (e.g., Is. 30:12–14; Jer. 5:1–17). The inevitability of judgment does not stop the prophets from calling for repentance. Even Amos, a prophet of doom, admonishes the people to turn from their evil ways (5:14–15). Even if punishment is inevitable, perhaps a few of God's chosen people—a remnant—who remain faithful to the LORD will be saved (see Is. 3:12–13; 4:2–6; 7:3; 10:20–22; 11:10–16; 28:5; 37:32; Zeph. 3:13; Hag. 1:12–14; Zech. 8:6; 11–12).

The prophets also look beyond the time of judgment to a period of restoration or new beginning. After announcing the inevitable destruction of Israel, the Book of Amos draws on the promise to David to envision a restoration (9:11–15). Isaiah 40–55 is the most sustained section developing the theme of restoration. Sometimes the new beginning includes a picture of an age of universal peace, as in the vivid picture of the nations coming to Jerusalem to learn the ways of the LORD and inaugurate a time when swords will be beaten into plowshares and spears into pruning hooks (Is. 2:2–4 and Mic. 4:1–3). Other vivid images of universal redemption can be found in Is. 11:6–9; Hos. 2:18–23; and Is. 49:6.

THE PROPHETIC BOOKS

Our survey of the Latter Prophets will examine each book in the canonical order: Isaiah, Jeremiah, Ezekiel, and the Scroll of the Twelve. There are two reasons for this nonchronological approach. First, it is less complicated for readers who are trying hard to integrate their reading of this account with a reading of the Bible. Second, the Book of Isaiah, which is first in the canonical order of the Latter Prophets, is an anthology of the work of a school of prophecy descending from the great eighth-century prophet Isaiah of Jerusalem. In working through the contents of the scroll of Isaiah, one receives a survey introduction to almost the entire age of the Latter Prophets.

The Isaiah Anthology

The evidence within the Book of Isaiah makes it plain that the material it contains cannot all have issued from a single eighth-century prophet, Isaiah of Jerusalem. Isaiah himself mentioned a circle of disciples who would treasure his teaching in an unfavorable era (Is. 8:16). Apparently, they did more. The continuity of themes through the scroll, despite evidence that various parts of it could not have come from the eighth-century master, is most readily explained by the hypothesis that the school of disciples persisted for more than three hundred years, not only treasuring up the words of

The Dead Sea Scroll of Isaiah. Two scrolls of the Book of Isaiah from the Hebrew Bible were among the first scrolls to be discovered at Qumran, near the Dead Sea. This one, known to scholars as 1Q Isaiah A, is the oldest known complete copy of a biblical book in Hebrew, or in any language. It was copied about 200 B.C.E. Its text closely resembles that of the traditional rabbinic (Masoretic) text, proving that the Masoretic text (with the oldest existing manuscripts from about 1000 C.E.) accurately preserves an ancient form of the Hebrew text. *Source:* David Harris/Israel Museum Jerusalem

Isaiah but also adding their own prophetic insights from generation to generation, in Jerusalem, in Babylonian exile, and again in Jerusalem.

Biblical scholars conveniently refer to the principal blocks of material in the sixty-six chapters of Isaiah as First Isaiah, Second Isaiah, and Third Isaiah. To be sure, no Hebrew manuscript is so divided. This division is a theory that will stand only so long as none better comes along to explain the data. The following outline is one way the parts of the book can be associated with the three different levels.

Isaiah 1–12; 20; 22; 28–33. First Isaiah, material issuing from Isaiah of Jerusalem in the eighth century.

Isaiah 36–39. First Isaiah, historical appendix (a slightly edited recapitulation of 2 Kgs. 18:13–20:19, from the eighth to the sixth centuries).

Isaiah 35; 40–55. Second Isaiah, material issuing from the "Isaiah" of Babylon, an anonymous prophet of the Isaiah school (sixth century).

Isaiah 34; 56–66. Third Isaiah, a collection of oracles from various postexilic members of the Isaiah school (sixth to fifth centuries).

Isaiah 13–23. Oracles against foreign nations, probably issuing from a broad spectrum of history. Except for Isaiah 20 and 22, all are probably later than First Isaiah.

Isaiah 24–27. A visionary section, called the *Isaiah Apocalypse* because of some colorful apocalyptic imagery. It is considered by many to be the latest section of the book (a fourth Isaiah?), but by others to be earlier.

FIRST ISAIAH   The earliest datable material in the Book of Isaiah is the Temple vision of Chapter 6, which supplies a date in the year of Uzziah's death, 742 B.C.E. This vision underscores a basic theme of First Isaiah that became a trademark of the entire school: the holiness of the LORD.

The decree Isaiah was to carry as ambassador of the divine court was one of condemnation, but the LORD would not strike without warning. Most of the first five chapters of Isaiah (except 1:1–9 and 2:1–5) belong to the next few years, before the human agency of doom was clearly visible. Isaiah probably seemed as odd in these years as Jeremiah did a century later, proclaiming a doom that never seemed to materialize. Isaiah singled out the greedy and the proud for special condemnation: absentee landlords (5:8–10), the Jerusalem debutante cotillion (3:16–4:1), and self-indulgent, self-deceived leaders (5:11–30). Like other great prophets, Isaiah insisted that justice, righteousness, and compassion, especially toward the poor and weak, were essential aspects of communal life. And obedience to the Torah was indissolubly connected with religious fidelity to the LORD as the only appropriate repository of trust.

Crisis arose about 735 B.C.E., with a new king, Ahaz, on the throne of Judah. Assyrian expansion was the problem. King Pekah of Israel and King Rezon of Syria decided to try to repeat the strategy of the previous century, when the Levantine coalition, including Ahab, had held Assyria at bay. When Ahaz held back, the Samaria–Damascus alliance schemed to depose Ahaz and install a puppet. Isaiah found King Ahaz inspecting the Jerusalem defenses. Isaiah 7–8 narrates the prophet's response to the crisis (the Syro-Ephraimite war). At first Isaiah offered hope based on trust in the LORD, but Ahaz, in a mock show of piety, declined Isaiah's sign. The prophet gave it anyway: the sign of a child, Immanuel (God with us). By the time the child attained the age of responsibility, Pekah and Rezon would long since be in history's ash heap, and Judah would be enjoying Eden-like prosperity (7:10–17).

In 735, Isaiah had a son old enough to accompany him on a royal interview. The prophet gave him a symbolic name, Shearjashub, which means "a remnant shall repent (or return)." Thus, Isaiah already had developed at this early period the notion of a *remnant* that became another of the central ideas of the Isaiah school.

Ahaz had already sent messengers to the Assyrian king Tiglath-Pileser III, begging aid. So Judah became Assyria's voluntary vassal, and Ahaz dutifully introduced Assyrian religious objects into the Temple of the LORD in Jerusalem. With the addition of a single phrase to the Immanuel oracle—"the King of Assyria" (7:17)—its thrust was changed from hope to doom.

Isaiah withdrew from public life after Ahaz's treachery (8:16–17), but returned about 715 B.C.E. to advise a new king, Hezekiah, in a new crisis. There was widespread rebellion against Assyria, but Isaiah warned against it. He made the point symbolically by walking around Jerusalem dressed as a war slave (Isaiah 20). Apparently Hezekiah listened.

The materials in Isaiah 36–39 (*cf.* 2 Kgs. 18:13–20:19) are almost certainly not in strict chronological order. The embassy of the Babylonian king to Hezekiah certainly precedes the war with Assyria. Fortunately, we are aided by the records of the Assyrian king Sennacherib in understanding what happened. Hezekiah joined a rebellion, fomented in part by the Babylonians. Sennacherib dealt with the rebels in a series of ruthless campaigns. It was Judah's turn in 701 B.C.E. Every fortified city of Judah was destroyed. Sennacherib was so proud of his conquest of the great Judean fortress city of Lachish that he made the siege of that city the subject of the stone relief decorating the throne room of his palace in Nineveh. Jerusalem seemed doomed. In desperation, King Hezekiah turned to Isaiah. Isaiah's message was consistent: Trust in the LORD. Miraculously, the Assyrian army withdrew. Judah was ruined, but Jerusalem was spared, its walls intact. Why did Sennacherib let Hezekiah off so lightly with a payment of tribute and a promise of good behavior, as both 2 Kgs. 18:14–16 and the Assyrian records record? Assyrian records are mute. The biblical accounts mention sickness in his army, but from their perspective, the power of the LORD was the real answer.

The remaining materials associated with 1 Isaiah 28–33 probably issue from the years surrounding the crisis of 701, and they underscore the basic themes of faithfulness and trust in the LORD and scorn for all false sources of confidence. The very first words of the scroll (1:1–9) portray the conditions of those sad days after Assyria's withdrawal.

SECOND ISAIAH   The historical notes in Isaiah 40–55 seem to set this block of the scroll off from the earlier chapters (except for Chapter 35). Jerusalem is in ruins (44:26–28). The Judeans are suffering at Babylonian hands, some as exiles, but Babylon herself is on the verge of doom (47:1–15). Cyrus of Persia is named as the deliverer (indeed, he is called the Messiah of the LORD in 44:28–45:7). The sufferings of war and exile have paid for the guilt that stood under judgment in 1 Isaiah (40:2). This evidence suggests that Second Isaiah speaks near the end of the Babylonian Exile, about 539–538 B.C.E.

The historical evidence accords with the literary data. The style of Isaiah 40–55 is distinctive. These chapters contain long, complex poems, unlike the short prophetic sayings typical of earlier chapters. The theme of hope and redemption has replaced the mood of doom. In 40:1–11 the prophet, hearing the decrees of the heavenly court as his master did, receives a commission to announce a message of hope and redemption.

Still, these materials share more with First Isaiah than the same scroll. Second Isaiah continues the theme of the holiness of the LORD (using the Holy One as a name for God). Perhaps influenced by Babylonian creation mythology, Second Isaiah places the great event of the LORD's redemption of Israel, the Exodus, on a par with the creation of the cosmos (e.g., Is. 42:5–9). Second Isaiah speaks of a "new exodus" through which the LORD will bring the exiles out from bondage in Babylon (40:3, 41:17–20, 42:16, 43:16–19, 51:9–16).

Second Isaiah also develops the theme of holiness into a theoretical assertion of monotheism. Earlier prophets had been *practical monotheists* who did not explicitly say that only the LORD existed as god. For Second Isaiah, the LORD is the only deity. The LORD is god of all peoples. Second Isaiah combines this with the old ancestral motif of the LORD's blessing being extended to all nations (Gen. 12:1-3). It declares that Israel will be "light to the nations," carrying the truth of the LORD to all peoples. Second Isaiah can be cutting in its satire on idolatry (44:9–29; 46:1–13). The final chapter of Second Isaiah might well be called "The Gospel According to Isaiah." The prophet cordially invites everyone to partake of God's gracious bounty. The invitation is united with Davidic hope and infused with the universalism of Is. 2:2–4/Mic. 4:1–5. The invitation is repeated, again in universal terms offering redemption to all penitents. Then the poet turns to a meditation on the nature and power of the Lord's word, perhaps reminiscent of Isaiah 40:8. Second Isaiah concludes with a final word of assurance to the exiles in Babylon.

The mission of Israel is portrayed in a series of *servant songs* (42:1–9, 49:1–7, 50:4–9, 52:13–53:12). Elsewhere, Israel is clearly the servant of the LORD (41:8–10, 42:18–25, 44:1–5), and traditional Jewish interpretation has always held that the prophet is personifying the nation in the figure of the servant. Some interpreters think the servant must be an individual, perhaps the prophet, especially in 52:13–53:12. In any event, Second Isaiah introduced a motif that became important for the development both of the thought of the Tanak on the matter of suffering and of later Christian thought (see Chapter 11). The servant vicariously bears in his or her suffering the sins of the nations.

THIRD ISAIAH Isaiah 56–66 does not exhibit the same consistencies of theme and style as First and Second Isaiah. Rather, it is unified by a common historical setting, the situation of Jerusalem after some of the exiles have returned. Third Isaiah is probably an anthology within an anthology, a collection of prophecies of the Isaiah School produced after about 515 B.C.E. The Temple has been rebuilt (56:5–7; 60:7; 66:6), and sacrifice has resumed (66:3). The Second Isaiah–like oracles in 60:1–3 and 61:1–4 contrast with the vindictive song directed against Edom in 63:1–6, but most of the material is of a classical prophetic style. The exception is the concluding oracle in 66:22–23. It envisions a "new heaven and new earth," exhibiting apocalyptic flavor similar to Isaiah 24–27.

ORACLES AGAINST FOREIGN NATIONS Archaeologists have unearthed numerous texts from ancient Near Eastern cult sites in which curses are leveled against foreign enemies. Thus, it is not surprising that Israelite prophets sometimes proclaimed the wrath of the LORD on Israel's foes. Of the oracles in Isaiah 13–23, which are drawn from a range of historical settings, one is of particular interest. It is a taunt song over a dead Babylonian king (14:4–20). It gives us one of our more graphic biblical descriptions of the underworld (*sheol*) where the dead dwell, and it includes one of the few biblical allusions to the motif of a fallen god/angel.

THE ISAIAH APOCALYPSE Isaiah 24–27 seems more attuned to apocalyptic than prophetic literature (resurrection, universal judgment, a cosmic battle between the LORD and mythic foes, and a banquet heralding a new age of peace). Because other apocalyptic motifs are missing (such as visions and symbolic numbers; see Chapter 9), this section is sometimes called *proto-apocalyptic* and is used as an example of a transitional form between prophetic and apocalyptic writing.

Jeremiah

The Book of Jeremiah transmits more information about the prophet who stands at the head of its tradition than any other. There are descriptive data about the activities of the prophet and subjective information from the prophet himself. This gives us insight into the activities and attitudes of at least one, if not all, prophets. With the note (Jeremiah 36) that Jeremiah's secretary Baruch wrote down a collection of Jeremiah's oracles, we have a bit of evidence about the development of prophetic books.

Jeremiah's activities spanned the most calamitous decades of Judean history prior to the Christian era. The years from 620 to 609 B.C.E. had been years of nationalism, reform, expansion, and prosperity under Josiah (see Chapter 5). But from Josiah's death in 609, disaster piled upon disaster, culminating in the destruction of Jerusalem and its Temple by the Babylonian army in 587–586 B.C.E.

Scholars have long debated the role Jeremiah may have played in the deuteronomic reform. The earliest datable oracle in Jeremiah (22:10–12) issues from 609, the year of Josiah's death and the effective end of the reform. If Jeremiah was active in the reform, we have no concrete evidence.

Unlike Isaiah of Jerusalem, Jeremiah was an unwilling prophet. He protested his youth at the time of his call (1:1–10). Later in his career he tried, but failed, to quit prophesying. His reluctance is understandable, for his prophetic activity made him the target of an assassination plot (involving members of his own family). A priest, he was barred from the Temple. He was without friends and alone much of the time, and he was forbidden by the LORD to marry. He was put in stocks, beaten, left in a muddy cistern to die, and imprisoned through much of the Babylonian siege. To keep at his prophetic mission under these circumstances suggests rather remarkable courage.

The early oracles of Jeremiah spoke of doom and made him the butt of mockery when, as in Isaiah's time, the catastrophe was slow to materialize. From a secular viewpoint, Jeremiah was a lackey of the pro-Babylonian party at court, opposing the pro-Egyptian party. From a prophetic viewpoint, the LORD had commissioned him to announce that the Babylonian yoke was divine judgment on the sins of the nation, especially its unworthy rulers. The burden was to be borne with patience until the LORD lifted it, as Jeremiah dramatically illustrated (Jeremiah 28). Other prophets expressed contrary views, which Jeremiah roundly condemned (23:9–40). He accused his prophetic adversaries of being phonies who had never stood in the LORD'S court.

The "Confessions of Jeremiah," mentioned earlier, are unique in prophetic literature. These utterances not only mourn the prophet's fate but also challenge the LORD, accusing God of deception and unfair use of the deity's greater power. Then they swing to the realization that the LORD is the prophet's only source of hope. There are no specific divine answers to these laments, only the LORD's promise that if Jeremiah is steadfast, God will not allow the prophet to be totally overwhelmed.

When the doom of which Jeremiah had spoken arrived, a new side of the prophet emerged. Like Second Isaiah, he turned from the time of judgment to envision hope for Israel. It was not the naive hope he had condemned other prophets for voicing. It was a long-range hope grounded in a deep faith in the love and fidelity of the LORD. Three examples of this side of Jeremiah must suffice:

1. Jeremiah wrote the exiles of the 597 deportation, warning them against superficial hopes of an early restoration, but with the promise that the LORD would ultimately restore Jerusalem (Jer. 29).
2. While he languished in prison during the Babylonian siege, Jeremiah took the seemingly illogical step of buying property in his hometown, Anathoth, near Jerusalem. Appropriately, Jeremiah was redeeming family property, as he expected God to redeem Judah (Jer. 32: 6–9).
3. Finally, the "new covenant" passage (Jer. 31:31–34) promises a renewal of the LORD'S relationship with Israel and Judah based on a covenant inscribed on the heart (i.e., on the consciousness and will) of people. The passage had great influence on later Jewish groups, including the Dead Sea community and early Christians.

Jeremiah survived the fall of Jerusalem. He declined a Babylonian sinecure to share the lot of his people in a ravaged Judah, joining the court of Gedaliah, the Jewish governor appointed by King Nebuchadnezzar of Babylon. Gedaliah was murdered, and a group of fearful refugees forced

Jeremiah to go with them to Egypt. He is last seen continuing his courageous prophetic work, an exile in a foreign land (Jeremiah 40–43).

A note of concern for individual responsibility emerged in Jeremiah's oracles. Everything cannot be blamed on the sins of the fathers. People will reap the benefits and misfortunes of their own behavior. The buck cannot be passed to others (Jer. 31:29–30; *cf.* Ezek. 18:1–4).

Ezekiel

The autobiographical introduction to the Book of Ezekiel (1:1–3) presents him as a priest among the exiles of the first Babylonian deportation (597 B.C.E.). His prophetic activity is dated from the fifth year of Jehoiachin's exile (592 B.C.E.). His datable oracles extend to the late 570s.

The rabbis of the late first century C.E. debated whether Ezekiel really was canonical. The "problem" with Ezekiel was apparently two-fold:

1. Ezekiel's vision of the Chariot of the LORD (1:4–28; *cf.* 9:3–10:22) was a source of mystical speculation. As with other objects of mystical speculation, many authorities felt the use of Ezekiel should be restricted.
2. Ezekiel's envisioned plan for the reconstruction of the Temple in Chapters 40–48 differed from the rules for the Tabernacle–Temple in Leviticus.

Ezekiel's own reported trance states have been a source of controversy among modern students. However, his reported levitations, transports, visions, trances, catalepsy, and other phenomena are all well documented in the literature of anthropology. One need not propose elaborate editorial theories for the book or consider the prophet psychologically unstable.

The Book of Ezekiel locates the prophet's primary activity among the exiles in Babylon, but he claimed access to Jerusalem by vision and levitation and seemed well informed about the situation there. The contents of the book are topically arranged into four blocks. Chapters 1–24 are mostly oracles denouncing the sins of Israel and Judah (even though the Northern Kingdom had been gone for over a century). Chapters 25–32 contain oracles against foreign nations, and Chapters 33–39 mainly oracles of hope. The latter section concludes with the elaborate Gog–Magog oracle, possibly proto-apocalyptic (Ezekiel 38–39). Chapters 40–48 contain a highly idealized plan for the reconstruction of the Temple, and of the national life of Israel, on lines more congenial to the priesthood than to the secular nobility.

Ezekiel exhibits more colorful symbolic actions than any other prophet. He ate a scroll (2:9–3.3; *cf.* Rev. 10:8–11). Chapter 4 recounts his lying first on one side, and then on the other for long periods, drawing war comics on a brick, and subsisting on the foul diet of a siege victim or war slave. He shaved his head and beard and did some strange things with the hair (Ezekiel 5). He dramatized the fate of Zedekiah, perhaps bemusing his neighbors in the process (12:1–16). He cooked meat in a rusty pot (24:1–14). At the death of his wife, he did not mourn (24:15–27). These actions are, in context, graphic prophetic messages.

The career of Ezekiel, like that of Jeremiah, may well have reached a turning point with the fall of Jerusalem. When judgment struck, the prophet of doom became the prophet of hope (e.g., 28:24–26, 33:1–48:35). The vision of the resuscitation of bones (37:1–14), symbolic of the restoration of the nation, is the most famous of Ezekiel's prophecies of renewal.

Again like Jeremiah, Ezekiel denounced those he considered false prophets, saying they plastered and whitewashed a faulty defensive wall (13:1–16). He stands in the classical prophetic tradition with his condemnation of ethical transgressions, violence, corruption, and bloodshed (see Ezekiel 22). But idolatry and religious infidelity were the most serious sins to this priestly prophet, for they begat all other transgressions (Ezekiel 8, 14, 16). Like Jeremiah, Ezekiel emphasized the idea of personal responsibility (Ezekiel 18). He also applied the idea of responsibility to the work of the prophet, "the watchman" (3:16–21; 33:1–20).

Two other themes in Ezekiel deserve our attention. The term *son of man* is God's favorite title for the prophet. It means *human being*. The clear meaning of this phrase here cannot be ignored when considering its meaning in other biblical documents. Finally, Ezekiel's life-giving stream, which issues from the restored Temple in his reconstruction, not only had roots in Gen. 2:10 and other Near Eastern lore but is also the probable source of the similar image in Rev. 22:1–2.

The Scroll of the Twelve

This section of the canon is known to modern Christians as the books of the *minor prophets*. They should be considered minor only in terms of length. They are united, because all twelve together roughly equal the length of one of the three major prophets, thus bringing the Latter Prophets up to four scrolls, balancing the four scrolls of the Former Prophets (Joshua, Judges, Samuel, and Kings).

There is no clearly discernible scheme underlying the arrangement of materials within the Scroll of the Twelve. Certainly the twelve sections do not stand in chronological sequence (see Table 6.1).

HOSEA   The evidence within the Book of Hosea suggests that this prophet witnessed the disintegration of the era of prosperity in the Northern Kingdom under Jeroboam II and in the south under Uzziah as well as the Syro-Ephraimite war that followed. The most likely dates for Hosea's prophetic career are 745–725 B.C.E. He is unique among the Latter Prophets as a native of the north.

Extremes of wealth and poverty were abhorrent to the egalitarian values of the Torah tradition. Thus, Hosea vigorously denounced oppression and exploitation of the poor, especially through the perversion of the courts by the wealthy and powerful. Hosea also shared the prophetic repugnance at religious apostasy, including cultic aspects of foreign diplomatic alliances. Hosea equated such with adultery, an apt image given the fertility overtones of most pagan ritual at the time and the religious aspect of the Sinai Covenant (*cf.* Chapter 4; Hos. 4:11–14). Hosea also denounced unworthy priests, some of whom he accused of brigandage (6:8–10).

Hosea's private life was intertwined with his prophetic message. At the LORD'S instruction, he married a common prostitute (as opposed to a cultic prostitute who participated in pagan ritual). She left him, which became a metaphor for the LORD'S relationship with Israel. Like Hosea's Gomer, Israel had gone "whoring" after other husbands (in Hebrew, *baals*). And just as Hosea continued to love his wayward spouse, the LORD continued to love Israel and, in the long run, wanted to win her back and purify her. There are many questions about how to untangle the events alluded to in Chapters 1–3, but this is the substance of the action and its symbolism.

Hosea was not preoccupied with only a single metaphor. He also used the picture of a stubborn domestic animal (4:16) and a rebellious child (11:1–9) to speak of the LORD'S deep love for his wayward people. The key to Hosea's understanding of the LORD is the Hebrew term *hesed*, which, as noted, means "steadfast love," "faithfulness," and "devotion." It describes the covenant relationship between the LORD and Israel, portraying both the LORD'S intention toward Israel and his expectation for the people (6:6). Hosea apparently thought of the sufferings of war and exile as the path to penitence. The saving purpose of the LORD'S love for the people would not be thwarted.

JOEL   Internal evidence from the Book of Joel suggests a postexilic date (fifth or fourth century B.C.E.) for Joel's prophecy. The sacrificial practices mentioned seem to reflect the priestly code (see 1:9, 13; 2:14; *cf.* Ex. 29:38–42 and Num. 28:3–8). The dispersion of Jews seems to be a fact of life (3:1–3). The Temple stands with a functioning priesthood (which means after 515 B.C.E.). Joel seemed to know the prophetic tradition. Joel 3:10, for example, contains a parody of Is. 2:4 and Mic. 4:3. The influence of Amos may elsewhere be discerned. The most likely time for the Book of Joel is about 400–350 B.C.E.

The prophecy begins with an account of a severe locust plague accompanied by drought. The prophet suddenly realizes that the disaster may be a harbinger of cosmic catastrophe, the dreaded Day of the LORD. The LORD interrupts the litany of doom, commanding a fast, one undergirded by genuine penitence. The lament of priest and people is answered by an oracle of assurance. The Day of the LORD has become a day of fulfillment for Israel. Israel's enemies will suffer, but Israelite exiles will return home and Judah will become both fertile and secure, with the LORD in the midst of Zion (2:28–3:21).

In fuller canonical context we could examine the citation of Jl. 2:28–32 in the Pentecost sermon of Peter in Acts 2:17–21. Form criticism has pointed to the Book of Joel for the "setting in life" of the laments so common in the Psalms. Theologians point to Joel's expression of true repentance: "rend your hearts and not your garments" (2:13).

AMOS   The Book of Amos contains the earliest collection of oracles in the Scroll of the Twelve. Like Hosea, he lived in the time of Jeroboam II and Uzziah (1:1). Amos can be placed at about 750 B.C.E.; he does not reflect the chaos of the 730s.

The superscription introduces the collection as the words that Amos *saw.* More typically, the word of the LORD is described as *coming* to a prophet. Some of Amos's visions are narrated: a locust plague, a drought so severe that the cosmic deep was consumed, and a wall (Israel) hopelessly out of plumb. Amos interceded after the first two visions, and the LORD "repented." Amos was silent after the third, and the LORD proclaimed irrevocable doom (7:1–9). Later, doom was portrayed as a basket of summer fruit (a pun in Hebrew; Am. 8:1–2). Amos's visions, like those of Jeremiah (see Jer. 1:11–14), may reflect the perception of profound significance in ordinary sights rather than mystical experiences.

Amos's first set of oracles (1:2–2:16) reflects the rhetorical skill of the prophet (or the compiler). He used the 3 + 1 formula of wisdom teaching ("for three transgressions, and for four . . . "; *cf.* the three visions of Am. 7:1–9). Amos played upon the prejudices of his Israelite audience by denouncing the surrounding nations, culminating in an oracle against his own Judean homeland (he was from Tekoa, south of Jerusalem). Then, with the audience in the palm of his hand, the prophet swatted, pronouncing a detailed condemnation of Israel's Torah violations.

In his condemnation of foreign nations, Amos appealed to a sense of common morality. In his denunciation of Israel and Judah, he held them accountable to the Mosaic covenant. Repression and exploitation of the poor and the perversion of justice called forth wrath. He excoriated the religious hypocrisy that substituted ritual for ethical behavior (4:4–5; 5:21–27). Amos the radical went so far as to suggest that the sacrificial cult was a human innovation, not a Mosaic institution!

Amos was not a professional prophet, as his encounter with Amaziah the priest makes clear (7:10–17). He was minding his own business when God sent him north to denounce covenant dereliction. Amos did not hold out hope for his audience. Although repentance could bring redemption (5:4–6, 14–15), he did not expect it to happen. The prophecy of restoration in 9:11–15 has the marks of a later addition. The booth of David (Jerusalem) had not yet fallen in Amos's day (9:11).

OBADIAH   The Book of Obadiah is only one chapter long. It belongs to the *oracles against foreign nations* category of prophetic sayings. Obadiah's wrath was directed against Edom (Esau). Prior to the Babylonian wars, the Israelites apparently looked upon Edom as cloddish kinsmen, fit targets for ethnic humor (Gen. 25:27–34; 27:1–28:9). However, Edom took advantage of Judah's prostrate condition after 587 to loot, pillage, and annex territory in the Negev. Thereafter, Edom became the object of the wrath reflected by Obadiah (and Third Isaiah in Isaiah 34 and 63:1–6). A date during the Exile or the early postexilic period is generally accepted. The vision (1:1) may have been offered on a cultic occasion.

JONAH   There *was* a prophet named Jonah of the eighth century B.C.E. (2 Kgs. 14:25–27), but the book called Jonah is quite unlike any other block of tradition in the Latter Prophets. It is not a collection of oracles with narrative interludes; it is a narrative with only one oracle (3:4). It is more like the short stories of the Tanak (see Chapter 9) than the other books of the Latter Prophets.

It is hard to miss the satire and irony in this delightful tale. This prophet, who knows better than God, is drawn with broad and absurd strokes. Everything he does is inappropriate, and his only correct action occurs under duress. Even his pious psalm from the belly of the great fish (Jonah 2) is more appropriate for a near-drowning victim. Everyone in the story turns out to be more devout than the self-righteous prophet: the pagan sailors, the king and people of Nineveh, even the domestic animals. The story illustrates how a comic art form can be a powerful vehicle for religious meaning. Jonah is the archetype of hypocritical persons who would reserve God's love for themselves and their own and consign their enemies to God's wrath.

A precise date for this work is nearly impossible to defend. The popular notion that it was propaganda against the "exclusivism" of Ezra and Nehemiah distorts their policies (*cf.* Chapter 9). The sympathetic and ahistoric view of Assyria strongly suggests a postexilic date.

MICAH   Micah is the only canonical prophet quoted by name in another section of the Latter Prophets (*cf.* Mic. 3:12 and Jer. 26:18). His career fits between the Assyrian campaign against Samaria (mid-720s) and Sennacherib's siege of Jerusalem (701 B.C.E.). Micah was from a rural village (Moresheth-Gath) southwest of Jerusalem, and may have been a member of Isaiah's school. The most direct evidence is the Zion oracle common to Mic. 4:1–4 and Is. 2:2–4. A number of other oracles seem similar (such as Mic. 1:10–16 and Is. 10:27–34, and Mic. 2:1–3 and Is. 5:5–30).

Like Isaiah, Micah denounced the exploitation of the rural poor (2:1–5; 3:1–3) and saw the cities as repositories of evil (1:5; 13). He had little use for mercenary prophets (3:5–8), and he felt that many of his contemporaries would rather hear a windy temperance preacher than a true prophet of justice (2:6–11).

The most famous passage in Micah (6:6–8) takes the form of a covenant lawsuit. Its conclusion as to what the LORD requires of people is sometimes taken as a summary statement of eighth-century prophetic themes: Do justice (Amos), love mercy (Hosea), and walk humbly with God (Isaiah).

NAHUM   Nothing is known of Nahum of Elkoah, whose vision stands next in the Scroll of the Twelve. Its superscription even lacks the usual association with a king. Nahum's prophecy is concerned solely with the fall of Nineveh, the Assyrian capital, to the Medo-Babylonian coalition in 612 B.C.E. His words have the character of a taunt song over a defeated foe rather than an oracle against a foreign nation. Nahum's prophecy may have been part of a liturgical recreation of Nineveh's downfall, the end of the "bloody city" that had visited such grief on so many.

HABAKKUK   The setting for this work is suggested by the reference to the Chaldeans, the aristocracy of the neo-Babylonian empire (Hab. 1:6). The Babylonian armies are active, but Jerusalem has not yet fallen, suggesting a period between 605 and 600 B.C.E.

Like his contemporary, Jeremiah, Habakkuk dared to question the LORD about the moral operations of the world (1:2–4). The LORD responded that he was raising up the wrath of the

Chaldeans to punish Judean sinners (1:5–11). Habakkuk quickly concluded that the cure was worse than the disease (1:12–17). Here, the prophet literally challenged God to give him the answer he had been seeking. He took his stand in the watchtower until the answer came (2:1).

Habakkuk did not have to wait long. The LORD instructed him to write the answer so plainly that it could be read on the run. The answer itself was, "Look at the proud! Their spirit is not right in them, but the righteous live by their faith" (2:4). The Hebrew word (*amunah*) means "fidelity," "faithfulness," not simply belief. In a canonical and theological context, Paul's use of this verse in Gal. 3:11 and Rom. 1:17, and Martin Luther's use of Paul, makes this one of the more influential prophetic utterances in Christian interpretation.

Habakkuk 3 is a lament with indications of liturgical use. The poem draws on the mythic imagery of the cosmic combat between the LORD and sea monsters (3:8). It offers another response to Habakkuk's question from the watchtower. The LORD, creator, is the master of all chaotic powers (3:17–19).

ZEPHANIAH The superscription of this book locates the prophet in the reign of Josiah (640–609 B.C.E.). He stands in the classical prophetic tradition, denouncing religious apostasy (1:4–6), social syncretism (1:8), religious indifference (1:12–13), violence and oppression (3:1–2), official corruption (3:3–7), and pride and lying (3:11–13). Most notable is his awesome account of the approaching Day of the LORD, which eclipses even the visions of Amos and Joel (1:12–18). It appears that everything on the face of the earth will be swept away. The medieval hymn *Dies Irae* ("A Day of Wrath") was inspired by this oracle.

But the Zephaniah tradition is not totally bereft of hope, despite the radical language. A few of the humble and lowly will be spared (2:1–3; 3:11–13). Zephaniah does not use the term *remnant*, but the concept is present.

HAGGAI Ezra 5:1–2 reports that Haggai prophesied at the time that Zerubbabel, the governor, and Joshua, the high priest, began to reconstruct the Jerusalem Temple. His work is dated to the second year of Darius I, 520 B.C.E., which accords with Ezra's reference.

Haggai's prophecies offered strong support for the Temple program. He promised that the restored house would exceed the glory of its predecessor, despite current appearances. The wealth of nations would flow into Jerusalem (2:1–9; 20–22). He also promised Zerubbabel (a Davidic descendant) nothing less than the throne of David (2:23; *cf.* Jer. 22:24). Soon thereafter Zerubbabel disappeared from the records.

Haggai has been criticized for his practicality, but his prophecy is a counterweight to romantic idealism. As any anthropologist or sociologist can testify, no human idea, however worthy or spiritual, will long survive without embodiment in some sort of institution.

ZECHARIAH Although Haggai and Zechariah made no mention of one another, they were contemporaries. Zechariah shared Haggai's zeal for a rebuilt Temple and a purified community, and he held out the hope of divine intervention to create an ideal age.

Zechariah 1–8 records a series of *night visions* (1:7–6:8), followed by a description of the crowning of Joshua as messianic leader (there were originally two crowns, one for the missing Zerubbabel; 6:9–15). Zechariah 7–8 offers classical prophetic oracles. Satan makes his only appearance in the Tanak (other than in Job 1–2) in 3:1–10. As in the Book of Job, Satan is the heavenly prosecutor, failing to make a case against Joshua (3:1–10). Satan as leader of a heavenly rebellion against God is a later tradition.

Zechariah 9–14 seems to be later than 1–8. Chapters 9–11 are called "an oracle," and they announce the restoration of Israel, with the messianic king entering Jerusalem on a colt (9:9–10; *cf.* Mt.

21:4–5). Chapters 12–14, also called simply "an oracle," announce the coming Day of the LORD, when Jerusalem will be purified, the covenant will be renewed, and there will be a universal kingdom centered in Jerusalem. There seem to be links between this material and apocalyptic literature.

MALACHI   The name Malachi (drawn from Mal. 3:1) may actually be a title, "my messenger." Reflections of religious customs in the book suggest that Ezra's work still lay in the future. However, the fervor stirred up by the Temple rebuilders had cooled, and Malachi devotes much of 1:6–2:9 and 3:6–11 to attacking religious indifference. Among the oracles of judgment in Chapters 3 and 4, we find a reference to a coming messenger who will prepare the way for the LORD. Elijah is named as the forerunner of the Day of the LORD, performing the remarkable task of reconciling the generations. These oracles have deeply influenced Jewish and Christian eschatology.

Malachi's penultimate words constitute an apt point on which to conclude a consideration of the prophets of Israel. Every one of them would have echoed his call to Torah fidelity:

> Remember the teaching of my servant Moses, the statutes and ordinances that I commanded him at Horeb for all Israel. (4:4)

Summary

The books of the Latter Prophets are mostly collections of the utterances of charismatic figures who lived between the eighth and sixth centuries B.C.E. They are divided into so-called major prophets (Isaiah, Jeremiah, and Ezekiel) and minor prophets or the Scroll of the Twelve. These prophets were not so much predictors of the future as ambassadors of the divine king, bringing messages of judgment and hope to the covenant people and other nations. In addition to the writing or classical prophets, Latter Prophets, other prophets such as Nathan and Elijah are prominent figures in the Former Prophets.

In our treatment of the prophets in this chapter, we discussed prophecy as a social phenomenon, stressing its spontaneous, charismatic character. We also traced the history of prophecy from its origins in premonarchic Israel. Our literary analysis highlighted the form of individual prophetic sayings and narratives and the recurrent themes of covenant, judgment, and redemption.

Following the canonical rather than chronological order, we then examined each prophetic book to try to reconstruct its most likely original context and to emphasize its most important themes.

Although the period of classical prophecy ended and the prophetic canon closed before the New Testament era, the phenomenon continued, as we shall later see. For that matter, contemporary voices, speaking words of judgment and hope, claim to speak with divine authority, like prophets of old. Many choose to call such charismatic figures modern prophets. One way to evaluate these contemporary prophets is to measure their messages against the standard established by the classical prophets of ancient Israel.

The Contemporary World

Case Study

What Would the Prophets Say?

Through the marvels of time travel, imagine that some of the prophets of ancient Israel are present at a gathering of heads of state of the world's most wealthy nations. Drawing on your study of the literary and historical worlds of the works associated with these prophets, reflect on/discuss what they might say to these leaders about the following: the tremendous gap between the rich and the poor; the spread of a consumerism that values the accumulation of material things above all else; the deterioration of the environment as a result of human actions, especially overconsumption and waste in the wealthy nations; the breakdown of families due to selfish individualism and immorality; the warehousing of the elderly; luxurious houses of worship built by congregations that pay little or no attention to the plight of the poor and homeless. What would they say about the future of these nations and what the leaders and people of these countries must do? How would the leaders respond to them? How would members of Jewish and Christian congregations in these countries respond? How would the prophets' confrontations with the leaders be reported by the press?

What do you think are the qualities necessary to be recognized as a modern prophet? Can you think of any figures who should be considered twentieth- or twenty-first-century prophets, men and women whose conduct and messages follow the example of the biblical prophets? Here are just a few possible candidates to research (in alphabetical order): Dorothy Day, Mohandas Gandhi, Martin Luther King, Jr., Pat Robertson, Rosemary Radford Ruether, Mother Teresa, Desmond Tutu, Jim Wallis, and Rick Warren. Which of these men and women, or others you can think of, should be recognized as prophets?

Questions for Discussion and Reflection

1. *Read the Book of Amos:*
   a. According to the prophecy of Amos, God holds all nations accountable, but especially the nation Israel. Why? Do you think the same holds true today? If so, which nations are especially liable for their actions?
   b. Imagine a contemporary Amos appearing suddenly in your hometown. What would he say about the behaviors he observed among the most well-to-do and powerful members of society? What might be the response of religious and political leaders? How would the news media respond to him? Are there any "Amoses" today?
   c. In the Book of Amos, as in a number of the other prophetic works in the Hebrew Bible, God seems to show special regard for the poor and ire against those who oppress them. Why? Is this still the case?

2. *Read Isaiah 1–11, 40–55:*
   a. Isaiah 6 is a description of the prophet's commissioning by God. Do you think such direct encounters with the sacred still occur today? Are people still "called by God" to particular careers or for special missions?
   b. Is the vision of the future in Isaiah 2:1–4 naive? If not, what must happen to bring about a peaceful world?
   c. What are the environmental implications of another of Isaiah's visions of the future—11:6–9?

   d. In Christian tradition certain passages in Isaiah are understood as prophecies fulfilled in Jesus (e.g., 7:14, 9:2–7, 11:1–5, 40:1–11; 52:13–53:12). Do you think this is an appropriate interpretation of the prophet's words, written hundreds of years before Jesus was born? What is the basis for your position on this issue?
   e. "Second" Isaiah parodies the "idols" made by human hands to represent other gods, claiming that the LORD alone is the only God (e.g., 46:1–11). What "idols" might the prophet satirize in contemporary American culture?
   f. One implication of the strong monotheistic theology expressed in "Second" Isaiah is that the one and only God is the ultimate cause behind all that happens, fortunes and misfortunes (*cf.* Is. 45:5–7). The Holocaust, in which millions of innocent Jews and other people were slaughtered, has caused some Jewish and Christian theologians to question the type of monotheism expressed by "Second" Isaiah. Discuss "Second" Isaiah's portrayal of an all-powerful God, who determines the course of events, and the arguments of those who challenge that this way of understanding God is no longer persuasive in the modern world.

3. *Read Jeremiah 1–7, 20:7–12:*
   a. When did Jeremiah believe God called him to be a prophet? Do you believe that our destinies are determined before we are born? If so, what is the role of free will?

b. Jeremiah 1:5 is another text that has figured
    in the contemporary debate over abortion. In
    your view, what is its relevance today, if any?

c. Despite the reform of King Josiah, which
    attempted to restore the proper worship of the
    LORD (see Chapter 5), Jeremiah mounts an at-
    tack on the attitude he finds among the people
    of Judah toward the Jerusalem Temple (Jer.
    7:1–34). According to Jeremiah, what will be re-
    quired of the people if the LORD is to dwell with
    them? What might Jeremiah have to say about
    the religious institutions and people's attitudes
    toward them that he would find in America
    today?

Chapter 7

Israel's Sacred Songs

Psalms, Song of Songs, and Lamentations

(The Writings I)

The Old City of Jerusalem. This view of the Old City of Jerusalem looks from east to west across the city and the Temple Mount, identified by the prominent Muslim Dome of the Rock (Haram es Sharif). Jerusalem is frequently mentioned in the Psalms as Zion. The destruction of Jerusalem by the Babylonians in the sixth century B.C.E. inspired the Book of Lamentations.   *Source*: Danita Delimont/ Alamy

The third section of the Hebrew canon is the Writings (*Ketuvim* in Hebrew). It was the final section of the Tanak to be incorporated into the canon. Inclusion of some of the books (especially Esther, the Song of Songs, and Ecclesiastes) was the subject of serious discussions within the Jewish community. Several types of literature are found in the writings: songs, wisdom literature, short stories, historical narrative, and apocalyptic literature. Except for the historical narratives (Ezra, Nehemiah, and the Chronicles), the rest are types of literature that we have not yet encountered in the biblical books. We will organize our discussion of this section of the canon in the next three chapters around these different literary forms.

The Book of Psalms, the Song of Songs, and Lamentations represent different types of songs of ancient Israel. The Psalms is a collection of various types of poems, most of which were sung in the context of worship. The Song of Songs is an anthology of love poetry from ancient Israel, and Lamentations is a group of poems of anguish that were all motivated by the destruction of Jerusalem in 587 B.C.E.

A PEOPLE'S POETRY: THE BOOK OF PSALMS

Introduction

The Book of Psalms (also called the Psalter) is a collection of 150 poems, most addressed to God. The twentieth-century Catholic mystic Thomas Merton called the Psalms "the most significant and influential collection of religious poems ever written."[1] They are the substance of daily worship in Jewish and Christian practices to this day, a staple of Sabbath or LORD's Day celebrations in nearly all Jewish and Christian communities, and a source for private devotion and reflection for millions. People who know nothing else about the Bible are familiar with quotations from the Psalms. In short, it may be the most influential single book of the Bible and therefore deserves our careful attention.

To orient you to the Psalms as literature, we will examine (1) the types of poems found in the Psalter, (2) the Psalms as unique poems, and (3) the relational world of the Psalms. To introduce the historical world of the Psalms, we will discuss their original setting in the worship of ancient Israel.

The Literary World: The Psalms as Poems

THE TYPES OF PSALMS   Although the Psalms are not organized in the Psalter according to literary types, twentieth-century interpreters have recognized several different literary categories, based on the psalms' form and content. We will briefly describe the major types of psalms, discuss an example of each, and list the psalms that probably should be considered part of each category.

The most frequent type of psalm is the *lament*—a prayer to God that describes a situation of distress (the lament proper), cries out to God in anguish, and calls upon God to act to relieve the situation (the petition). Laments usually express confidence in the LORD's mercy and promise to praise God for the anticipated deliverance. However, some laments do not have such expressions. Frequently, the psalm includes reasons intended to motivate God to intervene.

Approximately one-third of the psalms are *personal laments* describing the situation of a single person, although in such a general way that it is difficult to identify the specifics of the distress or the personal identity of the one in anguish. Some apparently personal laments may in fact be prayers of a personified community. Psalm 13 is a brief example of an individual lament. Its structure illustrates the typical three-fold focus of the description of distress: God (v. 1), "me" (v. 2a), and enemy (v. 2b). In this psalm the petitioner's appeal to God is combined with the motives for action (vv. 3–6).

---

[1]Thomas Merton. *Bread in the Wilderness.* London: Hollis and Carter, 1953, p. xi.

Dead Sea Psalm Scroll from Cave 11. Among the Dead Sea Scrolls was a selection of Psalms concluding with a Hebrew text of Psalm 151, which appears in the Greek (Septuagint) Psalter, but not the Masoretic Hebrew. *Source*: David Harris/Israel Museum Jerusalem

In addition to Psalm 13, the following psalms and a few other scattered psalms can be considered individual laments: 3–7; 10–12; 14; 22; 25–28; 35–36; 38–40; 51–59; 61–64; 140–143. Outside the Psalter there are examples of this type of poem in Lamentations 3, Jeremiah (the "Confessions"), and Job (especially Chapter 3).

There are a few *communal laments* in the Psalter that focus on the plight of a sometimes ambiguous "us." They have a similar structure and also use stereotyped language to address God and describe the plight of the people. Psalm 79 is an example of this type. The situation is described in terms of enemies (vv. 1–3), "us" (v. 4), and God (v. 5). A petition (vv. 6–12) is followed by a promise of praise (v. 13).

One element of the individual laments not found in the communal laments is a clear-cut expression of confidence. Instead, there are reminders to God of the deity's gracious acts in the past (e.g., Ps. 44:2–3; 74:12–17; 80:8–11). Other examples of communal laments in the Psalter include Psalms 44, 74, 80, and 83. Outside the Psalter, communal laments are found in Lamentations.

The next most common type of psalm is the *song of praise*, a poem that acknowledges and affirms God, in terms of either who God is or what God has done. Some psalms of this type give thanks to God for specific deeds of deliverance and could be called *songs of thanksgiving*. Others praise God in general. This type of psalm is usually called a *hymn*.

Among the songs of thanksgiving, the most frequent is that voiced by an "I" and relating to a personal situation, exemplified by Psalm 138. Other examples are 9; 18; 22:22–31; 31; 32; 34; 40; 66; 92; 116; and perhaps 107. Outside the Psalter, this type of psalm can be found in Jonah 2 and Lam. 3:52–57. Most of the psalms found among the Dead Sea Scrolls are of this type. There are only a few communal songs of thanksgiving in the Psalter, among them Psalms 66:8–12, 124, and 129.

The *hymns* include some of the most beautiful poems in the Psalter. A good example of the simple and straightforward hymnic form is found in Psalm 113, in which a call to praise (vv. 1, 9b) surrounds descriptive praise of the LORD's majesty and mercy (vv. 2–9a). Characteristic of hymns is praise of the majesty of God, evidenced in nature, and of the goodness of God, manifested in God's treatment of the poor and needy. Other hymns in the Psalter include 8; 19; 29; 33; 57:7–11; 65; 66; 89:5–18; 93; 95–100; 103; 104; 111; 113; 117; 134–136; 139; and 145–150. Outside the Psalms, hymns are found in Isaiah 40–55, the Book of Job, and Chronicles.

Beyond laments and songs of praise, attempts at classification of the psalms become more problematic. Scholars have not developed a generally accepted set of types. There is disagreement over which psalms fit which type. As we have noted, some psalms do not address God at all, in praise or lament. Some of them are didactic, designed to instruct (e.g., 34:11–22; 37; 112; 128), while others reflect on human mortality (90), the suffering of the righteous (73), or both (39, 49).

Because of the similarity between these psalms and the wisdom books (Job, Ecclesiastes, Proverbs), they are sometimes grouped together as *wisdom psalms*. Still other psalms seem to have in common a concern with the king and are called *royal songs* (2, 18, 20, 21, 45, 72, 89, 101, 110, 132, 144). However, they are diverse poetically and could, using different criteria, as easily be placed with other types. Similar observations could be made about the so-called *liturgical psalms*, which give indication of some specific use in public worship (e.g., 15, 24, 107, 122), the *Zion psalms*, which focus on Jerusalem (46, 48, 76, 84, 87, 132), or psalms of divine kingship (47, 93, 95–99).

Psalm 119, the longest psalm in the Bible, is an example of another common type—the *acrostic* (alphabetic) poem. In a typical acrostic (such as Psalm 37) the first line or strophe (stanza) begins with *aleph*, the first letter of the Hebrew alphabet, the second with the second letter, *beth*, and so on through the twenty-two Hebrew letters of the alphabet. Other examples of acrostic psalms include 9–10, 25, 34, 37, 111, 112, and 145. However, Psalm 119 is constructed in a more impressive fashion, in twenty-two eight-line strophes. All eight lines in each stanza start with the same letter, *aleph* in the first stanza, *beth* in the second, and so forth. All modern translations clearly divide the stanzas. *Tanakh: The Holy Scriptures*, the new Jewish Publication Society translation,[2] prints the respective Hebrew letters in the margin, a touch that may be appreciated even by people who do not know Hebrew. Psalm 119 is a celebration of God's teaching, his Torah, and thus, like Psalm 1, may also be classified as an example of a *Torah psalm*. Trivia fans will want to remember that, at 176 verses, Psalm 119 is not only the longest psalm but also the longest chapter in the entire Bible.

The assignment of one psalm to various categories should alert us to the limits of literary classification. It is helpful to realize there are different kinds of psalms, but merely "typing" a psalm does not tell us what it means. We must also consider the Psalms as unique poems.

THE PSALMS AS UNIQUE POEMS   Thomas Merton also wrote in his meditative study of the Psalms, "A good poem . . . stands by itself, graced with an individuality that marks it off from every other work of art."[3] Although the Psalms do reflect typical patterns, they should also be appreciated as individual poems that create worlds of their own. The best way to make this point is to explore the unique world of one of the psalms.

Psalm 8 is classified as a hymn, for it is a psalm praising the LORD as creator. However, merely to classify it does not do justice to its richness. That is apparent when we treat it not as a hymn but as a unique poetic utterance. This psalm, which uses a poetic meditation on the creation of humanity as a basis for praising the LORD, is structured to communicate a sense of order that is in harmony with its theme. The frame of the meditation on the place of humanity is the ascription of praise in verses 1 and 9. This sense of symmetry underlies the theme of a divinely created order, and it frames the expression of awe at the majesty of humankind within the context of the sovereignty of the LORD. Within the body of the poem (vv. 2–8) there is a balance between the heavenly bodies ordered by God (v. 3) and the creatures of earth, sky, and sea, for which humankind has responsibility (vv. 6–8). In the center of this symmetrical pattern is the pivot, the question and answer in verses 4 and 5. At the center of the psalm is verse 5, making the point that the glory and honor of humanity derive from the majesty and splendor of the creator. The distinct sense of movement in the psalm includes a flow from acclamation of God's majesty to the seeming insignificance of humankind measured against God and the creation; a pivot at the affirmation of the centrality of humankind in God's plan; a movement back through creation, now focusing on that for which humankind is responsible; and a return to the beginning and the acclamation of God's sovereignty.

---

[2] *Tanakh: The Holy Scriptures*. Philadelphia: Jewish Publication Society, 2007.

[3] Thomas Merton. *Bread in the Wilderness*. London: Hollis and Carter, 1953, p. xi.

The imagery of the psalm is built on a series of contrasts. The basic contrast is between the majesty of God and the insignificance of humankind, mediated by the glory bestowed on humanity by the creator. In verses 1–2 the praising of God "above the heavens" is contrasted with that which comes from the mouths of babes and infants. It is an image of God being praised by the mightiest to the weakest of creatures, but with an ironic twist, for it is from babes and infants that the power to still the forces of chaos comes. At the heart of the psalm is an even more ironic twist. The divine king, who controls all hostile powers, who needs no "help" managing the cosmos, assigns to mere humanity a royal status. (The "glory" attributed to the LORD is shared with humankind, vv. 1, 5.) It is this paradox at which the psalm marvels. Its pivotal verse goes so far as to place humanity in the company of the *elohim* (the divine beings who serve and praise the LORD in the heavenly court).

Like other Hebrew poems, the psalms utilize *parallelism* as the basic poetic technique. For example, Ps. 8:3 is a good example of *synonymous parallelism.* The second half of the verse balances the thought of the first half, element for element. However, it is not enough merely to note the type of balancing used. The question is: How does it function in the poem? In Ps. 8:3 we note that, despite the synonymous parallelism, the second line drops the *I* after contrasting the human *I* with the divine *your.* By not repeating the *I,* the second half of the verse sharpens the sense of human insignificance toward which the poem is building. This is a subtle nuance contributing to the effect of the psalm as a whole. Another good example of the function of parallelism in a psalm is Ps. 29:1– 2. Here, *stair-like parallelism,* in which an element is repeated and the thought extended, serves to build a crescendo, climaxing in the voice of the LORD on the waters (v. 3), like a thunder roll leading to the thunderclap that follows.

These examples must suffice to support the point that the student who desires a full appreciation of the poetry of the Psalms must treat each psalm as a unique poem.

THE RELATIONAL WORLD OF THE PSALMS   Although each psalm is unique, all of them come from a poetic tradition with a common stock of imagery. That imagery reflects a basic view of life that we might call the *relational world of the Psalms.* Each psalm focuses on one of the following basic relationships: God and I, God and other divine beings, God and Israel, and God and nature.

God and I.[4]   Most of the psalms are written from a first-person perspective, speaking to God. Usually the identity of *I* is ambiguous, so that it might be an individual, a representative of the people (priest or king, e.g.), or a symbolic expression for everyone. The situations described are so general that we can identify only two basic patterns: dislocation and reorientation.

In many psalms (especially the laments), *I* articulates a situation of dislocation. Often vivid, but general, images of physical distress are present (e.g., Ps. 22:14–15). Either directly, as in this psalm, or indirectly, the infirmity is linked to God; thus, the physical distress becomes a relational problem, a situation of dislocation or disorientation in the relationship between God and *I.* This creates a tension that only divine action can resolve.

Sometimes the disorientation is linked to the moral failure of *I* (e.g., Ps. 25:11 or Ps. 51), and often it is linked to the persecution of "foes" whose identity is always ambiguous, allowing the psalm to be adapted to a variety of situations (e.g., Psalm 3). Invariably, *I* portrays the situation as hopeless without divine intervention. The imagery is often that of life and death. Unless there is action by God, *I* is, in effect, as good as "dead." In ancient Near Eastern mythology, the dead were thought

---

[4]See Lawrence Thompson. *Introducing Biblical Literature: A More Fantastic Country.* Englewood Cliffs, NJ: Prentice Hall, 1978, pp. 53–66.

Cherubim. Mentioned nearly one hundred times in the Tanak (e.g., Ps. 18:10, Ezek. 10:6-8)) and once in the New Testament (Heb. 9:5), *cherubim* (plural of *cherub*) are mysterious supernatural beings with two or four wings often associated with the Ark of the Covenant, the chariot of God, and the Temple of Solomon. In western art *cherubim* are often represented with the faces of children, as in these carvings at St. Paul's Cathedral in London, England. *Source:* D Silva/Shutterstock

to go to an underworld (in Hebrew, as mentioned, called *sheol*, "the Pit") where they continued a minimal shadow existence cut off from the relationships that give meaning to life. In particular, it is a place where people no longer have a relationship with the divine, and from which they are unable to praise God. Thus, the *I* of the psalms uses the image of death and sheol to speak of the complete dislocation from the deity toward which *I* feels "myself" moving (e.g., Ps. 88:3–7). Another image of separation from God is the waters, symbolic of the chaos God has not yet ordered (e.g., 69:2), which is saying that "my world has collapsed and the forces of chaos are overwhelming me."

Balancing dislocation imagery, often within the same psalm, is reorientation imagery. Although rarely described within Psalms, an act of divine deliverance is assumed, which has restored the *I* to harmony with God, reversing the previous disorientation (e.g., Ps. 30:1–3). The result of the reorientation is often expressed in terms of the re-identification of the individual *I* with the larger worshipping community. For example, in Psalm 22 the *I* moves from a situation of isolation and persecution by enemies to an anticipated reorientation expressed in terms of participation in the worshipping community (22:22–31).

Many psalms give a spatial identification to reorientation, using the Temple in Jerusalem as a symbol of harmony with God. In the Temple the community gathers for worship, and the individual feels a sense of orientation. In distress, *I* is alienated from the Temple (e.g., Ps. 28:2). The joy of feeling oriented and in harmony is expressed in the imagery of either going up to or being in the Temple (e.g., Ps. 122:1–2). The ascent imagery of going up to the mountain of God reflects the fact that in ancient Near Eastern mythology the dwelling of the divine king is always symbolized as a mountain (in the imagery of the Hebrew Bible, first Mount Sinai [Horeb], and then Mount Zion in Jerusalem). In contrast is the descent imagery of going down into sheol.

For most *I* psalms, the tension and movement, then, is within these poles. Some psalms (such as the famous Psalm 23) are fully on the side of orientation, although a past disorientation is almost always acknowledged, and some (such as Psalm 10) are almost totally focused on disharmony, although there is virtually always some anticipation of restored harmony.

God and Other Divine Beings.   Often confusing to modern readers of the Psalms are references to other divine beings besides the LORD. Although many English translations mute this mythological imagery, it is important to understand if the relational world of the Psalms is to be fully appreciated. As we have noted in our discussion of prophetic literature, the LORD is sometimes portrayed as the king of a divine court, surrounded by a heavenly entourage of other beings (e.g., 1 Kings 22, Isaiah 6). This same imagery is present in the Psalms. For example, Psalm 82 opens with a picture of God in the role of administrator of cosmic justice, addressing the divine court (vv. 1–2). Psalm 29 begins in the heavenly court with a call for the "sons of God" to praise the LORD. Other examples of divine beings surrounding the LORD as servants appear in Ps. 89:5–8 and 103:21.

In addition, the Psalms draw on the imagery of a primeval battle between the divine warrior–king and cosmic foes (e.g., Ps. 74:13–14; 89:9–10; 104:5–8). Invariably, the imagery serves to herald the might and power of the LORD, sometimes as the basis of an appeal for the divine warrior to engage contemporary, historical foes as the LORD did the primeval, mythic ones. Imagery such as this raises the question of the attitude of the Psalms and other biblical literature toward the mythology of the cultures surrounding Israel. It is apparent that biblical writers could both attack the other gods who were the actors in these myths, such as the Canaanite Ba'al, even denying they existed, and also adapt the myths of other cultures to their view of the LORD. This conflict might bother us, but it was apparently not a problem for those who originally wrote or read the Bible. Although the LORD, unlike other ancient Near Eastern deities, was portrayed as a god who was known through historical events (such as the Exodus), this did not stop biblical writers from using the imagery of the nature myths of surrounding cultures to speak of the LORD. Sometimes (as in Ps. 74:13–14 and Exodus 15) the imagery of what was an ahistorical fertility myth is used to suggest the cosmic significance of one of the LORD's deeds within history.

God and Israel.   The Psalms stand within the same covenantal tradition as the Prophets, and Torah, alluding to the special relationship of the LORD with the nation Israel, manifests in acts of deliverance in fulfillment of the ancestral promises, the covenant at Sinai, and the promise to David of an everlasting dynasty. Within the Psalms there are sometimes general references to the "deeds you performed in . . . the days of old" (e.g., 44:1–3), which call forth the imagery of ancestors, exodus, wilderness, and conquest. In several psalms (66, 78, 105, 106, 135, 136), these deeds are recited in detail, not only so that they may not be forgotten, but also so that they may be made present (see, e.g., 66:1–7, especially v. 5), just as Deuteronomy places a later generation at the Exodus.

God and Nature.   In a number of psalms the "earth" in general is admonished to praise the LORD (e.g., 66:1; 96:1; 97:1), and various elements of nature are called to join in exultation of the kingship of the LORD (e.g., 96:11–13). When God appears, nature convulses (e.g., 29:5–8; 68:7; 114). In the world of the Psalms, nature is not inanimate matter, but alive, a dynamic part of the web of relationships to be taken seriously (see, e.g., Psalms 148–150). Thus, Psalm 104 lauds God's provision not only for humankind but also for all of nature.

The Historical World: The Psalms in Israel's Worship

There can be no doubt that many, if not all, of the psalms were associated with acts of worship in ancient Israel, in the Temple at Jerusalem, and perhaps at other shrines before sacrificial worship

Model of the Second Temple, Jerusalem. The Jerusalem Temple, first built by Solomon in the tenth century B.C.E., was rebuilt on its original site after being destroyed by the Babylonians in the sixth century B.C.E. A reconstruction project, originated by Herod the Great in the first century B.C.E., continued into the first century C.E. This model of "Herod's Temple" at the Holy Land Hotel in Jerusalem is based on both literary and archaeological evidence. The rabbinic literature preserves memories of the use of biblical psalms in the worship of the Second Temple.   *Source*: Boris Diakovsky/Shutterstock

was centralized. Some of the titles added to the psalms give instructions for their use in worship (e.g., Psalms 4 and 5). The repetition of the word *Selah* probably is a notation concerning performance of the psalm, although its precise meaning is a mystery. There is also evidence in the Bible outside the Psalms of their use in Temple worship (e.g., 1 Chr. 16:7–36). Moreover, some psalms seem to reflect a specific liturgical event. Psalm 24, for example, was probably used in association with a procession of the Ark of the Covenant into the Temple. These hints of the cultic use of the psalms have sparked a great deal of speculation on the types of services or festivals with which various psalms may have been associated. Rabbinic literature records the liturgical use of a number of psalms in the worship of the Second Temple. For example, Mishnah Pesahim 5:7 notes that the hallelujah psalms (Psalms 113–118) were chanted by the Levitical choir while the Passover lambs were being sacrificed (see Chapter 10).

Because many psalms acclaim the LORD as king (e.g., Ps. 96:10), and there is evidence in the culture surrounding Israel of yearly festivals in which a god was enthroned as king, many interpreters believe that these psalms reflect an *enthronement festival* in Israel. At this festival, associated with the beginning of the new agricultural year in the autumn, the LORD's enthronement as divine king would have been reenacted in the Temple, the earthly representation of the heavenly palace. Unfortunately, there is no evidence within or outside the Bible of any such festival in ancient Israel, so it must be considered only a hypothetical possibility. A modification of this hypothesis holds that, in association with the enthronement of the divine king, there was a yearly Royal Zion festival in which the earthly, Davidic king was also enthroned. But these psalms may be equally well understood as proclamations of the LORD's continuing kingship.

Because of the importance of the remembering–reenacting of the LORD's mighty deeds of deliverance for Israel and of the evidence of covenant renewal festivals in ancient Israel (e.g., Joshua 24), some interpreters theorize that many psalms were originally associated with an annual *covenant renewal festival.*

It is also possible to conceive of worship events that might have been the context for the individual and communal laments. In many laments there is, as we noted, a transition from the situation of distress and petition for help to an expression of confidence. Perhaps this transition reflects the giving of an oracle of assurance by a priest or other religious leader (see, e.g., 1 Sam. 1:17). There is also some evidence in the Bible of communal fasts at times of crisis such as crop failure, pestilence, or attack from enemies (e.g., 1 Kings 21:9; Am. 5:16; Is. 22:12; Jer. 14:2). Thus, it is possible that communal laments originated as songs used at times such as these. The prophetic book of Joel illustrates at least one cultic situation in which communal laments might have been used, a fast day proclaimed in the light of some great disaster (Jl. 1:13–2:29). Indeed, Jl. 2:17 contains a highly condensed lament using very typical language. The ninth day of the month Ab, when the Babylonians destroyed the Temple, and anniversaries of other such great tragedies probably were occasions of annual fasts. Because the Romans destroyed the Temple a second time on the ninth of Ab, in 70 C.E., this is one of the saddest days on the Jewish liturgical calendar.

Interpreters have also associated the Songs of Ascent (Psalms 120–134) with the journeys to Jerusalem that would have been a part of the pilgrimage festivals identified in the Torah. Whether any of these particular festivals might have been occasions for enthronement or covenant renewal festivals has also been the source of much speculation.

Although there is little clear evidence as to particulars, we can assume that most psalms originated as songs associated with corporate worship. In that sense they were the product of the life of the community as much as the work of individual poets. However, some psalms may well have originated as religious poems by individuals, apart from a liturgical setting. For example, the psalms that are reflections on the importance of the Torah of the LORD (1; 19:7–14; 119) might not imply a background of worship. The so-called *wisdom psalms* (such as 36, 37, 49, 73, 112, 127, 128, 133) have no obvious connection with worship.

The many attempts to date particular psalms have proven largely futile because of the lack of external evidence and the ambiguity of their imagery. Liturgical languages in most cultures tend to be conservative and traditional. It also must be general enough to be used on more than one occasion. Even when a psalm pictures a specific situation (such as the destruction of the Temple in Psalms 74 or 79), too few details are given to link the psalm with a concrete historical event. Although King David may have composed some of the seventy-three psalms attributed to him in the titles added to the psalms, the traditional assumption that David is the author of all the Psalms is inconsistent with the editorial superscriptions of many psalms, let alone with the internal evidence of the Psalter. Some psalms are attributed to other famous persons such as Moses (90) and Solomon (72, 127). Psalm 72:20 indicates that the Davidic collection has concluded. Moreover, the phrase translated into English "of David" in the titles of the Psalms does not necessarily imply authorship. The relation of David to the Psalter is probably like that of Moses to the Pentateuch and Solomon to Proverbs and the other works attributed to him: original inspiration but not necessarily authorship of the books. It is likely that psalms were composed throughout the biblical period, certainly from the time of David and Solomon onward. The present collection comes from the postexilic period, although individual psalms may have been composed much earlier.

THE MEGILLOTH

Five of the short works among the Writings are grouped together as the Five Megilloth, the Five (festival) Scrolls. They are Ruth, the Song of Songs, Ecclesiastes, Lamentations, and Esther. The custom developed of reading one of these scrolls on each of five important festivals or days of religious observance through the year. The connection of Esther with Purim is obvious, because it explains the origin of the feast. Similarly, Lamentations, which bemoans the Babylonian destruction of Jerusalem and its Temple, fits well with the fast of the ninth of Ab, the anniversary of that tragedy. The connection between the Song of Songs and Passover may reflect the influence of the allegorical reading noted in a later discussion here. However, the association of Ruth with Shavuot (the Feast of Weeks) and Ecclesiastes with Sukkot (the Feast of Tabernacles, or Booths) appears somewhat arbitrary.

THE SONG OF SONGS

The Song of Songs (also known as the Song of Solomon, or Canticles) is a collection of erotic love poetry. Quotations from this work, which frankly celebrates physical passion, have inspired incredulous responses such as "Is *that* in the Bible?" It is not surprising that many have interpreted the poems allegorically since rabbinic times. For Jewish interpreters, the Song was taken as an allegory of the LORD's relationship with his "bride," Israel. Christian commentators saw in the imagery a symbol of Christ's love for the church. From our perspective, these interpretations are part of the historical world of the Book. However, as we shall see, they are not especially helpful in leading us into the literary world of the Song.

The Literary World: An Anthology of Love Poems

In its final form the Song of Songs is an anthology of between eighteen and thirty-one separate poems, depending on how they are divided by the reader.[5] (They are not distinguished in the text.) Despite their common interest in erotic love, they are in fact quite diverse in subject matter, tone, and situation. The poems are *lyric* in the sense that they are subjective expressions of the feelings of a speaker addressed to a particular listener. Several types of poems can be distinguished. In *love monologues* an *I* (male or female) speaks either to or about his or her beloved, for example:

> My beloved is mine and I am his; he pastures his flock among the lilies.
> Until the day breathes and the shadows flee, turn, my beloved, be like a gazelle, or a young stag on the cleft mountains. (2:16–17)

Other love monologues are 1:1; 1:9–11; 2:4–7; 2:14; 3:1–5; 4:1–7; 4:8; 4:9–11; 6:4–10; 6:11; 8:1–4; 8:5b; and 8:6–7. Another type is a love dialogue, in which there is conversation between two lovers, for example:

> Ah, you are beautiful, my love; ah, you are beautiful; your eyes are doves.
> Ah, you are beautiful, my beloved, truly lovely.
> Our couch is green; the beams of our house are cedar, our rafters are pine. (1:15–17)

Others of this type are 1:7–8; 2:1–3; 2:8–13; 4:12–5:1; and 8:13–14. In addition, there are monologues by an *I* in a love relationship with an audience outside the relationship (1:5–6 and

[5]We are indebted in our literary analysis to Marcia Falk. *Love Lyrics from the Bible: A Translation and Literary Study of the Song of Songs.* Sheffield, England: Almond Press, 1982.

8:11–12), monologues by a group to an unspecified audience about love (2:15; 3:6–11; 8:5a), dialogues between an *I* and a group about erotic matters (7:1–6 and 8:8–10), and one composite poem (5:2–6:3).

Several of the poems are *wasfs* (from the Arabic word for "description"). A *wasf* is a poem or section of a poem that describes the parts of the human body through a series of metaphors. In ancient Hebrew literature these are unique to the Song of Songs. Song 4:1–5 is a partial *wasf*, describing a woman from her eyes down to her breasts. Each part is described with an agricultural image. In 5:11–16 a female speaker describes her beloved, from his head down, with various images. In 7:1–6 there is another complete *wasf* describing a female body.

Despite ingenious efforts to find an organic structure uniting these poems, it is very likely that the Song of Songs is simply a group of love songs gathered together without any overarching pattern of organization.

In these poems male and female speakers voice freely their affection and desire for one another in passionate, but never lurid, expressions of erotic love. As a whole, then, the poems are a celebration of the love a man feels for a woman and the love a woman feels for a man. This is quite in keeping with the understanding of sexuality in both the creation accounts in Genesis and elsewhere in Scripture. In the dramatized relationship there is no sense of one of the lovers being possessed or dominated by the other. The physical expression of love is portrayed with a mutuality and caring often missing in erotic literature. The mood of the Songs can perhaps best be expressed in an utterance by one of the females, speaking to an audience of the "daughters of Jerusalem": "This is my beloved and this is my friend . . . " (5:16b).

The Historical World: Authorship and Original Function

Although the first verse identifies the work as Solomon's, and Solomon is remembered for his proverbs and songs (1 Kgs. 4:32), it is unlikely that Solomon is the author of these poems. Some of the poems do refer to him. In 1:5 a woman compares her dark beauty to the "curtains of Solomon." The poem in 3:6–11 speaks of Solomon on the day of his wedding, and 8:11–12 refers to the vineyards of Solomon (his harem) in contrast with the speaker's own vineyard (his beloved). These third-person references are internal evidence that Solomon did not author these poems. The maiden, the Shulammite (6:13), has been associated with Abishag the Shunammite, David's virgin bedfellow (1 Kgs. 1:3–4). Because Solomon did not give her to Adonijah (1 Kgs. 2:13–17), the presumption is that he kept her for himself. But Shulammite and Shunammite look no more or less alike in Hebrew than they do in English. It is most likely that the attribution of the Song to Solomon was added to lend authority to it by linking it to the king renowned for his wisdom and his many loves. Given the variegated nature of the anthology, it may be more appropriate to speak of an editor or collector who gathered a variety of love poems together.

There have been numerous attempts to reconstruct the original setting of the Song, some of them highly imaginative but none of them very convincing. As mentioned, early interpreters viewed it allegorically. Unfortunately, unlike Isaiah 5, an allegorized harvest song, there is no evidence within the text for this interpretation. Modern commentators have suggested a dramatic interpretation with two or three main characters, such as Solomon and one or two lovers. But there is absolutely no hint of a plot or a setting, and a drama can be detected only by a very imaginative reading. Other theories hold that the Song has been adapted from an ancient fertility ritual involving a god and goddess or that it is a cycle of wedding songs used at marriage ceremonies in ancient Israel (with the bride, groom, and guests as speakers). However, none of these theories has won a consensus of scholarly opinion, suggesting that they are all attempts at forcing the Song into a mold it does not fit. Until there is further evidence supporting these or some other as yet unforeseen view of the Song's original function, we should probably hold our imaginations in check and take the song for what it is—an anthology of sensuous love poetry celebrating human love.

As a whole the Song echoes the view of human sexuality that Genesis presents as the way God intended it to be (Gen. 1:27–28; 2:24–25) before the rebellion of man and woman led to the embarrassment and manipulation that still plague the expression of physical love today.

LAMENTATIONS

The Book of Lamentations is a collection of five poems mourning the destruction of the city of Jerusalem (see 2 Kings 25:8–12). Originally composed after Jerusalem was sacked and the Temple destroyed by the Babylonians in 587 B.C.E., the poems became a part of the yearly remembrance of this terrible event in the Jewish liturgical calendar. In the Writings it is the only one of the five festival scrolls associated with the yearly fast on the ninth of Ab. Although tradition assigns it to Jeremiah (see 2 Chr. 35:25), and this is the title and location of the book in Christian Bibles (following the LXX), it was probably an anthology of poems by several poets.

The Literary World: An Anthology of Laments

The first four poems (Lamentations 1–4) are *acrostics*, that is, each stanza begins with a subsequent letter of the Hebrew alphabet. Because there are twenty-two letters in the Hebrew alphabet, there are twenty-two stanzas. The final poem in Chapter 5 also has twenty-two stanzas but does not follow the acrostic form. This acrostic pattern is fairly common in the Hebrew Bible (e.g., Nahum 1, Psalm 119, Proverbs 31), and it was most likely a device to assist memorization when the poems were circulated orally. The acrostic form also creates a sense of thoroughness; everything from A to Z is covered in them. This artifice might seem to limit the spontaneity of feeling in the poems; however, reading Lamentations gives no such sense of artificiality.

The poem in Chapter 2 gives a vivid, first-person (some think eyewitness) description of the anguish of the residents of Jerusalem under siege (2:11–12; *cf.* 4:2–10). The poems in Chapters 1, 2, and 4 utilize the rhythm associated with funeral dirges, in which the first line receives three beats and the second two. This is one of the few clear-cut examples in biblical poetry of this *qinah* meter, as it is called. Even in translation we can sense the difference in length and accentuation of the lines in these chapters. Reading them aloud gives a sense of rhythm.

Not only are the poems vivid descriptions of the horrors of the total destruction of Jerusalem by the Babylonians, but they also step back and reflect on the meaning of the event. Jerusalem was not merely the capital of the nation; it was Mount Zion, the symbol of the LORD's presence with the covenant people. In the symbolic universe of ancient Israel, Jerusalem was the center.

As modern studies have shown, the first step in facing the loss of someone or something essential to life is often to express the volatile emotions aroused by the loss. The poems in Lamentations first of all verbalize the feelings of the community and individuals who have seen their loved ones killed and the symbols at the center of their existence destroyed. But grieving also involves trying to place the loss in some framework that makes sense out of it. Lamentations finds that context in the belief that Jerusalem and its inhabitants were being punished by the LORD for their disobedience. The LORD allowed the Babylonians to destroy the Temple and the people because of divine indignation (see, e.g., 2:17). The poems give voice to this explanation, but they do not simply accept it meekly. Speakers also urge the survivors to cry out in anguish to the LORD for allowing this to happen (e.g., 2:18–22), and the collection ends with an impassioned plea to the LORD to "remember."

At the center of the anthology (Lamentations 3), the tone abruptly changes. The speaker expresses a hope based on trust in the unceasing, steadfast love (*hesed*) of the LORD (3:22–51). The basic tension of the collection is apparent here. It is between the experience of the presumed anger of the LORD and a stubborn faith that God is merciful. This hope is anchored in neither the covenantal nor the creation traditions; it is based on a fundamental perception of the divine character that both good and evil come from God (3:38) and "although he causes grief, he will have compassion according to the abundance of his steadfast love" (3:32). Despite this general hope, there is no anticipation that circumstances will soon change, as in many of the laments of the Psalms. Our attention is also drawn to Chapter 3 by the form. Not only does every stanza begin with a subsequent letter of the alphabet, but also every verse in each stanza begins with the same letter.

The Historical World: Original Setting

There is biblical evidence of acts of lamentation carried out soon after the destruction of Jerusalem in 587 B.C.E. (Jer. 41:5). Zechariah 7:3–5, written about 518 B.C.E., suggests that a fast had been held during the fifth month (Ab) ever since the city fell. On the basis of these data, we can legitimately argue that the poems of Lamentations were used liturgically in the exilic period. This practice was probably the reason for making Lamentations one of the festival scrolls, associated with the annual fast on the ninth of Ab in the Jewish liturgical calendar.[6]

Although there is a change of speakers (from the first-person singular to the first-person plural), there is no substantial evidence of any dramatic setting for the collection. This has not stopped some interpreters from trying to reconstruct one.

---

[6]The apparent contradiction in language here goes back to ancient rabbinic usage. Fasts were treated along with feasts in one section of the Mishnah, which bore the title *Moed* ("feasts").

Summary

The songs included in the Tanak range from the impassioned love poetry of the Song of Songs to the anguished laments of the Psalter and the Book of Lamentations. In this chapter, we considered the literary character and most likely original historical settings of the songs of ancient Israel.

The 150 poems of the Book of Psalms are a rich anthology of the best of ancient Israelite religious poetry, most of it associated with worship in the Jerusalem Temple. In treating the psalms as literature, we surveyed the types of psalms and offered a reading of Psalm 8 to illustrate the importance of recognizing the unique as well as typical features of the psalms. We then described the basic relationships within the psalmic world. Our historical analysis identified the various acts of worship with which the psalms may have originally been associated.

Although most traditional interpreters read the Song of Songs allegorically, we chose to present this anthology of love poems in terms of their implicit speakers and audiences. We assessed the mood of the Song as a frank and sensitive celebration of the physical expression of human love.

Lamentations is an anthology of five poems, inspired by the destruction of Jerusalem, traditionally associated with the prophet Jeremiah. We found these poems not only moving evocations of the horror associated with the annihilation of a city but also carefully crafted meditations on the significance of the event. The laments almost certainly appeared in the liturgies of cultic events marking this pivotal event in Israel's history.

Poetry is the literary medium by which we express our deepest emotions. Although the style and imagery of many of these songs may make them seem impenetrable to the modern reader, they reward any who allow themselves to feel the moods they evoke.

The Contemporary World

Case Studies

Settings for Biblical Songs

Select poems from the Books of Psalms, Song of Songs, and Lamentations that best suit the following contemporary situations: a marriage celebration, a memorial service for the victims of the terrorist attacks of September 11, 2001, a gathering of people who have successfully completed a drug rehabilitation program and are preparing to go home, a terminally ill person facing the end of life, and an outdoor worship service in the mountains of Colorado. How has your study of the literary and historical worlds of Israel's sacred songs enhanced your ability to choose appropriate poems?

Royal Songs

We noted previously that the Psalms may be classified in type categories by form and/or subject. But we also noted that each Psalm is an individual poem, to be understood in its own right. Psalms 2, 45, 72, 89, and 110 are all royal psalms, concerned with the person, welfare, duties, and so on, of the Davidic king. Analyze these unique poems. What particular occasions, situations, or circumstances in the king's life do they illuminate? Profile the life, office, and functions of the king as portrayed in these poems. Which of these could be applied to a modern head of state/government, a monarch, president, or prime minister, and which could not?

Questions for Discussion and Reflection

1. *Read Psalms 1, 8, 13, 23, 24, 29, 44, 51, 73, 90, 104, 121, 137, 139, 150:*
   a. Think of the songs in the Book of Psalms as the popular music of ancient Israel. Psalms gave expression to a wide range of human emotions—joy, anger, pride, guilt, fear, hope, despair, and so on. Do the popular songs with which you are familiar fulfill a similar purpose today? Can you identify with the feelings expressed in any of the above psalms?
   b. Many psalms were used in worship in ancient Israel. Some were sung or enacted in public worship; others may have been used in individual prayer. Which of the above psalms seem best suited for public and private worship? Imagine creative ways in which some of these psalms might be used in contemporary worship.
   c. One interpreter of the Book of Psalms[7] suggests they reflect the three "seasons of life" through which almost all people pass. The seasons include times of orientation (as in the creation psalms), times of disorientation (as in the laments), and times of reorientation (as in the songs of thanksgiving). Can you identify with any of these "seasons of life" as you reflect on your own experience or that of others you know? Assess this approach to relating the psalms to the contemporary world.

2. *Read the Song of Songs:*
   a. A law student had just begun to date a very religious young woman. He asked a friend who was a graduate student in biblical studies to recommend a biblical passage about love he could read to the woman to impress her. His friend said, "The Song of Songs is a love poem. Read her that." The law student did, and the relationship ended on the spot. How might the discussion of the Song of Songs in this chapter have helped the law student clarify what he was reading to the woman?
   b. Compare the view of sexuality in the Song of Songs to the attitudes prevalent in American popular culture.

3. *Read the Book of Lamentations:*
   a. Most of us are accustomed to seeing television reports of wars and violence with graphic images of death and destruction. How does

---

[7]Walter Brueggeman. *The Message of the Psalms.* Minneapolis: Augsburg, 1985.

being bombarded with such pictures on the evening news affect one's reading of the images of violence in Lamentations? What effect has the portrayal of violence in modern movies had on contemporary society? Have we become desensitized, callous, and uncaring? At what cost?

b. In order to face a tragedy, why is it often necessary to express the intense feelings aroused? Do you think Lamentations and the rituals with which the book was associated served that function for ancient Israelites? What outlets are available today in religious or secular settings for the expression of feelings of anguish? Why do many people keep such feelings within?

c. The Book of Lamentations most likely contains poems reflecting the experiences of men and women who lived through the destruction of the Jerusalem Temple in 587 B.C.E. Compare reactions of those who survived the terrorist attacks on New York and Washington on September 11, 2001. Do any of the utterances in Lamentations express your own feelings about what happened that day?

Chapter 8

The Way of Wisdom

Proverbs, Job, Ecclesiastes (The Writings II)

Scene from the Book of Job. The English poet, artist, and mystic William Blake (1757–1827) created a set of woodcut illustrations for the Book of Job. He caught the mythological symbolism in the background of the Behemoth and Leviathan passages (Job 40:15–41:34) and here renders these beasts as marvelous, but relatively benign, creatures. *Source:* The Pierpont Morgan Library/Art Resource, NY

Although the Books of Proverbs, Ecclesiastes, and Job are not a distinct subgroup within the Writings, they are the Tanak's examples of a type of literature common in the ancient Near East (and throughout history)—*wisdom literature.* They are distinct from the rest of the Tanak (except for isolated examples, particularly among the Psalms) in their style and their view of the world. Stylistically, these works are dominated by short observations and instructions about life and how to live (Proverbs, Ecclesiastes), poetic dialogue (Job), and poems focusing on the nature and meaning of life (Ecclesiastes, Job).

In these books, themes such as Torah and the covenant that recur in the rest of the Tanak are missing. The concern is not the LORD'S involvement in history with Israel and other nations and the hope of fulfillment of God's promises. Instead, the wisdom writings treat the human search for and maintenance of order. This is a practical search for happiness through living with propriety and decorum, that is, in accord with the natural and social order. But the search goes on at a deeper, more speculative level too, for these works (especially Job and Ecclesiastes) reflect the quest for an underlying order in the world and the answers to such basic questions as: Why do the innocent suffer? Is there justice in the world? If we all die, what is the meaning of life? As a whole, the Bible tells the story of God's involvement with people in history. These works must be bracketed off from the major story line. They stand on their own as a set of writings whose concerns are always contemporary. For that reason they are probably the most widely read books in the Tanak.

As mentioned, the wisdom books are unique in the Hebrew Scriptures, but they stand squarely within a literary and intellectual tradition pervasive throughout history. Every culture produces proverbs that gain authority through usage (such as, "The early bird gets the worm") and literary works that reflect on basic human questions. Wisdom works are found in the Deuterocanon (Ben Sirach, the Wisdom of Solomon; *cf.* Chapter 10) and the New Testament (James and many of the sayings of Jesus within the gospels). They are also present among Egyptian and Mesopotamian works unearthed by archaeologists. Our introduction to these writings will be divided into a literary analysis of each book and a historical discussion of the wisdom tradition in Israel and the ancient Near East.

THE LITERARY WORLD

Proverbs: The Blessings of Wisdom

The Book of Proverbs is divided into a series of collections of short sentences and admonitions, with a few longer poems interspersed.[1] The short sayings are usually in poetic form as well. Most of the collections have titles (see next page).

Therefore, as a whole the book is an anthology of sayings and poems, in the same way as the Song of Songs is an anthology of love poems, Lamentations of laments, and Psalms of sacred songs.

The first collection is much different from the others, which are sets of individual, loosely connected sayings (except for the final poem). In Chapters 1–9 we find sayings, but they are linked together into short "essays" on various themes such as the dangers of association with the wicked (1:8–19) and the blessings associated with wise living (3:1–18). They are presented in the form of a father speaking to "my son." Also included are poems in which a personified Wisdom speaks to indict the fools who ignore her instruction (1:20–33) and to proclaim her worth, authority, and place in the creative process (8:1–36). In contrast, Folly is personified uttering her enticements to the foolish (9:13–18). This collection begins with a preface, probably intended for the book as a whole, suggesting the variety of audiences and levels of meaning to be derived from the work (1:2–6)

---

[1]Our interpretation of the literary world of Proverbs is indebted to James Crenshaw. *Old Testament Wisdom: An Introduction.* Atlanta: John Knox, 1981, pp. 66–99.

1	Chapters 1–9	The Proverbs of Solomon, son of David, King of Israel
2	Chapters 10:1–22:16	The Proverbs of Solomon
3	Chapters 22:17–24:22	The sayings of the wise
4	Chapter 24:23–34	More sayings of the wise
5	Chapters 25–29	More proverbs of Solomon transcribed by the men of Hezekiah, King of Judah
6	Chapter 30:1–9	Sayings of Agur, son of Jakeh from Massah
7	Chapter 30:10–33	Numerical proverbs (no title)
8	Chapter 31:1–9	Sayings of Lemuel, King of Massah, that his mother taught him
9	Chapter 31:10–31	An acrostic poem in praise of a "good wife" (no title)

and stating its basic theme (1:7a): "The fear of the LORD is the beginning of knowledge." This might be paraphrased as "Reverence for the LORD is the starting point and essence of knowledge."

The second collection gathers together 375 sayings covering a wide range of observations and maxims on everyday life, each of them two lines in length (except for 19:7). There is no evident thematic unity in the collection. In the first half (10:1–15:33), the second line generally contrasts the first, suggesting a stylistic principle of organization. Of the two basic types of proverbs (sayings that make observations on the way things are in life and instructions that give advice or admonish), the first is dominant:

> Fools mock at the guilt offering
> but the upright enjoy God's favor. (14:9)
> The crooked of mind do not prosper,
> and the perverse of tongue
> fall into calamity. (17:20)
> One's own folly leads to ruin,
> yet the heart rages against the LORD. (19:3)

The third collection, part of which is nearly identical with an ancient Egyptian collection of proverbs (discussed later), has one brief essay on the plight of drunkards (23:29–35), along with such admonitions as:

> Do not wear yourself out to get rich;
> be wise enough to desist. (23:4)

The fourth collection is a brief set of exhortations and admonitions and includes a short essay on laziness (24:30–34), concluding with the observation:

> A little sleep, a little slumber,
> a little folding of the hands to rest,
> and poverty will come upon you
> like a robber,
> and want, like an armed man. (24:33–34)

The fifth collection is marked by the frequency of comparative statements such as:

Better is open rebuke
than hidden love. (27:5)
Better to be poor and walk in
integrity
than to be crooked in one's way
even though rich. (28:6)

It also includes a proverb quoted by the Apostle Paul in Rom. 12:20 (Pr. 25:21–22) and the proverb that has given many children throughout history tender posteriors, wounded egos, and, in some cases, much worse (29:15).

The sixth collection is a dialogue between a skeptic and an unquestioning believer in God and a poem asking that the speaker be kept from these two extremes.

The seventh section is a miscellaneous set of numerical sayings, using a form similar to the opening chapters of the Book of Amos, prefaced by an admonition and a list of types of sinners.

The eighth section is advice given by the Queen Mother to her son, King Lemuel, concerning proper behavior for a king.

The last section is an acrostic poem (see Chapter 7) extolling the virtues of a good wife—hard work, good business sense, strength, compassion for the poor, constancy in trouble, a sense of humor, and kindness. This is the kind of woman who is to be praised because she "fears the LORD" (31:30).

In general, proverbs that make observations on the way life is and how to succeed dominate in sections 2, 4, and 5; and the proverbs that are instructional, giving advice or admonishing, are more prevalent in 1, 3, and 8.

The Book of Proverbs contains both practical wisdom, some of which is secular and some religious, and theoretical or speculative wisdom. The practical wisdom can perhaps best be understood in terms of several pairs of opposites that recur. One contrast is between life and death. Especially in the first section, the father admonishes his child:

My child, do not let these escape
from your sight
keep sound wisdom and prudence,
and they will be life for your soul
and adornment for your neck. (3:21–22)

The life that is promised is not life after death, but a long and fulfilling life on earth (3:15–18). Those who ignore wisdom and pursue wickedness will find themselves "dead," in the sense of lost, confused, and hopeless (1:18, 4:19).

Another image is the "way" or "path." The way of wisdom (that leads to life) is contrasted with the way of folly (that leads to death). The assumption is that wisdom is like a map that will assure that one keeps to the path of life and avoids the path of death (see, e.g., 4:18–19).

A related pair of opposites is the wise person and the fool. In the Book of Proverbs' view of the world, everyone falls into one of these two groups. Likewise, there is a dualism between good and evil. The world of Proverbs is quite black and white, with a clear choice between life and death, good and evil, and wisdom and folly. The individual proverbs are nearly all concerned with discriminating between these opposites and laying forth the consequences of behavior related to them. The instructions are designed to encourage behavior that is good, wise, and leading to life and discourage actions that are foolish, evil, and leading to death.

Many of the observations and much of the advice in Proverbs make no mention of God. They claim nothing more than the authority of experience. Much of the material can be considered textbook lore for the ancient counterpart of a school of business and public administration, training the scribes who would be the clerks, managers, executives, and ranking officials of government and cult. The prudence counseled is not unlike the conventional wisdom that has guided organization men and women through much of history. However, other proverbs are tied to belief in God as the power who desires and rewards good behavior and abhors and punishes evil actions, for example:

> Those who oppress the poor
> insult their Maker,
> but those who are kind to the needy
> honor him. (14:31)

Basic to the life-or-death orientation of Proverbs is the claim that "fear" (reverence) of the LORD is rewarded with "life," while disdain for the LORD leads to "death." Without this basic attitude, the final edition of Proverbs assumes, no one can be truly wise.

In addition to grounding its practical teachings in reverence for the LORD, Proverbs also asserts an authority for wisdom rooted in creation itself. Wisdom is personified as a principle associated with the creative process, present with God from the beginning (3:19–20 and 8:22–31). Wisdom is here heralded as the life-giving principle of cosmic order. This gives a theoretical foundation to the claim that wisdom is the order for everyday living. The personification of Wisdom in Proverbs introduces us to a type of speculation that we will encounter again in Job, the wisdom literature of the Deuterocanon (see Chapter 10), and the New Testament.

In conclusion, the Book of Proverbs presents wisdom in practical terms, contrasting the rewards of wise living with the perils of foolish behavior. It assumes that God generally rewards goodness and punishes evil. But if a choice must be made, righteous poverty is more desirable than wicked wealth. The book also speculates on the source of authority of wisdom, claiming that wisdom is the life-giving principle apparent in the very process of creation. These are the assumptions the Book of Job challenges.

Job: The Limits of Wisdom

At a conference, the authors had the opportunity to study with a teacher, who, in 1944 as a boy of fifteen, was taken to the Nazi death camp at Auschwitz, Poland. There his entire family died in the gas chambers, part of the Nazis' "final solution of the Jewish problem." He alone survived. After class one day, someone asked our teacher how he could retain his faith in God after what he had experienced at Auschwitz. His response was simply, "Have you read the Book of Job?"

Besides being widely considered the literary masterpiece of the Bible, the Book of Job speaks to some of the most profound questions of the contemporary world. Its meaning, perhaps more than any other book in the Bible, transcends the time in which it was written. Like other great literary works, it defies simple interpretation. This reading of the book should be considered only an invitation to enter the world of Job and marvel at its mysteries, not a final resolution of them.

The Book of Job, like so many other literary units we have examined in the Bible, has what might be called an *envelope structure*. It is a poetic drama (3:1–42:6) framed by the opening and closing scenes of a folk tale about Job (1:1–2:13 and 42:7–17). Many interpreters treat the two entirely separately. However, because in the final form they are bound together, we must ask how they are related to one another.

The legend about Job (probably linked to the ancestral figure Job named in Ezek. 14:14, 20) is a tale about a righteous, blameless man tested by God at the urging of the member of the divine

The Sufferer Job. One of a series of mosaics in front of the church on the Mount of Beatitudes at the Sea of Galilee in Israel shows the sufferer Job. The Latin phrase on the mosaic alludes to Job's response in the Prologue to the Book of Job after his property and children have been taken from him: "the LORD gave and the LORD has taken away," to which Job adds "blessed be the name of the LORD" (Job 1:21). *Source:* Zvonimir Atletic/Shutterstock

court who was charged with earthly intelligence work—the Satan. The scenes in the story move back and forth between earth and heaven. In the first scene, we are introduced to Job as a non-Israelite, Transjordanian sheik who practices the advice of Proverbs. He reveres God and shuns evil. His ten children and plenteous herds are a sure sign that, from the perspective of Proverbs, he is being blessed with "life" because of his following the path of wisdom. Job is so righteous that he even tries to intercede for his sons, lest they sin and be punished. Meanwhile, at the heavenly court, on the day when divine beings are received by the divine king, the Satan (here the term is a title, not a proper name, meaning "accuser," or in other words, "prosecuting attorney") appears. Apparently the LORD is very proud of Job, for the LORD asks the Satan if he has observed this righteous man. The Satan responds with a question of his own, showing that he is clever, "What do you expect? You have given him everything." He challenges the LORD to take everything away and then see what happens. Without comment, the LORD takes the wager and allows the Satan to remove the "hedge" around Job's faithfulness but not to touch Job himself. This establishes the basic theme of the story: Is there disinterested piety (righteousness), or do people revere God only because it pays? Job is to be the guinea pig in a divine experiment. There is no vendetta against him. Ironically, there is nothing personal in his suffering.

Having established the basic theme, we can move quickly through the rest of the story. Job's servants, flocks, and children are all killed, but he remains faithful. Even when the screws are tightened, and Job himself is afflicted, he refuses to give in to his wife's advice to "Curse God and die," calling her (in good wisdom style) "a foolish woman." Job is willing to accept both good and evil from the LORD without question. Three friends come to comfort him and sit in silence. When the story resumes, after the long poetic interruption, the righteous Job has his fortunes restored, receiving twice as much as before his ordeal. In other words, after Job has proven he will remain faithful even when everything is taken away from him, and the LORD has won the divine bet, Job is rewarded. Implied in the story are at least two answers to the questions of undeserved suffering: (1) if you keep your faith throughout a time of suffering, you will ultimately be rewarded and (2) suffering may be a test of one's faith and fidelity. The story has given rise to the idea of the "patience of Job," the image assumed in the New Testament Book of James (5:11).

However, when we turn to the poetic section of the work, the sufferer is hardly patient. As his friends sit silently, Job speaks in Chapter 3. His words astonish his companions, for they are totally out of character. Job utters not trust in God, but a bitter lament. He comes perilously close to cursing God by deprecating the day of his birth and the night of his conception. Included in the lament is the first of a number of mythic images. In calling for darkness to replace the light of his birth, the sufferer appeals for the arousal of two of the monsters of chaos who opposed the divine king in primordial combat, Yamm (Sea) and Leviathan (a sea serpent) (3:8).[2]

Job's curse arouses his friends, who take it upon themselves to go beyond merely comforting him. It is obvious to them that he needs instruction, which they feel qualified to give. Three "cycles" of speeches follow, with Job responding each time a friend speaks. In fact, each utterance is more a monologue than part of a dialogue, for both the friends and Job talk right past one another. Although there are various subtleties to the friends' arguments, their general approach is a defense of the doctrine of retribution, found both in Proverbs and in the Sinai Covenant tradition. According to this teaching, God rewards the righteous and punishes the wicked. That is the moral law the LORD has established and guarantees. The friends seem to reason that, because sin causes suffering, all sufferers must be sinners. From this perspective, Job must be suffering because of sin. He is being punished or disciplined. He is obviously the problem. Assuming this view of Job's predicament, the friends first gently, and then with increasing vigor and venom, argue that Job must have sinned, because he simply would not be suffering if he had not. Their remedy is for Job to repent, even if he is unaware of what he has done. Eliphaz, the first friend, sets the tone when he argues that:

> For misery does not come from the earth,
> nor does trouble sprout from the ground;
> but human beings are born to trouble
> just as the sparks fly upward. (5:6–7)

All three friends assure Job that God will be merciful and deliver him, if only he will acknowledge his wrongdoing. They grow increasingly angry as Job steadfastly refuses to accept their advice.

Job's replies are hardly responses to the friends. He rejects out of hand their arguments, maintaining that he is innocent, and, at the very least, his sufferings are completely out of proportion to any minor sin he may have committed (6:1–7). His friends have ceased to be friends, and they thus show that *they* are the ones who do not revere God (6:14). Job challenges them to show him his

---

[2]The Hebrew world translated "day" (3:8) in many translations could, with different Hebrew vowels, read "sea" and be an allusion to Prince Yamm, who, like Leviathan, is one of the gods in Semitic mythology.

sin, but as the replies progress, he increasingly turns his attention away from the friends and toward the one whom he accuses of unjustly causing his anguish—God. Again, using mythic imagery, Job accuses God of treating him, a mere mortal, like one of the monsters of chaos (7:12). He bitterly parodies the question at the heart of Psalm 8 (8:4), asking God:

> What are human beings, that you make so
> much of them?
> that you set your mind on them,
> visit them every morning,
> test them every moment? (7:17–18)

On the one hand, Job longs for vindication and clings to the hope that a vindicator will arise to intercede for him (9:33–35; 16:18–22; 19:25–27). On the other hand, he recognizes that he is powerless before the might of the one who created everything and vanquished the forces of chaos (9; 12:7–25; 26). He reluctantly recognizes that:

> It is all one; therefore I say,
> he destroys both the blameless and
> the wicked. (9:22)

Only if God stops this arbitrary punishment will Job and God be able to speak to each other. Still, Job stubbornly maintains his innocence and his anger at God's unjustified treatment of him. He sarcastically points out that while he, an innocent and righteous man, suffers, the wicked go unpunished while they spurn God. The problem is that God is not living up to the LORD's own moral law! Job remains bold in his belief that, if he could somehow get a fair hearing, he could prove his innocence.

After the cycle of speeches, a poem on the inaccessibility of wisdom (28) appears without introduction. The poem is built around the refrain:

> But where shall wisdom be found?
> And where is the place of understanding? (28:12)

The answer is that despite the marvelous achievements of human ability, wisdom is beyond humanity's reach. Only God knows its place. The poem ends with the familiar motto from Proverbs, "the fear of the LORD, that is wisdom" (28:28). In its current context the poem functions as an interlude.

When Job speaks again it is to bring the matter to a head. If God will not grant him a hearing, Job will force the issue. This he does by offering an "oath of clearance" (31), a legal device in which the accused lists the alleged crimes and invokes a curse if guilty. Because no charges have been filed against him, Job makes his own list of possible offenses, ranging from lust to failure to help the poor. In a final, dramatic flourish, he signs the oath, saying that if he had an indictment from his adversary, he would wear it like a crown and come before him like a prince (31:35–37).

Before the climax of the poem, there is another interlude (Job 32–37). A new speaker enters the stage, the arrogant young Elihu. (Elihu is a variant of Elijah, the one who "prepares the way for the coming of the LORD.") Elihu is angry with both Job and the three friends. Although younger, he claims that he speaks with authority because the Spirit of God is upon him. Like the friends, he defends God's ways, accusing Job of speaking without knowledge. It is not really clear whether Elihu really adds anything to the defense of God or simply repeats the arguments of the friends. He does stress one line of argument only touched on by the others, that God uses suffering to strengthen people's character. In any event, the speeches of Elihu heighten the tension, for when Elihu moves off stage, there is another voice that booms from behind the scenes.

The voice is the LORD, speaking from a storm. Interestingly, the special name for the deity appears only in the legend framing the poem and in the divine speeches. (The Hebrew *eloah,* a form of the same noun that appears more frequently in the Tanak as *el* or *elohim,* is the most typical term for God in the poetic section.) There are actually two speeches of the LORD from the tempest (38:1–40:1 and 40:6–41:34), each followed by a statement from Job. Although the introductions say the LORD "answered" Job, the divine speeches are questions rather than answers. Nowhere does the deity respond to Job's impassioned plea for a justification of his suffering. Instead, the speeches put the sufferer on the defensive. In the first, the LORD challenges Job to explain the mysteries of the natural world. The LORD wastes no time making the point about the limits of Job's understanding:

> Where were you when I laid the
> foundation of the earth?
> Tell me, if you have understanding. (38:4)

The implication, of course, is "How can Job demand answers from God, when he cannot even understand the world God has created?" In the LORD's description of the creation and control of the cosmos, there is, interestingly, no mention of humanity! The universe is quite complete without humankind! As Job had feared, when God speaks Job is overwhelmed. In response, Job can only admit that there is nothing more for him to say (40:2–5).

But this does not stop the LORD from blasting Job once more. This time the LORD accuses Job of attacking the creator in order to justify himself (40:8–9). The LORD asks Job if he is able to control wickedness in the world. Then the deity refers to two creatures—Behemoth and Leviathan—that are described ambiguously as a hippopotamus and a crocodile, but, especially in the case of Leviathan, with the characteristics of mythic dragon-like beasts. Job is unable to control these creatures that the LORD has made. How then can he try to challenge their creator?

In his final words (42:1–6), Job admits that the LORD is right. The divine purposes are beyond his understanding. He has spoken without knowledge about things beyond his ken. He has made assumptions about God based on what he had been told; now, having seen the LORD, he "melts into nothing" and "repents in dust and ashes."

The last phrase indicates that, in one sense, Job is back where he started—a sufferer sitting in dust and ashes, unaware of why he is afflicted. However, the story resumes immediately. The friends are condemned by God because they have "not spoken of me what is right, as my servant Job has" (42:7, 8). Job intercedes for them, and his fortunes are restored—in double.

The question that bedevils interpreters who wrestle with this book is "What is the meaning of the Book of Job?" Can we make sense out of this highly complex, ambiguous book, or is it hopelessly confusing? Of course, as with all great literary works, there is not just one meaning but many levels of meaning. What follows should be seen as an attempt to understand the book at one level.[3]

The basic issue raised by the poem is the question of divine justice; in particular, if God is just and powerful, why do innocent people suffer? Philosophically, this is the question of theodicy—how can evil (such as the suffering of an innocent person) exist in a world under the control of a just and

---

[3]We are indebted here to the perceptive reading of Job by Matitiahu Tsevat. "The Meaning of the Book of Job." *Hebrew Union College Annual,* 37 (1966), 73–106.

powerful God? Interpreters have wrestled with the problem of whether the poem answers this question. Some have suggested that there is no answer, because Job is as confused at the end of the poem as he is at the beginning. He is simply overwhelmed by God's power and wisdom. According to this view, the poem is an "anthology of doubts" that are expressed but not resolved. Others have argued that the answer is indirect. The LORD's questioning implies that he has the cosmos under control. By analogy, we are to assume that God will take care of human affairs. Simply by speaking to Job, the LORD shows his compassion for humanity. In the end, each person will get a just reward. The epilogue would seem to confirm that. Humankind must learn to accept what seems like temporary injustice, secure in the knowledge that there is divine justice that will ultimately prevail. Another approach is to say that even though the question is not answered, Job learns through the appearance of the LORD to trust in a God he cannot understand. It would be well for readers to evaluate each of these possibilities and think of others before continuing.

Another possible answer emerges when we consider the poem in the context of the story that frames it. In the story we are clearly told that Job's suffering is not a matter of divine justice; it has nothing to do with punishment of Job. His suffering is merely a test of the issue of disinterested piety, conducted to settle a heavenly wager. Of course, unlike the reader, Job and his friends are unaware of this bet. The friends assume that Job is in error by stubbornly maintaining his innocence; Job assumes that God is in the wrong. Both take for granted the doctrine of retribution.

God's response indicates that both are wrong, because of their assumptions about the deity's ways. To assume that God's involvement with the universe revolves around the issue of retributive justice for humans is to place humankind at the center of the cosmic stage. Morality is a human problem, not a divine one. God's first speech implies that there is no guarantee of retribution in the cosmic order. The rain, often portrayed as an instrument of justice, falls in the desert where there is no human (38:25–27). When properly translated, 38:12–15 suggests that the sun shines not only on the righteous but also on the wicked. The universe does not revolve around humanity; therefore, retribution is not a part of the cosmic order. Job is chastised for making erroneous assumptions about God's ways based on too narrow a viewpoint.

There is another dimension to the divine speeches, when we consider the basic arguments Job tries to raise.[4] He has tried to hold God to the doctrine of retribution and is told that this is not a part of God's ways. Job has also appealed to the mythic view of the deity as a divine warrior who establishes control of the universe in combat with cosmic foes. He has even suggested that God is treating him like a monster of chaos (7:12). The implication is that God is not discharging the deity's cosmic responsibilities. God is not controlling evil in the world. Instead of restraining the forces of chaos, God is venting rage on hapless Job, a mere mortal. The LORD's speeches blast this mythic assumption. In the first one, the LORD speaks of Sea (Yamm) not as a cosmic foe, but as a huge baby whom God has delivered and wrapped in swaddling bands (38:8–9). In the second speech, the LORD suggests that Behemoth and Leviathan are not the cosmic monsters Job has implied (see 3:8). They are a part of God's creation, of no threat to the cosmic sovereign. Only humanity confronts them as powerful enemies. In effect, the LORD deflates the mythic explanations Job has attempted to use, even as the moral argument is compromised.

According to this interpretation, the "answer" in the Book of Job is a redefinition of the questions. If God does not guarantee the moral order and retributive justice for humankind, then the question of justice is thrown back into the lap of humanity. Will humans find ways to control evil and to promote goodness? That is your problem, the LORD is saying in the Book of Job. And will people

---

[4]See William A. Young. "Leviathan in the Book of Job and *Moby Dick.*" *Soundings: An Interdisciplinary Journal,* 65 (1982), 388–401.

be able to believe in God without myths that assume God has control of chaos in the world? What if the truth is, as Job reluctantly realized, "It is all one; therefore I say, he destroys both the blameless and the wicked" (9:22)? Indeed, if morality is a human concern, then the truth of this statement is not an indictment of God. That is where Job erred. Unlike the friends, he spoke rightly of God (even though he did not realize it himself until after the divine speeches). The friends, on the other hand, spoke wrongly, because they presumed to speak for God in defense of the divine ways, which they distorted.

By dealing with the question of justice in this way, we are led back to the underlying question—Can there be disinterested piety? Will a person really maintain faith in God after realizing that there is no automatic reward for righteous behavior or punishment for evil deeds? The legend gives a simple answer. Of course, Job remained firm in his faith despite his suffering. The poem moves to a deeper level. The journey to disinterested piety is not so easy for the Job of the poem. He wrestles with the problem and comes perilously close to rejecting God. He expresses a bitterness toward God that becomes quite ugly. It takes a theophany (appearance of God) for Job to learn the lesson taken for granted in the story, that he must revere God even though he does not understand why he is suffering. Job has poured out the depth of his anguished soul to God, and God has responded, but not on Job's terms. The Job of the poem clings by a very thin thread to his faith in the God who seems to be his enemy. But in the end the thread holds.

So, in the final analysis, the Book of Job dramatizes two quite different roads to the basic truth that faith in God cannot be a conditioned response to the expectation of reward or the fear of punishment. God is not a heavenly behavioralist who practices operant conditioning on humankind!

Ecclesiastes: The Futility of Wisdom

Like the Book of Job, Ecclesiastes reflects a search for meaning amid a world in which evil flourishes and good goes unrewarded. However, the style and tone of the book are much different. Whereas Job is a poetic dialogue surrounded by a story, Ecclesiastes is an anthology of the reflections of an old sage. The Joban poem reverberates with the cries of an anguished sufferer and the blast of the divine voice from the storm. It is immediate and impassioned. Ecclesiastes is detached and philosophical. It looks back over life and shares the findings of someone who has "seen it all." In Job we come hard against the limits of wisdom; in Ecclesiastes we feel the futility of wisdom. That is not the end of this book, but the beginning.

Despite the ingenious attempts of interpreters to find structural unity in Ecclesiastes, it is most likely simply a collection of proverbs, brief essays, and poems, which can be grouped as follows (see next page).

A few structural observations can be made. The work begins and ends (before the editorial epilogue) with poems. In 1:14–6:9 the refrains "emptiness (vanity)" and "striving after wind" dominate, while in 6:10–11:10, the refrains are "cannot find out," "do not know," or "no knowledge."[5] In addition, the work weaves throughout these collections the recurrent motif that "there is nothing better for mortals than to eat and drink, and find enjoyment in their toil" (2:24; cf. 3:12–13; 5:18; 9:9–10).

The anthology begins and ends (1:2 and 12:8) with a statement of the underlying conclusion the old sage has come to about life:

> Vanity of vanities, says the Teacher,
> vanity of vanities! All is vanity.

---

[5]Crenshaw. *Old Testament Wisdom: An Introduction,* p. 145.

1:2–11	Poem: The futility of life
1:12–2:2	The search for meaning
3:1–15	Poem: The pattern of life
3:16–4:3	The problem of evil
4:4–16	The folly of fame and fortune
5:1–7	The folly of religiosity
5:8–6:9	The folly of wealth
6:10–7:12	The futility of trying to change life
7:13–21	The way of moderation
7:23–8:1	The futility of seeking wisdom
8:2–9	Obedience to the king
8:10–9:12	The failure of retribution
9:13–10:20	Observations on life and wisdom
11:1–6	Action in spite of uncertainty
11:7–10	Relishing youth
12:1–8	Poem: The allegory of old age
12:9–14	Editorial footnotes

"Teacher" is one way to translate the Hebrew term *Qoheleth* (in Greek, *Ecclesiastes,* the name or title the author uses for himself). It literally means "one who gathers together." The Hebrew term translated "vanity" literally means "without substance, empty," like a puff of air, present only for an instant, and then gone without a trace. According to Qoheleth, life is empty, there for a moment, and then gone forever.

The first poem states the thesis, and then produces evidence from human life and nature to support it. Everything moves in cycles but is never complete. "The more things change, the more they remain the same" is a modern proverb with the same point. Moreover, whatever is done is soon forgotten.

Next, Ecclesiastes puts himself temporarily in the position of King Solomon (to whom the title attributes the collection). As First Kings describes him, Solomon was heralded for his wealth, luxurious lifestyle, and wisdom. Yet, as Ecclesiastes portrays him, Solomon discovered that the search for wisdom leads to the conclusion that all is emptiness. Likewise, he found that pursuit of pleasure, accumulation of possessions, and devotion to work all are the same—empty. The wise man and the fool have the same fate: They die and are forgotten. This led "Solomon" to despair but also to the conclusion that it is best to find enjoyment in life day by day rather than to try to find some overarching purpose.

The well-known "catalogue of the seasons" in 3:1–9 suggests a predetermined pattern of life that is beyond human ability to understand or to alter. This too leads to the conclusion that there is nothing better than to enjoy life moment by moment.

Like Job, Ecclesiastes challenges the doctrine that the righteous are rewarded and the wicked are punished, which is found in Proverbs and other traditional wisdom teaching. Here we find the fatalistic attitude that humans are like any other animals, with no advantage, for all die. This also leads to the conclusion that the best we can hope for is the enjoyment of daily work.

As the outline suggests, Ecclesiastes sees folly and futility in those things often put forward as the answers to life's frustrations: fame and fortune, religiosity, changing one's life, and seeking wisdom. Time and again, his "answer" is to seek satisfaction and fulfillment in the daily activities of work, eating, and family life. The fullest expression of this sentiment is found in 9:7–9:

> Go, eat your bread with enjoyment, and drink your wine with a merry heart; for God has long ago approved what you do. Let your garments always be white; do not let oil be lacking on your head. Enjoy life with the wife whom you love, all the days of your vain life that are given you under the sun, because that is your portion in life and in your toil at which you toil under the sun.

This sounds similar to the popular philosophy to which many have turned over the centuries: Eat, drink, and be merry, for tomorrow you may die. Or, to quote a modern commercial: "Grab all the gusto you can; you only go around once in life." However, Ecclesiastes is not counseling the pursuit of pleasure for pleasure's sake, or gluttony. That too is vanity. Rather, moderation is the key (7:13–22). Despite the similar fate for the wise man and the fool, there is still a difference between wisdom and folly (10:12–20). Even though everything, including the pursuit of wisdom, is futile, that is no reason to give up. Go ahead and do your best, the old sage advises (11:1–6). Enjoy your youth (for the time will come when you cannot find such enjoyment). That is what life (and God) has to offer.

As should be obvious by now, the Book of Ecclesiastes is iconoclastic. It refuses to accept the traditional verities such as, "If you work hard, you will be rewarded." One technique used to question traditional teachings is to quote a popular proverb, and then immediately refute it with a second (see 4:5–6). At the speculative level, Ecclesiastes challenges the assumption traditional wisdom takes for granted—that there is an order to life that humans can understand and follow (e.g., 1:15; 3:11).

Apparently, the intended audience for Ecclesiastes was young people (11:9). The old sage is trying to spare youth the bitterness and disillusionment that he passed through as he tried to find the meaning of life. The search is futile; better to face the meaninglessness of it all and find joy day by day. It is often said that Ecclesiastes is a pessimistic and skeptical book. It might be better to say that it tries to face life realistically, so that life can really be enjoyed *for what it is*. Nor is Ecclesiastes an antireligious work. It does caution against hollow religiosity (5:1–7), but throughout it maintains belief in the God who is the creator and judge of humanity. Like Job, however, Ecclesiastes claims that the ways of God are beyond human understanding and that humans must not assume justice is guaranteed by God. Unlike Job, Ecclesiastes has no direct encounter with God. Qoheleth's God may be closer to the Force of *Star Wars* fame than to any description of the deity in Scripture. However, Ecclesiastes edges back from such an impersonal understanding of the divine when he says that God's "gift" is to enjoy life. Nevertheless, Qoheleth's understanding of God is considerably different from the God of compassion, mercy, and justice who intervenes in history, which most of the rest of the Bible portrays.

The anthology ends as it begins, with the theme of "emptiness"; however, two editorial footnotes are appended. The first (12:9–12) describes Ecclesiastes in the third person. This note interprets the sayings as "goads" (i.e., provocations) and "pegs" to hang things on. That is to say, their limitations should be recognized. They are *not* the whole story. The second note says in effect that the last word is "Revere God and keep his commandments, for he is the ultimate judge." That brings the collection back within the circle of traditional wisdom and, for that reason, is almost certainly the addition of an orthodox editor intending to qualify the fatalism of the book.

To sum up, the theme of Ecclesiastes, an anthology of proverbs, poems, and brief essays of an old teacher that is intended primarily for young people, is that there is no great meaning or purpose to life. The truth is that we live for a while, die, and are forgotten. Whatever humans do to try to accomplish or discover meaning leads only to frustration. God is in control of life, but God's purpose is beyond human comprehension, despite our deep yearning to know it. The best we can hope for is enjoyment of the daily routine of life, shared with others. For Ecclesiastes, that is all there is, but, as the gift of God to humankind, it is enough.

THE WISDOM MOVEMENT IN ISRAEL AND THE ANCIENT NEAR EAST

In a verse that apparently speaks of the situation in the sixth century B.C.E., the prophet Jeremiah quotes his opponents as saying, "Come, let us make plots against Jeremiah—for instruction shall not perish from the priest, nor counsel from the wise, nor the word from the prophet" (18:18). This revealing statement recognizes three learned professions in ancient Israel—priests, who had charge of the Torah; prophets, who spontaneously spoke messages from the LORD; and sages, who gave advice based on their observations of the way things were. In order to place the wisdom writings in their original historical context, let us try to reconstruct briefly the role of the wise in ancient Israelite society and in the wider ancient world.

In Israel there were probably three separate settings for wisdom teaching: the clan, the court of the king, and the school.[6] In the clan the father and the mother were the sages, teaching their children how to behave in society and how to look at the world. Remnants of this type of teaching are found, as noted, in Proverbs' references to the instruction of a father to "my child." Proverbs also gives evidence of maternal wisdom in the counsel to heed the mother's teaching as well as the father's (7:8; 5:20) and in the poem of Chapter 31. Typically, these teachings are oriented toward the practical—how to succeed in work, whom to seek out and whom to avoid, how to be ready for life's pitfalls, and how to recognize the basic morality by which all should seek to live.

There is evidence of the place of wisdom in the court of the king in the historical narratives. Solomon, especially, took note of the importance of wise counsel and of searching for wisdom himself, but other kings are associated with sages who advised them (see 2 Sam. 16:23–17:14; 20:14–22). Women as well as men are portrayed as sages consulted by monarchs (e.g., 2 Sam. 14:1–20). Second Samuel 20:16–22 records an instance when a wise woman saved her town from great harm.

Later wisdom writings give evidence of a house of learning, that is, a school setting in which sages instructed the young (Sirach 51:23). As noted, it is likely that Ecclesiastes emerged from the setting of school instruction.

Whether trained by apprenticeship or by schooling, the sages of the ancient Near East constituted the bureaucracies of their respective societies, the clerks and secretaries of the governments and the temples as well as the schoolmasters for the next generation. The most successful became government ministers and diplomats. They shared a common outlook that was basically pragmatic and secular. Here was the one point where Israelite wisdom was unique. They linked wisdom and piety, as we noted in our previous discussion of the Book of Proverbs. From this perspective, one had to be pious in order to be genuinely wise. The sages of the region also shared a common language, which could be called "diplomatic Aramaic."

[6]Crenshaw. *Old Testament Wisdom: An Introduction*, pp. 42–65.

Wise men and women played significant roles in the royal court in several events narrated in the Tanak. For example, a clear subtext in the story of Absalom's Rebellion (2 Samuel 15–19) was the contest between Ahitophel, wisest of the wise, who sided with King David's son Absolom, and Hushai, who remained secretly loyal to David. Hushai's "disinformation" campaign and his fleet-footed messenger service undercut Ahitophel's advice, abetting David's victory and Ahitophel's suicide.

In another example of the influence of sages in the court, the prophet Isaiah exulted over the fall of the proud cabinet minister, Shebna, and rejoiced in his replacement by Eliakim, son of Hilkiah. However, Eliakim proved to be no improvement, and Isaiah announced his fall in turn (Is. 22:1–25). Both of these worthies, along with Joah the son of Asaph (Eliakim is the senior minister in the narrative), went out to negotiate with the Assyrian authorities during the 701 B.C.E. siege of Jerusalem. The Judean representatives wanted to conduct the negotiations in Aramaic, which as good sages they could do. But the Assyrians insisted on conducting the negotiations in Hebrew for the benefit of the defenders on the walls, presumably to demoralize them. Did they have a hand in the fact that Hezekiah came off better than he, a rebel, had a right to expect? He paid tribute, but remained on the throne, Jerusalem's walls unbreached.

In all its contexts, wisdom teaching tended to be conservative, cautiously accumulating observations of the ways of nature and society. The teaching of wisdom was a way to foster commitment to the perceived order at various levels of society. In traditions such as wisdom, which tend to justify the *status quo,* change tends to come spasmodically. Pressures build up until a new idea breaks the hardened shell of accepted teaching. It is fascinating that, of the three wisdom writings in the Tanak, two come from the "rebels" who challenged the assumptions of their traditions.

Israelite wisdom was part of a much wider movement that directly influenced the wisdom literature of the Bible and that manifests similar, but also different, forms of wisdom writing and thought. We can only give a hint of this huge corpus of literature here.

In Egypt there are a number of examples of instructional literature in which a father addresses a son or a teacher speaks to a pupil, with advice on behavior in various settings, frequently the court. One of these, the instruction of a minor official of the New Kingdom (thirteenth to twelfth centuries B.C.E.) named Amenemopet, was probably the source for Pr. 22:17–23:14. Also present in Egyptian wisdom were *onomastica,* lists of the names of various natural phenomena such as flora and fauna. This example of early science is similar to the divine naming of phenomena in Job 38–39. There are also examples in Egyptian wisdom literature of speculative literature with a pessimistic bent, most from the chaotic Twelfth Dynasty. There are also several fables and debates.

In Mesopotamia we also encounter instructional literature. One piece, the so-called *Book of Ahikar,* may have inspired Pr. 23:13–14 and 27:3. Similar to the custom in Israel, sages collected proverbs, which were published for the benefit of students. Like the Book of Job, several Mesopotamian compositions wrestle with the problem of the suffering of the righteous. There are also a number of fables and debates and one example of a skeptical and pessimistic dialogue.

Attempts to determine authorship and times of origin for wisdom writings have yielded only limited results. Although there is no reason to doubt that some of the sayings collected in Proverbs stem from the time of Solomon, the book probably continued to develop well into the exilic period. Some scholars think they have found stages of development in which secular collections within Proverbs have been given a religious bent. The Book of Job includes both a narrative frame that is probably based on ancient traditions of a righteous ancestral figure named Job and a poem so sophisticated in style and so dependent on other poetic forms that it is generally assumed to have come from the exilic or perhaps postexilic period. The author of Job was one of history's finest writers. Unfortunately, we do not have a trace of reliable evidence to determine who that person was.

There is a somewhat firmer basis for dating Ecclesiastes. The language of the book is late, probably from the fourth to the third centuries B.C.E. Although the title links the work to Solomon, and Solomon's experience is used in the first two chapters, this is a literary device that is soon dropped. The book later refers to the king in the third person. The author of Ecclesiastes was probably a scribe or teacher who lived in Jerusalem. Some of the teachings might mirror such Greek views as Stoicism (the sense of fatalism), suggesting that the book was written sometime after the beginning of the Hellenistic period. However, such ideas also occur in much earlier Mesopotamian wisdom lore.

Why were such skeptical books as Ecclesiastes and Job included in the canon? While there is evidence that the suitability of Ecclesiastes for the canon was challenged, the inclusion of the Book of Job was apparently not contested. Several reasons have been suggested. The frame of the Book of Job, with its emphasis on Job's faithfulness and God's restoration of Job's fortunes, moderated the more problematic portrayal of the questioning Job of the poetic dialogue. Also, God speaks directly in the Book of Job, giving it an aura of divine authority. Finally, Jewish leaders who might find the questioning in Job troubling would have recognized and admired its literary appeal.

Those who opposed including Ecclesiastes in the canon claimed that its skepticism was incompatible with the call to faith central to the rest of Scripture. Furthermore, opponents noted that Ecclesiastes is a collection of "sayings" of an old, disheartened sage, not wisdom with divine authority. They feared Ecclesiastes could lead the young away from a life of obedience to the commandments of God because the sage says there is no reward for following them. However, the tradition that the wisdom of Ecclesiastes comes from the paragon of wisdom in ancient Israel, King Solomon, found in the superscription added to the work (1:1) outweighed these arguments and was likely the principal reason this skeptical collection made it into the canon. Many modern readers of the Bible, who find the wisdom of the old teacher helpful as they wrestle with the ambiguities and contradictions of life, are grateful!

Summary

The wisdom books of the Tanak (Proverbs, Job, and Ecclesiastes) are examples of a corpus of literature found throughout the cultures of the ancient Near East. Unlike other books of the Hebrew Bible, the wisdom writings do not center on the history of the people of Israel and the LORD's involvement with the covenant people. Instead, these writings raise timeless questions, both practical and speculative, about the conduct and meaning of life in the world.

The Book of Proverbs is largely an anthology of collections of short sayings and admonitions on the way life is and should be. Interspersed we find several longer, more speculative poems. In Proverbs, wisdom orders life and is accessible to those who have reverence for the LORD. Proverbs assumes that the LORD rewards goodness and punishes evil.

The Books of Job and Ecclesiastes balance this understanding of wisdom by questioning whether life always follows the pattern of retribution Proverbs assumes. In our reading of Job we emphasized that the book challenges the assumptions that God necessarily guarantees justice for humans and that God's ways can be explained in human terms. The collection of proverbs, poems, and short essays attributed to a sage called Ecclesiastes (in Hebrew, *Qoheleth*) suggests that life is vanity and challenges readers to find joy in spite of life's emptiness and futility.

The evidence for understanding the original historical context of the wisdom books comes from hints in the Tanak about the role of wisdom in the clan, court, and school as well as a rich collection of practical and speculative wisdom writings from ancient Egypt and Mesopotamia.

Many modern readers find the wisdom books of the Tanak the most interesting and accessible books in the Tanak. They identify with the practical wisdom of Proverbs and find the questioning, skeptical spirit of Job and Ecclesiastes an attitude easy to affirm in our time.

The Contemporary World

Case Study

What Is the Meaning of Life?

The group of friends, introduced in Chapter 1, is once again discussing the Bible, asking whether the wisdom books they have been studying in their Introduction to the Bible course answers the question, "What is the meaning of life?" John says that the answer is found in particular verses from the Book of Proverbs such as 1:7 and 3:5–6. Mary, who admits that she is finding more relevance in the Bible than she thought she would, says that preference should be given to Ecclesiastes, who says that the search for the meaning of life is futile and leads only to frustration. Joyce says that, while both Proverbs and Ecclesiastes provide useful insights, the journey of Job seems the most honest in coming to grips with such a profound question. Based on your study of the literary and historical worlds of these wisdom books of the Hebrew Bible, and the three friends' reactions, reflect on/discuss the question of whether life has any discernible meaning and purpose.

Questions for Discussion and Reflection

1. *Read Proverbs 1–8:*
   a. List a few modern proverbs. How do they compare with the sayings in the Book of Proverbs?
   b. The Book of Proverbs might well have been a textbook for the ancient counterpart of a school of business and public administration. How does its advice compare with the education offered in parallel modern textbooks and schools? Is there any religious component in contemporary business education? If so, what is it? If not, do you think there should be?
   c. Feminine "Wisdom" in Proverbs 1–8 is portrayed as a prophet (1:20–22), a tree of life (3:18), with God before creation began (8:22–31), and the agent of divine creation (3:19–20, 8:22–31). In reflection on the role of women and feminine aspects of God, what role should Wisdom play? Is she, in effect, a goddess? If so, why have interpreters largely ignored her? Or is Wisdom in Proverbs mere poetic imagery?

2. *Read Job 1–7, 28, 38–42:*
   a. Do you know of situations in which an innocent person has suffered like Job? How did the person respond? Does the Book of Job offer comfort or confusion, or both, for people struggling to make sense out of seemingly meaningless suffering?
   b. According to Job 28, where is wisdom to be found? Compare this perspective with the portrayal of wisdom in the Book of Proverbs. Can the two be reconciled? Where is "wisdom" to be found today? Have Bill Gates and the other gurus of the "information age" shown us the "way to wisdom?"
   c. According to your reading of the Book of Job, what is the nature of the relationship between God and humans? Is the divine/human relationship portrayed differently in other biblical books? If so, how can (or should) those differing perspectives be reconciled by modern readers?
   d. This chapter mentions a survivor of the Holocaust who answered the question, "How can you believe in God after your experience in the Nazi death camps?" by saying, "Have you read the Book of Job?" Discuss what this response might mean.

3. *Read Ecclesiastes 1–3; 8:16–9:18; 12:*
   a. Some interpreters call the Book of Ecclesiastes the most modern book in the Hebrew Bible. Why might they say that? Do you agree?
   b. The Teacher (Qoheleth, Ecclesiastes) has been described as a "believing skeptic" who questioned the common assumptions of his day about God and religion and yet still affirmed faith in God. Do you know any such "believing skeptics?" What might their role be today?
   c. On the basis of your reading of Ecclesiastes, which adjectives would you apply to the book: challenging, disturbing, cynical, pessimistic, reassuring, insightful, warm, disrespectful, or others? As you think about the meaning of life, is Ecclesiastes a helpful book? Why or why not?

Chapter 9

The Rest of the Writings
Chronicles, Ezra, Nehemiah, Ruth, Esther, and Daniel

Reading from the Torah Scroll. The "Book of the Law of Moses," which Ezra read to the people in Jerusalem (Neh. 8:1–12), was probably part or all of the Torah. Today, the reading from the Torah scroll is an important part of the Sabbath morning service in Jewish synagogues. These worshippers are assembled at the Western Wall ("Wailing Wall") of the Temple Mount in Jerusalem. The masonry of the wall is part of Herod the Great's reconstruction of the Temple in the first century B.C.E. *Source:* Eitan Simanor/Alamy

The remaining books of the third section of the Hebrew canon, the Writings, represent three different types of literature: historical narrative (Chronicles, Ezra, and Nehemiah), short story (Ruth and Esther), and apocalypse (Daniel). The historical narrative is another version of events from the time of Saul through the period of the Babylonian Exile, with a genealogical introduction that links the story to the beginning of time (Chronicles) and a narrative concerning life after the return from the Exile in 538 B.C.E. (Ezra and Nehemiah). We will confine our historical discussion here to the postexilic period (see Table 9.1). We will then analyze Chronicles, Ezra, and Nehemiah as literature. Ruth and Esther provide us with an opportunity to examine two Hebrew short stories, both of which focus on a courageous woman. Daniel introduces us to apocalyptic literature and invites historical reflection on apocalyptic movements and apocalyptic thought.

THE HISTORICAL WORLD: AFTER THE EXILE

Cyrus and the Fall of Babylon

When we interrupted our historical discussion to examine the poetic sections of the Writings, the Babylonian Exile was the topic. That is where the historical narrative of the Former Prophets (paralleled in Chronicles) leaves the people of Israel. The leaders of Judah have been taken to Babylon, leaving behind Jerusalem in ruins and a disheartened populace. The Exile was interpreted by theological historians and prophets alike as judgment for national sins. But prophets such as Second Isaiah (Isaiah 40–55), Jeremiah, and Ezekiel held out hope for a restoration.

Internal dissension played a significant role in Babylon's sudden decline. Nabonidus, who seized the throne in 556 B.C.E., became embroiled in a program to reduce the power of the Marduk priesthood in Babylon. When he withdrew to Tema on the caravan route to Arabia, apparently to police against menacing raiders, administration in Babylon was left to his son, Belshazzar. The rise of Cyrus the Great counted for a great deal more than the decline of Babylonian power. Cyrus began his royal career as king of the small kingdom of Anshan in Persia. About 550 B.C.E. he began his advances, which ultimately produced the Persian Empire. Classical writers such as Herodotus tended to idealize Cyrus, but his reputation was not undeserved. Apparently, Cyrus was the first great master of propaganda, and he preferred intrigues such as bribery to pitched battles. He was able to march into Babylon "without firing a shot" and take the throne. The Cyrus Cylinder acquaints us with some of his propaganda. For instance, as part of his propaganda he claimed that Marduk had called him to come and rescue Babylon from the evil clutches of irreligious usurpers.

Cyrus was a tolerant overlord, patronizing the Babylonian worship of Marduk. We have already seen the positive reception given to Cyrus in (Second) Isaiah 45:1, where he is called the messiah (anointed one) of the LORD. Indeed, Cyrus allowed foreign exiles in Babylon (including the Judeans) to return to their homes and to take with them their images and religious objects, which had been seized by the Babylonians as war prizes. The Judeans had no images, of course, but the sacred vessels of the Jerusalem Temple were returned to them.

The Return

Many exiles from various places elected to remain in Babylon, where they had made homes. For the Jewish exiles, return home meant an arduous journey, much of it across desert, to a land still in ruins. As a consequence, the successive companies of Jewish returnees from about 539 B.C.E. onward tended to be high-status persons coming to assume leadership roles or to be the more deeply religious exiles. Some fell into both categories. This should not be taken as a slight to those who remained. Babylon became the center of some of the most important Jewish religious scholarship

TABLE 9.1 Political Situations in the Ancient Near East after the Fall of Judah

Date (B.C.E.)	Egypt	Judah/Palestine	Babylonia	Persia
600		Fall of Jerusalem (587) Third deportation (582)	Nebuchadnezzar (605–562)	
	Falls to Persia (525) Persian rule (525–401)		Nabonidus (556–539)	Empire begins (550) Cyrus (550–530)
		Edict of Cyrus (538) and return to Judah	Fall of Babylon to Persia (539)	Darius I (522–486)
		Zerubbabel (520–515) Temple rebuilt (536–515)		
500		Ezra (458?)		Xerxes (486–465)
		Nehemiah (445–?)		Artaxerxes I (465–424)
				Darius (423–404)
400	Independence (401)	Ezra (398?)		Artaxerxes II (404–358)
	Reconquered by Persia (334)	Falls to Alexander (333)	Falls to Alexander (battle of Gaugamela, 331)	
	Falls to Alexander (332)			
300	Ptolemy rule (323–116)	Ptolemy rule (301–198)	Seleucid rule (312–63)	
		Seleucid rule (198–167)	Parthian (neo-Persian) Empire (250 B.C.E. to 225 C.E.)	
200		Maccabean revolt (167–164)	Antiochus IV (Epiphanes) (175–163)	
		Maccabean rule/ Hasmonaean Dynasty (167–63)	Parthians establish a frontier on the Euphrates (155 B.C.E.)	
100		Falls to Rome (63)	Syria falls to Rome (63). Abortive Roman campaigns against Parthia (53 and 36)	
	Falls to Rome (30)			

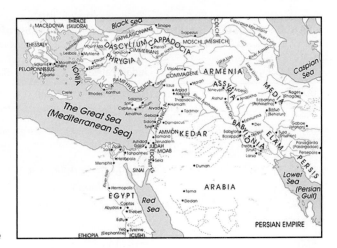

Persian Empire

over the next thousand years and more. The Babylonian community flourished under the titular headship of the exilarch, a descendant of King Jehoiachin.

The land of Judah had been ravaged, but it had not been depopulated. The Book of Jeremiah, which seemed to have access to the best data, put the total number of deportees at 4,600 (52:28–30). Jerusalem was a ruin without a defensive wall. But it is again Jeremiah who informs us that even northern Israelites still made pilgrimage to Jerusalem to present offerings on the Temple site (41:4–5). The Babylonians had deported the people considered most likely to make trouble or the most useful for their purposes. These included members of the royal family, prominent priests, other aristocrats, soldiers, and skilled artisans. Those survivors left behind were largely of the lower orders. The society that emerged from the ruins of Judah probably resembled the village–tribal culture of the premonarchic period. Archaeology shows that the Babylonians did take over some Judean royal estates and operated them for their own imperial profit. But for the most part, small farmers and husbandmen probably appreciated the absence of royal revenue agents and the collection of tithes by the established priesthood. Some of the frictions experienced by the postexilic prophets and Ezra and Nehemiah are probably rooted in this time.

The reconstruction of Jewish life in the homeland under the leadership of exilic repatriates may be conveniently viewed in three stages. First, the Temple was rebuilt, and then the walls of Jerusalem. Finally, the Mosaic Torah, either the Priestly Code or perhaps even the completed Pentateuch, was embraced as the national constitution of the Jewish people. Each of these was, in its own way, essential to the survival and integrity of the community.

The Temple

A foundation for the Temple was laid almost immediately after the first group of returnees arrived in Jerusalem. Then the project languished until taken up again in 520 B.C.E. by the Jewish prince and Persian governor, Zerubbabel; the high priest Joshua; and the prophets Haggai and Zechariah.

It is not surprising that a leadership group composed of a substantial proportion of priests regarded the reconstruction of the Temple as the top priority. Judaism had not yet become, although it was becoming, "the religion of the Book." At this time, the Temple still constituted the common focus of Jewish loyalty. That continued until the Roman period. It was only when the Temple was destroyed in 70 C.E. that Jews discovered it could be *replaced* by Torah piety centering in the synagogue and the house of study.

Historians conveniently refer to the building raised on the site of Solomon's Temple between 520 and 515, and its successors, as the *second temple,* despite the fact that there were several extensive renovations and a total reconstruction by Herod the Great.

Nehemiah: The Wall

The reconstruction of the Temple provided a center for the reorganization of life in Judah and Jerusalem. But so long as Jerusalem remained defenseless, it was at the mercy of all comers. The jeopardy was enhanced by the rebuilt Temple, the growing wealth of which tended to attract covetous eyes.

This need was taken up by Nehemiah, a Jewish civil servant who had risen high in Persian service. Becoming aware of the situation in his homeland, he requested and received from the emperor a warrant to serve as royal governor in Jerusalem and to rebuild (refortify) the city. Back in Jerusalem he organized the task of rebuilding. But his project was opposed, particularly by the neighboring peoples, and, above all, by Sanballat, the governor of Samaria. The danger was such that laborers were armed, but the project was carried through to completion. It appears that Nehemiah served two terms as governor, or took a leave during his term of service, as the case may be. On his return, he instituted religious reforms and expelled Sanballat's ally, Tobiah, from an apartment in the Temple complex.

The Torah

Ezra, an Aaronid priest and a "scribe skilled in the Torah of Moses" (Ezra 7:6), was the central figure of the third major aspect of the restoration of Jewish life in the homeland. He went to Jerusalem armed with royal warrants to revivify the worship of the Jerusalem Temple. Ezra carried out a series of social and ritual reforms. He did not hesitate to use the coercive power at his disposal. The high point of Ezra's work was a great ceremony of covenant renewal, narrated in Nehemiah 8–10. Ezra read the Torah, his Levitical associates interpreted it for the congregation, and the assembled citizens of Judah and Benjamin affirmed it. It is probable that Ezra had a complete Torah, or at least the priestly section, whether he read every word of it or not. Ezra's activity marked a significant step on the road toward Torah-centered piety as it emerged in the second century B.C.E. and later. Israel was a province of the Persian Empire, not an independent nation, but the three-fold reconstruction of Temple, city, and Torah provided the means to maintain identity and integrity.

Nehemiah, Ezra, and prophets such as Malachi were vexed by Israelite marriages to foreign women. The two reformers obliged citizens of Jerusalem to rid themselves of foreign wives. This policy was not racist. The women who troubled the reformers were those who *remained* pagan and foreign. Women who converted to Judaism were no longer foreigners. Before the Exile, Israel, as a flourishing independent state, could permit marriages to foreigners. But in the postexilic period, the Judean community was small and threatened. They could not afford losses. The seemingly harsh marriage policy was motivated by a realistic concern for survival.

We have not yet attempted to date Ezra and Nehemiah. Taking the dating notations of the books at face value, Ezra came to Jerusalem in 458 and Nehemiah in 444. But on closer reading, we see that Ezra found the wall rebuilt (Ezra 9:9), and the two influential leaders never seem to have interacted. Further, they dealt with different high priests. The standard solution among historians is to move Ezra to 398–397, by placing him in the reign of Artaxerxes II rather than Artaxerxes I. Because the biblical text does not differentiate monarchs by Roman numerals, this is a convenient resolution of the conflict; however, it has been challenged by other historians. It must suffice for us simply to say there is a dating problem.

After the Exile, the Jewish high priest began to fill the functions of both chief magistrate and chief priest. Government by the major religious leader in a city or small province represents a situation fairly widespread in the Persian Empire. The Persian period is the "Dark Age" of biblical history. From the end of the time covered by the Books of Ezra and Nehemiah to the early years of the second century B.C.E., there is almost no documentary evidence on the affairs of the restored Jerusalem community. The recently discovered *Samaritan Papyri* (found in a cave in the Jordan Valley below Samaria) are largely commercial and legal documents that do not fill the narrative gap. There is a legend that when Alexander the Great marched through Israel on his way to Egypt in the fourth century B.C.E., he was greeted by the Jewish high priest in full regalia and, being much impressed, showed kindness to the Jews. The legend cannot be confirmed.

The Hellenistic Age

Alexander's meteoric imperial career, from the assassination of his father, Philip II of Macedon, in 336 B.C.E. to his own death at age thirty-three in 323 B.C.E., was fraught with consequences for the Jewish community. During that brief period, Alexander marched his army from Europe into Asia, swept southward into Egypt and Libya, turned back north to gain Babylon, and then invaded Persia proper. He fought his way eastward to the Indus, before a reluctant turn homeward. If he wept, it was not because there were no more worlds to conquer, but because his trusted soldiers would go no further.

After Alexander's untimely death, his empire was divided among four feuding generals. The two who loom largest in biblical history were Ptolemy, who established a dynasty in Egypt, and Seleucus, who established a dynasty in Babylon and Syria. The land of Israel first fell to Ptolemy, but, following battles at Gaza and Paneas (200–199 B.C.E.), the Seleucids gained control.

On the surface, things seemed not to change much when first Alexander, then the Ptolemies, and then the Seleucids took control. In Jerusalem the hereditary high priesthood stayed within the Aaronic Zadokite family. Taxation was left to a local aristocratic house, the Tobiads, but change was under way. Alexander was an evangelist for Greek language and (Hellenistic) culture, as were his successors. They built their cities in the Greek fashion, with Greek temples, theaters, gymnasiums, stadiums, libraries, and Greek-style dwellings. When Alexander established Alexandria in Egypt, the most splendid city to bear his name, and one destined soon to eclipse Athens as the intellectual capital of the Greek-speaking world, he invited Jews to settle there under favorable conditions. The Alexandrian community became (with the Babylonian) one of the two most brilliant and prosperous Jewish Diaspora communities. The Greek-speaking Jews of Alexandria spawned both the Septuagint (LXX) translation of the Scripture and Philo, one of the most creative philosophers and biblical interpreters of antiquity.

Greek culture also infiltrated Jewish life in the homeland. By early in the second century B.C.E., some prominent Jewish priests were beginning to use Greek names. There was a theater, a stadium, and a gymnasium in Jerusalem. In due course this Hellenizing tendency came into bruising contact with traditional Jewish belief and practice, and this collision coincided with tumultuous political developments (see Chapter 10). A glance ahead at the discussion of these developments will make the impending study of Daniel clearer.

THE LITERARY WORLD: THE CHRONICLER'S HISTORY (CHRONICLES, EZRA, AND NEHEMIAH)

In the Tanak, the Books of Ezra and Nehemiah are considered one work, as are First and Second Chronicles. Although, in the Hebrew canon, Chronicles is placed after Ezra as the last book in the Bible, there is internal evidence to support the theory that Chronicles originally preceded Ezra–Nehemiah. Ezra begins precisely where Chronicles ends, with a note about the decree of Cyrus that allowed the restoration to Jerusalem and the rebuilding of the Temple. Considered together, Chronicles and Ezra–Nehemiah tell a story that begins at creation and ends with the establishment of the Jewish province of Judea under priestly leadership. Because of stylistic similarities, many contemporary biblical scholars view this block as the work of a single author (or school), the "Chronicler." In any event, we can speak of Chronicles and Ezra–Nehemiah conveniently as the *Chronicler's History.*

The Chronicler's History portrays the rise and fall of the nation Israel and its limited resurgence after the Exile. Beginning with Creation, but skipping quickly to David, the Books of Chronicles show how the nation prospered when there were rulers who were concerned with the proper worship of the LORD in the Temple in Jerusalem, who supported the priesthood, and who lived piously. When this high level of devotion to the LORD faltered, the nation weakened, until disaster struck and the Temple was destroyed. Ezra–Nehemiah portrays the restoration, not only of people to their land but also of the level of devotion to the LORD reminiscent of the time of David. Against considerable opposition, the Temple was rebuilt, the priesthood was allowed to function again, and devotion to the Torah of the LORD was renewed. Now, under a hierarchy, there was new hope for Israel.

TWO SHORT STORIES: RUTH AND ESTHER

The Book of Ruth: A Woman of Valor

In the Hebrew canon the Book of Ruth is one of the festival scrolls (*megilloth*) read annually at Pentecost (Shavuot, the Feast of Weeks). In the Christian canon it appears in its presumed chronological setting (Ru. 1:1), after the Book of Judges.

The first verse and the last verses (4:17–20) give the book a historical context. Set during the period of the judges, it is the story of the foreign woman who was the great-grandmother of King David. Between these historical notes, however, the story moves from the history of the nation to a smaller stage. Between its beginning and its ending, Ruth is a story of the struggle and triumph of two women in a male-dominated society. Before trying to place the Book of Ruth in its historical context, let us seek to enter the world of Ruth and her mother-in-law, Naomi, as it is created in one of the short stories of ancient Israel.

THE LITERARY WORLD   On two levels Ruth is a story of redemption. On the one hand, it is the story of how two courageous women succeed in winning the legal right of redemption. Under the so-called *levirate law* (or law of redemption) of ancient Israel (see Dt. 25:5–10), if a man died without any sons, it became the responsibility of the nearest male relative to marry his widow and sire a son who would be the legal son of the deceased kinsman, so that the deceased man's heritage could continue and his immortality be assured. How far this responsibility extended, when the dead man had no brothers, is not clear. Apparently, sometimes a relative had to be convinced to exercise

Ruth. One of a series of mosaics in front of the church on the Mount of Beatitudes at the Sea of Galilee in Israel shows Ruth as she is gleaning in the fields of Boaz to provide food for her mother-in-law Naomi and herself (Ruth 2:1–23). *Source:* Zvonimir Atletic/Shutterstock

his role as "redeemer." This is what Naomi and Ruth did, cleverly creating the circumstances that caused Boaz to recognize and to fulfill his kinship responsibility.

However, at another level, another kind of redemption takes place in Ruth. At this level, the Book of Ruth is the deeply moving tale of the selfless love of Ruth, who "redeems" a broken and bitter Naomi. There was no law requiring Ruth to stay by Naomi's side. In fact, prudence dictated that when her husband, Naomi's son (who was an alien sojourner in her homeland of Moab), died, she should return to her family. Because of her stubborn devotion to Naomi, Ruth violated custom and common sense to comfort her mother-in-law during her time of grief and restore hope when all seemed lost.

The story moves quickly, as is the style in Hebrew narrative, with only the most essential details and few indications of the inner thoughts and feelings of the characters. Through what the characters say and do, we catch glimpses of the inner drama. The story is structured in four scenes (conveniently reflecting the four chapters). In the first scene, the central dilemma is identified; in the second and third, the tension increases as solutions are sought; and in the final scene, resolution occurs.

THE HISTORICAL WORLD   The Book of Ruth not only highlights the devotion and faith of a foreign woman but also makes the remarkable claim that the great King David descended from a Moabite great-grandmother. When might such a story have been written, and why? Many modern scholars feel that the Book of Ruth was written to attack the postexilic policy in the restored community of Judah against marriages with foreign women (Ezra 10:1–5; Neh. 13:23–27). Ruth is generally set alongside Jonah as fifth or fourth century B.C.E. reactions against the narrow nationalism and exclusivism that some have attributed to this era. There can be no doubt that Ruth is a critique of such attitudes.

The question being raised by some recent interpreters is whether exclusivism and responses to it were characteristic of only the postexilic period. The fact that Ruth accepted Naomi's God, the

God of Israel, places her in the role of a proselyte, a convert to Judaism. As we have already noted, it was only wives who remained pagan foreigners that the reformers of the restoration regarded as dangerous. So, in fact, Ruth may be construed as propaganda in favor of the Ezra–Nehemiah policies. In any case, the evidence for dating Ruth to the postexilic age is somewhat less than convincing. The clean narrative Hebrew prose could well be pre-exilic. Some have even suggested that the tradition of David's alien female ancestor is in fact anti-Davidic propaganda, of a piece with the tale of Judah and Tamar in Genesis and the seamier parts of the Succession Narrative. This case might be made stronger if it could be shown that Ruth is written in a northern dialect, but no general agreement exists on this issue. Here, as at other points in the historical study of the Tanak, the final conclusion must be that the evidence does not warrant final conclusions.

The Book of Esther: A Dream Fulfilled

There are a number of similarities between the Books of Ruth and Esther. Besides being among the festival scrolls in the Hebrew canon, both are found among the historical books in the Christian canon (Esther is after Ezra and Nehemiah). Both are short stories about courageous women whose actions have far-reaching consequences for their people. Both are set rather loosely in historical contexts (Esther in the Persian period). In both books God is not an onstage character. However, unlike in Ruth, in the Book of Esther the name of God is not even mentioned (unless the additions found in the Deuterocanon are included). It is not surprising that the canonical status of Esther was debated in both Jewish and Christian circles.

THE LITERARY WORLD   Whereas the Book of Ruth is a sensitive portrayal of women in a time of crisis, Esther is a potboiler, a tale full of intrigue, violence, and dramatic action. There are several major themes in the book—the gaining of power by Jews in a situation of powerlessness, the importance of loyalty to the Jewish community over fidelity to unjust civil powers, and the underlying

Hebrew Scroll of the Book of Esther. The Book of Esther is one of the five books of the Tanak known as *Megilloth* ("scrolls"), all associated with Jewish festivals. Esther is closely linked with the festival of *Purim* (Est. 9:16–23), which celebrates the liberation of the Jews from a persecution in Persia that threatened to annihilate them.   *Source*: Arkady Mazor/Shutterstock

pattern beyond the level of human intrigue. Throughout the story, reversal and irony are used to develop these themes. The following observations are based on the literary analysis of Esther by Sandra Beth Berg.[1]

A story that begins with a feast showing the power of the Persian king ends with a feast celebrating the power of the Jewish people over their enemies. Jews in a situation of powerlessness have attained power. The reason for this dramatic change is Jews showing loyalty to the community over loyalty to those in power. At first this seems foolish and costly. Mordecai's disobedience in refusing to honor Haman precipitates the planning of the annihilation of the Jews. This crisis causes Esther to take a risk she might otherwise have avoided. It is her disobedience that initiates the series of actions that lead to deliverance for the Jews and victory over their enemies. Both Mordecai and Esther are motivated by their identity as Jews to disobey civil authority (3:4; 4:13–16); yet their disobedience jars with their typical concern to be loyal to those in power. In disobedience they are willing to accept the consequences of their actions (4:16), and when the crisis is past, they are again obedient to their king. Indeed, they argue that their disobedience was in the king's interest.

The story is full of reversals and ironies supporting these themes. For example, Queen Vashti is punished for refusing to appear before the king when he has requested her presence. Queen Esther is rewarded for appearing without being asked. Haman, thinking he is honoring himself, chooses and bestows honors on his archenemy. Haman's plot to kill Mordecai backfires. Instead, Haman is hanged on the gallows built for Mordecai, and Mordecai receives Haman's office and Esther his house. The planned destruction of the Jews is reversed, and their enemies pay a price in blood.

The Book of Esther is full of "coincidences," such as the king's just happening to be reading the report of Mordecai's loyalty when Haman is plotting to kill him. These coincidences suggest an underlying pattern to events that will lead to the deliverance of the Jews, raising the question of whether a subtle hint of divine providence is present. The unexpected reversals that permeate the story are just too overwhelming to be a matter of chance. Even though God is never mentioned in Esther, the story could still be pointing toward the divine patterning of events, with the purpose of release and fulfillment for the people of God. The precedents of the Joseph story, the Succession Narrative, and Ruth can be cited in this connection.

THE HISTORICAL WORLD   Interpreters disagree on the question of whether the events described in Esther actually took place. Some feel that the wealth of details about Persian court life and Ahasuerus (Xerxes I) make the story credible. Others argue that there are too many historical improbabilities and inconsistencies for the story to be considered historical. Most importantly, there is no extrabiblical record of a Jewish queen at the Persian court. When Esther was supposed to have been queen, the Greek historian Herodotus names another. Still others take a middle ground, suggesting that there is a historical kernel in the story that has been embellished with nonhistorical legends.

Many interpreters who question the historical nature of the Book of Esther suggest that it arose as an explanation for the origin of the feast of Purim, originally a non-Jewish festival that was adapted for use in the Jewish community. The names Mordecai and Esther might be adaptations of the names of two central Mesopotamian deities—Marduk and Ishtar—and might hint at a myth behind the story. Because of indications such as this, speculation abounds about the possible mythical background of the story. However, there is little concrete evidence in support of any of the imaginative hypotheses about the type of myth involved.

---

[1]Sandra Beth Berg. *The Book of Esther: Motifs, Themes and Structure.* Missoula, MT: Scholars Press, 1979.

THE HORIZON OF HISTORY: THE BIRTH OF APOCALYPTIC (DANIEL)

Introduction: Apocalyptic Literature and Movements

In the Book of Daniel we encounter a new type of literature—*apocalyptic* (from the Greek word for "a revealing"). Apocalypses are unveilings of things to come, revelations of the pattern of events that will lead to the end of the present historical epoch (*aeon*) and the beginning of a new age. Because of the use of highly symbolic language, apocalyptic literature is both difficult to understand and susceptible to manipulation by interpreters who feel they have discovered *the* key to unlock its mysteries. Although Daniel is the only apocalyptic book in the Tanak, there are apocalyptic-like sections in some of the prophetic books, for example, Isaiah 24–27, Ezekiel 38–48, Zechariah 9–14, and Joel 3. In the New Testament there is also one apocalyptic book, the Revelation to John, and there are apocalyptic passages in the gospels (Mark 13, Matthew 24–25, Luke 21) and the letters (1 Corinthians 15, First and Second Thessalonians, Jude, and Second Peter). There are also a number of apocalyptic works in the Jewish literature after the Tanak (see Chapter 10).

As literature, apocalyptic has a number of characteristics, not all of which are necessarily present in every apocalyptic writing. Apocalyptic literature reports visions from God concerning events that will climax in the vanquishing of the forces of evil and the establishment of a new age of righteousness. This is similar to the theme noted in the prophets of a time of judgment (the Day of the LORD), to be followed, according to some prophets, by the establishment of the LORD's universal rule and a new age of peace. However, apocalyptic moves beyond this view of an ending to a new beginning in several respects. Most importantly, apocalyptic works portray the end of the present aeon and the dawn of a new aeon, as a radically new beginning beyond history as currently experienced. The present age is perceived to be under the dominion of evil, whether human or demonic in origin. This renders God's saints helpless, pending divine intervention to set things right. The new age is sometimes called the Kingdom of God in apocalyptic writings. Apocalyptic visions typically reveal a series of cataclysmic events leading to a final climax in which God acts directly to end the old age and begin the new.

There are a number of paired opposites in apocalyptic literature—between this age and the next, between the forces of good and evil, and between heaven and earth. The visions are of the heavenly events that will determine the course of history at the earthly level. They are full of highly symbolic, mythic imagery of angels, God, and dragons and other animals representing the forces of chaos. This imagery constitutes a secret code that, when deciphered, reveals to the faithful the truth about the end and the events leading to it. This veiled language also serves to conceal the truth from the reprobate, whether they are foreign enemies or native quislings. When the recipients of these visions are named, they are invariably heroes of the faith who have demonstrated their righteousness (such as Daniel). They receive the visions, usually in a trance state, often with interpretations by an angel. They are usually instructed to seal them up until the time of the end. Sometimes the visions are "raptures," as the seer is transported into the heavens to see what will transpire. Apocalyptic writing focuses on reporting these visions recorded by the seer, and sometimes it establishes the "credentials" of the seer through stories demonstrating his faithfulness (as in Daniel 1–6).

Two other characteristics of apocalyptic literature should be mentioned. Apocalyptic writings often speak of life beyond death, ensuring that the righteous who die before the end of the present age will not be denied their place in the Kingdom (e.g., Dan. 12:2–3) and that the wicked will receive their just punishment. There is also, in apocalyptic literature, mention of the agent or agents who will rule in the new age for God (as in Dan. 7:13–15). In some apocalyptic writings this figure is harmonized with the messianic expectation of a new King David who will restore the fortunes of Israel. Sometimes the figure is the "son of man," with no apparent link to the messianic hope.

Apocalyptic movements (and literature) developed in Judaism at times of persecution and crisis, when hope seemed lost. Usually, alienated from traditional religious teachings and institutions, apocalyptic movements took refuge in the alternative, symbolic universe of the visions they believed predicted an imminent deliverance and a new age. Invariably, the apocalyptic movement interprets its own time as the age just before the end. For example, the Qumran community of the Dead Sea Scrolls was part of an apocalyptic movement that withdrew from society to purify itself in preparation for the final battle between the "sons of light" and the "sons of darkness" and the new age to follow. Some early Christian communities were apocalyptic groups, believing that Jesus would return soon to inaugurate God's kingdom. Some apocalyptic communities did not resist those persecuting them with force, believing instead that God would act to vanquish these foes directly. Victory was predetermined, so resistance was unnecessary. Others, such as the Qumran sect, were simply awaiting the signal to launch a holy war.

The relationship of the Zealot movement of the first century C.E. and the messianic claims of Simeon bar Cocheba in the second century C.E. to apocalyptic thought have not yet been clarified by scholarship. Because of their rejection of tradition and their esoteric teachings, apocalyptic movements were looked on with suspicion by most religious authorities. Apocalyptic movements within Judaism were rejected by rabbinic leaders who feared the consequences of militant enthusiasm.

Apocalyptic literature and movements have arisen throughout history at times of crisis and persecution. In the current age, although the Cold War confrontation between Western and Eastern blocs has subsided, a threat remains that a launch control failure or actions by smaller nuclear powers, rogue states, or terrorist groups might still unleash a nuclear holocaust. The danger of an accident such as Three Mile Island or Chernobyl that got completely out of hand also remains a worrisome prospect. Such prospects have elicited an apocalyptic response in many religious communities. Christian apocalyptic groups often strongly believe that the canonical apocalypses (Daniel and Revelation) point to the present era as the end time. The so-called *cargo cults* of the South Pacific represent the transmission of Christian apocalypticism to folk cultures victimized first by European colonialism and later by indigenous state-level organizations. The Native American Ghost Dance movement of the late nineteenth century is another example of an apocalyptic response to persecution.

The Book of Daniel

THE LITERARY WORLD   Although placed among the prophets in the Greek canon (the order adopted by the Christian churches), its placement among the Writings in the Hebrew canon indicates that Daniel was recognized as a different type of literature and completed after the prophetic canon was closed, a point made explicit in rabbinic sources.

The Book of Daniel has two easily distinguished sections. The first six chapters form a collection of legends about Daniel and three friends, who are presented as deportees to Babylon after an otherwise undocumented Babylonian siege of Jerusalem in the third year of King Jehoiakim (606 B.C.E.).

The elements of the story should have a familiar ring. Daniel, like Joseph, is a handsome young man who demonstrates his allegiance to God when tested and rises to influence in a foreign court because of his skill as an interpreter of dreams. Like Esther and Mordecai, Daniel and his friends are victims of court intrigue. Like these tales, the legends of Daniel 1–6 are instructive, giving a model of persons in situations of crisis displaying exemplary behavior. The message is that if you maintain loyalty in the face of persecution, everything will work out in the end. Even if you do not survive the immediate crisis, even if fidelity costs you your life, you will share in the final triumph (Dan 3:16–18, 12:2–3).

The second half of Daniel (7–12) is a collection of four apocalyptic visions, with interpretations by angels, received and written down by Daniel. At the conclusion Daniel is told that "the words are to remain secret and sealed until the time of the end" (12:9), when those who are wise will understand, but the wicked will not. The visions are graphic symbols of the unfolding of history from the time of Daniel to the end, when an everlasting kingdom will be established. The visions are rich in the mythic imagery that we have encountered before. For example, the description of "one like a son of man (or human being)" coming on the clouds of heaven to the throne of the Ancient of Days (7:13–14) is rooted in Canaanite imagery of the god Ba'al (rider of the clouds) coming before the high god El. This imagery is elsewhere applied to the LORD himself in the Tanak (e.g., Ps. 104:3). One of the classic problems of interpretation is the meaning of "one like a son of man." Although this phrase sounds like the description of an individual, later in the same chapter it is the saints (the community of the righteous) who seem to be in the situation attributed to the "son of man" (7:18, 22, 27). So "son of man" may be a corporate symbol here for the community of the faithful.

In another vision (Daniel 9), Daniel learns from the angel Gabriel that the "true" meaning of Jeremiah's prophecy of seventy years of exile (Jer. 25:11, 12; 29:10) is seventy *weeks* of years. This type of commentary on Scripture, which looks for a deeper meaning, is a typical apocalyptic technique, based on the assumption that hidden in Scripture are the keys that, when properly understood, will reveal the secrets of the end time. In Chapter 12, Daniel is reassured by Gabriel that when the present age draws to a close, Michael (Israel's guardian angel) will arise, and the righteous will be victorious. The dead will be raised—some to everlasting life and others to everlasting contempt. But for now Daniel is to seal the visions until the time of the end and "rest" until the time of resurrection. To this are added two separate attempts to determine when the end will come (12:5–13).

THE HISTORICAL WORLD   The second half of Daniel is dated by many modern interpreters more precisely than any other section of the Bible, on the basis of both external and internal evidence. Externally, the book is not among the Prophets in the Hebrew canon, so it is most likely post–fourth century B.C.E. It is first mentioned in a work that dates about 140 B.C.E. The book is not mentioned in Ben Sirach (c. 190–180 B.C.E.), where one might expect to find it. Internally, both the legends and the visions include unhistoric elements concerning Daniel's putative time, such as a Medean empire and a ruler, Darius the Mede, between the Babylonian and Persian empires. Meanwhile, the visions lead step by step to the year 165 B.C.E., but not to 164 B.C.E. Especially in Chapters 10 and 11, the detailed vision points to the profanation of the Jerusalem Temple by the Seleucid ruler Antiochus Epiphanes, which took place in December 167 B.C.E. (11:31). There is an allusion to the subsequent revolt of the Maccabees (the "little help" in 11:34), but the vision is somewhat misleading concerning the death of Antiochus and stops short of the rededication of the Temple in 164 B.C.E. This evidence leads to the conclusion that Dan. 7–12 emerged in 164 B.C.E. (*Note:* A fuller discussion of the Maccabean period is found at the beginning of Chapter 10.)

This method of dating reflects the modern view that apocalypses are frequently pseudonymous works, that is, attributed to one source but actually coming from another. In the case of Daniel, this means that the visions are a literary creation, written during the Antiochian persecution to inspire hope, using the device of visions received long before and sealed up until the present time. The visions are, according to this view, predictions after the fact. They have been combined with legends about the righteous Daniel and his friends, the models of piety in the face of persecution. The Prayer of Nabonidus, a document found among the Dead Sea Scrolls, confirms that the narratives in Daniel have a complex tradition history.

If this view of the origin of Daniel is accepted, what can be said of the apocalyptic movement of the second century B.C.E. with which the work was associated? By this time there was an identifiable group within Judaism known as the *hasidim* (faithful ones). They were dedicated to maintaining traditional practices (such as dietary laws) when many Jews, including religious leaders, were falling under the influence of Hellenistic (Greek) culture. When Antiochus enforced Hellenistic ways and outlawed Jewish practices, the hasidim practiced passive resistance. They felt that faithfulness to the LORD, rather than armed struggle, was the best course. Thus, they were unlike the Maccabees, who led a revolution against Antiochus. The hasidim believed that if anyone died refusing to compromise the faith, then that person was assured of resurrection when God brought victory and the divine Kingdom to earth. The consensus of modern historians is that the hasidim were the apocalyptic community for which Daniel was written.

Summary

In this chapter, we resumed our discussion of the history of Israel (see Chapter 5), picking up the story at the time of the Babylonian Exile. When the Edict of Cyrus in 539 allowed those exiled to return from Babylon to Judah, some did. They rebuilt the Temple in Jerusalem, constructed a new wall around the city, and embraced the Mosaic Torah as a basis of a renewed Jewish community. Unfortunately, historians of the postexilic period face a lack of solid evidence on which to construct as complete a narrative as they would like.

The Chronicler's History (First and Second Chronicles, Ezra, and Nehemiah) offers a different perspective on Israel's history from that found in the Torah and Former Prophets. Chronicles focuses on the rule of David, and the other two works highlight two prominent leaders of the postexilic community. The ongoing debate on how to date Ezra and Nehemiah reflects our historical uncertainty.

In this chapter we also analyzed the literary and historical worlds of two short stories—Ruth and Esther. Both works portray strong, heroic women who take the initiative to redeem others.

The Book of Daniel is a highly symbolic work, the only fully apocalyptic book in the Tanak. We provided in this chapter background information on the characteristics of apocalyptic literature and movements. We presented an interpretation of Daniel, reflecting the broad consensus of modern scholars that the book is a pseudonymous work written in 164 B.C.E.

The issues raised by the books of Ruth, Esther, and Daniel range from the role of women in societies dominated by men to the end of history as we know it. Discussion of them, guided by the following questions, should prove to be fascinating and perhaps somewhat intense.

The Contemporary World

Case Study

The Left Behind Series

After reading Chapter 9, John, Mary, and Joyce are discussing the popular *Left Behind* series authored by Tim Lahaye and Jerry Jenkins. John objects that the historical and literary approach taken to the Book of Daniel in Chapter 9 mocks the fact that it is a divinely inspired prophecy of the coming apocalypse. "Hauer and Young are obviously not Bible-believers," he said. "If they were, they wouldn't write about God's word in the way they do. The

Left Behind series is written by believers who trust God's word; the class would be much better off reading Lahaye's books to understand the Book of Daniel than this textbook!"

Mary says that she is glad Hauer and Young have used literary and historical methods to expose Daniel as a pious fraud and other books in the Bible as the works of humans blinded by their prescientific worldview. "Tim Lahaye is making a lot of money exploiting the fact that, unfortunately, lots of people today haven't left that naïve world behind."

"I think you're both missing the point," Joyce offers. "Since I don't agree with John's interpretation that the Book of Daniel is describing events in our time, I once had your view, Mary. However, understanding Daniel as an example of apocalyptic literature and learning about the historical context in which it was written has helped me appreciate that it does indeed relate to our times, though not as a predictor of events. Perhaps we should talk about the literary and historical worlds of the *Left Behind* books if we really wanted to understand them. That would be revealing!"

With which of the friends do you most agree and why? Is literary and historical study of the Book of Daniel helpful to you in coming to a position?

Questions for Discussion and Reflection

1. *Read the Book of Ruth:*
   a. Reflect on the main characters in this story: Ruth, Naomi, and Boaz. Are they believable? Compare Ruth with the portrayal of other foreign women who act decisively and play a role in the unfolding story of the covenant people (e.g., Rahab in Joshua 2 and Zipporah in Exodus 4:24–26). Do you find common themes?
   b. The Book of Ruth has been called "a story about and for women in any age." What do you think the story might have said to women in ancient Israel? Are its themes helpful for women in modern, American society? Does it speak in a different way to men?

2. *Read the Book of Esther:*
   a. Does it matter whether the events described in the story of Esther ever occurred?
   b. The Book of Esther (as it is found in the Tanak) does not mention God. Does that mean it has no religious value?
   c. Compare the portrayal of Esther with that of other women in the Bible. Do any attributes of Esther make her a more compelling character for modern readers?
   d. The Book of Esther is dramatized in the film *One Night with the King* (2006). After reading the Book of Esther, watch the movie and analyze its interpretation of the story.

3. *Read Daniel 7–12:*
   Inspired by the belief they have uncovered the key to interpreting the visions in the Book of Daniel (and other apocalyptic writings), some interpreters have predicted the imminent end of history and the beginning of a new age. The predictions usually involve catastrophes and conflicts as the end approaches. They see contemporary events hidden within the symbolism of the visions of Daniel and believe they have discovered the key to their interpretation. What in the modern world encourages such interpretation of the Book of Daniel, and what accounts for its wide popularity? In your opinion, is it appropriate to relate the symbols within the visions in the Book of Daniel to contemporary events? Are there other ways to understand the significance of this book for the modern world? For example, could the work be interpreted as reassurance for those who are struggling to affirm faith in God in an increasingly secular, materialistic world, rather than a literal revelation of the end of history?

Chapter 10

Jewish Life and Literature

(200 B.C.E. to 100 C.E.)

Cave 4, Qumran. This is the most famous of the caves near the Dead Sea in which the Dead Sea Scrolls were found. In this cave, carved out of the marl terrace between the rocky Dead Sea beach and the limestone cliffs in which the other caves were located, were found fragments of most biblical books, the deuterocanonical (apocryphal) and pseudepigraphical works, and the sectarian documents of the Qumran community. *Source:* Ellas Design/Shutterstock

The period between 200 B.C.E. and 100 C.E., and even beyond, was one of the most vital and creative periods in the history of Judaism, or any other religion for that matter. From a historical perspective this period witnessed the flowering of a number of movements within Judaism, one of which became the form of Judaism that continues to flourish to this day (the movement associated with the Pharisees), another of which became a new and influential religion in its own right (the movement associated with Jesus of Nazareth).

From a literary point of view, this period witnessed the creation of a number of works that, despite their failure to achieve canonical status in the Tanak, are worthy of our consideration. We will survey some of the variety of literature from this period. This chapter is one of the most important in this book because it supplies the framework essential to a full grasp of the wider historical and literary contexts of the Tanak and the New Testament.

THE HISTORICAL WORLD: VARIETIES OF CLASSICAL JUDAISM

The Maccabean Period

The deuterocanonical Book of Sirach (Ecclesiasticus) ends its famous passage in praise of the great heroes of Israel (44:1–50:29) with a reference to a contemporary of the author Joshua—Jesus, the high priest Simon II. According to tradition, Simon had one foot in an old order that was passing away and one in a new, emerging order. He was the last of the great Zadokite high priests and rulers of the principality of Jerusalem. In the eyes of rabbinic tradition he was also the patron of an emerging pietism that bore Judaism's ultimate future.

Early in the second century B.C.E. the Seleucids were still the overlords of Judea. Their loss to Rome at the Battle of Magnesia in 190 meant that they owed the Romans tribute, which they exacted from subject peoples. This probably explains an abortive attempt to loot the Temple treasury during the reign of Simon's successor, Onias. With the coming of Antiochus Epiphanes to the Seleucid throne in 175 B.C.E., the situation of the Jewish community deteriorated. According to some sources, Antiochus was very ambitious, highly eccentric, and possibly a bit mad. *Epiphanes* means "God (Zeus) manifest," and he may have believed his own label. He was approached by Onias's brother, Joshua (who took a Greek name, Jason), and bribed into deposing Onias and installing Jason as high priest. The tables were turned on Jason by the unscrupulous Menelaus (another Jew with a Greek name), who offered Antiochus a bigger bribe. This intrigue upset the customary inheritance of the high priesthood through the Zadokite line.

The process of Hellenization had been going on for at least a century by this time, as discussed in Chapter 9. However, it was not until the 170s and 160s that a strong reaction to Hellenization emerged. Then a variety of factors combined to produce polarization, persecution, and, ultimately, rebellion. Hellenistic culture came from a brilliant and attractive civilization. It was "where the action was" for young sophisticates throughout the Mediterranean world, including Judea. Ultimately, Rome conquered the Greek east, but Hellenistic culture conquered Rome. The polytheism and pluralism of Rome could better accommodate Greek customs than could Judaism. Greek gods could be given Roman names and absorbed (e.g., Zeus became Jupiter). That does not work in Jewish monotheism. Nor could one dress like a Greek and fulfill the customs of the Mosaic Torah, especially the requirement of the *zizith* (fringed robe). The Dead Sea Scrolls and rabbinic traditions alike suggest that there was an upsurge of Jewish pietism among both priests and laity in the early second century B.C.E. Perhaps this renewal of commitment to the Torah was motivated, at least in part, by reaction against Hellenization. In any event, this new pietism was a strong center of resistance to the inroads of offensive Greek customs. The cultural conflict came to the point of persecution and eventually rebellion, largely because the Seleucid government exploited it in the pursuit of an essentially political agenda. The Jewish community had accommodated Hellenistic influences peacefully for over a century, and would do so again during the Maccabean and Roman periods, in some cases revealed by archaeology to a degree shocking for later orthodoxy (including the use of pagan iconography in Jewish homes and synagogues).

After Rome thwarted an unsuccessful attempt to add Egypt to Antiochus Epiphanes' empire, Antiochus salved his ego by entering Jerusalem on the Sabbath, slaughtering innocent people, and looting the Temple, with the full cooperation of Menelaus. The Temple was converted to pagan worship, and by 167 B.C.E. customary Jewish practices were outlawed. The *hasidim* practiced passive resistance, suffering torture and death as a consequence.

A radical turning point came in the village of Modein, northwest of Jerusalem, on a day when an apostate Jew, supported by Seleucid troops, sought to compel a pagan sacrifice. An old priest of Modein, Mattathias, led his neighbors in sacrificing the interlopers instead. Mattathias did not survive to lead the resistance movement inspired by his act. Rather, the struggle was led by three of his sons: first Judas, called *the Maccabee* ("hammerer"), then Jonathan, and finally Simon.

Judas was a brilliant guerrilla fighter who, in December (Kislev) 164, liberated the Temple (although he failed to dislodge the Seleucid garrison in Jerusalem). The Temple was cleansed and rededicated, an action that is celebrated in the Jewish calendar through the annual Feast of Lights, or Dedication, Hanukkah.

The war was punctuated by truces, negotiations, and diplomatic exploration. Sparta and Rome pledged moral support for the rebels but gave no tangible aid. Judas fell in battle. Jonathan and Simon were capable warriors, but they were even more adept as masters of politics in an age when Machiavelli's *Prince* would have sounded tame. Both died as victims of treachery. But before Simon's death (135 B.C.E.), total political independence had been won, and he had taken the titles of high priest and king. He began the Hasmonaean Dynasty, named for the family patronymic, ben-Hashmon.

Simon had two strong successors, John Hyrcanus and Alexander Jannaeus. Thereafter, the dynasty weakened through squabbles over succession. In 63 B.C.E. the Roman general Pompey entered Jerusalem, and the Jewish homeland was thereafter subordinate to Rome either directly or indirectly.

The Hasmonaean family had given Israel nearly a century of political and religious independence. Most information suggests that they were generally popular with the masses. But more dedicated pietists were reserved or hostile toward the Hasmonaean line. From the second generation onward, the Hasmonaeans took Greek names. Though not Davidic, they claimed the throne, and, though not Zadokites, they assumed the high priesthood. Thus, they were usurpers on two counts for Jews who valued tradition. Their military activities also exposed them to corpse impurity, an outrageous ritual violation for an officiating priest.

Rome was not the only power to exercise its influence in the traditional sphere of biblical history during the last few centuries B.C.E. As early as the mid–third century B.C.E., a Parthian dynasty had begun the process of restoring Persian independence. Mithridates I, perhaps the greatest Parthian emperor, pushed the Parthian boundary to the Euphrates about 155 B.C.E. When Rome terminated the Seleucid empire in 63, the Romans became the masters of Syria and began to view the Parthians across their common frontier with suspicion and hostility.

Rome had been drawn to the east by instability in the Greek-speaking world, and by her own deep-vested interest in the eastern Mediterranean grain trade, particularly the Egyptian, to feed agriculturally deficient Italy. Both Crassus (53 B.C.E.), who died in the process, and Mark Antony (36) conducted abortive campaigns against Parthia, and the Parthians reciprocated with an invasion of the Levant (44 B.C.E.) that included an attempt to restore the Hasmonaean Dynasty to a position of effective authority. The Parthians lent encouragement and aided Jewish resistance to Rome, particularly during the two Jewish revolts (discussed later). Indeed, the neo-Persian Empire remained Rome's greatest adversary in the east until the Muslim invasions created a new international situation.

The wily Edomite adventurer Antipater had wormed his way into Hasmonaean affairs. He quickly made himself useful to the Romans when they appeared. As a consequence, his son Herod was named Rome's client–king of the Jews, although he was, to a substantial degree, left to his own devices to make the claim stick. Antony and Cleopatra lent him aid against the resurgent Hasmonaeans. When the famous lovers fell into disfavor with Augustus, Herod indulged in some fancy footwork to retain Roman favor and, as a consequence, enjoyed a long reign (40–4 B.C.E.).

Herod was an able ruler and an ambitious builder. His splendid reconstruction of the Jerusalem Temple was his most famous achievement, although his founding of Caesarea as the capital and main seaport of his kingdom and the rebuilding of Samaria under the name Sebaste rank close behind. Both names, the first Latin, the second Greek, honored Augustus. But Herod was also a paranoid who brought about the deaths of his own sons and of his wife Mariamne (a Hasmonaean), among others. Some writers attribute Jewish contempt for Herod to his being a "half-breed" with an Idumean (Edomite) father. To the contrary, because his mother was Jewish, Herod would be considered a Jew under developing rabbinic custom. Jewish dislike for Herod was based on the fact that he was a bloody tyrant who patronized paganism in other places (including building temples dedicated to Augustus) while he rebuilt the Jerusalem Temple. Through it all Herod remained the faithful servant of Rome.

Both Herod and his heirs were at least technically answerable to the Roman governor of Syria, although they fell into the category of the type of client–king to whom the Romans entrusted the security of many imperial frontiers. At Herod's death, his kingdom was divided among his surviving sons. The one entrusted with the southern portion of the kingdom, Archelaus, proved a disaster and was removed by Rome, with a procurator (Roman governor) assuming the reins of power. Thus, Jesus lived in a Galilee ruled by Herod Antipas. But when he came to Jerusalem, he was under the authority of the procurator, Pontius Pilate.

The emperor Caligula (best remembered for his madness) made Herod's grandson Herod Agrippa master of much of the original Herodian kingdom. But after Agrippa's death (44 C.E.), Roman procurators assumed full power. Poor judgment (or worse) on the part of some, the earlier threat by Caligula to install an image of himself as Zeus in the Jerusalem Temple, and the unbalanced behavior of yet another mad emperor, Nero, probably hastened the outbreak of open rebellion.

The Zealot uprising that began in 66 C.E., against the better judgment of many priestly notables and pharisaic leaders, gained major popular support through the success of early guerrilla ambushes of Roman forces. But Rome's fear of Parthia and its disinclination to permit colonial escapes meant that maximum power would be used to crush the rebellion, and so it was. Jerusalem was captured and the Temple destroyed in 70, and the last Zealot holdouts perished at Masada in 73–74. The Jewish population would not fully recoup its numerical losses until modern times, and Jewish political independence in the traditional homeland was dead until 1948. But anti-Jewish measures under Trajan and Hadrian produced a second revolution (132–135), led by the messianic claimant, Simeon bar Cocheba. Again, Rome brought its awesome power to bear, and Judea was ravaged. The center of Jewish life in the homeland shifted northward into Galilee, and Jerusalem was reconstructed under Hadrian as a pagan city.

The New Order

John Hyrcanus was friendly with the Pharisees until there was a falling out over his fitness to serve as high priest. Thereafter, he patronized the Sadducees. The appearance of these two names is a

Masada. The name means "stronghold." This natural citadel by the Dead Sea served Herod the Great well during his struggle to possess his crown. Later, he turned it into one of several heavily fortified palaces located in various parts of his realm. This view shows the step-like northern palace complex, and the royal pleasure house, sited to benefit from the prevailing northwesterly breezes. Zealot warriors seized Masada during the first war with Rome and held out against the Romans until 73–74 C.E., when they committed suicide rather than let themselves be taken as slaves.   *Source:* Nathan Benn/Alamy

clear-cut indication that the old order had passed and a new order was dawning. Neither group is mentioned in sources predating the Maccabean Wars. By the same sign, the prewar and wartime *hasidim* had disappeared from the record, as had the hereditary Zadokite high priesthood. Thus, this was a watershed time in Jewish history. The Hebrew Scriptures had now all been written, and the three-fold canon of Tanak was well along the way to completion. A flourishing array of competing viewpoints in Judaism was a fact of life. Still, Torah and Temple remained the central operative symbols for all forms of Judaism (including early Christianity, when it appeared).

A variety of terms have been used to designate these competing viewpoints in classical Judaism. The ancient Jewish historian Josephus used *parties* and *philosophies,* terms meaningful to the Greco-Roman audience to which he was writing. Others speak of *sects,* although this is not an appropriate term to apply to all of them from a sociological standpoint. We have decided to use the term *denominations* to describe these various groups. It is, of course, anachronistic, because the term *denominationalism* is strongly associated with American Protestant Christianity. However, American Protestantism offers a good analogy for understanding the varieties of early classical Judaism. In good denominational fashion, each and all thought of themselves as Jewish but were obliged to recognize the Jewishness of their rivals. To be sure, their own group were the truest Israelites. The harshness of their judgments on Jews outside their own group was a function of how sectarian they were in their outlook. We will confine our discussion to those groups that can be documented in some detail. Our account begins with the four groups described by Josephus and documented in other sources.

Judaism has always been a religion that emphasized deeds, not creeds. What a person did was more important than what he or she believed. The oneness of God has been the one theological or philosophical idea that Judaism has emphasized, a teaching rendered urgent in the early period of classical Judaism by the divine pretensions of Hellenistic and Roman rulers. Even here the *Shema',* sometimes called "the creed of Judaism," those biblical verses that became central to Jewish liturgy, link conviction to action: "Hear, O Israel: The LORD is our God, the LORD alone; and you shall love the LORD your God …" (Dt. 6:4–5).

Torah was the sum total of God's authoritative teaching, including laws, rules, customs, public health measures, and so on. Torah and the Temple, so long as it stood, were central to the loyalty of all classical denominations. Embodied within Torah or derived from it was *halakah,* "the way," the authoritative and binding customs. The term *mitzvaoth,* "commandments," was used of its obligatory principles. The disagreements among the classical Jewish denominations were, therefore, not about creeds and doctrines. They were about the extent of the Torah and what it ordained, about how it was to be interpreted, and about who had the authority to interpret it. Deuteronomy had long ago laid it down that God does not command impossible things (Dt. 30:11–16), nor is God unaware of human fallibility. As Professor Samuel Sandmel once put it, "God does not expect a perfect performance. Only a perfect effort."

An aspect of traditional Torah piety that is widely misunderstood today is the notion of ritual purity and impurity. Modern secular culture has few obvious counterparts, although most traditional cultures had a similar view of things. It roots in the notion that one must be in the correct state to approach the Holy, to enter holy space, to touch holy things. The first thing that must be noted about it, at least so far as Judaism is concerned, is that it has absolutely nothing to do with sin or virtue. A person in a state of ritual purity is not in a state of moral uprightness, nor is a ritually unclean person in a state of particular sin. Indeed, uncleanness may arise from virtuous actions. It is a highly virtuous act to bury the indigent dead, but the person who does so contracts corpse impurity (a notion in many cultures) and must go through certain cleansing acts before he or she can resume a normal social role. Similarly, many very natural and even unintentional circumstances may lead to uncleanness. A man who experiences a nocturnal emission of semen or a woman in her menstrual period is ritually unclean and must be cleansed. One must not equate ritual uncleanness with "being dirty" in a repulsive sense, or with the sort of aesthetic revulsion some people feel toward, say, eating fried rattlesnake. Perhaps the best modern secular analogy is the sort of cleansing a person undergoes before assisting in a surgical operation. One must "scrub" with germicidal soap and don sterile gloves and clothing. We are all bacterially contaminated. It has nothing to do with morals. Some of these bacteria are benign. Some are even beneficial. All are out of place in the surgical suite. One must get into the proper state for the activity at hand. Some hostile (and false) reconstructions of classical Judaism have had it obsessed with ritual purity. The Essenes may have been, but there were, in fact, a variety of views.

The Pharisees

In its most common usage today, "Pharisee" refers to someone who is obsessively concerned with rules, giving more attention to the outward forms of religion than its spirit, and who is self-righteous and hypocritical. Unfortunately, this stereotype distorts one of the most important Jewish movements of the period covered in this chapter. We shall attempt here a more balanced, objective description.

The Pharisees were in fact a pietist movement composed largely of laity. Their name comes from a Hebrew word meaning "the excluded" or "the separated." It was perhaps, like *Christian,* a slur that stuck as a public nickname and perhaps became a badge of honor to a group excluded from national counsels by Hyrcanus. Or it could refer to their self-separation in a quest for ritual purity. They apparently did not use this name among themselves, preferring instead the title of the ancient wise men, the *hakamim.*

It should be noted before proceeding that recent scholars have been less willing to offer unified overviews of the Pharisees than earlier generations of historians. The reasons are that while several ancient sources (the Dead Sea Scrolls [where they are called "Those Who Seek Smooth

Things"], New Testament, writings of Josephus, and later rabbinical writings) provide evidence of the Pharisees, there are no surviving descriptions written by the Pharisees themselves. Moreover, each of these sources had its own biased perspective on the Pharisees, and a single portrait based on these divergent views may not be possible. For example, the conception that the Pharisees were legalists and hypocrites comes largely from the New Testament description. Almost the opposite impression is created by the Dead Sea Scrolls, where they seem to be described as too lenient in their observance of the Torah. The best we can do, some recent scholars are saying, is to treat each source on its own terms rather than harmonizing them.[1] However, given the importance of the Pharisees for an understanding of the emergence of both rabbinical Judaism and Christianity, some general, albeit admittedly speculative, remarks about the movement are in order.

Ancient societies had no middle class in the modern sense. However, references to the occupations of pharisaic leaders suggest that they were recruited largely from the middle orders of society: tradespeople, artisans, merchants, farmers, and others, though a few, were of lower rank. They could not claim many priestly adherents. They were apparently led by a company of lay scholar–saints whose authority was their power to persuade through reason and example rather than hereditary office or charisma. The few wonder-workers who cropped up among them constituted a qualified embarrassment on occasion. Ideally, every Pharisee was a scholar, although in practice this would have been unlikely. Their origins probably go back to the lay scribes (religious scholars) who emerged in postexilic Israel. Ezra and his colleagues and successors, to whom the title *Men of the Great Academy (Synagogue)* was applied, loomed large in pharisaic tradition. But Moses was considered their founder and supreme teacher.

The Pharisees saw the necessity of adapting Jewish piety to the changed conditions of life in the Jewish homeland (and in Babylon where they had strong connections), to enable the ordinary Jew to be a good Jew and still live as a productive citizen in the modern world. They accomplished this adaptation through two radical devices. One was through free interpretation of Scripture by their scholarly leaders. As noted earlier, *halakah* (obligatory customs and observances) had to be derived from the Torah, but any part of the Tanak could yield *haggadah,* inspirational teaching. According to the Pharisees, all Scripture bore witness to Torah, and all sacred teaching embodied Torah in some sense. They may well have played an important role in the recognition of the three-fold canon, the Tanak.

Alongside their free interpretation of Scripture, the Pharisees likely introduced the even more radical notion of *two Torahs*, one *written* and the other *oral,* both handed down from Moses at Mount Sinai. The oral Torah was none other than the traditional teachings of the great pharisaic scholars. These two devices, free interpretation of the Bible and authoritative oral tradition, gave the Pharisees the means to adapt Jewish practice to a changed world and to keep pace with a changing world. No *midrash* (biblical interpretation), *mishnah* (oral Torah), or *targum* (translation of the Bible into Aramaic) was permitted to be written down during this period. In this way, the Pharisees retained flexibility while showing deference to the written Scripture.

The Pharisees introduced a third device to hold their two radical ones in moderate check: *the principle of authority.* An interpretation of the biblical Torah or a purported oral teaching of halakah could be accepted *only* if it could be attributed to a recognized and authoritative leader.

Part of the pharisaic program seems to have been to permit pious Israelites in Jerusalem, in the villages of Judea and Galilee, and the Diaspora to participate in the high piety that the written Torah reserved for priests serving at the altar. They could not approach the altar, but they could maintain the purity called for in the Torah.

---

[1]See, for example, Jacob Neusner and Bruce D. Chilton. *In Quest of the Historical Pharisees.* Waco, TX: Baylor University Press, 2007.

Wailing Wall. The remnant of the wall that once surrounded King Herod's first century B.C.E. reconstruction of the Temple in Jerusalem is known as the Wailing (or Western) Wall. Because the wall is the closest Jews may approach the site of the Temple, it is one of the holiest places in Judaism, and Jews come from all over the world to pray at its base. It is customary to insert prayers written on pieces of paper into the crevices of the wall. *Source: Johan_R/Shutterstock*

Phariseeism was centered in observance of the Torah. Actions and purposes were more important than words or doctrines. The Pharisees believed that God had given Israel the whole Torah (written and oral) as an express statement of God's will for the people. The keeping of Torah therefore was *not* a legalistic quest for the favor of a coldly demanding God, but a response to the goodness of a loving parent. To keep a commandment, the Pharisees taught, was a joy, not a burden. Given the flexibility of determining commandments, the number multiplied. Multiplication occurred in part to "build a fence around the Torah," so that major commandments were "surrounded" with lesser ones to give them a "protective shield." Someone could bump up against the fence, so to speak, without violating a major commandment. The *principle of intention* was central to the Pharisees. Basically, it held that the purpose a person had in mind when doing a deed determined its validity. This tended to lighten the burden of religious observance for lay people.

In the opinion of some scholars there were two major schools among the Pharisees, the free constructionist school of Hillel and the strict constructionist school of Shammai, named for the two great masters whose careers spanned the turn of the eras. The terms *conservative* and *liberal* are sometimes used of the houses of Shammai and Hillel, respectively, but this can be done only advisedly. To oversimplify, the house of Shammai was inclined to stick up for the letter of the Torah, while the house of Hillel sought out its spirit. The outcome was that Hillelite usage tended to put people ahead of the letter of the law. At first, the Shammaites were dominant, but then the Hillelites gained the upper hand.

The Galilean Pharisees who disputed points of law with Jesus (as remembered in the gospels) tended toward the Shammaite view. The teachings of Jesus inclined more toward the Hillelite position. Jesus's disputes with the Pharisees were not unlike their arguments among themselves. However, after the time of Jesus, Jewish Christian leaders found themselves locked in dispute with pharisaic leaders for recognition in the community. This antagonism is reflected in the editing of the gospels, especially Matthew and John, as we will see in Chapter 12. Later gentile Christians tended to go even further and read into these "family arguments" a "we versus they" hostility. This antagonism has persisted through the centuries and has, regrettably, been the cause of Christian persecution of Jews in many periods.

During this period, the Pharisees evolved what was to become the characteristic Jewish attitude toward civil authority. They were willing to put up with just about any government, so long as Jewish religious practices were not utterly repressed. Although they detested the Roman occupation, most Pharisees eschewed armed revolution. They shared the general expectation of a messianic age, which God would begin in his own good time. In the meantime, they believed their obligation was to create a congenial environment for King Messiah's coming by living a life of Torah faithfulness.

After the destruction of Jerusalem and the Temple in 70 C.E., the Pharisees emerged with a form of piety and an institution, the synagogue (which they had not invented, but which was an ideal setting for their piety), adapted to carry on Jewish life and religion. The Romans recognized the principal pharisaic academy at Yavneh (Jamnia) as the Sanhedrin (highest court of the Jews). After 70 C.E., pharisaic Judaism became rabbinic Judaism. All forms of Judaism that exist today (except for the few Samaritans) descend from rabbinic Judaism.

The earliest references to what later generations would call *kabbalism,* the peculiarly Jewish and rabbinic form of mysticism, are associated with the students of Hillel around the turn of the eras. The earliest well-documented mystical traditions date from the post–70 C.E. academy of Yavneh.

Mysticism is a religious discipline that leads to direct encounters with the holy. In Judaism, two basic forms of mysticism developed. One was Chariot (or Palace) Mysticism, which was the most popular. The chariot was the Divine Chariot of the visions of Ezekiel (see Chapter 6). The palaces were the wondrous structures beheld by the mystics as they moved through the seven levels of heaven. As will be noted in Chapter 14, the Apostle Paul may have been associated with this tradition. The other form of mysticism was Creation Mysticism, which made the light of the first day of creation (Gen. 1:3) the object of contemplation. The Johannine School in early Christianity (see Chapter 12) may have been associated with this tradition.

Study of Torah was central to the discipline of both schools. The great masters would generally not admit novices to mystical training until they were already well grounded in Torah studies. And mystical discipline itself involved intensive, probably esoteric, inquiry into the text of the written Torah. It was said that birds so unlucky as to fly overhead when one gifted early mystic performed his meditation were incinerated.

The Sadducees

This group was composed of prominent priests and other aristocrats. The high priest was ordinarily the titular head. Aristocratic religion is usually traditional and conservative, and this seems to have been true of the Sadducees. They insisted on a strict literal interpretation of the Mosaic Torah. They are said to have had books of such interpretations, but none has survived. They may even have restricted their biblical canon to the first five books, like the Samaritans (discussed later).

Josephus, the New Testament, the Dead Sea Scrolls, and the rabbinic literature all accuse the Sadducean leadership of violent and unprincipled behavior to attain its ends. These are all hostile witnesses, but there is probably enough smoke to suspect some sort of fire. The Pharisees had once been the political antagonists of the Sadducees, and they remained their religious adversaries. The Sadducees wanted the high priest to envelop himself in a cloud of smoke from incense before entering the Holy of Holies in the Temple on the Day of Atonement, lest he see God and die. The Pharisees insisted he light it inside the Holy of Holies. The Pharisees affirmed belief in resurrection from the dead and in angels, while the Sadducees rejected such ideas. It is recorded that the Sadducees had to defer to the Pharisees' interpretation of ritualistic matters because of popular pressure.

The Temple was the power base and source of wealth for the Sadducean movement. Because the high priest was among their ranks, and because the Romans placed him at the head of the Sanhedrin, there was undoubtedly close contact between the Sadducees and the Romans. They were obliged to collaborate with the Romans, or at least with their Herodian clients. The alternative was to give up their privileged position.

The Essenes

A sectarian movement called the *Essenes* ("purified ones" or perhaps "healers") is described by Josephus in his histories, by the philosopher Philo, and by the Roman naturalist Pliny the Elder. The Essenes were a sect in the sociological sense, that is, they withdrew from the "sinful world" to live their higher form of life uncontaminated. All three sources agree that the Essenes had a major sectarian center in the isolated wilderness of the Dead Sea area, near Jericho. Philo and Pliny emphasized their celibacy, but Josephus said some were married and some lived in villages. Celibacy would have been extremely unusual among Jews, given the commandment of Gen. 1:28.

Scholars generally give greatest weight to Josephus's account because he may have had first-hand knowledge of the Essenes. In his description, they sound more like a Hellenistic than a Jewish sect, possibly even a community of sun worshippers, or Jewish Pythagoreans, presumably another accommodation of Josephus to his pagan readers.

Covenanters

We interrupt our discussion of Josephus's "four philosophies" because the discovery of the Dead Sea Scrolls and the center of community life associated with them at Qumran (on the northwest coast of the Dead Sea) has caused the majority of historians to conclude the community that produced the scrolls was composed of Essenes. This widely held conclusion is based on the evidence the Essenes withdrew from Jerusalem to create a community dedicated to a purified Judaism during the period archaeologists have dated the settlement at Qumran.

However, some scholars have come to reject identifying Qumran as an Essene outpost, and we will defend here this minority position. The Qumranians never link themselves to the Essenes in the scrolls, calling themselves instead *Covenanters*, the men of the New Covenant or the Covenant Community who remained faithful while Israel went astray. Their writings suggest that they represented the radical priestly wing of the pietist movement that had been patronized by Simon the Just in the early second century B.C.E. They were once led by a charismatic priest whom they called the Teacher of Righteousness. He received from God the ability to discern all the secrets of the prophets. They applied the words of Scripture to their own time in apocalyptic commentaries.

The community was rigidly hierarchical with the sons of Zadok, the faithful priests, at the head. Each member had an assigned rank within his respective order (priests, Levites, and laity), which was reviewed yearly. The rule for communal meals ordained that even if the Messiah were present, he and his lay entourage must defer in all things to the priests.

Some scholars now believe the Covenanters held views concerning *halakah* (religious law), which the Mishnah identified as Sadducean.[2] The key document, known in Dead Sea Scrolls jargon as "4QMMT," seems to date from the second century B.C.E. Some think it was a letter from the early

---

[2]Lawrence H. Schiffman. *Reclaiming the Dead Sea Scrolls: The History of Judaism, the Background of Christianity, the Lost Library of Qumran.* Philadelphia: The Jewish Publication Society, 1994.

Common Room, Qumran. This hall in the sectarian complex at Qumran, which scholars believe was an Essene community, served as the refectory and meeting hall for the members. This view to the east looks across the Dead Sea toward the land of Moab, today part of the Kingdom of Jordan.   *Source:* Dr. Christian E. Hauer Jr., FSA

leaders of the sect to the (Hasmonaean) high priest. The fact that it survives in multiple copies shows why the sectarians had withdrawn, but offered to return if the high priest would observe the correct (i.e., Sadducean) interpretation of the Torah, rather than following the customs of the Pharisees. (Both the Hasmonaean and Herodian priesthoods, though Sadducean, apparently followed Pharisaic *halakah* most of the time, in response to popular pressure.) The term *Sadducee* is simply a Greek transliteration of the ancient Hebrew title *zadoki*, a descendent of Zadok, the high priest of David and Solomon. "Sons of Zadok" was a favorite Covenanter term for their priestly leaders.

Does this mean that the Covenanters should be identified as Sadducees? They had split with the Jerusalem priestly leadership, the Sadducees of Josephus, the New Testament, and the Rabbinic literature. It would be very confusing to call two such opposed groups by the same name. Most of the surviving early scrolls scholars who made the initial identification between the Covenanters and the Essenes continued to call them "Essenes." Most experts in Jewish studies were never too happy with that identification, and 4QMMT makes them even less so. Strained interpretations of Josephus, Philo, Pliny, and the Dead Sea Scrolls are required to continue to apply "Essene" to the Dead Sea sect. We suggest that they were "sectarian Sadducees," who, for reasons noted previously, are best identified by some term from their own literature such as "Covenanters."

The many scholars who continue to identify the sect as Essenes must recognize, in the light of the Scrolls, that most of what Josephus said about the Essenes has to be discounted as accommodation to Hellenized readers, and in the case of Philo and Pliny, the perceptions of Hellenized writers. In sum, they gave us a name for a sect that may be the Dead Sea sect, but very little additional useful data.

The Dead Sea Scrolls themselves present us with a conservative priestly pietist sect following ancient Sadducean *halakah,* but casting their future in terms of an apocalyptic reading of the prophets (and other Scripture) by a charismatic priest, the Teacher of Righteousness. Such combinations of highly traditional behavior coupled to radical visionary apocalypticism are not unknown even in the modern world.

Reevaluation of archaeological data from Qumran also casts doubt on some earlier conclusions. The "monastic" aspect of the group is jeopardized by female and child skeletons in the Qumran cemetery, and at a second sectarian installation further south. Luxury goods, such as fine Roman glass, suggest that, despite their communal property laws and self-description as "poor men," the Covenanters as a community were hardly impoverished. The luxury goods are not unexpected, however, in a high-status group (e.g., priests) even if they practiced community of goods. "Self-effacing elites" are hardly a new datum to anthropology!

There have been attempts to reinterpret Qumran as a luxurious villa, as a ritual purification center, a trading post, a secular fortress, or even a seaport on the Dead Sea, and the Scrolls as the library of the Jerusalem Temple. Judicious consideration of the pottery, coins, and other archaeological data makes it clear that these revisionist hypotheses are mistaken and the original investigators basically correct. Qumran was the headquarters of a late Hellenistic/Herodian period Jewish sectarian group under priestly leadership, and the Scrolls were connected with their occupation. Reconsideration of the archaeological evidence and continuing study of the sectarian documents among the scrolls has modified our understanding of the sect, and further qualifications will no doubt result from the publication of the entire corpus of Dead Sea Scrolls.

The Covenanters were radically separatist. They were the Sons of Light. Everyone outside the sect, Jew or Gentile, was a Son of Darkness, a man of Belial's lot (their favorite name for the Devil). The Jerusalem Sadducees were "wicked priests." The Pharisees were "seekers after smooth things" (they made religion too easy). The Romans (known as *Kittim* in the texts) were the great foreign enemy.

The Qumran sectarians believed a great apocalyptic war was about to erupt in which the Sons of Light would be victorious. Then the Sons of Zadok would be installed in the Jerusalem Temple, and Jewish life and institutions would be restored according to the sect's teaching. The Qumran compound and another related to it further south were built as fortresses in preparation for the war. There was a conflict, but it resulted in their being wiped out by Roman Legion X. Some Covenanters may have joined the resistance at Masada, but the sect did not survive the catastrophe of 70 C.E.

Apocalyptic expectations had a long history at Qumran. But on the whole, the Covenanters were much more interested in the Messiah of Aaron, the restored anointed high priesthood, than in the Messiah of Israel, the anointed king. From their viewpoint the high priest and his priestly entourage took precedence over the king and his retinue in all matters. Now that the entire Dead Sea Scrolls corpus is available for study, several scholars have begun to note a rising interest in militant Davidic messianism in the latest Qumran documents, perhaps related to the collapse of the Hasmonaean Dynasty and the Roman occupation of Jerusalem. Atkinson took this insight a step further. He noted that the Psalm of Solomon 117 is a classical portrayal of the militant Davidic messiah, and that the "Son of God" in Dead Sea Scroll 4Q246 is nearly identical to the messiah of Ps. Sol. 117. It may be grouped with four other Scrolls, which, along with Ps. Sol. 117, have been dated to the Herodian period (37 B.C.E. to 70 C.E.). These documents, Atkinson avers, reflect the horror that greeted Herod's ruthless and systematic extirpation of the Hasmoneans on his rise to power, and posit a Davidic messiah who will repay Herod (or the Herods) in kind.[3]

The Zealots

According to Josephus, the Zealots were a "fourth philosophy" among the Jews. He said that they agreed with the Pharisees on religious matters. What set them apart was their attitude toward Rome.

[3]Kenneth Atkinson. "On the Herodian Origin of Militant Davidic Messianism." *Journal of Biblical Literature*, 118 (1999), 435–460.

Looking back to the success of the Maccabean revolt, the Zealots, perhaps spurred on by apocalyptic fervor, counseled armed resistance. The Zealots exhibited the sort of contentious factionalism that often characterizes revolutionary movements. They dealt harshly with those they considered inadequately enthusiastic about their campaign against Rome, which flared into a war by 66 C.E., and they fought among themselves. However, the heroic defense of Masada by a handful of Zealots who committed mass suicide rather than surrender to the Romans is justifiably legendary. Some scholars would reserve the name "Zealots" for a smaller band among the rebels of the first war with Rome. We follow the alternative convention of applying it to Josephus's "fourth philosophy," and to the revolutionary bands he described in Judea and especially in Galilee.

The Samaritans

Tension between Jerusalem and Samaria goes back to the foundation of Samaria as the capital of the Northern Kingdom. It was intensified during the postexilic reconstruction when the Samaritans sought, on one side, to gain a foothold in the Jerusalem cult, and, on the other, to impede the re-fortification of Jerusalem and hence its independence. The final major event in the schism between the Samaritans and the established leadership was the destruction by John Hyrcanus of a "counter-Temple" the Samaritans had established on Mount Gerizim.

The Samaritans were a localized and generally conservative denomination led by hereditary priests. Their Scripture consisted of only the Pentateuch. Rabbinic practice treated the Samaritans as marginal and suspect keepers of the Torah. The Samaritans reciprocated by showing contempt for "the Jews" (i.e., "Judeans") as they called them, meaning those Israelites who acknowledged Jerusalem's priestly and rabbinic leadership.

The Samaritans survived the debacles of the classical age, but their numbers were much reduced over the years by Christian and Muslim ill treatment, so that only a small group survives today.

Common Judaism

Many writers have taken up the term *common Judaism,* coined by Professor E. P. Sanders, to designate the customs and usages shared by most self-conscious Jews of Judea, Galilee, and neighboring areas during the early classical period. One of these traits was some concern for ritual purity as witnessed by the numerous ritual baths *(miqvaoth)* archaeologists have found on Jewish occupation sites from this time. Indeed, a cluster of *miqvaoth* is indicative of a Jewish village or neighborhood. Many customs (such as maintaining standards of modesty, or men wearing the traditional fringed garment, the *zizith*) were so much a part of normal everyday life that they probably were done without conscious awareness that one was keeping a *mitzvah.* This common core was probably for many Jews the extent of their religious observance, in which case one might think of it as a sort of "folk Judaism." Again, this "folk Judaism" was probably the religion of a substantial part of the community.

The People of the Land

Rabbinic literature used the term *people of the land* to describe the less observant members of the Galilean and Judean communities. They probably stood outside identifiable denominational movements. Some were simply ignorant of the finer points of Torah piety. Others were excluded by choice, chance, poverty, or occupation. *Publicans,* those who collected taxes for Rome and lined their own pockets in the process; prostitutes; and persons whose work made them ritually contaminated would have been included under the last heading.

Were the adherents of a minimal folk Judaism included in this category, or was it reserved for the generally unobservant and for blatant "sinners?" One cannot be certain. Some Pharisees, like other persons who practice an elite piety, may have lumped all those less pious than themselves together as "people of the land." The phenomenon is not unknown today. Modern students who are at least moderately religious are sometimes miffed to discover that their most pious fellows place them among the lost and ungodly. Whatever may have been the case, the admiration of these moderately observant to unobservant Jews, probably a majority of the population, was responsible for much of the public influence of the Pharisees. Matthew, the most Rabbinic Gospel, suggests that Jesus directed much of his energy toward "the lost sheep of the house of Israel" (Mt. 10:6). Were these the unobservant, or were "folk Jews" included?

Hellenistic Judaism

This is a catch-all phrase for a variety of forms of Judaism that developed after the time of Alexander. In general, it refers to those Jews who continued to consider themselves Jewish after they had become native Greek speakers and assimilated other aspects of Hellenistic culture. These Jews lived for the most part in centers of the Diaspora such as Alexandria, but there was also a Greek-speaking synagogue in Jerusalem, in the very shadow of the Temple. Indeed, we should not overplay the valid distinction between Hebraic and Hellenistic Judaism. Much of Jewish life had become influenced by Hellenism to some extent. The real question was: How much? The operative issue was probably whether they spoke Greek as their first (or only) language. Perhaps birth outside the traditional land of Israel, whether they used Tanak or the Septuagint (LXX) as Scripture, and whether they followed some Jerusalem denomination were additional factors.

Hellenistic Judaism did not survive the classical age. Some of it was assimilated into Christianity, some passed into the pagan world, and some accepted rabbinic norms. The works of the great first century C.E. Alexandrian philosopher and mystic Philo are Hellenistic Judaism's finest surviving intellectual monument. Philo used Greek allegorical interpretation to show that the Mosaic revelation had anticipated and indeed excelled the truths later discovered by Greek philosophy. The historical writing of Josephus reflects the influence of Hellenistic historiography, as does Luke–Acts in the New Testament (see Chapter 13).

The Septuagint was Hellenistic Judaism's most influential legacy. The triumph of rabbinic Judaism meant that most of the LXX's influence would be on Christianity, specifically the Greek-speaking gentile church. As early as the New Testament itself, biblical quotations were often from the LXX. Indeed, the LXX gave Greek-speaking Christians access to Scripture.

In the Diaspora communities, gentile converts to Judaism were not uncommon. To convert required instruction, followed by self-baptism, reenacting the Exodus deliverance at the Red Sea. Men had to be circumcised, which may explain why many men remained "God-fearers," who participated to varying degrees in things Jewish but did not take the full step of conversion. But if their wives were Jewish, either by birth or conversion, their children were Jews.

The Nazareans

No discussion of the variety of denominations in classical Judaism would be complete without mention of the small messianic community that arose in the first century C.E. and went on to become the world's largest religion. The rabbis of the time called this movement *Nazareans,* because its adherents were followers of Jesus of Nazareth, known in rabbinic sources as "the Nazarene." They called themselves, according to the New Testament, *The Way.* In Antioch they were called *Christians,* the name that stuck. Five of the six remaining chapters of this book are devoted to the literary and historical worlds of this movement, so no more needs to be said here.

Conclusion

This survey should suffice to demonstrate that the first three centuries of classical Judaism were an age of variety and creativity. It was an age that hinged on two great crises for the Jewish community. The first, culminating in the Maccabean Wars, saw an old order pass away and a new order, rich, varied, and dynamic, emerge. The emerging new order survived the fall of the Hasmonaeans and the arrival of Rome and, with Rome, the House of Herod. The second great crisis was the Zealot War of national liberation against Rome (66–73 C.E.), in which the fall of Jerusalem and destruction of the Temple in 70 were the pivotal points.

The events of 70 led to the winnowing of the new order. Rabbinic Judaism emerged from the maelstrom as the normative form of Judaism, and the process of estrangement between traditional Judaism and the increasingly gentile Christian movement was exacerbated. The Second Jewish War with Rome (132–135 C.E.) widened the gulf. However, recent archaeological research, and the critical resifting of other historical data, suggests that final estrangement lay in the future, on the whole in the early Byzantine period, even later in the special case of Galilee. But that is far beyond the purview of this book.

THE LITERARY WORLD

During the period between 200 B.C.E. and 100 C.E., a variety of types of religious literature not found in the Jewish canon or New Testament emerged. Collectively, these works are sometimes labeled the "Intertestamental Literature" because, for the most part, they came into existence between the times in which the Old and New Testaments were written. In this section we will survey these various types and note some of the ways in which they reflect the literature of the Tanak and foreshadow the literature of the New Testament.

The Deuterocanon

The *Deuterocanon* ("Second Canon"), or *Apocrypha* ("Hidden Writings"), consists of works not found in the Tanak, but included in most Septuagint (LXX) manuscripts as well as most Greek and Latin copies of the Christian Old Testament.[4] It is widely assumed that these books were regarded as canonical by Hellenistic Jewish communities during this period even though they were not part of the Hebrew canon. As we have noted in Chapter 1 (see Table 1.1), the Roman Catholic and Eastern Orthodox Christian churches included works from this grouping in their canons. Most Protestant Churches consider the collection "apocryphal," because it was not part of the Hebrew canon. The designation "deuterocanonical" was adopted in the sixteenth century to reaffirm that although not part of the "first canon" (the Tanak), these writings should be regarded as having sacred authority. Scholars now prefer "Deuterocanon" as a more descriptive and neutral designation than the "Apocrypha," which has taken on pejorative connotations. We will summarize here all of the deuterocanonical works, both those found in Roman Catholic (and Anglican) Bibles and the additional writings most widely recognized by the Eastern Orthodox churches.

First Esdras and *First* and *Second Maccabees* are historical narratives. First Esdras (called Third Esdras in Roman Catholic Bibles) closely parallels sections of the Hebrew canon (2 Chronicles 35–36 and Nehemiah 7:38–8:12). First Maccabees covers the period from 168 to 134 B.C.E., when

---

[4]The New Revised Standard Version translation of the Deuterocanon, with introductions and notes for each of the books, is available in Bruce M. Metzger and Roland E. Murphy, eds. *The Oxford Annotated Bible with the Apocryphal/Deuterocanonical Books.* New York: Oxford University Press, 1991.

the Maccabean revolt threw off Seleucid control. A straightforward narrative, it is almost the only record of this important period. Second Maccabees parallels First Maccabees 1–7, but it stresses miracles and divine appearances. It develops a theological interpretation of history that holds that the persecution of the Jews by Antiochus was a form of discipline.

Tobit, Judith, Susanna, and *Bel and the Dragon* are, like Ruth and Esther, short stories that teach moral lessons. Like Ruth, Tobit shows how the righteousness of ordinary people is rewarded. Like Esther, Judith is a historical romance in which the heroic action of a woman saves her people from an oppressor. The other two works are among the additions to the Book of Daniel in the Apocrypha.

The *Wisdom of Solomon* and *Ecclesiasticus (the Wisdom of Jesus, the Son of Sirach)* are, like Proverbs, Job, and Ecclesiastes in the Tanak, examples of wisdom literature. The Wisdom of Solomon (sometimes called simply the Book of Wisdom) purports to be an address by King Solomon to the rulers of the world, showing that the ethical and religious wisdom of the Tanak is superior to the wisdom of the Gentiles. In fact, the work is a creative synthesis of ideas drawn from canonical wisdom writings (such as reward of the righteous and punishment of the evil) and Greek concepts (such as immortality of the soul). As in Proverbs 8 and Job 28, Wisdom is personified as an independent agent. Although there are no direct citations of the Wisdom of Solomon in the New Testament, the theme of a personified, pre-existent Wisdom (e.g., 9:1–4) may have been part of the background for the imagery of the pre-existent *Logos* in the prologue to the Gospel of John (1:1–18). In addition, the imagery of the "whole armor of God" (Wisdom of Solomon 5:17–20) was adapted by the Apostle Paul in several of his letters (Rom. 13:12; Cor. 6:7; Eph. 6:14–17). Ecclesiasticus (or Sirach), like Ecclesiastes, is an old teacher's collected wisdom. The work is an anthology of aphorisms, brief essays, hymns to Wisdom, reflections on existence, and advice on proper conduct. Its style and view of life are similar to those found in Proverbs. Its famous catalog of heroes (44:1–51:24) may be the inspiration for a similar passage in the New Testament Letter to the Hebrews (11:1–12:2).

The *Additions to the Book of Esther* gives Esther an overtly religious dimension lacking in the Hebrew story. *The Story of Susanna* tells how a virtuous matron was saved from execution as an adulteress by the young man Daniel. He exposed the false accusation by two sordid old men when he examined them separately before the court, and justice was done. (Some consider it propaganda for Pharisaic jurisprudence.) *Bel and the Dragon* shows Daniel exposing fraudulent pagan priests and killing a snake that pagans regarded as a god. The other *Additions to Daniel* (the *Prayer of Azariah* and the *Song of the Three Young Men*) is a collection of devotional poems. The *Letter of Jeremiah* uses the letter form, which became popular in the New Testament. It purports to be a letter from the prophet Jeremiah to the leaders of Judah about to be deported to Babylon, warning them of the dangers of idolatry.

Second Esdras (called Fourth Esdras in Roman Catholic Bibles) is, like Daniel, an apocalyptic work, with visions giving symbols of the end of history. Included is an interesting explanation of the origin of the canon and the extracanonical works that claims that Ezra restored by inspiration the "twenty-four" books of Scripture and wrote seventy more reserved for the "wise."

Baruch is a composite work, including a confession of sins (linked to Jeremiah's secretary, Baruch), a poem linking Wisdom and Torah (*cf.* Sirach 24), and poems of hope and comfort.

The *Prayer of Manasseh* is a poem the wicked King Manasseh (2 Kings 21) ostensibly composed while in exile in Babylon, repenting of his sins. The Council of Trent removed it from the Deuterocanon and made it, along with First and Second Esdras (Third and Fourth Esdras), an appendix to the canon.

The Larger Apocrypha

The *Larger Apocrypha* is the term we have selected to denote Jewish religious writings from this period that are not regarded as canonical by any substantial Jewish or Christian group today. They are most commonly collected and published under the title *Pseudepigrapha*. However, a pseudepigraph is a work attributed to a famous person (such as Enoch, Noah, Moses, or Isaiah) who did not actually write it, and only some of the works in this group are of that type (pseudonymous). The Larger Apocrypha is less a coherent collection than a set of writings brought together by modern scholars. The following summary is representative of the types of literature within the collection.

The *Letter of Aristeas* includes the legend of the translation of the Septuagint. *Third Maccabees* is a legend that, like Esther, explains the origin of a Jewish festival. *Fourth Maccabees* is a philosophical essay on the question: Can reason rule the passions? The two works attributed to Enoch exploit the Tanak's mysterious note that Enoch was taken by God and walked with the deity (Gen. 5:24), to spell out what Enoch saw while on his heavenly stroll. *First Enoch* (called *Ethiopic Enoch* because it was preserved in an Ethiopian Christian community) is a complex anthology of apocalyptic visions, theological history, primitive science (astronomy), sayings about the Messiah, announcement of judgment by one called the Son of Man (interpreting Daniel 7), and an interpretation of Genesis. *Second Enoch* (*Slavonic Enoch*, so named because it survived only in a Slavonic translation) reveals the mysteries of creation seen by Enoch.

The *Sibylline Oracles* uses the device of a sibyl (the Greek name for an inspired woman who utters predictions of imminent events) to continue the prophetic tradition of announcing judgment on idolatry and the climax of history. *The Greek Apocalypse of Baruch* (Third Baruch) is a description of Baruch's journey through five heavens, where he learns cosmic mysteries. *The Syriac Apocalypse of Baruch* (Second Baruch) is another report of visions, similar to Second Esdras and Revelation.

Jubilees is named after the division of world history into periods of forty-nine years of "jubilees" (see Leviticus 25). In form, it is a commentary on the first section of the Pentateuch. *The Psalms of Solomon* is a collection of eighteen sacred songs emphasizing Torah obedience and reflections similar to those in the Psalms found among the Dead Sea Scrolls. *The Testament of the Twelve Patriarchs* purports to be the last testaments of the sons of Jacob, with advice that seems influenced by Hellenistic moral philosophy and with several apocalyptic sections. *The Assumption of Moses* alludes to an ascension of Moses into heaven, but includes only exhortation ostensibly given to Joshua (including several apocalyptic predictions). *The Martyrdom and Ascension of Isaiah* is a compilation of three short works: a commentary on 2 Kings 21, a Christian prophecy, and a description of Isaiah's journey through the seven heavens. *The Life of Adam and Eve* is a tale that picks up the action after Adam and Eve have been expelled from Eden, coupled with an apocalypse attributed to Moses. A respected English translation of the Larger Apocrypha includes these with twenty other apocalyptic writings and thirty-one other miscellaneous works.[5]

The influence of themes and imagery found in the *Larger Apocrypha* on the New Testament has been noted, especially in apocalyptic passages. For example, the impact of imagery associated with the Son of Man who will come at the end of time to judge the world when the new age comes found in texts such as 1 Enoch 37–71 is evident in the gospels (e.g., Mark 8:38).

The Dead Sea Scrolls

The *Dead Sea Scrolls* are the writings found in about a dozen caves in the hills on the western shore of the Dead Sea, near the ruins of the Covenanters' community at Qumran. The scrolls include canonical and deuterocanonical works, but also a number of noncanonical writings from this period. The scrolls were most likely the library of the Qumran community. Many of the scrolls were copies of books from the Tanak, the Deuterocanon, and the Larger Apocrypha. Others were apocalyptic

---

[5]James H. Charlesworth, ed. *The Old Testament Pseudepigrapha*, 2 vols. New York: Doubleday, 1983 and 1985. *Note:* Affordable, paperback editions were published in 2010.

commentaries on biblical books, written from a sectarian viewpoint, and collections of biblical verses esteemed by the community. The biblical documents have been of great value for the study of the history of the text of Tanak. However, some scrolls were original sectarian compositions. These, along with the apocalyptic commentaries, supply historians with firsthand information about a group concerning which little was previously known. Our discussion of early classical Jewish denominations (above) showed that this group was quite distinct from rabbinic–pharisaic Judaism or from early Christianity, particularly on the crucial Jewish issue of *halakah*. They simply represent a very different part of the spectrum. Thus, the scrolls communicate no direct evidence on the origins of rabbinic Judaism or Christianity, but they contribute significantly to understanding the larger background of both.

The Community Rule and *The Damascus Covenant Document* were manuals of community organization and practice. The latter had been known since copies were found in a Cairo synagogue around the turn of the twentieth century, but fragments have also turned up at Qumran. *The War Scroll* describes the great final struggle between the Sons of Light and the Sons of Darkness that is to usher in God's Kingdom on earth. *The Temple Scroll* offers an idealized reconstruction of Jerusalem, especially the Temple, in the form of instructions from God to Moses. It may have been intended to be a sixth book of the Torah! A number of original sectarian *Thanksgiving Psalms*, reflecting intense piety, were found. *The Habakkuk Commentary* was the most complete of the apocalyptic commentaries that read Scripture like a current newspaper, an interpretative approach that is still used. This summary only scratches the surface of the total scroll inventory.[6]

All of the original scrolls found were quickly published by scholars at Hebrew University and at the American Schools of Oriental Research. All of the later discoveries that came directly to Israeli scholars (such as the Temple Scroll) and quite a few other documents (such as the Cave 11 Psalms scroll) were also published. But much of the fragmentary material from Cave IV, the richest trove of all, remained unpublished. A festering scholarly scandal was recently resolved when the Huntington Library in California released a complete set of photographs of the scrolls that had come into its collection. The established scrolls editorial team was also reorganized and enlarged with goals set for full publication. The delay in full publication has fed a number of conspiracy theories. (For example, the scrolls were being suppressed by Roman Catholic or Orthodox Jewish authorities who feared their contents.) The falsity of such views should soon be demonstrated. The generalization in our initial paragraph represents the views of the majority of scrolls scholars. However, any discovery as dramatic as the scrolls is likely to continue to generate far-fetched theories pandered to in sensationalist publications for years to come.

The influence of the sectarian scrolls on New Testament writings is a source of ongoing scholarly inquiry. For example, the imagery of "Sons of Light," which is found in a variety of New Testament books (e.g., Luke 16:8, John 12:36, 1st Thess. 5:5), is not found in the Tanak or rabbinic literature, but is common in the *Manual of Discipline* and *The War Scroll*.

Rabbinic Literature

Rabbinic literature refers to the body of traditions of pharisaic Judaism that were circulated orally throughout most of this period and first published in written form around 200 C.E., although private written sources had existed earlier alongside oral traditions. Its literary history is so complex that, like the documents of the Tanak and the New Testament, it cannot be used uncritically as historical data. Used with care, it provides a rich source for understanding the circles that created and preserved

---

[6]For an English translation of the scrolls, see Geza Vermes. *The Complete Dead Sea Scrolls in English,* rev. ed. New York: Penguin, 2004.

it and the historical world in which they lived.[7] An influential group of scholars had argued on the basis of form criticism that the entire Mishnah was created after the disaster of 70 C.E. and hence provided no accurate information about earlier times. The "assured results" of form criticism of the New Testament gospels were sometimes cited in evidence. But 4QMMT, the Dead Sea Scroll discussed previously, shows conclusively that Mishnaic traditions preserve accurate memories of halakic disputes back to the second century B.C.E. If some traditions, why not more? This does not prove the historic validity of all Mishnaic traditions, but it reminds us again of the tenacity of oral tradition. It warns against excessive reliance on techniques of literary historical analysis that lack external control. And it may suggest that some applications of form criticism in other studies should be reevaluated.

Rabbinic traditions, as noted, are divided into the two categories of authority, *halakah* and *haggadah*. Halakah (meaning "the way," "the path") lays down obligatory principles on the way people should order their personal and communal lives. Haggadah ("narration") is devotional, inspirational, edifying lore. It does not command, but it helps one understand God and the holy life. The literature itself can be sorted into three major categories: the talmudic, the midrashic, and the targumic.

The heart of the talmudic tradition is the *Mishnah*, which is simply the rabbinic oral Torah reduced to writing. Officially published about 200 C.E. by Rabbi Judah the Prince, its contents are not exclusively halakic, although halakah dominates. Eventually, the later rabbinic discussions of Mishnah, anecdotes about the rabbis of the Mishnah and traditions about how mishnaic decisions were reached, and a great variety of other lore were added to the Mishnah. This elaboration was known as *Gemara* ("tradition"). The combination of Mishnah and Gemara is the Talmud, the great repository of rabbinic lore. There are two editions of the Talmud, one with a Gemara edited in the academies of Babylon and one with a Gemara edited in the academy of Tiberias in Galilee, both dating from around 500 C.E. The former is the more authoritative.

Midrash, or biblical interpretation, is of two sorts. *Halakic midrash* may be made only on the legal sections of the biblical Torah. *Haggadic midrash* may be made on any part of the Tanak. Indeed, there are haggadic passages in what are regarded as halakic midrashim. The largest collection of midrashic lore, *Midrash Rabbah* ("the Great Midrash"), is haggadic and treats every book of the Tanak.

Targum describes the *ad hoc* oral translations into Aramaic that synagogue readers made of the lessons from Hebrew Scripture after Aramaic became the common language of Israel and neighboring areas. Greater care was required in translating the Torah lesson than the second lesson, but both types tended to be expansive and interpretive. Eventually several written targums on the Tanak were published.

The Babylonian Talmud and the classical halakic midrashim remain authoritative for traditionally observant Jews.

A number of the literary forms found in rabbinic literature were utilized by New Testament authors. For example, many of the parables of Jesus in the New Testament gospels are similar in style to rabbinic parables. The Apostle Paul, himself a rabbi (*cf.* Chapter 14), frequently draws on rabbinic literary forms and devices in his letters to churches. For example, Paul's retelling of the story of Abraham in Romans 4 is an example of *haggadic midrash*.

---

[7]English translations of rabbinic literature include Herbert Danby. *The Mishnah.* London: Oxford, 1933; Jacob Neusner. *The Mishnah: A New Translation.* New Haven: Yale University Press, 1991; the multivolume *Soncino Talmud* and *Midrash Rabbah* (London: Soncino Press, 1978); and Lawrence H. Schiffmann. *Texts and Traditions: A Source Reader for the Study of Second Temple Judaism.* New York: KTAV Publishing House, 1998. For introductions, see Jacob Neusner. *The Mishnah: An Introduction* and *The Midrash: An Introduction.* Jason Aronson, 1994, 1990; and Adin Steinsaltz. *The Essential Talmud.* Basic Books, 2006.

Summary

This chapter highlighted the significant historical developments and movements and the Jewish literature of the period between 200 B.C.E. and 100 C.E. Our thesis was that this was one of the most vital and creative eras in religious history.

Our historical commentary described the Maccabean revolt, climaxing in the liberation of the Temple in 164 B.C.E. and leading to a brief resurgence of Jewish independence in the homeland. Roman invasion and subjugation marked the end of this period.

In these tumultuous times, a number of new groups arose in Judaism. They included the Pharisees, a pietistic and scholarly lay party; Sadducees, aristocrats, and priests who often opposed the Pharisees; Essenes; Covenanters of the apocalyptic community near the Dead Sea, from whom the famous Dead Sea Scrolls came; militaristic Zealots; the marginalized Samaritans; and the group called by rabbis the Nazareans. In this chapter we discussed these groups as well as common Judaism and the so-called people of the land.

We also touched on the important influence of Hellenistic (Greek) culture on many Jews during this time.

Our literary analysis briefly surveyed the writings known to Christians as the Deuterocanon (or Apocrypha) and the Pseudepigrapha (or, more appropriately, Larger Apocrypha). We also identified the sectarian documents of the Dead Sea Scrolls and the types of rabbinic literature from this important period.

The importance of this era for the development of an understanding of both Judaism and Christianity cannot be overemphasized. The writings of this period (except Daniel) did not attain canonical status in the Tanak. (The Deuterocanon is Scriptural for a substantial part of Christianity.) Even so, some of this literature and the groups for which it was written shaped Judaism as it is still known today and provided the principal milieu for the origin and early development of Christianity. Any serious student of the Bible will find the material introduced in this chapter a fertile field for further study.

The Contemporary World

Case Study

The Contemporary Religious Spectrum

In this chapter, a comparison was suggested between various movements within Judaism during the period between 200 B.C.E. and 100 C.E. and the different Christian denominations today. Drawing on the historical discussion of these Jewish groups and the literature associated with them, attempt to translate them into the contemporary world. For example, might the Sadducees be compared with "high church" Christian denominations that emphasize purity of ritual? Might the Essenes be compared with groups such as the Old Order Amish? Could the Covenanters at Qumran be compared

with one of the many Christian groups that has withdrawn from society to prepare for the apocalypse by developing their own, unique interpretation of the Hebrew Bible (such as the Branch Davidians)? With whom today would you compare the Pharisees, the Zealots, the Samaritans, the People of the Land, or Hellenistic Jews? If you have studied modern Judaism, consider to what degree is the spectrum described in this chapter reflected in the Orthodox, Conservative, and Reform branches today. If you have studied other religions, compare the spectrum of movements within Judaism discussed in this chapter with movements within religions such as Islam, Hinduism, and Buddhism today.

Questions for Discussion and Reflection

1. *Read Daniel 1–6: Legends of Daniel and His Friends:*
   Note: The Book of Daniel (introduced in Chapter 9) illuminates Jewish life during the period covered in this chapter.
   a. What can you infer from these stories about Jewish customs and moral and religious teachings at the time these stories were told?
   b. What were some of the problems confronted by the Jewish community that are reflected in these stories? How does the book suggest that these problems be dealt with? Who confronts similar problems today?

2. *Read the Book of Tobit (in the Deuterocanon):*
   Note: Tobit is a quest tale, like the Holy Grail legends, or Tolkien's *Lord of the Rings.* It was probably written in the second century B.C.E., in the early classical period of Jewish history.
   a. Tobit and his family are all regarded as virtuous Jews. Note those aspects of their lives that the story portrays as virtuous. Based on Tobit, make a list of Jewish virtues. Do these virtues still seem appropriate today?
   b. Tobit incorporates many traditional themes of folklore, such as the quest, the hidden treasure, the mysterious companion, and the cursed bride. See how many of these themes you can identify. How does the story use them in a refreshing and sometimes humorous way, so the story does not become hackneyed?
   c. As a "morality tale," is Tobit still relevant today?

3. *Read First Maccabees 1–4 (in the Deuterocanon):*
   Note: The book of 1 Maccabees in the Deuterocanon is a work of history, like Samuel and Kings in the Former Prophets. As in Samuel and Kings, God's presence and influence are presumed, but God is not a character in the story. 1 Maccabees carries on the tradition of Hebraic historiography. But coming as it does from the early classical period in Judaism, it also reflects the influence of Hellenistic literature. Through the story of the purification and rededication of the Temple, the basis of the Feast of Hannukah is laid.

   Compare the accounts of the exploits of Mattathias and Judas and his brothers to stories about Saul, David, Joshua, and the Judges that you have read. How is it like those stories? What features do you note that differ from the narratives in the Former Prophets that may reflect Hellenistic literary influence? What themes and motifs do you note that may remind you of the Ancestor narratives or the Moses tradition?

4. *Read Tractate Aboth: Chapters 1–3 (in the Mishnah):*
   Note: The Tractate Aboth of the Mishnah is a collection of favorite aphorisms of the great teachers of Rabbinic Judaism from "The Men of the Great Synagogue (or Academy)," traditional scholars of Persian and Hellenistic times, down to the time of Rabbi Judah the Prince, the editor of the Mishnah. It is often published separately as "Sayings of the Jewish Fathers." Look for a copy in a library. Note the teachings attributed to some of the great masters you have read, or will read about in this book: Hillel, Shammai, Rabbi Judah the Prince, the high priest Simon the Just, and the charismatic Hanina ben Dosa.

   Which of these sayings do you find particularly appealing or potentially helpful? Which do you find confusing or troubling? (Save your notes on Aboth to compare with Jesus's teachings when you study Chapter 11.)

Chapter # 11

Jesus of Nazareth

Sunset on the Sea of Galilee. Much of Jesus's ministry was conducted around the shores of this freshwater lake. His disciples Andrew, Peter, James, and John had earned their livings as fisherman on the lake, known in Hebrew as Chinnereth. Herod Antipas built the lovely town of Tiberias (noted for its hot springs) on the western shore to replace Sepphoris as his capital. The great rabbinic academy relocated in Tiberias after a brief period in Sepphoris following the savaging of Judah during the second war with Rome. *Source:* Gordon N. Converse

Is it possible to write a life of Jesus? Many people would regard this as a silly question. The New Testament contains not one, but four lives of Jesus. Every historical era since the first century has seen the production of lives of Jesus of *some* sort. The shelves of bookstores and libraries are full of them. Of course one can write a life of Jesus, several if one pleases and has time. Before the end of this chapter we will offer our own "brief life of Jesus."

When we inspect the lives of Jesus that have been written, it turns out that there are several different sorts. We confine ourselves in this observation to serious attempts at history or biography. We can safely exclude from discussion fad works that try to connect Jesus with the latest trend in pop culture (such as several during the 1960s that tried to prove Jesus was the leader of a drug cult). We can also pass over devotional works portraying Jesus as the world's best salesman or using some other gimmick to attract readership.

Readers should also beware of books that seek to distance Jesus from the Jewish world of his time, or that give a very negative account of the Judaism of Jesus's time (presumably to make his teachings look better). Prof. Amy-Jill Levine has identified seven distortions and misconceptions of Jesus and first-century Judaism that continue to plague biblical scholarship[1]:

- That Jewish Law was so burdensome, no one could follow the commandments.
- That all Jews desired a militant Messiah who would defeat the Roman occupation and rejected Jesus because he taught a path of peace.
- That Jesus was a feminist in a Jewish culture that mistreated and despised women.
- That Jews at the time were obsessed with purity rules while Jesus broke through these barriers.
- That Judaism was dominated by a Temple system that oppressed poor people and women and promoted unbridgeable divisions between "insiders" and "outsiders."
- That Jews were clannish and xenophobic while Jesus and his followers reached out and embraced the "other."
- That the New Testament is referring to "Judeans," not "Jews," a misguided attempt by scholars to distance the New Testament from the charge it is anti-Jewish.

In fact, as Levine argues persuasively, Jesus cannot be understood unless he is understood through the lens of first-century Judaism. Jesus dressed like a Jew, prayed like a Jew, instructed other Jews on how best to be obedient to the commandments revealed by God to Moses, argued like a Jew, and, like many other Jews at the time, was crucified by the Roman government.

Readers should also be on guard for anachronistic portrayals that do not fit the Jewish village agrarian world recovered by archaeology (which also is the world portrayed in the canonical Gospels), such as making Jesus out as a Hellenized philosopher.

Before the advent of critical historical writing, serious attempts to reconstruct the life of Jesus were essentially harmonized retellings of the gospels, often following John's implied chronology and perhaps elaborated from extracanonical sources, usually the authors' imaginations. Such "traditional" biographies continue to be written.

The introduction of critical historiographic techniques into the study of the New Testament has led to several different sorts of treatments of the life of Jesus. During the nineteenth century, critical scholars engaged in the so-called *quest for the historical Jesus* sought to disengage the "Jesus of history" from that "creation of superstition," "the Christ of faith." Some concluded that Jesus was entirely a mythical creation and that there is no historical evidence a historical Jesus ever existed. This effort was somewhat embarrassed by an increasing recognition that its selection of data seemed

---

[1] See Amy-Jill Levine. *The Misunderstood Jew: The Church and the Scandal of the Jewish Jesus.* San Francisco: HarperSanFrancisco, 2006, 124–166, 20.

to be dictated by a particular ideological agenda and a lack of serious attention to the historical evidence. Although largely discredited by serious historians, the claim that there is no proof the Jesus of history existed is still being made by writers today.[2]

Some New Testament specialists reacted by going to the opposite extreme and declaring that the "Jesus of history" (if there was one) is unknowable. It was impossible, they held, to get behind the interpretation of Jesus in the gospels to any actual events. However, some scholars who were suspected (or accused) of such views had not in fact quite thrown in the historical sponge. Rather, a more circumspect account of the life of Jesus resulted, in which the historians "said what could be said" without trying to write a full biography. The so-called new quest for the historical Jesus fell into this pattern. Although we do not subscribe fully to this approach, our work may be grouped with it in a general way.

A group of scholars known as "The Jesus Seminar" has attracted a good deal of attention recently. The Seminar was originally an interest group formed in the Society of Biblical Literature to study the question of which (if any) of the sayings attributed to Jesus by the Gospels he actually said. We have noted some of the criteria used by scholars to determine authentic sayings of Jesus below. The Jesus Seminar developed a much more detailed set of criteria that are set forth in logical format in their publications. About a hundred New Testament scholars became regular participants in the study, and many more were occasional participants. Although it was not part of their original program, members decided to record their collective opinion of respective sayings by dropping colored balls in a box, rather like voting on members for a lodge or fraternity. A red ball meant Jesus definitely said it, pink that he probably said it, gray that he probably did not, and black that he definitely did not. The results of these votes, annotated by summaries of the discussions beforehand, were published as *The Five Gospels* (the four canonical gospels plus the Coptic Gospel of Thomas, an early sayings collection of great interest to modern scholars; see Chapters 12 and 15). There have been highly emotional outbursts against the work of the Seminar from various quarters. On a substantive level, the work of the Seminar suffered from two serious methodological flaws. First, a substantial number of Seminar members lacked the background in Jewish studies to make the judgments they attempted. Second, it is unlikely that anyone (other than a mainframe computer) could reliably manipulate the number of criteria identified by the Seminar, some of which seem in addition to be quite subjective. One should, however, note in defense of the Jesus Seminar that their publications have included extensive notes explaining the considerations that led to their conclusions so that persons of judicious temperament may arrive at their own judgment concerning particular texts. Having completed its work on Jesus's sayings, the Seminar has turned to the Gospel reports of things Jesus did.[3]

If the question "Is it possible to write a life of Jesus?" can be translated as: "Can you prove (or disprove) the theological claims that the gospels (or the Apostle Paul, or later Christians) make about Jesus?," then the answer must be no. Historical method cannot answer theological questions. It might clarify such questions. For instance, it can discover what such religious ideas as *messiah* or *son of God* could have meant to various groups of people in particular times and places. If some fraud or forgery had been committed in the formulation and transmission of traditions, it might be found out. But whether Jesus was *really* the Messiah or the Son of God (*whatever* those titles mean) is beyond the power of history to show.

---

[2]See, for example, Timothy Freke and Peter Gandy. *The Jesus Mysteries: Was the "Original Jesus" a Pagan God?* New York: Three Rivers Press, 2001.

[3]Robert W. Funk and the Jesus Seminar. *The Acts of Jesus: What Did Jesus Really Do? The Search for Authentic Deeds of Jesus.* San Francisco, CA: HarperSanFrancisco, 1998; *The Five Gospels: What Did Jesus Actually Say? The Search for the Authentic Words of Jesus.* San Francisco: HarperOne, 1996; and *The Gospel of Jesus: According to the Jesus Seminar.* Santa Rosa, CA: Polebridge Press, 1999.

Historians can reconstruct the lineaments of the world in which Jesus was supposed to have lived, the world of the first century in the Roman Empire, more precisely, the world of Judaism in the Jewish homeland of Israel. This picture can be enlivened by the stock of well-documented events from that general time and place. They can also sift available materials that purport to bear upon things that Jesus said or did according to critical historical canons. Out of building blocks such as these, a picture can be constructed, rather as the bits of data laboriously radioed back by a spacecraft can be assembled by a computer into a recognizable image. And, just as a computer program can erase the static from a spacecraft picture and enhance its imagery, so techniques of literary and historical analysis and models borrowed from the social sciences can enhance the historical picture. But it will not be a complete biography.

Responsible historians and biographers are guided by the data and report their findings dispassionately, whether those findings are congenial or not congenial to their own convictions. Writing Jesus's biography is a particularly challenging enterprise. It compounds the normal problems and hazards of ancient history and biography with the passion of religious belief or disbelief. It raises the temptation to press history into the service of personal doctrinal views, whether those views are friendly or hostile to religion in general or to Christianity in particular. The more radical reconstructions proposed by some scholars[4] has led to a riposte from evangelical quarters.[5] One must indeed suppose that some New Questers are primarily motivated by the desire to find a Jesus whom they could, without embarrassment, take down for a drink with their secular humanist colleagues at the University Club. Professor Paula Fredriksen, one of the most competent scholars in the New Quest, remarked that anachronism is the new docetism. (Docetism was the early heresy that denied Jesus was a real person.) She was referring to the way in which some scholars read the claims about Christ of the fourth- and fifth-century Church councils back into the New Testament. But not all anachronism is orthodox. Some of the better selling books on the historical Jesus portray him in ways that do not comport with our knowledge of Judaism in the early first century or with the overall evidence from the Gospels critically considered. Some transpose the social background of a Hellenized and more urbanized Galilee back into Jesus's time, although archaeology shows these developments came fifty to a hundred years after the time of Jesus. Some seem to try to distance Jesus from Judaism, although his Jewishness is a given in all the literary sources. Here, it is not improper to observe, "Not a bad theory, if facts don't matter."[6]

EVIDENCE OUTSIDE THE GOSPELS

It is no secret that the gospels lodge certain religious claims about Jesus and appear to have been written precisely to advance those claims. This requires the historian to approach them with care as historic sources. Because the prudent historian adopts a "worst possible case" mentality about the subject, it is advisable to approach the question of a life of Jesus independently of the gospels. That is, one can ask if there is information outside the gospels and, indeed, outside the New Testament that documents Jesus as a historical person. If the answer is affirmative, then one can proceed to see what can be learned of Jesus from these sources. Otherwise, one is thrown back on the canonical materials for whatever may be made of them.

---

[4]See, for example, James Tabor. *The Jesus Dynasty: The Hidden History of Jesus, His Royal Family, and the Birth of Christianity.* New York: Simon & Schuster, 2007.

[5]See, for example, Craig A. Evans. *Fabricating Jesus: How Modern Scholars Distort the Gospels.* Downers Gove, IL: Intervarsity Press, 2008; Richard Bauckham. *Jesus and the Eyewitnesses: The Gospels as Eyewitness Testimony.* Grand Rapids, MI: Eerdmans, 2008; and Ben Witherington III. *What Have They Done With Jesus?* San Francisco: HarperOne, 2007.

[6]E. P. Saunders has provided an excellent brief account of Galilee in the time of Jesus, *cf.* E. P. Saunders. "Jesus in Galilee." *Jesus: A Colloquium in the Holy Land,* ed. Doris Donnelly. New York: Continuum, 2001, pp. 5–26.

Church of the Nativity, Bethlehem. A small, decorated grotto in the Orthodox Christian Church of the Nativity in Bethlehem, Israel, marks the spot venerated as the birthplace of Jesus of Nazareth.   *Source:* Independent Picture Service/ Alamy

There are relatively few extracanonical references to Jesus in near-contemporary classical sources. This is hardly surprising. Jesus may have been supremely important among his circle of devotees, but they were few in number and not at all prominent in a world where wonder-workers, religious teachers, and martyrs to Roman authority were quite commonplace. However, for authentic history, the quality of sources is much more important than their number. Two of the early non-Christian references to Jesus stand out precisely because of their quality.

Josephus, who was mentioned in Chapter 10, was a young Jewish aristocrat who served the father–son team of generals and future Flavian emperors, Vespasian and Titus. He was captured during the first revolt against Rome. After the war, he embarked on a literary career, patronized by the Flavian house. He sought further understanding of his people and managed in his writings to be both pro-Roman and pro-Jewish. Josephus is generally regarded as a reliable reporter where his own reputation is not at stake. Indeed, his writings are treasured as the best source on the last few centuries of Jewish history prior to and during the first Jewish revolt against Rome in 67 C.E.[7]

Josephus's writings include several references to Jesus, as well as mention of John the Baptizer and James, the brother of Jesus. The reference to the Baptizer in the *Antiquities* (18:116–119) does not connect John to Jesus in any way. It differs in matters of interpretation (including Herod's motives) from the gospel accounts of the Baptizer's arrest and execution at the hands of Herod Antipas. But it is of interest in confirming the historicity of an important figure in the gospels and the manner and agent of his death.

---

[7]The works of Josephus are available in translation, See, for example, Flavius Josephus. *Josephus: The Complete Works,* trans. William Whiston. Nashville: Thomas Nelson, 2003.

The direct references to Jesus are more important, but (not amazingly) more controversial. A succinct account in the eighteenth book of the *Antiquities* (18:63–64) notes Jesus's role as a religious teacher, his Crucifixion under Pontius Pilate, the traditions of his Resurrection, and the notion that the prophets had foretold a great deal about him. Much of the language in this passage would be fitting from Josephus's pen only if he had become a Christian, *which he had not,* even decades after the publication of *Antiquities.* Thus, the passage, if authentic in its core, must have been retouched by later pious Christian editors.

A similar but much stronger judgment adheres to a longer and more fulsome account in the Slavonic translation of *The Jewish War* (204:1–45). Whether the passage in question was even a part of the original Greek or Aramaic text of the *War* has been disputed. If it does include an authentic core, its adulatory language about Jesus strongly suggests heavy Christian editing.

The most important reference to Jesus occurs in a passage about his brother, James, in the twentieth book of the *Antiquities* (20:199–203). Like the reference to the Baptizer, it is interesting for its confirmation of yet another New Testament character, thus lending general authenticity to that body of tradition. But its reference to Jesus is even more interesting. Josephus identified James as "the brother of Jesus, the *alleged* Christ." When the fourth-century Christian historian Eusebius cited this passage, he inverted Josephus's Greek word order so that it read something more like "Jesus, who is called Christ," rather than "the alleged" or "so-called" Christ.

Unlike the passages noted previously in Josephus, this is precisely the sort of reference to Jesus we might expect from a Jewish writer who was not a Christian convert. It informs us that there was a person named Jesus whom Josephus regarded as a messianic pretender, that is, for whom messianic claims were made that Josephus did not credit, and that this Jesus had a brother named James. All of this squares with information in the gospels and other parts of the New Testament. It is particularly impressive to the historian because of the innocent and offhand manner of its presentation. Forgers and interpolators are generally much more ponderous, serious, and heavy-handed.

The other important classical treatment of Jesus is found in the *Annals* of the Roman historian Publius Cornelius Tacitus, a near-contemporary of Josephus. Tacitus narrated the great fire in Rome in the fifteenth book of the *Annals,* his last and greatest work. He noted that when Nero was unable to allay the widespread suspicion that the fire had been started on an imperial order, the emperor blamed it on the Christians and subjected them to vile and vicious treatment in public spectacles. As a good, conservative senatorial moralist, Tacitus held oriental religions in deep contempt and wasted few tears on the victims, although he recognized that Nero's wanton cruelty produced public sympathy for the Christians. But Tacitus was also a good historian and therefore felt obliged to explain who the pitiful, if detestable, victims were. They were named, he said, from Christus (using the Greek title as a proper name) "… who suffered the extreme penalty during the reign of Tiberius at the hands of one of our procurators, Pontius Pilate, and the pernicious superstition was checked for a moment, only to break out once more not merely in Judaea, the home of the disease, but in the capital itself, where all things horrible or shameful in the world collect and find a vogue" (*Annals* 15:44).[8]

Tacitus did not cite his source or sources of information, but he was not a credulous individual. Further, given his negative attitude toward things Eastern, he would probably have included anything less favorable about the Christians than their connection with an executed criminal, such as fraudulent origins, had he known such. Tacitus's Tiberian date for Jesus corresponds with the explicit statement of Lk. 3:1 and the implications of Luke 2 and Matthew 2 that Jesus was born during the reigns of Augustus and Herod the Great, near the time of Herod's death. It is also congruent with the observation of Lk. 3:23 that Jesus was about thirty at the onset of his public career.

---

[8]Tacitus. *The Annals, Loeb Classical Library,* trans. John Jackson. Cambridge, MA: Harvard University Press, 1937, pp. 283 (*cf.* pp. 270–285).

The Synagogue, Capernaum.
Archaeologists now believe that
this handsome classical house of
prayer and study was constructed
in the fourth to fifth centuries C.E.,
rather than in the third century,
as previously thought. The
synagogue where Jesus taught
probably stood on this same site.
The traditional site of Simon
Peter's house was nearby and was
occupied early in Christian history
by a "house church" and later by
an octagonal Byzantine church.
That such a fine synagogue
could be built so near a church
after Christianity became the
established religion of the Roman
Empire suggests harmonious
relations between the Jewish and
gentile Christians and traditional
Jews in Israel   *Source:* William A.
Young

A more detailed study would consider the less important pagan references to Jesus and early Christianity and the implications that can be drawn from references in rabbinic sources, themselves too late to be considered direct evidence. The two central references we have discussed should be adequate to establish that Jesus was in fact a historic personage. At any rate, they would be considered adequate for anyone other than Jesus. And they anchor several important data about Jesus that can be gathered from the New Testament. He lived during the reign of Tiberius. He was executed on orders of the Roman procurator Pontius Pilate. Messianic claims were lodged on his behalf whether he made them or not. He had a brother named James, a pietist of some prominence who was killed in Jerusalem shortly before the outbreak of the first revolt.

THE GOSPELS AS SOURCES: WHERE DID JESUS "FIT?"

One must avoid the temptation to jump from this independent confirmation of New Testament material to a naive reliance on the gospels as historical sources. Form criticism and redaction criticism (see Chapter 2) offer evidence that the traditions contained in the gospels were shaped to meet the needs, concerns, and interests of the developing church. Redaction criticism tries to demonstrate how the respective gospels crafted traditions to emphasize their particular insights. These matters will be explored in Chapter 12. This preliminary note indicates why it would be irresponsible to take the gospels at face value as historic sources.

It would be equally irresponsible to ignore the value of the Gospels as historic sources. If only pristine, unbiased sources could be used by historians, there would be very little history written. As it is, historians know quite well how to use both friendly and unfriendly sources. Critical Jesus history could be written on the basis of the Gospels alone. Fortunately for New Testament historians, that is not necessary.

Some form critics seem to assume as an axiom that the church of the Hellenistic world was not only the place where the gospel traditions were shaped but also their place of origin. If this were the case, the gospels would be quite useless as historical sources on Jesus. However, recent research has suggested that a substantial proportion of the tradition units in the gospels reflects a background in first-century "homeland Judaism." Further, some larger units (e.g., the Q cycle, discussed in Chapter 12, and the Gospel of Matthew) might have been shaped against a background in or near the Jewish homeland. A recent work by James D. G. Dunn suggests that more can be learned from the Synoptic gospels about the actual words and acts of Jesus than some scholars of earlier generations had supposed (see the following text and Chapter 12).

There is a strong consensus among historians and New Testament scholars that the following historical assertions about Jesus are almost certainly true:

He was a Galilean Jew of the early first century C.E.

He was a teacher and wonder-worker and taught a love doctrine.

Messianic claims were made for him.

He was executed by Pontius Pilate during the reign of Tiberius.

These assertions are warranted from the non-Christian sources noted earlier and by critical use of the gospels. Additional historical assertions are of course made, but not with the same unanimity.

Gospel specialists have devised several criteria to judge which sayings attributed to Jesus by the gospels are authentic. Some of these criteria may also be applied to stories about Jesus. These include:

Multiple attestation	Reported in more than one *independent* source
Linguistic suitability	Readily translatable back into Aramaic or Hebrew
Coherence	Consistent with other well-authenticated traditions
Embarrassing reports	Sayings (or stories) not in the interest of the early church (disparaging Gentiles, e.g.; *cf.* Mt. 15:26)

A final criterion, dissimilarity, would find little support among historians or anthropologists and is questioned by many literary analysts. It basically says that a saying that can be paralleled in first-century Jewish or Hellenistic moral and religious teaching, or the teaching of the early church (!), is probably not authentic. In other words, Jesus's teaching has to be unique. This seems to assert some sort of theological belief, not a historical consideration.

We will not be able to demonstrate in this brief introductory text the critical sifting of each particular unit of tradition that might be used to reconstruct a portrait of Jesus, but we hope to raise the fundamental issue: Does the portrait of Jesus that emerges from a critical sifting of gospel lore present a person who fits into a background in first-century C.E. homeland Judaism? We have pictured that world in Chapter 10. That is the world in which Jesus would have found his place unless he was a unique "flying-saucer" man, literally an alien to his environment. Such a person would have found it quite difficult to communicate with anyone and would have been much more seriously misunderstood than the gospels suggest Jesus actually was. His disciples are represented as getting the general idea right, but misinterpreting it; Peter knew Jesus was the Messiah, but he could not understand why the Messiah must suffer. We propose to ask whether the resultant critical portrait of Jesus fits *historically, ideologically,* and *sociologically* into the first-century Jewish world. Preference will be given to information from the Synoptic gospels, Matthew, Mark, and Luke, in this process. Although the Gospel of John probably had independent and authentic sources of information about Jesus, the purpose of the Fourth Gospel had moved much further into the interpretation of Jesus's significance than the other three. Thus, John will be utilized more as an occasional supplement to the Synoptics. Other more refined issues, such as apparent differences between the Synoptic and Johannine chronologies, need not concern us in this introductory discussion.

The Historical Fit

Is the picture of Jesus derived from the gospels *historically* credible? Does it coordinate with independent information about the history and topography of Israel in the first several decades of the first century? If, for instance, a gospel passage claimed that Jesus amazed and confounded Alexander the Great, a historian would be suspicious to say the least. Similarly, if Jerusalem were placed east of the

Palestine in 30 C.E.

Jordan, there would be grounds for skepticism. There are, to be sure, some minor issues of historical detail that cannot be totally resolved. For instance, if Jesus was born during the reign of Herod the Great, as Matthew and Luke assert (apparently on the basis of independent sources), could Quirinius have been governor of Syria, and did the tax census ordered during his tenure fall at the right time to account for Jesus's being born in Bethlehem? The independent data may be ambiguous, but even if Lk. 2:1–2 errs on this matter, it is an error within the historical ballpark and does not impeach his general accuracy. Similarly, not all of the topographic references in the gospels are entirely clear and identifiable, but none of them raises glaring difficulties.

One recent scholar has argued that, as Luke indicates, Jesus was born in 6 C.E., and the Herod of his story was Herod Archelaus, son of Herod the Great, whose deposition opened the way for Quirinius to take charge and conduct his census. There is triple attestation for Jesus's birth at Bethlehem (Mt. 2:1, 5, 6, 8, 16; Lk. 2:4–15; Jn. 7:42) and no contrary traditions.[9]

The gospel traditions seem to have things pretty much in order. This does not mean that the final authors of the gospel documents had to be fully conversant personally with the geography or the history in question. It is enough for historical purposes that such information is embedded in the traditions they utilized.

Jesus is identified with the village of Nazareth, a minor hamlet in those days, located in lower Galilee, overlooking the Valley of Jezreel and a few miles southeast of the sometimes provincial capital of Sepphoris (which, like its successor, Tiberias, Jesus never visited, so far as we know). He was pictured during his public career circulating among various towns of the area, with Capernaum as his apparent headquarters. Mark's version of the story of the healing of the paralytic (2:1–12) seems to reflect accurate knowledge of first-century home construction. His various travels and the hometowns of other characters are authentic places plausibly located.

---

[9]Mark D. Smith. "Of Jesus and Quirinius." *Catholic Biblical Quarterly,* 62:2 (April 2000), 278–293.

Feeding of the Five Thousand. An ancient mosaic inside the Church of the Multiplication of the Loaves and the Fishes (Tabgha, Israel) commemorates the miracle in which Jesus took several loaves of bread and fishes and fed five thousand people. It is the only miracle of Jesus described in all four canonical gospels (Mt. 14: 13–21, Mk. 6:31–44, Lk. 9:10–17, and Jn. 6:5–15). *Source:* Tomasz Parys/ Shutterstock

Jesus lived and died in a land incorporated in the Roman Empire, and the gospel narratives record that fact. We noted earlier in this chapter that the match between gospel narrative and Jewish and Roman rulers was accurate. Jesus died by crucifixion, a Roman, rather than Jewish, mode of execution, condemned by a documented Roman procurator. And so on.

The gospels also reflect accurate knowledge of the organization of the Jewish community in the homeland during the first century. At least one of Jesus's disciples can be identified as a Zealot (Lk. 6:15; the form of the name in Mk. 3:18 and Mt. 10:4 might be a transliteration of the Hebrew noun). The Pharisees appear as the most frequent opponents of Jesus in arguments. The Sadducees also appear, but less frequently, as would be expected, especially in Galilee. The Essenes are not mentioned. If they guarded their purity, as the Hellenistic writers say and the Dead Sea Scrolls imply, this is not surprising. The tradition is aware of the dispute between Pharisees and Sadducees over resurrection. The Sanhedrin is the highest authority in Israel, but subject to the Roman authorities. It is headed by the high priest, but includes both Pharisees and Sadducees. The overall picture suggests sources well informed about the world of which they speak.

The Ideological Fit

We indicated earlier in this chapter that Jesus would not have received a responsive hearing had he been totally alien to his world. His teachings had to be close enough to the ideas current in his time to be comprehensible to his contemporaries. This would be true even if his repertory included some new ideas (which it probably did), and even if some of his teachings were misunderstood (which they almost certainly were). On a general level, he was familiar with the Hebrew Bible and drew heavily on it. Even though the Greek gospels frequently seem to assimilate his Scripture citations to the LXX, his usage reflects the Hebrew canon of Israel and Babylon, not the more extensive LXX canon. He declared the Torah valid and irrevocable. Jesus frequented the synagogue in his hometown and in other communities he visited. In Jerusalem he and his disciples seemed comfortable around the Temple, and the disciples continued to go there after the Crucifixion and the Resurrection experience.

Banias. Located at the foot of Mt. Hermon at the northern border of Israel is Banias. It is near the site of the ancient city of Caesarea Philippi where, according to the synoptic gospels (Mk. 8:27–30, Mt. 16:13–20, Lk. 9:18–21), Jesus asked his closest followers: "Who do you say that I am?" The site became known as Banias (also Paneas) after the Greek god Pan who was venerated at its picturesque springs and streams after the conquest of the area by Alexander the Great. *Source:* Rudolf Tepfenhart/Shutterstock

What were Jesus's ideological affinities? If he was not a flying-saucer prophet, was he yet perhaps a sort of religious Lone Ranger? Such notions appeal to romantic imagination, but too much of the gospels bears the mark of the Judaism of the day. Attempts have been made to connect Jesus with various groups in first-century Judaism. That both he and all of them were Jewish means that they should share more in common than with non-Jews. However, only if the evidence is used very selectively can Jesus be made to appear as an Essene—Covenanter, Zealot, or Jewish Gnostic. The closest relationship that can be shown is between Jesus and rabbinic–pharisaic Judaism. Such an observation might offend persons who wish to distance Jesus from his Jewish roots. But, in fact, no teaching attributed to Jesus in the Synoptic gospels is without its parallel in the rabbinic literature. This fact should be tempered by the equally true fact that the history of gospel tradition (about thirty-five years for Mark, about sixty years for John) is much shorter than the four hundred years for Mishnah, the additional three hundred for Talmud, and a similar amount for parallel midrashic lore (see Chapter 10). But then, two hundred years of Mishnah's history preceded the birth of Jesus! So there are really no points to be scored on these data; there are only counsels of caution to serious scholars.

An objection that will almost certainly be raised against these data is, as noted earlier, that most of Jesus's disputes in the Synoptics are with the Pharisees. Three things must be noted at this point. First, detailed arguments are possible only between persons who share some common ground. Second, Jesus's disputes with the Pharisees were largely over questions of the correct understanding of Torah, a matter of mutual concern. The other main issue was his personal authority, because he seems to have ignored the rabbinic practice of citing sources. Finally, persons familiar with the rabbinic literature are aware that most of the disputes between Jesus and the Pharisees in the gospels are similar to disputes *among* rabbinic authorities in their nature, subject matter, and intensity. In other words, Jesus's arguments with his pharisaic contemporaries were good Jewish family arguments and should be so understood. They are distorted when placed in the context of later Jewish–Gentile Christian or church–synagogue hostility. Incidentally, as noted in Chapter 10, rabbinic–pharisaic Judaism did not use the term *Pharisee* for self-identification. Sometimes it is used, in rabbinic lore as in the gospels, to criticize persons whose pretensions to piety outran their achievements.

We noted in Chapter 10 that pharisaism, at least prior to 70 C.E., could be divided into two wings: the strict constructionist house of Shammai and the freer constructionist house of Hillel. In those cases where distinction is possible, Jesus's Torah teaching almost invariably inclines toward the Hillelite, and most of his Galilean disputes seem to have been directed against the stricter Shammaite position. The denunciation of the cleansing of the outside of a vessel (Mt. 23:25–26) is directed against Shammaite interpretation. The rigid Sabbath rules that Jesus opposed were also Shammaite. It may be that the house of Shammai was stronger than the Hillelites in Galilee; some evidence points to that. There is a measure of irony in the fact that Jesus was challenged on the issue of divorce as he passed into Judea. The question was a "litmus paper" issue between the Shammaites and Hillelites, and for once, Jesus came down on the strict constructionist side (Mk. 10:1–2; Mt. 19:1–9). The Hillelites were much more permissive. It has been noted that the few instances in which Jesus sided with the Shammaites were those in which strict constructionism served humanitarian ends. In this case it offered a greater security for women in a patriarchal society.

The title *Rabbi* is closely associated with pharisaic Judaism and its successor. Actually, the word became a formal title only after the time of Jesus, but its application to him is indicative.

Does this mean, then, that Jesus was a Pharisee, albeit one at odds with some of his contemporaries? Any answer to this question must be qualified by the caveat of recent scholarship that our understanding of the actual beliefs and practices of the Pharisees is very limited (see Chapter 10). Thus, our answer is admittedly speculative. Jesus's closest ideological affinities did seem to be with pharisaism. If his contemporaries had been obliged to categorize him in terms of the major first-century Jewish movements, they might have described him as a Pharisee or perhaps a crypto-Pharisee. But Jesus's Sabbath teaching was even more permissive than the Hillelites. Also, he was apparently skeptical about the oral Torah. He based his own teachings on midrash to a greater extent than seems to have been customary among Pharisees of his time. Finally, he apparently eschewed the principle of authority (see Chapter 10). Instead, he stood for his own teachings, whether midrashic or *ad hoc* (Mk. 1:21–22; Mt. 7:28–29).

Despite the hostility of the Matthean circle toward the late- to first-century rabbinic leadership at Yavneh, the Gospel of Matthew transmits Jesus's endorsement of pharisaic authority, even while it transmits his (and their own) reservations about the depth of some pharisaic piety (Mt. 23:1–36). If there is an irony here, it is that Matthew is, at the same time, the most pharisaic of the gospels. Matthew seems, for example, to subscribe to the view of the near-contemporary Akiva that there are no surplus words in Scripture, so that every single one must be interpreted. Thus, Matthew suggests that Jesus must have ridden two animals in the triumphal entry story (Mt. 21:1–11; Zech. 9:9).

Jesus's affinity to contemporary Jewish centrism is further evidenced by his use of parables as a teaching device. He also typically utilized rabbinic forms of argument such as "if ... how much more ...." This is the *light-to-heavy* form common in rabbinic debates.

We may safely conclude, therefore, that Jesus stood in basic ideological harmony with the Pharisees. But he entertained enough differences to justify the view that he was not simply a slightly deviant Pharisee. His general ideological niche is established, but a more precise location in the world of first-century Judaism remains to be established.

The Sociological Fit

Was there a place in first-century Israelite society in which a figure like Jesus, as portrayed by the gospels, would fit? That is the sociological issue to which we now turn.

Mount of Transfiguration. The traditional location of the transfiguration of Jesus (Mk. 9:2–8, Mt. 17:1–8, Lk. 9:28–36) is Mount Tabor, located in lower Galilee at the eastern end of the Valley of Jezreel. It was also the site of a famous battle during the period when Deborah judged Israel (Jg. 4:12). *Source:* William A. Young

It has been observed that Jesus was accorded the title *Rabbi* by both his followers and others. Further, his relationship to his immediate circle of followers was organized on the model of a rabbi and his disciples. His appointment of a special company of twelve (Mk. 3:13–19; Mt. 10:2–4; Lk. 6:13–16) is probably of eschatological significance, relating to the twelve traditional tribes of Israel (Mt. 19:28). Matthew and Luke assimilate the twelve to the Company of the Apostles, although for the earlier Marcan tradition they are simply *The Twelve.* The existence of a smaller company of three—Peter, James, and John—could be connected with the organization of the Dead Sea Covenanters (see Chapter 10). But it was also typical for a great rabbi to have an inner circle of especially dedicated and beloved students (a sort of graduate seminar) with whom he was most closely associated and to whom he communicated the most confidential teachings, including secret mystical lore.

These general sociological data tend to confirm the affinity between Jesus and rabbinic–pharisaic Judaism or, at any rate, to locate them in the social world. Is a more precise definition possible? It has long been recognized that there was a particular class of holy men, or *hasidim,* around the turn of the eras in Israel. Recently, within this class of holy men, there has been identified a group of wonder-working saints whose religious expression can be described as *charismatic Judaism.*[10] The term *charismatic* is used here not in the popular sense associated with Pentecostal Christianity, but in Max Weber's sociological sense: empowered with a special spiritual gift. Weber noted three kinds of authority: the traditional, the rational, and the charismatic. The hereditary priesthood, descended from Aaron, was a form of traditional authority in classical Judaism. Genealogy gave the priests the exclusive right to sacrifice at the Temple altar, the right to interpret Torah, and priority in pronouncing the benediction (Num. 6:24–26). The authority of the lay scholar–saints, the rabbis, who led the Pharisees was an example of rational authority. It was based on their scholarship and saintly lifestyle. Jesus also possessed rational authority; he was addressed as "rabbi," "teacher." But his additional charismatic authority set him apart from the Pharisaic leadership. Rational and scholarly authority is often uneasy with charisma, and so it was with the rabbinic leaders. Some rabbinic tales emphasize the inferiority of miraculous events in comparison to sound scholarship. It was a settled matter that in the definition of a point of *halakah,* no miracle, however wondrous, could impeach a majority vote of the assembled scholars.

Jesus seems to have been associated with a charismatic form of Judaism that was to be centered in Galilee. At least one of the Galilean charismatics, Hanina ben Dosa, made it into the rabbinic chain of tradition. Like Jesus, he was a healer, even over long distances. Like Jesus, he was proclaimed "son of God" by a *bath qol* (voice from heaven; literally "daughter of a voice," i.e., an "echo of *the* voice [of God]"). And like Jesus, Hanina apparently caused some discomfort in conventional pharisaic ranks.

Unfriendly rabbinic propaganda following the schism between church and synagogue portrayed Jesus as a sorcerer. Recently, it has been speculated that he was a necromancer or magician. These were nontraditional ways of getting in touch with the spirit world. The data concerning charismatic saints in Galilee in the first century are therefore particularly valuable in assessing Jesus's place in a first-century Jewish context. It shows there was a place on the fringes of rabbinism at this time for a teacher who was also a healer and a wonder-worker. It also shows that one need not resort to only one model, portraying Jesus as a wonder-worker, *or* a rabbinic teacher, *or* a mystic, *or* an eschatological prophet exclusively and attributing other sorts of traditions about him to later editorial activity. Two or more roles could be, and were, combined in first-century Judaism in Israel.

---

[10]Geza Vermes. *Jesus the Jew: A Historian's Reading of the Gospels.* New York: Macmillan, 1973, pp. 58–82. See also Vermes' subsequent works on Jesus in the Annotated Bibliography.

This charismatic aspect of the ministry of Jesus—the healings, resuscitations, exorcisms, and the few nature miracles attributed to him—has created the greatest problems of credibility for modern readers. This has led some interpreters to try to explain the so-called *miracles* in scientific or philosophical terms, or else to simply explain them away. Of course, anthropologists know well that the holy men and women of most pretechnological societies were believed to work wonders. It would have been as difficult for members of that overwhelming majority of humanity to believe that someone who could not or did not work wonders was a holy person as it is for a modern skeptic to accept the wonders themselves. Ordinary folks have generally expected wonders of their holy people, and they have seldom been disappointed. This does not solve the problem of credibility for persons imbued with the modern technological outlook, but it does suggest that the issue is too fundamental to be swept away by a bit of theological legerdemain or a touch of modern scientific dogmatism. In any case, Jesus is not represented as lodging much confidence in wonders as religious persuaders. This seems to be the point of the tag line to the parable of the rich man and Lazarus. If people are not persuaded by the Torah and the prophets, they are unlikely to be convinced by a dead man (Lk. 16:19–31).

JESUS AND THE TITLES ATTRIBUTED TO HIM

Even when it has been shown that Jesus fits rather well into the first-century Jewish world, some persons may remain uncomfortable with the fact that the materials used by the historian are infused with a set of titles ascribed to Jesus that have been the substance of later Christian theology. It is not our purpose to question or to quarrel with the later theological understanding of these titles. Rather, we are obliged to raise the question of whether they were meaningful in classical Judaism, and if so, what they might have meant. Otherwise, they must be sifted out of any historical account of Jesus, although they would remain significant in understanding the convictions of the developing church. The titles we shall examine are Messiah (Christ), Son of God, Son of Man, and Lord. We have not included "prophet" among these titles. We recognize that many scholars have treated Jesus as some sort of prophet, and some of his contemporaries regarded him as a prophet (*cf.* Mt. 21:11). His charismatic actions would put him among those the first-century C.E. Jewish historian Josephus called prophets. However, the canonical Gospels do not assign the title to him, and his only reference to himself as a prophet (Mt. 13:57) is highly problematic at best.

Via Dolorosa. The Via Dolorosa (Latin for "Way of Suffering") is the path in the Old City of Jerusalem in Israel that Jesus may have followed when he carried his cross to the site of his crucifixion. Christian pilgrims follow the fourteen Stations of the Cross marked on the Via Dolorosa. The fourth station (shown here) features a carving of Mary, the mother of Jesus, encountering her son. *Source:* William A. Young

Messiah

The inscription Pilate had affixed to Jesus's cross, "Jesus of Nazareth, The King of the Jews," was supposed to inform passersby of the nature of the charge for which he was perishing in such agony. It reflects the datum found in both Josephus and Tacitus, that Jesus was regarded by some as the Messiah.

Not all Jews during the first century C.E. expected a messiah. Those who did most commonly believed that God would restore the anointed Davidic line to the throne of Israel and, in the process, restore the Israelite kingdom, and, in the process, change the world. In some schemes, the "days of the Messiah" were a period of preparation for the realization of the heavenly kingdom on earth, "the world to come." (The Christian apocalypse, the Revelation of John, shares this pattern, although the terminology is somewhat different.) The usage of some documents is also ambiguous, with "days of Messiah" and "world to come" used interchangeably. We have seen that the Dead Sea sect was more interested in the restoration of the anointed high priesthood ("the Messiah of Aaron") than in the monarchy. Other Jews likely expected the messianic age would be inaugurated by a heavenly figure, perhaps Enoch.

Other figures were associated with the messianic age. Elijah would return to announce it (Mal. 4:5; Mt. 11:14; *cf.* John the Baptizer's costume in Mk. 1:6; Mt. 3:4). A "prophet like [Moses]" (Dt. 18:15) might have played a part in some expectations. Some also looked for a Messiah of Joseph (i.e., the Joseph tribes), who would help prepare the way for the Davidic messiah. A general restoration of prophecy could have been expected in some circles, but folk religion apparently ignored the pharisaic notion that it had ceased in the age of Ezra. When "messiah" is mentioned without qualification in Jewish sources, it is the Davidic messiah who is meant. If Jesus claimed to be the Messiah, or his followers lodged the claim for him, this is the territory they were staking out and not some exotic other.

There can be no doubt that Jesus's followers proclaimed him the Messiah. His Greek title, *Christos* ("Christ"), is a literal translation of the Hebrew *meshiah* ("Messiah"). Did Jesus lodge such a claim on his own behalf? The gospels make Jesus appear at least a trifle cagey on the subject. Mark features the "messianic-secret" theme, in which those who recognize that Jesus is the Christ are told by him to keep it quiet. Jesus's answers to Pilate are (understandably) guarded. A case can be made that he never explicitly claimed the title Messiah for himself, which would turn his execution into a tragic case of mistaken identity.

However, there are several points at which Jesus appears clearly to have asserted his messianic identity. His answer to the high priest in the Gospel of Mark (14:62) is quite direct. Matthew 26:24 may appear more evasive, but in fact is not, as we shall presently see.

The clearest personal claim to messianic status lodged by Jesus is found in his actions in the triumphal entry and cleansings of the Temple stories, directly linked in Matthew and Luke and proximate in Mark (Mt. 21:1–17; Lk. 19:28–46; Mk. 11:1–19). The triumphal entry is presented as a deliberate dramatization (i.e., fulfillment) of the messianic prophecy of Zech. 9:9. It is probably significant that this passage portrays a peaceful Messiah, a theme to which we shall return. But the Temple-cleansing story is at least as direct a claim. The gospels do not present it as a vigilante assault by an outraged pietist. That Mark inserts a night in Bethany between the survey of 11:11 and the action itself particularly suggests a calculated move. But only two officers in traditional Jewish circles had the requisite authority to police the Temple: the king and the high priest. No claim that Jesus was of the house of Aaron was made before patristic times.

Finally, the Transfiguration vision (Mk. 9:2–8; Mt. 17:1–8; Lk. 9:28–36) is understood by all three Synoptics as a messianic confirmation experience. Mystical masters in rabbinic Judaism generally did not give their students direct answers to the more profound issues. Rather, they fed them clues, obliging the students to work their own way through to a personal discovery. (Perhaps all teachers could profit from their example!) If Jesus, like many of the rabbis, gave mystical as well as legal (halakic) and inspirational (haggadic) instruction to his disciples, the Transfiguration could be showing that Peter, James, and John passed their examinations. The Synoptics link the Transfiguration Narrative rather closely with the story of Peter's declaration of Jesus's messianic identity at Caesarea Philippi (Mk. 8:27–33; Mt. 16:13–23; Lk. 9:18–22). The disciples had worked their way through to a divine illumination that gave them the correct answer concerning Jesus's identity. They were rewarded with a confirming vision.

The question then becomes: How did Jesus plan to activate his royal prerogatives? Pilate's actions against him reveal the typical reaction of a colonial governor to a native pretender to power. The Gospel of John suggests, in a passage highly colored by John's theological concerns (which yet could contain an authentic reminiscence), that the high priest did not so much fear Jesus as a rival for power as he feared his capacity to stir up a public uproar that would lead to vicious Roman reprisals (Jn. 11:45–53). Some historians believe that Jesus's Galilean homeland was the hotbed and headquarters of a great deal of Zealot activity, creating a revolutionary tinderbox where the slightest messianic spark might touch off a conflagration. Again, John, the least historical of the gospels, could contain a valuable reminiscence. John's narrative of the feeding miracle, the only miracle story recounted in all four gospels (Jn. 6:1–15; Mk. 6:45–51; Mt. 14:13–21; Lk. 9:10–17), concludes with the note that Jesus withdrew to avoid being acclaimed king against his will. Some within his own circle were already squabbling over cabinet appointments (Mk. 9:33–37).

Anthropologist Marvin Harris has used the happy phrase "the peaceful Messiah" to describe the gospel picture of Jesus.[11] Indeed, the gospel traditions are so imbued with this theme

---

[11]Marvin Harris. *Cows, Pigs, Wars and Witches: The Riddles of Culture.* New York: Random House, Vintage Books, 1975, pp. 179–203.

Empty Tomb of Jesus. A modern reconstruction of the tomb of Jesus illustrates the massive stone that covered its opening. The accounts in the canonical gospels of the followers of Jesus coming to the tomb and finding the stone rolled away and the tomb empty are Mk.16:1–8, Mt. 28:1–8, Lk. 24:1–12, and Jn 20:1–10. *Source:* Tiffany Chan/Shutterstock

that it is plausible to assume that it was organic to them. An overlaid matrix of militant messianism is quite lacking. Illustration of the theme should begin with the Triumphal Entry, Jesus's most public messianic self-proclamation. He did not come as a triumphant warrior king in a chariot or on horseback, but on the mount of peace, a donkey, dramatizing a pacific prophetic oracle (Zech. 9:9). His explicitly anti-Zealot saying in Mt. 26:52 exemplifies the antimilitaristic flavor of his teaching. The Synoptic Apocalypse is, among other things, a warning against war with Rome (Mk. 13:5–37; Mt. 24:4–36; Lk. 21:8–36). *The War Scroll* and other documents reveal a militant strain among the Dead Sea Covenanters, whom many had considered quietists. The *Magnificat* (Lk. 2:46–53) and the *Benedictus* (Lk. 2:68–79) are radically revolutionary hymns, although they do not specify the means by which God will achieve his ends. Some of Jesus's disciples were armed when they went to the Garden, but you do not start a war with two swords (Lk. 22:35–48)! One of them, identified by John as Simon Peter, actually used his weapon (Mk. 14:47; Mt. 26:51–54; Lk. 22:49–51; Jn. 18:10–11). However, these incidents seem intended to show Jesus's rejection of violent means. Militant Christian messianism does emerge in the Book of Revelation, during a time of persecution. Some scholars are now suggesting that there was a political aspect to Pauline Christianity, which has been largely concealed by later Christian interpreters. In Paul, as in the Lucan hymns, the means that will achieve God's purposes are not specified.

It is possible to ground a peaceful messianism in the first-century world of homeland Judaism. Indeed, the notion that all Jews at the time of Jesus expected a militaristic messiah, and rejected Jesus when he did not fulfill the role, is the creation of Christian apologists and is a distortion of the facts. There was a notion abroad in rabbinic Judaism that the coming of the Messiah and the realization of the messianic kingdom could be advanced by devotion to Torah. (Paul entertained a related notion, as will be noted in Chapter 14.) This theory grew in popularity over the years, becoming especially strong in mystical circles. Jesus directed his ministry toward "the lost sheep of the house of Israel" (Mt. 10:26; *cf.* 9:36), which could tell in favor of his endorsing this idea. His remark about the sick rather than the well needing a physician has sometimes been read as an ironic condemnation of his critics (Mk. 2:16–17; Mt. 9:11–13; Lk. 5:30–32). It was probably a very straightforward observation. The Torah keepers did not have to be recalled to Torah for the kingdom to be realized. The sinners did. The point is that the return of the lost would catalyze the dawn of the messianic kingdom. Finally, the fact that Jesus chided both his disciples and others for their dullness in not grasping what he was about suggests that in his own mind, he was not confronting them with something absolutely strange and radical, but with something they should have been able to understand.

However, Jesus may have added at least one new theme to the repertory of Jewish messianic ideas—the notion of the Messiah as suffering servant. The servant songs of Isaiah 40–55 (see Chapter 6) had been interpreted collectively, the servant being understood as Israel personified. Jesus apparently annexed the notion of the LORD's servant, whose suffering and unjust death achieved vicarious good to his own messianic understanding. The king in most ancient cultures (including Israel) embodied the nation, in a sense, so that his actions were crucial to national fortunes. Thus, the Messiah was, of all persons, best qualified to execute such a responsibility. Some have proposed that the interpretation was a product of the developing church, another piece of the program to rationalize its own understanding of Jesus. But it appears so early in the traditions that it is at least as plausible to attribute the insight to Jesus.

The resurrection of the dead was a feature of pharisaic and apocalyptic theories of the messianic age. The death and resurrection of only one person, the Messiah himself, were not. That a dying and resurrected Messiah was an unprecedented notion in Judaism is the best evidence that the disciples of

Jesus in fact had the Resurrection experiences they reported. For the first Christians themselves, their experiences of the resurrected Jesus were God's irrefutable endorsement of his messianic status and the earnest of his return to establish the Kingdom of God once and for all.[12]

Son of God

The Egyptian pharaoh was extolled as the son of Amon–Re, the sun god. He embodied the god, and, at death, his *ka* ("soul") was reunited with his divine parent. Greek culture (and Roman after it) allowed not only that humans might be elevated to the status of gods and demigods, but also that humans could even have a god as a biological parent. Alexander had permitted such a report about himself to circulate, if he did not actually encourage it.

Persons in the pagan environment of the Roman Empire were therefore probably disposed to so understand the ascription of the title *Son of God* to Jesus. This sort of literalism ultimately caused (and still causes) Christianity a great deal of vexation. An elaborate body of philosophical explanation (for which the doctrines of the Trinity and the Two Natures of Christ are a shorthand summary) has been devised over the centuries in an effort to preserve both Judeo-Christian monotheism and the unique status of Jesus in Christian faith.

Jesus's Jewish contemporaries, at least those who were not extensively assimilated into Greco-Roman culture, would have had no such problem. The notion of a human becoming a God or having a *literal* divine parent would have struck reasonably sophisticated Jews as being somewhere between trivial and absurd. Among the Semitic peoples of the Bronze and Iron Ages, the best a king could hope for was to be the *adopted* son of a god. Some of the other Semitic peoples got over this compunction in later times. Not so the Jews. The LORD was God, humanity was humanity, and that was that.

Still, the term *Son of God* could be meaningfully used in first-century Jewish discourse, and was. We have already alluded to one use. The Davidic king was proclaimed God's son in the Scripture (see Ps. 2; 89; 2 Sam. 7:4–17). Thus, *Son of God* could have been meaningfully ascribed to Jesus in his own historical setting in relationship to the messianic claim.

The second documented usage of the term was to designate a particularly saintly person. The Son of God is the one who behaves in a godly fashion, who does God's work in this world. The title was ascribed to several holy men in the rabbinic literature, including the Galilean charismatic mentioned earlier, Hanina ben Dosa. The ascription was made in several cases by a *bath qol,* a heavenly voice (see previous discussion). This second sense of *Son of God* could also have been meaningfully applied to Jesus by his homeland contemporaries. It can be observed that on two notable occasions, a *bath qol* proclaimed Jesus the Son of God. The first was at his baptism (Mk. 1:9–11; Mt. 3:13–17; Lk. 3:21–22). On that occasion, the second usage would perhaps have been most fitting, especially if the reservations expressed by the Baptizer are historic. God endorses Jesus's act; he is indeed a saintly one. It can be noted that the term in this sense is also applied to faithful Christians by both Paul and John (Rom. 8:14; Gal. 3:26; Jn. 1:12; 1 Jn. 3:2). Jesus declared peacemakers to be God's children (Mt. 5:9). The second was after the Transfiguration experience. If we have correctly connected this event with Jesus's messianic role, the first usage would apply.

It can be noted that the most common use of the term in the Hebrew Bible is usually in the plural, *sons of God* (or *god,* or *the gods*), designating either angels or the deities of pagan polytheism. But this meaning is not applicable in the case of Jesus. All Israelites, including Jesus, were God's children according to Dt. 14:1.

[12]John P. Meier. *A Marginal Jew: Rethinking the Historical Jesus,* 4 vols. New York/New Haven: Doubleday and Yale University, 1990, 1994, 2001, 2009. The title *A Marginal Jew* is unfortunate in creating the impression to casual readers that Jesus was not firmly grounded in Judaism, a claim Meiers rejects. Indeed, *A Marginal Jew* is widely respected as one of the most scholarly and thoughtful, as well as one of the most voluminous, works in historical Jesus research. In the fourth volume Meier addresses the theme of Jesus as royal, Davidic messiah.

Son of Man

Son of Man is apparently Jesus's favorite term of self-reference in the gospels. Significantly, it is only used once of Jesus outside the gospels in the New Testament (Acts 7:56).

The most common meaning of *Son of Man* in the Hebrew Scripture is simply *human being*. It is God's favorite form of address to the prophet Ezekiel (e.g., 2:1). In Dan. 7:13, the "one like a son of man" turns out to be almost certainly the personification of the saints of the Most High (7:27). But the introduction of the term in an influential early apocalyptic work probably had an impact. The pseudepigraphic apocalypse of Enoch (see Chapter 10) introduces a heavenly savior figure who bears the title *Son of Man*.

Vermes has shown that in Aramaic writing, especially in letters, from around the time of Jesus, *Son of Man* was a euphemism for the first-person pronoun, to be used when to say *I* or *me* would sound overly self-important or to avoid linking oneself with language concerning unfortunate events (a common human taboo).[13] This is a particularly impressive point when trying to understand what the phrase may have meant in Jesus's usage, for Aramaic was the common spoken language of Jews in Israel and Babylon in Jesus's time. However, this does not necessarily account for every occurrence of *Son of Man* in the gospels.

It could be that in some cases the phrase is used as a title in the apocalyptic sense already present in Enoch. If so, the issue becomes whether Jesus considered himself the Son of Man who would return in glory to judge the earth and establish the Kingdom, or whether he used the term in reference to another besides himself who would come later. On this question the debate goes on among knowledgeable interpreters. We will not attempt to resolve it here. Certainly, each occurrence of *Son of Man* in the gospels should be evaluated in its own context rather than forced into one predetermined pattern.

Lord

Our task in evaluating the titles attributed to Jesus would be much simpler were the gospels written in Hebrew or in the Aramaic in which Jesus taught and conversed. We cannot be certain which Hebrew or Aramaic term lies behind the Greek *kurios* ("lord") that stands in the New Testament texts. Indeed, the Greek word itself apparently came into Aramaic as a loan word and was even used as a surrogate for the Hebrew name for the deity, YHWH, substituting for the Hebrew *'adonai*. The Aramaic *mar* was apparently interchangeable with *'adon* and *kurios* in various senses. Evidence from the Dead Sea Scrolls shows that *mar* could be used to refer to God. However, *mar* might also be used interchangeably as the title for a respected person, such as a rabbi. Indeed, the term *rabbi*, as already noted, had as a primary meaning "my great one," "my master," and hence might appropriately be rendered as *mar* or *kurios*. If this were not complication enough, the term *kurios* was the title of the savior deity in some of the Hellenistic mystery cults. But the Greek term, too, could simply be a title of polite or deferential address. The evidence for how the title *Lord* might have been used in reference to Jesus is both complex and confusing. However, some things can be asserted with reasonable confidence.

First, Jesus's Jewish contemporaries would not address him with the divine name, nor is it likely that as a Jew Jesus would have made such an attribution to himself. However, given the evidence from the Dead Sea Scrolls, it is possible that the use of the term "Lord" applied to Jesus in Aramaic-speaking Christian communities, if not claiming the status of divinity for him, was affirmation that the now risen Jesus represented the Lordship of God on earth.

---

[13]Vermes. *Jesus the Jew,* pp. 160–191.

Second, it is most likely that the application of the term to Jesus partook of two uses. It could have been a form of polite or deferential address, like the American southern *sir* and *ma'am,* or the British *m'lord,* as, for example, in Mk. 7:38. Or it could have been used as a title of honor, either translating or replacing that of *rabbi,* which was also addressed to him by persons within and outside his circle, as in Mt. 7:21.

Finally, it is in the highest degree unlikely that Hellenistic mystery usage affected the language of the Synoptic gospels (Mark, Matthew, and Luke). However, the fact that the Greek term *kurios* was current in the mysteries of the pagan world, referring to deities (and, as *kuria,* to goddesses), probably colored the way it was understood by Gentiles in that world. This might account for the fact that *Lord* became the most popular title for Jesus in the gentile churches. His messianic title in Greek, *Christ,* became something like a proper name (Jesus Christ or Christ Jesus). It would be the Apostle Paul who made the most of the term "Lord" as a title in referring to Jesus (e.g., Phil. 2:11), using it to project the authority of Jesus into the communities of believers in the Gentile world to whom he was writing (see Chapter 14).

A BRIEF LIFE OF JESUS

Having analyzed how Jesus "fit" in the first century C.E. historically, ideologically, and sociologically, and surveyed the titles attributed to him in their original context, it is appropriate to draw this discussion of the "historical Jesus" to a close with an attempt to reconstruct a brief outline of his life. It is based on our own "sifting" of the evidence in the New Testament gospels.[14]

Legends about the birth of Jesus (preserved only in the Gospels of Matthew and Luke) agree that Jesus was the son of a young virgin named Mary in Bethlehem, a small town several miles from Jerusalem in Judea. Her husband was a carpenter named Joseph, from Nazareth in Galilee.

All the gospels agree that Jesus lived in Nazareth in Galilee when he began his ministry, but they tell us almost nothing about his childhood. Jesus was about thirty when he left Nazareth and ventured to the Jordan River, where he encountered a prophet named John the Baptizer who was proclaiming a message of repentance. Jesus was baptized by John in the Jordan, apparently culminating a period of spiritual awakening for him.

Following his baptism Jesus spent time in the wilderness of Judea fasting. Three of the four gospels portray this as a forty-day period of testing, during which Jesus was tempted by Satan. He then returned to Galilee, where he began to challenge people to repent, telling them that the Kingdom of God (a symbol in Jewish apocalyptic teaching of a radically new age, in which people would live in harmony with God and with one another) was at hand. Jesus called together a group of close disciples; the gospels say that there were twelve. This number is symbolic of the twelve tribes of Israel and reflects the view of his followers that the disciples of Jesus were a "new Israel" with whom God was entering into a new covenant. In addition to these twelve men, there were also women in the close band of followers of Jesus, according to the gospels.

The length of the ministry of Jesus is disputed. Only the Gospel of John implies a three-year period; the other gospels portray events that could have taken place in one year. Nor is it clear how many trips Jesus made to Jerusalem during his ministry.

Like some other inspired Jewish teachers of the time, Jesus taught people that compassion for others was more important than meticulous observance of the commandments. He warned people of the perils of wealth and the importance of being ready for the coming Kingdom of God. Jesus often taught using the rabbinic device of parables—sayings and stories that drew on events and characters with which people could easily identify.

[14]William A. Young. *The World's Religions: Worldviews and Contemporary Issues,* 3rd ed. Upper Saddle River, NJ: Pearson/Prentice Hall, 2010, pp. 202–203.

Like other "wonder-workers" in first-century Judaism, Jesus also worked miracles. He healed the sick, the blind, and the lame. He fed the hungry and cast out demons. His followers believe that he walked on water, calmed stormy seas, and even raised the dead.

More amazing at the time, to those in the Jewish community at the time particularly concerned with righteous living, was the tendency of Jesus to associate with known sinners and social outcasts. He maintained that his message was especially intended for those who were not considered righteous.

Opposition to Jesus among some religious leaders and political authorities began to grow and, according to the gospels, he withdrew from his public ministry to spend time with his closest followers. He then went to Jerusalem for the Festival of Passover. The gospels say that he was enthusiastically greeted when he entered Jerusalem and was proclaimed to be the Messiah. He also taught at the Temple and challenged the religious authorities. After a last meal with his disciples, he was arrested and condemned to death by Pontius Pilate, the Roman procurator of Judea.

Jesus died on the eve of the Sabbath; his body was placed in a rock tomb. On the morning after the Sabbath ended, several of the women among his disciples came to the tomb to anoint his body, as the Torah required, and found it empty. According to the gospels, Jesus had been raised from the dead. In several different legends, recorded in the gospels, Jesus appeared to his disciples at various times during the next forty days before he ascended into heaven.

CONCLUSION

Jesus was addressed with respect by his followers and others, and his status as a recognized teacher was acknowledged. Some outside his circle apparently regarded him as an eschatological prophet. It was reported that a *bath qol* had confirmed his saintliness. The humility he taught to others he practiced himself, using a polite euphemism (Son of Man) in place of the first-person pronoun (and when "speaking the unspeakable," as when forecasting his own suffering and death). He understood himself to be the Messiah, the awaited Davidic king who would restore Israel and prepare for the full manifestation of God's reign among people (the Kingdom of God). He proposed to achieve this through spiritual rather than military force, including vicarious benefits brought about by his own action as God's suffering servant.

Jesus's own intentions as the peaceful Messiah were too far removed from the attractive militant messiah of popular expectation even for his own students to understand his purposes readily or fully. It may have been his challenge to Sadducean priestly authority that led to Jesus's arrest. Josephus suggests that being a charismatic who drew excited crowds was sufficient ground for Roman reprisals. Perhaps fear of Roman pacification measures in the event that his activities excited a public disturbance caused the high priest to move against him. Both factors may have been involved. In any case, messianic claims by or for Jesus could be used against him before the Roman procurator Pilate. To Pilate, *messiah* would have only one meaning: a militant rebel against Rome.

Like the Dead Sea Covenanters, like the other pious priests and innocent folk noted by the rabbis, Jesus fell afoul of Sadducean politics. The trial before the high priest (Mk. 14:53–72; 26:57–75; Lk. 22:54–71) was not conducted according to rabbinic rules of jurisprudence. The high priest dominated the Sanhedrin prior to 70 C.E. The charge of blasphemy was a red herring. A rabbinic court would have required a much more searching examination to sustain such a charge. In any case, disrespect for an oriental God was no crime under Roman law. And Rome, in the person of its accredited representative, pronounced the verdict and executed the sentence. Rome took the messianic claim literally and seriously!

New Testament documents reflecting a more extensive development of thought after the resurrection reports of the apostles, such as the Letters of Paul, the Gospel of John, and the Letter to the Hebrews, show that the interpretations that ultimately led to the orthodox theological view of Jesus were already in the making during the New Testament period. The resurrection experiences of the first Christians not only confirmed for them the messiahship of Jesus but also made him available as an immediate focus of religious devotion and a continuing fount of religious insight for future generations. The rest, as they sometimes say on the sports page, is history.[15]

A life of Jesus, a full biography, is probably not possible. It is possible, however, to see Jesus as a person in a real time and place. The gospels *can* serve as historical sources to this extent, if they are used carefully. However, they are much more than sources for our construction of the historical Jesus. They are portraits of Jesus, interpretations of the significance of his life, death, and resurrection. To see the gospels in this way, we will turn to a literary examination.

Summary

The focus of this chapter was the attempt by historians to reconstruct the life of Jesus. We started from the assumption that, although a full biography of Jesus is not possible, we can reconstruct in general the setting in which he lived and establish some facts about his life.

The most important evidence about Jesus from outside the New Testament gospels comes from the Jewish historian Josephus and several Roman historians. These references establish that Jesus was indeed a historical person who lived during the reign of the Emperor Tiberius and was executed under the authority of Pontius Pilate, procurator of Judea. The rest of what can be reconstructed about the historical Jesus comes from the New Testament gospels.

Instead of summarizing all that a modern historian might claim to be able to say about Jesus, after fully evaluating the sources, we demonstrated the general historical, ideological, and sociological settings in which Jesus lived. In general, the portrait of Jesus in the gospels is historically credible. Ideologically, Jesus "fits" what is known about the rabbinic–pharisaic movement, especially its liberal branch. Sociologically, Jesus seems to have been most clearly associated with a charismatic type of Judaism that centered during his lifetime in Galilee.

We also summarized what has been discovered about the most likely original meaning of the titles assigned to Jesus in the gospels—Messiah (Christ), Son of God, Son of Man, and Lord. Although these titles took on other meanings as Christian theologians reflected on the significance of the life, death, and resurrection of Jesus, in each case the title had particular meanings in classical Judaism that may have applied to the historical Jesus.

Finally, we offered an abbreviated life of Jesus, based on the broad consensus of modern historical scholarship.

Discussion of Jesus can be expected to arouse strongly held, conflicting beliefs and opinions that may be difficult to examine rationally. This chapter seeks to create some common ground that will enhance reflection on the ongoing significance of Jesus of Nazareth.

---

[15]For a comprehensive study of resurrection in general and the resurrection of Jesus in particular, see N. T. Wright. *The Resurrection of the Son of God*. Minneapolis, MN: Fortress, 2003. For a lively debate on the topic, see Robert B. Stewart, ed. *The Resurrection of Jesus: John Dominic Crossan and N. T. Wright in Dialogue*. Minneapolis, MN: Fortress, 2006. For another perspective, see Geza Vermes. *The Resurrection: History and Myth*. New York: Doubleday, 2008.

The Contemporary World

Case Study

Jesus of History and Christ of Faith[16]

As we have noted, a distinction is often drawn between the historical Jesus of Nazareth and Jesus as the Christ who is the object of faith for over two billion people. To help clarify the distinction, write down a list of adjectives that seem to you to best describe Jesus. Reflect on/discuss which adjectives in the list are best suited to the "Jesus of history" and which to the "Christ of faith." What do the adjectives you have listed suggest about how your contemporary world is shaping your understanding of Jesus? How might a historical study of Jesus, as has been attempted in this chapter, broaden and deepen your view of Jesus? How might it make your understanding of Jesus more complex and difficult? How did reading this chapter affect the adjectives you chose to list? In the final analysis, do you consider the distinction between the "Jesus of history" and the "Christ of faith" important?

Questions for Discussion and Reflection

1. Historical (or scientific) methods cannot verify or falsify theological claims. In our world, then, what is the value of historical investigations of religious literature, leaders, movements, and other phenomena? Is it just an interesting pastime for history buffs, or does it have some value for religious thought and practice today?

2. If Jesus were a twentieth-century American rather than a first-century Galilean Jew, where do you think he would choose to go and with whom would he associate? What might he be saying and to whom would he be saying it? How might he respond to the many churches that claim to be his disciples in the world today? How do you think he would respond to people of religions other than Christianity and people who are not religious at all?

3. Various motion pictures have been made about Jesus. Some of the more famous are *The Greatest Story Ever Told* (1965), *The Gospel According to St. Matthew* (1965), *Godspell* (1973), *Jesus Christ Superstar* (1974), *The Last Temptation of Christ* (1988), and *The Passion of the Christ* (2004). Reflect on and/or discuss the portraits of Jesus in movies you have seen and the difficulties in attempting to make films about Jesus.

4. How much do you think a modern historian can say with confidence about the life of Jesus of Nazareth? What would you add to or delete from the abbreviated life of Jesus offered in this chapter?

---

[16]See J. R. Porter. *Jesus Christ: The Jesus of History, the Christ of Faith*. New York: Oxford University Press, 2007.

Chapter 12

The Four Gospels

Mark, Matthew, Luke, and John

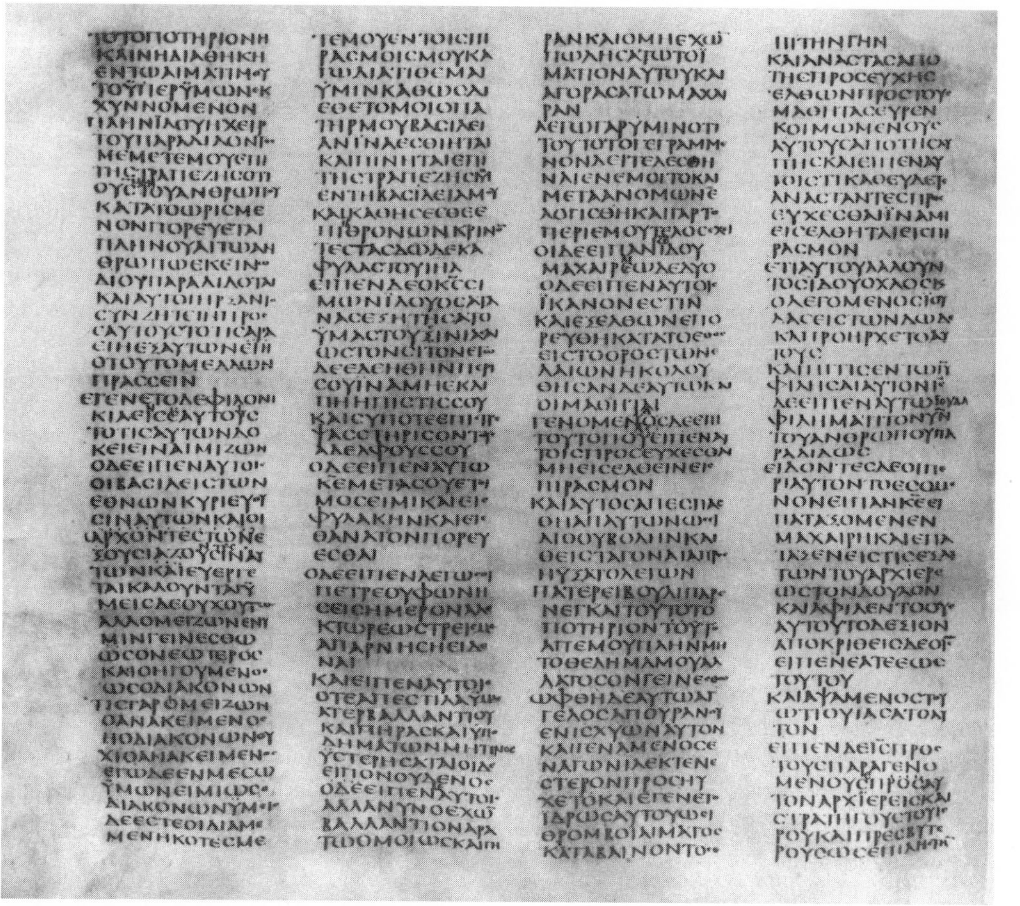

Codex Sinaiticus. One of the earliest Greek manuscripts of the Bible (fourth century C.E.) is called Codex Sinaiticus because it was preserved by the monks of St. Catherine's monastery on Mount Sinai. It was taken to Russia in the nineteenth century and sold to the British Library after the Russian Revolution, purchased with money raised by British schoolchildren. This picture shows part of Luke 22. *Source:* The British Library Board

239

If the gospels of the New Testament are not merely reconstructions of the life of Jesus, what are they? Why are there four gospels in the New Testament? Are these gospels fundamentally the same, or are there basic differences among them? To answer these questions, we must first apply the literary historical method to discovering what we can about the growth of the gospels. Then we will examine the literary world of each one. Finally, we will try to place them in their most likely historical settings.

THE GROWTH OF THE GOSPELS

Gospel as a Literary Genre

The term *gospel* comes from the Anglo-Saxon word *god-spell*, a story from or about a god, or about something good, a rendering of the Latin *evangelium*. The Latin term derives from a similar Greek word, *euangellion* ("good news"). As the New Testament employs the term, it connotes the divine announcement of the final stage of God's plan for salvation.

Sometime in the first or second century C.E., Christians gave a literary application to *gospel*. The "Gospel of Jesus Christ" came to refer to a literary work proclaiming the essential role of Jesus, the Christ (Messiah), in God's saving work. To lend credibility and authority to the works, they were sometimes associated (perhaps accurately) with apostles or persons close to apostles of Jesus. A number of gospels were produced, four of which were incorporated into the New Testament canon. Extracanonical gospels include the Gospels of Peter, Thomas, Judas, Mary, and many more. They will be discussed in Chapter 15.

From the perspective of the literary world, gospel is a genre, a grouping of works of similar form, style, content, function, and perspective. However, scholars have struggled to identify just what type of genre the gospels represent. Although each has a biographical framework, narrating the life of Jesus from his encounter with John the Baptist to his final days in Jerusalem, the four New Testament gospels are clearly not biographies in the modern sense. They are schematic and selective, covering only a relatively small portion of the life of Jesus, and they are theological rather than historical in their orientation. The gospel writers are clearly more concerned with proclaiming what they perceive to be the truth about Jesus in the context of God's plan of salvation than in placing him precisely in the context of his times. Their primary objective is to show that Jesus was the Messiah, the Son of God, the Risen Lord to whom readers should respond with faith. As we have seen in Chapter 11, modern historians using the gospels as historical sources for the life of Jesus have a challenging task.

Various attempts have been made to compare the gospels with contemporary Jewish and Greco-Roman genres. For example, the Jewish community preserved tales of religious heroes. However, these memoirs typically do not focus on the death of the hero as do the gospels. The gospels have also been compared with Greek tragedies where the emphasis often is on the death of the lead character. However, Greco-Roman tragedies do not portray the hero as sent from the divine world. Other possible literary antecedents include the Greco-Roman biographical form known as the "life" (Greek *bios* or Latin *vitae*) and encomiums, eulogistic accounts of the lives of great men.

Given a lack of consensus among scholars on literary parallels, it is probably best to describe the New Testament gospel as a unique genre. In any event, the four gospels were almost certainly included in the canon not because of their literary form, but because their particular perspectives were deemed to be the authentic testimonies of apostles of Jesus.

The Synoptic Problem

During the past two centuries critical study of the New Testament gospels has yielded a wealth of insights on their origin and development. We now have a widely accepted theoretical picture of the stages of development during the years between the death of Jesus and the writing of the gospels.

First, scholars confronted what became known as the *synoptic problem*. When broad outlines and specific contents of the four canonical gospels are compared, two intriguing features appear. For one, the Gospel of John is quite different from the other three. Important events in the life of Jesus that Matthew, Mark, and Luke recorded are absent from John (e.g., the Gethsemane scene [Mt. 26:36–46, Mk. 14:32–42, Lk. 22:39–49]), and *vice versa*. There are significant chronological and geographic differences as well. At the same time, comparison of the other three gospels shows a common structure underlying the differences. All three share a general chronological and geographic outline, namely:

the baptism of Jesus in the Jordan (Mk. 1:2–11, Mt. 3:1–17, Lk. 3:1–22);

temptation in the wilderness (Mk. 1:2–13, Mt. 4:1–11, Lk. 4:1–13);

ministry in Galilee (Mk. 1:14–9:50, Mt. 4:12–18:35, Lk. 4:14–9:50);

journey to Jerusalem (Mark 10, Matthew 19–20, Lk. 9:51–19:27);

last week in Jerusalem (Mk. 11:1–16:8, Mt. 21:1–28:15, Lk. 19:28–24:12).

Furthermore, long passages are paralleled in all three gospels. Because of their significant agreement in content and outline, Matthew, Mark, and Luke came to be called the *synoptic gospels* (*synoptic* means "to take a common view"), and the problem of explaining their interrelationship, the synoptic problem.

Although still challenged from time to time, the most widely accepted solution to the synoptic problem is the *Two-Source Hypothesis*, named after the two major sources the theory claims were used in the writing of the Gospels of Matthew and Luke. The first leg of the theory is that the entire gospel of Mark served as a source for Matthew and Luke. Except for a handful of passages, which are largely Mark's editorial contribution rather than substantive traditions, all of Mark is duplicated in the other two synoptic gospels, and, when a Marcan passage is missing from Matthew or Luke, it is almost always found in the other. The outline of Mark also seems determinative for the other two gospels. When Matthew or Luke varies from Mark's sequence, the other follows Mark. Except in a few minor instances, Matthew and Luke do not agree against Mark in wording. Considered together, the evidence for the dependence of Matthew and Luke on Mark is difficult to refute.

The second leg of the hypothesis is somewhat more conjectural but is still almost universally accepted among critical scholars. It is the notion that Matthew and Luke share a second common source besides Mark, the so-called Q source (from the German *Quelle*, meaning "source") or "sayings source." More than one-third of Matthew and one-fourth of Luke consist of material they share in common that is absent from Mark. Although it is possible that Matthew used Luke as a source, or *vice versa*, the shape of the shared material makes the Q hypothesis more plausible. The common material consists largely of sayings of Jesus such as Mt. 6:22–23 and Lk. 11:34–36. The high degree of verbal agreement between Matthew and Luke in Q sections makes it likely that Q was a written, rather than an oral, source. The discovery of the apocryphal Gospel of Thomas (see Chapter 15), which is *not* Q, but is a collection of sayings much like scholars think "Q" was, makes this notion increasingly plausible.

The third and fourth legs of the Two-Source Hypothesis are the most speculative, and the least important. To account for the sections in Matthew and Luke that are unique, it is assumed that each gospel had a special source, designated M for Matthew and L for Luke. Whether Matthew and Luke had separate sources or drew on different oral or written traditions circulating in the early Christian Church, M and L are convenient symbols for the special sections of each gospel. Following is a graphic and helpful summary of the Two-Source Hypothesis.

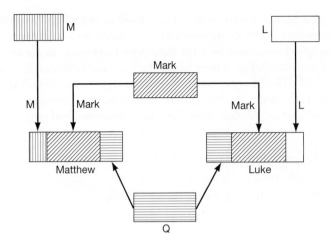

The principal critical rival of the Two-Source Hypothesis is the Griesbach Hypothesis, named for the eighteenth-century scholar who devised it. Griesbach argued that Matthew, not Mark, was the first written gospel (a view first propounded by St. Augustine). According to Griesbach, Luke used Matthew as a source along with other material at his disposal, and Mark used both Matthew and Luke as sources. The Griesbach Hypothesis is advocated by a thoughtful group of scholars who point to alleged weaknesses in the Two-Source Hypothesis, such as the hypothetical nature of the Q source. However, a majority of scholars conclude that the Two-Source Hypothesis solves more problems more simply and raises fewer new problems than does the Griesbach Hypothesis. In fact, the best alternative to the Two-Source Hypothesis may be a theory offered by the British scholar, Austin Farrer. He argued that Mark wrote first. Then Matthew developed an expanded narrative based on Mark. Luke then adapted and supplemented both Mark and Matthew. This view has the virtue of preserving the priority of Mark, which a comparison of the three Synoptic gospels demands. And it explains the presence of "Q" materials in Matthew and Luke. The Farrer Hypothesis seems to be gaining a belated following in Britain. All three hypotheses represent attempts by modern literary historians to understand, in descriptive terms, how the Synoptic gospels assumed their present form. They remain subject to revision or replacement if and when a better explanation is devised.

The research into the synoptic problem clarified the literary relationship of Matthew, Mark, and Luke, but it left untouched other crucial questions. The traditional view that the gospels were eyewitness accounts of the life of Jesus was upset by the realization that the gospels were edited collections of sources and traditions. What evidence is there that these traditions circulated independently before the stage of sources and written gospels? And what situations in the life of the early Christian Church caused these traditions to develop and to be transmitted?

Form criticism was applied to the question of the transmission of the individual traditions about Jesus and their settings in the life of the early Christian community. The assumption of form criticism is that the stories about, and the sayings of, Jesus were not kept alive merely to perpetuate his memory but also to serve the needs of the community seeking to follow him as LORD. In general, these situations would have included communal worship, teaching of children and converts, debate with Jews and Gentiles, community organization and discipline, and reassurance in the face of persecution. This method gives us insight into the general social situation of the early Christian community.

The next step beyond form criticism may have been taken in the work of English scholar James D. G. Dunn.[1] Drawing on regional ethnographies, he argues that the key point in a story or saying is quickly established in oral memory, perhaps even rehearsed at the moment or soon after, although peripheral details may remain relatively fluid. Among early Christian circles in Galilee there were people who had known Jesus, and who could correct someone who erred in a "performance" of Jesus tradition. Dunn does not deny the existence of Q, but does suggest that some parallels attributed to Q may, in fact, be oral parallels. This still relatively new work holds the promise of increasing the quantity of historical information about Jesus that can be drawn from the gospels through careful critical inquiry.

From a literary historical perspective, we have come to recognize that the writers of the gospels were probably neither eyewitnesses nor mere collectors of sources and traditions. They were creative authors who placed their own distinctive literary and theological stamp on their works. Each gospel is a literary unit with a coherent plan and purpose. This awareness resulted in the development of redaction criticism, which focuses on the stage in the growth of the gospels when they were given their final written shape. This method allows us to appreciate the distinctive theological perspectives of each of the gospels. Redaction criticism can be combined with intrinsic literary study to help us understand the unique worlds of each of the four gospels.

THE LITERARY WORLDS OF THE GOSPELS

Mark: The Secret Revealed through Suffering

Although the Gospel of Mark is the shortest, and probably the earliest, gospel, it is by no means the easiest to understand. One reason is that we cannot, as with Matthew and Luke, examine how the writer has interpreted the sources used. Our understanding of Mark's world depends on finding the key or keys to the gospel's portrayal of Jesus in the writing itself. The problem is that in Mark's gospel Jesus is often portrayed as a puzzling, mysterious presence surrounded by confusion and misunderstanding.

A careful reading of the first chapter of Mark reveals several of the crucial themes recurrent throughout. The opening verse establishes for the reader the truth that is only revealed to the participants in the drama of Jesus at the end of the narrative. This Jesus *is* the Christ, the Son of God. As we shall see, this announcement does not reveal the full truth about Jesus. Even the reader is kept in the dark at first. The rest of the gospel's prologue (1:1–13) identifies a continuity stretching back to the prophet Isaiah. A quote from Is. 43:3 (combined with an adapted text from Mal. 3:1) shows that the prophet prepared the way for John the Baptizer. By his testimony, John prepared the way for "he who is mightier than I" (1:7). Although John gives no special attention to Jesus when he baptizes him in the Jordan, it is made clear to the reader that Jesus is the one for whom John is preparing the way. The theme is power and authority, and their continuity and increase from the prophet Isaiah to the messenger to Jesus. At once, the unfolding drama is given cosmic significance, as Jesus is tempted in the wilderness by Satan and ministered to by angels (1:12–13).

However, the point toward which all is moving is not the earthly Jesus, for he proclaims in a saying that comes as close to a statement of Mark's theme as any in the gospel: "The time is fulfilled,

---

[1]James D. G. Dunn. "Jesus in Oral Memory." *Jesus: A Colloquium in the Holy Land*, ed. Doris Donnelly. New York: Continuum, 2001, pp. 84–145. *Cf.* James D. G. Dunn. *Christianity in the Making, Vol. 1: Jesus Remembered*. Grand Rapids, MI: Eerdmans, 2003.

and the Kingdom of God has come near; repent, and believe in the gospel" (1:14–15). The earthly Jesus prepares the way for the Kingdom of God.[2] The present age is ending; a new age in which God's rule will be fully manifest is imminent. The reign of evil will be replaced by the dominion of God. The time has come to turn away from the path of evil (i.e., repent) and embrace the gospel, the announcement of God's salvation. The earthly Jesus has come to proclaim the good news of the arrival of God's Kingdom with a power greater than earth or heaven has seen.

After the stage of the messenger has ended, with the arrest and imprisonment of John, Jesus at once sets about his work. It soon becomes clear that in Mark, Jesus proclaims the gospel not so much by what he says as by what he does. He begins to gather disciples, who leave their secular lives to follow him. According to Mark, when the call goes out, "immediately" they leave their nets. The recurrence of "immediately" (eight times in the first chapter alone and forty times in the gospel) reflects an urgency in the story being told. The reason for the urgency is eschatological. The end is at hand. The time is now, not only for characters in the story but also, by implication, for those hearing or reading this gospel.

The second section of the gospel (1:21–3:6) contains vignettes exemplifying the mysterious power of the man Jesus. He astonishes the people at the synagogue at Capernaum, "for he taught them as one having authority, and not as the scribes" (1:22). He displays the power to cast out evil spirits and to heal the sick. However, he does not stay in one place long enough to establish a reputation, and he instructs exorcised demons and healed people to keep quiet about him. When word spreads, he flees. Again and again, the question is raised: Why? (2:7, 16, 18, 24). As his ministry continues, the Galilean people respond enthusiastically to him, while the hostility of the scribes, Pharisees, and members of Herod's entourage intensifies.

Mark's next section (3:7–8:21) emphasizes the formation of an inner circle of disciples by Jesus, climaxing in their failure to grasp the significance of their master's teaching. Opposition from the Herodians and the Pharisees forces Jesus to withdraw to the Sea of Galilee, followed, Mark says, by multitudes from what had once been the nation Israel and beyond. In the hills above the lake, Jesus selects twelve (a symbolic *new Israel*) and sends them out to proclaim the Kingdom of God with acts of power. Then he returns to Nazareth, where he is rejected by the townspeople and even by his own family. Returning to the Sea of Galilee, he tells parables of the Kingdom to the gathered crowds, parables stressing the fact that, from meager and sometimes obscure beginnings, the Kingdom will grow and ultimately flourish. His explanation of the parables is that, to those outside the inner circle, everything is in riddles. Only those on the inside are taught directly, with "everything" explained to them. Miracles continue, as does the admonition of Jesus to keep silent about them. The Twelve are sent out again, return, and, with the feeding of the five thousand, begin to show their lack of understanding (see especially Mk. 6:51–52). Because of hardness of heart, not even the inner circle, to whom Jesus has explained "everything," grasps the truth. The section climaxes with a rebuke by Jesus to the Twelve: "Do you have eyes, and fail to see? Do you have ears, and fail to hear?" (8:18).

Now the impending suffering and death of Jesus become the dominant focus. Finally in Caesarea Philippi, one of the Twelve has his eyes opened (after the story of the healing of a man with physical blindness). In response to the question of Jesus "Who do you say that I am?," Peter gives the answer the readers of the gospel know to be true, "You are the Messiah." But again Jesus counsels secrecy.

---

[2]"Kingdom of God" is not a place, but a symbol expressing the apocalyptic hope of a new, final age of peace and righteousness (see Chapter 9) or, in a more general sense, God's redemptive activity on behalf of the covenant people. See Wendell Willis, ed. *The Kingdom of God in 20th-Century Interpretation.* Peabody, MA: Hendricksen, 1987.

With this glimmer of understanding, Jesus then reveals to the Twelve that:

The Son of Man must undergo great suffering, and be rejected by the elders, the chief priests, and the scribes, and be killed, and after three days rise again. (Mk. 8:31)

But they do not understand. Peter, who has sensed the truth that Jesus is the Christ, rebukes Jesus for speaking of suffering, drawing from him the stinging rebuke: "Get behind me, Satan!" (8:33). The identification of Jesus as the Son of Man has generated intense debate among interpreters (see Chapter 11). Some argue that the phrase is a title for the apocalyptic figure who will come at the end of the age to inaugurate the Kingdom of God. If *Son of Man* is an apocalyptic title, the remarkable claim is being made that before the new age begins, the one sent to inaugurate it must suffer and die. Of course, it may simply be a euphemism for *I* or *me*. The emphasis is on the *necessity* of suffering. Three times this *passion prediction* is repeated by Jesus (Mk. 8:31–33, 9:30–32, 10:32–34), emphasizing its importance. Surely it gives us our first clue to Mark's basic interpretation of Jesus. Jesus *must* suffer before the Kingdom of God can come. His ministry of teaching and healing is not sufficient. Acclaiming him as Christ is not sufficient. Not even his disciples grasp the irony. The one who comes with awe-inspiring power and authority will be the one who is humiliated and killed by those whose authority he surpasses. Recognition is more than hearing the words. The bottom line is not only that Jesus must suffer but also that if they are his disciples, they will suffer too (8:34–38). The message they cannot grasp is the irony of his kingship. The man of power will be glorified in suffering! So must they.

This gospel has been called a passion narrative with an extended introduction, not only because the story of the final week in Jerusalem occupies one-third of it (11:1–16:8), but also because, with the passion, the secret is revealed. His entry into Jerusalem is a public pronouncement of the messianic nature of Jesus's ministry. He fulfills a prophecy for the entry of the Messiah into Jerusalem, but it is an entry of humility, not belligerent power. He cleanses the Temple but then refuses to discuss with the chief priests, scribes, and elders the nature of the authority by which he has acted. He makes no effort to use the incident as a catalyst for an open confrontation with the power of these religious leaders or the power of Rome. Only when he has been taken captive, and his fate has been sealed, does he accept the title of Christ. To the end, his closest disciples seem baffled. They desert him when the time comes to suffer and are absent when the empty tomb reveals the vindication of that suffering. At what is usually assumed to be the original ending of Mark's gospel (16:8), the women who have come to the tomb are overcome with awe and keep to themselves what they have seen and heard. On the cross, a suffering Jesus cries out, all alone, "My God, my God, why have you forsaken me?" (15:34), quoting Ps. 22:1, a lament. When apocalyptic signs herald the new age at his death, it is not the disciples, but a Roman centurion, who makes a confession of faith, "Truly this man was God's son!" (15:39).

As we look back over Mark's gospel, a pattern emerges behind the shadows. It begins with John the Baptizer. He proclaimed the message of a new age and, as a result, suffered. Jesus, too, announced the coming Kingdom with his words and deeds. But only at his suffering does the Kingdom begin to break into history. In the apocalyptic section of Mark (Chapter 13), we find the prediction that those who follow Jesus will likewise suffer, with the promise that "the one who endures to the end will be saved" (13:13). God's plan of salvation is now apparent. The way has been fully prepared by a suffering Messiah. He had to suffer, for this was necessary to God's plan. Now those who truly understand the meaning of his coming must likewise take up their crosses and suffer. Like their master, their suffering will lead ultimately to the glory of the Kingdom.

Matthew: A Higher Righteousness

The structure of the Gospel of Matthew is nearly as overt as the Gospel of Mark's is hidden. Interpreters of Matthew have long recognized the five-fold pattern of organization in the gospel, with a Birth Narrative and a Passion Narrative serving as introduction and conclusion:

Introduction: The New Obedience (Mt. 1–2);

1. The Higher Righteousness (Mt. 3–7);
2. True Discipleship (Mt. 8–10);
3. The Kingdom of Heaven (Mt. 11–13);
4. The New Israel (Mt. 14–18);
5. The End of the Age (Mt. 19–25);

Conclusion: With You Always (Mt. 26–28);

Within each of the five central sections of the gospel, a narrative is followed by a discourse on the same theme. Each of these discourses ends with a phrase such as "When Jesus had finished saying these things …" (7:28; 11:1; 13:53; 19:1; 26:1). Clearly this gospel is concerned, in contrast with Mark, not only with proclaiming the authority of Jesus as teacher and preacher but also with giving the content of his teaching. The five-fold division of the gospel seems patterned after the Five Books of Moses in the Tanak.

Another pattern in the gospel indicates concern for the relationship between Jesus and the Tanak. Many times Matthew introduces quotations from the Hebrew Bible with a formula that, with some variations, says: "All this took place to fulfill what was spoken by the LORD through the prophet …" (see 1:22; 2:5; 2:23; 4:14; 8:17; 12:17; 13:35; 21:4; 27:9–10). According to Matthew's gospel, prophecies of Scripture were meticulously fulfilled (i.e., dramatized) in the life and ministry of Jesus.

While the other gospels and other early Christian writings reflect the belief that Jesus was the fulfillment of the hopes of Israel, in this gospel "fulfillment" may be understood as the dominant theme. As New Testament scholar R. T. France has written, "Where others might be content to quote a few rather obvious texts as 'fulfilled' in Jesus, Matthew explores the nature of fulfillment with remarkable ingenuity, and with a systematic attention to the place of Jesus' ministry within the unfolding purpose of God which affects and controls his presentation of all aspects of the story and teaching of Jesus."[3] As France demonstrates, Matthew's focus on "fulfillment" is evident not only in the trademark formula for quoting the Tanak just cited but also in a preoccupation with the relation between Jesus and the Hebrew Bible in a host of other passages. For example, in the story of Jesus and his disciples breaking the commandments by eating on the Sabbath, found in all three Synoptic gospels, Matthew's version (12:1–8) adds to the Marcan account references to the Tanak in vv. 5–7 (Numbers 28:9–10, Hosea 6:6) that justify breaking the law for a higher cause.

Having observed some of the gospel's main structural characteristics and the central theme of "fulfillment," let us attempt to further reconstruct the literary world of Matthew's gospel, looking for another, related key to this gospel's portrayal of Jesus. While Mark's gospel begins with the Baptism of Jesus by John, Matthew provides a preface of special material related to the ancestry and birth of Jesus (Mt. 1–2). Careful attention to this introductory section shows that it, like the prologue to Mark's gospel, foreshadows the essence of the gospel.

The genealogy with which the gospel begins (Mt. 1:1–17) links Jesus to two key figures in the history of Israel and also in the LORD's relationship with Israel—Abraham and David—and the

[3]R. T. France. *Matthew: Evangelist and Teacher.* Downer's Grove, IL: InterVarsity Press, 1998, pp. 166–167, and entire chapter entitled "Fulfillment" (pp. 166–205).

promises given to them. He is a son of Abraham, to whom God promised a land, many descendants, and blessing. He is also a son of David, recipient of the promise of an everlasting dynasty, root of the messianic hope. Linking Jesus to these heroes is a way of claiming that through him the promises of God, given to his ancestors, will be fulfilled. Yet into this genealogy breaks the unexpected. In the ancient world, genealogies were typically patrilineal, but in Matthew's lineage of Jesus, five women are included—Tamar, Rahab, Ruth, Bathsheba, and Mary. Moreover, each of the first four women either bore children under suspicious circumstances or was of disreputable character. The point seems to be that behavior questionable from a moralistic perspective turned out to be justified by the fact that God's plan was fulfilled.

Against this background the story of the birth of Jesus is recounted. The first scene focuses on Joseph's response to the pregnancy of his betrothed wife, Mary. Joseph has a dilemma. Knowing that he has not fathered the child, he is obligated by the Torah to separate himself from the shame of Mary. However, as a righteous man, Joseph resolves to divorce Mary quietly and not call public attention to her sin. Already Joseph shows himself to be a humble and compassionate man who does not demand total legal satisfaction. Through a dream (linking him to another Joseph) he learns of a still more radical form of obedience rooted in a new act of God. The child in Mary's womb is of the Holy Spirit, a savior of his people. Joseph is challenged to respond by going beyond the letter of the law to faith, or obedience to God. In the first of the fulfillment formulas, Matthew interprets this event as the realization of Isaiah's prophecy of the birth to a virgin (although it is dubious that "virgin" is what the Hebrew text of Isaiah literally says) of a son who shall be called Immanuel. Because God is present with his people in a new way, a new, radical form of obedience, a higher righteousness, is expected.

The fact that the Gospel of Matthew in a sense ends as it begins, with a call for obedience and the assurance of the continued presence of Jesus (28:20), lends support to the view we will now develop more fully. The key to Matthew's world, the gospel's portrayal of Jesus, is a call to a radical obedience, a higher righteousness, linked to the assurance that God is present with those who take this step in a new, definitive way.

Joseph, a Jew, responds to God's new initiative, and so do a group of gentile "wise men from the East." They respond to a sign (the star) that marks a new beginning, even when it requires them to violate their responsibility to abide by the authority of the ruler in whose country they are guests. They too model a new, higher righteousness.

Righteousness, as Matthew uses the concept, means living in a way compatible with God's will, or simply rightness of life before God. It is not a series of things to do to qualify for God's blessing; it is Torah righteousness, a way of life that is the essence of the Kingdom.

In Matthew, Jesus not only calls for a higher righteousness but also models it himself. Although he has no need to be baptized by John, he undergoes this act of repentance, personifying the people he will call together as the New Israel, in Matthew's words "to fulfill all righteousness." In the Temptation in the Wilderness Jesus demonstrates complete and accepting obedience of God's will.

The narrative moves quickly to the Sermon on the Mount. Like Moses, Jesus delivers an authoritative teaching from a mountain, which fulfills the law and the prophets. However, the point is not that Jesus is a new Moses. Whereas at Sinai God spoke through Moses, Jesus teaches on his own, direct, authority. "You have heard of old, … but *I* say to you …." And the teaching is not really a new Torah, but the old clarified.

If there is a single cornerstone to Matthew's gospel, it is probably 5:17–20. There the Matthean Jesus emphasizes the continuing validity of the Hebrew Scripture. Until everything has been accomplished—that is, until the Kingdom of Heaven is fully realized—not even the tiniest letter in the Torah may be overlooked. Those who reduce the demands of Torah cannot expect high position in the Kingdom, although they will not be excluded. However, the person who both teaches and does as the Torah commands (a typically rabbinic emphasis on action as well as thought) will be great in the Kingdom. Indeed, Jesus demands that his followers exceed the righteousness of the spiritual elite of the time, the scribes and Pharisees. Later the Gospel of Matthew draws on a Marcan story to make clear the nature of this higher righteousness that fulfills the Torah (22:34–40). *All* the law and prophets hinge on two commandments—the great commandment to love the one God (Dt. 6:4–5) and the second, to love one's neighbor (Lev. 19:18).

Matthew now turns from word to deed. The second section (Mt. 8–10) begins with ten miracle stories (Mt. 8–9) illustrating Jesus acting in obedience out of love for God. The gospel then moves to the calling of the disciples and climaxes with emphasis on the response of faith as essential to healing. This sets the stage for the so-called *missionary discourse*, in which Jesus instructs his followers on the nature of true discipleship. Importantly, at this stage of the gospel, the mission is limited to Israel (10:5–6). Only after the Resurrection does the time come for disciples to go to all nations.

The narrative and discourse of the third section (Mt. 11–13) focus on the Kingdom of Heaven. Apparently influenced by rabbinic usage, this gospel avoids the phrase *Kingdom of God* (which Mark uses), substituting the circumlocution *Kingdom of Heaven*. The meaning, however, is the same. The Kingdom of Heaven is not a place but an eschatological situation in which God's sovereignty is fully manifest. In contrast to the portrait Mark paints of reluctant disciples who fail to grasp the truth, Matthew implies understanding and obedience. For example, Mark's rebuke after the parable of the sower (4:13) is given a positive note in Matthew (13:15–16).

In the fourth section (Mt. 14–18) the church is highlighted. The Marcan order of stories is rearranged so that accounts of the rejection of Jesus by people of his own home, by his family, and by the scribes and Pharisees can be contrasted with the enthusiastic response to Jesus by those he heals, by a gentile woman, and finally by Peter and the other disciples. In this section, as elsewhere in the gospel, Peter has a heightened role, in comparison with the other gospels. Jesus also lays down rules concerning discipline within the Christian community, including the possibility of exclusion for those unwilling to repent. Jesus is represented as conferring on the church the powers of a *beth din*, a rabbinic court, "to bind and to loose," to reach authoritative decisions by majority vote, not by special revelation or by charismatic biblical interpretation. (Rabbinic lore insists that not even a *bath qol*, a heavenly voice, can overturn a majority!) Matthew 16:19 and 18:18 taken together show that this was a collective power, not something given to Peter alone.

The last of the five Matthean sections has as its theme the final judgment, especially in terms of how this affects the church (Mt. 19–25). Like the other synoptics, Matthew includes an apocalyptic section stressing the imminence of the end. In Matthew's version an explicit indication of delay in the coming of the end is the insertion of the following statement: "this good news of the kingdom will be proclaimed throughout the world, as a testimony to all the nations; and *then the end will come*" (24:14; emphasis added). After the discourse, there is a series of parables counseling watchfulness. For this gospel there is no question that the coming of the end will involve a judgment on the basis of actual deeds of mercy rather than of protestations of faith (7:15–23; 25:31–46; *cf.* 21:28–46). The test of discipleship is doing God's will, not one's own, as Jesus models in the dramatic conclusion to the gospel.

Matthew's version of the Passion Narrative does not, like Mark's, highlight the actual suffering of Jesus. For Matthew the emphasis is on Jesus's acting out a radical obedience to the will of God. For example, Matthew adds to Mark's account of Jesus accepting the cross (Mk. 14:36), a further affirmation of obedience (26:42). The Resurrection opens the door for the inclusion of all in the Kingdom. During his public career, Jesus's commission to the disciples was to carry the gospel to Israel. Now, the Risen Lord sends his disciples into all the world to baptize and teach the kind of obedience they have learned from his teaching and his life (28:16–20). The descendant of Abraham has now become the fulfillment of the promise to Abraham that through Israel all nations of the earth shall be blessed.

The Gospel of Matthew turns a complete circle. The initial emphasis on radical obedience, introduced in the Birth Narrative, is explained through the earthly teaching of Jesus (3:15; 5:6, 20; 6:33; 7:21; 21:28–32; 25:31–46) and finally enacted by him on the cross. How is such a higher righteousness possible? Because, in the words of the angel to Joseph, Jesus is Immanuel and, in the final words of the Risen Jesus in the last verse of the gospel (28:20), "Remember, I am with you always, to the end of the age."

Luke: Good News for All

With the Acts of the Apostles, the Gospel of Luke forms a two-volume history of the origin and expansion of Christianity throughout the Mediterranean world (see Chapter 13). The gospel is the first volume, containing a narration of the life of Jesus from a distinct theological perspective.

Literary analysis of Luke is assisted by the fact that, unlike either Matthew or Mark, this gospel begins with a preface stating its purpose (1:1–4). The contribution of this gospel, the preface claims, is not originality. Others have compiled narratives of the words and works of Jesus. This is possibly a reference to Mark and Q, the two major sources of the gospel. Luke is aware of the process of transmission of tradition, from eyewitness to ministers of the word to those who, like the writer of the gospel, compile these traditions. The stated purpose of this narrative is "an orderly account" that will seek to point to the "truth" about the story of Jesus. A preface to justify the writing of the work is a common device in Hellenistic historical writing.

Unlike the other gospels, Luke identifies the intended recipient of the work—Theophilus, which means "friend of God." Whether Theophilus is an individual (a Roman official or eminent citizen), a group of persons, or a literary device, Luke's intended audience is clearly (a) gentile, (b) aware of the story of Jesus, and (c) among the so-called God-fearers who were interested in the Jewish God.

Broadly speaking, Luke adopts Mark's basic order. Although Luke's gospel is a more sophisticated literary work than either Mark or Matthew, the world it creates is another variation of their worlds. Like the other gospels, it weaves a pattern highlighting not only what Jesus once said and did but also what it all means for those reading the gospel.

As with Mark and Matthew, this gospel begins with a section foreshadowing the major themes that dominate the portrayal of Jesus throughout the work. Like Matthew 1–2, Luke 1–2 is a Birth Narrative. However, Luke draws on an entirely different set of traditions to tell the story of the birth of Jesus. The major Lucan motifs introduced in this "prologue" and developed in the rest of the gospel are universalism, social justice, compassion for those rejected by the establishment, the crucial role of women in the story of Jesus, the importance of the spirit, the joy that envelops those who respond to Jesus, and the confession that Jesus is LORD. By examining these motifs and how they function in the infancy account and the gospel as a whole, we can develop a sense of Luke's unique world.

UNIVERSALISM Luke places the birth account of Jesus in the context of the events of world history (1:1; 2:1–2), suggesting that here is an event of universal significance. Whereas Matthew traces the genealogy of Jesus to Abraham and David, to emphasize Jesus's role as the fulfiller of the promises to Israel, Luke's genealogy begins with Adam, relating Jesus to all humanity. According to the angels who herald the birth of Jesus, the good news associated with his coming is for "all the people" (2:10).

This emphasis on the universal scope of the salvation Jesus has come to announce is woven throughout the entire gospel. As the story of the ministry of Jesus begins, it is with another reference to the events of world history (3:1–2). In the account of Jesus's baptism, Luke extends Mark's quotation from Isaiah to include the clearly universalistic prophecy that all flesh shall see the salvation of God (3:6; *cf.* Is. 40:5). In Luke's version of the parable of the banquet (14:15–24), which Matthew had adapted to highlight judgment (Mt. 22:1–10), the emphasis is on the inclusiveness of the invitation. Luke's apocalyptic discourse also adds a phrase stressing the universal implications of the events that will signal the end (21:25). Matthew withholds the universal emphasis until the Risen Christ commissions his disciples. Luke includes such a reference in the final commissioning (24:47), but as the capstone of a theme that has pervaded the entire gospel.

SOCIAL JUSTICE   Closely related to the universalistic emphasis is a clear concern for social justice. It is already present in the Birth Narrative in the hymn of praise (the Magnificat) Mary sings (1:46–55). The prophetic theme recurs frequently in the heart of the gospel, as, for example, in the stirring sermon at the synagogue in Capernaum (4:16–30) and in the concern of Jesus for justice for one of the criminals crucified with him (23:39–43). Luke's special concern for justice for the poor and oppressed can most clearly be seen in a comparison of the beatitudes in this gospel with those in Matthew (Lk. 6:20–21; Mt. 5:3, 6).

COMPASSION FOR OUTCASTS   Similar to the emphasis on social justice in the Gospel of Luke is the motif of compassion for those of low social esteem. The Birth Narrative introduces this concern in the account of Mary, who, as a woman without a husband, is of low social prestige in the ancient world. To her the angel Gabriel says, "Greetings, favored one! The Lord is with you!" (1:28). The motif continues with the account of the night of Jesus's birth. The baby himself is born in the humblest of surroundings. He is attended not by wealthy wise men, but by shepherds who have come from the flocks and who return to them after seeing the baby. Whereas Matthew makes no mention of Nazareth as the family home of Jesus, Luke alludes to the fact that this backwoods hamlet in the hill country of Galilee was indeed Jesus's hometown.

In the body of the gospel there are further references to the concern of Jesus for those of low social station, as well as those despised by "proper" society. The well-known parable of the good Samaritan, also found only in Luke's gospel, focuses on the fact that a social outcast from Samaria is more in tune with the will of God than established religious leaders. Moreover, in the ministry of Jesus as recounted by Luke, it is often those who have been branded with social disapproval who receive his attention (e.g., 7:36–50; 17:11–19; 19:1–10).

THE ROLE OF WOMEN   Luke also demonstrates an interest beyond that of the other gospels in the place of women in the story of Jesus. In the Birth Narrative of Matthew, the chief character (besides Jesus) is Joseph, but in Luke's account the focus is on the women of the story. Not only is Mary the principal actor, but it is also she who grasps the true significance of the birth of Jesus (1:47–56) and who is sensitive to the underlying meaning of events (2:19, 51).

Later in the gospel (and in the continued narrative in Acts), women occupy central positions among the disciples of Jesus. Luke names Mary Magdalene (*not* a prostitute in the gospels!); Joanna, wife of a high government official; and Susanna among prominent members of Jesus's entourage. Luke stresses the fact that in the last days of Jesus's life, it was the "women who had followed him from Galilee" who stood by him (23:49, 55). Unique to Luke is the account of Mary and Martha, two sisters who received Jesus into their home, Mary becoming a member of Jesus's coeducational seminar (10:38–42).

THE HOLY SPIRIT   The Holy Spirit plays such a crucial role in Luke's account that it is sometimes called, as we have noted, the *Gospel of the Spirit*. During the Birth Narrative the Spirit is frequently mentioned (1:15, 17, 35; 2:25, 26, 27). At the Baptism Luke offers the most graphic and public picture of the descent of the Holy Spirit on Jesus (3:21–22). Jesus begins his ministry "full of the Holy Spirit" (4:1, 14, 18). Interestingly, there is no further mention by Luke of the Spirit coming on Jesus or anyone else during his ministry, as though the descent of the Spirit was a singular event in the life of Jesus. Once empowered, Jesus was led by the Spirit. The next, and final, reference to the Spirit in Luke is at the end of the gospel, when the Risen Jesus instructs his disciples to remain in Jerusalem until "you are clothed with power from on high" (24:49). The allusion, of course, is to Pentecost, when, according to the narration in Acts, all the disciples were "filled with the Holy Spirit" (Acts 2:4).

RESPONSES TO JESUS: JOY AND RECOGNITION OF HIS LORDSHIP   The most frequent response to the coming of Jesus is simply "joy." When the angels announce the birth of Jesus, they call it an event of "great joy" (2:10; *cf.* 1:14). During his ministry (10:17; 15:7, 10) and after the Resurrection (24:41), persons respond with a joy that is sometimes overwhelming. The very last verse of the gospel records the "great joy" of the disciples who had seen the Risen Lord (24:52).

The other typical response to Jesus in Luke is the confession of Jesus as Lord. Beginning with the Birth Narrative (1:43; 2:11), Jesus is acknowledged at least eighteen times in the gospel as Lord. Like *Son of God, Lord* is an acclamation of power and authority that would have been more meaningful in gentile contexts than the Jewish ascription *Christ*.

THE "ORDER" IN THE GOSPEL   These recurring motifs help us enter Luke's world, but they do not represent the "order" Luke claims to have found that manifests the truth about Jesus. We come closer to seeing this pattern when we observe the implicit structure of the gospel. In the view of many modern scholars, Luke's "orderly account" is a reinterpretation of the history of God's plan of salvation as "three ages of the Spirit." The first age, presupposed by the gospel's tracing of the lineage of Jesus from Adam, is that which lasted from the creation, when the Spirit hovered over the waters of chaos and life was breathed into Adam, to John the Baptizer. The second age is the ministry of Jesus, beginning with the descent of the Spirit at his Baptism and continuing through the Resurrection and the promise of the Spirit's coming on the disciples. The third age, the Age of the Church, is the subject of Acts, beginning with the Pentecost account of the Spirit's descent and pointing toward the movement of a spirit-filled church throughout the known world. The purpose of the gospel's account of Jesus is to reveal the nature of the kingdom that will come when all the earth is full of the spirit and Jesus returns in power. During this period Jesus will embody the compassion, justice, joy, and universal scope of the Kingdom.

John: The Journey of Jesus

Like Matthew, Mark, and Luke, the Gospel of John is a proclamation of the "good news" about Jesus Christ, Son of God, meant to inspire a response of faith. The gospel states this purpose as follows (20:31):

> … these [signs] are written so that you may
> come to believe that Jesus is the Messiah, the Son of God,
> and that through believing you may have life in his name.

However, even the most casual explorer of the world of John's gospel senses that it is very different from the Synoptics in content, style, and mood. In 200 C.E. Clement of Alexandria distinguished John from the others as a "spiritual" gospel. That is a good description.

JOHN AND THE SYNOPTICS   Unlike Matthew or Luke, John has no Infancy Narrative. Instead, this gospel begins with a prologue that takes the story of Jesus all the way back, before the creation of the cosmos. In the interaction with John the Baptizer, there is no indication Jesus was actually baptized by John. Instead, Jesus and his disciples are portrayed baptizing people themselves and in tension and conflict with John and his disciples.

Whereas the Synoptics suggest that Jesus made only one journey to Jerusalem and conducted most of his ministry in Galilee, John portrays several journeys to Jerusalem. The Synoptics imply a one-year ministry. Because John refers to three Passovers (2:13; 6:4; 11:55), a three-year ministry is suggested. The Synoptics describe Jesus's last supper with the disciples as a Passover meal. John indicates that it took place on the day before Passover, and the crucifixion of Jesus occurred on the day the Passover lambs were sacrificed. In the Synoptics the cleansing of the Temple takes place during the final week. In John it is at the beginning of Jesus's ministry (2:13–25).

Most important in comparing John with the Synoptics is the difference in the way the teaching of Jesus is portrayed. In the Synoptics the sayings of Jesus are either individual units or loosely grouped series. The focus is on each saying. In contrast, the teaching of Jesus in John is in the form of long discourses on a single theme such as his relationship with God the Father, and the bread of life. In the Synoptics Jesus talks about his identity as the Son of God only in oblique terms. In John, Jesus declares who he is in bold assertions, using the formula "I am ...." These assertions are reminiscent of the form of divine self-revelation used in Exodus 3 and Second Isaiah (Is. 40–55). While parables about the Kingdom dominate the synoptic portrayal of the teaching of Jesus, there are no parables in John. In the Synoptics the metaphors typically point to the Kingdom of God or of Heaven. John is full of symbols, but they point to the mystery of who Jesus is and the nature of his relationship with those who believe in him.

In the Synoptics there is a mood of expectancy rooted in the hope of the return of Jesus (*parousia*) and the new life to come. In John that hope is maintained, but the tone is dominated by a feeling of realization, not expectancy. For believers the new life has already come. Through belief in Jesus they already experience the power of the Resurrection (e.g., 5:24). John delights in paradoxes such as this, between a sense of *already* and that of *not yet*. Another paradox is present in John's description of the Crucifixion and the double meaning of the term *lifted up*. Although Jesus is "lifted up" on the cross to die a shameful death (8:28), through the same act of "lifting up" he is exalted by God (12:32–34). Sometimes, John seems to be saying, you must look beneath the apparent meaning to see a deeper significance.

THE STRUCTURE OF THE GOSPEL OF JOHN   This "layering" of meaning is evident in the structure of John. It follows a rather straightforward outline to tell the story of Jesus. However, at a deeper level, the structure of the gospel is expressed in one of the self-revelations of Jesus: "I came from the Father and have come into the world; again, I am leaving the world and am going to the Father" (16:28). The gospel can be viewed in terms of three stages of this cosmic journey: the life of Jesus with the Father from whom he comes; his life in the world, revealing the glory of his Father to those who believe; and his return to the Father to a life of glory. The gospel focuses especially on his life in the world. Chapter 1 begins the story by revealing the origin of the journey and foreshadowing his revelation in the world. Chapters 2–12 contain the seven signs by which Jesus revealed to the world the glory of the Father. In Chapters 13–17 Jesus prepares "his own" for his return to the Father. In Chapters 18–20 the Son returns to the Father in glory.

This is the *horizontal* structure of the gospel. The journey itself, and the response of "believing" in order to have "life," implies a *vertical* dimension as well. In fact, the journey of Jesus is both vertical and horizontal, from the Father to the world and back. At any point along the journey, he manifests the "glory" (full nature) of his Father so that people can see God's presence breaking into time and space. The "eternal life" he brings is a status of existence through which the believer breaks free from the horizontal continuum of birth, life, and death. Through transformation wrought by God, the believer shares the unity that the Son has with the Father. We will now look more closely at the stages of Jesus's journey as presented in John.

THE JOURNEY: STAGE ONE (JOHN 1)   The Gospel of John begins with a poetic midrash (free interpretation) on the creation account in Genesis 1, as if to say, "To tell the real story of Jesus, we must begin at the *very* beginning." Genesis 1:3 says that creation began as God said, "Let there be light." This poem looks into that verse to explore the nature and significance of the divine utterance. The key term is Word (*logos*), which has a background in Greek philosophy and also a variety of possible biblical and rabbinic references, all of which the poem could very well be affirming.

In Greek philosophy, especially Stoicism, the *logos* was the principle of order, or reason, lying beneath the seeming chaos of the world. Jewish philosophers such as the Platonistic Philo of Alexandria had associated *logos* with the personified Wisdom of Jewish wisdom speculation. In that tradition, Wisdom is portrayed as the agent of God's creative power, present at the origin of the cosmos, bringing order out of chaos (for example, Prov. 8:22-31). The Torah plays a similar role in rabbinic thought. In the prophetic tradition, the Word of God was a means of revealing the divine will, as was the Word in the Torah tradition (as in the Ten Words [Commandments]). Thus, *logos* is a term with a number of layers of meaning that bring together basic themes from both Greek and Jewish intellectual traditions.

For the poem, this synthesis is a starting point; it opens up an even fuller range of meaning than the Greek and Jewish traditions suggest. The Word is paradoxically with God, yet "is" God. The *logos* to which this poem points is not merely a cosmic principle or agent of God; the Word mysteriously shares a common identity with the one God, yet it is also mysteriously present in the creation as "life." The *logos* is identified with the light of creation (Gen. 1:3–4) and is the true source of religious illumination. John does not use the term *logos* after his prologue. But light and light/darkness are recurrent themes.

The prologue and other passages in the gospel dealing with the motif of light reflect John's apparent contact with Jewish *Creation Mysticism* (see Chapter 10). But John is not a gospel merely for mystics. It is also a gospel by a mystic for a larger Christian community. The full significance of the creation of light is that "darkness" (a symbol for the chaos and evil threatening the divine order and will) is held in check. Darkness is present, but it cannot overcome the light, and by implication, the life that is the source of the light.

A brief narrative interlude (vv. 6–8) introduces the motif of witnessing to the life-giving light and begins to intertwine the mythic with the historical, for the witness is not a divine being but a man named John sent from God. He recognizes the light in a *person*, but he is not himself the light.

In verses 9–10 the poem resumes. The light-Word is a person who has come into the world. In verse 10 "world" takes on a double meaning as the creation but also as that which fails to recognize the "true light." The focus narrows from the "world" to "his own home" and "his own people," who do not receive him. Chapters 2–12 of the gospel develop this motif of rejection by "his own." In contrast, those who do receive him "by believing in his name" (which means not merely verbally acknowledging but also trusting in who and what he is) will become "children of God," not in the apparent, physical sense, but at the deeper, spiritual level. Chapters 13–17 focus on the community of those who respond in this way.

Now comes the climax toward which the poem has been moving. How is the *logos* present in the world? The Word is incarnate (in-fleshed), in a way in which "we" can see it. "We have seen his glory" points to a community bearing witness to the glory of God manifest in this person. This "enfleshment" stands in stark contrast to the world-rejecting ideologies of Hellenism and may be an explicitly anti-gnostic statement. Meanwhile, in Jewish tradition the glory of God was said to dwell in the Temple. There the believer could behold, indirectly through the high priest, the holiness of God. This poem is saying that the "Word made flesh" manifests the divine reality. The stage is set for a confrontation between the Temple and the Son. The comment (vv. 17–18) makes clear that in this gospel's view, the effect of the Word becoming flesh is that a new means of access to God has been opened. Finally, he is named: Jesus Christ.

THE JOURNEY: STAGE TWO (JOHN 2–12)   John tells the story of the public ministry of Jesus through seven accounts of signs (wondrous events pointing to a larger meaning) by which Jesus manifests his glory. Typically, the miracle is followed by a dialogue between Jesus and someone else, and then a monologue by Jesus. The seven signs are:

> turning water into wine at the marriage feast in Cana (2:1–11);
> curing an official's son at Cana (4:46–54);
> curing a paralytic in Jerusalem (5:1–15);
> feeding the five thousand in Galilee (6:1–15);
> walking on water (6:16–21);
> curing the blind man in Jerusalem (9);
> raising Lazarus from the dead in Bethany (11).

Scholars call this section of John the *Book of Signs.* The first, third, sixth, and seventh miracles have no parallels in the Synoptics, while the rest do. There are no exorcisms in John. The signs are woven into a narrative by inclusion of transitional segments that move Jesus from place to place.

As the prologue has indicated, those who believe are empowered to be born of God and receive new life. This is developed in a dialogue between Jesus and Nicodemus, a Pharisee and member of the Sanhedrin, on the theme of being born "anew" or "from above" (both translations of 3:3 are possible) and in a monologue on the theme of the power of the Son to give eternal life to those who believe in him (3:1–21). In the latter, the future expectation of judgment and the hope of new life are brought into the present. Jesus's reference to being born of the water and the spirit almost certainly means the church's rite of Baptism with the laying on of hands, symbolizing the gift of the Spirit. Elsewhere John alludes to both Baptism and the Lord's Supper (Eucharist), usually referring to the elements of water, bread, and wine.

Balancing the dialogue with Nicodemus, one of the rulers of Israel, who does *not* grasp the real behind the apparent, is a dialogue with a Samaritan woman who recognizes who Jesus is (John 4). A drink of water becomes the occasion for the revelation that Jesus brings the water of eternal life. And a comment by the woman about worship becomes an opportunity for a monologue about true worship in "spirit and truth."

The third to sixth signs are grouped together around the theme of Jesus and the Jewish festivals. First, Jesus and the Sabbath are taken up in Chapter 5. While in Jerusalem, Jesus heals a paralyzed man on the Sabbath. As in the Synoptics, this causes a controversy. Rabbinic practice authorized emergency, but not elective, medicine on the Sabbath, the day that prefigures the Kingdom of God. John typically generalizes the interaction between Jesus and religious leaders, so that here "the Jews" chastise him for working on the Sabbath. This becomes the occasion for Jesus to reveal his identity as the Son of God who does the work of his Father. The Son has the power to give life and to judge. He makes clear that to honor the Father, one must honor the Son.

John's use of the term "the Jews" for Jesus's adversaries constitutes an enigma. It cannot mean all the Jewish people. For example, Jesus and his disciples were Jews all their lives. Jesus acknowledged his Jewishness in the story of the Samaritan woman at the well (Jn. 4:1–42). It may be that John uses the term for those among the religious leadership who opposed Jesus. Samaritans used the term for those who acknowledge the religious priority of Jerusalem. Finally, the Greek (and Hebrew and Aramaic) words that underlie it meant "Judeans," people of Judah, although the term had acquired a religio-ethnic meaning in the Greco-Roman world.

In Chapter 6 Jesus and the Passover are the subject. The synoptic miracles of the feeding of the five thousand and the walking on water occur. Again, a distinction is drawn between the real and the apparent. The *real* bread of life is not that which the Israelites received in the wilderness, Jesus says, for "I am the bread of life." Those who receive the true bread are those who believe in Jesus. In Chapters 7–10 both the Feast of Tabernacles and the Feast of Dedication (Hanukkah) are used to reveal who Jesus is.

Periodically, John has mentioned the intention of "the Jews" to kill Jesus (5:18; 7:1). Now, the death of Jesus moves to the fore as the concern dominating the narrative. In a "rounding off," the public ministry of Jesus is described as ending (11:54) where it began, at the place where John baptized (10:40).

The last sign, the raising of Lazarus, leads to the crucifixion (11:45–53) and Jesus's revelation that "I am the resurrection and the life" (11:25). In a deeply ironic statement, the high priest, Caiaphas, unwittingly affirms the significance of the death of Jesus (11:49–50). And Jesus is symbolically anointed for death (12:1–8). As the Book of Signs draws to a close, Jesus literally "cries out" the significance of what he has done and the response of belief his acts should elicit (12:44–50).

THE JOURNEY: STAGE THREE (JOHN 13–20)   The public ministry and the revelation of his glory to "the world" complete, Jesus turns to his disciples to prepare them for his "glorification" and return to the Father (Jn. 13–17). At a last supper with his disciples he washes their feet, in an act of humility, as an example of how they should act and a prelude to his own action on the cross.

In a farewell discourse (Jn. 14–16) Jesus tells his disciples that he is going to "prepare a place for you" (14:1–2). In John's world the journey of the believer should model the journey of Jesus. Jesus uses journey imagery, saying "I am the way, and the truth, and the life. No one comes to the Father, except through me" (14:6). If the believer wishes to follow Jesus, he must "do the works that I do" (14:12) and "keep my commandments" (14:15). To guide and teach them, God will send the Holy Spirit (helper, advocate) to dwell in the believers (14:16–17, 26). Using the image of a vine, Jesus speaks allegorically of "abiding in me" like branches in a vine, which are to "bear fruit" (15:1–11). The believers are to enter into a relationship of love with one another (15:12–17) and to separate themselves from the "world" (15:18–27). They are to expect persecution, even death (16:1–4). He then reveals to them the journey he is on (16:28).

Turning now to heaven, Jesus offers a "high priestly prayer" (John 17). He prays for himself, that the Father might glorify him with "the glory that I had in your own existence before the world existed" (17:5). He prays for his disciples, asking not that they be taken "out of the world," but kept from the "evil one" (17:6–19). Finally, he prays for all believers everywhere (17:20–26), asking that they might share in the unity he has with the Father so that the world might believe.

Although the Passion Narrative in John roughly follows the same order as in the Synoptics, there are significant differences in emphasis. For one thing, the role of Jewish leaders in the death of Jesus is heightened, while the role of the Roman procurator Pilate is softened (see 19:11). In fact, in John, Pilate is portrayed as a sympathetic figure who is only interested in the welfare of Jesus. In addition, Jesus moves through his trial and crucifixion without a sign of anguish or despair. This is the moment of his glorification, according to John.

At the trial before the high priest we encounter a disciple (18:15), who is the so-called beloved disciple (20:2) referred to elsewhere in the gospel (13:23–26; 19:25–27; 21:7, 20–24). In 21:24 this disciple is identified as the source of the tradition on which this gospel is based.

Missing in this gospel are any of the apocalyptic signs associated with the crucifixion. At the crucifixion, Jesus says, with dignity, "it is finished," and dies. In the resurrection appearances, the emphasis is on seeing Jesus as a spiritual presence. Thomas is reprimanded for insisting on physical proof in order to believe. "Blessed are those," the Risen Jesus says, "who have not seen [physically] and yet have come to believe" (20:29). Once Jesus has returned to his Father, he can no longer be seen. Belief must be based on the testimony of others. The gospel ends with a statement of its basic purpose (20:31).

Balancing the prologue is an epilogue (John 21) that narrates a post-resurrection appearance of Jesus in Galilee. It highlights the restoration of a chastened Peter, after his earlier denial, to a position of leadership in the community, taking the role of shepherd. It also refers to the "other disciple" and his role as a writer of the traditions about Jesus.

THE HISTORICAL WORLD: THE SETTINGS OF THE GOSPELS

We return now to the historical world. On the basis of available evidence, what are the most likely historical contexts in which the four canonical gospels were written?

Mark

We have already accepted the theory of the development of the Synoptic gospels, which holds that Mark was the earliest. Traditions that can be traced to approximately 150 C.E. attribute authorship of this gospel to John Mark, the companion of the apostle Paul and, perhaps, of Peter. This tradition influenced the titling of this work as "The Gospel According to Mark." However, we must realize that this gospel, like the others, is anonymous if only internal evidence is considered. None of the gospels includes the name of the author. All the titles came from later church traditions, which may or may not have historical validity. Association with apostles or those close to apostles gave credibility and authority to the gospels and was a common practice in the ancient world.

It is possible that someone called John Mark wrote the Gospel of Mark but by no means certain. First Peter 5:13 does mention an associate named Mark, whom the author calls "my son." However, most modern scholars do not believe the New Testament Letters of Peter were written by the apostle Peter (see Chapter 15). Furthermore, the itinerary in the Gospel of Mark (e.g., 7:31) suggests a lack of familiarity with the geography of Palestine. The author of Mark most likely lived outside Palestine.

Both the Acts of the Apostles and the Letters of Paul identify an associate of Paul named Mark (Acts 12:25, Col. 4:10) and Acts 12:12 names a John Mark who is a member of the Jerusalem community of followers of Jesus. However, there is no trace of Paul's theology in the Gospel. In addition, the Gospel's confusion about the practices of the Pharisees in relation to other Jews (e.g., 7:3) renders an association with Paul or Peter unlikely, given the fact that Paul himself was a Pharisee and Peter knew well the distinctive character of the Pharisees. The safest conclusion is that the author of the Gospel is anonymous.

The date of the Gospel can be determined with more confidence. According to tradition, the gospel was written after the death of Peter and Paul in Rome about 63 C.E. Modern scholars focus on the Jewish revolt against Rome (66–70 C.E.) in their dating. The gospel itself seems to indicate the destruction of Jerusalem is either imminent or has just taken place (13:2, 14), so a dating just before or after 70 C.E. appears most likely.

Mark the Evangelist. Traditional representations of the author of the Gospel of Mark frequently show him holding a book to represent his gospel, as in this mosaic. He is often accompanied by his symbol, a winged lion. *Source:* Zvonimir Atletic/Shutterstock

The tradition of Roman origin for the Gospel of Mark is credible, for the gospel seems to have a general Christian audience in mind. Since the gospel is written in Greek, the audience was presumably Greek-speaking. The audience was more likely Gentile than Jewish, since the gospel assumes readers are not familiar with Hebrew and Aramaic words and Jewish practices (e.g., 5:41; 7:3–4, 22, 34; 12:18; 15:22).

Matthew

Like other gospels, Matthew has no direct reference within the work itself to its author or place of origin. A report usually dated about 130 C.E. seems to attribute origin of the gospel to the apostle Matthew, although the reference is to a Hebrew writing (the original Q?), and this gospel (like the others) was almost certainly composed in Greek. Because it used Mark as a source, it is hard to accept that the gospel as it stands is an eyewitness account of an apostle, even though it is the only one to name the tax collector called by Jesus as Matthew (9:9; 10:3).

Matthew the Tax Collector. In one of a series of statues of the twelve apostles in the Lateran Basilica in Rome, the apostle Matthew is represented as a tax collector (see Mt. 9:9, 10:3) in a work by the Baroque sculptor Camillo Rusconi (1658–1728).   *Source:* Jozef Sedmak/ Shutterstock

The familiarity of the gospel with Jewish law and customs and its concern over the "law and prophets" have caused some to view the author as an anonymous Christian scribe or perhaps a member of a school of Christian interpreters. For example, in substituting the phrase "Kingdom of Heaven" for "Kingdom of God," Matthew shows sensitivity to the Jewish practice of using circumlocutions such as Power, Glory, or Heaven for the divine name. The concern for church order and discipline suggests someone active in the leadership of a Christian community.

Because the gospel seems to assume the destruction of Jerusalem (22:7), a date after 70 C.E. is likely. If Mark was composed about 70 C.E., then Matthew could date to 80 C.E. or later. Because the earliest witness to Matthew's gospel is Ignatius, bishop of Antioch in Syria about 110 C.E., and because Antioch was an important center for early Christianity, with a mix of Jewish and gentile Christians, it seems a likely place of origin for the gospel.

The gospel clearly presupposes tension between traditional Jews and Christians (some of whom are Jewish), and perhaps between Jewish and gentile Christians, so the need to define Christian teaching as distinct from traditional Judaism is one obvious motive for its being written. As we have suggested, it may have served as a manual of instruction and discipline for a Christian community. Our observation that Matthew may have been a sort of Christian scribe or rabbi suggests that the author would have needed to defend his authority against the rising influence in the Jewish world of the rabbinate centered in Yavneh. The intended audience surely included Jewish Christians who needed to be reassured that the Christian gospel was not a negation of their heritage, but rather a fulfillment of it.

Luke

As early as 200 C.E. commentators recognized that the Gospel of Luke and Acts were written by the same author. As we have seen, this is almost certainly the case. Another tradition dating from about 180 C.E. is the source of the title of the gospel. It holds that the gospel was written by an associate of the Apostle Paul, a physician named Luke, who is mentioned in Col. 4:14 and 2 Tim. 4:11. However, at least two factors mitigate against identifying the author of the gospel as a companion of Paul named Luke the physician. If this Luke was the author of Luke–Acts, would not the gospel and Acts more clearly reflect the influence of Pauline theology? In addition, the author of Acts claims no direct association with Paul nor quotes the letters of Paul.

Luke the Evangelist. Traditional representations of the author of the Gospel of Luke often show him with his symbol, the ox. Another tradition is that he was one of the first Christian artists.   *Source:* Zvonimir Atletic/ Shutterstock

Because the Greek vocabulary and style of the Gospel of Luke are more refined than those of Mark and Matthew, it is likely that the author was an anonymous, educated gentile or Hellenistic Jewish Christian. The preface reflects awareness of Greek style. Attribution to Luke the physician gives the gospel the authority of one believed to be close to Paul.

Like Matthew, Luke used Mark as a source and seems to presuppose the destruction of Jerusalem in 70 C.E. (21:24). Because the gospel's preface looks back at two earlier stages of development of the tradition, we can assume a date about the same as or shortly after Matthew, about 85–90 C.E. The fact that Luke suggests a dampening down of the expectation of an imminent end time (e.g., 19:11) may also be seen as evidence for a date later in the first century C.E.

Because Luke does not seem to have a very good grasp of Palestinian geography, a gentile Christian setting outside Palestine is suggested. Of all the gospels, Luke seems to be addressed to a general audience to explain the universal implications of the story of Jesus, especially educated Romans already aware of and drawn to the Christian message.

John

According to this gospel the traditions on which it is based stem from the "beloved disciple" (21:24). The Christian Church traditionally has assumed that this was John, the son of Zebedee, who went to live in Ephesus, where he wrote the gospel. However, the epilogue to the gospel hints that this disciple did not live too long (21:23). A more general problem with identifying John, or any of the immediate disciples of Jesus, as the author is that the gospel seems to reflect a process of theological development. It is difficult to believe that the level of theological sophistication present in this gospel would have been reached so quickly.

An attractive theory of authorship is that of a *Johannine School*, which perhaps began with the beloved disciple and his reflections. As was the custom in Judaism, followers may have been attracted to this teacher and preserved his teachings about Jesus. The Johannine School theory is supported by the existence of other Johannine writings—the Letters of John. These are similar enough to the gospel in language, style, and thought to suggest common origin. We have already witnessed the phenomenon of a school preserving and developing a master's teachings in the Isaianic school associated with the Book of Isaiah (see Chapter 6).

If the gospel was written in the context of a "school," then there is not necessarily a single date of composition. The question remains of the time frame within which it developed. The latest evidence of a date comes from a papyrus fragment of several verses of the gospel (18:31–33, 37–38) found in Egypt and dated by scholars to the first half of the second century C.E. If the gospel was circulating in Egypt by about 125 C.E., it must have been written by about 100. In addition, a reference to expulsion from the synagogue in 9:22 probably reflects a ruling not adopted until 80 or 90 C.E. This points to a date for the final redaction of John about 80–100 C.E. However, earlier editions of the gospel may have existed prior to this time. An early time of origin for the gospel in some form is supported by some of the evidence concerning its intended audience.

In its final redaction the intended audience is surely the general Christian Church. However, there is a good possibility that there was originally a unique Christian community in which the gospel circulated in some form. Was there a Johannine community composed of "children of light," which, like the Qumran sect, withdrew from the world to prepare for the coming (again) of the Messiah and a new age? If there was, it probably did not withdraw into the wilderness, nor was it as exclusive as the Qumranian Covenanters. John indicates that there is antagonism with the world, and the community is not "of the world," but, like Jesus, the community is sent into the world to bear witness to Jesus. The community is not restricted to the purified, but is open to all willing to "come and see"—Jew and Gentile alike. Moreover, it was apparently not an apocalyptic community

John the Evangelist. The author of the Gospel of John is represented on a stained-glass window in St. George's Anglican Cathedral in Perth, Australia. *Source:* Tupungato/Shutterstock

awaiting the end, as was the Qumranian sect. The *parousia* was, as we have seen, deemphasized, and the stage was set for the community to exist for some time. If anything, its orientation was mystical, teaching persons how to experience the presence of God through the church sacraments and meditation on God's Son, who was, after all, the unmediated light of creation (1:4–5). Some members of the community may have practiced a Christian version of Creation Mysticism (see Chapter 10).

The Gospel of John portrays Jesus as the Redeemer who came from the Father to reveal God's glory on earth and then returned to the Father. On the surface this is a gnostic interpretation of Jesus, for Gnostics spoke of a divine figure who descended from heaven in order to liberate a selected group of spiritual people from their entrapment in the evil material world. However, it is clear that the gospel uses gnostic imagery in a polemical manner, to attack the gnostic point of view. Gnostics viewed the world as inherently evil, created by a fallen divine being. They viewed the Redeemer as a divine being who entered the evil world but was not part of it. The gospel makes clear that the world as created is not evil. It is the creation of God through the Redeemer himself. And the Redeemer is not purely a divine being, for the Word became flesh. Although there is a dualism between spirit and flesh, good and evil, life and death, and the world and the heavenly realm, the gospel portrays Jesus as the mediator between these polarities so that they lose their power.

In a more positive sense, the gospel was written not to counter, but to enhance, a school of thought with its roots in the Hebrew Scriptures—Jewish wisdom. As observed in Chapter 8, one dimension of Jewish wisdom was speculation on the principle of order in the world. In Proverbs 8 and Sirach 24, Wisdom is portrayed as a "person" who participated with God as an agent of creation and who "dwelled" in Israel. She is also the communicator of the divine will and purpose. In the Wisdom of Solomon this is especially apparent (9:9–10). Although John shifts from the feminine *Sophia* (Wisdom) to the masculine *Logos* (Word) to speak of Jesus (and draw in Greek philosophical imagery), the gospel is squarely within the wisdom tradition. As Sirach 24 developed Proverbs 8 to identify the place of Wisdom's dwelling as the Torah, John 1 takes a step beyond to assert that the Word–Wisdom had become human and "dwelled among us."

So, the intended audience of the gospel was probably originally a mixed community of Jewish Christians who withdrew from Temple worship to form a new community of believers in Jesus, led by the Spirit. They were perhaps joined by Gentiles. It is certainly possible that this community and its gospel existed very early in Christian history. In its first stages John may have been the earliest gospel!

Summary

The previous chapter analyzed the New Testament gospels as historical sources for the life of Jesus of Nazareth. In this chapter we summarized the results of literary historical study of the gospels and offered interpretations of the literary worlds of each of the gospels. We also considered the original historical settings of the gospels.

Gospel is a type of literature that developed in the first century C.E. as Christian writers sought appropriate ways to interpret the meaning of the life of Jesus. Comparison of the four canonical gospels reveals close similarities among Matthew, Mark, and Luke; hence, we call them the *Synoptic* gospels. The most widely accepted theory of how the Synoptic gospels are interrelated is the Two-Source Hypothesis, which holds that Mark and a *sayings source* (called *Q*) were the main sources used by the authors of Matthew and Luke.

Although similar in many ways, each Synoptic gospel has a unique interpretation of Jesus. The theme of Mark's gospel seems to be that the secret of Jesus's identity was revealed only when he suffered as a part of God's apocalyptic plan. Matthew stresses the radical obedience exemplified by Jesus and expected from those who would be his disciples. Luke emphasizes

that the gospel is intended for all and highlights special concern for social outcasts, the poor, and women.

The Fourth Gospel (John) is significantly different from the Synoptic gospels in content, style, and mood. In this chapter we argued that John's portrait of Jesus follows the pattern of a three-stage cosmic journey, through which the Word (Logos) of God became flesh, revealed the Father's glory, and returned to the Father to be glorified.

We concluded this chapter by speculating on when, how, why, and by whom the four canonical gospels may have been written. The inclusion of four canonical gospels in the New Testament suggests that the early Christian community recognized the inevitability, and perhaps desirability, of different interpretations of the meaning of Jesus. Still other perspectives on Jesus will be found in other New Testament books. The refusal to accept other gospels being written (see Chapter 15) implies limits to the range of interpretations of Jesus that early Christian leaders were willing to acknowledge. Readers would do well to reflect on and discuss the question of the range of interpretations of Jesus current today, and how broad the criteria of legitimate perspectives should be.

The Contemporary World

Case Study

Is There Only One Jesus?

Once again, the three friends are discussing their reactions to their Introduction to the Bible course. "Multiple portraits of Jesus! That's hogwash!" John says angrily, throwing down his copy of the textbook after reading Chapter 12. "There's only one Jesus in the New Testament, the savior who died on the cross for our sins, who rose from the dead and ascended into heaven! To see him any other way insults the divine author of the Bible!"

"Why are you so defensive?" Mary asks condescendingly. "You just need to accept the fact that the gospels contradict one another, showing they are not reliable as historical sources. Your view is childish nonsense. What a hodge-podge the Bible is once you understand it from a literary and historical perspective! Why so many are so obsessed with it is beyond me."

"You two!" Joyce says, with evident exasperation. "I'm really fascinated by the literary and historical worlds of each of the four gospels. I feel as though I am really seeing them for what they are for the first time in my life. Knowing that the New Testament has various images of Jesus, associated with different authors and groups of Christians, makes me much less anxious about the different perspectives on Jesus in the world today."

After your literary and historical study of the gospels, with which of the friends do you most agree and why?

Questions for Discussion and Reflection

1. *Read the beginning section of each of the gospels (Mk. 1:1–20, Mt. 1:1–4:17, Lk. 1:1–3:38, Jn. 1:1–51):*
   a. Note that each gospel has a unique introduction to its story of Jesus. Compare and contrast these introductions, noting similarities and differences. What does this comparison suggest about the distinctive themes of each of the gospels?
   b. Does the introduction to each gospel support the view that the gospels are seeking to provide "biographies" of Jesus, or do the writers have other objectives? How might a modern historian who is attempting to write a biography of Jesus treat these passages?
2. *Read Mk. 10:17–31, Mt. 19:16–30, Lk. 18:18–30: The Rich Young Man:*
   a. How do these passages illustrate the "synoptic problem" described in this chapter? (Note that the Gospel of John does not have a similar story.)
   b. Carefully compare these three passages. Note how each passage has a somewhat different version of the story. Do the particular emphases of the gospel writers account for the differences?
   c. This is one of a number of sayings of Jesus in the gospels about the dangers of attachment to wealth and concern for the poor (*cf.* Mt. 11:4–6 [Lk. 4:16–21], 25:31–46; Lk. 6:20, 10:29–37, 12:13–21, 14:12–24, 19:1–10; Jn. 12:6, 13:29).

   What, if any, contemporary implications might be drawn from these sayings?
   Note: A valuable tool for comparing the four gospels is a book (called a "synopsis," "harmony," or "parallel" of the gospels) that puts similar passages from the gospels in parallel columns. If your library has one, you will find it quite useful!
3. *Read Mt. 5:3–12 and Lk. 6:17, 20–23: The Beatitudes:*

   These passages provide an example of evidence that points to what some source critics call the "Q" or "sayings" source. Neither the Gospel of Mark nor the Gospel of John has parallels to these sayings or the collections ("the Beatitudes" in Matthew's "Sermon on the Mount" and Luke's "Sermon on the Plain") in which they are found.

   Carefully compare the passages. Look for indications of the particular emphases of each of the gospel writers in the way the sayings are expressed. Which, if any, of these beatitudes speak to us today? How do they speak differently to various audiences (e.g., a group of economically impoverished people as opposed to a congregation composed of persons of considerable means)?
4. *Read Mk. 15:33–16:8, Mt. 27:45–28:15, Lk. 23:44–24:35, Jn. 19:28–20:29: The Crucifixion and Resurrection of Jesus:*

a. Note the similarities and differences in the accounts of the death, resurrection, and ascension of Jesus in the four gospels, using the chart below.

b. Some contemporary interpreters have suggested that the significance of the resurrection of Jesus is found in the transformed lives of the disciples, the birth of Christianity, and the continuing potential of faith in the risen Jesus to change people. They say the meaning of the resurrection does *not* reside in whether the events described in these passages actually occurred. Others argue that if the Resurrection of Jesus was not historical, then the Christian faith is without foundation. Still others say that like the original creation, the Resurrection of Jesus occurred outside time and space as a "transhistorical" event apparent only to those with faith in God's power to bring life out of nothingness or death. As suggested in Chapter 11, some historians focus on the likelihood of the Resurrection experiences of the disciples, apart from the question of the substance of the Resurrection event itself. Reflect on and discuss these interpretations of the significance of the Resurrection. Can you think of others?

Death of Jesus	Mk. 15:33–39	Mt. 27:45–54	Lk. 23:44–48	Jn. 19:28–30
Witnesses	Mk. 15:40–41	Mt. 27:55–56	Lk. 23:49	Jn. 19:25–27
Side pierced				Jn. 19:31–37
Burial	Mk. 15:42–47	Mt. 27:57–61	Lk. 23:50–56	Jn. 19:38–42
Guard at tomb		Mt. 27:62–66		
Women at tomb	Mk. 16:1–8	Mt. 28:1–8	Lk. 24:1–12	Jn. 20:1–13
Appears to women	Mk. 16:9–11[*]	Mt. 28:9–10	Lk. 24:10–12	Jn. 20:14–18
Report of guard		Mt. 28:11–15		
Road to Emmaus	Mk. 16:12–13[*]		Lk. 24:13–35	
Appears to disciples	Mk. 16:14–18[*]		Lk. 24:36–43	Jn. 20:24–29
Appears in Galilee		Mt. 28:16–20		Jn. 21:1–14
Ascension	Mk. 16:19–20[*]		Lk. 24:44–53[*]	

[*]Note the controversy over whether Mk. 16:9–20 was part of the gospel originally or a later addition.

5. *Other questions:*

a. Each of the four gospels is a "portrait" of Jesus. Which of these portraits do you find most compelling and most believable?

b. To what degree should the four portraits of Jesus be harmonized today into a single description? How important is it to recognize and respect the different portraits as we seek to understand the significance of Jesus today?

c. The literary analysis of each gospel in this chapter is framed between a literary historical account of gospel origins and an attempt to understand the historical setting to which the gospel was first addressed. How important are historical observations such as these to understanding the gospels?

d. Jesus designated two passages from the Torah as the greatest commandments (Dt. 6:4–5; Lev. 19:18; *cf.* Mk. 12:28–34; Mt. 22:34–40; Lk. 10:25–28). Like the rabbis, Jesus emphasized Torah teaching and the principle of intentionality. Reflect on and discuss Jesus's emphases on these and other themes in Mt. 5:17–20, 7:15–23, 25:31–46.

e. Stereotypes of the women in Jesus's company, especially his mother, ordinarily portray them as quiet, submissive, and dependent. Make your own conclusions about the character of the women portrayed in the following units: Lk. 1:26–56, 8:2–3, 10:38–42; Mt. 28:1–10; Jn. 20:1–18.

f. "Gentle Jesus, meek and mild," is a popular stereotype of Jesus: a person who never spoke a strong word, never let his temper show, never bothered anyone else, and never enjoyed himself. Compare that stereotype and others to the picture of Jesus in the following passages: Mt. 11:1–19, 21:1–13; Mk. 3:13–35.

6. Mel Gibson's film about the last 12 hours of Jesus's life, *The Passion of the Christ* (2004), has inspired some impassioned debate. Gibson, a "traditionalist" Catholic, has said the film is consistent with the accounts of the arrest, trial, and crucifixion of Jesus in the four New Testament Gospels. However, scholars have noted that some of the scenes and characters (e.g., the "demon" children who drive Judas to suicide) come from non-biblical sources such as the recorded visions of Anne Catherine Emmerich, a nineteenth-century German nun, in a work entitled *The Dolorous Life of Our Lord Jesus Christ* and the popular "passion play" format (which emphasizes Jewish responsibility for the death of Jesus). In addition, historians note that Roman officials and officers serving in the eastern part of the Roman Empire would have spoken Greek, not Latin as they are portrayed doing in the movie. The film aims at creating an atmosphere of verisimilitude by having the dialogue in Aramaic and Latin with subtitles. Many viewers have described the graphic depictions of Jesus's suffering as touching and the most realistic screen depictions of what he experienced. However, many biblical scholars contend the film warps reality in portraying Jews as more responsible for Jesus's death than the Roman governor, Pilate. Some critics, including devout Catholics, express concern that the film's slanted depiction might revive the stereotype of Jews as "Christ killers," which has sparked acts of violence and discrimination against Jews throughout Christian history. Some Catholic theologians and biblical scholars have said the film distorts Catholic doctrine. Protestant and Jewish scholars have joined Catholic scholars in pointing out historical inaccuracies.

Reflect on and discuss the film and the controversy surrounding it, drawing on your study of the historical Jesus and the gospel portrayals of Jesus in your own reading of the gospels and in Chapters 11 and 12 of the text.

Chapter 13

The Birth of Christianity

The Acts of the Apostles

The Acropolis, Athens. The Acropolis was the ancient citadel of Athens. In classical times it became the great cultic center of the city, graced with a number of elegant temples and crowned by the Parthenon, which was dedicated to Athena Parthenos ("Athena the Virgin"), patroness of Athens. By the time Paul preached on the nearby Areopagus (Acts 17), Alexandria had eclipsed Athens as a center of learning. But Athens' symbolic status as a fountainhead of culture endured. *Source:* Martin D. Vonka/Shutterstock

THE UNITY OF LUKE–ACTS

As their introductions indicate, the Gospel of Luke and the Acts of the Apostles are two volumes of the same work. Acts also begins with a preface addressed to Theophilus that refers to the "first book" that dealt with the words and deeds of Jesus through his Resurrection and Ascension. Together, they are a history of the birth of Christianity. In this chapter, we examine the literary world of Acts and use the evidence from this historical narrative and other sources to reconstruct the life of the early Christian community in the decades after the death of Jesus.

As we noted in discussing Luke (Chapter 12), Luke and Acts together also form a historical narrative reinterpreting the history of salvation. According to Luke–Acts there are three epochs in the history of God's plan of salvation. Each of these is marked by the descent of the Holy Spirit: at creation, on Jesus, and on the apostles. The latter two periods both begin with baptism—of Jesus in the Jordan and of the apostles in a baptism by fire (e.g., Acts 1:5).

The first period is the subject of the "law and prophets" (the Hebrew Bible, with the third section of the canon still open). The Gospel of Luke tells the story of the middle age: the time of Jesus and his manifestation of the life of the Kingdom (see Chapter 12). Acts tells the story of the third phase of the salvation history, from the descent of the Spirit at Pentecost in Jerusalem through Paul's carrying of the gospel throughout the Mediterranean world, ending with Paul preaching "openly and unhindered" in the heart of the empire, Rome.

Luke–Acts is Hellenistic history, not modern critical history. But by the standards of historical writing of the time, Luke–Acts is good history. Like other historical works, it is not a mere recounting of events but also an attempt to find the underlying meaning and purpose of them. But what use may the modern historian make of Acts as a source on the early church? Majority judgment on this score has shifted back and forth through time and remains a matter of controversy. Perhaps these observations will suffice:

1. Luke's redaction critical interests and emphases are known from the comparative study of the Synoptic gospels. These may be taken into account in evaluating materials from Acts.
2. Luke seems to get things right on a *general* level where he can be checked. His version of the earliest Christian preaching, which will be discussed shortly, is coherent with the letters of Paul and other early documents. The sermon assigned to the Hellenist Stephen is similar to later Alexandrian Christian polemic. Paul's address in Athens sounds much like Hellenistic Christian apologetics.
3. Acts is not always in accord with other early sources, such as Paul's letters. The primary source (Paul) would ordinarily take precedence in such instances.

The schematic nature of Acts must be kept in mind. The general picture it gives may be fairly accurate, but reports of specific actions, speeches, and conversations must be evaluated with caution. Before using Acts as a historical source, let us examine the literary world it creates.

THE LITERARY WORLD: ACTS OF THE APOSTLES AS LITERATURE

The title *Acts of the Apostles* is drawn from Hellenistic literature, where narratives recounting the deeds of great leaders (like Alexander the Great) were common. Acts does focus on the activities of two principal leaders of early Christianity after the death of Jesus—Peter and Paul. However, it is not a chronicling of the lives of these two men. It is a historical– theological essay that weaves narratives of the lives of these and other leaders into a story of the spread of the Christian message from Jerusalem to Rome.

The structure of the narrative is geographic. Paralleling the journey motif of Luke (the journey of Jesus from Galilee to Jerusalem), Acts portrays the journey of the message about Jesus from Jerusalem to Rome. After the prefatory note to Theophilus, Acts links up with the end of the Lucan narrative (Lk. 24:51) by recounting the Ascension of Jesus (1:6–11). This passage establishes both the theme and the mood of the work. Jesus tells the disciples that once they have been empowered by the Holy Spirit they will be "my witnesses in Jerusalem and in all Judea and Samaria and to the end of the earth" (1:8). This is the theme of Acts, the carrying of the message of Jesus to the "end of the earth" under the guidance and power of the Holy Spirit. In response to the disciples' question of when Jesus will return, they are told that it is not for them to know the time (1:6–7). The concern of the disciples is not to be the return of Jesus but the work of carrying the gospel throughout the world. The expectation of the *parousia* is maintained (1:11), but emphasis is shifted from preparing for the end to mission in the world. The apocalyptic urgency of some other New Testament writings is not the mood of Acts.

The descent of the Spirit at Pentecost (2:1–42) closely parallels the beginning of the ministry of Jesus as narrated by Luke. It has been called a baptism (1:5); so the church begins, as did the ministry of Jesus—with baptism and the descent of the Spirit. The gift of tongues is a vivid symbol of the reality of the Spirit's presence and the worldwide implications of what has begun here. The image of the Tower of Babel (Gen. 11:1–9) is reversed. Language will become a means of bringing unity to mankind rather than separation. Description of the event gives way to an illustration of the unifying power of language—a speech purportedly given by Peter on the occasion (2:14–36, 38–39). This is the first of a number of speeches by Peter and Paul in Acts. In fact, nearly one-third of the content of Acts is comprised of such speeches. When the speeches are compared, it is apparent that a number of themes are repeated, regardless of who is speaking. These include the following:

1. Jesus is descended from King David.
2. Jesus's ministry was validated by mighty acts performed in the Spirit.
3. Jesus was put to death in fulfillment of the Scriptures.
4. God raised Jesus from the dead and exalted him as Messiah and LORD.
5. God sent the Holy Spirit through Jesus.
6. All people should repent and receive salvation through the name of Jesus, who is the judge of all mankind.

The similarities between these speeches suggest that they were not exact transcripts of the things literally said on each occasion. The frequent occurrence of all or most of the aforementioned elements in most of these speeches and in other early Christian writings such as the letters of Paul (cf. Rom. 1:1–6; 1 Cor. 15:3–11), where the subject is the preaching of the early church, has led many modern critical scholars to conclude that these elements made up the earliest Christian proclamation. The Greek word *kerygma* (meaning "proclamation") is used as a technical term for this early Christian preaching. We will note the probable historical settings of such preaching later. Hellenistic historiography sanctioned the use of such appropriate and typical speeches, particularly when the historian was not aware of a speaker's exact words. They might also serve to underscore an author's perspective on the significance of the narrative.

The first summary statement (2:43–47), like the others, describes the success of the church in carrying out the commission of the Risen Jesus. Just as the earthly Jesus had done (as recounted in Luke), the apostles performed signs and wonders that demonstrated their authority, we are told. A community was created that broke down social and economic distinctions (as Jesus had called for in Luke), and their numbers grew.

Empowered by the Spirit, the apostles continue in Jerusalem, the ministry of Jesus. Like him, they participate in the Temple ritual. They heal the sick (3:1–10). They are persecuted by the Sadducean religious leaders (4:1–31; 5:1–24), but they "obey God rather than any human authority" (5:29) and are defended by the Pharisaic leader, Gamaliel (5:34–39). They speak the Word of God with boldness (4:31). They share their goods and care for those in need (4:32–5:11). The account is rich in detail of name and place, giving it the appearance of an account based on eyewitness testimony. Whether this is actual realism or part of the "real-life" style of the essay is debated by interpreters. As a result of the apostles' ministry, the community grows from about 120 (1:15) to several thousand (2:41). The point is clear: empowered by the Holy Spirit, the church is growing.

Although Acts paints an idyllic picture of Christian life in Jerusalem, the narrative acknowledges disputes, the most prominent between the Hellenists and the Hebrews (Jews who spoke Aramaic or Hebrew, and were more conservative in keeping the traditions of their native culture).

Among these Nazarean Hellenists was Stephen, whose eloquence in debate sparked the enmity of certain other Hellenistic Jews in Jerusalem, whose accusations brought about his arrest and trial. But Stephen's own defense, presented as an inflammatory sermon not unlike the propaganda with which later Hellenistic Christianity sought to discredit Judaism, was his real undoing. What began as a trial ended as a lynching, with the young man Saul an approving bystander (Acts 6:8–8:1).

Stephen's death sparked persecution (in which Saul was one of the Jewish leaders). The Hellenists seem to have been the main targets. Ironically, persecution provided the opportunity to begin the movement of the Christian message into Judea and Samaria (in fulfillment of Jesus's instruction). As Jesus had reached out to draw social outcasts into the Kingdom, so do the leaders in Acts. The most marginal of the Jews, the Samaritans (cf. Lk. 10:25), hear the gospel. A eunuch hears the message and is baptized (8:30–40).

Saul, a young Pharisee from Tarsus in Asia Minor, had a vision of the Risen Messiah while on his way to Damascus armed with letters from the Sadducean high priest to facilitate his persecution of the Nazareans there. This illumination changed him from a persecutor to a partisan of the fledgling messianic community. This is such a crucial turning point in the narrative that it is repeated in three slightly different versions (9:1–30; 22:3–21; 26:9–23). It is Saul (also known by the Latin name of Paul) who will carry the gospel to the Gentiles (9:15). In contrast with Paul's own account in Gal. 1:1–20, Acts maintains that Saul went soon after his illumination to Jerusalem and began to preach there. At first he was suspected, then apparently supported by, the Twelve Apostles (9:26–30).

The Areopagus, Athens. The Areopagus ("Mars Hill") rose near the Athenian Acropolis. It was the original meeting place of an important Athenian council. According to Act 17:21–33, the Apostle Paul spoke to the "men of Athens" from the Areopagus. *Source:* Arthur C. Young

With the church established in Judea, Galilee, and Samaria (9:31), the Christian gospel moves into the gentile world. Acts portrays Peter converting the first Gentiles, showing that from the outset he did not disagree with a mission to the Gentiles that was not based on strict observance of the Torah (10:9–16; 11:1–18). The first church in the gentile world was established at Antioch (11:19–30). There Paul came at the urging of the Jerusalem church's delegate, Barnabas. In Antioch, according to Acts, those who followed the Way (of Jesus) for the first time were called "Christians" (11:26). The harmony between gentile and Jewish Christians is illustrated by the Antioch church's sending relief to the "believers" in Judea, where famine had struck (11:27–).

The rest of Acts focuses on the missionary activities of Saul (now known as Paul). This work is presented by Acts as three distinct missionary journeys (13–14:28; 15:36–18:21; 18:23–19:19). Given the penchant of Luke–Acts to organize the narrative by journeys, it is an open question whether these three journeys are a literary device to structure the presentation of Paul's work or an accurate description of what actually happened.

According to the patterning of events in Acts, Paul and Barnabas left from Antioch for the first missionary journey into Asia Minor. Paul preached in synagogues where "God-fearers" were especially responsive to his message. When challenged by Judean teachers who said that unless a man was circumcised he could not be saved, Paul and Barnabas returned to Jerusalem. There, according to Acts, certain Christian Pharisees argued the necessity of keeping the Law of Moses, but Peter opposed them, and his support of accepting Gentiles without prior condition won out. Once again, Acts shows Peter and Paul in full agreement, in keeping with the harmonious mood in the church that dominates the work.

The second journey carries Paul, joined by Silas and later by Timothy, back through Asia Minor and on to Macedonia. He preaches in synagogues and is received by God-fearers, but he is persecuted by the leaders of the Jewish community, who accuse him of treason before Roman authorities. This is another aspect of Acts' concern to blame Jewish, not Christian, leaders for the emerging split between Judaism and Christianity. Led by the Spirit, Paul takes the gospel into Europe, via Macedonia, at Philippi. Then he moves to Greece, where he makes a rational defense of the gospel in Athens (17:22–31) and establishes the church at Corinth. The narrative makes clear that Paul commits no offense against Rome (18:12–17).

On the third journey Paul goes to Ephesus for a long period (over two years), then back to Macedonia, Greece, and, finally, Palestine.

Led like Jesus by the Spirit, Paul resolves to go to Jerusalem and then on to Rome (19:22). Just as Jesus carried the gospel to the heart of the Jewish world, Paul will take the message to the center of the gentile world. Like Jesus, he has a hearing before the Sanhedrin (22:30–23:10) and the Roman governor (24:1–27). Like Jesus, he is accused of blasphemy and profaning the Temple. Unlike Jesus, Paul mounts a defense that convinces the scribes (Pharisees) in the Sanhedrin but not the Sadducees and the Roman governor. Only when Paul insists on his right as a Roman citizen to appeal his case to the emperor is he sent to Rome for trial.

The narrative shifts without warning to the first-person plural and uses it especially in the last phase of the story (16:10–17; 20:5–15; 21:1–18; 27:1–28:16). From a literary perspective these so-called *we* passages heighten the excitement of the description by giving first-person authenticity and drawing the reader into the story. Whether this is a literary device or an indication of the inclusion of a section of Luke's (or someone else's) travel diary is a historical issue. Certainly, the detail and realism of these passages are impressive.

The narrative concludes with an air of confidence and anticipation. Paul is active in the imperial capital, even though under house arrest. His work continues and the promise of the gospel's reaching the "end of the earth" is on the verge of fulfillment. The theme, stated in 1:8, has been fully developed.

Luke–Acts tells a story in which the gospel is carried from "nowhere" (Nazareth) to the city that is the greatest power center in the world (Rome) in journeys by persons led by the Spirit. Christianity should now be recognized as a legitimate world religion that reluctantly broke from its Jewish heritage. To its readers, Luke–Acts gives examples of how to live in the world by presenting heroes to emulate—Jesus, Peter, Mary, the mother of Jesus, Mary Magdalene, Stephen, Paul, and others.

THE HISTORICAL WORLD: THE EARLIEST CHURCH

The Resurrection experiences of the immediate followers of Jesus gave them both a message to proclaim and the courage to proclaim it. The main documentary source for this earliest stage of the Christian Church is Luke's book of Acts. As we have noted, the portrayal in Acts, although an excellent example of Hellenistic historiography, is selective and schematic. Luke is supplemented by the letters of Paul, other early Christian writings, and such archaeological data about the early church as exists (though very little can be pushed back this far).

This section will review the history of the church down to about 70 C.E., a few years beyond the coverage of Acts (see Table 13.1). It will reserve comment on Paul for the following chapter. But 70, the year the Romans destroyed Jerusalem and its Temple, serves as a significant watershed for both Jewish and Christian history. The events of that year probably hastened the estrangement of the early Christians from their original Jewish matrix. The flourishing community life of prewar classical Judaism could afford the richness and variety of the numerous denominations and sects that prospered to a greater or lesser degree (see Chapter 10). The community that emerged from the crisis was besieged and threatened. The rabbis at Yavneh, who inherited the task of reconstruction, had less room for toleration and maneuver. The truth is, surviving rabbinic documents pay very little attention to the emerging Christian movement. The archaeological record suggests that traditional Jews, Jewish and gentile Christians, and pagans lived in relative harmony in such Galilean cities as Sepphoris and Capernaum on into the fifth century, or longer. On the Nazarean side, where it had been advantageous to be identified with the Jewish community before the war, it became desirable to be recognized as distinct after it began. The increasingly gentile composition of the Christian group in the Roman world outside the Jewish homeland probably made separation inevitable over the long haul. In any case, once the church spread beyond Israel and opted for gentile conversions, this outcome was a demographic inevitability. The process was nevertheless a lengthy one, and developed at different rates depending on occasion, situation, and the respective Christian and more or less traditionally Jewish groups involved.

The Jerusalem Church

The earliest Jerusalem church pictured in Acts was centered among Galileans who had come to Jerusalem with Jesus and remained in the holy city, the most logical place to await the return of the Davidic messiah. The gospels suggest that Jesus had also acquired Judean followers prior to the crucifixion, including Joseph of Arimathea, a member of the Sanhedrin who provided the tomb in which Jesus was buried. The community organized itself in a fashion that was apparently an accepted model for Jewish sectarian communities. The Dead Sea Covenanters shared some of these same customs, which proves nothing more than that both were roughly contemporaneous Jewish groups. The churches of Galilee, and of the Diaspora, opted for the model of a synagogue congregation.

One of the first actions of the Jerusalem group in the Acts narrative was to replace Judas, the lapsed member of the Twelve, by lot from among the original disciples. One Matthias was chosen.

TABLE 13.1 Events Related to the New Testament before 70 C.E.

Date	Event	Roman Emperor
B.C.E.		
44	Parthian invasion	
40–4	Herod the Great appointed "King of the Jews" in Judea by Romans	Augustus Caesar (30 B.C.E.–14 C.E.)
20	Temple rebuilt by Herod	
Between 8 and 4	Jesus born	
4 B.C.E.–39 C.E.	Herod Antipas (son of Herod the Great) tetrarch of Galilee	
4 B.C.E.–6 C.E.	Herod Archelaus (son of Herod the Great) ethnarch of Judea	
C.E.		
18–36	Caiaphas high priest	
26–36	Pontius Pilate procurator of Judea	Tiberias (14–37)
27–29 (?)	Ministry of John the baptizer	
Sometime between 27 and 33	Ministry of Jesus	
Sometime between 30 and 33	Crucifixion and Resurrection of Jesus	
Sometime between 33 and 45	Illumination of Paul	
		Caligula (37–41)
37–44 (?)	Herod Agrippa, king of Judea, imprisons Peter	
41–49	Jews banished from Rome	
		Claudius (41–54)
About 47–56	Missionary activity of Paul	
About 49	Jerusalem Council	
56	Paul arrested in Jerusalem	
Between 60 and 63	Paul under arrest in Rome	
About 62	James, brother of Jesus, martyred	
Mid-to-late 60s	Peter and Paul martyred in Rome	Nero (54–68)
64–65	Christians persecuted under Nero after Rome burns	
66–73	Jewish revolt against Rome; Christians flee Jerusalem	
70	Jerusalem captured; Temple destroyed	Vespasian (69–79)

The Twelve, the inner circle of leadership established by Jesus, were, as noted, symbolically related to the twelve tribes of Israel, emphasizing further the Jewishness of the community. From the time of Jesus, there had been an inner-inner circle of three within the Twelve, Simon Peter and the two sons of Zebedee (probable cousins of Jesus), James, and John. They apparently continued to hold positions of particular importance. Peter, who had been the spokesman and leader of the Twelve in Jesus's public ministry, became the chief figure in the Jerusalem group. After James, the son of Zebedee, was executed on orders of Herod Agrippa (37–44), James, the brother of Jesus, appeared as one of the three "pillars" of the Jerusalem church (confirmed by Paul; Gal. 1:18, 2:9). In due course, James seems to have been recognized as the chief leader of the community, with Peter assuming the role of itinerant missionary. The group practiced a community of goods, pooling all their property in a common fund. Their Jewishness was further evidenced by their continued frequenting of the Temple, a custom going back to Jesus's ministry.

Luke attributed a sudden surge of growth in the community to a miraculous occurrence, the speaking "in other tongues" at Pentecost described in Acts 2. What may be behind the story is the astonishment that unlettered Galileans, noted for their strange accent and limited literacy, were speaking such a message. The first Hellenistic Jewish converts may date from this time.

The Jerusalem church was never a wealthy community. If the later Jewish Christian group called the *Ebionites* ("poor folks") were their descendants, they probably prided themselves on their poverty (as did the Dead Sea Covenanters). But their need for a relief offering like those collected in the gentile churches by Paul was due to the ravages of famine, not the failure of their communal and collective economic practices. Still, if the Jerusalem church was not affluent, it was influential. Other churches looked to it as the mother church, the arbiter of difficult issues.

Gentile Converts

Did Gentiles who wanted to enter the Way, the Christian circle, first have to become converts to Judaism? That was a question with which the Jerusalem church was asked to wrestle. Two matters must be grasped to understand the issue and its ultimate resolution. First, how did these first Christians understand their situation? The early Jewish Christians apparently understood the *kerygma,* the basic proclamation of their community, to be that the long-awaited Messiah, the once and future Davidic ruler, had appeared in the person of Jesus. All doubt was removed by the fact that, although he had been killed by his enemies, God had raised him from the dead, proclaiming him once and for all his agent of redemption. The Risen One would return to restore the fortunes of Israel and usher in the full realization of the reign of God on earth. Those who signified their trusting confidence in the Messiah thereby established their citizenship in the messianic kingdom.

This is almost certainly the way the *kerygma* was understood by early Jewish Christians and by their early gentile converts who had been "God-fearers" and, hence, were conversant with Jewish modes of thought. The dominant Jewish view of the destiny of non-Jews was enunciated in the generation after Paul by the great rabbi Joshua: "The righteous of all the nations have a portion in the world to come." This view was inherent in the Tanak and had been expressed in the school of Rabbi Hillel. Its gist was that, while God held the Israelites to their covenant promises, he expected of those without more detailed revelations only that they would behave according to their best lights. Still, for the gentile proselyte, there must have been a sense of special belonging to God's people through the step of conversion.

As the church moved further afield and made converts among Gentiles whose acquaintance with Jewish lore was more limited or nonexistent, the *kerygmatic* proclamation was heard more in terms of personal salvation—deliverance from a decaying world, from death, and from demonic powers. Familiarity with the revealer–redeemers of gnostic myths and the savior deities of Greco-Roman mystery religions colored the way the gracious offer of the *kerygma* was (and to a large extent still is) understood. Paul's mystical and highly personal formulation of Christian revelation lent particularly to this more Hellenized form of understanding (see Chapter 14). The identification of the *kerygma* does not imply the existence of a unified orthodoxy at this early stage. The gospels and letters of the New Testament and much extracanonical literature, including the New Testament Apocrypha (cf. Chapter 15), make it clear that a variety of interpretations of the significance of Jesus as the Messiah flourished in the early church.

However, emphasis in the early church's understanding of its basic message may have shifted. There was a common belief that the church was in, or at least on the threshold of, the messianic age. This leads to the second matter relating to gentile converts. As we have noted, Judaism had always accepted converts. Before the Exile, it had been more a matter of assimilation into a national population. After the Exile, the customs of proselytism evolved more as a religious exercise. But from the time of the prophets, and above all in texts with messianic, or at least eschatological, overtones, the notion had been abroad that, in the ideal future, the pagan nations would turn from their idolatry and to the God of Israel without ceasing to be Gentiles. (The terms *Gentile* and *nations* are the same.) The Messiah had come. Gentiles were showing an interest in the Way. Scripture was being fulfilled.

By creating a link between the first gentile converts and Peter, inspired by a vision, Acts diverts any allegation that the mission to the Gentiles initiated by the church in Antioch was a conspiracy. The mass gentile conversions by Paul and his associates were also regularized in Acts by the Jerusalem church (Acts 15). The only Torah-like observance required of gentile Christians resembled the rabbinic *Covenant of Noah;* that is, a few general moral and dietary observances.

Persecution

It appears in the early chapters of Acts that the principal adversaries of the church were the Sadducean high priest and his cohorts, who resented public attention being called to their role in the judicial lynching of Jesus. The pharisaic leadership, according to Luke, opposed the Sadducees on this score and urged toleration. The stoning of Stephen smacks of a spontaneous outburst of mob violence after he was interrogated by the Sanhedrin. It was not typical. Persecution was mainly directed against Hellenists such as Stephen. Peter and the "Hebrews" continued relatively unmolested in Jerusalem. The High Priest Ananus's killing of James, the brother of Jesus, and Herod Antipas's action against James, the son of Zebedee, were also isolated actions, the former act condemned by many influential Jews, according to Josephus.

A similar judgment must be made in connection with the treatment accorded to the church after it spread into the Roman world. The Greco-Roman world was generally tolerant and pluralistic. Despite the stereotypical view of "Romans seeking Christians under every stone and lions licking their chops waiting for them, the Romans were probably more tolerant of alternative religious practices than most of today's societies."[1] But Judaism, and its emerging daughter-religion, sat ill with the easygoing polytheism of that society. Neither would trade at the pagan temple butcher shops. Neither would participate in public occasions in which pagan religious overtones were too obvious. Neither would sacrifice to the divine emperor.

---

[1]Robert B. Kebric. *Roman People*, 3rd ed. Mountain View, CA: Mayfield, 2001, p. 250.

Ruins of Roman Aqueduct. The Romans built an elaborate raised aqueduct system to carry water to the port city of Caesarea, built in the first century B.C.E. by Herod the Great to honor Caesar Augustus. According to the Acts of the Apostles, Paul was imprisoned in Caesarea for two years before being sent to Rome for trial (Acts 25:1–26:30). *Source:* William A. Young

It is sometimes said that the unforgivable sin is to be *too* different from everybody else. In the Roman world, Jews and Christians were sometimes thought guilty of that sin and paid a price for it. The price was not constant violence and harassment, though it occasionally came to that. Nero's persecution in Rome was a special case of scapegoating. For the church in the latter part of the century and later, failure to participate in the emperor cult became a serious problem and resulted in individual arrests and executions and occasional local or regional persecutions, such as the one in the eastern provinces that led to the writing of the Revelation to John during the reign of Domitian (see Chapter 15). A famous exchange of letters between Pliny the Younger, governor of Bithynia in the early second century, and the emperor Trajan sanctioned Pliny's policy toward the Christians. Pliny held that the Christians were a relatively harmless lot, and he could not see that much really needed to be done about them. He did not search them out. Still, he did his duty and executed the hardheads among them when they were accused before him, Trajan endorsed the policy. Though the sufferings of those Christians who did end up in the arena or in the hands of the executioner are

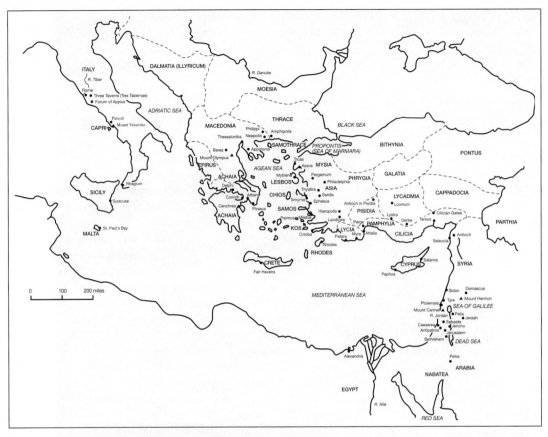

Roman World of the First Century C.E.

not diminished, it does not seem to be the case that the baptism of blood and fire of popular legend really belonged to this period.

As the church gained converts, the hostility against Christians increased. Among the charges leveled against Christians, according to one-third century C.E. source, was that they consorted with "the lowest dregs of society and credulous women" and "met in dark and despised the temples." "In loving one another as family, they committed incest, and cannibalism, and indulged in orgies after shocking love feasts . . . they threatened the whole world with destruction." In general, the Christians "were quite rightly perceived to be antisocial: they were creating their own society. . . . The [Christian] apologists could repeatedly point out that the Christians were peaceful members of the community, but in Roman eyes, if they did not correctly observe at least the imperial cult, they were not good citizens. They were alienating the *pax deorum*, the peace that the gods brought to the empire."[2]

The vicious and systematic persecutions occurred on the threshold of the church's final triumph, after it had become prominent enough to constitute a serious force in the Roman order. These persecutions began under Decius in 250 C.E., with the last and worst being mounted by

---

[2]Joyce E. Salisbury. *Perpetua's Passion: The Death and Memory of a Young Roman Woman.* New York: Routledge, 1997, pp. 78–79.

Diocletian until he abdicated in 305 C.E. In 311 there was an imperial decree of toleration followed by Constantine's Edict of Milan in 313, which legalized Christianity. Within a few decades Christianity was the established imperial religion, and non-Christians were persecuted! But all this lies far beyond the horizon of the biblical period.

Leadership

We have seen that the Twelve were the prominent leaders of the Jerusalem church, with the smaller number of three "pillars" exercising even greater influence. But the somewhat larger group, known as *apostles,* were the pre-eminent figures in the spread of Christianity through the Roman world. To clarify, the pillars and the Twelve were apostles, but the total company of apostles was more numerous. There is no clear indication of how many apostles there were. They were not identical with the disciples, the apparently larger number yet of Jesus's students and later, apparently close followers of the apostles.

The thing that made a person an apostle was a personal commission by the Lord Jesus. The Greek word *apostolos* means "one sent." Apostles were ambassadors of King Messiah, understood to have extraordinary authority in the church. Later church teaching associated *apostolic succession* with a power passed from Jesus to the apostles, then to the bishops. But documentation from the earlier history of the church shows that the concern was not for the passing of power, but for correct teaching.

In the world beyond Jerusalem, the church generally assumed the structure of a synagogue, that is, a congregation. The Greek word for church (*ekklesia*) means a group of people called together. They were governed by a group of elders (Greek, *presbuteros*), one of whom was chief. The organizing apostle would appoint the first *presbytery* (company of elders). With the passage of time, the office of chief elder evolved into that of *episcopos* ("overseer" or "bishop"). Ultimately, the bishops of the most important churches began to exercise authority over lesser churches in their neighborhoods (although this takes us beyond the period covered in this text).

Ephesians 4:11 lists prophets, evangelists, pastors, and teachers after apostles among the spiritually gifted leaders of the early church. Apostles stand first in 1 Cor. 12:28, followed by prophets, teachers, miracle workers, healers, helpers, administrators, tongue speakers, and presumably interpreters thereof (see 1 Cor. 14:1–9). In keeping with the order of both rosters, Paul assigned particular honor to the office of prophet. Acts 11:27–28, 15:32, and 21:10–11 show prophets in action among the early Christians. The authority of the apostle was derived from a connection with the Lord Jesus, while that of the church prophet was entirely charismatic. Apostles could also be charismatic, but their authority did not depend on it. The apostles were, of course, irreplaceable. In keeping with the development noted between 1 Corinthians and the later Ephesians, the charismatic offices in the church apparently waned progressively. This, as observed by anthropologists and sociologists, is in keeping with the typical development of leadership in religious organizations.

A Time Whose Idea Had Come

Traditional theology has held that Christianity arose providentially at just the right time to prosper. Even disbelievers in providence are obliged to agree that circumstances in the Roman world were rather well suited for the spread of a new religion of personal salvation at the time Christianity came on the scene. The legacy of Alexander in the east, combined with the Roman use of many Greek slaves as teachers and the mobility of free Greek traders, all meant that Greek could be understood in every quarter of the Roman Empire. The Roman highway system remains legendary. The *Pax Romana* (Roman peace, 27 B.C.E.–180 C.E.) enforced by Rome's legions and navy meant that travel was safer than it had ever been before. The Roman peace also created a common market extending

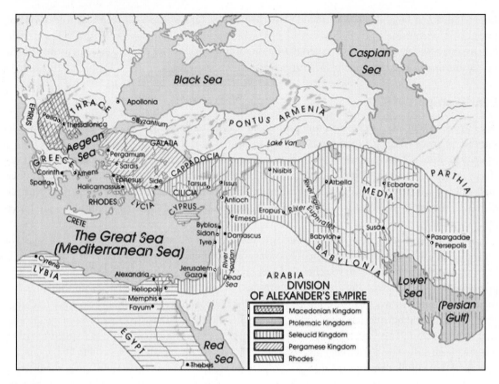

Alexander's Empire

on both sides of the Mediterranean from Arabia to Spain and northward into France, the German lands south of the Danube and west of the Rhine, and Britain. Cities grew as commerce waxed. Thus, Roman peace also brought Roman prosperity. People had places to go, business to conduct, and the relatively safe means to do so. Missionaries of the new faith could get about the world and count on making themselves understood with greater facility than at any earlier time. And not least, as noted before, Judaism had preceded the early Christians into the Greco–Roman realm. There were nuclei of people throughout the empire who knew the Scriptures, in most cases the LXX, and grasped some basic concepts of Judaism.

Cultural factors also favored the introduction of new religious options. The conquests of Alexander, followed by those of Rome, cut the roots to the past in a way that the predecessor empires had never done. They introduced attractive new cultural options, whereas the emperors of Persia, Babylon, Assyria, and Egypt had been content to let people rock along in their conventional ruts so long as tribute was paid on time.

Old religions also suffered from the new order. Most ancient religions were either the state cult of a kingdom or, in the case of the Greeks, a *polis* ("city-state") or family or tribal affair. Even the victors were vanquished, for the old cult of the city of Rome proved quite inadequate to the needs of the empire. The emperor cult arose as the needed surrogate, glue for a disconnected entity. Increasing numbers of people were moving from the countryside into the growing and prosperous cities. For many, the move was not voluntary; they came as slaves or displaced workers. Urban folks have always been rootless in comparison with rural populations, and, in this case, they provided a ready market for new religious ideas.

To judge from both the religious and the philosophical options exercised, as well as the superstitions cultivated, the age of the early Roman Empire was an age of anxiety. The blind goddess, fate, and the faceless goddess, chance, were figures of iconography. Astrology and augury flourished. It was widely assumed that not just these impersonal forces menaced human existence, but that potentially capricious gods and a variety of malign spiritual entities (including the "principalities" and "powers" of Rom. 8:38 and Eph. 3:10) threatened life and welfare both in this life and the hereafter.

If any single category summarizes the intellectual outlook and religious perspective of classical antiquity from the time of Alexander onward, it is *dualism.* This notion divides reality into two opposite and irreducible essences, the mental (or intellectual or spiritual) and the material. In the Greek version, the former is greatly to be preferred over the latter. It was Plato who drew the distinction most decisively, but the odds are it would have been drawn even if he had never lived. This characteristic attitude stood in stark contrast with the world-affirming optimism of the Hebrew Scriptures and Judaism, thus also of Jesus. The world, created by God, including people, sex and all, was pronounced in the Jewish tradition "very good."

The most popular philosophies of later classical antiquity shared a concern with personal salvation. Cynicism liberated people from stultifying convention. Epicureans sought the higher (intellectual) pleasures. Stoicism, particularly in its Roman versions, taught self-control, devotion to duty, and salvation through harmonizing one's own inherent *logos* (reason) with the cosmic *logos* that permeated the entire universe. Originally Pythagoreans combined a celibate, highly ascetic, coeducational monastic rule of life with a mystical quest that began with mathematical knowledge. Neo-Pythagoreanism was eclectic. Neoplatonism, with its theory of overflowing being, taught a mystical discipline designed to work through the levels of being to God. Although it did not emerge as a distinct movement until after this period, the work of Philo of Alexandria shows that the fundamentals of Neoplatonism were already well in place.

The term *mystery religions* is used to describe a class of religions that flourished in Graeco–Roman culture. They all promised the gift of immortality (or at least profound illumination) from a benefactor deity who had achieved the gift in question and had the right to distribute it. Persons were initiated into the mystery in rituals often adapted from ancient fertility cults. Some were not unlike modern fraternity, sorority, or lodge initiations. The Great Mystery was the cult of Demeter and Persephone at Eleusis in Greece. Two of the more widespread and popular mysteries, celebrated throughout the empire, were those of Isis and Mithra. Isis, the great Egyptian goddess, was the archetype of the faithful wife, and her cult was especially popular with women. The cult of Mithra, the Persian hero–god and bullslayer, was especially popular in the army and was dominated by males.

Later Christian apologists heaped abuse on the mysteries, calling them inventions of the Devil. However, the mystery cults almost certainly influenced the way people in the pagan world understood Christianity, and Christian missionaries may have borrowed mystery terminology to interpret their message to pagans unfamiliar with Jewish ideas.

Gnosticism (from the Greek *gnosis* [knowledge]) stands somewhere between religion and philosophy. Any discussion of Gnosticism is rendered more difficult by the fact that there were numerous gnostic sects and that until recently most of our information about them came from hostile sources, the polemical writings of early Christian leaders who saw gnostic versions of the Christian gospel as a dangerous heresy.[3]

However, in 1945, near an Egyptian village called Nag Hammadi, a local citizen found a pottery vessel containing thirteen leather-bound papyrus codices transmitting a total of fifty-two ancient texts, most of which were gnostic. It would be more than thirty years before these texts were

---

[3]See Birger A. Pearson. *Ancient Gnosticism: Traditions and Literature* Minneapolis: Fortress Press, 2007.

properly edited and published.[4] The discovery blew the lid on gnostic studies. Here, for the first time, modern scholars had a collection of authentic gnostic texts to study.

Gnosticism, like many religions and philosophies in the Graeco–Roman world, was dualistic, dividing reality between mind/spirit (good) and matter (evil). As its name suggests, it taught that salvation (the liberation of good souls from their material prison) was gained by mastering esoteric knowledge, frequently communicated by a heavenly messenger. Some gnostic sects were elitist, teaching that only a gifted few, the Gnostics, could grasp the revealed gnosis. Ordinary people might gain a lesser salvation by faith. Fleshly people were beyond redemption, hopelessly mired in the material.

A generic version of the great gnostic myth taught that the Pleroma, the fullness of being, contained thirty Eons, matched male–female pairs which had been emanated from Being Itself. One Eon (frequently it was Sophia [Wisdom]) fell, being enamored of matter, and created the material world. This was a disaster, because good souls were trapped in matter, setting the stage for a savior being from the Pleroma to come down and bring the secret saving knowledge.

The Nag Hammadi writings document the existence of gnostic Christianity as early as the first century C.E. Christianity, with its developing notion of a divine savior, a Son of God, provided a ready vehicle for gnostic interpretation. Christian Gnostics taught that the true gospel of Jesus was a saving knowledge rather than the message of the liberating power of his death and resurrection as most of the books in the canonical New Testament emphasize. At least in the first several centuries of the Christian era, gnostic Christianity was a serious contender in the struggle among rival interpretations of the meaning of the gospel of Christ, but by the fourth century state patronage and the ecumenical councils sealed the triumph of what became Christian orthodoxy.

In their attack on gnosticism as a dangerous heresy, some church theologians attributed gnosticism to the evil work of the Samaritan magician, Simon Magus (Acts 8:9–24), but the story is not so simple. Historians suspect that gnosticism emerged from the admixture of dualistic Hellenistic philosophy and local religious traditions in the region between Mesopotamia and Egypt during the pre-Christian era.

The Nag Hammadi documents include the Gospel of Thomas (see Chapter 15), the sayings source which has parallels to Synoptic sayings, but others with a gnostic cast. There are also documents which report conversations between Jesus and his disciples. Some of these have attracted the attention of feminist theologians because of the prominence assigned to women, especially Mary Magdalene. The Gospel of Philip makes Mary Jesus's closest disciple and the one who understood him best.

Many experts believe that most of the Nag Hammadi texts were from the gnostic sect known as the Sethian school, but that some came from the Valentinian school. The Gospel of Judas (see Chapters 15 and 16) comes from the Cainites. It confirms that for some Gnostics, salvation is found in liberation from the (material) body. So today there are primary texts from at least three gnostic sects. However, this has not made things simpler. One of the Nag Hammadi texts is the Gospel of Truth, which many experts think is the work of the great second-century gnostic thinker, Valentinus. It contains none of the more exotic gnostic speculations. It is not a gospel but a mystical meditation on the Gospel in Paul's sense, the Christian good news. It does not mention Eons or emanations. It does not name Sophia. God is the creator. It speaks of the Father and the Son, and, a couple of times, the Spirit. Where are all the "delerious melons of Valentinus," the Eons and

---

[4]James M. Robinson and Martin Meyer. *The Nag Hammadi Scriptures: The Revised and Updated Translation of Sacred Gnostic Writings in One Volume.* San Francisco: Harper One, 2009. See also, Stephen A. Hoeller, *Gnosticism: New Light on the Ancient Tradition of Inner Knowing.* Wheaton, IL: Quest Books, 2002; Willis Barnstone and Marvin Meyer, ed. *The Gnostic Bible: Gnostic Texts of Mystical Wisdom from the Ancient and Medieval Worlds,* rev. and expanded ed. Boston, MA: Shambhala Press, 2009; Elaine Pagels, *The Gnostic Gospels: A Startling Account of the Meaning of Jesus and the Origin of Christianity Based on Gnostic Gospels and Other Secret Texts.* New York: Random House, 2004.

emanations denounced by Iranaeus in his clever late second-century satire? At least at this stage of his career, Valentinus was not all that far from orthodoxy, lending substance to reports that he was almost elected a bishop about 150 C.E.

Thus, just as Christianity was not spawned amid a sterile and moribund Jewish matrix, but within a richly creative one, so it did not emerge into a pagan world bereft of vital spiritual options. Christianity, like the other newer religions and philosophies, found its market in the burgeoning cities of the Roman Empire and made its original urban inroads among Hellenized Jews and God-fearers. But it found the largest number of recruits among the urban masses of the gentile cities. Writers of an earlier time pictured the emerging Church as a community of the impoverished. A close reading of Paul's letters and the Book of Acts suggests it was probably more like a cross section of the urban world. Some members owned houses large enough to host Church meetings. A few were public officials. The upper orders of society, particularly the old Roman aristocracy, were underrepresented, as were the very lowliest, especially the rural poor. Membership may have been skewed in the direction of the less affluent. But the rhetoric of the early Church, like that of closely related Jewish piety, treated poverty as a virtue, which may have led to occasional exaggeration. The conversion of the countryside was slower (*pagan* comes from the term meaning "country person"). Christianity's competitors during this stage were probably not so much the philosophical schools as the mystery and gnostic sects, popular local cults, and purveyors of various forms of astrology and occultism. Also, Christianity was not localized, and was a "family religion," and while many Hellenistic religious groups provided a mutually caring community for their members, Christians were apparently seen as excelling in this regard, and this was part of their mass appeal.

In a well-populated religious environment, Christianity prevailed and ultimately became the religion of the empire. Faith attributes the outcome to providence. Anthropologists point out that Christianity turned out to be the most adaptive competitor. History simply notes the outcome. In the next chapter, we will take a somewhat closer look at the process, and in Chapter 15 we will carry it through the end of the biblical period.

Summary

This chapter dealt with the birth of Christianity as portrayed in the Acts of the Apostles and in light of available historical evidence.

The literary world of Acts includes the Gospel of Luke, for the two are part of a single historical work. The two volumes combined tell the story of the spread of the Christian gospel from its origins in the isolated hill country of Galilee to the very nerve center of the vast Roman empire. Luke recounted the role of Jesus. Acts is an account of the creation and growth of the community that proclaimed Jesus the Messiah and their LORD. Both stress the role of the Holy Spirit.

Like other historical sections of the Bible, Luke–Acts is more concerned with lifting up the underlying pattern of divine purpose in events than in merely describing them. Acts stresses that the early Christian Church was a community of social justice and universalism, embodying what Jesus himself taught according to Luke's gospel. Acts also emphasizes that the spread of the message about Jesus into the gentile world carried the endorsement of the original apostles, including the first leader of the emergent Jerusalem church—Peter. Paul, first a persecutor and then a partisan of the church, is used as the vehicle to portray the gentile mission. Much of Acts relates the missionary journeys of Paul and various companions throughout the Mediterranean world, climaxing in his arrival in Rome.

Our historical analysis in this chapter covered the period from the death of Jesus to about 70 C.E. We focused on the Jerusalem church; the conversion of Gentiles; early persecution of Christians; leadership in the early Christian churches; and the political, economic, cultural, and religious factors that enhanced the development and spread of Christianity throughout the Roman world. We discussed the reasons for the split between the followers of Jesus and the Jewish community and the various philosophies and religions of the Roman Empire, such as Cynicism, Stoicism, the mystery cults, and Gnosticism, which are significant for an understanding of this period. The important role of the Apostle Paul in the development of Christianity will be treated in the next chapter.

Although Acts presents an idealized picture of the early Christian Church, it can be interesting to compare the characteristics of the first Christian communities with those of churches today. As any movement matures, it becomes more and more institutionalized. This happened to Christianity, as we shall later see. At various times revitalization and renewal groups spring up, seeking to restore the original vitality of the movement. This is also true in Christian history.

The Contemporary World

Case Study

Intentional Christian Communities and the Acts of the Apostles

Today a number of intentional Christian communities seek to live as the followers of Christ described in the Acts of the Apostles by sharing their resources in common (see Acts 2:44). Follow some of the links in the Directory maintained by the Fellowship of Intentional Communities (http://directory.ic.org/records/christian.php) to find some of these communities. Choose one or two intentional Christian communities to research. To what degree are they successful in living as the early Christians described in Acts? Are they utopian communities out of touch with modern life, or are they a model of how more Christians (and others) should be living in the twenty-first century?

Questions for Discussion and Reflection

1. *Read Acts 1–2: The Ascension and Pentecost*
   a. The empowerment of followers of Jesus by the Holy Spirit is a significant theme in the Acts of the Apostles. Today some Christian believers in pentecostal churches or charismatic movements within other churches also claim to experience the power of the Spirit. Reflect on and discuss these claims and their relationship to the role of the Spirit in this passage.
   b. Note that women are included in the naming of the active leaders of the earliest Christian community in Jerusalem (Acts 1:14). Does this have any implications for the role of women in leadership positions in Christian churches today?
2. *Read Acts 9: The Enlightenment of Saul*
   a. This account has traditionally been called the "conversion" of Saul. Is it more accurately described as an "enlightenment" or "illumination" experience? What difference does the "label" the passage is given make today?
   b. The "Damascus road experience" of Saul has had a great impact on the way many Christians over the centuries have understood their own spiritual journeys. Do religious texts sometimes shape experiences? If so, what are the implications for the validity of the experience?
3. *Read Acts 17:16–34: Paul at Athens*
   The Apostle Paul is portrayed here using some of the philosophical concepts of his day to speak to the people of Athens about God. Do you think it is appropriate for contemporary Christians to use current philosophical and scientific concepts in speaking about God and Christ?
4. *Other Questions*
   a. What indications have you picked up that early Christianity was shaped by the social world in which it emerged? What are the hints in the Book of Acts? How are the modern expressions of Christianity (and other religions with which you are familiar) affected by the social settings in which

they occur? How are you affected in your own perspective on the Bible by your present social world?

b. What are the strengths and weaknesses of the Book of Acts as a source for a modern historian writing the history of early Christianity?

c. How do the creative purposes of modern artists, writers, musicians, and filmmakers shape their works? Is a "creative purpose" evident in the shaping of Acts?

d. Acts suggests that the early Christians were perceived as "different." Which religious groups are viewed as "different" in contemporary America? How are they treated?

e. Do we live now in a period of greater institutionalization or revitalization of Christianity and other religions?

Chapter 14

Paul: Apostle to the Gentiles

The Letters of Paul

Ephesus: The Main Street between the Harbor and Marketplace. The marketplace (agora) was the hub of life in any ancient city. It was probably in the agora of Ephesus that the uproar recorded in Acts 19:23–41 began. Ephesus was apparently a center of activity of the Apostle Paul in Asia Minor and Greece. *Source:* Arthur C. Young

It is both easy and extremely difficult to exaggerate the importance of the Apostle Paul. It is easy to exaggerate his importance in his own time. He is the central figure in over half of the Book of the Acts of the Apostles. Traditionally, he was considered the author of thirteen or fourteen of the twenty-seven books of the New Testament. He did write at least seven, and probably more, in the judgment of literary historians.

Legend has Paul preaching the gospel as far away as Spain, Gaul, and even Britain. A super-ficial reading might lead to the conclusion that Paul was a sort of apostolic Lone Ranger, single-handedly spreading Christianity throughout the Roman world. Paul himself never made such a claim. His own letters make it quite clear that he was only one among many early Christian mission-aries. Romans, ordinarily considered his most important letter, was written to a church he had not founded or visited at that point. In the context of his times, Paul was an important and controversial leader in the church from sometime in the 30s until his death in about 65 C.E., but he did not domi-nate the church of that time.

It is extremely difficult to exaggerate Paul's importance in the history of the interpretation of the New Testament and the development of later Christianity, particularly in the Western church (Roman Catholicism and Protestantism). St. Augustine (385–430 C.E.) was deeply influenced by Paul, especially in his relatively pessimistic view of human nature. Not only was Augustine the official doctor of the Western church through much of the medieval period, but also Pauline–Augustinian thought has fired many of the revitalization movements and many of the great leaders of Western Christendom. A partial list would include the Protestant Reformation, the Jansenist movement in seventeenth-century Roman Catholicism, neo-orthodoxy in the twentieth century, and leaders such as Martin Luther, John Calvin, Blaise Pascal, John Wesley, Karl Barth, and Reinhold Niebuhr.

It was once easy to write a life of Paul. The historian simply took the account of Paul's activities in Acts and harmonized it with the contents of his letters as much as possible. Then there was a period of extreme skepticism concerning the historical reliability of Acts. Today, historians feel that they may lodge qualified confidence in Acts (see Chapter 13). But at best, Acts covers only a small part of Paul's life. It does not supply as many chronological anchors as one might like. It is not clear how the letters that can be attributed to Paul with some confidence correlate with the Acts narrative. It is difficult, if not impossible, to square what Paul says about his visits to Jerusalem in Galatians with the visits men-tioned in Acts. This chapter follows the lead of the primary witness, Paul's letters, in cases of apparent divergence. But when all has been said, we simply lack the information to write a biography of Paul, just as we lack the information to write a biography of Jesus. However, as in the case of Jesus, there are some things that can be said with confidence even if a "life" is beyond our reach.

Indeed, it is in some respects becoming easier to place Paul in his original historical context. In the past, many critical studies of Paul emphasized the apostle's background in Greek thought, especially Stoicism and the mystery religions. Recently, scholars have recognized more fully Paul's debt to his Jewish heritage. That will be apparent in our treatment of where Paul fits in the first century C.E. We will honor his own claim to being "a member of the people of Israel . . . as to the law, a Pharisee" (Phil. 3:5).

THE QUEST FOR THE "HISTORICAL" PAUL

Paul and Judaism

There is no reason to doubt the assertion of Acts (9:11; 22:3) that Paul was born, and probably grew up, in Tarsus. Tarsus was an important Roman city, the gateway to the hinterland of Asia Minor (Galatia), a seaport and a university town. Paul's Hebrew name, as mentioned, was Saul. His Latin name doubtlessly related to the fact that he was by inheritance a citizen of Rome, and not just a citizen of a prominent provincial city. Our narrative will use his Latin name, simply because it is more familiar.

Paul's background made him a native of the Hellenistic world of the Roman Empire. His family must have retained a grasp of its Jewish heritage and genealogy, to judge from some of Paul's later autobiographical remarks. It is impossible to ascertain, however, whether Paul's was a family of Hellenistic Jews or a family of displaced rabbinic loyalists. Two things are plain, though. Whatever his original Jewish loyalties, Paul was a child of the Roman world, and he was, or became, a very devoted Jew. According to the Book of Acts, he sought higher Jewish learning in Jerusalem at the feet of Rabbi Gamaliel, the presiding officer (*nasi*) of the now-Hillelite academy.

At this point, anomalies begin to emerge. Both by his own testimony and by that of Luke in Acts, Paul was a fanatical persecutor of the earliest Christian Church. But Luke shows Paul's teacher, Gamaliel, defending the apostles against the murderous intentions of the Sadducean high priest and his cohorts (Acts 5:33–39). Here, Luke the historian reveals a grasp of the standard rabbinic–pharisaic operating procedure toward religious deviants. Luke also quickly acquaints his readers with the fact that the young fanatic from Tarsus sought and received credentials to root out the Nazarean deviants in Damascus from the Sadducean high priest, not from his teacher, the leader of the pharisaic academy. For whatever reason, the bright young student from the provinces had broken with the more tolerant policies of his teacher and made common cause with the Sadducees, even if he was ". . . as to the Law, a Pharisee."

Another anomaly concerns Paul's attitude toward the Law-Torah. Here, let it be noted that Paul wrote in Greek, not Hebrew. When he wanted to refer to the Mosaic Torah, he did so by the Greek word *nomos,* which comes into English as "law." *Nomos* is not quite so rich and comprehensive a term as *Torah,* but certainly closer to the Hebrew than the inadequate English term *law.* Moreover, a careful reading of Paul's letters suggests that he did not use *nomos* univocally. Sometimes, as in Romans 7, he seemed to use the term in two or more senses. However, the problem is more than one of ambiguity, for Paul seemed clearly to suggest that he once believed that the Torah was an instrument of salvation, that is, by keeping the Torah, one could be saved. This assertion is puzzling, because, as we have seen (Chapter 10), rabbinic Judaism never claimed that the Torah *was* an instrument of salvation. Rather, Torah was God's gift to the people, Israel, whom God had already taken. It was one of God's gifts of love to the people and a means of responding to that love, not a device for gaining God's acceptance.

It may be that Paul's notion of "salvation by works of the Law-Torah" was an idea he brought with him to Jerusalem from his Hellenistic background. This possibility gains credibility from the widespread popularity of such views in Hellenistic gentile Christianity from the late first century onward. Romans 7:7–25 implies that Paul was, and to some degree remained, deeply vexed by his near success and inevitable failure to live a perfect life of Torah faithfulness. The revelatory awareness that in Jesus the Messiah (Christ), God had freely given all that Paul sought and more, not only resolved his personal religious problems but also changed his perspective on the Torah, though not his respect for it. Following his revelation, Paul's notion of the function of Torah was in some respects closer to that of Hillelite phariseeism than it had been before. English speakers may be misled by the usual translation of the Greek word *telos* in Rom. 10:4, "Christ is the end [*telos*] of the law." This word means "goal," "purpose" (including, continuing purpose), or "fulfillment." A scholar who has led the way in study of Paul's background in rabbinic Judaism, W. D. Davies, has suggested that, for Paul, Messiah Jesus embodied the Torah. Paul's new understanding of Torah would hardly be fully congenial to his mentors in Judaism, whether Hellenistic or rabbinic. But it should be equally clear that his experience of the Risen Christ did not lead him to the out-of-hand rejection of Torah encountered in some oversimplified accounts of his thought.

The Apostle Paul. A statue by Adamo Tadolini (1788–1868) in St. Peter's Square at the Vatican in Rome shows the Apostle Paul holding "the sword of the Spirit" (Eph. 6:17) and a book, on which is inscribed: "I can do all things in him who strengthens me" (Phil. 4:13). *Source:* Jozef Sedmak/Shutterstock

Another possibility for understanding Paul's attitude toward the Torah arises from analyzing his relationship to mysticism. Although too much should not be made of it, the deliberately veiled reference to himself in 2 Cor. 12:1–10 seems to connect Paul with the practice of Chariot–Palace Mysticism (see Chapter 10). His affinity with early kabbalism suggests two possible explanations for Paul's attitude toward Torah.

The notion developed in regular rabbinic circles and, with the passage of time, became particularly strong in Jewish mysticism, that the coming of the Messiah could be hastened by devoted living of the Torah. Had Paul as a younger man tried to force the messianic age into being by living a perfect life of Torah, only to have the Messiah come graciously to him while he was still a fully self-conscious sinner? It cannot be proven, but it is a provocative possibility that should not be ignored.

A second and related possibility arises from the fact, noted in Chapter 10, that intensive study of Torah was an important part of mystical discipline. Was it in a profoundly personal way that the Torah, conventionally approached, failed Paul? Unable to achieve mystical illumination in the prescribed fashion, had he received his mystical vision unbidden, at the hands of the Risen Messiah Jesus? Again, a confident answer is not possible. But this conjecture, based on recent progress in research, warns against oversimplified views of Paul.

Paul never renounced his own Jewishness or the Jewish people as a whole. His own love was encompassing enough to include both Israel after the flesh and Israel after the spirit, those "honorary Jews" God had grafted onto the rootstock of Israel through Messiah Jesus (see Rom. 11:17–20). He was confident that God's love and providence were equally comprehensive.

Paul, the Apostle

Luke's account of Saul/Paul's vision of the Risen Messiah on the road to Damascus (Acts 9:1–22) is one of the most colorful narratives in the book of Acts. Popularly known as "the conversion of St. Paul," it has become a favorite theme of Western art, and the model of true Christian conversion for the more devotional forms of Christian piety. But in truth, the term *conversion,* in its usual sense, is a misnomer. It misrepresents Paul's experience, dramatic as it was, and it is anachronistic at this stage of history.

Paul did not stop being a Jew, or stop thinking of himself as a Jew, when he recognized Jesus as the Messiah of Israel. He seems rather to have thought that he was a *better* Jew as a consequence. Both his own writings and Luke's portrait in Acts make this quite evident. Further, it would be decades after Paul's time, centuries in some circles, before it was considered that a Jew who became a Christian thereby ceased being Jewish. It would be much more accurate to speak of Paul's transforming experience as an *illumination,* particularly in the light of his probable connection with Jewish mysticism.

Luke narrated his version of Paul's illumination twice more (Acts 22:4–16; 26:9–18) after his initial account. Paul's own description of what most historians take to be the same event (Gal 1:11–17; 1 Cor. 15:8) is much more modest. Luke had Paul launching his missionary career the moment he recovered from his trauma. Paul himself was less specific. He said simply that he went into Arabia and later returned to Damascus (Gal 1:17). These data would counsel caution in the use made of the Acts narratives. In any case, it is dubious that either Paul or Luke would have described his experience as a "conversion" from Judaism to a different and distinct faith.

Paul's illumination apparently took place in the early to mid-30s, that is, not too many years after the first Resurrection experiences. Whether he ever saw or heard Jesus before his death is beyond demonstration, though most Pauline experts think not.

A chronology of Paul's subsequent career is also difficult, though Luke's narrative portrays an itinerary and implies a chronology. But even Luke does not explicitly name three missionary journeys that can be shown on a map with dotted, dashed, and dot-and-dashed lines. That is a product of the interpretation of Acts. We simply do not know how many missionary journeys Paul made. It may have been more than three, probably not fewer.

The one event in Paul's career that seems to be closely datable is his death. The tradition that Paul and Peter were jointly martyred in Rome during Nero's postfire persecution of 65 C.E. is supported by a number of early sources, including the First Letter of Clement, then bishop of Rome, to Corinth in about 95 C.E. Whether Paul's death was the outcome of the imprisonment and forthcoming trial at the end of Acts is disputed by experts. There are legends that he was acquitted and released on that occasion, resuming his missionary activities. Some think that the contents of the so-called prison letters (to be discussed) demand two Roman imprisonments and another lengthy jailing in the east, probably at Ephesus.

Despite our inability to reconstruct a chronology, there can be little doubt what Paul was doing in the years between his illumination and death. He journeyed by land and by sea, from city to city in Syria, Asia Minor, and Greece. He had planned to visit Rome, which he eventually did as a prisoner, on his way to Spain (Rom. 15:24), and perhaps his travels eventually led there. Arriving in a town, he would take his stand in a public place and begin his proclamation or visit the synagogue, if there was one. There he could be sure of a nucleus of persons familiar with the Hebrew Scriptures, if only in the Greek version, and conversant with Jewish messianic hopes. These forays into Jewish congregations probably created friction, for though messianic enthusiasm was not unheard of, and certainly was not against the Torah, Paul's activities would almost certainly have appeared as a challenge to local leaders and, in due course, an attempt to split the congregation or make off with members and fellow travelers (the God-fearers). But through whatever approach, Paul's goal was the establishment of a Christian Church, probably meeting in the homes of adherents and attracting to itself additional members. Paul's stay in a community was usually governed by circumstances. If things went well, he might remain to instruct converts or perhaps move on, leaving the task to colleagues.

Paul was at least as likely to run afoul of public hostility and government zeal from gentile quarters as he was of Jewish resentment, any of which could lead to a hasty departure. Acts 19:9 may be taken to mean that Paul rented a hall during his rather long stay in Ephesus and lectured after the manner of a Stoic teacher. Luke noted two occasions when Paul got into trouble because his activities infringed on local business interests (Acts 16:16–24; 19:23–41).

Paul tried to revisit the churches he had established, though, as we learn from his exchange with the Corinthian church, he was not always welcome. Paul's letters were almost certainly intended as his surrogate presence with the churches he had established. He took care not to interfere in the affairs of congregations he had not started, his letter to the Romans being the one known exception to his rule of writing only to his own congregations. At least one letter is mentioned in the Pauline corpus that seems to have been lost, Laodiceans (Col. 4:16). It is quite likely that more were lost than survived.

No physical description of Paul survives in credible sources, though his remarks about himself to the Corinthians suggest that he was neither an imposing presence nor an impressive orator. He suffered from some sort of chronic illness or disability. He alluded to this disability as a "thorn in the flesh" that prevented him from becoming too intensely affected by his mystical experiences (2 Cor. 12:7–10). With the passage of years, he doubtless displayed more and more visible signs of the physical hardships he had endured in pursuit of his holy vocation: beatings, stonings, shipwrecks, prison terms, years on the road in all kinds of inclement weather. Whatever his physical limitations may have been, Paul more than made up for them through his courage, tenacity, and enthusiasm.

Paul comes across in his letters as a man of passion. His wrath blazed when he felt himself crossed, and his vocabulary of invectives knew few bounds. But he relished reconciliation and forgiveness more than victory. He seems to have been more of an intuitive thinker than a logical and discursive reasoner.

As we have seen in Chapter 13, the rank of apostle was the most prestigious office in the early church. Paul insistently maintained his claim to apostleship. To make his claim, he appealed to two basic arguments (see Galatians 1–2). Like all other true apostles, he was directly commissioned by the Lord Jesus, but in a revelatory encounter with the Risen Messiah, not during Jesus's physical ministry. And the most important leaders of the mother church in Jerusalem accepted him and his gospel. He could also have a dispute with them and win, he says, reporting his showdown with Peter over making Gentiles observe the dietary restrictions of the Torah (Gal. 2:11–14).

Paul also strongly maintained that he had received his gospel (i.e., the good news of Jesus's resurrection) not from any human agency, but directly from God through the Messiah. It was this gospel that received the approval of the Jerusalem church (again Galatians 1–2). This does not mean that Paul was claiming direct revelation as the source of everything he knew or taught. He quotes and cites sayings of Jesus. Twice in the latter part of First Corinthians alone he appeals to tradition (11:23–26; 15:1–11).

Paul, along with John, stands as one of the two most creative thinkers in the early history, perhaps the entire history, of the church. In terms of influence, Paul stands next after Jesus himself. But to portray Paul as the "real" founder of Christianity, the one who turned the religion of Jesus into a religion about Jesus, is a misrepresentation. It misunderstands both the impact of Paul and the timing of that impact, as well as the other currents flowing in the early church. By the time Second Peter was written, Paul's letters were being read with respect in the church, but he was not the only authority (2 Pet. 3:15–16). It is also true that Paul's formulation of Christianity lent itself particularly to the shift away from the Jewish messianism of the earliest church to the emphasis on personal salvation of later Christianity. One may suspect, though, that in his own mind, Paul was not so far removed from the traditional Jewish view of things as later readers have perceived. Indeed, some modern commentators have proposed that messianism, with its promised radical revision of the political and social order, was a factor in the appeal of early Christianity in the gentile world.

Sir Christopher Wren's epitaph in the great London cathedral he rebuilt, of which St. Paul is claimed patron, reads: "If you would see his monument, look about you." Something of the sort might equally be said of Paul himself, the Jewish–Christian apostle to the Gentiles.

THE LITERARY WORLD: LETTERS AS LITERATURE

Of the twenty-seven books of the New Testament, twenty-one take the form of letters. Thirteen are attributed to the Apostle Paul, seven are general ("catholic") letters attributed to James, John, Peter, and Jude, and one is anonymous, bearing the title "To the Hebrews." Most are "occasional" letters, that is, written to a particular person or group in response to a specific situation. All of the letters that designate Paul as author (except Ephesians and perhaps Colossians) are occasional letters. Third John is the only other occasional letter. Most of the rest of the letters can be called general because they are not addressed to any particular audience but to a broad group (such as "the saints" in the case of Ephesians or "the twelve tribes in dispersion" in James). Two of the letters (Hebrews and First John) are "open letters" or tracts, not addressed to any specific or general group, and called letters only because of their closing salutations.

The form of the New Testament occasional letters was similar to that used in the correspondence of the period. Consider, for example, a typical Greek papyrus letter of the first century C.E.:

> Irenaeus to Apollinarius his dearest brother, many greetings. I pray constantly for your health, and I myself am well. I wish you to know that I reached land on the sixth of the month of Epeiph and we unloaded our cargo on the eighteenth of the same month. I went up to Rome, on the twenty-fifth of the same month and the place welcomed us as the god willed, and we are daily expecting our discharge, it so being that up till today nobody in the corn fleet has been released. Many salutations to your wife and to Serenus and to all who love you, each by name. Goodbye.[1]

The writer begins by identifying himself and the one to whom the letter is being sent (salutation), prays for the well-being of the recipient (prayer), and talks of his own situation. The message is communicated (body), and the letter closes with greetings to others, more wishes, and a final word to end the letter (conclusion). The letter is a substitute for the more preferred form of oral communication; thus, its language is informal and free flowing (except for the stylized opening and closing). In contrast with a narrator, the author of a letter is an onstage participant in the writing. The "world" of the letter is the relationship presumed by the letter, and the letter is like a snapshot showing us the status of that relationship at a particular time. To understand the world of the letter, it is essential to know the nature of the relationship and the expectations of sender and recipient.

The occasional letters of Paul adapt this common form to the relationship between an apostle (Paul) and the Christian churches he has founded or intends to visit (Romans). The letters also assume a broader relationship between God and these churches and individuals, which has been established, both sender and recipient assume, through the Crucifixion and Resurrection of Jesus Christ. In his role as apostle (one commissioned by Christ to proclaim the gospel authoritatively), Paul presumes both his relationship to the churches and the relationship he and they have entered into

---

[1]C. K. Barrett. *New Testament Background*. New York: Harper & Row, 1961, p. 29.

with God through Jesus Christ. The modifications in the form of the typical Greek "familiar" letter reflect this broader relationship. Thus, Paul incorporates into his letters extended discussions of what God has done through the Crucifixion and Resurrection of Jesus and the implications of these events for his readers and others. He also includes exhortation (called *paraenesis*) concerning the obligations of this relationship. This was the counterpart of the behavioral advice given by rabbis.

Paul's correspondence is not very carefully patterned for literary effect. Where literary polish is evident (as in Phil. 2:6–11), it is usually the result of inclusion of a sacred song from Christian worship. The letters read, not surprisingly, like letters; that is, like a conversation between persons who know each other. The Pauline letters show a refinement of this conversational style, especially when making points about the nature of the divine–human relationship, and Romans reflects a more carefully patterned structure, as we shall see. But we should not try to make the letters more literary than they are, for, in Greek, Paul was a master of the run-on, or life, sentence. The basic elements of Pauline letters can be outlined as follows:

Salutation	(identification of sender and recipient and greeting)
Thanksgiving	(prayer)
Body	
Closing commands	(paranaesis)
Conclusion	(peace wish, greeting, kiss, benediction)

We should try to place ourselves within the context of the relationships, so that we can imagine what Paul is trying to say and why, and what his audience is hearing.

Themes in The Letters of Paul

Before we begin an analysis of each of the letters of Paul in their original historical contexts, let us consider three of the major theological themes in the correspondence considered as a whole. These are:

The ultimate triumph of God foreshadowed in the coming of Jesus, Christ and LORD.
The righteousness of God revealed in Christ, which brings all humans into harmony with God.
The new life of freedom of those who respond with faith to God's grace revealed in Christ.

It is important to acknowledge that these themes are not consistently stated in the Pauline letters. As we shall see, the letters reflect the ad hoc nature of Paul's thought as he responds to the situations of his various audiences and the change in his thinking over time. At best, these themes are one reader's construction of recurrent concepts, which may be seen to form the core of Paul's message.

All of Paul's letters affirm Jesus as Christ (Messiah) and Lord. With the death and resurrection of Jesus, Christ and Lord, God's final victory over all opposing forces was assured, Paul believed. Reflecting identification with the apocalyptic sense of expectation and urgency associated with the community that produced the Dead Sea Scrolls, Paul looked to the imminent end of the present age of history, the return of Christ, and the full implementation of the messianic kingdom. He called on people to prepare themselves for this new age.

According to the Pauline letters, all efforts by humans (both Jews and Gentiles) to live as God intends, and has made clear in the Torah and in the human conscience, inevitably fail because all are under the power of sin. Even though all humans know what God expects, they are all unable on their own to fulfill the divine commandments, whether they be those of the Jewish law or the dictates of conscience. Therefore, all humans are alienated from God and deserve condemnation. However, God's own righteousness creates a new situation. Through the death and Resurrection of Christ, God has brought sinful humanity into right relationship with God. In other words, justification (or righteousness) is not earned by good deeds, but by trust (faith) in God's free gift (grace).

Those who respond with faith to God's grace in Christ enter a new life of freedom. They are freed *from* the power of sin and life "according to the flesh," and freed *for* life in the Spirit, in obedience to the law of love. They are freed for life in community with others, forming the "body of Christ." The community's common meal, the Lord's Supper, is a powerful expression of the continuing presence of Christ and an anticipation of the new age, which will come fully when Christ returns.

THE HISTORICAL WORLD: THE LETTERS OF PAUL IN CONTEXT

In our discussion of the letters, we will combine literary and historical observations in an effort to understand the particular relationships forming the context of each letter. We have arranged the letters in the order of their most probable historical development, rather than following their canonical order (see Table 14.1).

Some thirteen or fourteen letters in the New Testament were ascribed to Paul by the fourth and fifth centuries. But how many, and which ones of them, did Paul actually write (or dictate)? The

---

TABLE 14.1 A Possible Reconstruction of the Life and Letters of Paul

c. 10 c.e.	Paul is born in Tarsus of Cilicia.
c. 16–34	Paul attends synagogue school, beginning a lifelong study of the written and oral Torah. He also probably studies Greek philosophy, perhaps among the Stoic teachers of Tarsus. He learns from his father the trade of tentmaking. Eventually, he goes to Jerusalem, perhaps to study under Rabbi Gamaliel. He becomes associated with the persecution of followers of Jesus.
c. 34–35	The "illumination" of Paul. He receives a mystical vision of Jesus, and thereafter enters into a period of meditation.
c. 37	Paul visits Jerusalem and meets Cephas (Peter) and James, the brother of Jesus. Thereafter, he goes to Antioch and from there begins his work proclaiming the gospel in the Mediterranean world.
c. 50–51	The "Jerusalem conference" (Gal. 2:1–10, Acts 15:1–21).
c. 50–52	First and Second Letters to the Thessalonians.
c. 52–54	Paul resides in Ephesus.
c. 53–54	Letter to the Galatians.
c. 54–56	First and Second Letters to the Corinthians. (Residing in Corinth c. 55–56).
c. 56–57	Letter to the Romans.
c. 58–60	Prison (Captivity) letters—Philippians, Colossians, and Philemon.
c. 65	Sometime during the mid-60s Paul is executed in Rome.

earliest canon lists mention "seven of Paul." There is a strong consensus among Pauline experts that a "solid seven" are indeed from Paul. These are Romans, First and Second Corinthians, Galatians, Philippians, First Thessalonians, and Philemon. When statistical studies have been done on various linguistic features of the entire traditional Pauline corpus, the "solid seven" correlate with one another much more highly than do the remainder. The consensus continues by noting three additional letters, sometimes called "Deuteropauline": Second Thessalonians, Colossians, and Ephesians. Many Paulinists will argue Second Thessalonians is by Paul (and we agree). Fewer will argue for Colossians and fewer yet for Ephesians. Next, the consensus regards the Pastoral epistles as "post-Pauline," though some would suggest they incorporate authentic Pauline fragments. Finally, the consensus notes that Hebrews is definitely not by Paul. His name does not appear in the best manuscripts (though some editions of the Bible add it in an editorial title). The literary style and thought of the letter are very un-Pauline. The Western church, which prized Paul most highly, refused to accept the Pauline ascription until the late fourth or fifth century, and then only as a compromise in which the Eastern church accepted Revelation as part of the canon.

First Thessalonians: Like a Thief in the Night

This is Paul's earliest surviving letter, which makes it a likely candidate for the oldest book in the New Testament. It was written about 50–51 C.E. to the church at Thessalonica, capital of Macedonia (in northern Greece), which Paul, Timothy, and Silas (Silvanus) had recently founded (see Acts 17:1–10), after Paul's imprisonment at Philippi (1 Th. 2:2). Paul had been forced to flee from Thessalonica (Acts 17:7), so he was naturally concerned about the well-being of the fledgling church. He sent Timothy to Thessalonica (1 Th. 3:1–10), and this letter is based on what he learned from his co-worker about the congregation and their concerns.

In his thanksgiving (1:2–10) Paul praises the Thessalonians for being an example to other believers (1:7) and hints at the themes he will develop in the letter—the validity of their ministry among other Thessalonians, the ethical implications of the gospel, and the coming again (*parousia*) of Jesus.

Apparently, Timothy had brought word of opponents who challenged Paul's work, saying that he was motivated by guile and a desire for gain, for the apostle mounts a vigorous defense of his work among them (2:1–16). Next he turns to what is bothering the Thessalonians (4:1–5:11). First, he exhorts them to "abstain from immorality" in order to attain "holiness" (4:1–8). Then, he reassures them that those who have died before the *parousia* will be raised from the dead when Christ appears (4:17). But he cautions them against trying to determine exactly when this will happen, for Christ will come when he is least expected, "like a thief in the night" (5:2). Therefore, Christians should be ever ready, armed with faith and love (5:8). This apparently is to counter the view of some that they should sit back and wait passively for the end to come.

After a final exhortation to "respect those who labor among you" (5:12), "admonish the idlers" (5:14), "rejoice always" (5:16), and not "quench the Spirit" (5:19), he closes with his typical blessing and a request to have the letter read to the whole church (5:27–28).

The letter is delicately balanced between encouragement and chastisement. Paul both applauds their exemplary faith and warns them about failure to respect his ministry and giving in to the vices of the world and laziness in the belief that the end is at hand. Paul makes use of apocalyptic imagery to describe his position on the parousia (4:16–17; 5:5), yet seems to reject the penchant to identify when the end will come, apparent in Daniel and other apocalyptic works.

Second Thessalonians: Stand Firm

Not all scholars agree on the date of this letter. Some think it was written shortly after (perhaps even before) the previous letter. Others argue it is not a Pauline letter at all but was written in the style of one and attributed to Paul after his time. Regardless, its major concerns—encouragement of the Thessalonians and correction of their understanding of the *parousia*—echo those of First Thessalonians.

Apparently, a spurious letter has come to the Thessalonians claiming to be from Paul, saying that the day of the Lord has already come (2:2). In response, Paul lays out some specifics about the signs of the end that seem to contradict his teaching in First Thessalonians that the end will come unexpectedly. He says that before the end there will be a "rebellion" and a "son of perdition" who will occupy the Temple of God. He has not come because there is someone who is "restraining" him. When the "man of lawlessness" comes, many will be deceived. Paul gives thanks for the Thessalonians' faith and exhorts them to "stand firm." As in the first letter, his final exhortation relates to those who refuse to work, apparently believing that the end is near.

First Corinthians: Unity in the Spirit

Corinth was one of the most important cities of Greece. It was a wealthy port city, a commercial center where all the cultures and religions of the Mediterranean world collided. Paul had established a church there, spending about a year and a half in the city. He worked principally among the poor. After leaving, Paul settled in Ephesus, across the Aegean Sea from Corinth. While there he wrote a letter (see 1 Cor. 5:9) that is now lost (or perhaps partly represented in 2 Cor. 6:4–7:1) in which he expressed concern about immoral behavior in the church. In response he received word that the church was perilously close to rupture because of rival factions within the community who made claims to have the only truth. He also received a letter from the congregation with questions about marriage, contact with the world, worship, the Resurrection, a collection for the church in Jerusalem, and a Christian teacher named Apollos, who had followed Paul to Corinth.

First Corinthians is Paul's response to both the oral and the written correspondence. At the same time as he sent the letter by sea, he dispatched Timothy with an oral message by land (4:17). On the question of factions, Paul urges the Corinthians to put aside dissensions and recognize that Christ is not divided (1:10–4:21). He reminds them of the gospel he preached,

> . . . Christ crucified, a stumbling block to Jews and foolishness to Gentiles, but to those who are the called, both Jews and Greeks, Christ the power of God and the wisdom of God. (1:23–24)

Although neither Paul nor the Corinthian Christians are wise or strong on worldly standards, God has chosen them both to show up the learned and powerful of the world. Factions are the result of their acting like "ordinary men" or, in Paul's vocabulary, "of the flesh" (3:3). Leaders like Paul and Apollos should be seen as "fellow workers" (3:9) in God's field, stewards of the "mysteries of God" (4:1). All the work of the leaders will be tested on the final day; it is not up to the Corinthians to judge.

A recurrent theme is the "unity" of the community. Paul uses the human body as a metaphor to describe the church as the "body of Christ" in which all are members though with various functions. Ideally, all work together for the common good. The parts of the body that seem the weakest are often the most indispensable (12:12–31). His concern about the ecstatic spiritual gifts, especially "speaking in tongues," is that this mysterious utterance be used to build up the community as much as other more intelligible gifts (14:1–12). According to Paul, the best way to unity is not through any of the various gifts, but through self-giving love, which he extols in his famous "Ode to Love" (1 Corinthians 13). Unity is also his concern when he condemns the Corinthians for turning the meal that commemorates the death of Jesus into a drunken orgy, making the problem of factions worse. Apparently, the wealthier members would arrive early and consume too much, leaving nothing for the

Bema at Corinth. In the ruins of the Greek city of Corinth archaeologists found this *bema* (platform) used for giving public addresses. According to the Acts of the Apostles (18:12–17) Paul was brought to this platform (built in 44 C.E.) to defend the message he was proclaiming, but the charges were dismissed. *Source:* Arthur C. Young

poorer members who came later. He reminds them of the instructions for observance of the meal and of its sacred significance that "I received from the Lord" (11:23). Paul's account of the Last Supper (1 Cor. 11:23–26) is the basis of the traditional Christian eucharistic liturgy. It differs only in minor ways from the Marcan version (Mk. 14:22–25; Mt. 26:26–29; Lk. 22:17–19).

In this letter, Paul gives his clearest statement of his view of life after death. In keeping with his pharisaic roots, Paul affirms resurrection of the body at the last judgment. Perhaps influenced by Greek teaching on the immortality of the soul, the Corinthians have questioned Paul's teaching. Paul's vigorous defense shows how important he considered this teaching. In his view, if there is no resurrection from the dead, then Christ has not been raised, and if Christ has not been raised "your faith is futile" (15:17). But if Christ has been raised from the dead, this is the "first fruit" of the resurrection of all believers. Paul explains the resurrection by using the argument of different types of bodies, including the "spiritual" bodies of the resurrection. Only when the resurrection occurs will the final victory over death be won.

Second Corinthians: From Bitterness to Joy

The majority view of scholarly opinion today is that Second Corinthians is not one, but at least two letters editorially combined. The principal reason is a markedly different tone in 2 Corinthians 10–13 from that of 1–9. We can also reconstruct a chain of events that accounts for two letters.

Upon Timothy's return to Ephesus, Paul learned that First Corinthians had failed to turn the community away from factionalism. Instead, new Christian missionaries hostile to Paul had come and made the situation worse (2 Cor. 11:1–15). In Paul's view these interlopers were "false apostles" (11:13) who preached "another Jesus" (11:4). They apparently performed "signs and wonders" to claim authority for their message, and they accused Paul of being forceful in his letters but inarticulate and uninspiring in person (10:10). Paul's response was to rush to Corinth himself, but it was by his admission a "painful visit" (2:1). He had been insulted (2:5–8; 7:12) and forced to leave in humiliation.

Against this background, it is easy to understand the anguished and bitter tone of the letter he wrote in response (2:3–4, 9; 7:8–12). Most interpreters believe this letter is preserved at least in part in Second Corinthians 10–13, the "severe letter." Here, Paul sarcastically attacks his opponents and boasts of his own apostleship. His defense of his Jewish background (11:21–22) suggests that the opponents are Jewish Christians. His claim of mystical experiences (12:1–10) implies that the opponents claim heavenly visions.

The response to the "severe letter," brought by Titus, was encouraging. The opponents had been dealt with, and a chastened church had new zeal for Paul's leadership (7:6–7). Paul then sent them another letter (8:16–24), which also might very well be partially preserved in Second Corinthians 1–9. These chapters climax in an expression of joy by Paul at the restoration of his relationship with the church (7:2–16).

In this letter, Paul develops his view of the "spiritual body," which he had mentioned in 1 Corinthians 15. He had spoken of the spiritual body that the faithful would inherit in the resurrection. He qualifies this position somewhat by speaking of a process of ongoing spiritual renewal (4:16–5:10) that begins in the earthly life, so that when the time comes to put on the "heavenly dwelling," "we will not be found naked" (5:3). This point of view relates to becoming a "new creation" in Christ, a concept he will develop in other letters, and taking up the "ministry of reconciliation" (5:16–21).

Galatians: "The Gospel Which was Preached by Me"

The origin of this letter is disputed, although there is consensus that it is an authentic Pauline writing. The uncertainty surrounds the location of the recipients and the date of its writing. "Galatia" could either be the old tribal kingdom in north central Asia Minor or the Roman province further south. Wherever they were, Paul had started the Galatian churches when he was confined by sickness to the area (4:13). Because of similarity to the major themes of Romans, many scholars think it was written about 54 C.E., perhaps while Paul was at Ephesus. Other scholars date the letter to 48–49 C.E., making it the earliest extant Christian writing. This dating resolves apparent conflicts with the Book of Acts on the place of the Jerusalem Council in the Pauline chronology (see Acts 15).

The letter is a vigorous defense of the legitimacy and basic themes of the gospel Paul is proclaiming. However, his presentation is, as usual, shaped by the situation he is addressing. The situation in Galatia is grave, Paul feels. These churches have turned to a "different gospel" (1:6) from that which Paul had taught them. There is an urgent need to reaffirm the true gospel, which is from Jesus Christ, not man. So Paul dispenses with his typical flowery thanksgiving and instead begins abruptly. For several verses, the words pour out and Paul's ire is painfully evident.

Apparently, his opponents have accused Paul of preaching a message received from men, specifically the apostles in Jerusalem (1:16–17). In response Paul describes his dramatic encounter with Jesus Christ and his commissioning by God to preach to the Gentiles (1:11–24). His is not a gospel of men, but from God via God's son Jesus. His apostleship was recognized by the Jerusalem apostles, and he was entrusted with the gospel to the uncircumcised (Gentiles), as Peter was entrusted with the gospel to the circumcised (Jews) (2:1–10). He intrudes an account of a confrontation with Peter over kosher customs that occurred earlier at Antioch, perhaps to underscore his own apostolic authority (2:11–14). He moves smoothly from his experience with Peter to a basic theme of the letter: "a person is justified [made right with God] not by the works of the law but through faith in Jesus Christ" (2:16). As we shall see when we turn to Romans, "justification by faith" is one of the key concepts in Paul's interpretation of the significance of Jesus Christ.

To the "foolish Galatians" Paul appeals to Scripture to defend "justification," by quoting Gen. 15:6, Hab. 2:4, and other proof texts. The true heirs of Abraham, he maintains, are not those who keep the law, but those who live by faith. That was already true in Abraham's time; now through Christ this truth is to be universally proclaimed. The law had a purpose, to restrain people (be a "custodian") until Christ came, opening to all the way of justification by faith. Christ's coming, Paul says, frees people from bondage to sin and the law and allows them to become children of God, heirs of the promises made to Abraham. To make the point, Paul uses the allegorical method to interpret Scripture (4:21–31). Developing the theme of "freedom," he confronts the issue of whether being liberated from the law means license to do what the law forbids. He argues that freedom from the law leads to life in the Spirit, which is a life, not of gratifying physical desires, but of "love, joy, peace" (5:22–23).

From Paul's concerns, we can assume that his opponent(s) at Galatia had tried to convince the gentile Christian men that they must be circumcised in order to be heirs to the promises to Abraham in the Scriptures (see Gen. 17:9–14). Because this position was based on scripture, Paul put to use his skills as an interpreter of the Bible to refute it. He also let his anger boil over (5:12).

In addition, some Galatian Christians were returning to worship of "elemental spirits of the universe" and to observance of pagan festivals (4:9–10). Paul appeals to the trust they once placed in him and begs them to listen to him and return to the true gospel.

Uncharacteristically, in the closing he signs his own name (6:11) and reiterates the basic themes of the letter in a postscript (6:11–18).

Romans: The Power of God for the Salvation of All

Unlike Paul's other letters to churches, Romans was written to a church he had not founded himself. It was a church he had not even visited. So Romans does not read like the other correspondence. Missing are the answers to specific questions and the responses to particular problems. Paul wanted to enlist the support of the important Roman church in his planned mission to Spain. Because this is a "letter of introduction," it is a more carefully developed basic statement of Paul's understanding of the Gospel of Jesus Christ than we find in his other letters. It was probably not written until about 56–57 C.E., from Corinth, so it also reflects a maturing of Paul's thought.

The general nature of Romans should not be overemphasized. Paul was certainly aware of the dynamics of the Roman church, and his message to them is shaped by that church's situation. In particular, Paul knew of the disputes between Jewish and gentile Christians in the church. The Jewish Christians would have emphasized observance of the commandments of the Torah, while the gentile Christians (who were in the majority) would have stressed freedom from these regulations and placed their emphasis on faith in Christ. The Jewish Christians would have labeled certain gentile practices immoral, and the Gentiles would have considered the Jewish members of the church overscrupulous and too wedded to the traditions of the past. In Romans, Paul addresses this conflict.

Paul begins his letter with an expanded greeting (1:1–6), to establish his right to communicate with the Romans (he is an apostle to *all* the nations) and his basic understanding of the Gospel of Jesus Christ. (Of Davidic ancestry, Jesus was designated Son of God by the power of the Resurrection.) The thanksgiving (1:8–15) includes a petition that he and the Romans may be "mutually encouraged by each other's faith" (1:12).

In 1:16–17 Paul in effect states the theme of the letter. He will demonstrate to the Romans that the gospel is the "power of God for salvation to everyone who has faith, to the Jew first and also to the Greek." In Paul's world, there are only two types of people: Jews and others (Greeks or Gentiles). Thus, in Romans he will make clear that everyone (Jew and Greek) with faith (trust) in the power of God will have salvation (be delivered from that which holds them in bondage). He will show how God's power for salvation has been made available—to the Jew first and then to everyone else—through faith and also what holds everyone in bondage. Through the gospel the "righteousness of God" (a state of harmony in which there is a proper relationship between God and humanity) is made available through faith.

First, why is salvation needed by "everyone?" In 1:18–3:20 Paul states his understanding of the fundamental human dilemma. Through the creation, God has revealed himself to all humanity, but to no avail, for humans fail to honor the God they instinctively know. All are aware of the proper way to live to honor God. Gentiles have an inner law written on their hearts (conscience), and Jews have the revealed law (Torah). The basic problem is that "both Jews and Greeks are under the power of sin" (3:9). This Paul substantiates with a list of no less than seven quotations from the Tanak. His conclusion is that, "no human being will be justified in his [God's] sight by deeds prescribed by the law, for through the law comes the knowledge of sin" (3:20). For Paul, sin is an insidious force, whose power thwarts the human ability to live as God intends (according to the natural or revealed law). Because of sin, a proper relationship between God and humanity is impossible.

If humans cannot justify themselves, how is a proper relationship with God possible? In 3:31–4:25 Paul explains that harmony with God is available as a free gift (by God's grace) through faith in Jesus Christ. For in Christ there is redemption (a buying back or ransoming of someone in bondage) through the expiation of his blood (the Crucifixion), seen as a sacrifice for sin, with the death of Christ wiping out the effect of sin on humanity. Thus, the way is open to justification. Neither Jew nor Greek has cause to boast. The gospel is not a new innovation, according to Paul. Abraham, father of the Jews, through whom blessing was promised to all nations (Gen. 12:1–3), which makes him in a sense father of all nations, was justified by faith before he received the sign of the Jewish covenant, circumcision. Therefore, all who have faith are the true descendants of Abraham, not just the heirs of the Torah. Paul again shows his mastery of rabbinic methods of scriptural interpretation in Romans 4, with an extended commentary on Gen. 15:6.

Having established the necessity of the gospel and how it is accessible to all, Paul describes the consequences of "justification by faith" in 5:1–8:39. As one man's disobedience (Adam's) brought death, one man's righteousness (Jesus's) leads to "acquittal and life for all" (5:18). As we have noted in our discussion of the Garden of Eden story in Genesis 3 (cf. Chapter 3), it was the interpretation of this passage by the fifth-century C.E. theologian, St. Augustine, that led to the Christian doctrine of "original sin," the view that all humans after Adam and Eve inherit their sin. Scholars dispute whether that is a possible, not to mention necessary, interpretation of the Greek of these verses. In the view of many, it is more likely that Paul was stipulating that all humans are prone to sin, not that Adam's sin is passed through inheritance, like a genetic flaw. Where sin increased, grace abounded all the more. Paul can hear the Romans asking whether this means Christians should keep on sinning so that grace will increase, and he preempts the question by developing the theme of "new life in Christ," which begins with baptism (symbolically dying with Christ and being raised with him). This "death" that leads to new life brings freedom from sin, replacing the bondage of sin with "righteousness for sanctification" (a harmony with God that leads naturally to ever greater devotion).

The new life also involves death to the law. This does not mean the law is evil. On the contrary, the law is holy. It is sin, Paul says, that dwells in my flesh (my human nature, which is not, per se, evil), making me incapable of following the law and doing good. When, by the grace of God received in faith, we are delivered from sin and death, we are also freed from having to try to follow the law, for instead we will act according to the Spirit of God, which dwells in us. By the Spirit we are God's children. The Spirit's regenerative power is present in all creation, which will, like God's children, be set free from its bondage (to decay, in the case of the natural world). In conclusion, Paul summarizes the gospel as he understands it and, in a rhetorical flourish, the consequences of the gospel (8:31–39).

In Chapters 9–11 Paul turns to the problem his Jewish roots cannot let him avoid. Does his message not imply that God has turned away from unconditional promises made to the nation Israel? Paul follows several lines of argument to explain what God is doing, buttressing his views with frequent biblical quotations: (1) He reiterates his contention that the true heirs of father Abraham are spiritual, not physical, descendants—those who live by faith; (2) he defends God's right to choose whomever God will; (3) the missing ingredient in Israel's response to God was the realization that righteousness is through faith, not works of the law; and (4) the Jewish failure to respond in faith is providential, for through the disobedience of Israel, the door has been opened to the Gentiles. In any case, God has not rejected the people whom "he foreknew" (11:2). The time will come when "all Israel will be saved" (11:26), for the gifts and the call of God are irrevocable (11:29). In the meantime, gentile Christians, wild branches grafted onto the rootstock of Israel, are warned not to exalt themselves over their hosts. The paradox at the center of Paul's interpretation is that "God has imprisoned all in disobedience, that he may be merciful to all" (11:32).

Moving to practical advice and exhortation (Romans 12–15), Paul echoes the body metaphor used in 1 Cor. 12:4–8. He urges respect for those civil leaders "to whom respect is due," saying that God creates governments. Human relationships should be guided by but one law: Love one another. He urges the strong in the community to respect the scruples of the weak and bear their burdens.

The letter closes with personal notes, greetings, and a benediction. Among those Paul greets are several women in positions of leadership, including Junia, whom he seems to address as an "apostle" (16:7). The extended greetings in Chapter 16 seem out of place in a letter to a church Paul has not yet visited. It may be that they were part of a different letter (to the Ephesians?) and were appended here editorially.

Philippians: My Joy Complete

Paul's letter to the Philippians is one of his "captivity letters" (as are Colossians, Philemon, and perhaps Ephesians). He wrote it either while in jail at Ephesus (before 55) or Rome (about 56–58 or 61–63). If written during his final imprisonment in Rome about 62, it is his last surviving letter.

Philippi was probably Paul's favorite church, as this letter implies (4:1). He was undoubtedly proud of it, because it was the first in Europe (Acts 16:11–45). It was the only community from which Paul accepted financial support. In contrast with the anger and bitterness he often felt in his relationship with others of his churches, Paul felt affection for the Philippians, which makes this his warmest letter.

When the Philippians received word that Paul was in jail, they sent Epaphroditus with money to aid him and to remain with him as a helper (4:18). When Epaphroditus became ill, Paul sent him back, perhaps with this letter (2:25–30).

The words that characterize the apostle's mood throughout this letter are "rejoice" (1:18–19; 2:28; 3:1; 4:4; 4:10) and "joy" (1:4; 1:25; 2:2; 4:1). He "rejoices" knowing that whether he lives or dies, Christ will be honored through him. He rejoices that those who oppose him still proclaim Christ. He calls on the Philippians to "complete my joy" by living a life of humility, following the example of Christ. His exhortation is to "rejoice in the Lord" as he does. Even though he is in prison, Paul is confident about his present situation, for even in jail he is advancing the gospel.

In his call for unity and humility among the Philippians, Paul utilizes a Christian hymn (2:6–11) that (according to our own translation) speaks of Christ as the "servant who though in the form of God emptied himself and took human likeness and was totally obedient, even to the point of dying on the cross. Therefore, God exalted him and gave him the name above every name—LORD."

While he rejoices, even in his opponents' preaching, Paul nonetheless has a word of caution about those who are misleading the Philippians. His joyful tone lapses as he denounces as "dogs" (3:2) those who "mutilate the flesh" (who insist that gentile men must be circumcised in order to be Christians), those who renounce the cross (3:18), and those whose god is their belly (who participate in the gluttonous rites of pagan, probably mystery religions, 3:19). It is difficult to see these opponents as one group, for some seem to argue for stricter observance of the Torah and others advocate self-indulgence.

For Paul, the process of salvation is not yet complete. His present sufferings are a sharing of the suffering of Christ, and they will ultimately lead to a sharing of Christ's glory (3:10–14). He is concerned that the Philippians not claim too much too soon in their faith, as a result of false teachers, and instead "imitate" him (3:15–17). Thus, Paul stresses that whether in poverty or plenty he is content.

Philemon: No Longer a Slave

While he was in prison, Paul met a fugitive slave named Onesimus. Paul converted him to the Christian faith and became his spiritual father (10). Apparently, Onesimus had been the slave of a man named Philemon, who had become a Christian himself as a result of Paul's preaching (19). Onesimus had fled Philemon's home, taking money with him (18).

Paul writes to Philemon, not to instruct him, but to appeal to him out of love (8). Although Paul would like to keep Onesimus with him, he is sending him back to Philemon. His appeal is that Philemon receives him no longer as a slave but as a beloved brother (16). Paul appeals to his relationship with Philemon as a "partner" (a fellow servant of Christ), to receive Onesimus as he would receive Paul himself, and to charge any debt the slave owes "to my account."

Paul uniformly showed respect for the ordering of society. He did not challenge the institution of slavery. But he did direct a Christian slaveholder to a higher law, the law of love, which should cause him to forgive a runaway slave and accept him as a brother in Christ. This letter shows how Paul put into practice in a particular instance his belief that in Christ there is neither slave nor free person (Gal. 3:28).

If this letter was written during Paul's final imprisonment in Rome, it dates to 60–62 C.E. However, it could also have been written during another, earlier confinement.

Colossians: Christ Is All in All

In most of the Pauline letters, the apostle focuses on the crucifixion and resurrection of Christ as the heart of the gospel. Paul stresses individual believers' conforming to the image of the one who gave himself fully for others that they might receive new life through Him.

In this letter to a church in a small town in Asia Minor, about one hundred miles from Ephesus, Paul emphasizes another aspect of his understanding of who Christ is. To the Colossians, Paul writes that Christ is not merely the firstborn of believers, to whom obedience unto death opens the way to their salvation. He is also the firstborn of all creation. In fact, he is the goal of all creation, for "all things were created through him and for him" (1:16). This portrait of a "cosmic Christ" in whom "all things hold together" (1:17) adds a new dimension to the Pauline view of the nature of Christ and causes some scholars to question whether Paul really wrote Colossians.

The reason for appealing to this different understanding of Christ was the nature of the opposition in the Colossian church. Apparently, there had sprung up a group who worshipped the "elemental spirits of the universe" and taught an elaborate system of festivals and rules as to what believers must avoid, even to the point of injuring themselves, in order to attain "wisdom" (2:8, 20–23). This may have been an early form of Gnosticism, which taught that the world is under the control of spiritual powers hostile to God that must be placated if their influence is to be overcome.

Gnostics believed that a redeemer had brought a true knowledge of God and that only those who purified themselves from this evil world and its powers would experience it.

Colossians challenges this teaching by attacking the "elemental spirits" themselves with a different understanding of the cosmos. The world has been brought into existence through Christ and continues to exist through him. There is no place for "elemental spirits." To be in Christ is to die to such beings (2:20) and to recognize any philosophy based on them as "empty deceit" (2:8). The true mysteries of the cosmos and knowledge are not in such speculation, but in Christ (2:2–3). Cleverly, Paul adopts the imagery of the teaching of his opponents and applies it to Christ (as the authors of the Tanak had done with the mythologies of their day).

As in Philippians, Paul again adapts an early Christian hymn (1:15–20) speaking about who Christ is. However, its theme is almost the opposite of the theme of the hymn in Phil. 2:6–11. There Christ was praised as the one who "emptied himself." Here Christ is praised as the one in whom "all the fullness of God was pleased to dwell" (1:19). "Fullness" is the Greek term *pleroma,* possibly a key gnostic concept.

The exhortation to the Colossians (3:1–4:6) follows from this teaching. If they have died with Christ through baptism (2:12), then they should be concerned not with earthly matters (the rules and regulations opponents are teaching), but with living a life in Christ, reflecting a "new nature." The ethics of the new life focus, not on rituals and rules, but on the virtues of human relationships. Their ritual should be simple, teaching one another and singing sacred songs (3:16). In the exhortation Paul adapts a literary form typical of Hellenistic moral teaching—a list of virtues for ordinary people. Except for the references to "the Lord" there is nothing particularly Christian in them, although they are clearly adapted to the purposes of the letter.

A case can be made for challenging the traditional assumption that Paul wrote this letter, in part because it portrays a development of church offices beyond his time (1:7, 23, 25). However, an equally strong case can be made for the view that Paul did indeed write it. Unless and until clear evidence emerges to resolve the issue, the vote should probably go to the apostle.

Ephesians: He is Our Peace

Although the Letter of Paul to the Ephesians is similar in many respects to Colossians, it is also quite different, not only from that letter, but from any attributed to Paul. In terms of literary form, Ephesians is not an occasional letter like the rest of the Pauline correspondence. It is an *epistle;*

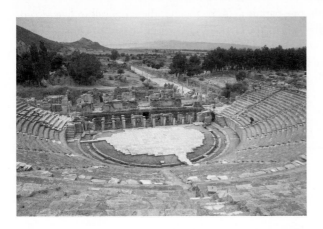

Ephesus: The theater at Ephesus seems to have been a hub for the work of the Apostle Paul in Asia Minor and Greece. According to Acts 19, some of Paul's colleagues were dragged into the theater at Ephesus by an irate mob, disturbed that sales of copies of the famous image of Artemis (or Diana) might be hurt by Paul's preaching. *Source:* Alex Khripunov/Shutterstock

that is, a general letter, which, instead of responding to particular concerns or opponents, develops a theme of its own. The greeting in the earliest known manuscripts is not even addressed to the Ephesians but to the "saints" in general. In its earliest form, Ephesians was probably an open letter addressed to no one church in particular.

The verbal parallels with Colossians are so pervasive (73 out of 155 verses) that many literary historians think Ephesians used Colossians as a source. Missing, however (except for 4:21, which is virtually the same as Col. 4:7), are the personal references and responses to specific opponents that make Colossians an occasional letter. Because of these many parallels with Colossians and other Pauline letters, some scholars feel that Ephesians was a sort of "cover letter" attached to the collected Pauline letters when they began to be circulated as a collection sometime toward the end of the first century. If this be the case, the letter may not have been written until 90–100 C.E. Others would identify it with the otherwise lost Letter to Laodicea (Col. 4:16).

The theme this epistle develops is that the unity of the cosmos through Christ (Ephesians 1–3) should be reflected in the unity of the church (Ephesians 4–6). Echoing Colossians, this letter asserts that the hidden mystery now revealed is that "things in heaven and things on earth" are united in Christ (1:10). To this it adds the Pauline view of "justification by faith" (2:5, 8–9), giving a rounded "introduction" to Paul's theology.

The letter looks upon the unity of Jews and Gentiles as an accomplished fact (2:11–12), utilizing a Christian hymn that begins

> For he is our peace;
> in his flesh he has made both groups into one
> and has broken down the dividing wall that is
> the hostility between us . . . (2:14)

This is the mystery of Christ now revealed (3:4–6). This "dividing wall" could be an allusion to the wall in the Jerusalem Temple that separated the Court of Israel from the Court of the Gentiles. It was physically destroyed in 70 C.E. According to this letter's interpretation of the hymn, it was symbolically destroyed when obedience to the Torah was abolished as a condition for being a part of God's people. Because division among Jews and Gentiles was an unsolved problem in Paul's time, its "resolution" implies a later era.

The theme of cosmic unity, now revealed in the unity of Jew and Gentile (that is, everyone) in Christ, leads smoothly to the exhortation. First there is an appeal for unity in the church (4:1–16), where there is but "one LORD, one faith, one baptism" (4:5). Second, there is a call to live according to the "new nature," renouncing the ways of the Gentiles in favor of being "imitators of God" (4:17–5:20). Third, there will be unity in the home (5:21–6:9) if all live by the principle: "Be subject to one another out of reverence for Christ" (5:21). Finally, there will be victory in the battle against the "principalities and powers" of this world and the spiritual world (6:10–20), achieved by putting on the "whole armour of God" (6:11).

Summary

Next to Jesus, the Apostle Paul is the most prominent character in the New Testament. He is a main figure in the Acts account of Christian origins. According to tradition he was the author of over half of the books of the New Testament.

In this chapter, we assessed Paul's importance in the historical world of the New Testament and in subsequent history. We placed the apostle in his original historical context, emphasizing the importance of his pharisaic and Hellenistic background and his self-understanding as an apostle of Jesus. We explained the difficulty of reconstructing the life of Paul. Instead of a detailed account of his life, we characterized his missionary work in general.

Our literary analysis began with the issue of whether the twenty-one letters in the New Testament should be considered literature. Most of them are occasional letters written in response to specific situations and to a particular audience. Others are more closely argued treatises intended for broader audiences. We suggested that the most fruitful literary approach to the occasional letters is to combine literary and historical observations in an effort to re-create the relationship between sender and recipient implied in the correspondence.

We treated those letters that are most likely authentically Pauline, following a likely chronological order of composition. This enabled us to see in general the development of Paul's thinking as he worked to spread the Christian message, but to respect the particular situation implied by each letter.

Interpreters disagree on the relevance of Paul's understanding of the meaning of Jesus for our age. In the following questions, we will raise some of the more significant issues.

The Contemporary World

Case Study

The Ordination of Women

Drawing on your literary and historical study of the Letters of Paul, reflect on/discuss the ongoing debate over whether women should be allowed to be priests or ministers in Christian churches. What guidance, if any, do Paul's Letters provide for confronting these divisive issues? If Paul were to reappear today, on which side of this dispute do you think he would stand?[2]

Questions for Discussion and Reflection

1. *Read First Thessalonians*
   a. If you were in the young, struggling church at Thessalonica, how would reading this letter from Paul make you feel?
   b. The return of Jesus was an issue much on the mind of the Thessalonians, to which Paul responded. Is this letter today relevant only for those who believe in the "second coming" of Jesus?
2. *Read First Corinthians 1–2, 12–14*
   a. According to Paul, the most serious problem the Corinthians faced was factions within the Christian community. Is this still the most serious problem in contemporary Christianity?
   b. First Corinthians 13 was probably an early Christian ode to "love." Among the contemporary "love songs" you have heard, do any evoke a similar image of the meaning of love?
   c. Should the restriction on the role of women in worship (First Cor. 14:34–36) be understood to mean that women should not speak in churches today?
   (***Note***: Many commentators believe that these verses were added by a later writer, perhaps the "pastor" of First Tim. 2:12. Elsewhere, Paul exhibits a positive attitude toward female church leaders; e.g., First Cor. 16:19 and Rom. 16:1–16.)
3. *Read Galatians 3–6*
   a. What does it mean to be "free?" Compare the description of freedom in Galatians with

[2]On the diversity of views on this topic in Christian churches, see Victor C. Pfitzner and Cathy Thomas, eds. *The Ordination of Women: Interdenominational Perspectives.* ATF Press, 2007.

contemporary understandings of freedom (including your own).

b. In Galatians, Paul uses the Hebrew Bible to develop his interpretation of the significance of the gospel. Note, for example, his interpretation of Abraham in 3:6–18 and the allegory in 4:21–31. Do you find his interpretation persuasive or are the readings forced?

4. *Read Romans 1–3, 8–13*

a. Romans 1:18–32 is often cited in the discussion of biblical teaching about homosexuality. Discuss the passage and its relevance, or lack thereof, to contemporary debate about homosexuality and the rights of gay and lesbian persons.[3]

b. Is the perspective in Romans 8:18–25 helpful in reflecting on the current environmental crisis?.

c. Reflect on and discuss Paul's position that Christians should be subject to the civil governments of the lands in which they live (Romans 13). Is this always the case?.

d. Some interpreters think that, in Romans, Paul supports God's "predestination" of only some to eternal life, emphasizing passages such as 8:29–30. Others stress texts like 11:30–32 in asserting that Paul's view includes universal salvation. Which, if either, position is most convincing to you? Why?

5. *Read Ephesians*

a. A principal theme in Ephesians is the breaking down of walls of hostility that divide people and finding unity. What are the most serious divisions to be overcome in the world today?

b. Some interpreters have blamed Paul's instruction to women (Eph. 5:22–24; Col. 3:18) for creating a climate of the subordination of women in which some husbands have resorted to abuse and violence to gain the "submission" of wives. Do these verses (note the context) really support the unqualified subordination of women? How should contemporary Christian women and men be guided by the instructions in this passage?

6. *Other Questions*

a. How do you think Paul's letters would be viewed if they, like the Dead Sea Scrolls, had not been found until recently, instead of being part of the New Testament?

b. Which, if any, of the teachings in Paul's letters do you find most compelling and relevant in the twenty-first century? Which do you have trouble with?

c. There is much discussion of the need today for "character education." Throughout the letters attributed to Paul, there are many exhortations to live virtuously (e.g., Gal. 5:16–25, Eph. 4:25–5:20). Do you agree that more attention is needed to educate people in basic virtues? How useful are Paul's instructions in this regard?

---

[3]For different perspectives on this and other texts cited in the ongoing debate over the Bible's teachings on homosexuality, see Robert A. J. Gagnon. *The Bible and Homosexual Practice: Texts and Hermeneutics.* Nashville: Abingdon, 2001 and Jack Rogers. *Jesus, the Bible and Homosexuality,* rev. ed. Louisville: Westminster John Knox, 2009.

Chapter 15

The Growing Church

The Pastoral and General Epistles, Hebrews, and the Revelation to John

Armageddon. *Harmagedon* (Hebrew for "Mount Megiddo") is made known in the Revelation to John (16:16) as the site of the final battle "on the great day of God the Almighty," before the coming of a "new heaven and new earth." Megiddo was a strategically located city in ancient Israel, at which a number of historic battles were fought (see Chapter Five). *Source:* Stavchansky Yakov/Shutterstock

In this chapter, we continue the story of the developing Christian Church, in the period known to historians as the postapostolic era (70–150 C.E.) (see Tables 15.1 and 15.2). We will then survey the group of writings known as the Pastoral Epistles (First and Second Timothy and Titus) and the General (or Catholic) Epistles (James; First and Second Peter; First, Second, and Third John; and Jude). Although the Pastorals are attributed to Paul, there is a strong case for associating them with a later period. We will also examine the Letter to the Hebrews and the one apocalyptic book in the New Testament, the Revelation to John. We will also devote attention to the noncanonical Christian writings from the early centuries of Christianity known collectively as the New Testament Apocrypha.

TABLE 15.1 Events Related to the New Testament after 70 C.E.

Date	Event	Roman Emperor
70	Temple destroyed	Vespasian (69–79)
	Major Rabbinic Academy and Sanhedrin at Yavneh (Jamnia)	Titus (79–81)
		Domitian (81–96)
		Nerva (96–98)
110–115	Some persecution of Christians	Trajan (98–116)
	Martyrdom of Ignatius	
132–135	Jewish Revolt of Bar Cocheba	Hadrian (117–138)
	Rabbinic Academy moves from Yavneh to Ussha	

TABLE 15.2 Suggested Dates for New Testament and Other Christian Writings after 70 C.E

68–70	Mark
75–100	Ephesians
85–100	Matthew, Luke-Acts
90–95	First Peter, Hebrews, Revelation
90–100	John (Gospel)
90–100	James
90–110	Letters of John
95	First Clement
100–130	Didache, Pastoral Epistles
100–140	Shepherd of Hermas
110–117	Epistles of Ignatius
110–130	Jude
130–150	Second Peter

THE HISTORICAL WORLD: TOWARD A POSTAPOSTOLIC CHURCH (70–150 C.E.)

Internal Changes

Church tradition held from an early period that John the son of Zebedee was both the youngest of the Twelve and the last to die. Irenaeus of Lyon, a great Christian writer of the second century C.E., cited the eyewitness authority of Polycarp for John's residence at Ephesus in Asia Minor. Irenaeus seemed to imply that John died during the reign of Trajan (98–116). The fourth-century historian Eusebius says so explicitly. It really does not matter for our immediate purposes whether this tradition is totally accurate. It is in any case a clear reminder that, as the church moved forward through time, there was an inevitable change in its form of organization and leadership. The apostles, unique in their authority because of their relationship to the Messiah-Christ, the bearers of treasured firsthand testimony to gospel events, inevitably had to pass from the scene. John's brother James died early on. Peter and Paul were martyred in the mid-to-late 60s. By the crisis of 70, four decades after the Crucifixion, the majority were probably gone. If one apostle survived to near the century's end, that would have been as remarkable as those two American architects of the Declaration of Independence, Thomas Jefferson and John Adams, living until July 4, 1826, half a century beyond the great event.

Loss of the apostles would not have been the only change. With the passage of time, less and less is heard of prophets in the church. And some of what is heard is not favorable. The Pastoral Epistles reflect developments in church offices beyond the data of Acts, First Corinthians, and Ephesians. The office of bishop became very significant (1 Tim. 3:1–7; Tit. 1:7–9). It is not clear whether the offices of bishop and elder were yet differentiated the way they eventually would be (1 Tim. 5:17–22; Tit. 1:5–9). The order of deacons had also apparently been regularized (1 Tim. 3:8–13).

Ignatius, who was martyred at Rome about 115, wrote letters to churches he knew or visited on his relatively leisurely journey to meet his destiny. Among other things, in his letters he urged fidelity to the bishops, who had received the authentic traditions from the apostles and who passed them on to true and faithful Christians. It appears from Ignatius's writings that by the early second century C.E., though the emergence of bishops over large areas, let alone a papacy or ecumenical patriarchate, remained a future development, the outline of the ministry in three orders (deacons, elders or priests, and bishops) was progressively defining itself. The bishop of each community was definitely the chief over the elders and deacons, as well as the laity, in Ignatius's view. This pattern would become the norm for most of Christendom thereafter.

The Teaching of the Twelve Apostles, also known by its Greek title, *Didache* (Teaching), is a church instruction book that probably emerged in Syria toward the end of the first century C.E. It expresses suspicion of itinerant prophets and suggests moral tests of their authenticity. Apparently, various sorts of crooks were exploiting the faithful. Of particular interest are the detailed instructions for executing such ritual actions as baptism and the regulations for ritual meals. These would strike many moderns as excessively meticulous. Some think that the first section of the document, a collection of moral teachings emphasizing the theme of "two ways, one of life and one of death," was the nucleus around which the remainder of the text was collected.

The gist of these data, and other facts that could be added, is that, in sociological terms, the church was developing in a less charismatic, more bureaucratic direction. This should not be understood as a negative observation. Ideas and aspirations, however noble they might be, require institutional embodiment to survive beyond one generation, if indeed they make it that far on a spontaneous basis.

The Church and Judaism

Recent research suggests that the process leading to the ultimate divorce between the church and traditional Judaism was much lengthier than was once supposed, and developed at different rates depending on local conditions and the particular communities involved. Paul's letters reflect a situation in which church and synagogue had drifted some distance apart, but there remained a sense of common relationship. By contrast, the Gospel of Matthew, while recognizing the historical fact of Jesus's Jewishness and the Jewish context of gospel events, reveals substantial hostility toward the pharisaic rabbinic leadership of post-70 Israel. The friction is not over theology (Matthew recognizes the validity of the "law and prophets"), but over ultimate authority. The leaders, sometimes called the "Christian rabbinate" of the Matthean circle, challenged the rabbinate of traditional Judaism while recognizing their right to "sit in Moses' seat." Meanwhile, the Johannine circle adopted the Samaritan term *the Jews* to reject traditional Jewish authority. In studying the evidence, one may begin to suspect that differentiation was largely a Christian interest, particularly an interest of the developing church bureaucracy and theologians.

At the official level, the 30s of the second century C.E. probably mark the break in a great part of the Roman world. Still, a sort of symbiotic relationship may have continued. Some historians suggest that, up to the fourth century, Christianity only took root in those parts of the Roman empire where Jewish communities already existed. And in the Jewish homeland, coexistence, if not cordiality, was the rule in parts of Galilee well into the Byzantine period between various mixtures of Jewish and gentile Christians and more traditional Jews. But this carries us well beyond the purview of this book.

Rabbi Gamaliel II, while leader of the major academy of rabbinic Judaism, attempted to deal with the problem of deviancy (Christian and otherwise) in a manner worthy of his distinguished namesake (Acts 5:34–39). He enacted the addition of a nineteenth prayer to the Eighteen Benedictions, the prayers that, along with the Shema (Dt. 6:4–5), constitute the core of the synagogal liturgy. It is sometimes called the *exclusionary benediction.* It prays, "For apostates may there be no hope, and may the Nazareans and the deviants suddenly perish." No Christian, Samaritan, or other deviant could lead in prayer or, in good conscience, worship with a congregation where such a curse was part of the liturgy. Thus, in a skillfully nonviolent manner such potential troublemakers were excluded.

Such nonviolent solutions were not to be found during the time of the Jewish revolutionary Simeon bar Cocheba, who accepted messianic acclaim for himself. During his abortive uprising, the Second Jewish War with Rome (132–135), devotees of other messiahs were given a simple choice: Recant or die. Christians were not the only skeptics where Simeon's claims were concerned, and they were thus not the only non-Roman victims of his wrath. But they were the advocates of a counter-Messiah and thus objects of special attention. Following Simeon's defeat and death, and the widespread ruin that befell Judah as a consequence, Christians had their revenge, mocking the catastrophes produced by false messiahs.

The Church and Rome

Difficulties with the Roman administration also increased with the passage of time. We noted earlier that the Romans had originally regarded the first Christians as simply more Jews, which most of them were. Frictions between Christians and traditional Jews were likely to be seen as "domestic quarrels." But as Christians grew more numerous, and gentile converts came to outnumber Jewish adherents by a growing percentage, such confusion was no longer possible.

Although some historians have tried to find in Roman law the reasons why the government began to pay more attention to the church, the simple fact is that the Christians were probably regarded as up to no good, whether or not they violated any specific legislation. Those officials who took time to investigate usually came to the conclusion that these Christians were a bit daft, but not dangerous.

Christians were objects of prejudice, which inclined the government against them. From the standpoint of the conservative aristocrats who occupied many of the seats of power in the Roman world, they were an oriental import, and that was damning enough. The satirist Juvenal exclaimed, "The Orontes [a river near Antioch, where Christians first emerged outside the homeland] has emptied into the Tiber [in Rome]." At least metaphorically, he held his nose.

Street gossip accused both Jews and Christians of atheism, because they had no images in their shrines. Christians were alleged to worship an ass. They were also alleged to be cannibals, no doubt a garbled understanding of the Lord's Supper. Such popular prejudice tends to encourage and justify official repression.

Still, the reaction of Roman officialdom was not generally vicious. Trajan, one of the legendary "good" emperors, endorsed the policy followed by Pliny the Younger of not seeking Christians out but of dealing with them if they were accused before him or one of his officials.

At one point, devout Christians were obdurate in their resistance to Roman policy. This was the cult of the divine emperor. Actually, the emperor cult was a bit of an anomaly. Augustus had built a temple to the Divine Julius in the Forum, but his uncle and patron was long since dead. The cult of the emperor was more popular in the provinces than in Rome itself. Augustus himself was honored with provincial shrines, and Claudius had a temple dedicated to him, the podium of which still supports the medieval castle at Colchester, in England. Caligula, his predecessor, had insisted on divine honors and claimed to be Zeus. The emperor cult enjoyed its greatest popularity in those provinces with a history of divine kingship, particularly in the eastern Mediterranean. And these were the areas where Christianity had a substantial foothold.

To most inhabitants of the empire, accustomed to polytheism, the offering of a pinch of incense to the emperor was an act as innocuous as saluting the flag today. Not so to Christians. And their refusal elicited a reaction not unlike a public refusal to salute the flag today. Their loyalty was under heavy suspicion. Despite the opportunities to be persecuted, and the church's honoring of its victims, Christians were discouraged from seeking out persecution and martyrdom. The martyr's crown was a gift to be received with joy, but if one went out of the way to get martyred, it did not count.

Other changes were occasioned by a shift in the apocalyptic orientation of the church. From its foundation, Christianity had been more charismatic and eschatological than rabbinic Judaism, because of the belief that the Messiah had come and would return soon to initiate the Kingdom of God on earth. This is not to say that all early Christian communities were whipped up in apocalyptic frenzy. Such sects are usually short lived or experience a high rate of membership turnover, and neither seems to be true of early Christianity. Probably not all were quite as literal about apocalyptic symbolism as that. Almost certainly, though, many early Christians expected a relatively early return of the Messiah and the consummation of the Kingdom. Some may have perceived the First War with Rome as the messianic woes of common expectation, "the birth pangs of the Messiah," as they were called by the rabbis. In the aftermath of the war (after 70), the realization must have settled in with almost everyone that the church might just be in business in this world for quite some time.

Religious movements that attract members of the lower orders of society to a more disciplined mode of life frequently have the effect of producing upward social mobility among their members.

In the case of "personal improvement" cults, the effect is deliberate. But in most cases it is probably serendipitous, and in some cases, contrary to the wishes of the leaders. We have noted that the appeal of the church in the Roman world was principally to the disenfranchised of the urban centers, though membership included persons having some wealth and social standing. Some had houses large enough to host meetings of the churches. But the Roman world was a prosperous world and one that had been experiencing extensive social change, an ideal environment for upward social mobility. Thus, it is likely that with the passage of time, not only did the church attract more affluent members, but it also moved up in the world with the improved condition of its previous members, which would render membership more palatable to persons of higher status. One consequence of the church becoming more "respectable" (that is, of assimilation into the larger culture) was a decline in the status of women in the church. Jesus had female disciples and both Acts and Paul mention prominent female leaders (Rom. 16:7 may even refer to a female apostle). Sociologists note that women frequently occupy significant leadership positions in religious movements like early Christianity. But over time, the church assumed the patriarchal model of the larger Roman world. (There were women's religions in classical paganism, but Christianity was never gender or age exclusive.)

No less a person than Augustus had legislated against social mobility, especially the rights of freedmen (freed slaves), who were often persons of talent and enterprise. The two older aristocratic orders of the city of Rome, the senatorial class at the top and the equestrian class immediately beneath, were not destined to restrain the tide. The conflicts accompanying the demise of the Republic and the rise of the Empire, the savaging of the aristocrats by the more eccentric emperors of the Julio–Claudian line, and subsequent upheavals must have exacted a substantial cost. Further, the demands of administration in the complex world of empire were such that a man who might occupy a seat in the Senate, live in a big house, or look good on a horse was completely beyond his depth. The recruitment of the provincial nobility, who of course remained persons of note if they were not expropriated by the Romans as an allied class, some of whose members were ultimately elevated to the equestrian or senatorial rank in Rome itself, was not adequate to stem the inevitable.

Beneath the aristocracy in Rome were the plebeians (the local proletariat), freedmen, and slaves. The latter two groups, gathered by Rome's conquests, were particular repositories of talent. The most gross of all the gross characters in Petronius's *Satyricon* (dating from the age of Nero) was a nouveau riche old freedman who was also the wealthiest character in the story. Other denizens of the lower ranks (again, especially freedmen) made their way upward by proven ability as administrators in the machinery of empire. And what was true in Rome was also true in the provinces. The introduction of new blood into the higher orders, by wealth or by title, and the introduction of foreigners into the official aristocracy probably made it easier for Christians and others who would have been objects of contempt to Cicero or Tacitus to rise to very high status, which made it easier for others who enjoyed similar backgrounds to join them. But in the last analysis it was Christianity's mass appeal that led Constantine to conclude that it was the perfect element to supply coherence to an empire.

The Outcome

It is probable that most of the books of the New Testament had been completed by 100, and all of them by 150. Hadrian, whose plan to rebuild Jerusalem as a pagan Roman city helped to touch off the Second Jewish War with Rome (132–135), had succeeded Trajan as emperor. The apostles had passed from the scene, replaced by an increasingly ordered ministry under the bishops. Clement of Rome and Ignatius of Antioch, in their writings, pointed toward the new class of gentile Christian intellectuals. In the second century, these would include the troublesome Marcion; the immensely influential Tertullian, whose dogmatic tendencies ultimately led him into heresy; and such champions of orthodoxy (as they understood it) as Justin Martyr, Irenaeus, and Clement of Alexandria. By the end of the second century, the main part of the New Testament canon would be established. That is an appropriate point at which to draw the line in this historical survey.

THE LITERARY WORLD: THE PASTORAL EPISTLES—BE STRONG IN THE FAITH

The Letters to Timothy and the Letter to Titus are attributed to Paul and included in the canon (with Philemon) as Pauline letters to individuals (after the letters to churches). These letters are usually called the *Pastoral Epistles* because they express pastoral concern for the well-being of churches and their leaders. They are similar in structure. After compact introductions and before brief conclusions, the bodies of the letters consist mostly of warnings against false teachers and advice on the organization of the churches.

Because the letters differ markedly from other Pauline letters in vocabulary, style, and mood, and especially because of the developed church structure the letters imply (bishops, elders, and deacons), they were almost certainly not written by Paul himself. Rather, they were written by a person or persons appealing to the authority of the apostle to deal with general developments among Christian churches in the period after 70 C.E. By their being addressed to companions of Paul, the literary device of pseudonymity (writing in the name and spirit of some earlier figure) is given greater plausibility. "Timothy" and "Titus" are effective symbols of church leaders trying to preserve the traditions of the past in a new situation. "Paul" is the voice of apostolic authority in a postapostolic age. These letters are not personal, despite their personal addresses and isolated references. They are general tracts written in response to the problems of a growing church.

First Timothy

This epistle takes up the problem of false doctrine focused on "myths and endless genealogies" (1:4), suggesting the gnostic view of hierarchies of spiritual beings with which humans must cope. Either the same, or other, teachers distorted the Jewish law (1:6–11). Like the troublemakers of Colossians, they practiced various forms of abstinence (4:1–3). To counter this false teaching, "Timothy" is to be an example by teaching the true doctrine he has received (4:6–16). He is to be guardian of the faith entrusted to him (6:20–21).

To serve as a "pillar of the truth" there must be a well-ordered church with officers—bishops, elders, and deacons are here mentioned—who live exemplary lives. And the various types of church members—such as widows, slaves, masters, heads of household, and other women—must recognize their places and submit to the proper authority. Women have clearly been excluded from important leadership roles and subordinated to male authority.

Second Timothy

Of the three pastorals, this letter is closest in tone to the authentic Pauline letters. Like the other pastorals, it focuses on false teaching and urges "Timothy" to be true to the faith he has received (3:14–15). However, it gives more of a sense of an actual relationship between sender and recipient.

The letter is written to urge "Timothy" to "rekindle the gift of God that is within you through the laying on of my hands" (1:6). He is urged to testify to Christ without shame (1:8–18) and be willing to suffer as a "good soldier of Christ Jesus" (2:1–13).

Two false teachers are named who teach that the Resurrection is past (and therefore salvation has been fully attained and we may "do what we please"). In particular, concern is expressed about "stupid, senseless controversies" which only breed dissension (2:23). In the final age, there will be great stress. People will be "lovers of self" (3:2) practicing the form of religion while denying its power (3:5). People of "counterfeit faith" will mock the truth. They are to be avoided.

To combat error, "Timothy" is urged to attend to "the sacred writings [Hebrew Scriptures] which are able to instruct you for salvation through faith in Christ Jesus" (3:15). This suggests that a more formal attitude toward Scripture was developing both in Jewish and Christian circles.

The letter ends with a personal note (4:6–8) and greetings (4:9–18), which give it a realistic one.

Titus

According to this letter, after accompanying Paul (Gal. 2:1, 3; 2 Cor. 8:6), Titus was entrusted with the organization of a church on the island of Crete (1:5). However, like "Timothy," "Titus" is probably a symbol for the *church leader* in general.

As in First Timothy, the two concerns of this letter are church order (elders and bishops) and false teachers. It is frustrating to church historians that, as in First Timothy, the focus is less on what these officers did than the moral qualifications for those who serve. Here, the two names seem to describe the same position, suggesting a stage in the growth of the church when they were not clearly separated. Bishops, at least, are to be able to give instruction in "sound doctrine" by holding firm to what they have been taught.

The false teachers are variously described as "empty talkers," members of the "circumcision party" (who insist that Gentiles must be circumcised before they can become Christians), and people who teach for base gain (1:10–11).

THE LITERARY WORLD: THE LETTER TO THE HEBREWS—CHRIST AS HIGH PRIEST AND MEDIATOR OF A NEW COVENANT

Except for an ending that reads like the closing of a Pauline letter (13:18–25), the Letter to the Hebrews makes no pretense of being a letter at all. It begins abruptly with a prologue stating the theme (1:1–5), then develops what may be the longest sustained argument in either the Old or New Testaments. Much of the argument is subsumed in two extended artistic allegories or typologies drawn from the Tanak, the figure of Melchizedek (Hebrews 7; cf. Gen. 14:17–20, Psalm 110) and the priestly directions for the observance of Yom Kippur, the Day of Atonement (Hebrews 9; cf. Lev. 16:6–34). The author of Hebrews was clearly influenced by Greek philosophy. The platonic contrast between the heavenly realm of eternal realities and the physical world of transitory phenomena is also discussed. Much of this is reminiscent of the approach of the Hellenistic Jewish philosopher Philo and of later Alexandrian biblical interpretation. The author's Greek is, along with Luke's, the best in the New Testament. The rhetorical skills of Hebrews are similarly well honed. All of this is quite un-Pauline, though later Christian tradition ascribed the "letter" to Paul at a time when an apostolic connection had become an essential factor in canonical credentials. The main body of the work makes no such claim.

The closing (13:20–25) was probably appended by an editor, and it was probably classed as a "letter" simply because the great majority of other New Testament books are letters. In fact, it is a religious treatise or sermon that was written to encourage Jewish Christians who were on the verge of giving up on the Christian faith and returning to traditional Judaism. It mixes proclamations about Jesus with exhortations. It probably originated during the period when there was not yet a clear distinction of church, synagogue, and temple or between Christianity and Judaism; perhaps even before the Temple was destroyed in 70 C.E.

The theme of Hebrews is the supremacy of God's revelation through his Son, "whom he appointed the heir of all things, through whom he also created the worlds. He is the reflection of God's glory and the exact imprint of God's very being, and he sustains all things by his powerful word." He is the heavenly priest who made "purification for sins" and is "superior to angels." In former days, God spoke through prophets; in the "last days he has spoken to us by a Son" (1:1–4). With this imagery Hebrews relates Christ to the priestly tradition, the prophetic tradition, and the wisdom tradition. In each case, Christ is superior to his precursor.

In subsequent sections, Hebrews supports these contentions with evidence to show that (1) Christ is superior to the angels (1:5–2:18); (2) he is superior to Moses (3:1–6); (3) Jesus is the great high priest (4:14–9:10) who is in the line not of the Aaronid or Levitical priests but of the great Melchizedek (7:1–8:13); and (4) the sacrifice of Jesus on the cross is incomparably superior to the sacrifices at the Temple (9:11–10:18). Alongside the argument there are exhortations to renewed faithfulness, maturity in the faith, and endurance (2:1–4; 3:7–4:13; 6:1–20). The work ends with admonitions to constancy in faith and endurance (10:19–39; 12–13), supported by a listing of the Jewish heroes and heroines who exemplify living "by faith" (Hebrews 11), climaxing with Jesus "the pioneer and perfecter of our faith" (12:1–2).

To defend the assertion that Christ is superior to the angels, Hebrews begins with a list of seven quotations from the Old Testament, asking the rhetorical question "For to what angel did God ever say . . . ?" After an exhortation to "pay the closer attention" to the message "declared at first by the Lord, and . . . attested to us by those who heard him" (cf. Lk. 1:2), Hebrews interprets Ps. 8:4–6 as a veiled reference to Christ, emphasizing the paradox that the one whom God made Lord over everything was "for a little while" (a translation that agrees with the LXX, but not the Hebrew, text of the Psalm) lower than the angels. This opens the way for a discussion of Christ's suffering, its saving purpose, and the necessity of Jesus's becoming human. We see here the early stages of theological reflection that ultimately led to the assertions of the two natures of Christ—fully divine and fully human.

Hebrews then introduces the phrase that dominates the treatise—Jesus as "high priest." In the organization of the Jerusalem Temple, the high priest represented the people before God and God before the people. On the yearly Day of Atonement (Yom Kippur), the high priest entered the Holy of Holies with the blood of the atonement sacrifices, thus assuring God's pardon and the reconciliation of the people with God for another year (see Leviticus 16). This gave the high priest a special role as mediator of the covenant between God and Israel and an aura of divinity that no other human shared. According to Hebrews, Jesus perfects both the human and the divine in the office of the high priest. He is in the very image of God and has "passed through the heavens" (4:14); thus, he is superior to any other in representing God to humankind. Yet, because of his humanity and his suffering, he is able to "sympathize with our weaknesses" (4:15).

Again Hebrews employs scriptural exposition to reflect on Jesus as a "new" high priest. In the ancestral narratives, a mysterious figure, Melchizedek, the priest-king of Salem (later Jerusalem), makes a brief appearance (Gen. 14:17–20). No ancestors or descendants for Melchizedek are named in the Genesis text. Psalm 110:4 names the Davidic king "a priest forever, after the order of Melchizedek." Hebrews uses both texts to argue that Jesus, the Davidic Messiah, is therefore an eternal priest, not in the line of the Israelite priests, the heirs of Levi, but after the order of the eternal priest, Melchizedek.

As an eternal priest, Jesus offered one sacrifice effective for all time. Thus, the sacrifice of Jesus, not with the blood of animals but with his own blood, replaces the Temple ritual. Just as the covenant through Moses was ratified by blood, Jesus has become the mediator of a new covenant (9:15). The perfect priest has made one perfect offering in the perfect (heavenly) tabernacle. The assurance of what Jesus, the heavenly high priest, has done should give the faithful confidence and hope even in the face of persecution.

Alongside the dualism of time (the limited duration of the earthly high priest versus the eternal nature of the priesthood of Jesus), there is a dualism of space in Hebrews. The earthly Temple is a copy of the heavenly Temple where Jesus serves as high priest. This distinction between seen and unseen, appearance and reality, material and spiritual, temporal and eternal might reflect the influence of Greek (especially platonic) philosophical thought on Hebrews. However, as we have seen, dualism is a characteristic of the apocalyptic (and mystical) traditions that sprang up within Judaism itself. Although the polished Greek style of Hebrews suggests an author familiar with Hellenistic culture, some recent scholars point to a tendency to overemphasize the Greek nature of the writing. Like the writings of Philo, it exemplifies Hellenistic Jewish thought.

Adapting the Jewish practice of appealing to a catalog of heroes (see Sirach 44), Hebrews names men and women from the Tanak who were given promises by God but did not live to see them fulfilled (Hebrews 11). This illustrates the definition of faith as the "assurance of things hoped for, the conviction of things not seen" (11:1). The fulfillment was, Hebrews has shown, to come through Christ. This list of heroes and, above all, the example of Christ should inspire the faithful to "run with perseverance the race that is set before us" (12:1).

The rhetorical power of the author blazes forth in a concluding peroration (12:18–29), which uses an awesome portrayal of the Sinai revelation as a foil for the even more profound revelation in Jesus, concluding, ". . . for our God is a consuming fire!" In sum, ignore at your own peril!

THE LITERARY WORLD: THE GENERAL (CATHOLIC) EPISTLES—FOR THE WHOLE CHURCH (JAMES; FIRST PETER; JUDE; SECOND PETER; FIRST, SECOND, AND THIRD JOHN)

Several "letters" are grouped together because (except for Third John) they take the form of letters but are written to Christians in general, not to specific churches or individuals. In this context *catholic* refers to the *universal* church. Grouping them together is somewhat misleading, for, from a literary perspective, they are quite different. What they share is a relatively late time of origin in comparison with other New Testament writings. Because Second Peter probably used Jude as a source, we will consider Jude out of its canonical order, before Second Peter.

The Letter of James

A one-verse salutation (1:1) gives this writing the form of a letter from James to the "twelve tribes in the Dispersion." The reference is to the "new Israel," the Christian Church spread throughout the Mediterranean world. In fact, the work is an anthology of admonitions and observations on various topics, with no single theme. This style and its concern with wisdom (1:5; 3:1–18) place it within the tradition of the wisdom literature of the Tanak and Apocrypha and the Greek tradition of ethical exhortation. It includes the Greek literary device of diatribe (a dialogue between the writer and an imagined questioner) in 2:18–26 and 5:13–15.

Despite its attribution to James, the brother of Jesus and a leader of the Jerusalem church, the work makes almost no mention of Jesus or the gospel. It apparently presumes that its readers are already familiar with who Jesus is and the meaning of his coming, and focuses instead on the question of how Christians ought to live. Its closest parallel in the New Testament is probably the Sermon on the Mount. Throughout, the tone is pragmatic. In contrast with the theological concerns of the Pauline letters, the Pastorals, and Hebrews, James is practical advice without much theological reflection. Jesus is, in fact, mentioned only twice in the work (1:1; 2:1), causing some to speculate that it was originally a non-Christian work adapted to a Christian setting.

Although there is no overarching unity to the collection, some topics receive repeated emphasis. In contrast to the Pauline stress on "justification by faith apart from works of the law," James observes that "faith by itself, if it has no works, is dead"(2:17). Because James quotes the same passage from the Abraham story that Paul uses in Romans to defend "justification by faith" to support justification by works "and not by faith alone" (2:24; cf. Rom. 4:1–8), it is possible that this is a self-conscious response to a perceived overemphasis on faith that might have resulted from Paul's teaching. The contrast, however, in James is not really the same as in the Pauline correspondence. In James, faith means *belief,* and the contrast is between merely believing and acting on that belief. In Paul's letters, faith is trusting in God's grace revealed in Christ, and the contrast is between trying to attain justification, reconciliation with God, through one's own efforts (works) and recognizing that it is only by faith (confident trust) in God's power that anyone can be justified. For James it is not enough merely to hear the gospel; the hearer must act on the gospel, which James calls the "perfect law, the law of liberty" (1:25). Practically, James and Paul seek the same end.

What sort of works should Christians undertake? James emphasizes acts of compassion for the weak and poor as the essence of true religion (1:26–27; 2:15–16). The letter also stresses, in traditional wisdom fashion, restraint in speech and control of anger and the passions (1:19–20, 26; 3:1–12; 4:1–12). Like Ecclesiastes, James highlights the transience of life (1:9–11). As in the prophets and the sayings of Jesus, there are warnings to the rich who oppress the poor (1:9–11; 5:1–6). James also counsels patience in the face of trials and sufferings, coining the phrase the "patience of Job" (1:2–4; 5:7–11). There is also advice on the practical benefits of prayer (1:5–8; 5:13–18). James advises Christians to keep themselves "unstained from the world" (1:27; 4:4–8).

It is difficult to determine a time of origin for a work like James. It could be an early response to misunderstood Pauline teaching or a later compilation.

First Peter

This work presents itself as a letter of the Apostle Peter, written from Rome (Babylon in 5:13 is a symbol for Rome; cf. Rev. 17:5, 9) to Christians in Asia Minor at a time of persecution. This means that it would have been written about 64–65 C.E., during Nero's persecution of the Christians in Rome. Many modern literary historians have questioned whether the letter originated with Peter at such an early date. The strategy of the letter, whoever wrote it, is to take a theological foundation stone, by reminding readers what God has done in Christ, and build on it with exhortations on how Christians are to live in the world. Some historians suggest that the letter was actually a baptismal sermon (see 3:21).

In the first section (1:13–2:10) readers are reminded of their having been "born anew to a living hope through the Resurrection of Jesus Christ" (1:3). Thus, they are called to a new life of holiness. Structurally, 1:21–25 rounds off the first section by returning to the image of 1:3. This is the gospel the letter is proclaiming (1:25). On this basis, the challenge is made to come to the "living stone" (Christ) and, like "living stones," be built into a spiritual house, a new Israel. The letter applies the imagery of the Sinai Covenant (Ex. 19:5–6) to the church.

The next section (2:11–4:11) is an appeal to good conduct that even Gentiles (which has come to mean non-Christians, because the church is the new Israel) will recognize as good (2:12). Like Paul in Romans 13, this letter counsels submission to the state. A recurrent theme in this section and throughout the letter is that endurance of unjust suffering at the hands of evil people is a necessity for Christians, and that through suffering they win God's approval, because they are following the example of Christ (2:20–23; cf. 1:6; 3:13–18; 4:1, 12–19; 5:10).

The final section (4:12–5:11) appears to be an afterthought or an addition after the letter has been ended (4:11). It reiterates the theme of enduring unjust suffering (4:12–19) but with the implication that it has already begun. The letter concludes with exhortations to the "elders among you" to lead through example, not domination (5:1–5).

Like Paul and Mark, First Peter reflects the apocalyptic view that the present age will end soon (4:7), and Christ will be revealed (1:7). During this time before the end, there will be persecutions that Christians must endure, but those who have been persecuted will receive a crown of glory (5:4). This apocalyptic perspective might help explain the enigmatic reference to Christ's preaching to the spirits in prison (3:19). Some consider this a reference to the fallen angels of Gen. 6:1–4. But it could equally well refer to condemned humans. The "generation of the Flood" were notorious sinners for rabbinic lore. The theme of Jesus preaching to the souls in hell was a favorite of some New Testament apocrypha (cf. also Eph. 4:8–10). But the fallen angel theme is developed in such apocalyptic works as Enoch (where the fallen angels are the heavenly counterparts of earthly rulers). Because the apocalyptic perspective was popular early in the development of the New Testament, this may support an early dating for First Peter.

Jude

Presented in the form of a letter from Jude (the brother of James and Jesus; cf. Mk. 6:3) to Christians in general (v. 1), this work is a polemic against a group of false teachers who have made their way into the church. Because the letter looks back on the time of the apostles (v. 17), it is almost certainly pseudonymous, assigned to Jude to lend it authority. It probably was written in the early second century C.E.

The heretics are described only in general terms. They are immoral men who reject authority, spurn the angels (vv. 4, 8), and carouse during the "love feasts" (v. 12). It is possible that they were Gnostics who argued that, because they were liberated from the flesh, they were free to engage in any actions.

In good polemical style, Jude is more interested in denouncing these heretics than debating with them. Their wickedness merits the punishment inflicted on the Egyptians, the fallen angels, and Sodom and Gomorrah (vv. 5–7).

Jude alludes once directly (vv. 14–16) and twice indirectly (vv. 9, 13) to the Jewish apocalyptic works, the Assumption of Moses and Enoch. These are the only references to the Larger Apocrypha (Pseudepigrapha) in the New Testament (see Chapter 10). The heretics are so perverse that they revile angels (v. 8). The Assumption of Moses includes the midrash that when Moses died, Satan came to claim his body, and the angel Michael rebuked him, but not with a "reviling judgment." So not even Satan deserves the kind of abuse from a fellow angel that these mere mortals are directing against good angels. Enoch assures the judgment of the wicked when God appears at the end of history. The motif of fallen angels (v. 16) is also apocalyptic.

Second Peter

This "letter" is a manifesto against false teaching and a defense of the return of Christ despite the delay. After a stereotypical greeting from Peter to Christians in general (1:1–2), there are no more characteristics of the letter form. For several reasons, this letter is often judged the latest of all New Testament writings, possibly composed as late as around 140 C.E. It uses Jude vv. 4–16 as a source in 2:2–17. It seems to know the Pauline correspondence as a collection, equating it with "other scriptures" (3:15–16). It quotes the synoptic account of the Transfiguration (1:17–18; cf. Mt. 17:1–8), and it also knows 1 Peter (3:1).

A key motif is the "knowledge of God and of Jesus Christ" (1:2, 3, 5, 6, 8; 2:20; 3:18). The authentic "knowledge of God" is manifest in righteous living (1:3–11), while the claimed knowledge of the false teachers shows it is unauthentic because of the perverse behavior of those who claim to have it (2:20–22). Apparently, the false teachers Second Peter is concerned about, like those condemned in Jude, are Gnostics who claim to be purified from the world but are in fact entrapped in it through their immoral behavior. They apparently twist the letters of Paul to support their views (3:15–17). Quoting a proverb, Second Peter calls them dogs who return to their vomit (3:22).

The letter uses the device of a Petrine origin to give validity to its teaching, reminding readers that "we had been eyewitnesses of his majesty" (1:16). Peter has had a mystical experience of true divinity every bit as powerful as the Gnostics claim to have had, and he teaches not licentiousness but purity.

The Gnostics would also have disputed the parousia, saying that the full revelation from Jesus had already come. So Second Peter reemphasizes the coming judgment by fire (3:7, 10). It will come in God's good time; its delay is so that more may repent and be saved (3:8–9). Christians must lead blameless lives so that they will be prepared when the new heaven and the new earth come.

Interestingly, Second Peter reflects the development of the canonical process. In quoting Jude, it purges all references to works outside the Hebrew canon, expunging the allusions to the Assumption of Moses and Enoch.

First John

This writing lacks even the pretense of being a letter, having no opening or closing greetings. Only the title, added later, claims that this is the first "letter" of John. It is actually a tract or sermon on the incarnation of Jesus, his coming in the flesh. Like a letter, it is written in the personal style of direct address (cf. 2:12–14, 26; 5:31). It may very well have been written to counter a teaching (called *docetism,* from the Greek word for "appear") that held that Jesus was fully divine, but only appeared to be human. This point of view was apparently associated with gnostic forms of Christianity. The vocabulary, literary style, and theological perspective of this letter (and Second and Third John) are similar enough to those of the Fourth Gospel to cause many to conclude that the letter and the gospel came from the same author, or from the Johannine School (see Chapter 12). Although attributed to the Apostle John, it is now widely agreed that this is a pseudonymous claim. The actual author is unknown and the time of origin disputed, although the scholarly consensus favors the first decade of the second century C.E. Tradition holds that all the letters of "John" were written in Ephesus.

The tract moves between instruction and exhortation, with no apparent unity of structure. In the prologue (1:1–4; cf. Jn. 1:17), the Incarnation is affirmed, and a mood of closeness with the readers is established. Apparently the opponents have claimed that they are free from sin, for the tract begins by saying that those who claim not to have sinned are liars (1:5–10). The ultimate goal of Christian living is to avoid sin, but that is possible only by keeping the commandments of God. The opponents presumably thought they were liberated from such obedience.

The opponents are called antichrists, whose appearance shows that the end is near (2:18). The term *antichrist* is unique to the letters of John (1 Jn. 1:2, 18, 25; 4:3; 2 Jn. 7), but the idea of an opponent or opponents of God (or his Messiah) appearing as a prelude to the coming of the end is fairly common in Jewish and Christian apocalyptic writing. The teachers about whom First John is concerned show themselves to be the antichrists by their denial that Jesus is the Christ and that he has come in the flesh (that is, the Incarnation). These are the "children of the devil" who, in contrast with the "children of God," persist in sin and hatred toward fellow Christians.

In perhaps the most famous passage, First John challenges readers to "love one another; for love is from God; everyone who loves is born of God and knows God. Whoever does not love does not know God, for God is love" (4:7–8).

Thus, the letter establishes a twofold test (summarized in 5:1–5) for distinguishing between truth and error—obedience to the commandments of God, which are centered in the command to love, and adherence to the true teaching that Jesus Christ has come in the flesh. The distinction is not only between truth and error, but also between life and death (5:12).

The dualism of the Gospel of John, between truth and error, life and death, the "world" and the believer, light and darkness, the spirit and the flesh, is quite apparent throughout.

Second John

This writing claims to be a letter from one called "the Elder" to the "Elect Lady," perhaps a church congregation or the whole church. Or possibly, as some feminist interpreters have suggested, the Elect Lady is a prominent female leader (bishop?) who hosts a "house church" in her home. All the thoughts of this letter echo First John: truth, love, following the commandments, the antichrist (false teachers who deny Jesus came in the flesh), eternal life. Here the "lady" is advised to deny membership in the church to any who deny true "doctrine." This suggests the development of standards of belief in the Christian churches and, therefore, a rather late date.

Third John

Here "the Elder" writes to an individual (Gaius) on specific matters of church life. There are no references to the motifs of First and Second John (except for v. 11). The Elder commends Gaius for receiving hospitably traveling missionaries (perhaps in order to ensure a good reception for another, Demetrius, named in v. 12). He contrasts another leader, Diotrephes, who refuses to acknowledge "the Elder's" authority or receive his emissaries. Apparently, when this letter was written, lines of authority were not yet clearly established, and church leaders competed with one another.

There is evidence of a church leader named Elder John who lived sometime during the late first or early second centuries C.E. It is tempting to see him as the author of the Johannine letters (and perhaps the Gospel of John), but there is too little evidence to establish the connection with confidence.

THE LITERARY WORLD: THE REVELATION TO JOHN—WHAT MUST HAPPEN SOON

The Revelation to John is the one complete apocalyptic work in the New Testament. There are apocalyptic sections in other works (such as Mark 13 and the parallel chapters, Matthew 24 and Luke 21) and an apocalyptic mood in many of Paul's letters (especially First and Second Thessalonians) and other writings (Second Peter and Jude especially). But, like Daniel 7–12 in the Tanak, the Book of Revelation is a report of highly symbolic visions purporting to reveal the secrets of the end time to a seer.

In at least two respects, the Book of Revelation is unique in literary form. Superficially, it presents itself as a letter. After a prologue that makes clear its apocalyptic thrust, there is an opening greeting (1:4–6). In addition, the work closes with a benediction (22:21) similar to Pauline closings. The first full section is composed of "letters" to seven churches in Asia Minor (2:1–3:22). The blessing upon those who read the book aloud and those who hear and keep its instruction is also reminiscent of the role of the apostolic letter.

Unlike most apocalyptic works, Revelation is not pseudonymous. The writer identifies himself as a man named John who had been exiled to the tiny Aegean island of Patmos because of his Christian faith (1:9). According to tradition, this John was the son of Zebedee mentioned in the gospels. However, there is no internal evidence to support this assumption. Nor is there solid evidence for the view of some modern interpreters that the author was the John the Elder who lived in Ephesus around 100 C.E., as the early church historian Eusebius maintained. The fact is we do not know who "John" was, though apparently his first readers did (1:9). He obviously wrote during a time of persecution that he himself had experienced. He may have been banished during the persecution of the Emperor Domitian in 95 C.E. At this time, Christians were under attack for their failure to worship the emperor as god, an act implied in Revelation 13. Finally, the work claims to reopen the tradition of prophecy (1:3; 22:6, 9, 19) that had been closed in rabbinic tradition. Like Isaiah (Isaiah 6), John's visions of heaven validate the message he is announcing. As in other prophetic works, the Word of God is received in the present and reveals what is about to unfold. The device of an ancient worthy who predicts the course of history up to the author's actual present time and beyond is not used.

The theme of Revelation is "Persevere!" The writer's visions reveal that the present evil epoch of history will end soon. Jesus will return. Although the forces of evil seem to prevail, they will be vanquished by the returned Messiah. After the final battle, a new age will begin. If the faithful continue to resist the powers trying to force them to compromise, they will be rewarded, as certainly as the evil will be punished. The impact of the visions as a whole is to assure the faithful that God has the course of history firmly in hand. God's plan is for the judgment of evil and the reward of righteousness.

In keeping with apocalyptic style, the "action" of the visions is at the heavenly level, with the effects felt on earth. This results in graphic but cryptic imagery that only the "initiated" would be able to understand. It also makes the Book of Revelation an exceedingly rich and enigmatic

John of Patmos. According to Rev. 1:9–11 John received the visions recorded in the Book of Revelation on the island of Patmos in the Aegean Sea. John is represented here in a mosaic in the Monastery of St. John the Theologian on Patmos. He may have been banished to the island as a form of persecution for his Christian preaching.   *Source:* Pierdelune/Shutterstock

piece of literature. The substance of the visions reflects imagery from a variety of canonical (Daniel, Ezekiel, Joel, Zechariah, and Jeremiah) and noncanonical sources. By the end of the first century C.E., the apocalyptic tradition had a large stock of symbols and images, and Revelation includes many of them. There are many parallels in this symbolism to the symbolism of early Jewish mysticism, particularly the Chariot school, in Revelation (cf. Ch. 10). John shared the Chariot school's interest in Ezekiel. The four beasts who bore the Divine Chariot are present in John's vision of the empyrean heaven; they have acquired some traits of Isaiah's seraphim (see Isaiah 6). The throne and the Presence upon it are not unlike the vision of Ezekiel (see Ezekiel 1). And John, like Ezekiel, ate a scroll (Rev. 10:8–10; Ez. 2:8–3:3). John, like the Chariot mystics, also ascended to heaven while in trance ("in the spirit," Rev. 4:1–3). It also reflects the liturgy of the early Christian Church, drawing on hymns and prayers probably current in Christian worship (for example, 1:5–6; 4:8, 11; 5:9–10; 7:10, 12; 11:15, 17–18; 12:10–12; 15:3–4; 19:1–2, 5–8; 22:13).

The structure of Revelation is so complex it has inspired many varying and conflicting interpretations. As with other subtle and imaginative literary works, there may be a variety of structures at different levels. We have already observed the letter structure of the whole work and the first section. In the rest of the book, after introductory visions of the heavenly court (4:1–5:14) and before the epilogue, interpreters generally see seven (the perfect number) visions: (1) seven seals (6:1–8); (2) seven trumpets (8:7–11:19); (3) the dragon's (Devil's) rule (12:1–13:18); (4) those who worship the lamb (Christ) and those who honor the beast (14:1–20); (5) seven bowls of divine anger (15:1–16:21); (6) Babylon's (Rome's) fall (17:1–19:10); and (7) the end of Satan's power and the creation of a "new heaven and a new earth" (19:11–21:8).

The symbol of triumph over oppression in Judaism is the seven-branched lampstand, the *menorah,* which goes back to the time of Solomon's Temple (1 Kgs. 7:49; cf. Ex. 37:17–24). The menorah was particularly associated in later times with the festival of Hanukkah (see Chapter 10), which commemorates the rededication of the Jerusalem Temple in 164 B.C.E., at the end of the persecution of Antiochus Epiphanes. The menorah was a popular Jewish symbol during the first century C.E. Archaeologists have discovered menorahs in synagogues and as decorations in funerary contexts. Revelation may be a Christian menorah, symbolizing in its sevenfold structure the end of the persecution of the church. The clue may be the several references to lampstands in Revelation (such as 1:12–13).

The seven churches to which John writes symbolize the whole church. In general, the letters commend, exhort, and chastise, like the Pauline letters. However, in all the letters, John singles out from the churches the righteous few who will persevere in the face of persecution—like the prophetic "remnant." "He who has an ear let him hear . . . " is present in each letter, indicating that only a few get the message (2:7, 11, 17, 29; 3:6, 13, 22). The letters allude to those who "conquer" (2:7, 17, 26; 3:5, 12, 21), promising the blessings of the new age to them—eating of the tree of life (2:7), escaping the second death (2:11), receiving the hidden manna and a new name (2:17), power over the nations (2:26), the morning star (2:28), white robes (3:5), becoming a pillar in God's temple (3:12), and sitting with Christ on the throne (3:21).

Against this background, the visions that follow become a validation of the seer's authority to make these promises and a preview for those righteous few who have "ears to hear" of the rewards beyond the present and impending struggle.

Like others in the prophetic tradition (see 1 Kings 22, Isaiah 6, and Ezekiel 1), John speaks of being transported "in the Spirit" to the heavenly throne room, where he experiences directly the majesty of the divine king surrounded by beings who glorify God with hymns (Revelation 4). Then he sees the slain lamb (Christ), who has already conquered and who is worthy to open the scroll (containing the divine plan).

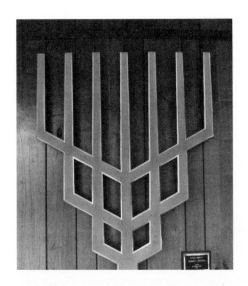

A Menorah. The Menorah, the seven-branched lampstand, is the earliest documented symbol of Judaism. The abstract modern form of this representation is reminiscent of wall drawings from the Maccabean period. Menoroth (plural) were a feature of the wilderness Tabernacle, the Temple of Solomon, and the postexilic Temples down to the Roman destruction. The Menorah figures in the legend of Hanukkah, when a single flask of pure oil sufficed to fuel the lamps through the entire festival. It also figures in the symbolism of the Book of Revelation. The Menorah could be represented as a candlestick only after the medieval invention of the candle. *Source:* The Herbert P. Eckstein Memorial; courtesy Temple B'nai Shalom, Hunsstville, Alabama. Photograph by Dr. Christian E. Hauer, Jr., FSA

Then come the three sets of seven visions, with the seventh vision of the first two sets transitional to the next. Their imagery is much too complex to explore in detail here. Some of the more famous images are the "four horsemen," who symbolize warfare, slaughter, famine, and pestilence (6:1–8); the dragon (identified as Satan), described in imagery reminiscent of the beasts of chaos who oppose the divine king in myths such as those found at Ugarit and Babylon (12:1–17); the beasts who do the dragon's bidding on earth (Revelation 13), one of whom is given the symbolic number 666 (13:18); and the drunken harlot (Revelation 17).

Revelation, Chapter 12, offers graphic illustration of John's knowledge and interpretation of biblical and postbiblical Jewish, Christian, and pagan symbolism. It illustrates the worldly and historic side of apocalyptic expectation; it was not exclusively or even principally ethereal and otherworldly. Chapter 12 stands at a strategic point in the book. The seven trumpets have sounded, concluding the second of three sets of seven woes. Now a portent appears in heaven: a woman clothed in the sun, with a crown of twelve stars, and the moon beneath her feet. She is pregnant and in labor. A red dragon (the devil we soon learn) is poised to devour at birth the child destined for the messianic role proclaimed in Psalm 2:9. The child was caught up to God, leaving the dragon to make war on the woman's other children.

The solar robe indicates the Queen of Heaven, as does the lunar symbolism. The lunar crescent was associated with many great goddesses: the Semitic Ishtar/Asherah, the Egyptian Isis, the Greek Artemis. But the Great Goddess wore the crescent as a headdress. Our lady in Chapter 12 has the moon beneath her feet. There has been a revolution. The Queen of Heaven is no longer a goddess but a human Jewish mother. Her crown of twelve stars points to the twelve tribes of Israel (as does the Christian symbol of the Twelve). The Queen Mother was an officer of state in the government of the Davidic kings; the annals in the Book of Kings name nearly every queen mother of Judah. The point of the Annunciation story in Luke 1:26–38 is that a courageous young woman embraced the angelic offer to become queen mother in a messianic (and therefore from the Roman viewpoint, seditious) government. The dragon's effort to devour the infant puts one in mind of Herod's attempt to kill the baby messiah, Herod being Rome's lackey and Rome being for John, Satan's deputy (Matthew 2:1–18). Denied the messiah and his mother, the dragon went off to make war on her other children, that is, the citizens of the messianic kingdom. There arise in the next chapter the beast from the sea (Rome, Satan's deputy) and the beast from the earth (the priesthood of the emperor cult), literally recruited from the soil (the local aristocracy), the agents for the persecution of the Churches addressed by John.

The demand for submission to the beast and the order that those refusing to worship the image of the beast are to be slain (13:15) strongly suggest the cult of the Roman emperor and the requirement that all in the empire pay homage to his statue. Not all emperors ordered such worship, as we have seen, so there are a limited number of circumstances available as a context for this demand.

The course of events as revealed in the subsequent visions is the reign of the beasts, followed by a series of disasters climaxing in the last great Battle of Armageddon (a Greek transliteration of the Hebrew term for the strategically located Mount Megiddo; see Chapter 4). Then Babylon (Rome) will fall, Satan's forces will be defeated, and he will be thrown into the "pit" for a thousand years (the millennium), during which Christ and the martyrs will reign. Satan then will be loosed and defeated forever. There will be a final judgment, and death and Hades (the temporary abode of the dead) will be destroyed. This reflects the pattern of rabbinic eschatology in which "the days of the Messiah" prepare the way for "the world to come," the eternal kingdom. Thus, there will be a new heaven and a new earth in which God will "wipe away every tear from their eyes. Death will be no more; mourning and crying and pain will be no more, for the first things have passed away" (21:4). Then John sees the heavenly Jerusalem coming to earth and the river of the water of life.

In the epilogue John is told *not* to seal up the words of this "prophecy," for the "time is near" (22:10). This contrasts with the instruction to Daniel to seal up his visions until the end (Dan. 12:4).

The enigmatic symbolism of the visions of Revelation has inspired persons in every generation, including the current one, to see their time as the end time prophesied by the seer. In any age, impressionable people can be led to read current events into the symbols of the visions. These interpreters are especially successful during times of high anxiety. Given the very real threats and conflicts of the modern world, it is not surprising that many have sought reassurance through interpreting Revelation as an ancient, inspired prediction of what is happening now. The authors will leave it for readers to discuss and decide whether this type of interpretation, similar to the way in which the sectarians of the Qumran community read the Hebrew prophets in the first century C.E., is a proper way to read Revelation in the twenty-first century. The alternative is to read Revelation as a prophecy to persons living in the first century, announcing God's judgment on wickedness and reassuring the faithful of God's ultimate Lordship in history.

Regardless of its historical reference point, Revelation dramatizes a world in which the conflict between good and evil ends with the triumph of goodness. In any circumstances in which evil seems triumphant, it is reassuring to feel such a world can still be projected. Jewish victims of the Nazi Holocaust framed similar worlds. It is not surprising that visions like those of John, of J. R. R. Tolkien in *Lord of the Rings,* of the Harry Potter books, and of movies like *E.T.* and the *Star Wars* saga strike such a responsive chord among so many.

THE NEW TESTAMENT APOCRYPHA

The designations "New Testament Apocrypha" or "Apocryphal New Testament" (see Table 15.3) refer to a wide-ranging group of Christian writings that present themselves as preserving memories of the life and/or teachings of Jesus and the apostles of the canonical New Testament and other early Christian leaders. Literary historians say that they were written between the second and ninth centuries C.E.[1]

---

[1]Wilhelm Schneemelcher. *New Testament Apocrypha (Vol. 1: Gospels and Related Writings; Vol. 2: Writings Related to the Apostles, Apocalypses, and Related Subjects),* revised edition, trans. A. J. B. Higgins and others. Louisville: Westminster John Knox Press, 2006. See also J. K. Elliott, ed. *The Apocryphal New Testament: A Collection of Apocryphal Christian Literature in an English Translation.* Oxford: Oxford University Press, 2005; Bart Ehrman. *Lost Scriptures: Books that Did Not Make It into the New Testament.* Oxford: Oxford University Press, 2005; Amy-Jill Levine and Maria Mayo Robbins. *Feminist Companion to the New Testament Apocrypha.* T & T Clark International, 2006.

TABLE 15.3 Selected Works of the "New Testament Apocrypha"

Gospels

Gospel of Thomas

Gospel of Peter

Gospel of Mary of Magdala

Gospel of the Hebrews

Gospel of the Nazareans

Gospel of the Ebionites

Gospel of the Egyptians

Secret Gospel of Mark

Gospel of Nicodemus

Gospel of Judas

Gospel of Philip

Birth and Infancy Gospels

Protoevangelium of James

Infancy Gospel of Thomas

History of Joseph

Infancy Gospel of Matthew

Arabic Infancy Gospel

Latin Infancy Gospel

Postresurrection Gospels (Dialogues and Revelations)

Questions of Bartholomew

Testament of our Lord

Testament of our Lord in Galilee

Apocryphon of James

Book of Thomas

Sophia of Jesus Christ

Dialogue of the Saviour

First Apocalypse of James

Coptic (Gnostic) Apocalypse of Peter

Gospel of Mary

Pistis Sophia

Books of Jeu

(Continued)

TABLE 15.3 Selected Works of the "New Testament Apocrypha" *(Continued)*

Apostolic Acts

Acts of Andrew

Acts of John

Acts of Paul

Acts of Peter

Acts of Thomas

Acts of Peter and the Twelve Apostles

Apostolic Epistles

Epistle of the Apostles

3 Corinthians (part of Acts of Paul)

Laodiceans

Letter of Peter to Philip (First part)

Correspondence of Paul and Seneca

Epistle of Titus

Other Apostolic Literature

Preaching of Peter

Prayer of the Apostle Paul

Second Apocalypse of James

Pseudo-Clementine literature

Accounts of the Dormition/Assumption of the Virgin

Apocalyptic and Prophetic Literature

Apocalypse of Peter

Ascension of Isaiah

Apocalypse of Thomas

Apocalypse of Paul

Coptic (Gnostic) Apocalypse of Paul

Coptic (Gnostic) Apocalypse of Peter

(Christian) Sibylline Oracles

5 Ezra

6 Ezra

Coptic Apocalypse of Elijah

Apocalypses of the Virgin Mary

Greek Apocalypse of Ezra

Apocalypse of Sedrach

Latin Vision of Ezra

Questions of Ezra

Apocalypses of Daniel

Seventh Vision of Enoch

Wisdom Literature

Teachings of Sylvanus

Hymnic Literature

Odes of Solomon

According to many contemporary scholars, the label "New Testament Apocrypha" is misleading for a number of reasons. The title implies a fixed collection of sacred writings, like the Old Testament Apocrypha/Deuterocanon (see Chapter 10). It also implies that the works were all actively considered for inclusion in the Christian canon, as the works in the Deuterocanon were for the Hebrew canon. In fact, only a handful were. In addition, "Apocrypha" is associated with "spurious" works that were rejected by the mainstream. While some of the works in this group (especially the so-called gnostic books) were rather vigorously suppressed by Christian leaders, most were not seen as in conflict with Christian teaching. Indeed, some (such as the infancy gospels) were very popular in Christian communities for centuries, though they were not deemed canonical. Finally, the designation "New Testament" implies that these works are of the same literary type as the works of the New Testament canon. Although most do claim to be of the same genres (gospels, acts of apostles, letters, and apocalypses), very few are. For example, most of the works of the "New Testament Apocrypha" called "gospels" bear little relationship in literary form to the Gospels of Matthew, Mark, Luke, and John. However, no substitute for the designation has won broad acceptance among scholars.

Gospels

The preface to the Gospel of Luke (1:1–4) implies the existence of many narratives about Jesus. Therefore, it should not be surprising that the "New Testament Apocrypha" includes a number of works claiming to present stories about Jesus and collecting sayings attributed to him.[2]

Many of the so-called gospels claim to provide information on Jesus not found in the canonical gospels, including details of his birth, youth, and activities after his resurrection. Interestingly, unlike the canonical gospels, few have stories about his death.

Probably the most important noncanonical "gospel" is the Coptic Gospel of Thomas, a collection of 114 sayings and parables attributed to Jesus as dictated to Judas Thomas ("the Twin").[3]

---

[2]Alan Jacobs and Very N. Nersessian. *The Essential Gnostic Gospels*. Watkins, 2009. See also Ron Cameron, ed., *The Other Gospels: Non-Canonical Gospel Texts* Louisville: Westminster John Knox Press, 1982; Elaine Pagels. *The Gnostic Gospels*. New York: Random House, 2004.

[3]Martin Meyer. *The Gospel of Thomas: The Hidden Sayings of Jesus* San Francisco: Harper San Francisco, 1992. See also Elaine Pagels. *Beyond Belief: The Secret Gospel of Thomas* New York: Random House, 2004.

Some of the sayings are similar to those in the canonical gospels. For example, Saying (Logion) 41 in the Gospel of Thomas ("Jesus said, 'All who have in their hand, to them shall be given; and all who do not have, from them shall be taken away, even the little they have") is echoed in Mt. 13:12, 25:29, and Lk. 19:26. The Gospel of Thomas claims these are "secret sayings" of Jesus to his followers, which enable those who understand them to "not experience death." Although the Gospel of Thomas has been stereotyped as a gnostic gospel because of its concern with a saving knowledge Jesus taught and because it was part of the Nag Hammadi gnostic library in northern Egypt discovered in 1945,[4] it may indeed preserve authentic sayings of Jesus which enhance our understanding of the historical Jesus and the composition of the gospels. The Gospel of Thomas could be described as a "Q"-like document (see Chapter 12). Although it is not Q, it looks much as scholars think Q did.

In addition to the Gospel of Thomas, two other "apocryphal gospels" have come to public attention in recent years. Because of fascination with the follower of Jesus known as Mary Magdalene generated by the bestselling novel *The Da Vinci Code* (see Chapter 16), the *Gospel of Mary of Magdala*, first published in the 1950s, has enjoyed new interest.[5] This work implies that Mary was not merely a member of the entourage that followed Jesus from Galilee, but that he chose her as one of his closest apostles. From the two known fragments of the gospel, a story emerges of Mary encouraging the male apostles of Jesus after his resurrection appearances by sharing with them hidden teachings he had given to her alone. However, Peter and the others refuse to believe that Jesus would have given such esoteric teachings to a woman. The Gospel of Mary of Magdala provides evidence that women were important teachers in early Christian communities.

The publication in April, 2006, by the National Geographic Society of another "gnostic" gospel, *The Gospel of Judas Iscariot*, has sparked a controversy that is still swirling.[6] The scholars who worked with the Society in publishing the text claim it portrays Judas, the betrayer of Jesus according to the canonical gospels, not as a villain, but rather a devoted follower who turned Jesus in to the authorities not out of greed or confusion but because it was the directive of his master who believed it was a necessary prerequisite to the fulfillment of God's purpose. According to these scholars, Judas was a leader of the apostles and the closest to Jesus. He was the only apostle Jesus could trust to carry out the dangerous mission.

The fragile manuscript, dated by scholars to as early as the second century C.E., has a colorful history that was played up in the film and book produced by the National Geographic Society. Like the Gospel of Thomas, it was a Coptic text (probably translated from Greek) found in a cave in Egypt. It made its way through a series of collectors until it ended up in a bank vault in the United States, before it was purchased and published by the Society.

Within months, scholars, including a few who had been involved with its publication, began to question how the Gospel of Judas was being presented. They claimed that in the rush to publish the gospel, mistakes in translation and interpretation were made and that it does not undermine the traditional view of Judas nearly as much as was being claimed. Five years later the controversy continues.

---

[4]James M. Robinson and Martin Meyer. *The Nag Hammadi Scriptures: The Revised and Updated Translation of Sacred Gnosic Writings in One Volume.* San Francisco: HarperOne, 2009.

[5]Karen L. King. *The Gospel of Mary of Magdala: Jesus and the First Woman Apostle* Santa Rosa CA: Polebridge Press, 2003; Martin Meyer and Esther A. DeBoer. *The Gospels of Mary* San Francisco: HarperOne, 2006.

[6]Rodolphe Kasser, Martin Meyer, Gregor Wurst, ed. *The Gospel of Judas*, 2nd ed. Washington, D.C.: National Geographic, 2008. See also Karen L. King and Elaine Pagels, *Reading Judas: The Gospel of Judas and the Shaping of Christianity.* New York: Penguin, 2008; Herbert Krosney and Bart Ehrman. *The Lost Gospel: The Quest for the Gospel of Judas Iscariot.* Washington, D.C.: National Geographic, 2006; James Robinson *The Secrets of Judas: The Story of the Misunderstood Disciple and His Lost Gospel.* San Francisco: Harper San Francisco, 2006; and, for a critical view, N. T. Wright. *Judas and the Gospel of Jesus: Have We Missed the Truth About Christianity.* Ada, MI: Baker Books, 2006.

Other Works

There are a variety of "acts" of the apostles among the apocryphal writings, such as the Acts of Paul, John, Peter, Andrew, and Thomas. They typically describe the heroic activities of the apostle and end with an account of his martyrdom.

Only a few letters are included among the works of the New Testament Apocrypha. Like some of the New Testament letters, most are tracts and treatises rather than actual correspondence.

There are apocalypses in which figures like Peter, Mary (the mother of Jesus), James, Stephen, and Thomas are transported into the realms of heaven and hell to see the fate awaiting the faithful and the unbelievers. An Apocalypse of Paul was probably inspired by Paul's reference to the experience of being taken up into the "third heaven" (2 Cor. 12:2).

There has been prejudice even in modern scholarship about the value of these works as historical sources. Indeed, many *are* fanciful writings. The story in the Infancy Gospel of Thomas describing Jesus as a child making clay sparrows on the Sabbath, then commanding them to fly away when he is chastised for playing on the Sabbath, hardly sounds realistic. However, each writing should, and now is, being carefully studied by itself to determine its value as a source for early Christian piety. Studies are also needed of the literary worlds of these writings.

In addition to the works classified as *New Testament Apocrypha,* some other writings of the early Christian Church were close to the New Testament both chronologically and in terms of their importance for the Christian community. A few were apparently considered canonical for a time. For example, one of the best ancient New Testament manuscripts (the *Codex Sinaiticus*) includes the Shepherd of Hermas (a visionary composition). Hermas was so popular that some scholars think it would have achieved canonical status were it not so clearly postapostolic. Hermas, the Didache (Teaching of the Twelve Apostles, a manual of church discipline), and the Epistle of Barnabas (a moral treatise purportedly written by Paul's traveling companion) appear alongside the canonical works, in an index. The early church leader Clement of Alexandria considered the Didache canonical. Indeed, it may preserve traditions dating to the apostolic age.

Summary

In this chapter, we completed our historical overview of the New Testament period with a description of the postapostolic era (70–150 C.E.). We discussed the significance of the passing from the scene of the original apostles and the growing institutionalization of the church. We also reflected on the growing split between Christians and Jews during this period and the treatment of Christians by Roman authorities.

Although attributed to Paul, the Pastoral Epistles (First and Second Timothy, and Titus) reflect the postapostolic situation, especially the more complex church structure. The majority view in modern scholarship is that attributing authorship to Paul and identifying the recipients as young colleagues of Paul was a literary device used to heighten their authority. While they certainly reflect a Pauline perspective, they probably were written by followers of the apostle after his death. The Pastorals give advice on church leadership and warn against false teachers.

The Letter to the Hebrews is actually a religious treatise directed to Jewish Christians who are faltering in their newly proclaimed Christian faith. Drawing astutely on Hellenistic philosophy and biblical interpretation, the anonymous author of Hebrews skillfully crafted a defense of the superiority of Christ to the angels, Moses, the priesthood and high priest, and Temple sacrifices.

The catholic (general) epistles are a group of compositions of various literary styles, considered together because they are by tradition directed to no one church, but to the universal (that is, catholic) church. James is the New Testament example of a Wisdom book. It is an anthology of advice and observations, attributed to James, the brother of Jesus. Its most frequent theme is putting faith into practice by caring for the poor and hungry. The two letters attributed to Peter and a Letter of Jude (another brother of Jesus) concern themselves with Christian conduct and false teaching. Three short letters of John may come from the same school or tradition in which the Gospel of John originated.

The last book of the New Testament is its one fully apocalyptic work—the Revelation of John. Our treatment explained its unique literary form, touched on the question of authorship, speculated on the basic theme and structure of the work, and highlighted some of the more intriguing sections of this enigmatic writing. We left open for your discussion the question of how the fantastic visions of Revelation relate to our world.

The chapter concluded with a brief overview of the New Testament Aporcypha, early Christian writings not included in the New Testament canon.

Having completed this journey into the literary and historical worlds of the Bible and having reflected on and perhaps discussed issues in the contemporary world of the Bible, what are your main impressions? Has the journey been exciting, challenging, confusing, enlightening?

In the final chapter we will discuss in general how the Bible has impacted our world. We suggest that before reading Chapter 16 you consider how the Bible and this study of it have affected you.

The Contemporary World

Case Study

Has the Journey Been Worthwhile?

Having completed their journey into the literary and historical worlds of the Bible, John, Mary, and Joyce are discussing the value of what they have learned.

"I still believe, in my heart, that the Bible is the literal Word of God, but this literary and historical study certainly has challenged that faith," John says somberly. "I am afraid that this kind of study just might destroy the faith of Bible believers not as strong as I am. I'm certainly going to tell the others in the Bible study I attend not to take this course or read this book!"

"Ignorance is bliss, isn't it, John?" Mary responds. "How strong could your faith be if it can't stand up to an academic study of the Bible? I still think the Bible isn't that relevant to my life or the world today because it is so dated, but I have come to appreciate its literary value and its historical depth. I can really see why so many have been so enthralled with it for so long."

"I realize we've just scratched the surface of what there is to learn about the Bible," Joyce points out. "I've learned enough to know that the assumptions we have about the Bible, whether we are believers or nonbelievers, are hard to break! I'm hoping I have the opportunity to go beyond this introductory study to more advanced work."

As you complete your study of the literary and historical worlds of the Bible, with which of the friends do you most agree and why? How motivated are you to continue a serious study of the Bible along the lines to which you have been introduced in this text?

Questions for Discussion and Reflection

1. *Read First Timothy*
   a. Many women today find the instructions to women in First Timothy 2:11–15 insulting. Does this directive for worship in an early Christian setting have any relevance today?
   b. This letter warns against false teachers (4:1–16). What might the author designate as false teaching today?
2. *Read Hebrews 1–2, 11–13*
   a. This letter develops the idea that God once spoke by prophets but "in these last days" has spoken to

us by a Son (1:1–2). Reflect on and discuss the issue of whether and how God speaks in the contemporary world. Can the differing views in various religions of how God speaks be reconciled?

b. Reflect on and discuss this letter's statement about "faith" (11:1–40) and "suffering" (2:5–18, 12:1–11).

3. *Read James*

a. What does James have to say about "religion" (1:26–27)? What different impressions of "religion" have you gathered in your study of the Bible? Which do you find most compelling?

b. Compare what James has to say about "wealth" (2:1–7, 5:1–6) with other discussions of riches in the New Testament and Tanak. How is wealth viewed in the modern world?

c. Compare what James says about "faith" (2:14–26) and "suffering" (1:2–18, 5:13–15) with the ways the topics are treated in other biblical books.

4. *Read First John*

a. According to this essay, what is the test of whether God abides in a person? Is that still an appropriate test to determine whether God is present in a person's life? Does it mean God may be present in anyone's life, regardless of their attitude toward religion?

b. Only in First John is the "antichrist" mentioned (2:18, 4:3). According to First John, who is the "antichrist"? Is this an appropriate concept to use in the modern world? If so, who might be called the "antichrist" today?

5. *Read Revelation 1, 4–8, 12–14, 20–22*

a. According to some interpreters, the Book of Revelation should be seen as a prediction of events taking place now. How does the analysis of Revelation in this chapter affect your view of this type of interpretation? Is Revelation still relevant at the beginning of the twenty-first century? If so, how?

b. Movies based on Revelation (like *The Seventh Sign*) and coverage of the interpretation of the book by apocalyptic sects (like the Branch Davidian leader David Koresh during the 1993 standoff with federal agents at the Mount Carmel complex in Waco, Texas) are evidence of continuing fascination with the Revelation to John. What in the contemporary world accounts for this level of interest in a 2000-year-old book? Is such fascination healthy or unhealthy?

c. Compare the portrait of Satan in Revelation with the description of "the Satan" found in the Book of Job (Job 1–2). How has the character of Satan developed? In your opinion, is there any place for the figure of Satan in contemporary religion?

d. The vision of the new Jerusalem (Revelation 21–22) has symbols that recall the early chapters of the Bible. What are they? How are they reinterpreted here? How might this vision speak to someone dying of cancer or trapped in poverty?

6. *Other questions*

a. Should the apocryphal books of the New Testament be included alongside the canonical books in a study of the Bible? Why or why not? Which, if any, of the apocryphal books do you think you would like to read?

b. We have noted that pseudonymity was not regarded as fraudulent in antiquity. The purpose of pseudonymous writings was often to promote the goals of an earlier worthy, as in the Pastoral Epistles. Modern writers sometimes do the same thing by making historical persons characters in novels, plays, or movies. If you were going to assume the role of Paul, Peter, James, or John in the modern world, what art form or medium might you employ? What ideas would you emphasize? How would you state them?

Chapter 16

Journey On!

The Annunciation. The story of the Annunciation (Luke 1:26–38) has been a favorite theme of artists through the centuries. The modern African American painter Henry O. Tanner (1859–1937) registered the psychological complexity of the situation: an innocent, young, unmarried woman called to the hazardous role of queen mother in a revolutionary regime. Tanner's Madonna shows a mixture of awe and skepticism. And how does one picture an archangel? *Source:* The Philadelphia Museum of Art/ Art Resource, NY

We began this journey into the three worlds of the Bible by suggesting the metaphor of a student going abroad to study. The modern reader venturing into the historical and literary worlds of the Bible is like a student who studies in a foreign country. Having completed this study, you (like the student who has gone abroad for a term) should now have a basic familiarity with the territory. You are ready to move on toward more advanced investigations, perhaps at some point even to become a tour guide yourself. In the Annotated Bibliography, we offer you suggestions on how to continue your journey into the literary, historical, and contemporary worlds of the Bible.

If our discussion questions have done their intended job, you will not only understand the first two biblical worlds better, but you will also have begun to develop sensitivity to the variety of ways that the Bible enters into the world of modern experience. We will end our discussion of the three biblical worlds by discussing the impact of the Bible on contemporary religions as well as the values, institutions, and culture of Western civilization in general and the United States in particular.

THE BIBLE IN CONTEMPORARY RELIGIONS

The most obvious way in which the Bible impacts upon the modern world (in the West and beyond) is as the Scripture of Judaism and Christianity. No study of these religions, or any particular segment of them, is complete without attention to the way in which the Bible functions in shaping the life, teaching, and worship of their various communities. For example, what is the role of the Tanak in Reform Jewish settings in comparison with its function in Conservative or Orthodox Jewish communities? Or how is the Bible used in a Roman Catholic mass in comparison with its function in a Baptist revival? Every minute of every day, the Bible is being read, studied, taught, and used in religious contexts. It is virtually impossible to overestimate its importance within the religious communities that honor its authority, although there is widespread disagreement on the nature of that authority.

Judaism and Christianity are not the only religions that recognize the truth found in the Bible. The sacred text of Islam, the Qur'an, recognizes the legitimacy of various faiths and sacred texts, including the Bible. It asserts that Allah (God) created the diverse peoples of the world "that

Calligraphy from the Qur'an. In traditional Islamic art, verses from the *Qur'an* are painted or inscribed, as on the red sandstone *Qutb Minar*, a 12th century, 240-foot tower in Delhi, India. *Source:* William A. Young

you might learn to know one another" (Surah 49:13). Each has received its own revealed way to live (5:48). According to the Qur'an, there is to be no compulsion in religion (2:256).

The Qur'an teaches that Allah has revealed His divine will through a series of prophets whom he sent to the Jews and Christians, who are known in the Qur'an as People of the Book. According to the Qur'an, Allah revealed sacred texts to the People of the Book (e.g., 3:187, 5:19) before He made known the words of the final and definitive text (the Qur'an) via the "seal of the prophets," Muhammad. In addition, the Qur'an features a number of the principal figures in the biblical narrative, including Adam and Eve (e.g., 3:11ff), Joseph (e.g., 12:4ff), Abraham (e.g., 2:124ff), Jacob (e.g., 2:132ff), Moses (e.g., 2:87, 5:20ff), David and Solomon (e.g., 21:78ff), Jesus and Mary (e.g., 19:16ff). In Muslim countries, People of the Book are *dhimmis,* protected communities. Thus, rather than harboring hostility toward Jews and Christians, Muslims are counseled by the Qur'an to recognize the values and beliefs shared with these communities.

On the other hand, the Qur'an also maintains that in an effort to make the revelations of God less demanding, Jews and Christians altered their sacred texts, called the Torah and the Gospels in the Qur'an. Where the Bible and the Qur'an differ on biblical characters and incidents, Muslims believe that the Qur'an is the more authentic word of God because it had not been corrupted as was the case with the earlier texts.

Therefore, while the Qur'an counsels respect for the Bible and those who follow its teachings, it does claim to have more legitimacy as the final divine revelation. That a religion would consider its own sacred text more authoritative than others that came before it should not be surprising![1]

Many of the new religious movements springing up in the contemporary world also interpret the Bible. One such movement is the International Raelian Religion, founded in 1973 after a French journalist named Claude Vorilhon reported that he had been visited by extraterrestrial beings who identified themselves as Elohim (a Hebrew term found in the Bible meaning "God" or "divine beings," which Raël defined as "those who came from the sky"). According to Vorilhon, the Elohim gave him the name Raël and told him that he had been chosen to proclaim the truth about humans and the Elohim and prepare the way for the coming of the sky-beings to earth. The core of Raelian teaching is a creation narrative that reinterprets the Genesis account in accord with the message Raël received. The laboratories where humans were created are the Garden of Eden in the Genesis story. When humans became aggressive, the Elohim expelled them from the laboratories. All the biblical prophets, and contemporary prophets like Raël, are the product of the interbreeding of Elohim and humans to which Genesis alludes (6:2). The prophets carry messages adapted to the cultures in which they live.

By 1997, the Raelian movement had raised enough money to begin construction of the embassy the Elohim had instructed them to build in Jerusalem in anticipation of their arrival. However, Raelians have so far been unsuccessful in convincing the government of Israel to allow the embassy to be built.

According to the Raelian worldview, and as an interpretation of apocalyptic books like Daniel and Revelation, we are now living in the Age of Apocalypse. Innovations in human genetics and understanding of DNA have humanity at the threshold of creating life. On the basis of this belief, Raelians have taken a special interest in the science of cloning. In 2002, unsubstantiated claims of successful human cloning by Raelian scientists working in a company called Clonaid brought global attention to the Raelian movement.[2]

---

[1]See F. E. Peters. *The Voice, the Word, the Books: The Sacred Scripture of the Jews, Christians, and Muslims.* Princeton, NJ: Princeton University Press, 2007.

[2]See Susan Palmer. *Aliens Adored: Raël's UFO Religion.* Piscataway, NJ: Rutgers University Press, 2004.

THE BIBLE IN WESTERN LAW AND GOVERNMENT

However, the Bible shapes the contemporary world in many other ways beyond the groups that consider it canonical. For example, the impact of the Bible on Western law and government is so pervasive that most people do not realize it. The principle that governments are of laws, not people, upon which Western European and American societies are based, is biblical. According to the Bible, God, and not any human ruler, is the source of laws. Even kings and emperors cannot ignore the law, as King David learned. Although secularized, the principle that no one is above the law and all are equal before it is a fundamental premise of Western legal systems.

Another biblical principle pervading our system of values in the West is the worth and dignity of the individual. It is rooted in the view of human life expressed in the first chapter of Genesis and reaffirmed throughout the rest of the Tanak and the New Testament. Other social systems put the highest value on the good of the entire society, at the expense of the rights, freedom, and sometimes the life of the individual or on the well-being of some privileged elite. Although individuals are not permitted to compromise the common good for their own advantage, Western societies reflect a commitment to the worth and dignity of the individual citizen that traces ultimately to the Bible. In the latter part of the twentieth century, liberation movements throughout the world were inspired by the Bible's special concern for the poor and oppressed. "Liberation Theology," drawing heavily on the words of the prophets and the teachings of Jesus, provides the intellectual basis for some of the most powerful movements for constructive social change. Other interpreters today apply the principle of the sanctity of individuals to the issues of abortion and capital punishment.

In the summer of 2003, a dispute over how to acknowledge the dependence of the American legal system on biblical law gained national attention. Chief Justice of the Alabama Supreme Court, Roy Moore, had fulfilled a campaign promise by installing a two-ton granite monument with the Ten Commandments inscribed on it in the rotunda of the State Judicial Building in Montgomery. A suit was brought by groups who argued that the Ten Commandments monument violated the prohibition of government promotion of religion found in the First Amendment of the U.S. Constitution. When a federal judge ruled that Justice Moore must remove the monument, he

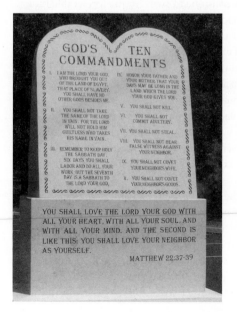

Ten Commandments Monument. The United States Supreme Court has made several recent rulings on whether government-sponsored displays of the Ten Commandments (Ex. 20:1–17, Dt. 5:1-21) and other biblical texts violate the prohibition against the establishment of religion in the First Amendment of the U.S. Constitution. *Source:* Bonnie Watton/Shutterstock

refused, citing his responsibility under Alabama law to acknowledge God and pointing out that the federal government itself, in its currency and in the Pledge of Allegiance, also acknowledges God.

Judge Moore's supporters claimed that removal of the monument would abridge their freedom of religious expression, also guaranteed under the First Amendment. Those who brought the suit to remove the monument claimed that to allow it to stand on public display in the Court building meant that the government was engaging in an unconstitutional promotion of the biblical religions (Judaism and Christianity) over other religions.

The dispute highlighted the tension in the two clauses of the First Amendment, one guaranteeing freedom of religious expression and the other forbidding the establishment of religion by Congress. Judge Moore's supporters argued that the removal of the monument was just one more example of courts going to the extreme in removing the biblical religion of the vast majority of Americans from the public sphere. They claimed that the First Amendment was intended by the Founding Fathers as a prohibition against a state religion, not a warrant for "taking God out of public life." They pointed out that the United States Supreme Court building itself has references to God on its walls. It is hypocritical, they claim, for a federal judiciary to mandate a state judge to remove public expressions of the religious heritage of the country.

Those who wanted the Ten Commandments monument removed asserted that, as the United States becomes more pluralistic religiously, it is all the more important to recognize the First Amendment's prohibition against government sponsored or endorsed religion in order to protect the minority who are members of other religions or who are not religious against the tyranny of the majority. They pointed out that the first three of the Bible's Ten Commandments were direct expressions of a particular religious faith not embraced by all Americans. They warned that the ultimate objective of those most vehement about keeping the monument was the creation of a theocracy in the United States, replacing the secular democracy that has served the country so well for over 200 years. The Ten Commandments monument was removed from public view in August 2003, as protesters vigorously objected on the steps of the Court building, promising to keep their cause alive. One poll reported that over 70% of the American public opposed the removal. The underlying controversy over the role of the Bible in American society, evident in the Ten Commandments monument dispute, will undoubtedly continue to swirl for the foreseeable future.

Over the years the U. S. Supreme Court has decided a number of cases involving display of the Ten Commandments by government bodies. Most recently, in 2005, the U.S. Supreme Court effectively ruled in a 5–4 decision that copies of the Ten Commandments could not be displayed in Kentucky court houses because to do so would violate the establishment clause of the First Amendment. Five years later the case was on its way back to the Supreme Court after being retried by lower courts. Supporters pointed out that the Commandments were but one part of a display called "Foundations of American Government" that placed them alongside other documents, like the Declaration of Independence, and that the purpose was not to promote religion but to acknowledge the various sources of the American system of government. Opponents argued that no matter how presented the display of the Ten Commandments constituted an unconstitutional government endorsement of religion.

We have already noted in Chapter 1 the role of the Bible in the debate over whether same-sex marriages should be made legal in the United States. Another disputed issue is whether the theory of "intelligent design" (also called "creationism"), which holds that the natural world cannot be explained without acceptance of the theory of a supernatural agency, should be taught alongside the theory of evolution by natural selection in public school science classes. Just before Christmas 2005, U.S. District Judge John E. Jones barred a Pennsylvania public school district from introducing the concept of "intelligent design" in a biology class, ruling the district was violating the constitutional ban on the government's "establishment of religion." Judge Jones said that the theory of intelligent design (which holds that there are aspects of nature that cannot be explained apart from the theory that they were designed by a supernatural intelligence) was really an attempt to introduce the biblical account of creation by God found in the biblical book of Genesis (see Chapter 3) into a public school science classroom, where it does not belong. Supporters of the decision called the decision a vindication of the "separation of church and state" principle in the United States while opponents asserted it was a manifestation of a disturbing trend in modern America to reject the country's biblical heritage and impose the secular, atheist ideology of evolutionary materialism.

Until the beginning of the twentieth century the most prominent book used to teach students to read in American schools, *The New England Primer,* drew heavily on biblical references. With increased sensitivity to religious diversity and the need to keep church and state separate, public schools began to remove the Bible from their curricula. However, in its famous 1963 ruling on religion in public schools, the U.S. Supreme Court called for "study of the Bible…, when presented objectively as a secular program of education," while ruling against required prayer and other religious observances in public schools. Various groups in the United States are now working hard to respond to the Court's directive by promoting greater attention to the Bible and its impact on Western institutions, culture, and values in public schools. One is the Biblical Literacy Project (BLP) founded in 2001 to foster and encourage the academic study of the Bible in public schools. The BLP published a guideline for public schools on how to include teaching about the Bible in their curricula without violating the constitutional prohibition on the government establishment of religion. In 2005, the BLP published a textbook entitled *The Bible and Its Influence* for use in classes in public high schools studying the Bible. Full of examples of how the Bible has impacted Western culture the book is a valuable resource for older readers as well. Though in 2010 fewer than 10% of public high school students had access to an elective course on the Bible, schools in more than forty states were teaching such courses, many using *The Bible and Its Influence.*

THE BIBLE AND THE ENVIRONMENTAL CRISIS

One area in which the impact of the Bible on modern Western culture has been very controversial is the contemporary environmental crisis. Many modern environmentalists believe that the biblical theme of humans as separate from, rather than part of, the natural community has been a major contributing factor in Western culture's exploitation of nature. Other biblical themes (particularly evident, it is claimed, in the first two chapters of the Book of Genesis) that have allegedly injured the balance of nature include: human dominion over nature as part of God's plan of creation; God's directive to humans to subdue nature and increase the human population; God as separate from nature, with nature viewed as either dead or at least not in God's image; emphasis on other worldly concerns, leaving the earth as a mere place of testing and preparation for a life beyond; and the wilderness as hostile and cursed, to be "tamed" and "humanized." This has led some concerned people to turn away from the Bible and to other sources of inspiration for living in harmony with nature.

However, other interpreters have pointed out that while the Bible has been used to justify abuse of the environment, responsibility and respect for nature is its dominant perspective and mandate for humans. For example, it is argued, rather than giving humans free reign over a separate nature, the first two chapters of the Book of Genesis actually portray humans as part of a natural community cared for and ordered by God. In this community of life, humans have a responsibility to act as good stewards of the earth and its inhabitants, cooperating with God's plan for the well-being of the planet. The human tendency to pollute the earth results from sinful rebellion against God; it is *not* a way of life sanctioned by the Bible.

Space Ship Earth. American astronauts on their way to the Moon aboard the Apollo 17 spacecraft made this now famous "Blue Marble" photograph of Earth. Revealing as it does the fragility of the planet with its oceans of water, blanket of air, and wisps of cloud, it has become a powerful symbol of the environment/ecological movement, and of the need to preserve peace in an era of weapons of mass destruction.   *Source:* NASA/Johnson Space Center

Both Jewish and Christian interpreters of the Bible have developed a biblically based ethic that promotes environmental responsibility. For example, Jewish interpreters of the biblical precept concerning protection of nature during a time of war (Dt. 20:19) have extended it to argue for strict limitation on wanton destruction of nature for human ends in all circumstances. Likewise, Christian interpreters have drawn on New Testament passages that point toward ecological awareness. One such text is Colossians 1:15–17 that suggests the presence of Christ in *all* reality. If such is the case, then divinity permeates the natural world. This means that nonhuman aspects of nature have intrinsic value, not merely worth as instruments of human manipulation. Modern church leaders ranging from Pope John Paul II to evangelist Billy Graham have called on Christians to take a leadership role in efforts to overcome the sinful abuse of nature and to care for the earth as God intends.

According to the National Aeronautics and Space Administration, the decade ending in 2009 was the hottest on record and 2009 was the second warmest year since 1880, when scientists began recording surface temperatures of the earth. The warmest year was 2005. Climate change resulting in global warming unprecedented in more than a century is not in doubt, but a debate rages over how disastrous the effects of global warming will be, whether humans are largely responsible for the elevation of temperatures, and what, if any, actions should be taken by humans to counter climate change.

As in virtually every other central issue of the twenty-first century, interpretation of the Bible figures prominently in the controversy. Some hold the view that the Bible shows global warming is part of the natural cycles that are identified as part of God's creation (Gn. 8.22) and should be accepted as such. Others contend the Bible predicts climate catastrophes such as global warming as indicators of the end times. They argue that just as God has used severe weather events in the past to affect the course of history (e.g., Genesis 6–9), the Bible reveals the beginning of the end of the current age of history will be marked by climate disasters such as droughts (Is. 24:3–6, Rev, 16:8–9) and mammoth storms (Lk. 21:25). Still others point to climatic chaos in the Bible as God's acts of judgment within history on human sinfulness. The prophet Jeremiah, for example, announced climatic upheaval, including desertification, because the people of God had rebelled against the commandments of God by perverting justice and morality (Jeremiah 4–5). In particular, those who hold this view emphasize that the abuse of the earth by the wealthiest and most powerful nations has resulted in devastation that continues to affect disproportionately the poor and powerless. A growing number of interpreters point to passages such as Gn. 1:26–28 to bolster the contention that God has given humans the power and responsibility to care for the creation, and in the twenty-first century that means the richest humans making the lifestyle sacrifices necessary to minimize the negative consequences of global warming.

THE BIBLE AND INDIGENOUS CULTURES

The impact of the Bible on indigenous cultures is also a subject of contemporary debate. For example, beginning with first contact with Native American cultures and continuing in some cases to the present, many Christian missionaries have sought to strip away from the Indians their traditional customs and beliefs, replacing them with a "biblical" lifestyle and values. Were these efforts at conversion motivated by a sincere concern for the spiritual welfare of the people? Was it necessary, as some nineteenth-century missionaries put it, to "kill the Indian" in order to "save the person?" Have those Indians who willingly adapted to biblically based religion fared better than those who have steadfastly clung to their traditional values? Or has the Bible been used to rationalize a pattern of cultural genocide that has taken and continues to exact a terrible toll on Native American and other indigenous peoples? Can the teachings of the Bible be adapted to non-Western settings, without undermining the distinctiveness of the culture? These are among the hotly disputed questions being discussed among those engaged in or concerned about the ongoing impact of the Bible among indigenous peoples in the United States and throughout the world.

Other contemporary ethical issues in which interpretation of the Bible plays a central role include the debates over how to end the incidents of global violence in which the Bible plays a prominent role (such as the Palestinian/Israeli conflict), how to cope with the population explosion, and how to confront and end discrimination based on race, ethnicity gender, sexual orientation and religion.

THE BIBLE IN WESTERN ART, MUSIC, AND LITERATURE

The impact of the Bible on Western art is also almost incalculable. A visitor to any major art museum in the world will be struck at once by the substantial amount of art based on biblical themes. Much of this, like Michelangelo's famed rendition of creation on the ceiling of the Sistine Chapel at the Vatican in Rome, was executed for religious leaders or houses of worship. Some of it still is. But the

Pro-Palestinian Rally. A June 2010 rally in Brighton, England protests the blockade of Gaza by the government of Israel and advocates an independent Palestinian nation. Various factions in the ongoing Palestinian-Israeli dispute draw on their interpretation of the Bible and the *Qur'an* to support their positions.   *Source:* Dutourdumonde/Shutterstock

great themes themselves seem to challenge the artistic imagination. The great Rembrandt, a sort of artistic entrepreneur who executed both secular and religious works in various media, seemed to find particular inspiration in biblical characters and events as is evident in works such as "The Woman Taken in Adultery" and "St. Paul in Prison."

The works of some modern artists interpreting the Bible have sparked much controversy. For example, a portrait of Mary, mother of Jesus, covered with dung inspired boycotts when it was displayed in an exhibition at a New York City museum. Some art critics, however, acclaimed the work as an honest representation of the religious hypocrisy in contemporary life. The debate over artistic works that some view as assaults on biblical values will surely continue in the twenty-first century. Art historians have pointed out that similar controversies once surrounded now revered works of art, such as the paintings of Michelangelo in the Sistine Chapel in the Vatican.

Popular art writer Sister Wendy Becket has published an essay, "Sister Wendy's Top Twenty Biblical Paintings," illustrated with sumptuous color plates.[3] The works span a period from 700 C.E. into the 1990s, with an unsurprising heavy load of Renaissance and Baroque paintings. The cover illustration of this book, the first text page from the Lindisfarne Gospel of John ("*In Principio Erat Verbum*"), is among her selections.

The stained-glass windows created by painter Marc Chagall in 1960 for a small synagogue at the Hadassah Hospital, Jerusalem, bring the poetic language of Genesis 49 and Deuteronomy 33 to life in images that speak in the mystical accents of eastern European Hasidic Judaism. Many of Chagall's other works, such as "The Dream of Jacob" and "Abraham Approaching Sodom with Three Angels," explore biblical themes and characters. A poignant realism informs the African American artist Edward Tanner's *Annunciation,* now in the Philadelphia Museum of Art. The British artist

---

[3] *Bible Review* 1995 (vol. 21, no. 1), pp. 15–35. See also *Sister Wendy's Story of Painting,* Enhanced and Expanded Edition. New York: Dorling Kinderslee, 2000 and Lynn R. Huber, Dan W. Clanton, Jr., and Jane S. Webster. "Biblical Subjects in Art," *Teaching the Bible Through Popular Culture and the Arts,* ed. Mark Roncace and Patrick Gray Atlanta: Society of Blblical Literature, 2007, pp. 187–228.

Edwina Sandys, a granddaughter of British leader Sir Winston Churchill, sculpted a feminist version of the Crucifixion, entitled *Christa,* with a female body. It is an interpretive work inspired by issues of our day. The point is that painters and sculptors today continue to draw from the rich reservoir of biblical themes, images, and characters in the styles and with the meanings to which the present age points.

The Bible has also inspired some of the most memorable musical creations in history. To cite but one familiar example, the entire text of Handel's *Messiah* is drawn from the Bible. Today, contemporary musicians continue the tradition. Arnold Schoenberg's opus 50 is a beautiful *de profundis,* that is, Psalm 130. Thus, he joins Ralph Vaughn Williams and a host of other modern composers who have set the Psalms and other biblical texts to music. Carlisle Floyd's contemporary opera "Susannah" claims to be based on the tale in deuterocanonical additions to Daniel. It thus carries on the tradition pioneered by such great composers of the past (and their librettists!) as Handel (*Joshua, Saul, Solomon*), Verdi (*Nabucco*), and Saint-Saens (*Samson*) in basing operas and dramatic oratorios on biblical materials.[4]

Popular music has also been substantially influenced by the Bible. For example, folk legend Bob Dylan has written and performed a number of songs reflecting the impact of the Bible on his music, including "Man Gave Names to All the Animals," "In the Garden," and "Are You Ready" to name but a few. Country music star Johnny Cash was inspired by the Bible in songs such as "If Jesus Ever Loved a Woman," "Spiritual," and "Matthew 24 (Is Knocking at the Door)." Rock music has also shown the influence of the Bible, in songs such as U2's "The First Time" (a retelling of the Parable of the Prodigal Son) and Bruce Springsteen's "Jesus Was an Only Son."[5]

The great English and American writers have also dealt extensively with biblical themes. Critical editions of Shakespeare often contain footnotes revealing the approximately 1300 biblical references and allusions of the bard. John Milton's epic poem *Paradise Lost* was his meditation on the story told in the early chapters of the Book of Genesis. Modern poets have also drawn on the Bible. T. S. Eliot's *The Wasteland,* a poem written in the 1920s and expressing the desolate mood of the twentieth century, weaves a number of allusions to biblical poetry together with hints of various Asian scriptures. The American poet Wallace Stevens used the deuterocanonical story of Susanna and the Elders in his "Peter Quince at the Clavier." Without an awareness of the biblical references, the reader's appreciation of these and other modern poems is hampered. The biblical allusions are more obvious in poems like W. H. Auden's "They Wondered Why the Fruit Had Been Forbidden" and Emily Dickinson's "A Word Made Flesh is Seldom."

Even without notes, the biblical connections of a substantial amount of modern poetry, drama, and fiction spring out at the reader with a solid background in the study of the Bible. The great nineteenth-century American writer Herman Melville drew on the Bible, especially the Book of Job, in telling his intricate tale of the search for the great white whale *Moby Dick.* Many interpreters feel that *Moby Dick* is, at least on one level, Melville's dialogue with the Bible, especially Job. He captured the impact of the mysterious meaning of that book for America in the early nineteenth century. In his later novella, *Billy Budd,* he wrestled with the theme of the fall from innocence in the story of Adam in Genesis and the New Testament question of redemption through suffering.

---

[4]For a fuller discussion of classical music inspired by the Bible, see Dan W. Clanton Jr. and Bryan Bibb. "Classical Music," *Teaching the Bible Through Popular Culture and the Arts,* ed. Mark Roncace and Patrick Gray. Atlanta: Society of Biblical Literature, 2007, pp. 53–83,

[5]These and many other examples of popular music inspired by the Bible are discussed in Mark Ronace and Dan W. Clanton Jr. "Popular Music," *Teaching the Bible Through Popular Culture and the Arts,* ed. Mark Roncace and Patrick Gray. Atlanta: Society of Biblical Literature, 2007, pp. 15–51.

One of the most influential books in American history, Harriet Beecher Stowe's *Uncle Tom's Cabin,* cannot be fully understood without awareness of its rich use of biblical references and symbols.

Twentieth-century writers have also engaged in imaginative interpretations of the Bible. Obvious examples would include Thomas Mann's rendition of the Joseph story from Genesis and Archibald Macleish's retelling of the story of Job in dramatic form in *J.B.* Much of the ambience of John Steinbeck's *East of Eden* is lost on those who miss its roots in the early chapters of Genesis. So also is the impact of the title of William Faulkner's *Absalom, Absalom,* a work based on 2 Samuel 13–18. Characters in Flannery O'Connor's novel *The Violent Bear it Away* show the mark of the biblical prophets. Recent novelists like John Updike (a Protestant), Graham Greene (a Catholic), and Bernard Malamud (a Jew), to name but a few, have used biblical themes in their works. They are often more subtle than the direct allusions to the Bible of earlier writers, but they are no less important to a full understanding of these authors' works.[6]

THE BIBLE AND CONTEMPORARY POPULAR CULTURE

Pop culture offers examples of imaginative use of the Bible; for instance, the hit musicals *Godspell, Jesus Christ Superstar,* and *Joseph and the Amazing Technicolor Dream Coat,* the first two based on the Gospels and the last on the Joseph story in Genesis. *Joseph* and *Superstar* are both by Andrew Lloyd Weber. All of these have enjoyed major professional revivals and have become staples for community theatres and college and school companies. Science fiction sometimes offers unorthodox interpretations of the Bible, as, for example, Robert Heinlein's *Stranger in a Strange Land.* The so-called *Christ figure* has become virtually a stock character in post–World War II literature and films. One was the convict of the title in *Cool Hand Luke,* effectively portrayed by Paul Newman. Other, more explicit movies about Jesus, such as *The Last Temptation of Christ,* have inspired heated discussion and led to public demonstrations. Jeffery Katzenburg's animated feature, *The Prince of Egypt,* offers a somewhat fictionalized account of the life of Moses.[7]

As we move through the twenty-first century, the influence of the Bible on popular culture is becoming more, not less, pervasive. A prominent example is *The Da Vinci Code,* a novel by American author Dan Brown, which combines the popular mystery/detective and conspiracy genres. First published in 2003, by March, 2006, the hardcover edition had sold forty million copies, been translated into forty-two languages, and appeared on the *New York Times* bestseller list for 155 continuous weeks. *The Da Vinci Code,* which Brown claimed in a preface was based on "facts," was considered by many readers a true account of aspects of the life of Jesus not mentioned in the New Testament. Other readers believed the novel to be an insidious assault on essential claims of Christianity. A number of books, inspired by the novel and the controversy that swirled around it, have been published.[8]

The novel's chief protagonist, Dr. Robert Langdon, is a Harvard University religious studies professor, implying to some that the work has a level of academic credibility despite its fictional nature. According to the story the novel tells, Jesus was actually married to one of the women mentioned in

---

[6]See Ira Brent Driggers and Brent A. Strawn. "Poetry" and Jaime Clark-Soles, Patrick Gray, and Brent A. Srawn, "Prose: Fiction and Nonfiction," *Teaching the Bible Through Popular Culture and the Arts,* ed. Mark Roncace and Patrick Gray. Atlanta: Society of Blbilcal Literature, 2007, pp. 251-327.

[7]See the Annotated Bibliography at the end of the book for a list of movies inspired by the Bible. For a fuller discussion of movies directly based on the Bible or influenced by Biblical themes, see Nicola Denzey and Patrick Gray. "The Bible in Film" and "Nonbiblical Narrative in Film," *Teaching the Bible Through Popular Culture and the Arts,* ed. Mark Roncace and Patrick Gray. Atlanta: Society of Blbilcal Literature, 2007, pp. 97–172.

[8]See, for example, Bart D. Eherman. *Truth and Fiction in the Da Vinci Code.* New York: Oxford University Press, 2004.

the New Testament, Mary Magdalene, by whom he fathered a daughter whose descendants became a royal dynasty of France. As the plot unfolds, readers are drawn into a centuries old struggle between *Opus Dei,* a mysterious Roman Catholic organization committed to keeping the story of the lineage of Jesus from being revealed, and a secretive society, the Priory of Sion, whose mission is to protect the bloodline of Jesus. The Catholic Church labeled Mary Magdalene as a prostitute, according to the novel, in order to discredit her, while the rituals of the Priory of Sion manifest the union of the masculine and feminine dimensions of God. The title of the novel, and its central mysteries, relate to its claim that the great artist and scientist of the Renaissance, Leonardo Da Vinci (along with a number of other famous figures in the European history), was a member of the Priory of Sion and symbolically expressed the intimate relationship between Jesus and Mary Magdalene in his famous painting, *The Last Supper,* and the union of the sacred masculine and feminine in the enigmatic portrait, *The Mona Lisa.*

The twists and turns and layered symbolism of *The Da Vinci Code,* which was turned into a Hollywood movie in 2006, are much too complex to summarize further here. From our perspective, the depth and breadth of interest in the novel and movie demonstrate the vitality of the contemporary world of the Bible in twenty-first century popular culture. Many of the novel's readers have been inspired to explore for themselves not only the New Testament gospels' accounts of Jesus, but the apocryphal gospels (see Chapter 15) and the various legends on which Dan Brown, and the works he drew on as sources, used to spin the tale of Jesus and Mary Magdalene and their descendants.

Brown was sued for plagiarism in a British court by authors of works from which he was alleged to have copied. Despite Brown's claim in the book's preface, that *The Da Vinci Code* was based on history, his successful defense in the plagiarism case was that the work was "pure fiction." Historians who analyzed the book have agreed that *The Da Vinci Code* should be considered imaginative fiction.

In 2009 filmmaker James Cameron (of *Titanic* fame) released the 3D movie *Avatar.* Not only was *Avatar* a blockbuster hit, the movie was seen by some viewers as yet another cinematic interpretation of key biblical themes. In *Avatar* Jake Sully, a paraplegic Marine, takes the form of the indigenous *Na'vi* people of Pandora in order to convince them to leave their homeland so it can be mined for precious minerals. However, Sully bonds with the Na'vi people and resists those out to destroy them. Some who saw the movie consider it a twenty-first century retelling of a central biblical story—the power of unconditional love to redeem those open to it when greed and arrogance corrupt. Sully, they say, is, like Adam, a symbol for all humanity, faced with the choice of living in harmony with creation or succumbing to the lust for power. Or, others suggest, Sully is a Christ figure, an incarnation who sacrifices himself that others may live, and, in the process, enters into life eternal. Others who saw *Avatar* take the opposite view and claim the movie was an attack on the Bible and its values. They contend it glorified the pagan practice of worshiping nature condemned in the Bible, and took its central theme not from the Bible but from Hinduism. *Avatar,* they point out, is a Sanskrit term that, in Hinduism, means the manifestation of the divine in material form. Jake Sully, they contend, is more like Krishna, the warrior in the Hindu epic *The Bhagavad Gita,* who is revealed to be an *avatar* of the god Vishnu, than Christ or any biblical figure.

Educational television and serious cable channels such as A&E, Discovery, and the History Channel regularly run documentaries on biblical topics and biblical characters. Such presentations vary widely in quality, ranging from popular accounts of respectable scholarship to deliverances from the lunatic fringe. The four-part PBS series *From Jesus to Christ* (1998) is a model of balanced presentation of the views of prominent historians and New Testament scholars. Television is also a source of information (and misinformation!) on biblical archaeology. Viewers should be suspicious from the start of the program that presents "the lone crusader," the scholar whose discovery or solution to a mystery is rejected by the "establishment." The viewer is led through an hour-long saga that culminates in the exoneration of the crusader in the film, but not in the real world. Maverick scholars have made important discoveries (see Chapter 2, on revisionism), but most frequently the maverick views simply are not supported by sufficient evidence or compelling arguments.

    Scholarly culture and popular culture enjoyed a most congenial encounter with The Gospel of Judas (see Chapter 15), thanks to the responsible behavior of the National Geographic Society. The Society put up the money to purchase the document and secured competent scholars to conserve, edit, translate, and interpret the document. The Gospel of Judas will be deposited in an appropriate museum where it may be studied by qualified scholars and viewed by the public. The Society correctly anticipated that, given its sensational contents—the relationship between Jesus and Judas Iscariot—there was the potential for great public interest. The Judas gospel was given the full treatment as a major media event, but always in a respectable scholarly fashion. There was a feature spread in the April 2006 edition of *National Geographic* with the exquisite photography for which the magazine is renowned plus additional historic and contemporary illustrations and carefully crafted text. Further comments from scholars were included in the May edition. The Gospel was featured in a television documentary (which has been issued as a DVD), and the Society released two reasonably priced books (*The Gospel of Judas* and *The Lost Gospel: The Quest for the Gospel of Judas*). While scholars may discover that, contrary to some claims, the Gospel of Judas does not include any new historical information about Jesus or Judas, it does provide a window into the Cainites, one of the gnostic groups in second century Christianity.

    The Discovery Channel screened a documentary, *The Lost Tomb of Jesus,* in 2007, the handiwork of filmmaker and star of the show, Simcha Jacobovici, and producer James Cameron, of *Titanic* and now *Avatar* fame. The film claims to have identified Jesus' Jerusalem family tomb and to have found a number of ossuaries that once preserved the bones of Jesus; his mother, Mary; his wife, Mary Magdalene; their son, Judah; and other members of the family, including a previously unknown Matthew. Six of the boxes had inscriptions, one of which read "Jesus son of Josepeh." The ossuaries have been in Israel Archaeology Authority storage since 1980, when the tomb in which they were placed was unearthed during a construction project in Talpiyot, a Jerusalem suburb.

    The Talpiyot Tomb, as it is known in the archaeological record, was fully published by archaeologist Amos Kloner, who identified it as the tomb of a fairly well-to-do Jerusalem family.[9] A documentary with similar claims as *The Lost Tomb of Jesus* was shown on BBC in 1996 and dismissed by scholars. The 2007 documentary does offer two new items. A sophisticated statistical analysis purports to show that the names on the ossuaries had to be Jesus' family. Archaeologists note that the names were so popular at the time that the statistics are not very meaningful. In addition, DNA analysis of residue in the "Jesus" and "Mary Magdalene" boxes showed the two were not related. However, this does not prove who they were or if they were married.

    Among scholars of note, only James Tabor of the University of North Carolina at Charlotte, a member of the production team, offers even qualified support for the thesis. Apparently, the remarks of some scholars who were consulted in the production were edited to suggest more support than they intended.

    Entertainment TV no longer shies away from biblical themes, even controversial ones, as it once did. One example is the wildly popular *The Simpsons,* an animated series that lampoons virtually every aspect of modern American life and culture, including the Bible and its interpreters. By the 2010 season *The Simpsons* had aired nearly 500 episodes in twenty-one years, making it the

---

[9]See, Simcha Jacobovici and Charles Pellegrino. *The Jesus Tomb: The Discovery, the Investigation and the Evidence That Could Change History.* San Francisco: HarperOne, 2008 for the argument that the Talpiyot tomb houses the bones of Jesus and his family and Don Sausa, ed. *The Jesus Tomb: Is It Fact or Fiction? Scholars Chime In.* London: The Vision Press, 2007 for essays by scholars disputing Jacobovici and Pellegrino's claims.

longest running entertainment series in the history of American television. Episodes revolve around an allegedly "typical" American family—the comically dysfunctional Simpsons (Homer, the father; his wife, Marge; ten-year-old, perpetual troublemaker Bart; eight-year-old, budding social activist Lisa; and pacifier-sucking, baby Maggie) and a host of other quirky characters. Some commentators have noted that while caricaturing biblical zealots like the Simpson's pious neighbor Ned Flanders the show often reflects a nuanced and positive interpretation of biblical stories and themes.[10] For example, a second-season episode entitled "Homer versus Lisa and the 8th Commandment," addressed the contemporary relevance of the Ten Commandments. Another, "Homer Badman," from the sixth season, brought the story of the innocent sufferer Job to life in a humorous but also engaging and thoughtful manner. "Simpson's Bible Stories," from the tenth season, shows the bored Simpsons daydreaming in church that they are characters in Bible stories like the Garden of Eden. A final example, first broadcast in the seventeenth season (2006), "The Monkey Suit," took up the issue of the conflict between a literal interpretation of the Genesis account of creation (represented by Ned Flanders) and Evolution (defended by Lisa). Other popular animated series, including *South Park* and *Family Guide,* feature episodes on biblical characters and themes.

These examples of the Bible's influence on popular culture only scratch the surface. As you read fiction and poetry, and go to plays and movies and watch television, be sensitive to the presence of biblical themes and allusions, and ask yourself how they contribute to the meanings of the works. It will be a rewarding endeavor, leading to a fuller appreciation of modern culture and the manifold ways in which the Bible is still influencing our perception of ourselves and our world.

THE BIBLE AND AMERICAN CIVIL RELIGION

Another interesting area in which the Bible is shaping modern life was opened up for exploration by Robert Bellah's provocative essay "Civil Religion in America" (1970). As a social scientist, Bellah realized that all political states develop some organized set of symbols to legitimate the nation. The nations of Europe drew on traditional Christianity in the form of established churches to achieve an underlying symbol system. But the diverse religious affiliations present at the birth of the United States made the establishment of any particular church denomination impossible.

Thus, by happenstance or design, a religious symbol system began to emerge that cemented and celebrated the national identity of America. Important aspects of this symbol system drew on biblical themes, especially from the Hebrew canon. These include the Exodus (from oppression in Europe) and the coming to a promised land in the New World. To the founders of the United States, America was a "new Israel" chosen by God to be his people in a noble new experiment. According to Bellah, the early versions of American civil religion avoided any allusions to the New Testament. However, the Civil War introduced such New Testament ideas as redemption through suffering, sacrifice, and rebirth.

Many interpreters feel that this biblically based civil religion, which is apart from any particular denomination, is still an important ingredient in understanding the special dynamics of American life. Some contemporary observers wonder whether an American Civil Religion can continue to function in the even more diverse religious climate of twenty-first century society. Actually, the largest number of "new Americans" are Hispanics, most of them Catholic, changing the Protestant/Catholic balance but not the prevalence of people sympathetic to the claims of Civil

---

[10]See Mark Pinsky, *The Gospel according to the Simpsons, Bigger and Possibly Even Better Edition.* Louisville, KY: Westminster John Knox Press, 2007. For an episode guide, with summaries, and a list of references in episodes to the Bible, see The Simpsons Archives (*snpp.com*).

Religion. Muslims, a new element in the American mix, are unlikely to be offended by the language of the Civil Religion and may find it congenial. The South and East Asian religions such as Hinduism, Sikhism, and Buddhism (some forms of which are in fact theistic, affirming a personal god at the center of life) are notably tolerant. If there is a threat to the Civil Religion, it is more likely to arise from homegrown sources, on the one hand a radical form of secularism that seems bent on extirpating the word "God" from all public discourse, and on the other extremist Christian fundamentalism which seeks to turn the country from a democracy into a theocracy. The Civil Religion flourishes best in an atmosphere of civility, and the culture wars in which these positions constitute the polar opposites that dominate public discourse are anything but civil. American Civil Religion flourished at a time of great national turbulence in the nineteenth century. Time will tell whether it can survive the social turbulence of the twenty-first.

CONCLUSION

The final conclusion must therefore be that the third world of the Bible, the contemporary world, is very much alive and well. An awareness of the Bible and its continuing influence remains essential for anyone who desires to grapple with the question of where we are and where we might be going. Whether from the perspective of a religious community or a more neutral vantage point, the Bible cannot be avoided, not merely for its historical and literary value, but for its continuing role in shaping our world. Journey on!

ANNOTATED BIBLIOGRAPHY

No one book or type of book can encompass all information that an explorer, even a beginning explorer, in the various biblical worlds might wish to have. We have assembled here a limited list of resources for further study of the three worlds of the Bible. Our intent is to be suggestive rather than exhaustive. Our bibliography includes only general works, not those that relate to specific books or passages.

GENERAL

Bibliographical Aids

To locate works on particular biblical passages in major English language periodicals in the field of biblical studies, consult the Humanities Index. Notes on virtually all published scholarly works in biblical studies may be found in the following: *New Testament Abstracts; Old Testament Abstracts;* and *Religious and Theological Abstracts.* These are now available in CD-ROM and/ or online format. Additional bibliographical guides include *Religion Index* and *Elenchus* (associated with the journal *Biblica*). There are now countless web sites on the Internet with discussion of biblical books and passages. Net "surfers" need to be cautioned that due to the unsupervised nature of the Internet, the truthfulness and reliability of comments will vary greatly. Let the reader beware! Here are a *few* web sites the authors recommend as ways to initiate a search for helpful information.

> *sbl-site.org—the web site of the Society of Biblical Literature (SBL), the major professional organization in biblical studies, with links to other biblical studies sites. An electronic version of the SBL's Review of Biblical Literature, with articles on recent works in biblical studies, is available at.bookreviews.org/.*

> *wabashcenter.wabash.edu/resources/guide_headings. aspx—a gateway to resources in the study of religion, including study of the Bible, maintained by the Wabash Center for Teaching and Learning in Theology and Religion. See especially the Internet Guide to Religion's section on Archaeology, Bible, and Classics.*

> *ntgateway.com—a gateway for the academic study of the New Testament, maintained by Dr. Mark Goodacre of Duke University.*

The following sites focus on archaeology in the ancient Near East:

> *asor.org—the site of the American Schools of Oriental Research.*

> *oi.uchicago.edu—the site of Oriental Institute at the University of Chicago, with links to resources in the study of the ancient Near East.*

> *english.imjnet.org.il/htmls/home.aspx—web site of the Israel Museum in Jerusalem.*

Bible Dictionaries

A Bible dictionary is an extremely useful tool for students of the Bible. It includes articles about words, topics, persons, and events in and relating to the Bible. Two very good one-volume Bible dictionaries are:

The HarperCollins Bible Dictionary, rev. ed. San Francisco: HarperSanFrancisco, 1996.

Eerdmans Dictionary of the Bible. Grand Rapids, MI: Eerdmans, 2000.

Two sets of Bible dictionaries are the most useful reference works for biblical studies in English. They are actually encyclopedias rather than dictionaries, for they include detailed articles by recognized experts.

Anchor Bible Dictionary, 6 vols. Garden City, NY: Doubleday, 1992. (Available in CD-ROM.)

The New Interpreter's Dictionary of the Bible, 5 vols. Nashville, TN: Abingdon, 2006–2009

Two dictionaries provide excellent descriptive theological studies of key words in the Bible. Although the words are in the original languages, these resources can be used even by students who do not know these languages.

Theological Dictionary of the New Testament, 10 vols. Grand Rapids, MI: Eerdmans, 1964–1984. Abridged edition, 1986.

Theological Dictionary of the Old Testament, 12 vols. Grand Rapids, MI: Eerdmans, 1978–2006. Abridged edition, 1986.

Specialized Bible dictionaries have also been published. The following are among the best:

Jacob Neusner and William Scott Green, eds. *Dictionary of Judaism in the Biblical Period.* Peabody, MA: Hendrickson, 1999.

Karel van der Toorn, Bob Becking, and Pieter W. van der Horst, eds. *Dictionary of Deities and Demons in the Bible,* 2nd edn. Grand Rapids, MI: Eerdmans, 1999.

Concordances

A concordance is an alphabetic listing of the words occurring in a particular body of literature. For example, concordances on the works of writers like Shakespeare have been prepared. A number of Bible concordances are available. They are a great help in studying a particular concept (such as *righteousness*) or in locating the appearances in the Bible of a particular person, word, or idea. Only those that list words in the original languages of the Bible (Hebrew, Greek, and Aramaic) are universally useful. However, for students studying the Bible in English, concordances keyed to various translations are available. Those called "analytical" concordances include helpful linguistic information. Here are two examples, keyed to the New Revised Standard Version, which we have utilized in this book. They include the books of the Deuterocanon.

John R. Kohlenberger, ed. *The Concise Concordance to the New Revised Standard Version.* Oxford: Oxford University Press, 1993.

R. E. Whitaker, et al., eds. *The Analytical Concordance to the New Revised Standard Version of the New Testament.* Grand Rapids, MI: Eerdmans, 2000.

A useful concordance based on the King James Version is:

Robert Young, ed. *Young's Analytical Concordance to the Bible.* (Available from several publishers, including Eerdmans, Nelson, and Hendrickson.)

An online concordance to a number of versions of the Bible is available at *biblegateway.com.*

Commentaries

A commentary is an extremely valuable tool when actually reading the Bible closely. Commentaries usually contain introductory articles on a number of relevant topics, followed by verse-by-verse explanatory notes to clear up difficulties in understanding the text at hand.

Several good one-volume commentaries, covering all the books of the Bible, are available.

HarperCollins Bible Commentary. San Francisco: HarperSanFrancisco, 2000.

The Oxford Bible Commentary. New York: Oxford University Press, 2007. Available on CD-ROM.

Commentary on the Torah with a New English Translation. San Francisco: Harper Collins, 2003.

The New Interpreter's One Volume Commentary. Nashville, TN: Abingdon, 2010.

The New Jerome Biblical Commentary. Englewood Cliffs, NJ: Prentice Hall, 1990.

Global Bible Commentary. Nashville, TN: Abingdon, 2004.

Africa Bible Commentary. Grand Rapids, MI: Zondervan, 2010.

The Women's Bible Commentary. Expanded edn. Louisville: Westminster/John Knox Press, 1998.

The IVP Women's Bible Commentary. Downer's Grove, IL: Intervarsity Press, 2002.

Eerdmans Commentary of the Bible. Grand Rapids, MI: Eerdmans, 2003.

Zondervan Bible Commentary: One Volume Illustrated Edition. Grand Rapids, MI: Zondervan, 2008.

Some commentaries devote an entire volume or more to a single biblical book. Such works are most useful to serious students or persons engaged in research projects. Commentaries too numerous to survey here on individual books by experts on that book are available. In addition, multivolume series, with volumes on most, if not all, biblical books, may also be found in most academic libraries. Some of the most widely used are:

The Anchor Bible (translations and notes).

Hermeneia.

Interpretation.

The Interpreter's Bible.

The Jewish Publication Society Torah Commentary.

The New International Commentary on the Old and New Testament.

The New Interpreter's Bible.

The Old and New Testament Libraries.

Word Biblical Commentary.

Introductions

The Bible in General

S. Daniel Breslauer. *Decoding Religion in the Bible: Learning to Recognize the Diversity of Biblical Texts.* Cornwall-on-Hudson, NY: Sloan, 2007.

J. Bradley Chance and Milton P. Horne. *Rereading the Bible: An Introduction to the Biblical Story.* Upper Saddle River, NJ: Prentice Hall, 1999.

John B. Gabel, et al. *The Bible as Literature: An Introduction,* 5th edn. New York: Oxford University Press, 2005.

Susanne Scholz, ed. *Biblical Studies Alternatively: An Introductory Reader.* Upper Saddle River, NJ: Prentice Hall, 2003.

The Tanak (Hebrew Bible, Old Testament)

Bernard W. Anderson, Steven Bishop, and Judith Newman. *Understanding the Old Testament,* 5th edn. Upper Saddle River, NJ: Pearson Prentice Hall, 2007.

Bruce Birch, Walter Brueggemann, and Terrence Fretheim. *A Theological Introduction to the Old Testament, 2nd edn.* Nashville: Abingdon, 2005.

James E. Bowley, *Introduction to Hebrew Bible: A Guided Tour of Israel's Library.* Upper Saddle River, NJ: Pearson Prentice Hall, 2008.

John J. Collins. *Introduction to the Hebrew Bible.* Minneapolis: Augsburg/Fortress, 2004.

Norman Gottwald. *The Hebrew Bible: A Brief Socio-Literary Introduction.* Minneapolis: Fortress Press, 2008.

Stephen L. McKenzie and John Kaltner, *The Old Testament: Its Background, Growth, and Contents.* Nashville: Abingdon, 2007.

John Tullock and Mark McEntire. *The Old Testament Story,* 8th edn. Upper Saddle River, NJ: Pearson Prentice Hall, 2009

The New Testament

Raymond E. Brown. *An Introduction to the New Testament.* New York: Doubleday, 1997.

Catherine A. Cory, *A Voyage Through the New Testament.* Upper Saddle River, NJ: Pearson Prentice Hall, 2008.

Luke Timothy Johnson. *The Writings of the New Testament,* 3rd edn. Minneapolis: Fortress Press, 2010.

Howard Kee. *Understanding the New Testament,* 5th edn. Englewood Cliffs, NJ: Prentice Hall, 1993.

Marla J. Selvidge. *Exploring The New Testament,* 2nd edn. Upper Saddle River, NJ: Prentice Hall, 2002.

Robert A. Spivey, D. Moody Smith, and C. Clifton Black. *Anatomy of the New Testament,* 6th edn. Minneapolis: Fortress, 2010.

The Deuterocanon (Apocrypha) and Larger Apocrypha (Pseudepigrapha)

G. W. E. Nickelsburg. *Jewish Literature Between the Bible and the Mishnah: A Historical and Literary Introduction,* 2nd edn., with CD-ROM. Philadelphia: Fortress, 2005.

Methodological Works

Several good introductory surveys on methods of interpreting the Bible are:

John Barton. *The Nature of Biblical Criticism.* Louisville: Westminster John Knox, 2007.

Marc Zvi Brettler. *How to Read the Bible.* New York: Jewish Publication Society of America, 2006.

Susan E. Gillingham, *One Bible, Many Voices: Different Approaches to Biblical Studies.* Grand Rapids, MI: Eerdmans, 1999.

Stephen Haynes and Steven McKenzie. *To Each Its Own Meaning: An Introduction to Biblical Interpretations and Their Applications,* rev. edn. Louisville: Westminster/John Knox Press, 1999.

Richard A. Soulen and R. Kendall Soulen. *Handbook of Biblical Criticism,* rev. edn. Louisville: Westminster John Knox, 2001.

A series of works for general readers on most of the traditional and more recent methods of biblical interpretation is available from Fortress Press.

Periodicals

The most recent research in biblical studies, as in other disciplines, appears in learned journals. These will be of use to students engaged in specific research projects.

Journals that include articles on both the Tanak and New Testament include the following.

Bible Review. Beautifully illustrated articles intended for general readers. Ceased publication, but available online through the Biblical Archaeological Society (*bibarch.org*).

Biblical Interpretation: A Journal of Contemporary Approaches. A European journal published by E. J. Brill Publishers.

The Catholic Biblical Quarterly. High-quality research from both Catholic and non-Catholic scholars.

Journal of Biblical Literature. The most prestigious journal in English.

Journals with articles on the Tanak and the Deuterocanon include:

Journal for the Study of the Old Testament. Published in England. Features articles that utilize innovative literary and social scientific methods.

Vetus Testamentum. Also published in England. Articles in English, French, and German.

Zeitschrift für die alttestamentliche Wissenschaft. A German journal with frequent articles in English.

Journals with articles on the New Testament include companions to the publications listed previously:

Journal for the Study of the New Testament.

New Testament Studies.

Zeitschrift für die neuestestamentliche Wissenschaft.

Journals with reports on the relationship between archaeology and biblical studies include:

Biblical Archaeology Review.

Bulletin of the American Schools of Oriental Research.

The Israel Exploration Journal.

Near Eastern Archaeology formerly *Biblical Archaeologist.*

Translations into English

We will mention here only three works, the most useful editions of the New Revised Standard Version. They are recommended for use by individual readers and in classes.

Walter J. Harrelson, et al., eds. *The New Interpreter's Study Bible.* Nashville: Abingdon, 2003.

Wayne A. Meeks, gen. ed. *The HarperCollins Study Bible: A New Annotated Edition by the Society of Biblical Literature.* San Francisco: HarperSanFrancisco, 2006.

Michael Coogan, et al., eds. *The New Oxford Annotated NRSV Bible with the Apocryphal Books,* 4th edn. New York: Oxford University Press, 2010.

LITERARY WORLD

General

Robert Alter and Frank Kermode, eds. *The Literary Guide to the Bible.* Cambridge, MA: Harvard University Press, 1990. Includes essays on each of the books of the Bible.

Jeanie C. Crain. *Reading the Bible as Literature.* Cambridge, UK: Polity Press, 2010.

Northrop Frye. *The Great Code: The Bible and Literature.* New York: Mariner Books, 2002.

A unique approach to the Bible by one of the most influential modern literary critics.

Northrop Frye. *Words with Power: Being a Second Study of "The Bible and Literature,"* ed. Michael Dolzani. Toronto: University of Toronto Press, 2008.

Leland Ryken and Tremper Longman. *A Complete Literary Guide to the Bible.* Grand Rapids, MI: Zondervan, 1993.

Amos Wilder. *The Bible and the Literary Critic.* Minneapolis: Augsburg/Fortress Press, 1991.

Formal Criticism

Robert Alter. *The Art of Biblical Narrative.* New York: Basic Books, 1983. All three of Alter's excellent and provocative works are on the Tanak.

Robert Alter. *The Art of Biblical Poetry.* New York: Basic Books, 1987.

Robert Alter. *The World of Biblical Literature.* New York: Basic Books, 1991.

Yairah Amit. *Reading Biblical Narratives.* Minneapolis Fortress Press, 2001.

James L. Bailey and Lyle D. Vander Broek, eds. *Literary Forms in the New Testament: A Handbook.* Louisville: Westminster Press, 1992.

Harold Bloom, *Jesus and Yahweh: The Names Divine.* New York: Riverhead Books, 2005

Harold Fisch, *Poetry with a Purpose: Biblical Poetics and Interpretation.* Bloomington: Indiana University Press, 1990.

Michael Fishbane. *Biblical Text and Texture: A Literary of Selected Texts.* Oxford, UK: Oneworld, 1998.

Jack Miles. *Christ: A Crisis in the Life of God.* New York: Vintage, 2002.

Jack Miles. *God: A Biography.* New York: Alfred A. Knopf, 1996.

Meir Sternberg. *The Poetics of Biblical Narrative: Ideological Literature and the Drama of Reading.* Bloomington: Indiana University Press, 1987.

Rhetorical Criticism

The following works offer good introductions to this method in the Hebrew Bible and New Testament:

Alan J. Hauser and Duane F. Watson. *Rhetorical Criticism of the Bible.* Leiden, Netherlands: Brill, 1994.

Dale Patrick and Alan Scult. *Rhetoric and Biblical Interpretation.* Sheffield, Eng.: Almond Press, 2009.

Phyllis Trible and Gene Tucker. *Rhetorical Criticism.* Minneapolis: Fortress Press, 1994.

Ben Witherington III. *New Testament Rhetoric: An Introductory Guide to the Art of Persuasion in and of the New Testament.* Eugene, OR: Wipf and Stock, 2008.

The following works combine rhetorical analysis with concerns of feminist interpretation:

Phyllis Trible. *God and the Rhetoric of Sexuality.* Minneapolis: Fortress, 1986.

Phyllis Trible. *Texts of Terror: Literary–Feminist Readings of Biblical Narratives.* Minneapolis: Fortress, 2003.

Narrative Criticism

Shimeon Bar-Efrat. *Narrative Art in the Bible,* Trans. Dorothy Shefer-Vanson. London: T&T Clark International, 2004.

Adele Berlin. *Poetics and Interpretation of Biblical Narrative.* Winona Lake IN: Eisenbrauns, 1994.

J. P. Fokkelman. *Reading Biblical Narrative: An Introductory Guide.* Louisville: Westminster/John Knox, 2000.

James L. Resseguie. *Narrative Criticism of the New Testament: An Introduction.* Grand Rapids, MI: Baker, 2005.

Jerome T. Walsh. *Old Testament Narrative: A Guide to Interpretation.* Louisville: Westminster/ John Knox Press, 2010.

HISTORICAL WORLD

Among the literally thousands of works that explore the original historical contexts of the Bible and reconstruct the history of the Bible, the following are a representative sample:

Histories

Ancient Israel

Thomas Cahill. *The Gifts of the Jews: How a Tribe of Desert Nomads Changed the Way Everyone Thinks and Feels.* New York: Doubleday, 1999.

Michael D. Coogan, ed. *The Oxford History of the Biblical World.* New York: Oxford University Press, 2001.

John Day, ed. *In Search of Pre-Exilic Israel.* London: T&T Clark, 2004.

J. Andrew Dearman. *Religion and Culture in Ancient Israel.* Peabody, MA: Hendrickson, 1999.

William G. Dever. *Who Were the Early Israelites and Where Did They Come From?* Grand Rapids, MI: Eerdmans, 2006.

Philip H. King and Lawrence E. Stager. *Life in Biblical Israel.* Louisville: Westminster/John Knox Press, 2002.

Victor H. Matthews. *A Brief History of Ancient Israel.* Louisville: Westminster John Knox Press, 2002.

Carol Meyers. *Household and Holiness: The Religious Culture of Israelite Women.* Minneapolis: Fortress, 2005.

J. Maxwell Miller and John H. Hayes. *A History of Ancient Israel and Judah,* 2nd edn. Philadelphia: Westminster, 2006.

Hershel Shanks, ed. *Ancient Israel: A Short History from Abraham to the Roman Destruction of the Temple,* rev. edn. Washington, DC: Biblical Archaeology Society Press, 1999.

The Intertestamental Period

George W. E. Nickelsburg. *Jewish Literature Between the Bible and the Mishnah.* 2nd edn. with CD-ROM. Minneapolis: Fortress, 2005.

The New Testament Period

Robert L. Anderson and Terry Giles. *The Keepers: An Introduction to the History and Culture of the Samaritans.* Peabody, MA: Hendrickson, 2002.

Gary Burge, et. al. *The New Testament in Antiquity: A Survey of the New Testament within its Cultural Context.* Grand Rapids, MI: Zondervan, 2009.

John Dominic Crossan. *The Birth of Christianity.* San Francisco: HarperSanFrancisco, 1999.

James G. Crossley, *Why Christianity Happened: A Sociohistorical Account of Christian Origins (26–50 C.E.).* Louisville: Westminster John Knox, 2006.

Bart Ehrman. *The Lost Christianities: The Battle for Scripture and the Faiths We Never Knew.* New York: Oxford University Press, 2003.

Elisabeth Schüssler Fiorenza. *In Memory of Her: A Feminist Theological Reconstruction of Christian Origins.* New York: Crossroad Herderd Herder, 1994.

Richard Horsley and Neil Asher Silberman. *The Message and the Kingdom: How Jesus and Paul Ignited a Revolution and Transformed the Ancient World.* Minneapolis: Fortress, 2002.

Hans Josef Klauck. *The Religious Context of Early Christianity: A Guide to Graeco-Roman Religion.* Minneapolis: Fortress, 2003.

George W. E. Nickelsburg. *Ancient Judaism and Christian Origins.* Minneapolis: Fortress, 2003.

Hershel Shanks, ed. *Christianity and Rabbbinic Judaism: A Parallel History of their Origins and Early Development.* Washington, DC: Biblical Aracheology Society Press, 1992.

Leif E. Vaage, ed. *Religious Rivalries in the Early Roman Empire and the Rise of Christianity.* Waterloo, ON: Wilfred Laurier, 2006.

The "Historical" Jesus

James Beilby, ed. *The Historical Jesus—Five Views.* Downers Grove, IL: Intervarsity Press, 2009.

Marcus Borg. *Jesus: Uncovering the Life, Teachings, and Relevance of a Religious Revolutionary.* San Francisco: HarperOne, 2008.

Marcus Borg and N. T. Wright. *The Meaning of Jesus: Two Visions,* 2nd edn. San Francisco: HarperSanFrancisco, 2007.

John Dominic Crossan. *Jesus: A Revolutionary Biography.* San Francisco: HarperOne, 2009.

John Dominic Crossan and Jonathan Reed. *Excavating Jesus,* rev. ed. San Francisco: Harper SanFrancisco, 2003.

James D. G. Dunn and Scott McNight, eds. *The Historical Jesus in Recent Research.* Winona Lake, IN: Eisenbrauns, 2005.

Bart D. Ehrman. *Jesus: Apocalyptic Prophet of the New Millennium.* New York: Oxford University Press, 2001.

Elisabeth Schüssler Fiorenza. *Jesus: Miriam's Child, Sophia's Prophet.* New York: Continuum, 1994.

Paula Fredriksen. *Jesus of Nazareth, King of the Jews: A Jewish Life and the Emergence of Christianity.* New York: Vintage, 2000.

Sean Freyne. *Jesus, a Jewish Galilean: A New Reading of the Jesus Story.* London: T&T Clark, 2004.

Amy-Jill Levine. *The Misunderstood Jew: The Church and the Scandal of the Jewish Jesus.* San Francisco: HarperSanFrancisco, 2006.

Hyam Macoby. *Jesus the Pharisee.* London: SCM, 2003.

John P. Meier. *A Marginal Jew: Rethinking the Historical Jesus.* 4 vols. New York and New Haven: Doubleday and Yale University Press, 1991, 1994, 2001, 2009.

E. P. Sanders. *The Historical Figure of Jesus.* New York: Penguin, 1996.

Robert E. Van Voorst. *Jesus Outside the New Testament.* Grand Rapids, MI: Eerdmans, 2000.

Geza Vermes. *Jesus in His Jewish Context.* Minneapolis: Fortress, 2003.

Geza Vermes. *The Religion of Jesus the Jew.* Minneapolis: Fortress, 2003.

Geza Vermes. *Who's Who in the Age of Jesus.* New York: Penguin, 2006.

The "Q" (Sayings) Source

Marcus Borg. *The Lost Gospel Q: The Original Sayings of Jesus.* Berkeley, CA: Ulysses Press, 1999.

John S. Kloppenborg. *Excavating Q: The History and Setting of the Sayings Gospel.* Louisville: Westminster/ John Knox Press, 2008.

Burton L. Mack. *The Lost Gospel: The Book of Q and Christian Origins.* San Francisco: HarperSanFrancisco, 1994.

Atlases and Geographies

Historical atlases on the Bible wed geographic and historical considerations and provide both maps and a narrative, bringing the two into conjunction.

Adrian Curtis. *The Oxford Bible Atlas,* 4th edn. New York: Oxford, 2009.

Anson Rainey, R. Steven Notlry, M. Avi-Yonah, and Ze'ev Safrai, eds. *The Sacred Bridge: Carta's Atlas of the Biblical World.* Jerusalem: Carta, 2006.

> The best work in providing geographic placement of each biblical event, replacing *The Macmillan Biblical Atlas.*

Historical geographies provide a more detailed narrative correlating history and geography.

Y. Aharoni. *The Land of the Bible,* rev. edn. Philadelphia: Westminster, 1979.

> Still the most authoritative work.

Denis Baly. *The Geography of the Bible,* rev. edn. New York: Harper & Row, 1974.

> The best source on physical geography and the geology of Israel.

Texts and Images Relating to the Bible from Ancient Near Eastern Cultures

Some of the many texts, discovered by archaeologists, that shed light on the historical context of the Bible have been collected and translated into English in the following volumes:

C. K. Barrett, ed. *The New Testament Background: Selected Documents,* rev. edn. San Francisco: HarperSanFrancisco, 1995.

Craig A. Evans. *Ancient Texts for New Testament Studies: A Guide to the Background Literature.* Peabody, MA: Hendrickson, 2005.

Victor H. Matthews and Don C. Benjamin. *Old Testament Parallels: Laws and Stories from the Ancient Near East.* 3rd edn. New York: Paulist Press, 2007.

Simon Parker. *Stories in Scripture and Inscriptions: Comparative Studies in North-west Semitic Inscriptions and the Hebrew Bible.* New York: Oxford University Press, 1997.

James Pritchard, ed., *The Ancient Near East: An Anthology of Texts and Pictures.* Princeton: Princeton University Press, 2010.

Jack M. Sasson, et al., eds. *Civilizations of the Ancient Near East* (4 vols). New York: Charles Scribner's Sons, 1995.

Kenneth L. Sparks. *Ancient Texts for the Study of the Hebrew Bible.* Peabody, MA: Hendrickson, 2005.

John H. Walton. *Ancient Near Eastern Thought and the Old Testament: Introducing the Conceptual World of the Hebrew Bible.* Grand Rapids, MI: Baker, 2006.

Archaeology

The following works introduce the history and methods of archaeology:

Ian Hodder, ed. *Theory and Practice in Archaeology.* New York: Routledge, 1995

Thomas E. Levy and Thomas Higham, ed. *The Bible and Radiocarbon Dating: Archaeology, Text and Science.* London: Equinox Press, 2005.

Colin Renfrew and Paul Bahn. *Archaeology: Theories, Methods, and Practice.* New York: Thames and Hudson, 1991.

Of the many works in biblical archaeology, the following are to be recommended:

Y. Aharoni. *The Archaeology of the Land of Israel.* Philadelphia: Westminster, 1982.

Obed Borowski. *Daily Life in Biblical Times.* Leiden: Brill, 2003.

Fabio Bourbon and Enrico Lavagno. *The Holy Land: Archaeological Guide to Israel, Sinai and Jordan.* White Star Publishers, 2009. An excellent guide for travel to archaeological sites.

William Dever. *Did God Have a Wife? Archaeology and Folk Religion in Ancient Israel.* Grand Rapids, MI: Eerdmans, 2008.

Israel Finkelstein, et. al. *The Quest for the Historical Israel: Debating Archaeology and the History of Early Israel.* Atlanta: Society of Biblical Literature, 2007.

Alfred J. Hoerth. *Archaeology and the New Testament.* Ada, MI: Baker Academic, 2009.

Ann E. Killebrew. *Biblical Peoples and Ethnicity: An Archaeological Study of Egyptians, Canaanites, Philistines and Early Israel. 1300–1100 B.C.E.* Atlanta/Leiden, Netherlands: SBL/Brill, 2005.

John McRay. *Archaeology and the New Testament. Ada, MI:* Baker Academic, 2008.

Eric Meyers, et al., eds. *The Oxford Encyclopedia of Archaeology in the Near East* (5 vols). New York: Oxford University Press, 1996.

Eric Meyers and James Strange. *Archaeology, the Rabbis, and Early Christianity.* Nashville, TN: Abingdon, 1981.

Ephraim Stern. *The New Encyclopedia of Archaeological Excavations in the Holy Land.* Jerusalem: Carta, 1993.

The Dead Sea Scrolls

The most readable translation of the Dead Sea Scrolls into English include:

F. Garcia Martinez and W. G. E. Watson.. *The Dead Sea Scrolls Translated,* 2nd edn. Leiden: Brill Academic Publishers, 1997.

Geza Vermes. *The Complete Dead Sea Scrolls in English,* rev. edn. New York: Penguin, 2004.

Michael Wise, *et. al. The Dead Sea Scrolls—Revised Edition: A New Translation.* San Francisco: HarperOne, 2005.

Among the many studies of the Dead Sea Scrolls and their importance for the study of the Bible, students may wish to consult:

Michael Thomas Davis, et al., eds. *Qumran Studies: New Approaches, New Questions.* Grand Rapids, MI: Eerdmans, 2007.

Maxine L. Grossman, ed. *Rediscovering the Dead Sea Scrolls: An Assessment of Old and New Approaches and Methods.* Grand Rapids, MI: Eerdmans, 2010.

Jodi Magness, *The Archaeology of Qumran and the Dead Sea Scrolls.* Grand Rapids, MI: Eerdmans, 2003.

Lawrence H. Schiffman, *Qumran and Jerusalem: Studies in the Dead Sea Scrolls and the History of Judaism.* Grand Rapids, MI: Eerdmans, 2010.

Eileen M. Schuller. *The Dead Sea Scrolls: What Have We Learned?* Louisville: Westminster John Knox, 2006.

James C. VanderKam. *The Dead Sea Scrolls Today,* rev. edn. Grand Rapids, MI: Eerdmans, 2010.

Geza Vermes. *An Introduction to the Complete Dead Sea Scrolls.* Minneapolis: Fortress Press, 2000.

Literary History

The major results of research on the literary history of the Bible are summarized in the introductions mentioned above and in works such as:

David Aune. *The New Testament in Its Literary Environment.* Philadelphia: Westminster, 1987.

Martin J. Buss. *Biblical Form Criticism in Its Context.* Sheffield, England: Sheffield Academic Press, 1999.

Richard Elliott Friedman. *Who Wrote the Bible?* San Francisco: HarperSanFrancisco, 1997.

Richard Elliott Friedman. *The Hidden Book in the Bible: The Discovery of the First Prose Masterpiece.* San Francisco: HarperSanFrancisco, 1999.

James L. Kugel. *The Bible as It Was.* Cambridge, MA: Harvard University Press, 1999.

Burton Mack. *Who Wrote the New Testament?* San Francisco: HarperSanFrancisco, 1996.

Canonization

The process of canonization is studied in:

Craig A. Evans And Emmanuel Tov, eds. *Exploring the Origins of the Bible: Canon Formation in Historical, Literary, and Theological Perspective.* Ada, MI: Baker Academic, 2008.

Lee Martin McDonald. *The Biblical Canon: Its Origin, Transmission and Authority,* 3rd edn. Peabody, MA: Hendrickson, 2007.

James A. Sanders. *Canon and Community.* Eugene, OR: Wipf & Stock, 2000.

Jed Wyrick. *The Ascension of Authorship: Attribution and Canon Formation in Jewish, Hellenistic, and Christian Tradition.* Cambridge: Harvard University Press, 2004.

Translation

F. F. Bruce. *History of the Bible in English,* 3rd edn. New York: Oxford University Press, 1978.

Bruce Metzger, *The Bible in Translation: Ancient and English Versions.* Ada, MI: Baker Academic, 2001.

History of Biblical Interpretation

Alan J. Hauser and Duane F. Watson. *A History of Biblical Interpretation. Vol. 1–2:.* Grand Rapids, MI: Eerdmans, 2003, 2009.

Henning Graf Reventlow. *History of Biblical Interpretation. Vols. 1–2.* Atlanta: Society of Biblical Literature, 2009.

John Sandys-Wunsch. *What Have They Done to the Bible? A History of Modern Biblical Interpretation.* Michael Glazier, 2005.

Richard N. Soulen. *Sacred Scripture: A Short History of Interpretation.* Louisville: Westminster/John Knox, 2009.

Social Scientific Interpretation

Here are representative examples of the growing numbers of studies that apply the principles and methods of modern sociological and anthropological analysis to the study of the Bible:

Anthony J. Blasi, Jean Duhamime, and Paul-Andre Turcotte, eds. *Handbook of Early Christianity: Social Science Approaches.* Lanham, MD: Altarmira Press, 2002.

Charles E. Carter and Carol L. Meyers, eds. *Community, Identity and Ideology: Social Science Approaches to the Hebrew Bible.* Winona Lake, IN: Eisenbrauns, 1998.

Ferdinand Deist. *Material Culture of the Bible: An Introduction.* Sheffield, UK: Sheffield Academic Press, 2000.

Philip F. Esler, ed. *Ancient Israel: The Old Testament in its Social Contexts.* Minneapolis: Augsburg Fortress, 2005.

N. K. Gottwald. *The Politics of Ancient Israel. The Library of Ancient Israel.* Louisville: Westminster/John Knox, 2001.

Louise J. Lawrence and Mario I. Aguilar, eds. *Anthropology and Biblical Studies: Avenues of Approach.* Leiden: Dech, 2004.

Bruce J. Malina. *The New Testament World: Insights from Cultural Anthropology,* 3rd edn. Louisville: Westminster/John Knox Press, 2001.

Victor H. Matthews. *The Social World of the Hebrew Prophets.* Peabody, MA: Hendrickson, 2003.

Wayne Meeks. *The First Urban Christians: The Social World of the Apostle Paul.* New Haven: Yale University Press, 1983.

Rodney Stark. *The Rise of Christianity.* San Francisco: HarperSanFrancisco, 1997.

John Van Seters. *The Pentateuch: A Social-Science Commentary.* Sheffield, England: Sheffield Academic Press, 1999.

CONTEMPORARY WORLD

A listing of works that arise from the devotional, ethical, and liturgical uses of the Bible in the contemporary world is beyond the scope of this bibliography. We include here a few examples of more traditional works in biblical theology and some of the recently developed methods that emphasize aspects of the contemporary world:

Hermeneutics

Suited for general readers, the following works introduce readers to the methods and problems associated with finding the meaning of the Bible in the contemporary world.

Walter C. Kaiser, Jr. and Moisés Silva. *An Introduction to Biblical Hermeneutics,* rev. edn. Grand Rapids, MI: Zondervan, 2007.

Alan G. Padgett and Patrick R. Keifert, eds. *But Is It All True? The Bible and the Question of Truth.* Grand Rapids, MI: Eerdmans, 2006.

W. Randolph Tate. *Biblical Interpretation: An Integrated Approach,* 3rd edn. Peabody, MA: Hendrickson, 2008.

Theological Works

The now-classic theological interpretations of the Bible include:

Rudolf Bultmann. *Theology of the New Testament,* 2nd edn. Trans. Kendrick Grobel Waco, TX: Baylor University Press, 2007.

Walter Eichrodt. *Theology of the Old Testament,* 2 vols. Trans. J. A. Baker. Philadelphia: Westminster, 1961–67.

Gerhard Von Rad. *Old Testament Theology,* Trans. D. M. G. Stalker. New York: Westminster/ John Knox, 2001.

More recent works that offer innovative interpretations include:

Walter Brueggemann. *Theology of the Old Testament: Testimony, Dispute, Advocacy.* Minneapolis: Fortress Press, 1997.

James D. G. Dunn. *New Testament Theology: An Introduction.* Nashville: Abingdon Press, 2009.

John Goldingay. *Old Testament Theology, 3 vols.* IVP Academic: 2003, 2006, 2009

Frank J. Matera. *New Testament Theology: Exploring Diversity and Unity.* Louisville: Westminster/ John Knox, 2007.

James K. Mead. *Biblical Theology: Issues, Methods, Themes.* Louisville: Westminster/ John Knox, 2007.

Dale Patrick. *The Rhetoric of Revelation in the Hebrew Bible.* Minneapolis: Fortress Press, 1999.

Reader Response Criticism

A. K. M. Adam. *Faithful Interpretation: Reading the Bible in a Postmodern World.* Minneapolis: Fortress Press, 2006.

George Aichele, et al., eds. *The Postmodern Bible: The Bible and Culture Collective.* New York: Yale University Press, 1995.

Note: This work includes discussion of reader-response criticism, poststructuralist criticism (deconstruction), psychoanalytic criticism, feminist and womanist criticism, and ideological criticism.

Robert Detweiler, ed. *Reader Response Approaches to Biblical and Secular Texts.* Harrisburg, PA: *Semeia* 31, 1985.

Robert Fowler. *Let the Reader Understand: Reader-Response Criticism and the Gospel of Mark.* Harrisburg, PA: Trinity Press International, 2001.

Edgar McKnight. *Post-Modern Use of the Bible: The Emergence of Reader-Oriented Criticism.* Nashville, TN: Abingdon, 1988.

Kevin J. Vanhoozer. *Is There a Meaning in the Text? The Bible, The Reader and the Morality of Literary Knowledge.* Grand Rapids, MI: Zondervan, 2009.

Liberation Criticism

Among the many provocative works on reading the Bible from the perspective of oppressed and marginalized peoples are:

David Tuesday Adamo, *Biblical Intepretation in African Perspective.* University Press of America, 2006.

Alejandro F. Botta and Pablo R. Andiñach, edn. *The Bible and the Hermeneutics of Liberation.* Atlanta: Society of Biblical Literature, 2009.

Carol J. Dempsey. *The Prophets: A Liberation—Critical Reading.* Minneapolis: Fortress Press, 2000.

Cain Hope Felder, ed. *Stony the Road We Trod: African American Biblical Interpretation.* Minneapolis: Augsburg Press, 1991.

Norman K. Gottwald and Richard Horsley, eds. *The Bible and Liberation: Political and Social Hermeneutics.* Maryknoll, NY: Orbis, 1999.

Jose Miranda. *Communism in the Bible.* Maryknoll, NY: Orbis, 1982.

D. N. Premnath, ed. *Border Crossings: Cross-Cultural Hermeneutics.* Maryknoll, NY: Orbis, 2007.

R.S. Sugirtharajah, ed. *Asian Biblical Hermeneutics and Postcolonialism,* Maryknoll, NY: Orbis, 1999.

R.S. Sugirtharajah, ed. *Voices from the Margin: Interpreting the Bible in the Third World,,* 3rd edn. Maryknoll, NY: Orbis, 2006.

Gerald O. West. *The Academy of the Poor: Towards a Dialogical Reading of the Bible.* Sheffield, England: Sheffield Academic Press, 1999.

Feminist Criticism

Hee An Choi and Kathryn Pfisterer Darr, eds. *Engaging the Bible: Critical Readings from Contemporary Women.* Minneapolis: Fortress Press, 2006.

Adela Yarbro Collins, ed. *Feminist Perspectives in Biblical Scholarship.* Chico, CA: Scholars Press, 1985.

Elisabeth Schüssler Fiorenza. *Wisdom Ways: Introducing Feminist Biblical Interpretation.* Obis Books, 2001.

Tikva Frymer-Kensky. *Reading the Women of the Bible: A New Interpretation of Their Stories.* New York: Schocken Books, 2004.

Tikva Frymer-Kensky. *Studies in Bible and Feminist Criticism.* Jewish Publication Society, 2006.

Carol L. Meyers. *Discovering Eve: Ancient Israelite Women in Context.* New York: Oxford University Press, 1988.

Ilona N. Rashkow. *Taboo or Not Taboo: Sexuality and Family in the Hebrew Bible.* Minneapolis: Fortress Press, 2000.

F. Scott Spencer. *Dancing Girls, Loose Ladies, and Women of the Cloth.* New York: Continuum, 2004.

Phyllis Trible, et al. *Feminist Approaches to the Bible.* Washington, DC: Biblical Archaeological Society, 1995.

Renita Weems. *Just a Sister Away: A Womanist Vision of Women's Relationships in the Bible.* San Diego: Luramedia, 1988.

The Bible in Western, Art, Music, and Literature

Roland Bartel, ed. *Biblical Images in Literature,* Nashville: Abingdon, 1975.

David R. Cartilidge. *Art and the Christian Apocrypha.* New York: Routledge, 2001.

Carol Crown, ed. *Coming Home! Self-Taught Artists, the Bible, and the American South.* Jackson: University Press of Mississippi, 2004.

David Curzon, ed. *Modern Poems on the Bible: An Anthology.* Philadelphia: Jewish Publication Society, 1994.

Chiara DeCapoa. *Old Testament Figures in Art.* Trans. Thomas M. Hartmann. Los Angeles: J. Paul Getty Museum, 2003.

John Drury. *Painting the Word: Christian Pictures and Their Meanings.* New Haven: Yale University Press, 1999.

Colin Duriez, ed. *The Poetic Bible: A Selection of Classic and Contemporary Poetry Inspired by the Bible from Genesis to Revelation.* Peabody, MA: Hendrickson, 2001.

J. Cheryl Exum and Ela Nutu, eds. *Between the Text and Canvas: The Bible and Art in Dialogue.* Sheffield, UK: Sheffield Phoenix Press, 2007.

David Jasper and Stephen Pickett, eds. *The Bible and Literature: A Reader.* Oxford: Blackwell, 1999.

K. R. R. Gros Louis et.al. *Literary Interpretations of Biblical Narratives.* Nashville: Abingdon, 1978.

Jules Lubbock. *Storytelling in Christian Art from Giotto to Donatello.* New Haven: Yale University Press, 2006.

Martin O'Kane. *Painting the Text: The Artist as Biblical Interpreter.* Sheffield, UK: Sheffield Phoenix Press, 2009.

Dorothy Sollee, et. al. *Great Women of the Bible in Art and Literature.* Grand Rapids, MI: Eerdmans, 1994.

Susan Wright. *The Bible in Art.* New York: New Line Books, 2005.

Terry R. Wright. *The Genesis of Fiction: Modern Novelists as Biblical Interpreters.* Ashgate, 2007.

The Bible in Popular Culture

Roland Boer. *Knockin' on Heaven's Door: The Bible and Popular Culture.* New York: Routledge, 1999.

Paul C. Burns, *Jesus in Twentieth Century Art, Literature, and Movies.* New York: Continuum, 2007.

J. C. Exum, *Plotted, Shot, and Painted: Cultural Representations of Biblical Women.* Sheffield. UK: Sheffield Academic Press, 1996.

Michael J. Gilmour, ed. *Call Me the Seeker: Listening to Religion in Popular Music.* New York: Continuum Books, 2005.

Mark McEntire. *Raising Cain, Fleeing Egypt, and Fighting Philistines: The Old Testament in Popular Music.* Macon, GA: Smyth & Helwys, 2006.

Mark Roncace and Patrick Gray, eds. *Teaching the Bible Through Popular Culture and the Arts.* Atlanta: Society of Biblical Literature, 2007.

Robin Sylvan. *Traces of the Spirit: The Religious Dimensions of Popular Music.* New York: New York University Press, 2002.

The Bible in Films

George Aichele and Richard Walsh, eds. *Screening Scripture: Intertextual Connections Between Scripture and Film.* Harrisburg, PA: Trinity Press, 2002.

Bruce Babington and Peter Williams Evans, *Biblical Epics: Sacred Narratives in Hollywood Cinema.* New York: St. Martin's, 1993.

Mark G. Boyer. *Using Film to Teach New Testament.* Lanham, MD: University Press of America, 2002.

Eric S. Christianson *et al. Cinéma Divinité: Religion, Theology and the Bible in Film.* London: SCM-Canterbury, 2005.

Stephenson Humphries-Brooks. *Cinematic Savior: Hollywood's Making of the American Christ.* Westport, CT: Praeger, 2006.

Larry Kneitzer. *The Old Testament in Fiction and Film.* Sheffield, Eng.: Sheffield Academic Press, 1994.

Adele Reinhartz. *Jesus of Hollywood.* New York: Oxford University Press, 2007.

Adele Reinhartz. *Scripture on the Silver Screen.* Louisville: Westminster/John Knox, 2003.

Erin Runions. *How Hysterical: Identification and Resistance in Bible and Film.* New York: Palgrave Macmillan, 2003.

David Shepherd, ed. *Images of the Word: Hollywood's Bible and Beyond.* Atlanta: Society of Biblical Literature, 2008.

Jeffrey L. Staley and Richard Walsh. *Jesus, the Gospels, and Cinematic Imagination.* Louisville: Westminster/ John Knox, 2007.

W. Barnes Tatum. *Jesus at the Movies: A Guide to the First Hundred Years.* Santa Rosa, CA: Polebridge, 1997.

Richard Walsh. *Finding St. Paul in Film.* New York: T&T Clark, 2005.

Civil Religion

Robert Bellah. *The Broken Covenant: American Civil Religion in a Time of Trial.* New York: Seabury, 1975.

Robert Bellah. *Varieties of Civil Religion.* San Francisco: Harper & Row, 1980.

Conrad Cherry, ed. *God's New Israel: Religious Interpretations of American Destiny,* rev. ed. Chapel Hill, NC: The University of North Carolina Press, 1998.

THE INTERPRETATION OF THE BIBLE IN MOTION PICTURES AND FILMS

Hebrew Bible (Old Testament)

Intolerance (1916, 178 minutes)

D. W. Griffith's epic film combining four stories of prejudice and inhumanity, beginning with one set in the Babylonian period. No rating.

Samson and Delilah (1949, 128 minutes)

A famous dramatization of the story of Samson (Judges 13–16), featuring his infatuation with the Philistine beauty Delilah. Starring Victor Mature and Hedy Lamarr. Directed by Cecil B. DeMille. Remade for television in 1984 (with Mature as Samson's father) and 1996. No rating.

David and Bathsheba (1951, 116 minutes)

Gregory Peck and Susan Hayward star in a dramatization of the adulterous relationship between King David and Bathsheba, and the subsequent tragedies (2nd Samuel 11–First Kings 2). Directed by Henry King. No rating.

The Ten Commandments (1956, 220 minutes)

Perhaps the most famous biblical epic, telling the story of the life of Moses. Starring Charlton Heston as Moses. Directed by Cecil B. Demille, who made a silent film with the same title in 1923. No rating.

Solomon and Sheba (1959, 120 minutes)

Yul Brynner and Gina Lollobrigida star in an expansion of the story of the Israelite king and the foreign queen (First Kings 10). Directed by King Vidor. No rating.

David and Goliath (1960, 95 minutes)

A badly reviewed Italian adaptation of the encounter between the youthful David and the Philistine giant (First Samuel 17). Directed by Richard Pottier. No rating.

The Story of Ruth (1960, 132 minutes)

An adaptation of the story of one of the many heroic women of the Bible. Directed by Henry Koster. No rating.

Sodom and Gomorrah (1963, 154 minutes)

An Italian film, expansively telling the story of the two biblical cities that symbolize evil and depravity (Genesis 19). Directed by Robert Aldrich. No rating.

The Bible (1966, 174 minutes)

Narrated by the film's director, John Huston, a made-for-television dramatization of most of the stories found in Genesis 1–22. Intended as the first installment of a series of dramatic movies on the Bible; no others were made. No rating.

The Fixer (1968, 132 minutes)

Based on Bernard Malamud's novel, a Joban story of a falsely accused Jewish handyman in Russia early in the twentieth century. Starring Alan Bates. Directed by John Frankenheimer. No rating.

Wholly Moses (1980, 109 minutes)

Dudley Moore stars in this comedy about a man who thinks God has chosen him to lead the Hebrew slaves out of bondage in Egypt. Directed by Gary Weis. Rated PG.

King David (1985, 114 minutes)

Breaking from the "epic" tradition of early movies on the Bible, a dramatic, but more straightforward, account of David's life from his boyhood encounter with Goliath through his Kingship of the united Israel. Starring Richard Gere as David. Directed by Bruce Beresford. Rated PG–13.

Prince of Egypt (1999, 129 minutes)

An animated version of the life of Moses, emphasizing his relationship with his sister Miriam and the young Pharaoh. Directed by Jeffrey Katzenburg. Rated G.

Joseph: King of Dreams (2000, 75 minutes)

An animated version of the story of Joseph (Genesis 37–50). Directed by Rob LaDuca and Robert C. Ramirez. Rated G.

One Night with the King (2006, 123 minutes)

A dramatization of the life story of Hadassah, who became Queen Esther, based on the Book of Esther. Directed by Michael.Sajbel. Rated PG.

Evan Almighty (2007, 96 minutes).

A sequel to *Bruce Almighty* (2003), Evan Baxter (Steve Carell) is directed by God (Morgan Freeman) to build an ark. Advertised as a "comedy of Biblical proportions." Directed by Tom Shadyac Rated PG.

New Testament

Gospels

King of Kings (1927, 115 minutes)

The most acclaimed silent film on the life of Jesus. Directed by Cecil B. DeMille. No rating.

The Robe (1953, 135 minutes)

An adaptation of the Lloyd Douglas novel about the Roman centurion in charge of the crucifixion of Jesus. Starring Richard Burton, Jean Simmons, and Victor Mature. Directed by Henry Koster. No rating.

Ben-Hur (1959, 212 minutes)

An epic film, based on Lew Wallace's novel about the Jewish slave Ben-Hur, who encounters Jesus. Won eleven Academy Awards. Directed by William Wyler. No rating. A 1926 silent film entitled "Ben-Hur: A Tale of Christ" was also made.

Barabbas (1961, 134 minutes)

Adaptation of a novel based on the Jewish revolutionary freed by Pontius Pilate, who gave the crowds the opportunity to call for the freedom of Jesus instead. Starring Anthony Quinn. Directed by Richard Fleischer.

The King of Kings (1961, 168 minutes)

Narrated by Oscar Wells, starring Jeffrey Hunter as Jesus. Acclaimed musical score by Miklos Rozsa. Directed by Nicholas Ray. No rating.

The Gospel According to St. Matthew (1964, 135 minutes)

Mostly amateur actors in a moving, straightforward presentation of the first New Testament gospel. Directed by Enrique Izazoqui, a Marxist. Italian, dubbed in English. No rating.

The Greatest Story Ever Told (1965, 141 minutes)

An adaptation of the gospel story of the life of Jesus. Featuring many of the major stars of the period, including Max von Sydow as Jesus. Directed by George Stevens. No rating.

Cool Hand Luke (1967, 126 minutes)

Story about a prison camp, with Paul Newman in the title role. Some interpreters see the protagonist as a "Christ figure." Directed by Stuart Rosenberg. No rating.

The Ruling Class (1972, 154 minutes)

Black comedy about a modern British heir to a lordship who thinks he is Jesus. Starring Peter O'Toole. Directed by Peter Medak. Rated PG.

Godspell (1973, 103 minutes)

Based on a popular musical play, a retelling of the story of the life of Jesus set in modern New York City. Directed by David Greene. Rated G.

Jesus Christ Superstar (1973, 103 minutes)

An adaptation of the acclaimed Tim Rice–Andrew Webber Broadway musical. Directed by Norman Jewison. Rated G.

Jesus of Nazareth (1977, 6 hours)

A made-for-television adaptation of the gospels' accounts of the life of Jesus, with Robert Powell as Jesus. Directed by Franco Zefferelli. No rating.

Jesus (1979, 117 minutes)

Filmed in Israel, a fairly straightforward retelling of the story of Jesus. Directed by Peter Sykes. Rated G.

Life of Brian (also *Monty Python's Life of Brian*) (1979, 93 minutes)

The satirical story of a man whose life parallels the life of Jesus. Features the Monty Python ensemble, including John Cleese and Terry Gilliam. An irreverent crucifixion scene. Directed by Terry Jones. Rated R.

The Last Temptation of Christ (1988, 164 minutes)

An adaptation of Nikos Kazantzakis' novel of the same title, speculating on the self-doubts of Jesus when he becomes aware that God had chosen him. Boycotted by some Christians who considered it blasphemous. Acclaimed by others moved by the portrayal of the humanity of Jesus. Willem Defoe as Jesus. Directed by Martin Scorsese. Rated R.

Jesus of Montreal (1989, 119 minutes)

In Montreal a group of actors stages an unconventional passion play. In the process they confront both religious hypocrisy and materialism, but also experience the power of the story. French, dubbed in English. Directed by Denys Arcand. Rated R.

Matthew (1996)

An ambitious project, based on the Gospel of Matthew. Directed by Regardt van den Bergh. No rating.

Jesus (1999, 120 minutes)

A made-for-television movie directed by Roger Young, with Jeremy Sisto as Jesus.

Mary, Mother of Jesus (1999, 105 minutes)

A made-for-television movie in the *Hallmark Hall of Fame* series, adapting the gospels' accounts of the relation between Mary and Jesus. Starring Pernilla August and Melinda Kinnaman as Mary, Christian Bale as Jesus of Nazareth, Geraldine Chaplin as Elizabeth, and David Threfall as Joseph. Directed by Kevin Connor and produced by Eunice Kennedy Shriver and Robert Shriver. No rating.

The Miracle Maker (2000, 90 minutes)

An animated feature. Directed by Derek Itayes and Stanislav Sokolov. Voice of Jesus by Ralph Fiennes.

The Passion of the Christ (2004, 90 minutes)

The last twelve hours in the life of Jesus. Directed by Mel Gibson. James Caviezel as Jesus. See the Questions for Discussion and Reflection at the end of Chapter 12 on the controversy surrounding this movie. Rated R.

The Nativity Story (2006, 101 minutes)

A dramatization of the gospel accounts of the journey of Mary and Joseph from Nazareth to Bethlehem and the birth of Jesus. Directed by Catherine Hardwicke. Rated PG.

The Son of Man (2006, 86 minutes)

One man's journey of love, deception and betrayal in contemporary South Africa, based on the story of Jesus in the gospels. Directed by Mark Dornford-May. Not rated.

The Da Vinci Code (2006, 149 minutes 174 minutes [extended cut])

Based on the bestselling thriller by Dan Brown, the novel and film draw on two extracanonical early Christian writings, *The Gospel of Mary* and *The Gospel of Philip*. See Ch. 16 for a full discussion. Directed by Ron Howard. Rated PG-13.

Other New Testament

The Four Horsemen of the Apocalypse (1921, 131 minutes)

Acclaimed silent film, telling the story of cousins who end up fighting on opposite sides in World War I. The title and theme relate to the apocalyptic devastation symbolized by four horses in Revelation 6:2–8. Directed by Rex Ingram. Remade in 1962. No rating.

The Sign of the Cross (1932, 118 minutes)

An account of the persecution of Christians under the emperor Nero. Directed by Cecil B. DeMille. No rating.

The Seventh Seal (1957, 96 minutes)

The classic story of a disillusioned knight returning from the Crusades, who plays chess with Death. The seventh seal refers to the last seal on the scroll to be opened at the time of the end (Revelation 8:1). Directed by Ingmar Bergman. No rating.

The Seventh Sign (1988, 98 minutes)

An "end-of-the-world" thriller, starring Demi Moore, loosely inspired by the seven signs of the end in the Book of Revelation. Directed by Carl Schultz. Rated R.

For information on ordering the above motion pictures for personal use, contact one of the following:

Facets (800/532–2387; *facets.org*)

Movies Unlimited (800/466–8347; *moviesunlimited.com*)

Documentary Films on the Bible

Apocalypse (1999, two hours)

A PBS-Frontline documentary on the history of interpretation of the Book of Revelation, with commentary by leading scholars of apocalyptic movements.

Ancient Secrets of the Bible

Explorations of some of the most controversial mysteries of the Bible, with claims of evidence to validate the stories. Scholars and skeptics debate. The series includes the following titles:

Ark of the Covenant: Lost or Hidden Away (1995, 24 minutes)

Battle of David and Goliath: Truth or Myth? (1994, 27 minutes)

Fiery Furnace: Could Anyone Survive It? (1995, 29 minutes)

Moses' Red Sea Miracle: Did It Happen? (1995, 28 minutes)

Moses' Ten Commandments: Tablets from God? (1994, 30 minutes)

Noah's Ark: Was There a Worldwide Flood? (1995, 34 minutes)

Samson: Strongman Hero or Legend? (1994, 32 minutes)

Shroud of Turin: Fraud or Evidence of Christ's Resurrection? (1995, 35 minutes)

Sodom and Gomorrah: Legend or Real? (1994, 24 minutes)

Tower of Babel: Fact or Fiction? (1995, 24 minutes)

Walls of Jericho: Did They Tumble Down? (1994, 22 minutes)

Biblical Archaeology Society Series

Hosted by Hershel Shanks, editor of *Bible Review* and *Biblical Archaeology Review*.

The Archaeology of Jerusalem from David to Jesus (1990, 74 minutes)

Biblical Archaeology: From the Ground Down (1996, 90 minutes)

From Jesus to Christ: The First Christians (1998, four hours)

A PBS-TV series on the life of Jesus and the history of the movement he started. Interviews with leading scholars of the historical Jesus are featured. A set combining the video and the book *From Jesus to Christ: The Origins of the New Testament Images of Jesus* by Paula Fredriksen is available.

Genesis: A Living Conversation

A group of biblical scholars, theologians, artists, and others in engaging conversations about stories in the Book of Genesis, hosted by Bill Moyers in a PBS—TV series. Each story is dramatically read by actors Mandy Patinkin and Alfre Woodard. Produced in 1996, 120 minutes each, with a total of ten 60 minute segments focusing on characters in Genesis.

In God's Image and Temptation (Adam and Eve)

First Murder and Apocalypse (Cain and Abel, Noah)

Call and Promise and A Family Affair (Abraham and Sarah, Sarah and Hagar)

God Wrestling and Exile (Jacob, Isaac, and Rebekah)

Blessed Deception and the Test (Abraham and Isaac, Joseph and His Brothers)

Accompanying volumes include Bill Moyers's *Genesis: A Living Conversation* (New York, Main Street Books [Doubleday], 1996) and *Talking About Genesis: A Resource Guide* (New York: Doubleday, 1996).

Holy Quest: In Search of Biblical Relics

Scholars in search of artifacts related to the Bible.

Castle of the Holy Grail (1996, 42 minutes)

Dead Sea Scrolls (1996, 41 minutes)

Quest for the Lost Ark of the Covenant (1996, 40 minutes)

Turin Shroud (1996, 42 minutes)

Jesus: From the Gospel

Based on the Gospel of Luke, shot in Israel. Narrated by Orson Welles and Alexander Scourby.

Birth (1994, 48 minutes)

Parables (1994, 48 minutes)

Passion (1994, 48 minutes)

Mysteries of the Bible

Drawing on contemporary biblical scholarship and the latest archaeological discoveries, a number of the "mysteries" of the Bible are explored. The episodes include:

Abraham: One Man, One God (1994, 50 minutes)

Apocalypse: The Puzzle of Revelation (1994, 50 minutes)

The Execution of Jesus (1994, 50 minutes)

Joseph: Master of Dreams (1994, 50 minutes)

Philistines: The Arch Enemy (1994, 50 minutes)

Prophets: Soul Catchers (1994, 50 minutes)

Queen Esther: Far Away and Long Ago (1994, 50 minutes)

Biblical Angels (1996, 50 minutes)

Cain and Abel (1996, 50 minutes)

Heaven and Hell (1996, 50 minutes)

Herod the Great (1996, 50 minutes)

The Last Revolt (1996, 50 minutes)

The Last Supper (1996, 50 minutes)

Archenemy: The Philistines (1998, 50 minutes)

The Bible's Greatest Secrets (1998, 50 minutes)

Who Wrote the Bible? (1998, 50 minutes)

Testament: The Bible and History

Shot on location, one scholar's search for the historical context of the Hebrew Bible and New Testament as well as the history of the interpretation of the Bible through the medieval period.

As It Was in the Beginning (1991, 60 minutes)

Chronicles and Kings (1991, 60 minutes)

Gospel Truth (1991, 60 minutes)

Mightier Than the Sword (1991, 60 minutes)

Paradise Lost (1991, 60 minutes)

Power and the Glory (1991, 60 minutes)

Thine Is the Kingdom (1991, 60 minutes)

Ancient Evidence (2004)

Produced by BBC-TV (500 minutes total)

Mysteries of the Old Testament

Mysteries of Jesus

Mysteries of the Apostles.

Digging for the Truth (History Channel, 2005–2008, 60 minutes each)

Host Josh Bernstein explores various historical mysteries and icons, including the following episodes linked to the Bible:

Quest for King Solomon's Gold (Season One, Episode 6)

The Lost Tribe of Israel (Season One, Episode 8)

The Real Queen of Sheba (Season Two, Episode 8)

The Real Sin City: Sodom and Gomorrah (Season Two, Episode 12)

Lost Treasures of the Copper Scroll (Season Three, Episode 10)

Searching for King David (Season Three, Episode 12)

God's Gold, Parts 1 and 2 (Season Four, Episodes 5 and 6)

Lost Worlds (History Channel, 2005–07. 44 minutes each)

Explorations of various "lost" locations, including the following episodes related to the Bible:

Jesus' Jerusalem (Episode 8, 2006)

The First Christians (Episode 12, 2006)

Herod the Great (Episode 19, 2007)

Lost Superpower of the Bible (Episode 24, 2007)

Armageddon (Episode 26, 2007)

Resurrection: A Search for Answers (ABC-TV, *20/20*, 2006, 45 minutes)

The Bible's Buried Secrets: Archaeology's New Theories (PBS-TV, *Nova*, 2009, 112 minutes)

The latest developments in biblical archaeology are analyzed.

Walking the Bible: A Journey by Land Through the Five Books of Moses (PBS-TV, 2006, 168 minutes on 2 discs)

Based on the best-selling book by journalist Bruce Feiler.

Secrets of the Dead: Battle for the Bible (PBS-TV, 2007, 60 minutes)

The intriguing story of the translation of the Bible into English.

Great Figures of the Bible (PBS-TV, 2004, 510 minutes on 4 discs)

Nobel-prize winner Eli Wiesel explores the compelling stories of great figures of the Tanak.

For the Bible Tells Me So (2007, 98 minutes)

The role of interpretation of the Bible in the debate over homosexuality.

For information on ordering the previous documentary films for personal use, contact the following:

Video Market Place (480/596–9970; *videomarketplace.com*

PBS Videos (877/PBS-SHOP; *shoppbs.org*

GLOSSARY

Note: Most proper names in the Bible and biblical books are not included in this glossary. See the Index for appropriate page references.

Adam Hebrew for "(hu)man." Formed by God from the earth (Hebrew *'adamah*), according to Gen. 2:7. In Paul's letters (see Rom. 5:12–21), "first" Adam (of Genesis) contrasted with "new" Adam (Christ).

Agape A Greek term for "good will." Used in the New Testament to refer to the unconditional love shown by God to humankind in the sending of God's son (see First Corinithians 13).

Alexandria Egyptian city named after Alexander. Largest Jewish population outside Palestine by the first century C.E. Tanak translated into Greek from Hebrew and allegorical method of biblical interpretation perfected here. Philo and other important Jewish and Christian philosophers worked in Alexandria.

Allegorical Referring to a narrative or method of interpretation in which the elements of a literary composition serve as symbols for other religious or moral truths. The allegorical method of interpretation is evident within the Bible (see, for example, Romans 4).

Amarna The modern name assigned to the ruins of the ancient Egyptian city of Akhentaten, capital in the fourteenth century B.C.E. In the ruins, archaeologists discovered over 350 letters, many from rulers of cities in Palestine (including Jerusalem and Megiddo). During the Amarna Age the Egyptian king Akhenaton experimented with the worship of a single god, the sun god Aten.

Anthropology The social science that focuses on the study of human origins, and the development and dynamics of human cultures.

Antichrist The final opponent of Christ. Found in the New Testament only in the Letters of John.

Antioch A Syrian city to which the Christian gospel was brought by Hellenists about 40 C.E. The name *Christian* first used here (Acts 11:26). Center of mission to Gentiles.

Apocalyptic From the Greek for "an uncovering." Refers to literature and movements that speak of the "uncovering" of the secrets of the end of history, the vanquishing of evil, and the beginning of a new age of peace and righteousness.

Apocrypha From the Greek for "hidden." A group of books or portions of books not found in the Jewish canon but included in the Septuagint and early Christian versions of the Old Testament. Most Protestant groups do not consider these works canonical. The Catholic Church considers them a Deuterocanon ("second" canon) to distinguish them from the Jewish canon. In Catholic usage, "Apocrypha" refers to the writings that have become known as the Pseudepigrapha, but that we suggest calling the Larger Apocrypha.

Apostles Greek for "one sent out." In the New Testament the inner circle of followers of Jesus commissioned to carry on his ministry. The "Apostolic Age" in early Christianity is usually dated from the death of Jesus to the Fall of Jerusalem in 70 C.E.

Aramaic A Semitic language closely related to Hebrew, evident from the ninth century B.C.E. onward. Several Tanak passages are in Aramaic (especially Dan. 2:4–7:28). In common use by the first century C.E., so it was the language spoken by Jesus.

Archaeology The scientific study of the material remains of the human past.

Archetype A literary term used to designate recurrent situations, characters, images, symbols, or plots. Often they function in opposites. Recognition of the archetypes in a literary work such as the Bible enhances understanding of the literary world of that text.

Ark of the Covenant The container for the tablets upon which the Ten Commandments were inscribed. A symbolic throne for Yahweh, and thus representative of the divine presence and protection. Placed in the Jerusalem Temple's Holy of Holies.

Armageddon Hebrew for "Mount Megiddo." Transliterated into Greek in Rev. 16:16 as a name for the place of the final, cosmic battle of the forces of good and evil.

Ascension The departure of the Risen Jesus into heaven (Acts 1:2–11).

Asia Minor The western peninsula of Asia, from the Black Sea to the Mediterranean, where Turkey is now located.

Assyria A major ancient Near Eastern empire, located in Mesopotamia, which dominated Israel and the entire region from the ninth through the seventh centuries B.C.E.

Atonement, Day of Ten days after the Fall New Year, a day set aside to confront and remove the sins of the past year. In the Jerusalem Temple the high priest entered the Holy of Holies only on this day, symbolically placing the sins of the people on an animal called the "scapegoat." See Lev. 23:27–32 and Hebrews 8–9.

Ba'al "Lord, Husband." A Canaanite deity associated with thunder-storms, god of fertility. Opposition to worship of Ba'al is a recurrent theme in the Tanak.

Babylonia Ancient Near Eastern empire, located in southern Mesopotamia, which dominated Judah in the later seventh and sixth centuries B.C.E.

Babylonian Exile See **Exile.**

Baptism From the Greek for "immerse in fresh water." A rite of religious purification and regeneration.

B.C.E. Before the Common Era. A neutral designation for the Christian B.C.

Bishop Translation of Greek word (*episcopos*), meaning overseer, guardian. An early Christian office mentioned in Phil. 1:1 and the Pastoral Epistles.

Canaan Name for the region and inhabitants of the land of Palestine, prior to its becoming "Israel." Grandson of Noah (Gen. 9:18–27).

Canon From a Greek term for "rule" or "standard." Any list of religious writings deemed authoritative. The process through which the writings become accepted as authoritative is called *canonization.*

Capernaum The town on the northwest shore of the Sea of Galilee that served as the center of the Galilean ministry of Jesus.

Catholic Epistles See **Epistle.**

C. E. Common Era. A neutral designation for the Christian A.D.

Charismatic From the Greek word for "gift." In general, refers to a spiritual power, and by extension, to the qualities of leadership that come not from office or inheritance, but that mark a particularly powerful, inspiring person. In the New Testament it refers to the particular gifts of the Holy Spirit (see 1 Corinthians 12 and Romans 12).

Christ From the Greek term *Christos,* which translates the Hebrew term *meshiah* (messiah), which means "anointed one." Specifically, the one anointed by God from the house of David to restore the

nation Israel. Became a title associated with Jesus of Nazareth. See **Messiah.**

Circumcision The removal of the foreskin of a male's penis. In ancient Israel a sign of God's covenant with Israel (Genesis 17). The merits of the necessity of the ritual were debated in early Christianity (see Acts 15).

Corinth A major Greek city, with ports on both the Aegean and Adriatic seas. Site of an important Christian congregation. Visited by the Apostle Paul for the first time in 50 C.E.

Cosmos Referring to the entire universe considered as an ordered whole, as opposed to the chaos that precedes and stands against cosmos.

Covenant A formal, sacred treaty or agreement between two parties with each assuming obligation. Refers especially to the relationship established by God with the nation Israel. Several covenants are important in the Bible, including the Noahic Covenant (Genesis 9), the Abrahamic Covenant (see Genesis 12–17), the Sinai Covenant (see Exodus 19–20), the Davidic Covenant (see 2 Samuel 7), and the "new" covenant mentioned in the prophetic books (for example, Jer. 31:31) and understood in the New Testament as the new relationship between God and humans begun with Jesus Christ (see, for example, Mk. 14:24).

Cultic Having to do with the organized, institutional aspect of religion.

D A designation by source critics for the book of Deuteronomy, considering it one of the written sources of the Torah.

Deacons One of the types of ministry and apparent officers in early Christian communities.

Dead Sea Scrolls The writings discovered in caves along the north-west shore of the Dead Sea, beginning in 1947, near a site called Qumran, including at least fragments of almost every book of the Tanak and many documents from the apocalyptic religious community that resided there. Important for understanding Palestinian Judaism and Christian origins as well as providing the earliest evidence of Hebrew texts of the Tanak.

Decalogue The Ten Commandments.

Deuterocanon From Greek for "secondary canon." See **Apocrypha.**

Deuteronomic Code The legal section of the Book of Deuteronomy (Deuteronomy 12–26).

Deuteronomistic History The historical narrative that runs from Deuteronomy through Second Kings. Many modern scholars think the framework of the narrative reflects a pattern of judgment by God on Israel because of the people's failure to follow their covenant obligations. Called Deuteronomic because of stylistic similarities, and because this theology is found in that book.

Diaspora From Greek for "scattered." The Jews who lived outside Palestine after the Babylonian Exile (587 B.C.E.).

Divided Kingdom The period between 922 and 722 B.C.E. when the once united Israel became a Northern Kingdom (Israel) and a Southern Kingdom (Judah). Ended with Assyrian conquest of Israel.

Documentary Hypothesis The theory advanced by modern source critics that the Torah came into existence through the combination of several originally separate "documents." See **J, E, D,** and **P.**

Dualism A perspective that divides a subject into two opposite categories such as good and evil, light and darkness, life and death, matter and spirit.

E The "Elohist," one of the hypothetical sources of the Torah. So named because of the preference for the divine name Elohim. Supposedly deriving from Northern traditions about the origins of Israel and dated to the eighth or ninth centuries B.C.E. Genesis 22:1–19 is a famous "E" passage.

Ebla Modern Tell Mardikh in Syria, site of an important ancient city-state, where a library of tablets was discovered in excavations beginning in the 1960s. The relevance of the finds for the study of the Tanak is debated by scholars.

El The common word for "God" in ancient Semitic languages like Hebrew. The father god and head of the Canaanite pantheon. Appears in personal names in the Bible, such as Elijah ("Yahweh is my God"). Worship of El in pre-Israelite Canaan is suggested in names for God that appear in the ancestral narratives (for example, Gen. 16:7–14).

Elders In ancient Israel, the notable persons of a tribe who were responsible for the maintenance of justice. In the New Testament, either Jewish leaders or officers in Christian communities (translating the Greek *presbuteros*).

Election A theological term used to refer to the belief that God chooses a particular agent (Israel and/or Christ) as an instrument and bearer of divine salvation. In the New Testament the "elect" are those who respond to Christ.

Elohim Hebrew for "gods" or "God." Common name for God in Tanak (occurring over twenty-five hundred times).

Enuma Elish The Babylonian story of creation of the cosmos, resulting from divine combat. So named after the account's first words, in the original language of the text.

Envelope Structure A pattern in which the opening and closing of a literary unit are similar in form, serving to round off and enclose the composition.

Ephesus An important port city in western Asia Minor. Visited on more than one occasion by the Apostle Paul, once for more than two years, according to Acts. Fourth largest city in Roman Empire in the first century C.E. The city has been extensively excavated, revealing many first-century structures.

Episcopos See **Bishop.**

Epistle From Greek *epistole,* letter. Modern scholars distinguish between the more personal and informal "letter" and the more literary, impersonal "epistle" that uses the form of a letter as a literary device.

Eschatological From Greek *eschaton,* last or final. A term used by modern scholars to refer to ideas about the end of history.

Essenes A Jewish sectarian group in existence from mid-second century B.C.E. until about 70 C.E. Most scholars think the group at Qumran that possessed the Dead Sea Scrolls were Essenes. Mentioned as one of several Jewish groups by Josephus.

Eve The first woman (Gen. 2:21–22). Meaning uncertain, but resemblance to Hebrew word for "living" relates to identification as "mother of all living" (Gen. 3:20).

Exile The period during the sixth century B.C.E. when part of the population of Judea was taken into captivity in Babylon.

Exodus The escape of Semitic residents of northern Egypt from forced labor under the leadership of Moses, described in the book of the same name. Becomes a powerful biblical symbol for God's deliverance of the chosen people from bondage. The "New Exodus" refers to the anticipated restoration of the people from Exile in Babylon.

Faith Trust in or reliance on God, in response to God's trustworthiness. One of the most basic and important biblical themes, found in both the Tanak and New Testament.

Forgiveness The "sending away," "covering," "removal," or "wiping away" of hu man sins.

Galatia Both the ancient territory in north central Asia Minor and the Roman province that included this area and others to its south. Thus, New Testament references to Galatia and the Galatians might be to either the territory or the province.

Galilee The forty-five-mile (north to south) region in northern Palestine in which Jesus grew up and conducted most of his public ministry.

Gehenna Hebrew term, meaning Valley of Hinnom, a place near Jerusalem where human sacrifices were once conducted. In the New Testament it was the city dump and thus a symbol for the place of judgment on sinners.

Genealogy A history of the descent of a person or group from an ancestor, or showing the boundaries of a kin group.

Genre A literary term designating literature according to basic, distinctive types.

Gentile From the Latin word for *nation.* A non-Jew.

Gilgamesh Epic A legend about the Mesopotamian king Gilgamesh (c. 2650 B.C.E.). The legend includes a flood account similar to the narrative in Genesis.

Gnostic Referring to a variety of religious movements of the early Christian period that claimed salvation came through *gnosis* (Greek for "knowledge").

God-fearers Gentiles who were attracted to the monotheistic teaching of Judaism and/or the Christian gospel in the Roman world.

Gospel English translation of Greek *euangelion,* "good news." Used in the New Testament to refer to the good news of God's Kingdom proclaimed by Jesus and the good news of what God accomplished for humanity through Jesus. By the second century C.E., referred to the literary genre represented in the New Testament canon by Mark, Matthew, Luke, and John.

Grace In general, that which brings joy or happiness. In the Bible refers to the divine mercy shown toward humans.

Habiru (or Khapiru) Sumerian term for "outcasts." In ancient Near Eastern texts from the third and second millennia, the term refers to various ethnic groups who stood outside the feudal system. The possible association with the "Hebrews" of the Bible is hotly disputed.

Hades Greek word used to translate Hebrew term *sheol,* the abode of the dead.

Haggadah Jewish term for interpretations of Tanak that are devotional, not legal in character (contrast *halakah*). Often supplement the scriptural narrative with stories about principal characters.

Halakah From the Hebrew term for "to walk, go." Refers to the rules that guide the faithful person's life, derived from interpretation of the Torah. The New Testament portrays Jesus engaged in *halakic* discussions with Pharisees (for example, Mt. 12:1–8).

Hanukkah The Jewish festival of dedication, celebrating the purification of the Jerusalem Temple during the Maccabean revolt (164 B.C.E.). During the eight-day festival, a candle is lit each night remembering the miraculous relighting of the Temple menorah (lampstand).

Hebrew The Semitic language in which most of the Tanak was written. Also used to designate the people of the nation Israel. Typically used by foreigners when speaking about Israelites and as a self-designation by Israelites when speaking to foreigners (for example, Gn. 40:15, 41:12, 1 Sam. 13:3).

Hellenistic Referring to the Greek culture that spread throughout the Mediterranean world (including Israel) beginning in the late fourth century B.C.E.

Hellenists A term found only in Acts 6:1 and 9:29, which probably denotes Greek-speaking Jewish members of the early Christian community in Jerusalem.

Heresy Deviation from accepted teaching or practice in a religious community.

Hermeneutics An area of study dealing with the principles and process of interpretation of the Bible or other literature.

Herod In general, a family that ruled Palestine from about 55 B.C.E. until the late first century C.E. The most famous was Herod the Great (40–4 B.C.E.), who was named "King of the Jews" by Roman authorities. His son, Herod Antipas, was ruler of Galilee from 4 B.C.E. to 39 C.E.

Holy of Holies The most sacred portion of the Jerusalem Temple, which housed the Ark of the Covenant. Entered only once a year on the Day of Atonement, and only by the high priest, during the Second Temple period.

Holy Spirit The mysterious power and presence of God within and among humans and nature.

Hymn Any poetic composition praising God. Found in the Book of Psalms and elsewhere in the Tanak (for example, Ex. 15:1–18). In the New Testament some hymns honor Christ (for example, Phil. 2:6–11).

Immortality Endless existence, life beyond death. A Hellenistic idea that influenced some biblical writers. See also **Resurrection.**

Incarnation Literally, "to become flesh." Refers to the Christian teaching that the Son of God was present with God at creation, indeed *was* God, and "became flesh" in the person Jesus (see John 1).

Inerrancy The belief that God inspired the writers of the Bible in such a way that their words are without error.

Irony A literary term for the incongruity that results when words are used to convey a meaning opposite of what they literally mean, and when what happens is contrary to what might logically be expected. A frequent literary device in the Bible.

Israel The name for the twelve tribes that the Tanak says descended from the patriarch Jacob (also called Israel). A political designation for the nation and people who inhabited the land of Canaan. After the division of the nation in 922 B.C.E., "Israel" referred to the Northern Kingdom. Also a synonym for the Jewish people. See also **Palestine** and **Canaan.**

J The designation used by source critics to refer to the Yahwist (from the German transliteration "Jahweh"), one of the hypothetical written sources combined to create the Torah or perhaps Hexateuch. Dated to the tenth century B.C.E. and thus the earliest of the sources of the Pentateuch.

Jehovah See **Yahweh (YHWH).**

Jericho A city in the Jordan River Valley, just north of the Dead Sea.

Jerusalem Literally, "city of peace." The key city of ancient Israel, located in the central hill country on the edge of the Judean desert. Under King David it became the religious and political symbol of the unity of the covenant people. Referred to as *Zion* in the Bible.

Jew A designation for the people of the Judean Kingdom, later province, and those in the Diaspora. Came into use after the Babylonian Exile. In the New Testament, used to distinguish descendants of Israel from the Samaritans and Gentiles.

Josephus A Jewish historian (c. 37–100 C.E.) whose works strive to make Jewish history and traditions understandable to Hellenistic readers.

Judah (1) A son of Jacob and Rachel, ancestor of the Tribe of Judah; (2) the region in southern Palestine associated with the tribe; (3) after the division of the nation Israel in 922 B.C.E., the Southern Kingdom, ruled over by the Davidic dynasty until the Babylonian conquest of the early sixth century.

Judea Greek for *Judah.* A political designation first used to describe the Jewish province created by the Persians around Jerusalem in the sixth century B.C.E. Under the Maccabeans came to refer to the whole of Palestine; later under the Romans to the area ruled by Herod the Great, then to the limited area around Jerusalem administered by procurators. Also one of the three geographic regions in Israel, in addition to Samaria and Galilee to the north.

Judgment God (or the Messiah's) punishment of the wicked and reward of the righteous, either during history or at a Day of Judgment at an "end time."

Justification To make or declare righteous. A recurrent concept in both the Tanak and New Testament. Refers to the bringing of persons into proper accord with one another and/or God, overcoming that which thwarts the right relationship. In the New Testament, used to explain what God accomplished through the sacrifice of Jesus, accessible to persons through faith.

Kerygma A transliteration of a Greek term, meaning "preaching." In the New Testament the focus is on the content of the preaching, the gospel.

Kingdom of God/Heaven The sovereignty or rule of God. A rabbinic and New Testament phrase, rooted in the Tanak's claim of God's universal sovereignty. The Synoptic gospels portray the announcement of the nearness of the kingdom and the necessity of repentance in order to prepare for it as the basic message of Jesus. It is sometimes used in apocalyptic contexts as a symbol for the expected new age. As a symbol, it relates also to God's redemptive activity for the covenant people.

Lament A literary term denoting personal and communal songs that cry out in anguish to God, imploring God to act to deliver the individual or people from the situation of distress.

Larger Apocrypha See **Pseudepigrapha.**

Levite In general, members of the priestly tribe of Levi. In the Book of Deuteronomy, a term for the priests who conducted sacrifices and administered the law. After centralization of worship in Jerusalem, the Levites were apparently reduced to a position subordinate to the Aaronide Temple priesthood. After the Exile, however, certain Levites constituted the Temple choirs.

Light Often a symbol for the presence of God and spiritual illumination.

Logos Greek for "word." In Stoic philosophy, reason. The principle that gives the world coherence and order. In the New Testament, Jesus is called the *logos* (see John 1).

Lord A title of respect and authority, used for God and prominent persons in the Tanak and applied to Jesus in the New Testament. See **Yahweh (YHWH)**.

Lord's Supper The last meal shared by Jesus with his disciples. Became the central sacrament in the Christian community.

LXX See **Septuagint (LXX)**.

Maccabees A family that led the revolt against Seleucid rule in Israel (167–164 B.C.E.) and established the Hasmonean dynasty, which governed throughout much of the second and first centuries B.C.E.

Marduk (or Merodach) A Mesopotamian deity, chief god of the city of Babylon. A storm deity portrayed as creator in the Babylonian creation poem. See **Enuma Elish.**

Mari An ancient Mesopotamian city that served as a center of trade in the third millennium. Archaeological excavations have revealed texts that shed light on the cultural background of some biblical customs.

Megiddo A city in northwestern Palestine in the Plain of Esdraelon, in a very strategic location controlling two major trade and military routes, above all the mountain passes leading to the coastal plain.

Melchizedek Hebrew for "my king is righteous." King of Salem (Jerusalem) called in Genesis 14 a priest. Interpreted later to mean "King of Righteousness." Came to be regarded as the ideal priest-king, a supernatural figure whose priesthood is eternal (see Hebrews 5–7).

Mesopotamia The geographic region bounded by the Tigris and Euphrates rivers, now modern Iraq. The Sumerian people occupied southern Mesopotamia around 3300 B.C.E. Later, the Babylonians were centered in this area, while the Assyrian Empire dominated northern Mesopotamia.

Messiah Hebrew for "anointed one." In general, anyone inducted into an office or given a responsibility through the ceremony of anointing with oil. In particular, the king of united Israel, or the Davidic monarchy of Judah. After the fall of the Davidic monarchy, associated with the notion that God would restore the Davidic line in the person of an ideal king. Some Dead Sea Scrolls also speak of a Messiah of Aaron, a restored high priesthood (see Lev. 9:30).

Midrash Biblical interpretation of the type found in rabbinic literature, in which the text is carefully explained, often verse by verse. Midrashic interpretation assumes the text has an inexhaustible store of meaning to be mined by the careful reader. May be halakic or haggadic.

Millennium In general, a thousand years. In the Bible, a thousand-year reign of peace. In Revelation, associated with a period in which Satan would be defeated and Christ would rule, before a final onslaught by Satan and the final defeat of evil (Rev. 20:1–3). Corresponds to the rabbinic "days of the messiah."

Minimalists A small group of Old Testament scholars, so-called because they radically reduce the historical content of the Tanak. Most Minimalists argue that the books of the Former Prophets as well as the Torah are late compositions, largely ideological in nature. They deny that there was a united monarchy of David and Solomon, though some would allow that a complex polity existed in Judah/Jerusalem in the eighth century B.C.E. Archaelogists note that many of their views are falsified by archaeological data.

Mishnah Rabbinic-pharisaic Judaism claimed that its oral traditions (in the New Testament, the "traditions of the elders") constituted an oral Torah, equal in antiquity and authority to the written Torah. Mishnah refers specifically to the written version of the rabbinic Oral Torah, completed in Palestine by about 200 C.E. Became the basic stratum of the Talmud.

Monotheism The belief in one all-powerful god to the exclusion of other deities.

Moses The leader of the people of Israel out of bondage in Egypt and the mediator between Yahweh and the people, through whom God entered into the Sinai Covenant with Israel. Considered the lawgiver and archetypal prophet.

Mystery Religions Hellenistic groups associated with various deities, all with the belief in initiation rites that united believers with the deity, with the promise of immortality. The influence of these groups on the formation of early Christian teaching is disputed.

Mysticism A disciplined quest for direct experience of the divine presence.

Myth In a narrow sense, an account of activities of the gods in eternity or in the spirit realm, though it may also denote accounts of divine–human interaction. In a more general sense, stories that embody the foundational traditions of a culture. May be reenacted in worship.

Nag Hammadi A town in Upper Egypt where (beginning in 1945) a cache of texts (such as the Gospel of Thomas), which shed light on early Christian history, were found. Some documents provide primary evidence for gnostic teachings.

Nazarene A Greek term used to refer to Jesus and his followers in the New Testament (for example, Acts 24:5). The Hebrew form "Nazareans" was a rabbinic term for the early Christians.

Nazareth A small village of lower Galilee, near the major trade route to Egypt, where Jesus grew up.

Nineveh Capital of Assyria during the height of its power.

Nuzi A Mesopotamian city, where a collection of texts that aid the reconstruction of the cultural context of early biblical history were unearthed by archaeologists. The texts date to about 1450 B.C.E.

Oracle A message from a god.

Oral Torah See **Mishnah.**

P A term used by source critics to designate the priestly source, one of the hypothetical sources of the Torah. Called "priestly" because of a special concern for ritual and the Aaronide priesthood. Thought to be the latest of the four "sources," dating from about the fifth century B.C.E.

Palestine From the Greek name for the area along the eastern coast of the Mediterranean Sea (after the Philistines). Also called Canaan, Israel, and the Promised Land.

Parables Brief stories that point beyond their literal meaning toward another truth or truths. The Synoptic gospels record over twenty-five parables of Jesus.

Parousia Greek for "coming," almost always referring to the expectation of the coming again of Jesus to judge the earth.

Passion Narratives The stories of the suffering and death of Jesus in the gospels.

Passover The Jewish festival commemorating God's deliverance of the people of Israel from bondage.

Patriarchs The male leader of a family or clan. In the Tanak, refers to the ancestors of Israel described in Genesis.

Pentateuch Greek term for the first five books of the Tanak (cf. **Torah**).

Pentecost Greek for "fiftieth," designating the Jewish Festival of Weeks (Shavuot) held fifty days after Passover, which came to be associated with the giving of the Torah on Mount Sinai. Because of events on Pentecost narrated in Acts 2, Pentecost has become an important Christian festival.

People of the Land In Tanak, originally notables among the lay yeomanry with militia responsibilities. Later, the humbler classes. Rabbinic-pharisaic term for the Jewish masses who were careless or indifferent in their religious practices.

Pharisees A predominantly lay–scholarly religious movement of particularly pious and influential Jews, in the classical period, described by Josephus and the New Testament.

Philippi A city in northeastern Greece, visited by Paul in about 50 C.E. Site of the first European Christian community.

Philistines A group that migrated to the southern coast of Palestine in the twelfth century B.C.E. and became one of the principal rivals of the Israelites.

Phoenicia Land of the Phoenicians; the name given to the coastal area to the north of Israel during the first millennium B.C.E. Tyre and Sidon were the most important cities in the region; known for its extensive trade.

Presbyters See **Elders.**

Prophet One who serves as an instrument of communication between God and humans.

Proverb A brief statement that communicates a familiar truth.

Psalm From the Greek *psalmos,* translating a Hebrew word meaning "song." However, among the 150 psalms of the canonical Book of Psalms, one finds prayers and other types of religious poems, in addition to songs.

Pseudepigrapha Approximately sixty-five noncanonical Jewish writings from roughly the third century B.C.E. until the second century C.E. They are called the Pseudepigrapha ("false writings") because many are connected with persons who are not the authors. However, this designation is being questioned by many modern scholars, who consider it unnecessarily misleading in its suggestion that the works constituted an ancient collection. The term *Larger Apocrypha* is preferred in this text.

Pseudonymous A literary convention in which an author assumes the name of another person, perhaps a famous person, to lend authority to the work.

Purim A Jewish holiday based on the Book of Esther.

Q A designation used by New Testament scholars for the material common to the Gospels of Matthew and Luke, but not found in Mark. From German *Quelle* (source). It is commonly assumed that the Q material comes from a source used by the writers of the Gospels of Matthew and Luke.

Qumran The site of a settlement along the northwest shore of the Dead Sea, where the Dead Sea Scrolls were found.

Rabbi Hebrew title that came to mean "my master" or "teacher." A title denoting respect for Jewish teachers. Used in New Testament in direct address to Jesus.

Redemption The release of someone or something in exchange for payment. In the Bible, also refers to the action of God in restoring sinful people.

Remnant In the Bible, the remainder of faithful people left over after divine judgment on a nation's sins.

Repentance Turning around from the wrong way toward the proper path. In the Bible, turning from sin to the Lord and the path in harmony with God.

Resurrection New life beyond death. In the Bible, a complete transformation of the human being or nation after the experience of death. For people, an event to take place at the end of history when the dead are raised and brought under divine judgment.

Retribution Repaying in kind. A principle that applies in various biblical writings both to human and divine justice. The belief that God will reward or punish people in proportion to their degree of loyalty to divine law.

Revelation Unveiling or disclosing. In the Bible, the making known of truths from God about enduring realities or the divine plan for the future. Often associated with apocalyptic teaching.

Righteousness The state of being right, or in proper relationship. In the Bible, God is portrayed as righteous, indicating the divine intent and action to bring humans and all creation into a state of harmony. Humans are also described as righteous when they are living in obedience to God or trusting in the divine righteousness. A pervasive theme in the Bible.

Sabbath From the Hebrew *shabbat,* seventh. The weekly seventh day of rest mandated for Israelites by God in the Ten Commandments. Observed as a memorial of God's resting after creation and to give workers an opportunity to rest. From sundown on Friday to sundown Saturday.

Sadducees Priests, descendants of Zadok. An aristocratic Jewish group that existed from the second century B.C.E. until the late first century C.E. Usually described as opponents of the Pharisees and thought to be from the priestly and wealthy families.

Samaria The capital city of the Northern Kingdom from the early ninth century B.C.E. until its destruction by the Assyrians in 721 B.C.E. Also, a district in the central hill country, north of Judah and south of Galilee.

Samaritans A religious community centered in Samaria, near Mount Gerizim, which Samaritans consider the holy mountain (in contrast to Mount Zion in Jerusalem). Although Samaritans and Jews shared a common heritage, differences in beliefs and traditions led to the animosity reflected in the New Testament. The community continues to exist today.

Sanctification Making holy or dedicating someone or something to God. Transferred from a secular, profane state to a sacred one.

Sanhedrin A Greek term for a council of leaders. The term may refer to a series or councils of courts, but principally the council of Jewish notables who were responsible for Jewish relations with Rome. In the Bible, the most famous sanhedrin is the council of Jewish leaders in Jerusalem during the New Testament period. The precise composition and powers of the Jerusalem Sanhedrin are the subject of intense scholarly debate.

Satan Hebrew for "adversary." Depicted in the Tanak as a member of the divine court whose duty is to report to the heavenly king on the faithfulness of humans. By the time of the New Testament, perhaps as a result of Persian influence, Satan (also identified as Belial, Beelzebub, or simply the Devil) is portrayed as the leader of forces hostile to God.

Second Temple Refers to the Jerusalem Temple from its rebuilding following the Babylonian Exile, until it was destroyed by the Romans in 70 C.E. The Temple was in fact refurbished several times, and completely rebuilt on the orders of Herod the Great.

Semitic A term developed by scholars to describe a group of peoples of the ancient Near East whose cultures and languages were very similar. Includes Assyrians, Babylonians, Canaanites, Hebrews, Phoenicians, Arabs, and others. Often refers to the languages of these peoples.

Septuagint (LXX) The Greek translation of the Tanak from Hebrew begun in Alexandria, Egypt, in the third century, to which the Deuterocanon was added. From the Greek for *seventy,* reflecting the tradition that the translation was done by seventy elders.

Sheol   The place where the dead go. See also **Hades.**

Sinai, Mount   The mountain in the Sinai Wilderness where, according to the Exodus narrative, God revealed the Torah to Moses and Israel entered into covenant with God. Also called Mount Horeb.

Social Sciences   Disciplines that study the dynamics of psychological, social, and cultural organization and change.

Sociology   The social science that focuses on the communal dimension of human behavior, whether in families, clans, tribes, nations, or the hosts of institutional settings in which humans are grouped.

Son of God   In general, a person or community with a special relationship with God. In the Tanak, angels or divine beings. Became a title applied to Jesus to denote his special relationship with God, and ultimately shared identity.

Son of Man   A phrase with meanings varying from simply "a human being" to an apocalyptic title for the one coming to judge the world. Also a euphemism for the first-person pronoun. In the New Testament, the meaning of Jesus's reference to himself as "son of man" is a subject of intense scholarly debate.

Stoicism   A school of Greek philosophy established in the fourth century B.C.E., emphasizing the logos that orders all things, and a life of discipline and duty.

Structure   In this text, a literary term for the pattern or patterns discernible in a literary unit.

Sumerians   A people who inhabited southern Mesopotamia and developed the first ancient Near Eastern civilization in the fourth millenium. According to Genesis, the ancestors of Israel came from Sumer.

Synagogue   Greek for "assembly." A Jewish place of gathering for prayer, reading and studying Scripture, and hearing its teachings expounded.

Synoptic   From the Greek for "from or with a similar perspective." Refers to the first three canonical gospels (Matthew, Mark, and Luke), which share a similar view of Jesus's public career.

Talmud   The authoritative compilation of rabbinic lore not directly dependent upon Tanak. Consists of Mishnah plus Gemara-comments and elaborations on the Mishnah. There are two editions of the Talmud: the Babylonian, edited in the rabbinic academies of Babylon, and the Yerushlami, edited

in the academies of Galilee, the former being more authoritative. Completed about 500 C.E. See **Mishnah.**

Tanak   An acronym created from the Hebrew words for the three canonical sections of the Hebrew Bible: Torah, Neviim (Prophets), and Ketuvim (Writings). Used in this text in preference to other possible designations, such as Old Testament or Hebrew Bible.

Temple   The house or palace of a god. A place of sacrificial worship. In the Bible, especially the place of worship constructed in Jerusalem, first by King Solomon, which was the center of the nation Israel and came to symbolize God's dwelling with the people.

Theology   The application of human reason to the study of God and divine revelation in an attempt to explain their meanings.

Theophany   The manifestation of God. In the Bible a number of stories about and poetic allusions to appearances of God are found (see, for example, Ex. 3:1–4:18; 19:1–20:21; Is. 6:1–8; Mt. 17:1–8; Rev. 4:1–11).

Torah   Hebrew for "instruction, teaching." Refers to God's instruction to the covenant people as well as to the first five books of the Tanak. In its broadest sense refers to all of the divine commandments, from both the Tanak (the written Torah), the Mishnah (the oral Torah), and other religious teaching, and thus to the total divine revelation of how the covenant people are to live.

Transfiguration   The event narrated in the Synoptic gospels when the "true nature" of Jesus was revealed to his closest followers (see Mark 9:2–8 and parallels).

Ugarit   An ancient city-state located along the Mediterranean coast in Syria opposite Cyprus, now known as Ras Shamra. Twentieth-century archaeologists discovered a library of texts at Ugarit that provide important information for the linguistic, cultural, and religious background of ancient Canaan, and of the Tanak.

Versions   Translations of the Bible into other languages, ancient and modern.

Virgin Birth   Refers to the tradition that Mary gave birth to Jesus by the power of the Holy Spirit rather than human agency.

Way   In general, a term used in the Bible to refer to the path of action in harmony with God's intentions. Also, one of the earliest designations for the Christian community (see Acts 9:2).

Yahweh (YHWH) The name for God, which, according to the narrative in Exodus, was revealed to Moses and thus was the "special" Israelite name for God. Jewish tradition considered the name too holy to pronounce; whenever the name appeared in the text the Hebrew word for Lord (*'adonai*) was pronounced. When vowels were added to the consonantal text of the Tanak, the vowels for *adonai* were placed with the consonants YHWH to remind readers not to pronounce the divine name. Some English translations therefore render Yahweh as Jehovah, reading YHWH with the substituted vowels. Represented in English versions in uppercase type, usually LORD, but also Lord GOD.

Zealots Refers to opponents of the Roman occupation of Israel, who sometimes engaged in violent revolution against the Romans.

Ziggurat A Mesopotamian stepped tower, usually with shrines both at its base and on its top, connected by a processional ramp. The Tower of Babel described in Genesis 11:1–9 was probably a ziggurat.

Zion Name of the "mountain" on which the Jerusalem Temple was located, hence Mount Zion.

TEXT CREDITS

Bible quotes throughout book: New Revised Standard Version Bible, Copyright 1989, Division of Christian Education of the National Council of the Churches of Christ in the United States of America. Used by permission. All rights reserved.

Chapter 1: Alan G. Padgett & Patrick R. Keifert, *The Bible and The Question of Truth*, Eerdmans Publishing Company © 2006. Used with permission.

Chapter 3: David J.A. Clines, "The Theme of The Pentateuch," *Journal of the Old Testament.* Copyright © 1978. Printed with permission from the Continuum International Publishing Company.

Chapter 4: Tullock, *The Old Testament Story,* 1st edition. Copyright © 1981. Printed and electronically reproduced by permission of Pearson Education, Inc., Upper Saddle River, New Jersey.

Chapter 10: *Fishers of Men,* photographed by Gordon N. Converse, text by Robert J. Bull and B. Cobbey Crisler. Prentice Hall Publishing © 1980. Reprinted with permission of the authors; Kee, *Understanding the New Testament,* 4th edition. Copyright © 1983. Printed and electronically reproduced by permission of Pearson Education, Inc., Upper Saddle River, New Jersey.

Chapter 14: *The New Testament Background: Selected Documents* (PPBK Reprint), edited by Charles K. Barrett. Harper & Rowe © 1961. Used with permission of SPCK Publishing.

INDEX